Ethics for Paralegals

The McGraw-Hill Paralegal List

WHERE EDUCATIONAL SUPPORT GOES BEYOND EXPECTATIONS.

Introduction to Law & Paralegal Studies
Connie Farrell Scuderi
ISBN: 0073524638
© 2008

Introduction to Law for Paralegals
Deborah Benton
ISBN: 007351179X
© 2008

Basic Legal Research, Second Edition
Edward Nolfi
ISBN: 0073520519
© 2008

Basic Legal Writing, Second Edition
Pamela Tepper
ISBN: 0073403032
© 2008

Contract Law for Paralegals
Linda Spagnola
ISBN: 0073511765
© 2008

Civil Law and Litigation for Paralegals
Neal Bevans
ISBN: 0073524611
© 2008

Wills, Trusts, and Estates for Paralegals
George Kent
ISBN: 0073403067
© 2008

The Law Office Reference Manual
Jo Ann Lee
ISBN: 0073511838
© 2008

The Paralegal Reference Manual
Charles Nemeth
ISBN: 0073403075
© 2008

The Professional Paralegal
Allan Tow
ISBN: 0073403091
© 2009

Ethics for Paralegals
Linda Spagnola and Vivian Batts
ISBN: 0073376981
© 2009

Family Law for Paralegals
George Kent
ISBN: 0073376973
© 2009

McGraw-Hill's Torts for Paralegals
ISBN: 0073376930
© 2009

McGraw-Hill's Real Estate Law
for Paralegals
ISBN: 0073376957
© 2009

Legal Research and Writing for Paralegals
Pamela Tepper
ISBN: 007352462X
© 2009

McGraw-Hill's Criminal Law for Paralegals
ISBN: 0073376930
© 2009

McGraw-Hill's Law Office Management
for Paralegals
ISBN: 0073376957
© 2009

Legal Terminology Explained
Edward Nolfi
ISBN: 0073511846
© 2009

For more information or to receive desk copies, please contact your McGraw-Hill Sales Representative.

Ethics for Paralegals

Linda A. Spagnola

Vivian B. Batts

Contributing Author
Bryant & Stratton College

McGraw-Hill
Higher Education

Boston   Burr Ridge, IL   Dubuque, IA   New York   San Francisco   St. Louis
Bangkok   Bogotá   Caracas   Kuala Lumpur   Lisbon   London   Madrid   Mexico City
Milan   Montreal   New Delhi   Santiago   Seoul   Singapore   Sydney   Taipei   Toronto

ETHICS FOR PARALEGALS

Published by McGraw-Hill, a business unit of The McGraw-Hill Companies, Inc., 1221 Avenue of the
Americas, New York, NY, 10020. Copyright © 2009 by The McGraw-Hill Companies, Inc. All rights reserved.
No part of this publication may be reproduced or distributed in any form or by any means, or stored in a
database or retrieval system, without the prior written consent of The McGraw-Hill Companies, Inc.,
including, but not limited to, in any network or other electronic storage or transmission, or broadcast for
distance learning.

Some ancillaries, including electronic and print components, may not be available to customers outside the
United States.

This book is printed on acid-free paper.

1 2 3 4 5 6 7 8 9 0 QPD/QPD 0 9 8

ISBN   978-0-07-337698-1
MHID 0-07-337698-1

Vice president/Editor in chief: *Elizabeth Haefele*
Vice president/Director of marketing: *John E. Biernat*
Sponsoring editor: *Natalie J. Ruffatto*
Developmental editor II: *Tammy Higham*
Marketing manager: *Kelly Curran*
Lead media producer: *Damian Moshak*
Media producer: *William Mumford*
Director, Editing/Design/Production: *Jess Ann Kosic*
Senior project manager: *Rick Hecker*
Senior production supervisor: *Janean A. Utley*
Designer: *Marianna Kinigakis*
Media project manager: *Mark A. S. Dierker*
Outside development: *Beth Baugh*
Cover design: *Studio Montage*
Interior design: *Jenny El-Shamy*
Typeface: *10.5/13 Times New Roman*
Compositor: *Aptara, Inc.*
Printer: *Quebecor World Dubuque Inc.*
Cover credit: © *Ken Glaser/Corbis*

Library of Congress Cataloging-in-Publication Data

Spagnola, Linda A.
  McGraw-Hill's ethics for paralegals / Linda Spagnola and Vivian B. Batts.
    p. cm.—(The McGraw-Hill paralegal list)
  title: Ethics for paralegals
  Includes index.
  ISBN-13: 978-0-07-337698-1 (alk. paper)
  ISBN-10: 0-07-337698-1 (alk. paper)
    1. Legal assistants—United States. 2. Legal ethics—United States. I. Batts, Vivian B.
II. Title. III. Title: Ethics for paralegals.
KF320.L4 S69 2009
174'.30973—dc22

                                                    2008007106

The Internet addresses listed in the text were accurate at the time of publication. The inclusion of a Web site
does not indicate an endorsement by the authors or McGraw-Hill, and McGraw-Hill does not guarantee the
accuracy of the information presented at these sites.

www.mhhe.com

Dedication

This book is dedicated to two very different people in my life who have taught me the importance of perseverance:

Matthew Thomas Filliman, my nephew, who was born at the beginning of the writing of this book. He was very premature and weighed under two pounds. He had the strength of a small bull, though, and every day grew stronger and stronger. He is a gorgeous, giddy toddler now. The lesson learned: Take each day as it comes.

Dr. Phillip Papas, my colleague and best friend. A true gentleman and scholar. He listened with patience and kindness and provided guidance during this endeavor. His support and confidence never faltered for a moment. The lesson learned: Try to control only what you actually can and just keep moving forward.

Linda Spagnola

About the Authors

LINDA A. SPAGNOLA

Linda Spagnola earned her BA in French with a minor in political science from Rutgers College and her JD from Seton Hall School of Law. She is admitted to practice in New Jersey, New York, Massachusetts, and North Carolina, where she now resides on a peaceful wooded acre with her husband, two beautiful little girls, and Winston, the yellow Labrador.

Upon graduation, she began working for a boutique law firm specializing in construction law. This area of law is its own peculiar creature whose practice requires attention to detail and perseverance to endure years of complex litigation. After leaving active practice in 2001, Dr. Spagnola began academic pursuits. She joined the faculty of Union County College in Cranford, NJ and was able to create the Paralegal Program from the ground up and in 2003 starting registering students. The spring of 2006 saw her first class of graduates earning their associate degrees in Paralegal Studies.

Never satisfied being confined to a single discipline, Dr. Spagnola has helped create two other programs at Union County College. She has served as chair of these two initiatives: Honors Studies and Women's Studies. She has also drafted initiatives for Experiential Education. Her latest academic interest has led her to pursue her master's degree in history, in the course of which she intends to study the United States Constitution in greater depth.

She is active not only on campus, but also on the national stage in paralegal education, as a member of the Editorial Committee in AAfPE (American Association for Paralegal Education). Dr. Spagnola is involved in professional development for paralegals as well. She has spoken and plans to continue to speak at various national paralegal conferences, where she presents on contract law and legal ethics.

VIVIAN B. BATTS

Vivian B. Batts is the Program Director/Subject Area Coordinator of Paralegal Studies at Bryant & Stratton College. She began her legal career as a legal secretary, progressing to executive legal secretary and legal assistant for several large law firms in New York City.

In 1995, Ms. Batts received her MS degree in education from Hofstra University. A few years after she relocated to Richmond, Virginia, she was hired as an adjunct instructor in the medical and paralegal programs at the Richmond campus of Bryant & Stratton College. Bryant & Stratton College is a career college emphasizing lifelong learning.

Since her association with Bryant & Stratton College began, the student population has tripled. Ms. Batts has increased the on-campus presence of guest speakers; established a campus chapter of Lambda Epsilon Chi (LEX—the National Paralegal Honorary Society, founded by AAfPE), revitalized the campus club (Legal Assistant Mentor Program), and, with the assistance of a dedicated and supportive adjunct faculty, increased retention in the paralegal studies program to over 75 percent.

Preface

When presented with the notion that paralegal students should study the attorney's code of professional ethics, the student's first reaction is probably: "Why?" It is a valid question. The two professions are distinct from one another; however, they are inexorably linked. While the practice of law has been around since the earliest codifications of a system of laws, which date back to the Code of Hammurabi in 1780 BCE, the paralegal profession developed in the early 1970s.

The development of this new profession was spurred by economics, both those affecting the clients and those of the practitioners. Many people have legal issues that need guidance from a legal professional in order to resolve them; however, the cost of attorney's fees may be prohibitive. Concurrently, legal practices have faced the hard economic choice either to increase fees to meet the financial requirements of running the practice or to turn clients away. The solutions to both needs can be found in the paralegal profession. With the proper education and training, paralegals acquire legal knowledge and skills to perform many tasks previously performed by attorneys. The cost of hiring a paralegal is far less than the cost associated with an attorney. This is the "access to justice" theory. As many potential clients cannot afford the fees and costs associated with obtaining the assistance of an attorney, they are denied access to the justice system. There have been many criticisms that in the justice system, the wealthy can "get away with murder" because they can afford the high cost of legal services and/or can pay to drag out the process and drain the other side of resources. Additionally, Legal Services attorneys are booked beyond their capacity to serve all those who qualify for public legal assistance. That is why paralegals have become indispensable members of the legal team in both the private and the public sectors.

As a vital member of the legal team, the paralegal performs tasks that, absent the paralegal, would have to be performed by an attorney. It follows logically, then, that the paralegal, in practicing law under the supervision of an attorney, needs to follow the same rules as an attorney. Otherwise, the delegation of these legal duties to a paralegal would not be proper or ethical. A mantra common in the ethics classroom is this: "A paralegal cannot do that which an attorney cannot do." So it follows that a paralegal must do what an attorney must do—and that is to conform to the ethics rules in every task performed.

The legal profession is self-policing: the rules of professional conduct are written by lawyers and judges and enforced by lawyers and judges. This is different from the situations in almost every other profession, as the latter are governed by rules written by the legislature (of whom about 50 percent hold law degrees). These rules are not a ceiling, but a floor. This means that the standards set forth in the ethics rules are the minimum acceptable actions. Attorneys and paralegals should strive for more—to not only meet, but exceed these requirements. Ultimately, these ethics rules should be considered alongside your own personal moral compass as well.

That being said, why do paralegals and lawyers need a separate and comprehensive set of rules if individual morality is to be considered as well? It is the nature of not only the relationship between the lawyer and the client but also the relationship to the justice system that requires a higher standard of care to be exercised by legal professionals. A client comes to the law office seeking help during an important time in his life. No one seeks out legal advice "for the fun of it." Consulting with a legal professional is expensive and often stressful. A client is in a vulnerable position, and the lawyer is under a special "fiduciary" duty to assist the client to the best of her individual capability. This fiduciary relationship requires that the attorney act with good faith and trust, maintain the confidences of the client, and be truthful and forthright in rendering an opinion regarding the representation of the client.

Now that the reasons a paralegal needs to study the ethics rules have been clarified, the job title "paralegal" needs to be clarified.

What is a paralegal? Many students encounter this question as they begin their studies. Indeed, even attorneys are not clear on what constitutes the practice of a paralegal. The many organizations that are involved in the profession have their own definitions. However, there are some common elements to all of them. A paralegal is a professional who works under the supervision of an attorney performing substantive legal work for which the time spent on these tasks is billable. In essence, the work performed by paralegals is work that, if the paralegal were not available to perform it, would have to be performed by an attorney. This brings me to the point of this textbook. If a paralegal is performing substantive legal work, that paralegal must also perform that work to the same ethical standards that apply to lawyers. This is why it is imperative that paralegal students learn not only how to perform their jobs well, but also how to perform them ethically. Almost every task performed in the law office, even one not necessarily substantive in nature, has an ethical reason behind the method of performance. Indeed, even filing systems conform to ethical standards, by preserving client confidentiality.

So far, no concrete picture of a paralegal has emerged. In an attempt to both clarify the duties of a paralegal and educate attorneys, the "consumers" of paralegal services, if you will, the ABA has prepared *Model Guidelines for the Utilization of Paralegals*.

Despite the public reputation of lawyers in general, the profession is held to the highest standards of integrity and candor. (The public's perception is easily revealed in a simple "Google" search of "lawyer jokes," resulting in over eight million hits.) These high standards apply to the paralegals working under the lawyers' supervision as well. Indeed, the ABA has created the Model Guidelines for the Utilization of Paralegal Services (MGUPS), which supplement the ethics rules, in that the MGUPS addresses the relationship between the attorney and the paralegal rather than the attorney and the client. The thrust of the MGUPS is the proper delegation and supervision of tasks to a paralegal and the clarification of the position of paralegal to third parties. While a paralegal performs legal duties, it is the lawyer who remains ultimately responsible for the end product. The lawyer must be sure that the paralegal has the proper skills in order to competently carry out the task assigned. Furthermore, the paralegal's conduct must be consistent with the lawyer's obligations under the relevant ethical codes; this emphasizes the need for the paralegal student to study the attorney's code of ethics.

With these guidelines, the ABA hopes to promote the growth of the paralegal profession by giving attorneys a way to confidently delegate duties for which the paralegals have been trained. Effective use of paralegals in the law office increases productivity, billable hours, efficiency, and client satisfaction. Paralegals, working in concert with their supervising attorneys, can find both career and personal satisfaction in knowing that they are a vital part of a team rendering legal services to a broader spectrum of clients and potentially increasing access to justice, with the utmost ethical integrity.

In order to promote the student's understanding of all of these various and numerous rules, a quick review of the Table of Contents is necessary. It reveals the general organization of this book. Ethics can be taught either as a stand-alone course or as an integral part of every legal specialty course—or as a combination of both—in the paralegal curriculum. The book is divided into three parts. Part One introduces the paralegal student to the basic tenets of legal ethics. Part Two covers the issues, rules, and regulations affecting the paralegal's practice of law and the relationships with clients. Part Three addresses the roles and ethical requirements that legal professionals play in the justice system. Codes of professional responsibility of both NALA (National Association of Legal Assistants) and NFPA (National Federation of Paralegal Associations) are presented for analysis. In some instances they are very similar, and in others they diverge. This side-by-side comparison provides the paralegal student an opportunity to exercise critical thinking skills.

Additionally, in an effort to make learning legal ethics interesting, comprehensible, and practical, I have included a variety of different learning tools at the end of every chapter.

1. **In Class Discussions** introduce scenarios with potentially diverse or surprising outcomes. This is an opportunity to talk about them with the instructor and other students in class.

2. **Review Questions** of many different kinds address the different learning styles of students. There are "Faulty Phrases" (the statements are false and the student must correct them), Explanations, Multiple Choice questions, and others. The emphasis is on critical thinking and problem-solving skills as they relate to the Rules of Professional Responsibility.

3. **Case in Point** is a section containing the text of a relevant case or ethics opinion, presented for you to read and discuss in class. A summary or case brief, if the students are familiar with that format, should be prepared by the student both to aid the student in active class participation and to reinforce strong writing skills.

4. **Spot the Issue** is an analytical tool wherein the student must identify the problem in a short fact scenario.

5. **Research This** attempts to strengthen the student's research skills by providing suggestions for more in-depth study of key issues.

6. **Surf's Up** addresses the current electronic globalization of the practice and problems associated with virtual communications, privacy, and confidentiality.

7. **Cyber Trips** direct the paralegal student to relevant Web sites for independent viewing outside the classroom.

8. **Reel to Real** turns the paralegal's critical eye on popular movies portraying the practice of law. The exercise asks the student to scrutinize Hollywood's portrayal of attorneys and ethical dilemmas.

Acknowledgments

The writing of this book would not have been possible without the support of many gracious and patient people.

I would like to thank, first, Tammy Higham, developmental editor from McGraw-Hill, for her enduring support. Amazingly, she signed on to assist me with another book. She is not only a friend but also a cheerleader and amateur psychiatrist. I certainly put her through her paces this time.

Thanks go to Natalie Ruffatto, sponsoring editor from McGraw Hill, for reading and responding to the rantings of a stressed-out author. One of us (it was not me) had to have a level head and steady nerves. Thank you for your patience and assistance in getting this book to print.

Freelance developmental editor Beth Baugh should be thanked for her invaluable input at the revision stages. She has always been so helpful, understanding, and gracious.

I was also fortunate enough to have a dedicated student who has turned into every professor's dream success story. Stacey Hazel assisted in finding relevant case law that conformed to the various specifications I set forth. I could not be prouder of her and all that she has accomplished.

I also wish to thank my colleagues who acted as reviewers of the draft of the manuscript. They spent a great deal of time to write valuable feedback to assist me in making this book the best it could be.

Elizabeth J. Beardmore
Colorado Technical University

Arlene A. Cleveland
Pellissippi State Technical Community College

Steven Dayton
Fullerton College

Darren Defoe
Andover College

Joseph F. McGowan
Middlesex Community College

Mercedes Medina
Miami Dade College

Hillary Michaud
Villa Julie College

Joan Stevens
Loyola University of Chicago

Julia Tryk
Cuyahoga Community College

Thomas E. Weiers, Jr.
Duquesne University

Bobby Wheeler
Highline Community College

Linda Spagnola

A Guided Tour

Ethics for Paralegals provides students with a primer on the ethical codes that govern the behavior of both attorneys and paralegals in the practice of law. The text shows that because attorneys and paralegals are inexorably linked, it is important for paralegals to understand the ethical codes of both professions. The book is structured around the American Bar Association's Model Guidelines for the Utilization of Paralegals, but focuses on the NALA (National Association of Legal Assistants) and NFPA (National Federation of Paralegal Associations) codes of professional responsibility for paralegals. The many practical features and exercises throughout and at the end of each chapter allow students to put into practice what they are learning about ethics in the practice of law. The pedagogy of the book applies three main goals:

- Learning outcomes (critical thinking, vocabulary building, skill development, issues analysis, writing practice)

- Relevance of topics without sacrificing theory (ethical challenges, current law practices, technology application)

- Practical application (real-world exercises, practical advice, portfolio creation)

Chapter Objectives

Provides a road map of the issues covered in each chapter and highlights the concepts students should understand after reading each chapter.

CHAPTER OBJECTIVES

The student will be able to:

- Compare the educational requirements for attorneys and paralegals
- Differentiate among the different types of regulatory plans for the paralegal profession and discuss the pros and cons of each
- Recognize the major associations related to the legal field and identify their mission and role in the paralegal profession
- Identify the various ethical sanctions that can be imposed upon attorneys and the conduct by either the attorney or the paralegal that would warrant those sanctions

This chapter will explore the formal educational requirements and regulations imposed upon the legal profession: WHO may call themselves attorneys or paralegals; WHAT steps they must fulfill to achieve that position; WHERE they may practice; and HOW they stay current in the field by taking continuing legal education and joining relevant legal organizations.

SPOT THE ISSUE

Pat Parkins has worked as a paralegal for the Godwin, Bailey and Ulmer Law Firm for years and knows a great deal about the practice and the expectations of the firm. Archie, the new associate, is under a tremendous amount of pressure to bill more hours and get more clients. He has begun to binge drink at lunch with potential new clients. One day at lunch, in a loud, obviously drunken voice, he began to complain about a well-known and well-respected judge. Pat was the only employee of the firm that was there to hear this. Three days after that incident, Archie was grumbling about his workload at the local pub with Pat. He claimed that the firm was giving him all the cases in front of this judge just to punish him; after all, the firm had this judge in its "back pocket" and the firm would ultimately win no matter how Archie performed, so this was all just "busy work." Pat knows that other pub patrons heard this comment. What should Pat do? Does Pat have any ethical obligations under your state's rules of professional conduct? What about under the paralegal association's rules of conduct? Is Pat obligated to say anything? If so, to whom?

Spot the Issue

Is an analytical tool that asks students to identify an ethical problem in a short fact scenario.

RESEARCH THIS

Find a case or ethics opinion in your jurisdiction that defines the "practice of law." What considerations did the court find important in describing what is or is not the practice of law (which is, therefore, confined to be practiced by attorneys)? Write your own definition for the "practice of law." After performing this task, write a paralegal job description detailing the duties and responsibilities of the position. Create a narrative of what the paralegals, both employees and freelancers, can and cannot do in order to stay within the UPL statutes of your jurisdiction.

Research This

Gives students the opportunity to investigate issues more thoroughly through hands-on assignments designed to develop critical research skills.

CYBER TRIP

Good "how-to" explanations are located at these sites:

http://www.lifehack. org/articles/ productivity/the -tickler-action-file. html (The Lifehack site offers many different organizational and productivity discussions.)

http://www.addre sources.org/article _tickler_roehl.php.

A virtual system is available for a small monthly fee at www. myticklerfile.com.

Cyber Trip

Encourages students to go to the Internet to learn more about a wide array of legal issues.

In Class Discussions

Describe scenarios with potentially surprising outcomes. This feature invites students to discuss relevant issues with the instructor and other students in class.

IN CLASS DISCUSSION

Discuss the following scripts from the television advertisements of law firms. Which do you think violate ABA Model Rule 7.1, prohibiting false or misleading communications? Why? Describe the elements of the commercial that are potentially misleading. What could you change about them to make them comply with the ethical constraints? (Ignore the fact that the name of the law firm has been omitted; assume there is one in the actual commercial.)

1. The advertisement, known as the "Strategy Session," depicts a conference room where actors portraying insurance adjusters are discussing a claim. An older man, the "senior adjuster," asks a younger man, the "junior adjuster," how the claim should be handled. The junior adjuster describes the claim as " . . . a large claim, serious auto accident" and suggests they try to deny and delay to see if the claimant will "crack." The senior adjuster then asks which lawyer represents the victim, whereupon the junior adjuster responds: "The XYZ Law Firm." A metallic sound effect follows and the senior adjuster, now looking concerned, states: "The XYZ Law Firm? Let's settle this one." At this point in the advertisement, a well-known actor appears on screen and advises viewers, "[T]he insurance companies know the name The XYZ Law Firm." He invites individuals who have been injured in an auto accident to tell the insurance companies they "mean business" by calling The XYZ Law Firm. The actor provides the firm's telephone number, which also appears at the bottom of the screen. *See In re Keller,* 792 N.E.2d 865 (Ind. 2003).

2. In four of the television commercials, former clients of the firm appear, talking about actual situations in which they have employed the law firm. In one of the presentations, a client says that the firm "fought the law all the way to the state Supreme Court and we won." A client in another presentation says, "They really fought for me. They were aggressive and settled things quickly. I never expected the large settlement they won for me." A third client says, "They made things happen. And they got results. If you have the right attorneys, you can fight City Hall." The fourth former client says, "They fought for me and got me a very good judgment. Take my word for it, they're the best." The attorney adds at the end of the commercial: "There's no charge unless we win your case. What could be fairer?" *See Disciplinary Counsel v. Shane,* 81 Ohio St. 3d 494, 692 N.E.2d 571 (1998).

Surf's Up

Addresses the electronic globalization of the practice and problems associated with virtual communication, privacy, and confidentiality.

SURF'S UP

Technology has increased attorneys' productive capacity and has made it possible to "short-cut" some tasks and to perform others from a distance, where previously this was impossible. File Transfer Protocol (FTP) sites allow attorneys to send electronic documents via the Internet; database and knowledge sharing sites make it possible to access information at the speed of sound instead of spending hours in the library; networked office computers gain access to the entire firm's work product. How has all this affected fees and billing practices? While the streamlined nature of technology has decreased the billable hours spent on a task, the expense of obtaining and maintaining the technology has increased the per hour earnings of attorneys.

Reel to Real

Uses popular movies portraying the practice of law and asks students to scrutinize Hollywood's portrayal of attorneys and ethical dilemmas.

REEL TO REAL

Runaway Jury (2003) starring John Cusack, Gene Hackman Dustin Hoffman, and Rachel Weisz illustrates how vulnerable juries can be. With a huge jury verdict in the works and major public policies on the line, the defendants (a gun manufacturer) hire jury consultants who turn out to be much more influential than is proper. View *Runaway Jury* and look for the jury tampering from both outside the courtroom and inside the jury.

Summary

The ethics rules regarding conflicts of interest are broad in scope and applicable to every attorney-client relationship or paralegal-client rapport, and last indefinitely. Where there is a doubt as to whether the attorney may take on a new client or should withdraw as counsel, the preferred choice (where there is not a prejudicial effect upon the client) is to defer to the conflicts rules and disengage from the relationship.

There are very specific requirements that must be fulfilled in order to enter into or maintain an attorney-client relationship or generally prohibited transaction. The requirement that is found in almost every rule is the concept of "informed consent." Because attorneys have superior knowledge of the law and legal relationships, they cannot use this to the detriment of their clients who look to them for advice. Clients generally assume that their attorneys and paralegals are looking out for their best interests, and this is generally a good assumption, because the ethics rules impose this burden upon them. However, in this chapter, we have seen that there are certain circumstances for which this premise may not be true. In these instances the client must be informed of the terms and consequences of the proposed arrangement in clear, easy-to-understand terms and must have the ability to consult with outside counsel for advice on those terms.

Summary

Provides a quick review of the key concepts covered in the chapter.

Key Terms and Concepts

Acquisition of clients	Legal documents
Attorney-client relationship	Management of the law practice
Fiduciary relationship	Multijurisdictional practice
Freelance paralegal	Negotiation and settlement
Gatekeeping function	Paralegal manager
Independent paralegals	Representation in court
Legal advice	Substantive legal tasks
Legal document preparer (LDP)	Unauthorized practice of law (UPL)

Key Terms and Concepts

Introduces students to basic legal terminology. Key terms are used throughout the chapters, defined in the margins, and listed at the end of each chapter. A common set of definitions is used consistently across the McGraw-Hill paralegal titles.

Review Questions

MULTIPLE CHOICE

Choose the best answer(s) and please explain WHY you choose the answer(s).

1. A frivolous claim
   a. extends or modifies existing law.
   b. is always permissible as a defense in a criminal case.
   c. is sanctionable unless supported by a belief that it is necessary.
   d. unduly burdens the process of litigation.
2. An attorney's ongoing duty of candor to the tribunal requires
   a. the attorney to submit all the case law found during his research process.
   b. the paralegal to call and update the court before trial if any facts change.
   c. the attorney to present only information which he reasonably believes to be true.
   d. All of the above
3. If an attorney wants to speak to a third-party witness, she must
   a. call him and identify himself as an attorney for the opposition.
   b. determine whether or not he is represented by counsel.
   c. subpoena the witness to testify.
   d. submit written interrogatories to opposing counsel.

EXPLAIN YOURSELF

All answers should be written in complete sentences. A simple yes or no is insufficient.

1. Explain an attorney's duty to reveal contrary legal authority to the court.
2. Why is it impermissible for an attorney to speak about a matter he is handling in public?
3. Describe the kind of courtroom behavior that would result in an ethical complaint against the attorney.
4. A frivolous claim is best described as . . . .

Review Questions and Exercises

Ask students to apply critical thinking skills to the concepts learned in each chapter and test the students' retention and understanding of the chapter materials.

Portfolio Assignments

Ask students to use the skills mastered in each chapter to reflect on major legal issues and create documents that become part of the paralegals' portfolios of legal research. The Portfolio Assignments are useful both as reference tools and as samples of work product.

PORTFOLIO ASSIGNMENT

Write Away

Compare the following scenarios and write a letter in response to each client. Assume you are a paralegal at a general practice firm and have been given three files to review:

- Client A is getting a divorce and his wife is trying to obtain sole custody of the children.
- Client B wishes to write her will.
- Client C is involved in a complex litigation that is currently in the discovery phase.

You have read all the relevant facts of these cases.

- Client A asks how many times women get custody of the children in these kinds of matters and what his chances are to obtain sole custody.
- Client B asks whether she can have her sister sign as a witness to the will and whether she should set up a trust for her children.
- Client C wants to know how much time is left for submitting answers to interrogatories served on him by the defendant and what his chances are at getting the counterclaim against him dismissed.

Case in Point

Exposes students to real-world examples and issues through a case chosen to expand on key topics discussed in the chapter. To demonstrate their understanding of the case, students should be asked to prepare a brief of the case.

CASE IN POINT

State Bar of Michigan
Standing Committee on Professional and Judicial Ethics
Opinion Number R-1
*1 December 16, 1988

SYLLABUS

A lawyer having direct supervisory authority over a nonlawyer shall make reasonable efforts to ensure that the person's conduct is compatible with the professional obligations of the lawyer.

A lawyer cannot adequately supervise the quality of legal services rendered by six civilian and eighteen prison paralegals to a prospective client population of 4,500 prisoners located in prisons throughout the State of Michigan, including the Upper Peninsula.

TEXT

The director of a legal services organization (LSO) is considering submitting a bid on a legal assistance program which the Michigan Department of Corrections may start pursuant to a recent federal court order. Under the program, LSO would provide assistance, not in-court representation, in post-conviction and conditions of confinement cases to prisoners at six locations in four Michigan prisons. The staff would consist of one lawyer/director, six civilian paralegals and eighteen prisoner paralegals. The duties of the lawyer/director would include the hiring, training and supervision of the six civilian and eighteen prisoner paralegals at six separate locations throughout the state. While the duties would include other aspects of administering the program, it is the hiring, training and necessary supervision of the paralegals which generate concern. The civilian paralegals would be entrusted with a variety of responsibilities which would include visiting and assisting prisoners in segregation units, responding in writing to requests for legal assistance and supervising an average of three prisoner paralegals and an unknown number of prisoner law library clerks. The prisoner paralegals would be entrusted with duties which would include providing legal research and drafting assistance to civilian paralegals and conducting conferences with prisoner clients.

Estimates of new caseloads range to 1,718 persons per year. Additionally, there are currently 226 open cases. Case estimates are difficult because, first, the prisoner population at any prison constantly changes, thus even though capacity for a given facility may be 500 prisoners, several thousand persons could pass through the facility each year. Second, the percentage of persons requesting assistance fluctuates depending on the quality and speed of the responses. The more efficient and better staffed the LSO becomes, the greater the number of requests.

May the lawyer/director of LSO ethically accept the responsibility of supervising 24 or more nonlawyers or any number of nonlawyers in so many locations? May civilian paralegals under the lawyer/director's control provide on-site supervision over the work of prisoner paralegals?

Any issue addressed relative to the activities of paralegals operating under the supervision of licensed lawyers must be viewed with *MRPC 5.3* and *5.5* in mind. *MRPC 5.5* forbids a lawyer from assisting a person who is not a member of the bar in the performance of activity that constitutes the unauthorized practice of law. The comment following *MRPC 5.5* specifies that paragraph (b) does not prohibit a lawyer from employing the services of paraprofessionals and delegating functions to them, so long as the lawyer supervises and retains responsibility for the delegated work.

What constitutes the unauthorized practice of law in a particular jurisdiction is a matter for determination by the courts of that jurisdiction. Questions of law are beyond the scope of the Committee's jurisdiction. The inquirer is referred to the following resources: *State Bar v Cramer*, 399 Mich 116 (1976); Vol 59 No 3 MBJ 173 (1980); Vol 62 No 8 MBJ 624 (1983); and Vol 56 No 8 MBJ 704 (1977).

MRPC 5.3 further defines and enhances the responsibility of the supervising lawyer by providing that not only does that lawyer have a responsibility not to aid in the unauthorized practice of law, but also must assure that the nonlawyer over whom he or she has direct supervisory authority does not engage in conduct incompatible with the professional obligations of the lawyer, or engage in conduct that would be a violation of the Michigan Rules of Professional Conduct if engaged in by a lawyer. The comment following *MRPC 5.3* notes that the measures employed in supervising nonlawyers should take account of the fact that they do not have legal training and are not subject to professional discipline. It also says a lawyer should give nonlawyers personal assistance, appropriate instruction, and supervision concerning the ethical aspects of their employment, particularly regarding the obligation not to disclose information relating to representation of the client, and that the lawyer should be responsible for the work product of the nonlawyer.

Given the parameters set forth in *MRPC 5.3* and *5.5*, for the lawyer/director to assume the responsibilities as outlined would be to invite a violation of *MRPC 5.5* and could lead to a violation of *MRPC 5.3*. While it appears as though the legal assistants under the terms of the plan described would not be expected to engage in the practice of law by making court appearances or providing actual, technical representation, there is a distinct possibility and, in all likelihood, a probability that they will be active in advising clients of their legal rights. The proposed legal assistance program will utilize the Technical Assistance Manual on Offender Legal Service prepared by the American Bar Association's Commission on Correctional Facilities and Services as a guide in delivering services. The

Brief Contents

Table of Contents

Part One

The Practice of Law

Chapter 1

Oversight: Regulation and Licensing of the Legal Profession

CHAPTER OBJECTIVES

The student will be able to:

- Compare the educational requirements for attorneys and paralegals
- Differentiate among the different types of regulatory plans for the paralegal profession and discuss the pros and cons of each
- Recognize the major associations related to the legal field and identify their mission and role in the paralegal profession
- Identify the various ethical sanctions that can be imposed upon attorneys and the conduct by either the attorney or the paralegal that would warrant those sanctions

This chapter will explore the formal educational requirements and regulations imposed upon the legal profession: WHO may call themselves attorneys or paralegals; WHAT steps they must fulfill to achieve that position; WHERE they may practice; and HOW they stay current in the field by taking continuing legal education and joining relevant legal organizations.

All professionals, those with education and/or experience in a certain field, are responsible to provide the public with the best services they can render. This duty may require compliance with formal guidelines or voluntary observance of standards of conduct. There are varying degrees of control exercised over a particular profession. The least constrictive are those professions in which a person may choose to become *registered*. The highest degree of control is exercised by a governmental body that issues *licenses* to perform certain services to the public. Between these two extremes lie *certified* professions. See Figure 1.1

FIGURE 1.1
Control of a Profession

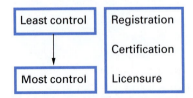

illustrating the relationship between these methods of control. The characteristics of both registration and licensure are blended in certification. The qualification is completely voluntary (like registration) but there are strict standards that must be complied with in order to use the designation (like licensure).

This text will speak to the generally accepted norms and guidelines regarding attorney and paralegal educational and practice standards across the nation. It will be up to the paralegal student to investigate the particulars of his individual state. This is an exciting time to be a paralegal. Students and professionals have the opportunity to be involved in the process of shaping the future of the paralegal profession, because it still is developing and growing. In order to be best armed for involvement in these issues, it is important for the student to understand the ethical and regulatory models that affect the practice of law for both paralegals and attorneys.

PARALEGALS

Education

There are currently no formal requirements for paralegal education. The local marketplace dictates the extent of education required by the candidate. Generally, the more metropolitan areas and the larger firms look for a four-year degree, while smaller firms may desire a two-year degree (in order to save costs in salary), and some firms are willing to train "in-house" without any formal coursework. Why this range in qualifications? The simple answer lies in the economics of supply and demand. The more qualified candidates there are in an area, the more an employer can demand from them. The best advice to a paralegal student? Know your market and pursue the appropriate level of education.

As a guide, both the American Bar Association (ABA) and the American Association for Paralegal Education (AAfPE) have set forth certain educational standards for paralegals. An institution's decision to comply with these standards and/or to apply for ABA approval is completely voluntary. Along with the ABA and the AAfPE, the International Paralegal Management Association (IPMA), formerly known as the Legal Assistant Management Association; the National Association of Legal Assistants (NALA); the National Federation of Paralegal Associations (NFPA); and the Association of Legal Administrators (ALA) have recognized that a quality paralegal education consists of at least 18 semester units of paralegal coursework, along with general education requirements earned from an educational institution accredited by a nationally recognized agency.

What is "paralegal coursework"? How does it differ from law school courses? Primarily, a paralegal's education focuses on gaining the **practical skills** needed to enter the workforce as a productive member of the legal team. Much of the coursework is "hands-on" and "how-to". Paralegals are taught not only the substantive and procedural law in various areas of practice, but also what to do with that information. Intricate theory is saved for in-depth law school courses. This is where the difference between law school and paralegal degree programs becomes clear. Many new lawyers enter the workforce, having passed multiple grueling exams, certain of their theoretical knowledge base, having no idea either how to prepare a legal document evidencing it or where to file it. The hours spent bent over a casebook deciphering court opinions and preparing for a day of Socratic interrogation does not prepare a law school graduate to fill out a HUD statement for a real estate closing. However, since most paralegal curricula do prepare those graduates to do just that, entry-level paralegals must hit the ground running.

practical skills
The ability to put theory into practice by performing the tasks necessary to achieve a desired result.

Regulatory Plans

Just as there are no formal educational requirements in place for paralegals, there is no mandatory authority regarding who may practice as a paralegal. There have been many attempts in the profession's history and in many parts of the country to somehow control the practice of paralegals. There are generally three means of monitoring and/or controlling a profession: (1) *public or private registration,* (2) *private regulation and certification,* and (3) *licensure.* The nomenclature is not nearly as important as the plan and method of controlling the profession, and it will vary from jurisdiction to jurisdiction. The processes may apply to either professionals at the entry level or those of advanced standing, or to both.

Registration

This is the least burdensome and least restrictive of the three main categories of oversight. Registration simply results in a list of persons who call themselves paralegals, and the list can be maintained by either a private or public entity. There are no requirements for being able to put your name on the list and registration is voluntary. If your name is not on the list, it has no impact on your right to practice as a paralegal.

Private Regulation and Certification

certification
The recognition of the attainment of a degree of academic and practical knowledge by a professional.

certificated
Describing a person who has completed a certain course of study and thus earned a certificate from the issuing institution.

First, the distinction between **certification** (or being certified) and being **certificated** must be made clear. Following a course of study may result in earning a certificate of completion from an entity. A person completing the requisites has become *certificated.* This is not the same as taking a comprehensive exam given by a private entity with the purpose of testing the candidate's knowledge base in a given area. Once the candidate has passed the exam, she is considered certified by that private entity. To put this in paralegal terms: there are many, many programs offered that will grant a certificate to a student after he has completed a set of courses; the student has earned a certificate of completion. However, there are only a few entities that sponsor a certification exam with an accompanying credentialing designation following the paralegal's name. The organizations that currently have certifications are NALA, NFPA, NALS (the Association for Legal Professionals) and AAPI (American Alliance of Paralegals, Inc). These certification designations include the following:

- NALA's Certified Legal Assistant/Certified Paralegal (*CLA/CP*) Exam and its newly introduced *APC* (Advanced Paralegal Certification)
- NFPA's *PACE* (Paralegal Advanced Competency Exam) permits those who pass to use the designation "RP", (Registered Paralegal)
- NALS's *ALS* (the basic exam for legal profesionals), *PLS* (the advanced certification for legal professionals) and *PPC* (professional paralegal certification)
- AAPI's *AACP* (American Alliance Certified Professional).

 CYBER TRIP

Please visit the following Web sites:

http://www.nala.org/cert.htm for more information about the Certified Legal Assistant/Paralegal Exam;

http://www.nala.org/APC.htm for more information on the Advanced Paralegal Certification;

http://www.paralegals.org/displaycommon.cfm?an=17 for more information about the Paralegal Advanced Competency Exam;

http://www.nals.org/certification/ALS/index.html for more information about NALS' (the National Association for Legal Professionals') basic certification;

http://www.nals.org/certification/PLS/index.html for more information about the advanced certification;

http://www.nals.org/certification/professionalparalegal for more information about the Professional Paralegal Certification; and

http://www.aapipara.org/Certification for more information about the American Alliance Certified Paralegal credentials.

The CLA/CP (Certified Legal Assistant/Certified Paralegal) Exam is an entry-level exam open to recent paralegal graduates that tests basic-level knowledge and skills, as well as particulars of legal specialties. NALA has recently adapted its advanced specialty exams to meet the needs of modern paralegals and reflect the trends in areas of legal specialty. An APC (Advanced Paralegal Certification) provides a curriculum-based measure of a paralegal's competency in a legal specialty. The APC is open only to paralegals already holding the CLA/CP designation. NFPA sponsors an advanced designation only. Those who pass the PACE exam are able to use the designation "RP" (Registered Paralegal), as the organization does not believe that an entry-level exam is necessary or beneficial to the profession. Its test is designed to test the competency level of *experienced* paralegals (two years' experience minimum) who have a certain level of education as well. To maintain the credential, the paralegal must also take continuing legal education courses.

NALS's exams are designed for both the entry-level and the advanced legal professional. The ALS and PLS are designed for any law office professional; it is not confined to paralegals. The tests are focused on law office procedures and general skills. This is where the PP (Professional Paralegal) differs greatly. This new test was created in 2004 and is targeted to the paralegal's knowledge base in substantive and procedural law and the skills to prepare substantive legal work products.

The AAPI exam is designed to credential the experienced paralegal (five years' experience minimum) with certain educational experience as well. The AACP exam requires continuing legal education and adherence to the AAPI Code of Professional Ethics.

The benefit to taking any one of these certification exams is the nationwide recognition of the standards. An employer has an idea of the incoming paralegal's knowledge base. In addition, although the contents of the exams vary, the common thread is the requirement of adherence to the ethical standards of the organization and the commitment to continuing legal education. See Figure 1.2 for NFPA's comparative chart of the major credentials offered by the various paralegal organizations. It can also be directly accessed at this Web address: http://www.paralegals.org/associations/2270/files/PACEComparisonChart.cfm.

NALS has a similar chart that can be accessed as follows: http://www.nals.org/certification/compchart.html.

Licensure

The most stringent of all the methods of oversight is **licensure**. Those professions that deal directly with the health, safety or welfare of the public are generally licensed. The system is designed to provide a safeguard to the public. In professions that are licensed, a governmental entity grants permission for certain persons to practice and use the name of the profession exclusively. Punishments for practicing without a license are also imposed under this scheme. Candidates for licensure must meet certain educational requirements, pass standardized tests and keep the license current. Each state, via its court system and/or bar association, maintains oversight of all licensed attorneys in its jurisdiction. Each state promulgates its own rules regarding all aspects of the practice of law, although most states have adopted or fashioned their codes on one or more of the ABA models. The ABA has promulgated several sets of models: the 1908 Canons, the 1964 Code, the 1977 Rules, and most recently, the "Ethics 2000" Recommendations and Rules. Territoriality reigns in the regulation of the practice of law; states are protective of their lawyers, and every state has particulars about education, admission to the bar, continuing legal education, and ethical review. There are many other licensed professions, but paralegal is not currently one of them.

licensure
The requirement of governmental approval before a person can practice a specific profession.

FIGURE 1.2   **NFPA's Comparison Chart for Paralegal Certifications**

Source: Reprinted by permission from The National Federation of Paralegal Associations, Inc., www.paralegals.org.

Note: NALS has a similar chart that can be accessed at http://www.nals.org/certification/compchart.html.

	Professional Paralegal (PP)-NALS	**PLS . . . the advanced certification for legal professionals (PLS)-NALS**	**Certified Legal Assistant (CLA) or Legal Paralegal (CP)-NALA**	**Paralegal Advanced Competency Exam (PACE)- Registered Paralegal (RP)**
Organization Established	1929, incorporated in 1949	1929, incorporated in 1949	1975	1974
Certification Established	2004	1960	1976	1996
Membership	5,000 individual members $100 new member7 ($90/yr after) $45 associate8 $19 student	5,000 individual members $100 new member7 ($90/yr after) $45 associate8 $19 student	6,000 individual members $99 new member-active2 $84 associate3 $40 student $50 sustaining4	15,000 (includes affiliate organizations, no information is available on individual members $70 new member (paralegal or paralegal supervisor) $60 associate5 $50 student $120 sustaining6
Number Certified	371 (eff 03/07)	5,430 (eff 03/07)	13,958 CLA (eff 02/07) 1,126 CLAS (advanced certification) (eff 02/07)	587 (eff 12/06)
Eligibility to Test Education and/or Employment	Five years' experience performing paralegal duties Partial waivers: 1. A two-year waiver for a candidate with a paralegal degree, or 2. A maximum one-year waiver for post-secondary degrees, successful completion of the PLS exam, or other certifications	Three years' experience in the legal field Partial waiver: A maximum one-year waiver for post-secondary degrees, successful completion of the ALS exam, or other certifications	1. Graduation from legal assistant program approved by ABA or associate degree program or postbaccalaureate certificate program in legal assistant studies, or bachelor's degree program in legal assistant studies, or legal assistant program of 60+ hours, 15 hours in substantive legal courses 2. Bachelor's degree in any field plus one year's experience as legal assistant (15 hours of substantive legal courses equivalent to one year's experience as legal assistant) 3. High school diploma or equivalent plus seven years' experience as	An associate's degree in paralegal studies obtained from an institutionally accredited and/ or ABA approved paralegal education program and six years' substantive paralegal experience; or bachelor's degree in any course of study obtained from an institutionally accredited school and three years of substantive paralegal experience; or bachelor's degree and completion of a paralegal program within an institutionally accredited school (which may be embodied in the bachelor's degree) and a minimum of two years'

Continued

FIGURE 1.2   NFPA's Comparison Chart for Paralegal Certifications *Continued*

	Professional Paralegal (PP)-NALS	PLS . . . the advanced certification for legal professionals (PLS)-NALS	Certified Legal Assistant (CLA) or Legal Paralegal (CP)-NALA	Paralegal Advanced Competency Exam (PACE)-Registered Paralegal (RP)
Eligibility to Test Education and/or Employment *Continued*			a legal assistant under supervision of attorney, plus minimum of 20 hours of CLE within two-year period prior to exam date	substantive paralegal experience; or four years' substantive paralegal experience completed on or before December 31, 2000
Examination Topics	Part 1 - Written Communications: Grammar and word usage, spelling, punctuation, number usage, capitalization, composition and expression Part 2 - Legal Knowledge and Skills: Legal research, citations, legal terminology, the court system and ADR, and the legal skills of interviewing clients and witnesses, planning and conducting investigations, and docketing Part 3 - Ethics and Judgment: Ethical situations involving contact with clients, the public, coworkers, and subordinates; other ethical considerations for the legal profession; decision making and analytical ability; and ability to recognize priorities Part 4 - All areas of substantive law, including administrative; business organizations and contracts; civil procedure and litigation; criminal; family; real property; torts; wills, trusts, and estates; admiralty and	Part 1 - Written Communications: Grammar and word usage, punctuation, number usage, capitalization, spelling, and composition and expression Part 2 - Office Procedures and Technology: records management, computer information systems, equipment/information services, office procedures and practices, office accounting Part 3 - Ethics and Judgment: Ethical situations involving contact with clients, the public, coworkers; ethical considerations for legal profession; decision-making and analytical ability; ability to recognize priorities Part 4 - Legal Knowledge and Skills: Legal knowledge of citations, legal research, and the ability to prepare legal documents based on oral instructions and materials; all areas of substantive law	Federal Law and Procedure: Major subject areas include communications, ethics, legal research, human relations and interviewing techniques, judgment and analytical ability, legal terminology. Section on Substantive Law includes five miniexaminations covering the American Legal System and four of the following areas: administrative law, bankruptcy, business, organizations/corporations, contracts, family law, criminal law and procedure, litigation, probate and estate planning, real estate	Domain I - Administration of client legal matters: conflict checks; developing, organizing and maintaining client files; developing and maintaining calendar/tickler systems; developing/maintaining databases; coordinating client services Domain II - Development of client legal matters: client interviews; analyzing information; collaborating with counsel; preparing, filing, and serving legal documents/exhibits; preparing clients/witnesses for legal proceedings Domain III - Factual/legal research: obtaining factual/legal information; investigating/compiling facts; inspecting/evaluating evidence; ascertaining/analyzing legal authority Domain IV - Factual/legal writing: communicating with client/counsel; drafting legal analytical documents Domain V - Office Administration: personnel management; acquiring technology; coordinating and utilizing

Continued

FIGURE 1.2   NFPA's Comparison Chart for Paralegal Certifications *Continued*

	Professional Paralegal (PP)-NALS	PLS . . . the advanced certification for legal professionals (PLS)-NALS	Certified Legal Assistant (CLA) or Legal Paralegal (CP)-NALA	Paralegal Advanced Competency Exam (PACE)-Registered Paralegal (RP)
Examination Topics *Continued*	maritime; antitrust; bankruptcy; environmental; federal civil rights and employment discrimination; immigration; intellectual property; labor; oil and gas; pension and profit sharing; taxation; water; workers' compensation			vendor services; creating and maintaining library of legal resources; developing/maintaining billing system (Ethics embedded throughout)
Length	One day	One day	Two days	Four hours - 200 questions
Sites	Nationally/most major cities	Nationally/most major cities	Nationally/most major cities	200+ Sylvan Learning Centers
Frequency	First Saturday in March Last Saturday in September (no waiting period to retest)	First Saturday in March Last Saturday in September (no waiting period to retest)	March April July December	Within 90 days of approval of application (six-month waiting period to retest)
Cost Member Nonmember	$200 (retake $50/section) $250 (retake $60/section) PLS Members Part 4: $150 (retake $50) PLS Nonmember Part 4: $200 (retake $60)	$150 (retake $40/section) $200 (retake $50/section)	$225 (retake $50/section) $250 (retake $50/section)	$225 (no section retake) $225 (no section retake)
Recertification Frequency	Every five years	Every five years	Every five years	Every two years
CLE Required	75 hours (five hours legal ethics)	75 hours	50 hours	12 hours (one hour legal ethics)
Topics	5 hours of ethics and 70 hours in substantive areas. Substantive areas should include those that reflect the substantive nature of a paralegal's work, enhance a paralegal's knowledge of the profession, update knowledge of the law, or relate to the	Education on PLS exam topics or teaching, lecturing, writing, earning college credit, earning other certifications	Legal assistant topics or teaching	Substantive law; specific nature of paralegal profession, i.e., computer skills, research techniques, management skills, etc.; ethics

Continued

FIGURE 1.2   NFPA's Comparison Chart for Paralegal Certifications *Continued*

	Professional Paralegal (PP)-NALS	PLS . . . the advanced certification for legal professionals (PLS)-NALS	Certified Legal Assistant (CLA) or legal Paralegal (CP)-NALA	Paralegal Advanced Competency Exam (PACE)-Registered Paralegal (RP)
Topics *Continued*	Professional Paralegal examination; including, but not limited to, procedural and communications skills, legal research and citations, and procedural and substantive law			
Costs	$75	$75	$50	$25 (if a topic is not pre-approved by NFPA, individual or speaker may request approval - $25 for a speaker or non-member; $10 for individual member)
American Council on Education College Credit for Certification	Application in process	Yes, up to 27 credits	None	None

Why are professions licensed? Why do states get involved in the livelihoods of their citizens? States are charged with protecting the welfare of all their citizens, and through licensing certain professions, a state can ensure competency levels in those professions. Additionally, the state can impose penalties on persons practicing without a license. How do states determine what professions they will license? A profession must come in contact with the public, and there must be a potential for harm to occur to the clients of that profession.

It is easy to see why doctors and lawyers are licensed professionals. Doctors hold people's health (sometimes life-or-death situations) in their hands; lawyers advise the public on matters that affect the legal rights associated with lives and property. What about other professions? Hairdressers and manicurists use volatile chemicals on their clients. Insurance salesmen and brokers deal with planning for the economic well-being of their clients. Nurses, members of a profession that supports doctors, must also be licensed, as they deal with public health issues daily. However, paralegals, members of a profession that supports attorneys, are not licensed—despite the fact that they also deal directly with the public.

The comparison between nurses and paralegals has been made often, and there are many similarities in their supportive roles. However, the licensing issue is the major difference between the two, and this issue has caused a great divide in the legal profession. The national paralegal organizations are not in agreement regarding the necessity for licensure. There are pros and cons to licensing and, so far, the cons are

FIGURE 1.3
The Positives and
Negatives of Licensure

Pro—Licensing Arguments	Con—Licensing Arguments
Standardization of educational requirements—all candidates would have to have similar degrees from approved programs	Barriers to entry-level paralegals: many paralegals are trained on the job, and forcing them to get a certain level of education in order to pass a licensure exam would deter some candidates from entering the field
Higher salaries for paralegals	Possible transfer of the cost of the salary increase to the client
Possibility for "independent paralegals" to provide a regulated set of services directly to the public	Limitations on the practice areas or tasks that paralegals could perform. Currently, lawyers may delegate a substantial amount of work without reference to a prescribed set of tasks allowed under regulations.
Recognition of the professional status of the paralegal profession in the eyes of both attorneys and the public	Practical difficulties in creating and administering a licensing board
"Quality control" by ensuring both mandates for continuing legal education and sanctions for malpractice and/or ethical violations Control over who may use the title of "paralegal"	Unnecessary control over an already regulated area; lawyers have discretion and first-hand knowledge as to what their paralegals are capable of doing. The use of the title has little impact on who is performing the work and who may engage in the unauthorized practice of law.

winning. This is evidenced by the fact that no state has enacted a licensing scheme, although a few have some regulations regarding the practice.

The primary argument against licensing is found in the generally accepted definition of a paralegal: a professional who works **under the supervision of an attorney** performing substantive legal work. The opponents of licensing advocate that the rules in place for attorneys satisfactorily regulate the paralegals working under their supervision.

The primary argument for licensing is found in the primary reason for the creation of the profession: an economically feasible legal profession that could provide **access to justice**. Please visit http://www.atjsupport.org/ for more information. A licensed paralegal can perform many of the tasks that would otherwise be performed by a more expensive attorney.

Further arguments on both sides are set forth in Figure 1.3. There are national organizations on both sides of the issue. Their positions will be discussed in the section below dealing with them.

Individual State Regulation

It is each state's prerogative to regulate the practice of any profession within its borders. The practice of law is no exception. The following states have taken "official" positions by specifically addressing the issue of paralegal regulation. This list is not all-inclusive, because the trend towards some sort of state oversight is continuing to grow and interest in it has experienced significant growth in recent years. By presenting this variety of regulatory schemes, the paralegal student can appreciate the dynamic nature of the profession and its recognition.

Arizona

While it does not have a paralegal regulatory scheme per se, Arizona has enacted a statute defining and certifying "legal document preparers" (LDPs). These legal document preparers must meet certain educational and practice requirements, one of which may be to hold a paralegal degree, and the candidate must pass a test administered by the

under the supervision of an attorney
A term used to describe the work of a paralegal, which must be assigned, reviewed and approved by a responsible attorney who takes responsibility for the content of the work.

access to justice
The full opportunity of all persons to use all the legal resources available to the public, without regard for their ability to pay or knowledge of the legal system or experience in dealing with lawyers.

court. LDPs may provide general legal information and assist in filling out the appropriate forms and documentation where the party is not represented by an attorney. An LDP assists in assuring that all the documents are filled out properly and completely. Under no circumstances can the legal document preparer give specific legal advice or render an opinion or recommendation "about possible legal rights, remedies, defenses, options or strategies." The LDP is subject to sanctions and ethical codes of conduct, including mandatory continuing legal education. This kind of oversight is substantially similar to the kind espoused by the proponents of paralegal licensing. The main difference is that LDPs do not work under the supervision of an attorney, and therefore, the main argument against paralegal licensing—the fact that they are properly supervised and the public is satisfactorily protected—does not apply to LDPs.

California

Preceding the statute enactment in Arizona, California pioneered the similar concept of Legal Document Preparers. These professionals, as noted above, assist with routine legal tasks, such as typing and filing the paperwork for uncontested divorces, bankruptcies, wills, and similar basic documents. *See* California Business & Professions Code § 6400.

California further regulates the practice of nonlawyers by setting legislative standards to define a "paralegal" as a person

> *who either contracts with or is employed by an attorney, law firm, corporation, governmental agency or other entity and who performs substantive legal work under the direction and supervision of an active member of the State Bar of California. . . . Tasks performed by a paralegal include, but are not limited to, case planning, development, and management; legal research; interviewing clients; fact gathering and retrieving information; drafting and analyzing legal documents; collecting, compiling, and utilizing technical information to make an independent decision and recommendation to the supervising attorney; and representing clients before a state or federal administrative agency if that representation is permitted by statute, court rule, or administrative rule or regulation.*

Id. at § 6450.

This legislation is in addition to, and clearly defines, the differences between California's "Legal Document Preparers." The state also sets minimal educational requirements for entry into the paralegal field, as well as continuing legal educational requirements, including ethical study. Perhaps most significant is the prohibition of anyone who is not directly supervised by an attorney from presenting herself as a paralegal. California paralegals are prohibited from being employed directly by consumers; *see id.* § 6451. Persons doing so can be found guilty of an infraction or misdemeanor punishable by fines starting at $2,500 and possible imprisonment for up to one year. *See id.* § 6455.

Florida

One of the most recent examinations of the necessity of a "regulatory" scheme has occurred in Florida. In the summer of 2005, the Bar appointed a committee to study the possible regulation of the profession. In November 2007 the Supreme Court of Florida approved the Amendments to the Rules Regulating the Florida Bar and instituted the Florida Registered Paralegal Program. This is a voluntary credentialing system that requires certain educational requirements and entrance exam requirements. The Florida Registered Paralegal designation can be acquired in one of three ways:

1. Through education and experience:
   a. A bachelor's degree in paralegal studies from an approved paralegal program and a minimum of 1 year of paralegal work;
   b. A bachelor's degree in any field from an accredited institution and a minimum of 3 years of paralegal work;
   c. An associate's degree in paralegal studies from an approved paralegal program and 2 years of paralegal work;

    d. An associate's degree in any field from an accredited institution and a minimum of 4 years of paralegal work;

    e. A Juris doctorate degree from an ABA accredited school plus a minimum of 1 year of paralegal work.

2. By obtaining a National Certification either from NFPA or NALA.

3. Through grandfathering by working 5 out of the last 8 years as a paralegal proven by an attestation of their supervising attorney.

The full text of the new rules can be accessed through the Web site: http://www.floridabar.org/TFB/TFBResources.nsf/Attachments/43709F4CEB5E4B9E85257155005CEBE1/$FILE/Ch%2020%20Paralegal%20Rule.pdf?OpenElement

New Jersey

Many years earlier, in 1992, the Supreme Court of New Jersey's Committee on the Unauthorized Practice of Law rendered Opinion 24, which examined the role of paralegals in the delivery of legal services. The Committee ultimately recommended that paralegals should be licensed and function under the direction of the New Jersey Supreme Court. In essence, the Committee suggested that paralegals should be treated in much the same way as attorneys. Opinion 24 was then studied for many years, and in 1999, the New Jersey Supreme Court decided against such a licensure scheme. "The Court has concluded that paralegal oversight is best conducted by the supervising attorneys who are responsible for all legal work done by paralegals." (N.J. Sup. Ct. C'tee on Paralegal Education and Regulation, Admin. Determinations Report, May 18, 1999).

North Carolina

North Carolina has taken an intermediate position with regard to the control of the profession. North Carolina, through the Bar Association and approval of the North Carolina Supreme Court in 2004, has adopted "voluntary certification." A paralegal who has graduated from a qualified paralegal program can apply to the State Bar in order to become a "N.C. Certified Paralegal." This program sets minimum educational standards and mandates continuing legal education for paralegals applying for the designation. Candidates must also sit for an exam administered by the State Bar. For the first two years after enactment, the Bar has provided an alternate way to apply for the certification; this second option requires a certain amount of work experience. Minimally, an applicant taking the alternate route must possess at least two thousand hours of experience working as a paralegal in North Carolina. These are recent enactments, and therefore, there was a need to implement this "grandfathering" clause whereby experienced paralegals could have the requirements waived and still qualify to use the certification designation. Of course, the exact details can be found on the N.C. Bar's Web site.

Ohio

Ohio has adopted a Bar Certification for Paralegals very similar to the North Carolina model, although it permits paralegals who do not have formal education in paralegal studies to apply, and there is no exam. The Ohio State Bar has the power to grant (or revoke) the "OSBA Certified Paralegal" credential. There are different work experience requirements that are dependant on the type of degree earned. Both a post-baccalaureate certificate of at least 20 semester hours and a baccalaureate degree in paralegal studies require one full year of full-time experience as a practicing paralegal, while an associate's degree in paralegal studies of at least 60 semester hours requires a minimum of five years of full-time experience. Any practicing paralegal without a higher degree in paralegal studies must have seven years of full-time experience accrued after December 31, 2006, in order to apply for this credential.

South Dakota

South Dakota has a similar statutory approach to those of Arizona and California. It provides oversight to the profession by defining a "paralegal" as a person having a certain education, working under an attorney, and committed to continuing legal education. There is some variation in the actual technical requirements; however, the spirit remains the same as that of the two other states.

Wisconsin

Before the Court of Wisconsin is the Final Report of the Paralegal Practice Task Force recommending and setting forth a true licensure scheme for paralegals. The proposal mirrors the general requirements for other paralegals under alternate schemes, in that it imposes minimum educational requirements, ethical obligations, employment by a supervising attorney, and mandatory continuing education. The main difference in licensure is the risk and responsibility that goes along with holding a license. Certain actions (crimes of moral turpitude, criminal activities, malpractice, etc.) can result in revocation of the license and, therefore, the elimination of a career path.

CYBER TRIP

There are many states that have considered or are currently considering a definition for paralegals or related professions, and/or regulation of the paralegal profession. A list of links for each state can be found in Appendix A. The links for the states referenced in this section are listed here:

Arizona:
http://www.supreme.state.az.us/cld/LDP.htm

California:
http://calbar.ca.gov/state/calbar/calbar_generic.jsp?cid=10157&id=1245

New Jersey:
A direct link to the New Jersey Supreme Court Committee on Paralegal Education and Regulation, Administrative Determinations Report: http://www.judiciary.state.nj.us/pressrel/admpara.htm

North Carolina:
http://www.nccertifiedparalegal.org/

Ohio:
http://www.ohiobar.org/pub/?articleid=785

Wisconsin:
Final Report of the Paralegal Practice Task Force:
http://www.wisbar.org/AM/Template.cfm?Section=Research_and_Reports&TEMPLATE=/CM/ContentDisplay.cfm&CONTENTID=50550

For general information on Legal Document Preparers, please visit the National Association of Legal Document Preparers at

http://www.naldp.org

To access your particular state's materials, remember to use the "McGraw-Hill State-Specific Paralegal Portal" at

www.mhhe.com/paralegalportal

From these examples, it is clear that individual states are taking or are contemplating one of these four methods of oversight: (1) no formal oversight procedures for paralegals; rather, leaving the oversight to the employing attorney; (2) statutory definitions, with prohibitions and penalties against others not holding these credentials but using the title "paralegal"; (3) court-supervised certification or registration; and (4) true licensure, mandated and implemented by the highest court of the state. Notably, no state has

IN CLASS DISCUSSION

States are considering four methods of paralegal oversight: (1) no formal oversight procedures for paralegals; rather, leaving the oversight to the employing attorney; (2) statutory definitions, with prohibitions and penalties against others not holding these credentials but using the title "paralegal"; (3) court-supervised certification or registration; and (4) true licensure, mandated and implemented by the highest court of the state.

Which state regulatory scheme do you most strongly prefer? Why? What implications does this have for the paralegal profession?

taken this last step as of yet to enact a true mandatory licensure scheme, such as the one in place in every state for the oversight of attorneys. To track an individual state's development in this area, the student should consult his state bar and local paralegal association Web sites. A list of these sites is supplied in Appendix A.

National and Local Organizations

As the profession is leaving its infancy, it seems that as an adolescent, it is searching for more independence and recognition of its individuality. But like any teenager, the profession is not quite sure which way is the best to develop. This angst is reflected in the above discussion regarding regulation, and the dilemma is further complicated by the fact that there is not a single uniform governing body for the paralegal profession. There are many diverse paralegal associations, and they each seem to have a slightly different position with regard to the development of the profession. There are currently seven national associations that address the paralegal profession:

ABA: The American Bar Association is the national voluntary bar association for attorneys. The ABA serves its members by providing accreditation of law schools, approval procedures for paralegal programs in higher education, and continuing legal education for the legal community; providing both the legal community and the general population with information about the law; and developing initiatives to improve the legal system for the public.

NALA: The National Association of Legal Assistants has a membership of over 18,000 paralegals. Members can have direct membership in the national association or through its 90 state and local affiliated associations. NALA endorses the proper utilization of paralegals in the law office and delivery of high-quality legal services. NALA promotes standards of excellence in paralegal education, training and experience, and ethical responsibility.

NFPA: The National Federation of Paralegal Associations is composed of more than 60 local and state paralegal associations, as well as individual members to total more than 15,000 paralegal professionals. The goals of the association include promoting the profession, providing leadership, exchanging and disseminating information, and maintaining ethical and educational standards.

AafPE: The American Association for Paralegal Education recognizes the need to increase and improve access to the legal system by promoting the highest educational standards for paralegals. To this end, the association encourages professional improvement for paralegal educators, and in collaboration with other paralegal associations, promotes professional growth in order to prepare graduates to perform significant roles in the legal community.

NALS: The Association for Legal Professionals (formerly the National Association of Legal Secretaries) stresses continuing education and offers certifications, information, and training to those choosing any of the occupations in the legal services field. NALS members represent a broad spectrum of legal practice, and the association offers expertise to make the programs offered valuable to all members of the legal community.

IPMA (formerly LAMA): The International Paralegal Management Association (formerly Legal Assistant Management Association) "promotes the development, professional standing and visibility of paralegal management professionals." IPMA advocates, through a strong communication network, the paralegal manager's viewpoint and the vital role that this individual plays in the delivery of legal services.

AAPI: The American Alliance of Paralegals focuses on the individual paralegal by establishing minimum educational criteria and ethical standards, providing networking opportunities, and serving as a resource center for its members.

SURF'S UP

Find the Web sites for all the previous paralegal associations. With which position statement do you most agree? Why? Try to locate your local paralegal association on the Web. Is it associated with any of the national organizations? Does it have student memberships available?

Each state has at least one paralegal association for members practicing in that state, and some large urban states have several. Many of these associations are local chapters of either NFPA or NALA. The above list includes only the major national associations, and is not conclusive or definitive in its scope. As a paralegal student, it is important that you explore the resources available to you in your own locality.

The diversity can either be a blessing or a curse. With no unified body, there can be no consensus as to the educational standards, ethical duties, and responsibilities of the position. Indeed, the very definition of "paralegal" remains unsettled. On the other hand, diversity can be celebrated; as the profession is still growing, it helps to have many viewpoints, in order to ensure that the very best of each can be incorporated into the perception of a paralegal. Similar to the "free marketplace of ideas" that founded our nation, the free marketplace of paralegalism may shape the profession for the better.

LAWYERS

The paralegal student will notice a difference between the educational requirements for an attorney and those for a practicing paralegal. This is due primarily to the great disparity in length of history between the two professions. Attorneys have been around for centuries, whereas the paralegal profession is relatively new. The legal profession has had a very long time to develop, hone, and implement the regulations imposed upon attorneys.

Education

In order to become an attorney, a person must meet the following educational criteria:

1. Graduate with a bachelor's degree from a four-year accredited college or university. There is no requirement that a student take any particular course of study. Students from many diverse backgrounds apply to and become successful in law school. The important factor is the development of good writing, comprehension, and analytical skills.

REEL TO REAL

The Paper Chase (1973) revolves around a Harvard Law School first-year student's struggle to keep up with the demands of law school, with its tyrannical professors and intense competition, while still maintaining a life. The main character, Hart, begins to question whether he really wants to enter such a high-demand profession. This film portrays the law school ordeal with honesty and accuracy. What do you think of this somewhat cruel process? Does it adequately prepare law students to enter the practice with the aggressiveness needed—or does it simply foster and perpetuate the hostility in our adversarial system?

Compare Hart to the main character, Elle Woods, in *Legally Blonde* (a little bit of a stretch, since the genres are completely opposite). Which student handles law school better? Which one, do you think, is more prepared to enter the legal profession?

2. Take the LSAT (Law School Admission Test), a standardized test used by all ABA (American Bar Association)–approved schools to assess potential candidates for admission. The test measures comprehension and analytical reading and writing skills. Successful results on the test do not guarantee admission into law school, as the schools use many other criteria for assessing the potential of the applicants.

3. Graduate from an ABA-accredited law school. Law school is a three-year, full-time (four-year part-time) endeavor (although some may describe it as an ordeal). The standard curriculum for law school includes courses in contracts, constitutional law, torts, property, professional responsibility, legal research and writing, civil procedure, evidence, family law, wills and estates, tax, business organizations, criminal law and procedure, and various electives.

Sitting for the Bar

After all of this academic rigor, the journey is still not over. The J.D. (Juris Doctor) degree does not qualify a person to practice law. More steps still lie ahead. The potential attorney must also do these things:

4. Apply to the state board of bar examiners in each jurisdiction in which she would like to take the bar exam. This often involves a lengthy written application requiring substantial personal history and letters of recommendation. The board may choose to accept or deny this application to take the bar exam.

5. Take and pass the state bar exam(s) of choice. A candidate may usually sit for two "bars," if he so chooses, within the prescribed test dates. Each state requires two days of examination: one day for writing essays and answering practical assignments specific to that state, and one day for the multistate multiple-choice exam.

Character and Fitness

6. Take and pass the MPRE (Multistate Professional Responsibility Exam). This exam is required in all but three jurisdictions in the United States. The purpose of the MPRE is to evaluate the candidate's understanding of the ABA Model Rules. The test requires application of all the rules to factual situations; the candidate must determine if an ethical violation has occurred and what the ramifications might be.

7. Perform other requirements, which may include undergoing a character and fitness personal interview and a background check. These requirements examine

the candidate's record for evidence indicating that the potential attorney is an upstanding citizen and making a positive contribution to society.

8. Be sworn in before a judge or other designated official and promise to uphold the Constitution and all applicable laws.

Continuing Legal Education

Even after these two significant hurdles have been overcome, the work of an attorney is still not complete. The now-admitted attorney must also

9. Attend the required CLE (Continuing Legal Education) courses as prescribed by the relevant state judiciary. Generally, this entails more extensive hours for newly admitted attorneys—on average, about 36 hours over a three-year period.

RESEARCH THIS

Find your state bar board of examiners' Web site and find the specific requirements with regard to steps 4-9 above, relating to the application to attain and maintain bar membership.

Ethical Review Boards

After an attorney has navigated this course, she still must bear all the rules in mind in every task she performs, in order to protect her clients' interests and maintain professional integrity. Every ethical board, however designated and controlled by the individual state, is able to hear complaints by persons affected by an attorney's unethical conduct. It is important to note that the grievance procedure does not give a complainant financial compensation for any potential loss. This is due to two factors: (1) the complainant generally does not have to prove any financial harm in order to bring a grievance against an attorney, and (2) the complainant has recourse to the courts for any harm incurred due to the attorney's misconduct as a malpractice claim.

Sanction Powers

If an attorney has been found to have committed a breach of the ethical code of conduct, the review board recommends the appropriate discipline to the state court for action. All of these actions, or **ethical sanctions**, are kept on the attorney's record. In order from least severe to most severe, an attorney can be disciplined in the following ways:

1. **Private reprimand**. A letter from the court is sent to the attorney admonishing him for the inappropriate conduct. In some jurisdictions the term "censure" is used in place of "reprimand." Habitual violations or repeat offenses of behavior that would normally result in a private reprimand may cause the discipline to escalate to a public reprimand or probation. *See Florida Bar v. Walker,* 2003 WL 23112702, 3 (SCTFL) ("This incident, standing alone, would probably merit an admonishment or private reprimand. It is only because the new violations occurred so soon after the initial reprimand and for similar conduct that a suspension is appropriate.")

2. **Public reprimand**. A notice, including the attorney's name and reason(s) for discipline, is posted in the appropriate forum, usually the legal newspaper. A common violation resulting in public reprimand is associated with lawyer advertising.

ethical sanctions
Methods of disciplining attorneys who commit a breach of the ethical code of conduct.

private reprimand
The minimum censure for an attorney who commits an ethical violation; the attorney is informed privately about a potential violation, but no official entry is made.

public reprimand
A published censure of an attorney for an ethical violation.

What constitutes "misleading" advertisements will be discussed later, in chapter 6; suffice it to say that attorneys do or should know where to draw the line. This is the reason they are censured more harshly and publicly for such a transgression. All of the following state ethics opinions resulted in public reprimands for the advertising conduct specified. *See, e.g.,* S.C. Adv. Op. 84–06, 1984 WL 272918 (S.C.Bar.Eth.Adv.Comm.) ("A lawyer should not participate in an attorney referral service established by a profitmaking organization that has not been approved by either the ABA or the local bar association in the geographic area served by the referral service."); OH Adv. Op. 2003–2, 2003 WL 1948000 (Ohio Bd.Com.Griev.Disp.) ("A law firm is not permitted to provide statistics as to the number of intellectual property matters won, lost, and settled by the law firm as it is considered both 'misleading and self-laudatory.'"); OH Adv. Op. 98–9, 1998 WL 312397 (Ohio Bd.Com.Griev.Disp.) ("A lawyer who advertises regarding contingent fees has an obligation under the rule to advise the public that contingent fee clients are responsible for costs and expenses of litigation and to disclose whether percentages are computed before or after deduction of costs and expenses.").

probation

A court-imposed criminal sentence that, subject to stated conditions, releases a convicted person into the community instead of sending the criminal to prison. Or, in the case of discipline of an attorney for unethical conduct, the monitoring of an attorney's conduct for compliance with ethical rules, sometimes accompanied by additional requirements.

3. **Probation.** For a prescribed period of time the attorney's actions and office procedures can be monitored for compliance with the ethical rules. The court (or other relevant disciplinary body) may also add any terms of probation as may be necessary to ensure ethical compliance. The Supreme Court of Florida sanctioned an attorney for mismanagement of his firm, including permitting a disbarred attorney under his supervision, who was operating in the capacity of a paralegal, to have direct contact with clients. The attorney was placed on probation and was compelled to attend ethics education courses from the state bar and to file quarterly reports establishing that he had not split any fees with his "paralegal" former lawyer. *See* 2003 WL 23112685 (SCTFL).

suspension

The prohibition of an attorney from practicing law for a specified period of time.

4. **Suspension.** An attorney can be prohibited from practicing law for a specified period of time. This suspension includes a prohibition against performing any legal work, even without receiving compensation. Additionally, the suspended attorney cannot hold herself out as an attorney during that time. The case law suggests that the potential for harm and breach of trust is a driving factor in dispensing this type of sanction. Two common bases for suspension are sexual relationships with clients and neglect of cases—sins of commission and omission, respectively.

> *The act of commission, sexual involvement with a client, warrants suspension because it is a violation of the attorney's fiduciary duty to take advantage of the potentially vulnerable position of the client and could compromise the independent judgment of the attorney with respect to the case.* See, e.g., *PA Eth. Op. 97–100, 1997 WL 671579 (Pa. Bar. Assn. Comm. Leg. Eth. Prof. Resp.); OK Adv. Op. 311, 1998 WL 808034 (Okl. Bar. Assn. Leg. Eth. Comm.); OR Eth. Op. 1991–99, 1991 WL 279201 (Or. St. Bar. Assn.).*
>
> *The act of omission, neglect of case, has the potential for harm and prejudice to the client in that the entire matter may be lost due to failure to prosecute or running of the Statute of Limitations. "The failure of an attorney to pursue representation on behalf of a client resulting in prejudice to a client's rights is an intolerable breach of trust."* Florida Bar v. Dabold, *2003 WL 23112705, 3 (SCTFL), citing* Florida Bar v. Morrison, *669 So. 2d 1040, 1042 (Fla. 1996).*

disbarment

Temporary suspension or permanent revocation of an individual's license to practice law.

5. **Disbarment.** An attorney's license can be revoked, and he will be permanently prohibited from practicing law in that state. The decision of the board or committee can provide for reinstatement after a period of time, upon application of the disbarred attorney supported by good cause.

While attorney advertising seems to fall under one of the least onerous punishments, prohibited in-person solicitation can and will result in disbarment. This "ambulance chasing" is considered horrific for two reasons: (1) it takes advantage of accident victims soon after their injuries, which "presents an opportunity for fraud, undue influence, intimidation, overreaching, and other forms of vexatious conduct." *In the Matter of Pajerowski,* 156 N.J. 509, 520, 721 A.2d 992, 998 (1998). (2) "It is a practice that tends to corrupt the course of justice, and so the more abominable and evil in its incidence." *In re Frankel,* 20 N.J. 588, 598 120 A.2d 603, 613 (1955).

The second and virtually guaranteed way to disbarment is misappropriation of client funds. There is a "zero-tolerance policy" with regard to the intentional misuse of client money and/or property. The violation does not have to actually cause harm to the client, nor does it have to financially benefit the attorney, to be a sanctionable offense.

These are only some of the kinds of ethical violations that will result in these various sanctions. The courts will take every violation seriously and conduct an investigation in order to determine the proper form of discipline to be imposed. There are many interesting situations that do not appear to be a direct breach of the ethical code's language, but have resulted in sometimes severe penalties. The courts keep three goals in mind when determining the degree of sanction to be imposed: (1) fairness to the client and society, (2) fairness to the attorney, and (3) the deterrent effect of the punishment on others. The client and society must feel redressed for the wrongdoing; the attorney must be punished in proportion to the offense; and the punishment must serve as a disincentive to other attorneys, so that they will not be tempted to engage in that type of violation.

Further, the courts will punish a lawyer for any criminal conduct; this should be relatively obvious. However, note that the judicial sanctioning is in addition to the criminal prosecution. Further, any allegation involving **moral turpitude** is taken very seriously. Moral turpitude has been defined as any conduct that reflects unfavorably upon the attorney's character—his honesty, integrity, and fitness to serve as an officer of the court. Essentially, this is the same examination for character and fitness that a candidate to the bar must pass. This is the way that the judiciary can maintain the character standards once the attorney has been admitted to practice.

The guilt of the attorney is not retried in the disciplinary proceeding. The finding of the trial court will be considered conclusive evidence that the attorney committed the conduct in question. *In re Rosen,* 88 N.J. 1, 438 A.2d 316 (1981). Conduct that is in contravention of any law is considered a sanctionable offense, as the lawyer has been sworn to uphold the rule of law. This can range from the most flagrant offenses to more minor infractions. For example, a lawyer found to have committed vehicular homicide while intoxicated will not only be punished through the criminal justice system, but also be sanctioned by the court.

Having read all this, it is a wonder that anyone goes through this Dantian[1] descent into these levels of Hell (herein referred to as the steps to obtain and maintain a license to practice law). It also should make the paralegal student re-evaluate the common misconceptions about the number of unethical lawyers. The

moral turpitude
An act or behavior that gravely violates the sentiment or accepted standard of the community.

---

[1]Dante Aligheri's *"Inferno"* (part of *"The Divine Comedy"*) is an epic poem written between 1308 and 1321 and is considered one of the greatest in world literature. The *"Inferno"* describes a journey of descent further into each level of hell. Dante describes eight levels, each more horrific than the next until finally reaching the ninth level where Satan resides. The poem describes in great detail the unfortunate occupants of each level and what sins and crimes they committed in their lives to deserve their eternal punishments.

SPOT THE ISSUE

Larry has been a practicing attorney, duly licensed in the state for 40 years. He has an ongoing business relationship with another attorney, Ruth; they mutually refer clients to each other. Larry practices only workers' compensation law, and Ruth only wills and estates law, and they share a portion of their fees with each other. Ruth was indicted under a federal fraud charge and was disbarred from practice in the state; however, Ruth continued to refer clients to Larry and Larry continued to pay a portion of the fee collected to Ruth for her referral.

Should Larry be sanctioned for his actions? Why? To what degree? Does the court have this power? Under what premise?

For a hint, *see In re Discipio,* 163, Ill.2d 515, 645 N.E.2d 906 (1995).

old adage "It only takes one rotten apple to spoil the bunch" is particularly true in the legal profession. Only a small percentage (generally 0.5% nationwide) of practicing lawyers are disciplined each year; most lawyers understand the serious ramifications of violating the rules of ethics.

Since paralegals do not hold a license to practice, they are not subject to the same disciplinary procedures and effectively forced out of practice. However, any paralegal that holds one of the national certifications can lose his membership status and right to use the corresponding credential. Further, serious infractions of professional responsibilities may subject the paralegal to civil or criminal liability. This will be discussed in further detail later in the text.

CONTINUING LEGAL EDUCATION

Professional paralegals and students should understand the importance of continuing legal education (CLE). Just as attorneys must strive to stay up to date in their practice areas, so should the paralegals upon whom the attorneys depend. A paralegal's education does not end after graduation from college or a certificate program, but continues throughout her career. While every day on the job is a learning experience, seminars, online programs, and conferences present the opportunity to expand a paralegal's knowledge and skill base. By participating in continuing legal education, these professionals can both ensure that they are performing to the highest degree of competence and enhance their careers. Both NALA and NFPA have endorsed this ideal in their respective guidelines and rules, as shown in Figure 1.4. (For the full text of NALA and NFPA guidelines, see Appendix C and Appendix D, respectively.)

There are numerous organizations offering CLE. Many state bars offer seminars just for paralegals, and the national and regional paralegal organizations not only

FIGURE 1.4
Continuing Legal Education Requirements of NALA and NFPA

NALA Guideline 4

In the supervision of a legal assistant, consideration should be given to:
   4. Providing continuing education for the legal assistant in substantive matters through courses, institutes, workshops, seminars and in-house training.

NFPA Ethical Considerations

   EC 1.1(b) A paralegal shall aspire to participate in a minimum of twelve (12) hours of continuing education, to include at least one (1) hour of ethics education, every two (2) years in order to remain current on developments in the law.

CYBER TRIP

A general Internet search reveals a host of opportunities for paralegal CLE. For more information, see the following:

Loman Education at http://www.lorman.com/paralegal.php

The National Business Institute at http://www.nbi-sems.com/instituteforparalegaleducation.html

Estrin Legal Education at http://www.estrinlegaled.com

The Washington Online Learning Institute at http://www.woli.com/?trackcode=bizcom

The Center for Advanced Legal Studies at http://www.paralegal.edu/about.html

The Center for Legal Studies at http://www.legalstudies.com/courses/clecourses.html

The Advanced Paralegal Education Group at http://www.apeglegal.com/

This list is just a sampling; there are many offered in each state as well.

offer their own CLE courses, but also refer to independent CLE conference providers that are approved to provide CLE credits. These various organizations provide a diverse array of topics for paralegals at any stage of their careers. Further, many colleges that offer undergraduate or certificate programs also offer CLE courses so that their graduates and other local professionals can further their careers. With the plethora of opportunities to take CLE courses, a paralegal who calls himself a professional would be remiss not to take advantage of them. Moreover, any paralegal holding a certification may be stripped of that designation for failure to comply with that organization's continuing legal education requirement.

Summary

The paralegal profession does not impose any mandatory, formal educational requirements in order to call oneself a "paralegal." Depending on the geographical and economical factors, a firm or practitioner may require either a bachelor's or an associate's degree, or may be willing to train "in-house." Both the ABA and the AAfPE have set forth the minimum educational requirements for an "approved" paralegal program. Additionally, all the national paralegal associations have taken positions with regard to the knowledge and skills required by a practicing paralegal. Many of these associations have certification credentials that paralegals may earn in order to demonstrate their proficiency in the profession. Moreover, many states and some paralegal associations have considered the pros and cons of the three main kinds of oversight mechanisms:

1. public or private registration
2. private regulation and certification
3. licensure

In an effort to protect the public, the practice of law by attorneys is governed by the court system and/or bar in their jurisdiction. Attorneys must satisfy several qualifying criteria before they are permitted to practice:

1. graduate with a four-year degree from an accredited institution
2. score well on the LSAT
3. graduate with a J.D. degree from an ABA-accredited law school

4. apply to take the state bar exam

5. pass the state bar exam

6. pass the MPRE (Multistate Professional Responsible Exam)

7. perform any other relevant character and fitness reviews in the jurisdiction

8. take the oath

9. attend mandatory CLE sessions

Any violations of the ethical codes applicable to the practicing attorney may result in the imposition of sanctions, which may be any of the following:

1. private reprimand

2. public reprimand

3. probation

4. suspension

5. disbarment

Although only attorneys may be sanctioned by an ethical board, both attorneys and paralegals may be subject to criminal or civil suits for their conduct. Further, paralegals who are certified by an association may lose their membership and forfeit their credential.

Key Terms and Concepts

Access to justice
Certificated
Certification
Disbarment
Ethical sanctions
Licensure
Moral turpitude

Practical skills
Private reprimand
Probation
Public reprimand
Suspension
Under the supervision of an attorney

Review Questions

MULTIPLE CHOICE

Choose the best answer(s) and please explain WHY you choose the answer(s).

1. Licensure schemes are designed to
   a. Collect fees from members
   b. Protect the public from criminals pretending to be something they are not
   c. Ensure that the professionals have and maintain a certain level of education and knowledge about their profession
   d. Permit members to use certain credentials after their names

2. The primary reason for the development of the paralegal profession was
   a. That attorneys have too much work to do
   b. To provide low-income citizens with legal services
   c. To increase the salaries of all members of the law office
   d. To enforce educational requirements on all non-attorneys in the law office

3. The worst sanction that can be imposed upon an attorney by the ethics board is
   a. Imprisonment
   b. Permanent suspension
   c. Disbarment
   d. Fines in excess of one million dollars

EXPLAIN YOURSELF

All answers should be written in complete sentences. A simple yes or no is insufficient.

1. What is YOUR primary argument for or against licensure?
2. Which exam sponsored by any of the national paralegal associations do YOU think has the most marketability in employment? Why?
3. How does paralegal coursework differ from that of the law school curriculum?
4. In your own words, describe the differences between regulation and licensure.
5. Why are the ethics boards of all jurisdictions particularly concerned about allegations of "moral turpitude" levied against attorneys?

FAULTY PHRASES

All of the following statements are FALSE; state why each one is false and then rewrite it as a true statement. Do not just make the statement negative by adding the word "not."

1. Once an attorney is disbarred, he can never practice law in any jurisdiction ever again.
2. An attorney should major in a pre-law curriculum when she is going to college so that she is better prepared to go to law school.
3. Once an attorney passes the national MPRE and the "multi-state," he can apply for admission to any bar he likes.
4. An attorney must be convicted of a criminal offense in order to be disbarred.
5. Being certificated and being certified are the same thing, as far as paralegal regulation is concerned.
6. All of the national paralegal associations agree that the paralegal profession should be licensed.
7. Mere accusations of questionable conduct on behalf of an attorney cannot be brought before the ethics board.

 PORTFOLIO ASSIGNMENT

Write Away
Informal fact gathering is a task normally assigned to paralegals. Your first assignment is to find all the paralegal education offerings in your state. What are the significant similarities and differences between them? Prepare an internal memorandum to your supervising paralegal manager advising her of your findings.

EXCERPTS FROM OPINION #24 OF THE NEW JERSEY SUPREME COURT COMMITTEE ON UNAUTHORIZED PRACTICE

The following contains excerpts from the opinion rendered by the New Jersey Supreme Court Committee on Unauthorized Practice of Law regarding the oversight of independent paralegals. This opinion was later challenged in the Supreme Court of New Jersey. The excerpt of that case will be discussed in the next chapter of the text.

NJ Unauth.Prac.Op. 24, 126 N.J.L.J. 1306, 1990 WL 441613 (N.J.Comm.Unauth.Prac.)

New Jersey Supreme Court Committee on Unauthorized Practice

INDEPENDENT LEGAL ASSISTANTS

Opinion Number 24

November 15, 1990

[...]

While the ABA definition imposes the requirement that a legal assistant be a person "qualified through education, training or work experience", no law or regulation would prohibit a person lacking that qualification from holding himself out to the Bar as an independent contractor offering to do paralegal work for attorneys. While most of the paralegals who testified do possess education, training or work experience, and many of them recommended that paralegals should have certain minimum amounts of experience or education or a combination thereof, all of the witnesses recognized that there is no supervisory body which would prevent untrained or otherwise unqualified persons from working as independent paralegals. While it may be suggested that there is no difference in levels of supervision by the attorney in the case of the employed paralegal as against the independent contractor paralegal, common experience and evidence presented to the Committee demonstrate that the contrary is true and, in the case of the independent contractor, the supervision is far less and, unfortunately in all too many cases, non-existent.

Rule of Professional Conduct 5.3 promulgated by the Supreme Court of New Jersey requires attorneys to maintain reasonable efforts to insure that the conduct of non-lawyers (retained or employed) is compatible with the attorney's professional obligations. [FN omitted] That rule makes the lawyer responsible for the conduct of a retained or employed paralegal that would violate the Rules of Professional Conduct if (i) the conduct is ordered or ratified by the lawyer; (ii) the lawyer has failed to make reasonable investigation that would disclose prior instances of misconduct by the non-lawyer; or (iii) if "the lawyer has direct supervisory authority over the person and knows of the conduct at a time when its consequences can be avoided or mitigated but fails to take reasonable remedial action." It is the view of the Committee that, where there is an employment relationship between the paralegal and the attorney, the attorney will have that direct supervisory authority and will be in a position to take steps to avoid or mitigate the consequences of improper bad actions by the paralegal. If the relationship is one of independent contractor, however, the lawyer cannot have the same direct supervisory authority over the

paralegal and is unlikely to learn of conduct in a way that would permit him to avoid or mitigate its consequences. R.P.C. 5.3, by limiting the attorney's responsibility to those circumstances wherein he knows of conduct and can avoid it, makes it clear that the protection afforded by the Rule will not extend to the independent paralegal with the same force and effect as it will to the employed paralegal. Since there is no body maintaining files or information with respect to misconduct by paralegals, it is difficult to determine how a lawyer could comply with R.P.C. 5.3(c)(3) by making "reasonable investigation" in instances of past misconduct.

As matters presently stand, there is no mechanism that would regulate the conduct of the paralegal other than the supervision of the attorney for whom the work is done, which, more often than not, may be sporadic, uneven or non-existent. That is demonstrated by the following:

1. While there are a number of different associations and organizations with which paralegals may affiliate, there have been no standards or guidelines set down by any body with regulatory authority to control and regulate the activities of independent paralegals.
2. At least one New Jersey college provides an American Bar Association-approved paralegal program and provides a Certificate of Completion to successful candidates. A Bachelor of Arts degree is a prerequisite to the obtaining of the Certificate of Completion. Those requirements are applicable only to matriculating students and it is clear that no law or regulation imposes the requirement of obtaining such a Certificate of Completion on those students who propose to practice.
3. Neither the State of New Jersey, any Bar Association, nor any organization or affiliation of paralegals or legal assistants provides for licensing procedure or any other procedure to regulate and control the identity, training and conduct of those who engage in the work. [FN omitted]
4. While the ABA definition states that a legal assistant should be "qualified through education, training or work experience" which will serve as a guideline for its members in the use of paralegal assistance, that requirement

is not imposed or binding upon a person who desires to engage in independent paralegal practice. Most of the witnesses testified that they believed there should be a requirement of a minimum number of years of training or education to permit one to practice as an independent paralegal. All of them agreed, however, that no such requirement presently exists.

5. There is no paralegal association or organization which functions in a way that can impose any uniform mechanism of standards of ethics, disciplinary proceedings, and rules and regulations to oversee the activities of paralegals. Those who function as paralegals, therefore, do so pursuant to standards and rules either of their own devising or of the devising of the variety of different groups or organizations, none of which have the power to impose adherence to standards or to control or discipline those who do not adhere to standards.

Problems raised by the absence of direct supervision and regulation of the independent paralegal are highlighted by the kind of work being undertaken by some independent paralegals. For example, one of the witnesses testified that she had become an expert in probate matters as a result of experience in the probate field and learned from that experience that many attorneys who do probate work do not specialize in estate work and are generally unfamiliar with the field. Many of those attorneys do not want to refer their matters to attorneys who are specialists, but desire to retain control of their files and clients. Accordingly, those attorneys retain the witness to handle the estates that come into their offices. She testified that she handles matters for approximately forty-five attorneys. She stated that she "ultimately takes full responsibility for making sure that I get done what needs to be done and, believe it or not, that the attorney gets done what he or she needs to get done." She signs correspondence for the attorneys, initialing it to make it clear that she has written the correspondence. She states that she never signs a letter "that contains a legal opinion, legal advice." She does, however, prepare many of those letters for her attorney clients and she has much client contact (Tr. at 24). [FN omitted] She handles safe deposit box openings, takes clients to motor vehicle departments to transfer vehicles, handles social security matters for them. She charges the attorneys at the rate of $45 per hour. She testified that she accepts work from many attorneys who have no experience or training in estate or probate work. [FN omitted] Therefore, as a result of her perceived expertise, she does all of the technical estate and probate work for the attorney and the attorney who participated in this practice and collects a fee over and above the charges of the witness faces the possibility of ethical problems. *(See, e.g., R.P.C. 1.5(a))*

Another paralegal described a different specialty which permits her to provide a service for attorneys who do not have in-house competence in that specialized area. She stated the following:

On occasion a matter will come into the attorney's office in a very specialized area of law that the in-house staff is unfamiliar with. Rather than send their client away, the attorney can call me to assist. For instance, one of my specialties is bankruptcy law and of late my work in assisting attorneys has been in that area. (Tr. at 69)

To the extent that paralegals such as the probate specialist and the bankruptcy specialist are providing expertise to attorneys who do not have that expertise in house, their work demonstrates that the concept of direct supervisory control by the attorney is illusory. It seems highly unlikely that an attorney who does not do estate work or bankruptcy work in his office would employ a full-time paralegal to perform that work in the attorney's office. There appears, however, to be some significant group of attorneys who do retain the services of an independent paralegal to fill in that area of specialty and expertise for the attorney that the attorney does not have in house. While the attorney who retains that specialist paralegal may, on the surface, appear to have responsibility for the work of that paralegal, it is difficult to determine how that attorney can utilize reasonable efforts to insure that the conduct of the paralegal, who is working in a field unfamiliar to the attorney, will be "compatible with the professional obligations of the lawyer" (R.P.C. 5.3). Based on the testimony and evidence considered by the Committee, the paralegal admittedly is performing legal services in an area not included within the attorney's range of expertise. It is difficult to see how the lawyer can either order or ratify the paralegal's conduct or provide that direct supervisory authority over the paralegal which would permit the avoidance or mitigation of improper conduct required by R.P.C. 5.3. In these areas, the paralegal is becoming a substitute for the attorney, not an assistant to the attorney, and that is a situation which comes about because of the independent nature of the paralegal's work relationship.

The nature of the work of independent paralegals presents other problems. Those paralegals employed in an attorney's office do prepare correspondence that is routinely reviewed and signed by the attorney. The independent paralegals made it clear through their testimony, however, that a much looser arrangement exists in their practices with respect to correspondence and communication. Some of the paralegals keep supplies of the attorneys' letterheads in the paralegals' offices. The paralegals acknowledge that they send out letters, signed in the name of the paralegal, but that they do so without prior review by the attorney. In some instances, the attorneys whose letterheads are used do not receive copies of the letters from the paralegals. The potential for misunderstanding by the public which may receive those letters, and the absence of supervision by the attorney in the use of the attorney's letterhead, is an example of the kind of problem that the practice of the independent paralegal presents.

[...]

The Committee is sensitive to the fact that the practice of law becomes ever more complex and that there is a need to provide legal services to the public. Some of the witnesses who appeared before the Committee expressed the view that the work of the independent paralegal would have the result of bringing legal services more extensively to the public and at fee levels that would be more affordable because of the lesser charges involved in the work of the paralegals. It is the view of the Committee that the need to bring services to the public and the need to provide legal services at more affordable rates should not be met by permitting legal services to be performed by non-lawyers who, by virtue of their independent status, cannot be subject to the kind of direct supervision by attorneys that is otherwise required. There certainly are differing levels of complexity in the legal issues and matters to be handled by attorneys and paralegals. When the paralegal is employed by the attorney, the nature of the employment relationship makes it possible for the attorney to make the decisions as to which matters are appropriate for handling by the paralegal and which matters require direct hands-on work by the attorney. When the attorney and the paralegal are separated both by distance and the independent nature of the paralegal's relationship with the attorney, the opportunity for the exercise of that most important judgment by the attorney becomes increasingly difficult.

This is not to say that there are not matters that could be handled by an independent paralegal with appropriate supervision by the attorney contracting with the paralegal. The problem is that the decisions as to what work may be done by the paralegal should be the attorney's to make but the distance between attorney and paralegal mandated by the independent relationship may result in the making of those decisions by the paralegal or by default.

It is the view of the Committee, moreover, that the paralegal practicing in an independent paralegal organization, removed from the attorney both by distance and relationship, presents far too little opportunity for the direct supervision necessary to justify handling those legal issues that might be delegated. Without supervision, the work of the paralegal clearly constitutes the unauthorized practice of law. We found, from the testimony and materials presented to our Committee, that the opportunity for supervision of the independent paralegal diminishes to the point where much of the work of the independent paralegal is, in fact, unsupervised. That being the case, the independent practice by the paralegal must involve the unauthorized practice of law. The fact that some of the work might actually be directly supervised cannot justify the allowance of a system which permits the independent paralegal to work free of attorney supervision and control for such a large part of the time and for such a large part of the work.

Without the direct supervisory control contemplated by R.P.C. 5.3, the attorney who utilizes the independent paralegal might not have professional responsibility for the paralegal's misconduct. With the separation of the independent paralegal from the attorney, both by distance and relationship, the ability of the attorney to make reasonable efforts to insure that the paralegal's conduct is compatible with the professional obligations of the lawyer must diminish. The danger of legal work being done without appropriate professional responsibility to the public increases to a point wherein it cannot be condoned.

The attorneys who use independent paralegals are not free of ethical problems. Where the specialized paralegal, for example handling probate matters, charges an hourly fee to the attorney, the attorney may well be put in a position to charge a fee to the probate client which will constitute a percentage of the estate. Most or all of the work will have been done by the paralegal. Since the attorney is not sufficiently skilled in the area to supervise properly the work of the paralegal, the attorney will be compensated for work done by the paralegal that, because of the lack of supervision, will constitute the unauthorized practice of law. That presents a clear ethical dilemma created by the existence of the independent paralegal. [FN omitted] Where the work of the independent paralegal constitutes the unauthorized

practice of law, the attorney retaining that paralegal will be in violation of R.P.C. 5.3(d)(2).

It is suggested that the availability of the independent paralegal makes paralegal services available to the single practitioner who might not be able to employ a full-time paralegal. While there might be merit to making some of the paralegals' time available to the single practitioner, that value does not, in the opinion of this Committee, override the very real problem of lack of supervision inherent in that relationship. There well may be mechanical things to be done by the independent paralegal for the single practitioner. Any part-timer could accomplish that kind of work for the attorney without the risk of unsupervised work that is created by the independent paralegal's distance from the attorney.

We are involved in this inquiry, moreover, with the work of a legal assistant which the ABA defines as being "substantive legal work" which "requires a sufficient knowledge of legal concepts that, absent such assistant, the attorney would perform the task." If the case is beyond the capacity of the single practitioner, whether by virtue of complexity or sheer volume of detail, this Committee does not believe that the problem is properly solved by work done by the independent paralegal who cannot properly be the subject of the kind of supervision that would be required. There are alternatives: The work could be referred to a specialist attorney or to a firm which has, in house, the personnel to handle the volume. This Committee finds, based on the presentation of both documentary and oral materials to it, that the use of the independent paralegal to do the substantive legal work which the attorney would otherwise do, represents an inappropriate level of delegation.

The Committee does not believe that the need for the supply of legal services requires that the Bar utilize independent paralegals whose work is unregulated either by an employment relationship with the attorney or through any systematic body of regulations.

If there is an argument that legal services have not been brought to the consumer over the past years, it is no answer to that argument to permit those legal services to be performed by persons not subject to uniform standards, not subject to training, and who can work independently of the supervision of attorneys which must be the keymark of paralegal work. The Committee believes that the increasing number of attorneys entering the practice, the availability of legal service programs, and the availability of attorneys to do pro bono work can fill those needs appropriately. It is inappropriate to suggest that there is such a void in the providing of legal services at reasonable rates that independent paralegals should move in to fill that void. At its best, the Committee believes that the remedy of providing legal services through the independent paralegal can create more harm than the perceived ill which it purports to be designed to correct.

The Committee recognizes that the bringing of legal services to the public must be an issue of continuing concern to the Bar. We believe, however, that it is totally inappropriate to suggest that legal services can better be brought to the public by a group that is not subject to any kind of uniform educational, training, professional or ethical standards.

[…].

Source: Reprinted with permission from ThomsonWest.

Chapter 2

The Unauthorized Practice of Law

CHAPTER OBJECTIVES

The student will be able to:

- Discuss the development of and necessity for prohibitions against the unauthorized practice of law

- Define the "practice of law"

- Compare the unauthorized practice of law as it relates to attorneys, paralegals, and other support staff

- Identify the various considerations in making a determination as to whether the conduct in question is the unauthorized practice of law

This chapter will focus on WHAT tasks may be performed by WHOM in the legal system and WHY there are restrictions on the practice of law. There are certain tasks which have been deemed the practice of law by definition, and are off limits to non-lawyers. Performance of these tasks is considered the "unauthorized practice of law" (UPL). Paralegals are particularly susceptible to overstepping the line during the course of their work, and must understand HOW to avoid UPL.

The dramatics of conducting a trial aside, what kind of work do lawyers do? What is the practice of law? It is important for a paralegal to understand the boundaries of the practice by being able to answer these vital questions. Unfortunately, there are not easy, clear-cut answers. The general population, through the *many* television shows and movies made about lawyers, has only a limited consciousness of what lawyers really do. The media limits itself to exposing or lampooning the exciting and/or controversial elements of the practice, usually involving litigation. This is understandable, as the ratings for shows titled *The Research Brigade* and *The Discovery Drudges* would be abysmal.

The boundaries of the practice are far-reaching and their edges are quite fuzzy. Indeed, it is in these border outposts that the practice of law by an attorney overlaps with that by a paralegal. Paralegals *do* engage in the practice of law within their own territories, the law offices where they work. The paralegal's work frees up the attorney's time so that she can concentrate on the core practice, that which only a lawyer can do. The analysis and strategy to be applied in a particular case, the maintenance of the client relationship, and the ultimate responsibility for all the work performed for a client—these tasks make up the heart of the practice of law. A paralegal may take on some of the **substantive legal tasks** that must be performed proper to or in support of this core. It is the "core" that is preserved solely for attorneys. Paralegals do not engage in the unauthorized practice of law as long as their work is "of a preparatory nature, such as legal research, investigation, or the composition of legal documents, which enable a licensed attorney-employer to carry a given matter to a conclusion through his own examination, approval or additional effort." *In re Easler,* 272 S.E.2d 32 (S.C. 1980).

HISTORY AND DEVELOPMENT OF THE UNAUTHORIZED PRACTICE OF LAW

The concern of the ethics rules is not the act itself of practicing law; it is the **unauthorized practice of law (UPL)**. Within the four walls of their offices, within their own territories, and given the proper instruction and supervision, paralegals are practicing law—and are authorized to do so. The authorization comes from the proper delegation of the legal task to the paralegal. It is when a paralegal leaves the supervision of an attorney and/or performs a task that is impermissible that she ventures into the potentially dangerous territory of the unauthorized practice of law. The unauthorized practice of law within the law firm can be either

1. the improper supervision of a paralegal who is performing a legal task, or
2. direction by and supervision of the attorney in the paralegal's performance of an improper or unethical task.

Of course, a student, a practicing paralegal, or an attorney would like a clear line of demarcation in the definition of the unauthorized practice. Unfortunately, that is not going to be possible. Numerous courts and ethics committees have been unable to write a concise and thorough definition of the practice of law. As with many questions of law, the answer lies in the facts of the case. In other words, "it depends." As the advice of attorneys grows more and more expensive, the temptation to engage in the unauthorized practice by those not licensed to do so grows.

The unauthorized practice ranges from the obvious, outright behavior of the imposter to behavior that is well-meaning and seemingly harmless (if not downright beneficial). *Louisiana Claims Adjustment Bureau, Inc. v. State Farm Insurance Co.* (La.App.Cir. 2004); 877 So.2d 294. A public insurance adjuster brought an action against a liability insurer to recover for defamation and intentional interference with business relations by telling the adjuster's clients that the adjuster was engaged in unauthorized practice of law. The public adjuster, which negotiated personal injury claims with insurance companies, engaged in the unauthorized practice of law when its representatives evaluated claims and advised clients of their causes of action; evaluating a claim and determining whether it had merit or was frivolous had to be done by a licensed attorney.

Non-lawyer parents, acting solely as a representative of their minor son, lacked authorization to maintain an appeal of their son's libel action against his school. The parents could not proceed pro se, although if their son had been of age, he could have done so. The "representation" in this instance required an attorney; the parents were not licensed to practice law as required to act on their son's behalf. *Lowe v. City of Shelton,* 83 Conn.App. 750, 851 A.2d 1183 (2004).

History

While the above case references are relatively recent, the *regulation* of the practice of law dates back very roughly to the ancient Greeks. As was their style, the Greeks formalized the litigation process, created complex procedural rules, and used legal terminology with aplomb. True to their form, the ancient Romans borrowed, further studied, standardized, and refined their Greek predecessors' work. Through this formalization of the practice of law, a class of professionals emerged which can properly be equated with modern attorneys. The Romans also turned their analytical, scientific eyes on the law and developed the science of jurisprudence, whereas before, the Greeks had only treated it as a philosophy. History has attributed Gnaeus Flavius with publishing the exact words for instituting and maintaining these ancient legal actions. This indicates that there were extensive rules of procedure that were, prior to their publication sometime around 300 B.C., known only to the aristocrats practicing law. These "secrets" now revealed, there was a substantial increase in the number of persons practicing and studying the law.

It is the same opening of doors, the letting out of "secrets," that has permitted the development of the profession of paralegal. Through the impetus of economics and the availability of education, students are able to study and ultimately practice law. Chapter 1 examined the educational qualifications and entry requirements an individual needs to be admitted to the practice of law or to be considered qualified to act as a paralegal. This chapter will focus on the definition of the practice of law, identifying those tasks that are fundamental to the profession of attorney and therefore off limits to non-lawyers.

What is it exactly that defines the profession of lawyer and makes it unique and isolated from other professions? The practice of law itself was isolated by the early colonial Americans, who restricted what lawyers could do in response to their general distrust of the traditional English elite. Indeed, the "Massachusetts Body of Liberties" of 1641 prohibited lawyers from receiving a fee for their services. Lawyers were merely to assist the party in preparing the case, only if the party were unable to carry it on himself. This reflects the ideals of the Puritans: recall the *Mayflower,* whose passengers felt that their faith would be their guidance and no lawyers would be necessary.

In such a utopian world, this may, indeed, be the case. However, the "melting pot" that became America is a dynamic and diverse group with different ideals and morality. The legal profession grew quickly in response to the need after the Revolution, and continued to grow at a rapid pace. Fortunately, the reputation of the lawyers also flourished.

Necessity

As the reputations and pocketbooks of the attorneys grew, so did the need to protect the profession. Controlling the practice of law can relate either to the cynical view of protectionism toward the livelihood or to the altruistic view that by regulating the practice we can better protect the public. By restricting access to the profession and thereby restricting access to the justice system, lawyers are ensured that they will always have an income. People must pass through the lawyer as "gatekeeper" if they want to accomplish their legal goals.

This **gatekeeping function** may also be described as a "safeguarding" mechanism. By ensuring that only those who are qualified appear before the court, the justice system can also ensure that the parties' interests are protected. Both substantive and procedural laws are very complicated and potentially stringent in their application. It can be a complex and convoluted journey from commencement of suit to final resolution. There are pitfalls along the way that may have serious consequences for the unrepresented party.

Economics

The increasing need for expert legal advice responded also to pure economics; as demand increases, so does the cost of the service. For the most part, the expense is justified; attorneys have received a very expensive education and usually have "paid

gatekeeping function
A restriction of entry into a profession to ensure that certain standards are met prior to admission. It serves to protect both the professionals inside and the public at large against unqualified persons performing the tasks associated with that profession.

CYBER TRIP

For the full text of the ABA Model Rules of Professional Responsibility, please visit:

http://www.abanet.org/cpr/mrpc/model_rules.html

A very interesting point. George C. Leef, "Lawyer Fees too High? The case for repealing unauthorized practice of law statutes."

Regulation: the CATO Review of Business and Government.http://www.cato.org/pubs/regulation/reg20n1c.html

Outsourcing Law.com, a Web site that offers insights on Effectice Outsourcing from Bierce & Kenerson, P.C., wrote "The Unauthorized Practice of the Law: What the Buyer Should Know about 'Legal Drafting' and other Services by Non-Lawyers" and it can be accessed at:

http://www.outsourcing-law.com/Unauthorized LawPractice.2005.04.18.htm

their dues" on the battleground of legal practice. However, many people simply cannot afford these services. There are some areas of practice in which those in most need of assistance are those least likely to be able to afford it. These areas include, but are not limited to, family issues (divorce, child custody and support, domestic violence, etc.), landlord/tenant matters, bankruptcy, and immigration. How can these citizens access one of the fundamental services provided by the government—have their "day in court"? This is where independent legal service providers entered the scene. They used various names: freelance paralegal, independent paralegal, legal document preparer, legal technician. The important difference between these providers and the traditional means of obtaining legal services is the lack of a supervising attorney. These providers work for themselves, outside of a legal firm headed by an attorney.

There are competing economic forces at play as access to justice increases by this means. The demand for these services increases, and therefore the charges for the services can increase. That is why paralegalism started in the first place—to lower the cost of legal services—but now they have become part of the "elite-in-demand." Additionally, law firms and in-house corporate legal departments have noticed the economic advantages of employing paralegals. A competent paralegal can demand a very high salary. It is a matter of balance. Paralegal professionals, no matter by whom they are employed, want to be paid what they are worth. This is not unreasonable. However, by increasing their worth, they may decrease their accessibility to those members of the public who need less expensive legal services. It's a catch-22. What everyone can agree upon was concisely stated by Robert D. Welden in his article "Defining the Practice of Law—Untying the Gordian Knot," Washington State Bar Association, January 2001.

All members of society should be able to afford/retain essential legal assistance from individuals who have the requisite skills and competencies and operate subject to an oversight/regulatory scheme that ensures that those whose important rights are at stake can reasonably rely on the quality, skill and ability to perform necessary appropriate tasks.

This statement returns to the issue of UPL. While it is hard to disagree with the access to justice argument, what remains undefined is those "necessary and appropriate tasks" that make up the practice of law, or conversely, those that do not.

DEFINING THE PRACTICE OF LAW

What tasks are routinely handled by paralegals that may involve the unauthorized practice of law? How can these practicing professionals protect themselves and their supervising attorneys? The practice of law is very, very broad. It is necessary to define that which is solely within the purview of an attorney to perform. Therefore, every task that is not within the particular realm of the attorney should be "fair game" for paralegals to practice within the strictures of the definition of the paralegal profession.

Unfortunately, there is no set definition of the practice of law. Courts have had a tendency to define it in the negative, meaning that they have decided what non-attorneys cannot do, rather than what only attorneys can do. It is important to note that each jurisdiction has its own set of UPL rules; for this reason, the paralegal should research the relevant statutes, case law, and ethics opinions in her jurisdiction. Both NALA and NFPA can only refer the paralegal to the general relevant prohibitions. (See Figure 2.1.)

About half the states have statutory and/or case law definitions of the "practice of law"; the others have avoided pinning down a definition in favor of a strictly case-by-case approach. Still, there are six generally accepted tasks that are solely attributable to attorneys as the "practice of law":

1. the acquisition of clients and establishment of the attorney-client relationship

2. giving legal advice

FIGURE 2.1
Unauthorized Practice of Law

NALA Guideline 2

Legal Assistants should not:
1. Establish attorney-client relationships; set legal fees; give legal opinions or advice; or represent a client before a court, unless authorized to do so by said court; nor
2. Engage in, encourage, or contribute to any act which could constitute the unauthorized practice of law.

NFPA EC 1.8(a)

A paralegal shall comply with the applicable legal authority governing the unauthorized practice of law in the jurisdiction in which the paralegal practices.

3. preparing legal documents
4. managing a law practice
5. representation in a court of law
6. negotiation and settlement of legal claims

The Acquisition of Clients and Establishment of the Attorney-Client Relationship

Taking a chronological approach to the practice of law, the very first step in practicing law is the **acquisition of clients**. This is also the first opportunity to practice law: the determination of whether to take on the particular client, evaluation of the merits of the case and possibility of success, and the establishment of the **attorney-client relationship**. Due to the fiduciary nature of the relationship between an attorney and a client, it is significant who establishes its terms. A **fiduciary relationship** is one in which there is, essentially, a "caretaker": one person agrees to look out for and act in the best interests of the other. This encompasses the benefactor's duties of good faith, trust, and honesty. Further, the duty of confidentiality attaches at the moment that this fiduciary relationship is created. Clients must trust attorneys with very sensitive information and disclose personal facts; they must be able to rely on a trained professional who is held to ethical standards of practice.

It is important to note that the establishment of the relationship does not rely on the actual signing of retainer agreements. Another aspect of creating the relationship is the setting of legal fees. Fee arrangements are complex enough to warrant their own chapter, and will be discussed later in the text. It is the intent of the client to enter into an attorney-client/fiduciary relationship that actually creates that relationship.

The existence of an attorney-client relationship does not depend on an express contract or the payment of fees, and may be implied from the parties' conduct. An attorney-client relationship is established when a party seeks and receives advice and assistance from an attorney on matters pertinent to the legal profession. The existence of an attorney-client relationship turns largely on the client's subjective belief it exists and looks to the nature of the work performed and to the circumstances under which confidences are divulged. The existence of an attorney-client relationship is a question of fact. *Moen v. Thomas,* 682 N.W.2d 738, 744–745 (N.D. 2004).

The relationship can be created under numerous circumstances, not just the conventional office meeting. An attorney-client relationship may be formed in the local diner over coffee or in the local pub over a pint. The test applied to the determination of whether the relationship is formed is whether the potential client reasonably believed that he was entering into such a relationship. This can be deduced from a positive

acquisition of clients
The approaching of people in need of legal services and the obtaining of their consent to represent them in a legal matter; this may be done only by an attorney.

attorney-client relationship
The legal relationship established between attorney and client. This relationship has many protective and confidential aspects and is unique in the legal context.

fiduciary relationship
A relationship based on close personal trust that one party is looking out for the other's best interests.

response to any of the following questions leading to a finding that the relationship was probably formed:

1. Did the attorney volunteer her services in the aid of the prospective client? This may involve identifying oneself as an attorney to the prospective client, thereby appearing to offer one's professional services.

2. Did the attorney agree to investigate the merits of the matter or render any legal advice specific to the facts given by the prospective client?

3. Did the attorney formerly represent the person in another matter? While each matter undertaken by an attorney requires a separate retainer, the fact that the attorney has done work for this person before tends to suggest that the attorney will take on the present matter.

4. Did the attorney accept payment or bill for fees on the work performed regarding the issue presented?

5. Did the prospective client approach the attorney in confidence? The cornerstone of the relationship is the client's reliance on the fiduciary and confidential nature of the relationship.

For example, in *Tormo v. Yormark,* 398 F. Supp. 1159, 1169 (D.N.J. 1975), the attorney told a potential client that he would "see what could be done with regard to settlement." This preliminary contact "was sufficient as a matter of law to impose upon him the duties owed by an attorney to his clients." The potential client was entitled to the same care from the attorney as any other who had formally been taken on as a client. From the moment that a person believes that the attorney is acting in the potential client's interest, the relationship can be found. In *Miller v. Metzinger,* 91 Cal. App.3d 31, 154 Cal. Rptr. 22 (1979), the attorney's "declaration[s] that his function was purely investigatory and that he did not agree to represent her, charge any fee for his services or secure a retainer agreement do not suffice to eliminate the existence of an attorney-client relationship." Even if the terms of the relationship have not yet been settled upon, the relationship itself may exist. The details can be determined later. "We may agree with [the attorney] that it was merely an accommodation or a pro forma relationship, but we find nevertheless that it was indeed an attorney-client relationship. The duties or specifics of the relationship in this instance might well be disputed, but the fact that an attorney-client relationship existed is clear." *Insurance Co. of North America v. Westergren,* 794 S.W.2d 812 (Tex. App. 1990). The court looks at the conduct of the attorney and the potential client "in light of the totality of the circumstances" and may find that there should be, in all fairness, an enforceable agreement for legal services between them. CA Eth. Op. 2003-161, 2003 WL 23146200 at 3 (Cal. St. Bar. Comm. Prof. Resp.).

Giving Legal Advice

legal advice
Generally, the provision of guidance regarding the meaning or application of the law or the rendering of an opinion on the possible outcome of a legal matter.

A client comes to the office looking for advice, **legal advice** on how best to proceed in any given circumstance. The rendering of legal advice to the public is the sole domain of an attorney. Clients are expecting to be counseled regarding their rights, potential liabilities, the effect of rules of law and of the court on their case, and the necessary steps to proceed with the matter. These are tasks that "reasonably demand the application of a trained legal mind." *People v. Landlords Professional Services,* 215 Cal.App.3d 1599, 1605, 264 Cal.Rptr. 548 (Cal.App. 1989) (citing *Agran v. Shapiro,* 127 Cal.App.2d Supp. 807, 818, 273 P.2d 619 (1954). Additionally, the determination relates to the strength of the defenses available to the other parties, possible counterclaims, and a potential challenge to the suit based upon failure to state a claim or filing a frivolous suit.

FIGURE 2.2
**Disclosure of
Paralegal Status**

NALA Guideline 1

Legal Assistants should:
1. Disclose their status as legal assistants at the outset of any professional relationship with a client, other attorneys, a court or administrative agency or personnel thereof, or members of the general public.

NFPA EC 1.7(a)

A paralegal's title shall clearly indicate the individual's status and shall be disclosed in all business and professional communications to avoid misunderstandings and misconceptions about the paralegal's role and responsibilities.

How do courts determine whether the line has been crossed between supplying information relating to the law and rendering legal advice? "Although there may be a 'twilight zone' between those acts that are and those that are not permissible for persons who are not lawyers, it is clear the core element of practicing law is the giving of legal advice to a client. In fact, merely entering into such relationship constitutes the practice of law." *Rhines v. Norlarco Credit Union,* 847 N.E.2d 233, 239 (Ind. App. 2006).

The answer lies in the specificity and expectations of the client. Answering detailed questions about a particular situation forms the base of the trust relationship between attorney and client. The client assumes (correctly or not) that the legal professional to whom she is speaking is knowledgeable and authorized to make legal conclusions. "Because defendant offers counsel in the form of professional guidance to persons seeking to extricate themselves from a legal relationship, the party represented, as well as the public in general, has a right to be assured that these interests are properly represented by members of the bar. To the extent that defendant provides personal advice peculiar to the dissolution of a specific [situation], she is engaged in the 'unauthorized practice of law.'. . . " *Landlords* at 1608 (citing *State Bar v. Cramer,* 399 Mich. 116, 137, 249 N.W.2d 1, 9 (1976). While only an attorney can create the relationship, the client may be unaware of either the paralegal's inability to create this relationship or the fact that the person to whom he is speaking is in fact a paralegal. For this reason, both NALA and NFPA espouse the full disclosure to the public of the paralegal's status. (See Figure 2.2.)

Preparing Legal Documents

After the determination has been made to take on a particular client, the next step usually involves preparing **legal documents** to initiate or respond to a legal proceeding or to secure the needs of the client in a legally recognizable format. Pleadings, motions, deeds, wills, contracts, briefs, and various other legal documents all secure and potentially affect the legal rights of the client and third parties to the transaction. It is imperative that these writings and instruments are scrutinized by a person trained to perform legal analysis. They are very often initially drafted by paralegals. This is one of the core duties of paralegals. However, their finalization, ratification, and submission must come by and through the supervising attorney. Independent paralegals or other non-attorneys who do not work under the supervision of an attorney (hereinafter simply referred to as "non-attorneys") cannot perform this last step. This is also the area in which most non-attorneys get into trouble. There are certain professions that do permissibly create documents that are legal in nature, but are so intertwined with and merely tangential to their primary business that the courts do not find that they are engaged in the unauthorized practice of law. For example, realtors prepare sales agreements, mortgage lenders prepare promissory notes, property managers prepare uncontested eviction notices—and the list goes on. There is a fact-sensitive fine

legal documents
Papers that are filed in furtherance of a court action or secure a legal right or grant legal recourse to a party.

line in these situations as to what crosses into the unauthorized practice of law. While there is no prohibition on the preparation of documents incidental to the business, the line is crossed where the employees of the business use their own discretion in selecting which forms to use, and in doing so, affect the legal ramifications of the selected documents.

The preparation of these documents also must not extend past a "form-fill" function on documents that have actually been prepared by an attorney. *Kim v. Desert Document Services, Inc.,* 101 Wash.App. 1043 (2000). It is this reliance of the clients on the representations of the businesses that they would choose the proper legal document for the client's individual situation that gets the document preparers in trouble. This is true even where the document preparers do not make any assertions that they are qualified to make legal decisions or render legal advice. Where is this line that should not be crossed? The court in *State v. Northouse,* 848 N.E.2d 668, 672 (Ind. 2006) stated it best:

> *Generally, it can be said that the filling in of blanks in legal instruments, prepared by attorneys, which require only the use of common knowledge regarding the information to be inserted in said blanks, and general knowledge regarding the legal consequences involved, does not constitute the practice of law. However, when the filling in of such blanks involves considerations of significant legal refinement, or the legal consequences of the act are of great significance to the parties involved, such practice may be restricted to members of the legal profession.*

A client has a right to expect that her "legal work" will be performed by an attorney or a person qualified to do so under the direct supervision of an attorney. *McMahon v. Advanced Title Services Company of West Virginia,* 216 W.Va. 413, 607 S.E.2d 519 (2004).

What is important to note is that the preparation of these documents is not (or should not be) the primary goal of these businesses; nor do these businesses presume to act in a role of legal advisor. The clients have no expectation that these businesses have or apply any particular legal knowledge to their situation. Compare this to *Cleveland Bar Assn. v. Sharp Estate Serv., Inc.,* 107 Ohio St.3d 219, 837 N.E.2d 1183 (2005). The company marketed and sold living trusts and estate plans that they prepared. They also explained the legal consequences of the clients' specific decisions relating to these plans. Although the actual trusts and wills were entered into the company's computer program by "review attorneys" who were under contract with the company, these attorneys did not counsel or come in contact with the clients. The attorneys provided merely a scrivener service rather than a counselor role; they were restricted to preparing documents as provided by the company. This requirement was a second infraction of the ethical rules. Attorneys must be free to exercise their independent professional judgment in legal situations. Taking direction from a non-lawyer as a result of the agents' unauthorized practice of law was "insult added to injury."

"Independent Paralegals," a.k.a. "Legal Document Preparers"

We have spoken earlier of paralegals who choose to practice as freelancers under term contracts and offer their services to attorneys. There are also those who are "independent" and offer their services directly to the public without the supervision of an attorney. The **freelance paralegals** essentially are under the supervision of an attorney, they work for themselves or a "paralegal firm." Their functions are carried out either in the hiring office or in the freelancer's own space. This freelancing offers paralegals a chance to work in many different environments with different attorneys. The only real difference between "traditional" employment and freelancing is who plays the role of "boss." In this type of practice, it is the attorneys who are the paralegals' clients.

On the other hand, **independent paralegals** do not provide services for use by an attorney; "independent" in this context means freedom from that kind of relationship. This type of practice has a great benefit, as it directly addresses the societal need for

freelance paralegal
A paralegal in business for him- or herself who contracts with an attorney or law firm to perform specific tasks for a designated fee.

SPOT THE ISSUE

Every person has the right to represent himself in court and to act on his own behalf in legal matters. What, then, can a corporation do on its own behalf? It needs to be represented by a person. Since that person is "representing" the corporation, does she have to be an attorney? Compare these two scenarios:

An investment company apartment manager (who was the company's 99 percent majority interest holder and actually owned the building) filed complaints seeking rent money from tenants in small-claims court. The court provided the proper forms for the manager to fill out and file. The manager then appeared in court and gave testimony; however, he did not engage in cross-examination or legal argument. At no time did the manager hold himself out as an attorney during any of the proceedings.

A director and CEO of a nonprofit organization filed a motion to dismiss a complaint filed against her organization for underpayment of wages to its employees. She also filed other motions relating to this representation of the organization. Her signature indicated she was "Attorney or Agent" of the organization.

Of these two scenarios, what would you characterize as the unauthorized practice of law: the first, the second, both, or neither? Why? What are the aggravating or mitigating factors in your decision? *Compare Cleveland Bar Association v. Pearlman,* 106 Ohio St.3d 136, 832 N.E.2d 1193 (2005), and *Disciplinary Counsel v. Givens,* 106 Ohio St.3d 144, 832 N.E.2d 1200 (2005).

access to justice. However, within this type of practice, there are many opportunities to cross the line into questionable territory, as the safety net of an attorney who is ultimately responsible for the work is absent. These independent paralegals are still prohibited from all the activities previously discussed as the unauthorized practice of law. This practice has evolved under another name in order to clarify the services performed by these professionals: **legal document preparers (LDPs)**. Two states which have standardized this profession in the law are California (Business and Professions Code §§ 6400-6415) and Arizona (Code of Judicial Administration § 7-208). Both statutes characterize the career as a self-help service; the client is in control of the decisions that would normally be made by an attorney thus preventing, in theory, the LDP from exercising legal judgment and rendering legal advice. LDPs primarily provide access to published legal documents from which the client may choose as most appropriate. The LDP may supply general legal information in order to allow the client to make a decision, but may not make any specific recommendations regarding that choice. The LDP can then follow through by completing the selected forms and file them at the direction of the client.

With this delineation of duties also comes responsibility. The statutes provide for legal remedies and penalties to be levied against the LDP who oversteps the bounds of ethical conduct. There is no job description as such for paralegals who practice under the supervision and direction of an attorney; there is merely a proscription against the unauthorized practice of law. In contrast to this "definition in the negative," the LDP statutes are very clear in defining the positive acts that may be taken by those practitioners. Infractions may result in warnings, fines, or, in severe cases, revocation of the right to practice as an LDP. In many ways this reflects the sanctioning structure of attorneys. Recall that once an industry is regulated, the state has the power to punish the offenders. The state has a substantial interest in protecting its citizens' interests and in ensuring that their legal rights are preserved.

This concern over the protection of the public is so high that it can take precedence over other individual legal protections. The Arizona Supreme Court has found that protecting the public and the integrity of the legal profession is paramount to a person's interest in protecting reputation through the tort of defamation. A certified legal document preparer sued an attorney for defamation because the attorney had sent a letter to the state bar association accusing the LDP of the unauthorized practice of law in

Independent paralegals and legal document preparers (LDPs)
Legal professionals who offer their services directly to the public. LDPs generally restrict their activities to assisting in preparing legal forms based upon the information obtained from their clients; they do not and cannot render legal advice or represent their clients in legal matters. In jurisdictions where there aren't separate formal designations for the profession of LDP, they are generically called "independent paralegals (LDPs)."

connection with a divorce proceeding. The court held that the attorney's communication to the ethics board of the bar was absolutely immune from suit by the LDP. This protection to express even ungrounded fears or accusations is reserved for circumstances where the public interest is so important that the speaker is granted complete freedom of expression that is not dependent on motive or supporting evidence.

> *In light of the role now permissibly played by certified legal document preparers in working with the public and providing the public with certain legal services, just as with the legal profession, public policy demands that absolute immunity be extended to members of the public who report alleged unethical conduct by certified legal document preparers. We can conceive of no reason why a person who reports allegedly unethical conduct by a lawyer should be protected by absolute immunity while a person who reports allegedly unethical conduct by a certified legal document preparer should be subjected to the risk of civil liability. Given the public's need for access to legal services and the importance of regulating those who provide such services, there should be no distinction. The proper, fair and efficient administration of justice demands no less.*

Sobol v. Alarcon, 212 Ariz. 315 ¶ 14, 131 P.3d 487, 490 (App. 2006).

As could be expected, California leads the pack in the number of businesses formed to supply these legal document preparation services, but as the demand for these services increases, so will the number of businesses. In the same vein, in October 2005, the NALDP (National Association of Legal Document Preparers) was created to address professional, consumer, and regulatory issues related to this new profession. A survey of the cases regarding independent legal service providers highlights the perils of this type of practice; and judging from the most recent cases, it is particularly perilous in Ohio (recall the *Legal Aid State Services* case; *see supra*).

- *Ohio State Bar Ass'n v. Cohen,* 107 Ohio St.3d 98 (2005): The office of DocuPrep USA advertised that it could "prepare and file the important documents of life without the services and expense of a lawyer." However, the court found that the office was engaged in the unauthorized practice of law when it selected the forms and causes of action. While the intent of the office may have been honorable (to protect its clients' interests), the clients' reliance on its services to protect their legal rights in court was impermissible and violative of the law.

- *Cleveland Bar Ass'n v. Para-Legals, Inc.,* 106 Ohio St.3d 455, 835 N.E.2d 1240 (2005): The company's services included legal research, document preparation, and other ancillary legal services. It touted on its letterhead: "We Are Not Attorneys, We Just Do All Of The Work!" The particular incident that resulted in the lawsuit was preparation of a petition in the domestic relations court of Ohio without a licensed attorney's oversight.

- *Ohio State Bar Ass'n v. Allen,* 107 St.3d 180, 181–182, 837 N.E.2d 762, 763–764 (2005): The court was particularly severe in its penalties assessed against the respondent due to his

> *repeated transgressions [of UPL] and his demonstrated disrespect for the relator and the board. . . . Respondent flouted our constitutional authority [...] to regulate the practice of law and to protect the public from interlopers not subject to the ethical constraints and educational requirements of this profession. Though given ample opportunity, respondent refused to cooperate in this process, flagrantly practiced law without a license, and caused unsuspecting and vulnerable customers harm by taking their money in exchange for providing inferior services with potentially disastrous ramifications.*

Four proven instances of UPL resulted in $40,000 in fines ($10,000 per occurrence).

- *The Florida Bar v. Miravalle,* 761 So.2d 1049 (Fla. 2000): The operator of a legal form preparation service was found to have engaged in the unauthorized practice of law by rendering services that the public relied upon to properly prepare and file legal documents, not merely provide a "form fill" service. The court also discussed the nature of the company's name "Express Legal Services, Inc." and advertisements as misleading, because they gave the impression that the company specialized in certain types of practice and described legal procedures.

- *Statewide Grievance Committee v. Patton,* 239 Conn. 251, 683 A.2d 1359 (1996): The Connecticut Supreme Court upheld a very broad interpretation of acts constituting the practice of law. "Doc-U-Prep" provided customers with a questionnaire pertaining to the type of service requested. The Connecticut Courts have consistently held that legal document preparation is the type of activity "commonly understood to be the practice of law." *Id.* at 254. "Although such transactions have no direct connection with court proceedings, they are always subject to subsequent involvement in litigation. They require in many aspects a high degree of legal skill and great capacity for adaptation to difficult and complex situations." *Id.* at 254–255, citing, *State Bar Ass'n v. Connecticut Bank & Trust Co.,* 145 Conn. 222, 234–235, 140 A.2d 863 (1958).

IN CLASS DISCUSSION

In light of the fact that legal document preparers/independent paralegals are regulated and must register with or be certified by the state, what is the benefit or detriment to regulating the paralegal profession as a whole? Do you think that "traditional" paralegals have more or less freedom in their practices with regard to the rules of UPL? How would you personally prefer to practice? Why?

Managing a Law Practice

Daily tasks are also performed slightly differently in a law office. There are day-to-day office activities that are common to all businesses, and these can be handled by non-attorney staff. However, the **management of the law practice** must be handled by an attorney. What is the difference between these two realms? The attorney (commonly called the "managing partner") handles the manner in which cases are distributed to the practice areas in the firm, billable hours, client protocol, trust funds, and other issues particular to the practice of law. "Management" also encompasses the ultimate responsibility for all the work that leaves the office and the proper supervision of all employees. This has important ramifications for UPL, as an attorney may not be consistently absent from the office or delegate duties of oversight.

While the courts in each jurisdiction determine what constitutes the unauthorized practice and could have differing opinions, it appears that the courts in Ohio have little sympathy for poor office management. An attorney who was bedridden for several months was suspended for six months for relying on his paralegal to help him manage the law practice. *Columbus Bar Association v. Watson,* 106 Ohio St.3d 298, 834 N.E.2d 809 (2005). Even worse, in *Matter of Thonert,* 693 N.E.2d 559, 561 (Ind. 1998), a suspended attorney instructed his staff to keep the lines of communication open with the clients, including advising them of court dates and other matters arising in their cases. Billing was ongoing, as the staff was instructed to send out new statements on accounts receivable. In his absence the staff was also told to organize the office and close out files. The court concluded that "the conducting of the business management of a law practice, in conjunction with that practice, constitutes the practice of law." *Id* at 563 (citing *Matter of Perrello,* 270 Ind. 390, 398, 386 N.E.2d 174, 179 (1979)). Generally, the courts do not divide the practice of law into practical matters and legal matters. The business elements merge into the legal elements so that there is one cohesive whole.

management of the law practice
Oversight of the purely business aspects of the law firm, as well as ensuring that the protocols conform to the ethical requirements placed upon the attorneys and support staff.

FIGURE 2.3
Structure and Functioning of the Law Office

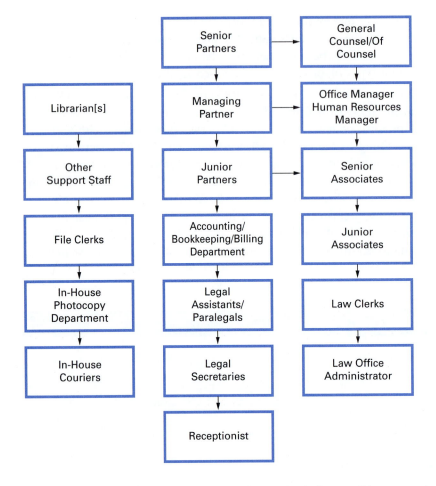

The unique attributes of the law practice make it impossible to conduct the business without knowledge and regard for the legal elements. *See Perrello* at 397. The fact that the non-attorney staff members are entirely competent to run the office is insufficient to overcome the mandate that an attorney manage the law practice.

The management of a law firm is distinct from the law office manager/paralegal position in many larger firms and corporations. This position coordinates the activities of the office and the other employees. Strong organizational skills are an essential asset a premium in this field, as the paralegal may also be made a project leader to ensure that certain tasks are performed optimally. Parallel to the managing attorney's role in the law office is the position of **paralegal manager**. Depending upon the structure of the firm or company, paralegal managers generally recruit, interview, and hire new paralegals and help to train them. They also oversee the distribution and progress of paralegal assignments. "In performing these tasks, the Manager plays multiple roles: leader, mentor, advocate, supervisor, trainer, financial watchdog, evaluator, problem solver, and resource manager." *The Value of a Legal Assistant Manager,* published by IPMA. This resource is available online at http://www.paralegalmanagement.org/ipma/docs/Value%20of%20a%20Manager.pdf. There are many players in the hierarchical structure of a law firm, not just the managing partner and paralegal manager along with their respective staff. The proper and efficient functioning of the law firm takes many people. Figure 2.3 provides a flowchart of these players.

Appearance before a Court of Law

After the matter has been commenced through some sort of legal document preparation, and the attorney has been managing the matter, the next logical step in the progression involves **representation in court** and other tribunals. There are some

paralegal manager
A position in a law firm usually held by a paralegal who generally recruits, interviews, and hires new paralegals and helps to train them.

representation in court
The right to speak and be heard by the court in a legal matter; a duly licensed attorney is the only person, other than the defendant or plaintiff, who is acknowledged to have this right.

agencies that permit non-lawyers to represent parties in hearings; however, this is the exception, not the rule. *See Sperry v. Florida,* 373 U.S. 379, 83 S.Ct. 1322, 10 L.Ed. 2d 428 (1963). A non-attorney was engaged in the practice of preparing and prosecuting patent applications in Florida before the United States Patent Office. Under Florida law, this constituted the unauthorized practice of law because the non-attorney was appearing before a tribunal. However, federal statutes and patent regulations authorized practice before this tribunal by non-attorneys. The federal rules preempted the Florida rules. State rules that are contrary to federal law are not enforceable. Therefore, the non-attorney practitioner was not guilty of the unauthorized practice of law before the federal patent office.

Paralegals can check their state office of administrative courts for the rules particular to their jurisdiction for non-attorney appearances. The rules will differ from state to state. There are some administrative agencies that perform judicial functions and hold hearings. These agencies can provide for non-attorney representation of the parties before them. In *Caressa Camille, Inc. v. Alcoholic Beverage Control Appeals Bd.,* 99 Cal.App.4th 1094, 121 Cal.Rptr.2d 758 (2002), the California Appellate Court concluded that a liquor license revocation proceeding before the administrative agency was not a "court of record." The non-attorney was permitted to represent the corporation that was the subject of the hearing. The New Jersey Office of Administrative Courts states this:

> *An attorney may represent a party or a party may present the case him or herself. Additionally, in some cases a non-lawyer may assist a party at the hearing. Some examples are, a paralegal or assistant employed by legal services; a principal of a close corporation; a union representative in a civil service case; and an individual who is permitted by federal law to appear in a Special Education case. In Family Development, Medical Assistance, and Youth and Family Services cases the non-lawyer can ask to be allowed to appear on the day of the hearing. In all other cases, the non-lawyer must complete a Notice of Appearance/Application form [available on this website] and return it to the OAL at least ten days before the hearing.*

"Appearance in court" is a term referring to the attorney's right to speak for his client and to be heard on the record. Paralegals often accompany their attorneys to court to assist them at trial, but this presence is not considered an official appearance in court.

The Supreme Court of Ohio found that a paralegal was guilty of committing UPL despite having registered as an "independent paralegal" with the probate court. The paralegal filed the required papers in order to represent a claim in the court; however, a responsible supervising attorney did not sign the registration document. The paralegal crossed out the word "attorney" on the form and inserted "paralegal." The probate court found that while paralegals are permitted to represent claimants, subverting the system by changing the form and acting without the supervision of an attorney was punishable as contempt of court. *Columbus Bar Ass'n v. Purnell,* 94 Ohio St. 3d 126, 760 N.E.2d 817 (2002).

In all judicial courts, a party may choose either to represent herself or to have a licensed attorney in that jurisdiction represent her interests. The constitutional right to have representation in court does not extend beyond these two classifications of parties. A person who is not an attorney licensed in that jurisdiction cannot represent the party, regardless of how knowledgeable the non-attorney is or how much the party wishes to be represented by that individual. It is well settled that "[t]here is no constitutional right to representation by lay counsel"; that is, a party does not have the right to have a non-attorney represent him. "Any other rule would in effect put this court in the position of sponsoring the unauthorized practice of law." *Rhines* at 239, citing *Terpstra v. Farmers & Merchants Bank,* 483 N.E.2d 749, 760 (Ind. Ct. App. 1985) (citations omitted), reh'g denied.

Interestingly, many courts have decided that an attorney who acts on her own behalf as a pro se litigant must follow the ethical rules and avoid contacting the opposing party, even though there is no prohibition against lay litigants from contacting each other. The rationale for this prohibition is grounded in the very concerns over who should be permitted to practice law. Attorneys are permitted exclusive rights to practice law because they have specialized knowledge of the intricate workings of the law and legal system. Using this knowledge when they are a pro se litigant against the opposing party, who may not have this degree of knowledge, would potentially give the pro se attorney an unfair advantage. Some courts have taken an absolutist position, where no harm needs to be shown from the contact in order to hold that the communication is prohibited by the ethical rules. *See*, for example, *Runsvold v. Idaho State Bar*, 129 Idaho 419, 925 P.2d 118 (1996); *In re Haley*, 156 Wash. 2d 324, 126 P.2d 1262 (2006); *Sandstrom v. Sandstrom*, 880 P.2d 103 (Wyo. 1994). Other courts will examine the facts of the particular case at hand to determine whether the communication was of a legal nature, or the type of contact that would ordinarily and permissibly take place between lay litigants. *Pinsky v. Statewide Grievance Committee*, 216 Conn. 228, 578 A.2d 1075 (1990). The Pinsky court's rationale indicated that contact between litigants is specifically authorized by the relevant professional codes. The restriction on direct communication with the represented opposing party is limited to the situations where the attorney is representing a client. Therefore, an attorney who is representing himself and not a client may communicate with the other litigant directly. ("While the [attorney]'s conduct may have been less than prudent, it did not violate Rule 4.2"). *Pinsky* at 236.

Negotiation and Settlement

negotiation and settlement
The alternative means to terminate a legal matter rather than full trial on the merits. As the settlement has the same force as a final adjudication, an attorney must perform the tasks associated with it.

Finally, negotiating and settling a matter is exclusively an attorney's job. **Negotiation and settlement** takes skill, tenacity, and experience to achieve the proper and just result for the client. Strategy regarding procedural and substantive law must be taken into account during this time. The courts have previously held that when a person who is not an attorney represents another in the negotiation and settlement of a personal injury claim for consideration, pursuant to a contingency fee contract, that person has engaged in the unauthorized practice of law. *Duncan v. Gordon*, 476 So.2d 896 (La.App. 2d Cir. 1985). It is the unauthorized practice of law because the person must advise the client of issues concerning the redress of a legal wrong. *Id.* Negotiation and settlement are functions solely performable by an attorney. Attorneys analyze the merit of a case's facts in light of the state of the current law. They apply law to fact to render a legal conclusion to gauge the value of settlement versus litigation; it is the trained, impartial analysis of an attorney's mind that can be relied upon to make that determination. This is not to say that others who are not licensed could not make that determination, but remember, again, that the courts and clients can hold an attorney accountable for imprudent actions taken in this regard.

Delegation of settlement negotiations to non-attorney staff will result in the finding that the supposedly "supervising" attorney assisted in the unauthorized practice of law. In an extreme case, an attorney completely renounced the essential role of the attorney in settlements. In *In re Sledge*, 859 So. 2d 671 (La. 2003), the attorney was absent from his law practice for approximately half the time, delegating complete control of the management of the law office to his staff. Most shockingly, he

> admitted there were often cases that were handled from the interview stage to the settlement distribution without any involvement on his [the attorney's] part. Respondent [attorney] conceded he authorized [his office manager] to negotiate settlements, and that he did not get involved in the non-litigation cases, reasoning it was "routine" and that non-lawyers deal with insurance adjusters better than lawyers. As convincing evidence of his adequate supervision

of his employees, respondent [attorney] referred to the existence of his "employee office manual," which according to respondent had the appropriate checklists and guidelines for his employees to process his cases. . . . Respondent conceded that he supervised [his office manager]'s performance exclusively based on graphs evidencing how many cases she settled and the gross income generated from the cases.

Id. at 682–683.

Needless to say, the Supreme Court of Louisiana did not find this to be either the adequate supervision of the attorney's staff nor the appropriate delegation of the practice of law. The attorney's characterization of settlement negotiations as "routine" or "cookie-cutter" was "clearly at odds" with the philosophy of the court that every client deserves the benefit of the lawyer's legal training and skill to resolve the particular issue before him. *Id.* at 686. It should be no surprise that Mr. Sledge was disbarred for this conduct.

A paralegal's claim that she was doing "nothing more than relaying information" will not shield her from prosecution for the unauthorized practice of law. *The Florida Bar v. Neiman,* 816 So.2d 587, 589 (Fla. 2002). The claims regarding the UPL committed by Neiman, a paralegal, were numerous. Although interviewing clients is perfectly acceptable paralegal practice, this paralegal took it a step further by commenting that it sounded like a "good case." *Id.* Legal research that is normally performed by a paralegal turned into UPL when Neiman reported the results directly back to the client. *Id.* It is good office protocol to return phone calls from other attorneys; however, again, Neiman took his role of paralegal one step too far, by not only speaking to opposing counsel, but also arguing about issues of liability, evidence, and settlement. *Id.* at 590. Neiman, a paralegal, was very successful in "running the show" at the law office where he was employed. *Id.* at 594. However, this is unacceptable under the laws concerning UPL. The recommendation to the Supreme Court of Florida was very specific as to what actions taken by this paralegal were to be enjoined, and it provides a comprehensive list of prohibited actions. Paralegals who have been found guilty of UPL should be prevented from

a. having direct contact with any client, opposing counsel or third party, unless it involves the [paralegal]'s own personal legal matters;

b. without limiting the above, discussing, construing or interpreting the applicability of any case law, statutory law or any other law with any opposing counsel or other third party;

c. speaking on behalf of third parties at settlement conferences, meetings, negotiations or mediations, even with an attorney present;

d. appearing on behalf of third parties at settlement meetings, negotiations or mediations without the attorney present for whom [the paralegal] is employed;

e. without limiting the above, providing third parties advice on the strengths and weaknesses of any legal matter, or making decisions on behalf of others that require legal skill and a knowledge of the law greater than the average citizen;

f. without limiting the above, advising third parties as to various legal remedies available to them and possible courses of action;

g. preparing pleadings, motions or any other legal documents for others, and, without limiting the above, explaining to third parties the legal significance of any document;

h. without limiting the above, having direct contact in the nature of consultation, explanation, recommendation, advice or assistance in the selection of any legal remedy or course of action;

    i. suggesting, directing or participating in the accumulation of evidence supporting any legal claim;

    j. holding [himself] out to third parties in such a manner that a third party places some reliance on [him] to handle legal matters;

    k. impliedly holding himself out as an attorney;

    l. without limiting the above, serving as a conduit or intermediary for the obtaining or relaying of any information for the preparation, consideration or evaluation of any legal matter from others who have never consulted with [the paralegal's] supervising attorney;

    m. soliciting or accepting attorney's fees;

    n. without limiting the above, corresponding with parties or attorneys of parties as the representative of any client relating to legal matters;

    o. signing any letter, pleading or other document on behalf of any attorney or under any attorney's signature, even with such attorney's consent. . . .

Id. at 595–596.

The reviewing court was careful to point out that this did not unnecessarily restrict a paralegal's practice. Many other tasks are necessary for a law office to run properly, and these are properly delegated to the paralegal. Further, note that these prohibitions were very strictly construed against Neiman because of his flagrant abuse of his position at the firm. The most important factor to be considered is real supervision of a responsible attorney, something that was clearly lacking in the above case. Paralegals whose roles and duties are clearly delineated and known to clients do not run the risk of failing the test espoused by the Neiman court. "In common parlance, Neiman's activities fail the 'duck' test. That is, in common parlance, one would expect that if it looks like a duck, and walks, talks, and acts like a duck, one can usually safely assume it is a duck. Unfortunately, while Neiman at all times acted like an educated and licensed lawyer, he was not." *Id.* at 599.

 RESEARCH THIS

Find a case or ethics opinion in your jurisdiction that defines the "practice of law." What considerations did the court find important in describing what is or is not the practice of law (which is, therefore, confined to be practiced by attorneys)? Write your own definition for the "practice of law." After performing this task, write a paralegal job description detailing the duties and responsibilities of the position. Create a narrative of what the paralegals, both employees and freelancers, can and cannot do in order to stay within the UPL statutes of your jurisdiction.

HOW PARALEGALS CAN AVOID THE UNAUTHORIZED PRACTICE OF LAW

The burden of preventing the unauthorized practice of law does not fall solely on the shoulders of the supervising attorneys. Indeed, every member of the legal team should strive for compliance. This is particularly true for paralegals, as they have significant client contact. Further, clients cannot appreciate the subtle differences between giving them general information regarding their case and its progress and rendering legal advice. To complicate matters even further, paralegals often know the correct legal answer or have prepared the legal analysis regarding the issue, but are not permitted to communicate that to the client.

The paralegal's rapport (avoiding the use of the term "relationship," since that is a term of art saved for use with the attorney here) with the client is essential in the delivery of legal services. Often the paralegal is present at or in charge of the intake interview; or perhaps she is fielding the first phone call from the prospective client. Even these preliminary tasks present an opportunity to cross that line into the unauthorized practice of law. From the outset, the client should be informed of the paralegal's status and role as a member of the legal team. This is to avoid confusion on the part of the client as to whom he can look to for certain types of information. Legal advice, of course, cannot be given by the paralegal, and this constraint should be explained to the client in order to "head it off at the pass." Clients will call to check on the status of their cases, and if the attorney is unavailable, will also look to the paralegal for legal guidance. Once the boundaries of the duties of the paralegal have been established, the client will have been advised of this prohibition. Again, it is not that the paralegal does not know the answer, but that the protections of the ethical codes do not allow her to convey them directly to the client.

Paralegals may be most at risk for crossing the line in the situations that need them the most. Legal Aid Services provide free legal services to low-income residents in the jurisdiction. Often paralegals are used for intake screening, to determine the nature of the matter in order to refer the issue to the appropriate attorney; to ensure that the party is eligible for the legal services requested; and to screen for potential conflicts. The conversations between the paralegal and the potential client may or may not contain sensitive information, and the client may feel that a confidential legal relationship has been formed. This is a fact-sensitive issue which can be avoided by clear communication to the potential client during screening of the purpose and limitations of the role of the intake paralegal. In these situations, paralegals may find it difficult to refrain from answering anxious clients' legal questions. The desire to help, which probably drove the paralegal into employment at Legal Aid Services in the first place, must be overcome by the paralegal's ethical obligations to refrain from the unauthorized practice of law.

The same holds true for paralegals engaged in other areas of law where anxiety runs particularly high. In bankruptcy, family law, wills/estates/trusts, landlord/tenant and other document-based practices, it is very often the paralegal who actually prepares the first drafts of these papers. The worried client may be aware of this fact and the paralegal, having the information at hand, may be tempted to provide information regarding the matter. What type of communication is permissible, and when does it cross the line? The court has typically held that decisions regarding the choice of document to be prepared, the ramifications of that choice, and the actions to be taken by the client in furtherance of that choice, are impermissible as the unauthorized practice of law. Conversely, paralegals have not stepped over the line when they have taken some of the above actions, but have sought the final review and approval of a supervising attorney.

Other preliminary tasks also present potential hazards. Paper is everywhere in a law office, and much of it is letters. Constant correspondence is sent out to so many different people and companies, not just the client. These entities are not familiar with the role of the paralegal in the matter. As first impressions are everything, law firms often list their attorneys on their letterhead, indicating their bar admissions and certified specialties. Firms may also choose to list the names of their paralegals, and this is perfectly acceptable, as long as the paralegals are clearly identified as such. Indeed, it may give some clients a degree of comfort to know that qualified paralegals, whom the firm is proud to list, are employed on their cases. This may be particularly true where the paralegal has earned certifications from any of the national paralegal associations. Firms may also choose to supply their paralegals with business cards. Again,

FIGURE 2.4
Signing
Correspondence

NALA Guideline 5

. . . A legal assistant may perform any function delegated by an attorney, including, but not limited to the following:

9. Author and sign letters providing the legal assistant's status is clearly indicated and the correspondence does not contain independent legal opinions or legal advice.

NFPA EC 1.7(b)

A paralegal's title shall be included if the paralegal's name appears on business cards, letterhead, brochures, directories, and advertisements.

NFPA 1.7(c)

A paralegal shall not use letterhead, business cards or other promotional materials to create a fraudulent impression of his/her status or ability to practice in the jurisdiction in which the paralegal practices.

this is beneficial, in that the various parties who need information regarding a matter upon which a paralegal is working will be able to have the direct link to her. Signing correspondence, whether on letterhead indicating the paralegal's status or not, should also note under the signature the title of "paralegal," "legal assistant," or whatever other title is appropriate in the particular firm. See Figure 2.4 for the paralegal codes regarding this issue.

These issues related to correspondence have been addressed by various courts and ethics boards. The New Jersey Supreme Court Advisory Committee on Professional Ethics put it very clearly:

> It is not and should not be our intention to hamstring the effectiveness of the non-lawyer assistant by placing artificial barriers in the way of the performance of his or her duties. Thus, for example, the non-lawyer assistant may, we believe, properly sign firm letterhead in connection with routine tasks in many fields of law such as the gathering of factual information and documents....

NJ Eth.Op. 611, 1988 WL 356368 at 1.

The committee's opinion went on to explain that other kinds of correspondence should not be signed by non-attorneys. Communications that include substantive legal issues or are sent to the court and opposing attorneys must be signed by the responsible attorney. The key to this issue is the substance of the correspondence. If the paralegal could not say or do what is accomplished in the letter without committing UPL, then the paralegal should not sign it.

> Such a rule has several beneficial effects including the following: It avoids the opportunity or temptation for the non-lawyer assistant to step over the line by rendering legal advice. . . . Second, it enables the responsible attorney to keep abreast of the matter by controlling important correspondence and so performing his essential function as the responsible attorney including his obligation of close supervision.

Id.

A paralegal's participation in pursuing a matter and its ultimate termination must comport with the aforementioned standards. *Any* action taken by a paralegal on behalf of the client impacting the client's legal rights and liabilities without an attorney's supervision will likely be found to be the unauthorized practice of law. Even if the conduct would have been permissible had it been overseen by an attorney who was ultimately responsible for the work product, it is an ethical violation in the absence of that oversight. The South Carolina Supreme Court rendered an opinion regarding the quality and type of oversight of a paralegal's conduct resulting in the unauthorized practice of law. The Court opined: "Meaningful attorney supervision must be present throughout the process [of solicitation and representation]. The line between what is and what is not permissible conduct by a non-attorney is oftentimes 'unclear' and is a potential trap for the unsuspecting client." *Doe v. Condon,* 341 S.C. 22, 26, 532 S.E.2d 879, 881 (2000), citing *State v. Buyers Service Co., Inc.,* 292 S.C. 426, 357 S.E.2d 15, 17 (1987). In *Doe,* the court found several different activities, one of which has not yet been discussed here, that constituted the unauthorized practice of law. The matter came before the court as the petitioner sought a declaratory opinion as to what proposed activities would be "out of bounds." Among other things, the paralegal intended to conduct educational seminars for the public on the topic of estate planning. Even answering "general" questions of the audience would involve the exercise of legal judgment, and therefore be prohibited.

ATTORNEYS AND THE UNAUTHORIZED PRACTICE OF LAW

Until now, the discussion has centered on the practice of law by non-attorneys; attorneys also can violate this rule, in two ways. First, the attorney can commit UPL herself in violation of ABA Model Rule 5.5, which prohibits an attorney from practicing in a jurisdiction in which he has not been formally admitted. Second, the attorney could violate the rule by assisting a non-attorney in committing UPL.

Multijurisdictional Practice

In today's trend toward globalization, many individuals and companies find themselves doing business across state lines and across national borders. This business model does not fit the way that attorneys have traditionally practiced law. As noted earlier in this chapter, attorneys must pass the bar for each state in which they practice. Traditionally, clients' interests were contained within the state in which they retained their attorneys. This simply is no longer the case. Engaging in the practice of law in a state where the attorney is not admitted is the unauthorized practice of law in that jurisdiction.

multijurisdictional practice
The practice of law by an attorney outside the state in which that attorney was originally licensed, because the clients' interests are interstate or national in scale.

The problem is serious enough that in 2000, the ABA created a task force, the Commission on Multijurisdictional Practice, to study and report on this issue. The former version of the Multijurisdictional Practice Rule contained essentially only one sentence: "a lawyer shall not: (a) practice law in a jurisdiction where doing so violates the regulation of the legal profession in that jurisdiction; or (b) assist a person who is not a member of the bar in the performance of activity that constitutes the unauthorized practice of law." The goal of the ABA commission was to find a balance between the interests of clients operating on national and international scales and of the states in protecting their citizens and maintaining the integrity of their own judicial systems. Clients have the right to retain the attorney of their own choosing; it places an undue burden upon them to have to retain an attorney for each state in which they operate.

While every state has accommodations for a "one-time-only" admission where the client requires out-of-state assistance, the reality is that clients need their lawyers to operate in other jurisdictions on a more frequent basis. The "one-time-only" special dispensation for practice in the jurisdiction in which the lawyer is not admitted is called "pro hac vice"—literally, "for this turn." The attorney is required to submit an application to the court in front of which she desires to appear. Usually, a state also requires that an attorney admitted to practice in that state agrees to "sponsor" the petitioning attorney. The petitioned court may request any other reasonable information from the applicant that it deems necessary to make a determination as to whether leave to appear before the court is granted. This may include a substantial amount

The Internet provides access to the entire world at the click of a mouse, making all users members of a virtual community without borders. UPL statutes and opinions have definite borders, as they are creations of individual states' legislatures and courts. The increase for the need to access to affordable legal services has resulted in several online service providers. Visit these sites, for example:

- www.wethepeopleusa.com: "We the People" is a national chain with individual state offices and websites
- www.nshlp.com: "National Self Help Law Project" is based out of California
- www.legalinfonetwork.com: "Self-Help Legal Information Network" is also based out of California
- http://www.seniorsapprove.com/legal-documents.html: This is a national document preparation service provider for seniors that specializes in documents relating to elder care

Note also that NALDP provides a listing of these service providers by state at www.naldp.org.

Crossing borders has significant impact on these practitioners, much like the multijurisdictional practice issues discussed regarding lawyers. The Ohio Supreme Court has recently addressed this very issue in *Trumbull County Bar Ass'n v. Legal Aid State Services, Inc.*, 109 Ohio St. 3d 93, 846 N.E.2d 35 (2006). The legal service provider ran an online business based in Las Vegas, Nevada that purported to have expertise in preparing legal forms to be consistent with individual state standards. The incident that brought the service firm before the Ohio court was an adoption petition filed in Trumbull County, Ohio. The court found that the business was engaged in the unauthorized practice of law in Ohio, regardless of its place of operation, when it prepared legal papers to be filed in an Ohio court on behalf of its clients.

of detail regarding the applicant's current practice and reasons why the applicant should be permitted to practice in the jurisdiction. If there isn't any benefit to the client in having the out-of-jurisdiction attorney appear for the party, then the court is likely to refuse the application and deem it in the best interest of the client to have an in-state attorney appear on the client's behalf. This may also be seen as a protective measure for the in-state attorneys against infiltration of "border attorneys" (those practicing near the state line) who are not admitted to the practice in that state.

The new ABA Model Rule 5.5 adds much clarity, explanation, and guidance for practitioners who find themselves involved in multijurisdictional issues. The number of lawyers, and therefore the number of paralegals also, who are going to find themselves in this situation will continue to rise. The multijurisdictional practice rules make more practical sense for attorneys and paralegals who are practicing law today. Attorneys and paralegals have been given a means to serve their clients' interests without violating the ethics rules. Each state remains territorial and the particular rules regarding out-of-state legal representation must be investigated, but at least such representation is now possible.

Assisting Others in Committing the Unauthorized Practice of Law

A significant change made by the ABA commission to Rule 5.5 was the expansion of the concept that a lawyer should not assist *anyone* in the unauthorized practice of law. The previous definition suggested that lawyers should not assist only those who were not members of the bar, giving lawyers from another jurisdiction (members of the bar) a potential loophole, depending on how closely one read the rule. This modification makes it quite clear that any person who is not admitted to practice in the relevant jurisdiction should not be assisted in the practice of law. How does this play out in the law office? Attorneys, like many others, move from state to state for various reasons. If they are to be employed in a law firm, they must be admitted to practice in their new state. In *Bluestein v. State Bar,* 13 Cal.3d 162, 118 Cal.Rptr. 175 (1974), a purported foreign attorney who was not licensed in California was listed on the California attorney's letterhead as "of Counsel," thus giving the appearance that he was an admitted, duly licensed attorney in that jurisdiction. The California attorney permitted the unlicensed person to consult with his clients regarding a matter arising in Spain. The California attorney was then held to have violated the ethical rules against aiding another in the unauthorized practice of law.

> Whether a person gives advice as to local law, Federal law, the law of a sister State, or the law of a foreign country, he is giving legal advice. . . . To hold otherwise would be to state that a member of the State Bar only practices law when he deals with local law, a manifestly anomalous statement. Giving legal advice regarding the law of a foreign country thus constitutes the practice of law, and the next question is whether such practice is unauthorized. Business and Professions Code, section 6125, provides, "No person shall practice law in this State unless he is an active member of the State Bar."

Id. at 174.

It appears that the courts have interpreted the practice of law as the practice of any law, regardless of the source of that law. The conduct of an attorney who holds himself out as being able to practice law in a jurisdiction where he is not admitted also reflects upon his fitness to practice and violates his duty of candor towards the tribunals of that jurisdiction and their clients. In *In re Jackman,* the New Jersey Supreme Court found that a large New Jersey law firm had aided in an associate attorney's unauthorized practice of law where the managing partner knew about the associate's lack of admission to the New Jersey bar. After about seven years at the New Jersey firm, the associate sat for the New Jersey bar exam. During this time, the associate was admitted to practice only in Massachusetts and had actually been put on inactive status in that jurisdiction. Further, the court supported the significant delay in the associate's certification to admission to the New Jersey bar after having taken the bar exam to "underscore to this candidate the seriousness with which we view his earlier improper practice and his failure to be responsible in discerning his personal obligation to satisfy our admission and practice requirements." 165 N.J. 580, 593, 761 A.2d 1103, 1110 (2000).

However, most relevant to paralegal students is how the rules affecting attorneys pertain to them, clearly persons who are not members of the bar in any jurisdiction. Paralegals offer very valuable services to attorneys, services that are legal in nature. It is up to the trained professional determination of the attorney to determine how best to use the paralegal without overstepping the boundaries of the practice. Recall that paralegals are essential in some areas of practice in order to be able to deliver cost-effective legal services to members of the the public who are most in need but sometimes least able to afford these services. This belief was highlighted in an ethics opinion of the Philadelphia bar. An attorney had requested an advisory opinion regarding his acceptance of referrals and interpretation services provided by a bilingual paralegal. The opinion could not address the attorney's concern over whether the independent paralegal was engaged in the unauthorized practice of law, because that is a fact-sensitive matter and would have to be determined by a court of law. However, the ethics committee did comment on the attorney's conduct with respect to these services provided by the paralegal. It found no ethical problem as long as the attorney did nothing that could be construed as aiding and abetting in the unauthorized practice of law by that paralegal. The attorney, by necessity, had to rely on the assurances of the paralegal that he was not giving any legal advice during those translation services. *See* 1988 WL 236395 (Phila. Bar. Assn. Prof. Guid. Comm.).

While it seems intuitive from the above rule that attorneys may not accept assistance from others in the practice of law, that is indeed what they are doing from the moment they employ a paralegal. If paralegals could not practice law, they would be of very little use in the office. Recall, it is the authorized practice of law that paralegals perform. For this reason, the ABA has created Model Rule 5.3. This rule requires that all responsible lawyers in the firm must ensure that there are ways of monitoring their assistants' conduct and make certain that it is compatible with the professional

FIGURE 2.5

Paralegals'
Knowledge of the
Attorneys' Rules of
Professional Conduct

NALA Guideline 3

Legal Assistants should:

#3 – Understand the attorney's Rules of Professional Responsibility and these Guidelines in order to avoid any action which would involve the attorney in a violation of the Rules, or give the appearance of professional impropriety.

NFPA EC 1.3(e)

A paralegal shall not knowingly assist any individual with the commission of an act that is in direct violation of the Model Code/Model Rules and/or the rules and/or laws governing the jurisdiction in which the paralegal practices.

obligations of the lawyers in the firm. This obligation underscores the importance of a paralegal's understanding of the Rules of Professional Responsibility that govern the attorneys in the relevant jurisdiction. See the Paralegal Codes regarding this issue in Figure 2.5.

The main thrust of ABA Model Rule 5.3 is to permit attorneys to effectively use their paralegals, while reinforcing the necessity of supervision and their ultimate responsibility for not only the work product, but also the ethical performance of that work. This is precisely why paralegals need to study the applicable rules of ethics for their jurisdiction. A paralegal's conduct must comport with the standards of the supervising attorney. Without this mandate, the paralegal can become the "weakest link" in the chain of the provision of legal services to a client. Knowledge of the ethical standards serves to protect not only the paralegal and the attorneys in the office, but also the client's interests. To the extent that a paralegal is properly supervised and held accountable to the standards of ethics, she can practice law without overstepping the line into the unauthorized practice of law.

 REEL TO REAL

Take a look, or a second look if you've already seen it in the theater, at *Erin Brockovich*; Julia Roberts portrayed this spunky legal assistant in the 2000 movie. The general plot follows the true story of Ms. Brockovich, who has lost a personal injury lawsuit and subsequently is employed by her attorney. During some routine filing, she finds some interesting connections between medical records and toxic leakage from the Gas and Electric Company that threatens the entire community's health. Examine the tasks assigned to and the actions taken by Ms. Brockovich, and evaluate whether any of them could be considered the unauthorized practice of law.

The duty of supervision is taken very seriously by the bar and the courts. An attorney's office must have all the proper procedures in place to ensure that a paralegal's actions are compatible with the attorney's ethical obligations. An attorney must ensure that the paralegal is performing tasks in the same manner that the attorney is required to, and to ensure that the attorney is able to fulfill her own tasks required under the ethical codes. While proper procedures were in place in the attorney's office in *People v. Smith*, 74 P.3d 566 (Colo. 2003), his paralegal failed to follow through in ensuring that all client communications were transmitted to the attorney. The delegation of substantial work to a paralegal is perfectly acceptable; however, the attorney must properly supervise that work to make certain that the paralegal is taking the requisite actions. Failure to do so can, and in the Smith case did, result in the paralegal's commission of the unauthorized practice of law. The Smith court had little sympathy for the attorney, who claimed that the case neglect would not have occurred had the paralegal brought certain matters to his attention. The court found that it was the attorney's affirmative responsibility to take positive steps in supervision of the paralegal. Inaction or neglect by the paralegal did not excuse the attorney of responsibility and the finding that he was in violation of his ethical duties. For that reason, the attorney was suspended from practice for a period of nine months. Needless to say, it behooves the professional paralegal to maintain his personal integrity and responsibility for his own work product and work ethic in order to protect himself and his supervising attorneys.

Much in the same vein, ABA Model Rule 5.7 addresses this issue with regard to other law-related services provided by the attorney. If an attorney is involved in other businesses that are separate from but related to the law practice, the attorney must still comport with the applicable rules of professional conduct. The significance of this rule relates to the idea that an attorney is always cloaked with "legal authority," wherever she might be. A business, although separate from the actual legal practice, will take on this aura if there is an attorney involved in its management. Clients may not be able to make this complete separation between practice and business. Therefore, the ethical standards will follow the attorney into the business and impose standards upon the attorney where there normally would not be any if the business were managed by a non-lawyer. It is in this setting as well that the attorney must control the output of his employees, so as not to give the impression that the business is rendering legal services. If that were the case, the attorney would be assisting in the unauthorized practice of law.

What are these other businesses that may cause this type of problem? Fields that are tangential to the provision of legal services, such as insurance, title searching, financial and estate planning, accountancy, medical consultations, political lobbying, and tax preparation, just to name a few, are susceptible to the ethical protections for clients. The list goes on, depending upon the specialty of the attorney. It is important for the staff of these tangential services to understand the nature of the proscriptions of the ethical rules in order to avoid the unauthorized practice of law.

Other groups of "practitioners" have the potential to be affected by UPL issues. Mediators and arbitrators are growing in number as the citizenry turns to alternate dispute resolution. In an effort to address this critical issue, the ABA Section of Dispute Resolution adopted a Resolution on Mediation and the Unauthorized Practice of Law in 2002. The resolution had four main points. First, it was determined that mediation is not the practice of law. Mediators do not represent the parties, but rather function as impartial negotiators to assist the parties in reaching a voluntary settlement. Second, while legal issues are addressed, these discussions do not constitute legal advice, and there is no fiduciary relationship created. This is true even where the mediator is an attorney. Third, drafting the settlement agreement for the parties is not the practice of law, as the mediator is acting more as a scrivener. If the mediator inserts terms not agreed upon by the parties, he may be liable for UPL. The mediator must be clear that the suggestions made are merely for informational purposes and are not legal advice. Finally, just like paralegals, the mediator must make his role clear to the parties. If any party needs legal advice, that party will need to seek independent legal counsel before proceeding. Through this resolution, the ABA was able to underscore the importance of alternate dispute resolution in the rendering of legal services to the public: it performs a cost- and time-saving function in addressing societal needs similar to those that gave rise to the paralegal profession. The burden on the court system can be alleviated by offering an efficient and effective means of handling legal disputes.

It is important for the paralegal to bear in mind the role she plays in the legal system as a whole, not just the law office where she is employed. The unauthorized practice of law can take place in a law office, where the paralegal is either unsupervised or improperly supervised, or outside of the firm or corporate setting, where paralegals or others perform legal services that are exclusive to the attorney's practice of law. While many paralegals may have the experience to answer the legal questions posed by their practice and clients, it is imperative that they understand the boundaries of their own profession and not cross the line into the unauthorized practice of law.

Summary

This chapter has examined the complexity and variety of situations that may involve the unauthorized practice of law. The judiciary has created a "self-policing" system that limits the authority of those who are not prepared by education and experience to secure or defend the rights of parties in the legal system. They have distinguished between the tasks which are permissible for a non-lawyer to perform and those which are solely within the purview of attorneys. If a non-attorney performs any of those tasks ascribed solely to attorneys, she has committed the unauthorized practice of law (UPL). The traditional tasks ascribed to attorneys alone include these:

1. the acquisition of clients/establishment of the attorney-client relationship
2. giving legal advice
3. preparing legal documents
4. managing a law practice
5. representation in a court of law
6. negotiation and settlement of legal claims

While the performance of these tasks by non-lawyers is clearly UPL, attorneys themselves can commit UPL in two situations: (1) practicing in a jurisdiction where they are not licensed, and (2) assisting others in committing UPL.

Understanding the rules relating to the unauthorized practice of law is essential for a paralegal in order to properly practice her profession within the boundaries of ethical conduct. Paralegals should be particularly vigilant in these areas:

1. communications with the client
2. identifying themselves as paralegals
3. writing and signing correspondence
4. ensuring proper supervision by their employers

Independent paralegals (also known as "legal document preparers") face unique issues relating to UPL as they deliver legal services directly to the public. These professionals may be regulated by state statute, and must be mindful of the civil and criminal penalties that may be imposed for either UPL or professional negligence.

Key Terms and Concepts

Acquisition of clients
Attorney-client relationship
Fiduciary relationship
Freelance paralegal
Gatekeeping function
Independent paralegals
Legal advice
Legal document preparer (LDP)

Legal documents
Management of the law practice
Multijurisdictional practice
Negotiation and settlement
Paralegal manager
Representation in court
Substantive legal tasks
Unauthorized practice of law (UPL)

MULTIPLE CHOICE

Choose the best answer(s). Please explain WHY you chose the answer(s).

1. "Legal advice" can best be defined as
   a. The opinions of a lawyer
   b. Explanations of rights and liabilities of a citizen under the laws
   c. Informing a client about any legal proceeding
   d. Describing the process of the judicial system
   e. All of the above
   f. None of the above

2. The judicial system prohibits non-lawyers from representing persons in court because
   a. Non-lawyers have not paid the necessary dues to practice law
   b. Non-lawyers cannot know the intricate workings of the legal system
   c. The court cannot guarantee that the non-lawyers know the proper law and procedure
   d. Everyone has the right to represent themselves in court

3. Attorneys may be admitted "pro hac vice"
   a. When they want to practice in another jurisdiction
   b. When an established client has a legal issue in a jurisdiction where the attorney is not admitted
   c. Into multiple jurisdictions to ensure that they can represent corporate clients
   d. Before they are admitted to practice in the jurisdiction where they live

4. Which of the following is NOT traditionally accepted as a "lawyers only" task in the "practice of law":
   a. Managing a law practice
   b. Acquiring clients
   c. Settling claims relating to a lawsuit
   d. Performing legal research

EXPLAIN YOURSELF

All answers should be written in complete sentences. A simple yes or no is insufficient.

1. In your own words, describe the difference between an attorney's practice of law and a paralegal's practice of law.
2. Why can't a paralegal negotiate and settle a matter for a client where the client has consented to that kind of representation?
3. Describe the problems associated with "multijurisdictional practice." Is there a good solution to the globalization problem faced by corporate counsel?
4. What is the biggest problem, in your opinion, faced by "independent paralegals"?
5. Explain an attorney's duty of supervision. Why is it so critical to the proper functioning of the legal system?

FAULTY PHRASES

All of the following statements are FALSE; state why they are false and then rewrite each one as a true statement; do not just make the statement negative by adding the word "not."

1. All legal actions taken by non-lawyers constitute the unauthorized practice of law.
2. Paralegals may not prepare legal documents without committing UPL.

3. Once a retainer letter has been signed by the client, the attorney-client relationship has been formed.

4. All law office managers must be attorneys.

5. Attorneys cannot practice in multiple jurisdictions.

6. Paralegals should avoid signing correspondence to clients in order to avoid UPL.

 PORTFOLIO ASSIGNMENT

Write Away

1. In an effort to clarify the role of the paralegals in the firm, the managing partner asks you to write a paralegal job description detailing the duties and responsibilities of the position. The manager wants a narrative of what the paralegals, both employees and freelancers, can and cannot do in order to stay within the UPL statutes of your jurisdiction.

2. Prepare a legal memorandum advising the managing partner of the firm's potential liability for the following actions taken by paralegals employed by the firm:

   a. Allen answered the law office telephone and recognized the client's voice. He told the client that she had nothing to worry about in her matter because the attorney was on the other line right at that moment with the opposing counsel, settling the case for her.

   b. Betty was out to lunch with the other paralegals in the firm and they began discussing the legal strategy of the biggest cases of product liability that the firm was handling.

   c. Carl met with new clients Mr. and Mrs. Smith to obtain some basic information from them. They have come to the firm to have their wills made. Carl took the liberty of suggesting that they see a financial advisor about their assets in order to protect them from estate taxes.

   d. Debbie drafted a will for her parents at their request. She told them they would have to see an attorney at her firm in order to have it finalized.

   e. Ernie spoke to opposing counsel regarding the discovery deadlines for a case he was working on. The other attorney became angry that Ernie was insisting that the firm receive the answers within the time required by the court rules and insisted that he be given an extension. Ernie said he would file a motion to compel seeking attorney fees if opposing counsel did not answer per the court rules.

State v. Atchley, 108 Haw. 77, 116 P.3d 719, 2005 WL 1793458 (Haw. App.)

CONSTITUTIONALITY OF UPL STATUTES

(Under Rule 35(c) of the Hawai'i Rules of Appellate Procedure, a memorandum opinion or unpublished dispositional order shall not be cited in any other action or proceeding except when the opinion or unpublished dispositional order establishes the law of the pending case, res judicata or collateral estoppel, or in a criminal action or proceeding involving the same respondent.)

Intermediate Court of Appeals of Hawai'i.

STATE of Hawai'i, Plaintiff-Appellee,

v.

Kitty L. ATCHLEY, also known as Kitty L. Ah Loy, Defendant-Appellant.

No. 25322.

July 28, 2005.

Appeal from the Circuit Court of the Second Circuit (CR. No. 02-1-0197(3)).

BURNS, C.J., FOLEY and NAKAMURA, JJ.

SUMMARY DISPOSITION ORDER

Defendant-Appellant Kitty L. Atchley (Atchley) appeals from the Judgment filed on August 13, 2002, in the Circuit Court of the Second Circuit (circuit court). [FN omitted] Atchley was a paralegal who operated a sole proprietorship known as Valley Isle Paralegal. She was not a licensed attorney and did not work under the supervision of an attorney. Between August and October of 2000, Atchley assisted Ellen and Richard Kamaka (the Kamakas) in obtaining an uncontested divorce, charging them approximately $300 for her services.

After a jury trial, Atchley was found guilty of practicing law without a license, in violation of Hawaii Revised Statutes (HRS) § 605–14 (1993).[2] Because Atchley had previously violated HRS § 605–14, she was subject to punishment for a misdemeanor. HRS § 605–17 (1993).[3] Atchley was sentenced to a one-year term of probation subject to conditions which included that she pay restitution to the Kamakas in the amount of $462.48[4] and perform 200 hours of community service.[5]

On appeal, Atchley argues that 1) HRS § 605–14 is unconstitutionally vague because it does not define what is meant by the "practice of law" and 2) the prosecutor engaged in misconduct in eliciting and the circuit court committed plain error in allowing testimony regarding Ellen Kamaka's conversation with a lawyer. After a careful review of the record and the briefs submitted by the parties, we conclude that Atchley's arguments have no merit.

I.

Atchley did not challenge the constitutionality of HRS § 605–14 on vagueness grounds in the court below. We agree with the State of Hawai'i (the State) that Atchley waived her right to raise this claim on appeal. *State v. Ildefonso,* 72 Haw. 573, 584–85, 827 P.2d 648, 655 (1992). But even if we consider her claim on the merits, Atchley is not entitled to relief.

In *Fought & Co., Inc. v. Steel Engineering and Erection, Inc.,* 87 Hawai'i 37, 46, 951 P.2d 487, 496 (1988), the Hawai'i Supreme Court indicated that the phrase "practice of law," as used in HRS § 605–14, entails far more than appearing in court proceedings. The court cited the legislative history of HRS § 605–14 which reflected the legislature's recognition that the practice of law is not limited to appearing before the courts. It consists, among other things of the giving of advice, the preparation of any document or the rendition of any service to a third party *affecting the legal rights. . . of such party,* where such advice, drafting or rendition of services requires the use of any degree of legal knowledge, skill or advocacy.

Id. at 45, 951 P.2d at 495 (quoting Sen. Stand. Comm. Rep. No. 700, in 1955 Senate Journal, at 661) (emphasis in original).

---

[2]Hawaii Revised Statutes (HRS) 605-14 (1993) provides, in relevant part: It shall be unlawful for any person… to do or attempt to do or offer to do – any act constituting the practice of law, except and to the extent that the person… is licensed or authorized so to do by an appropriate court, agency, or office or by a statute of the State or of the United States…. Nothing in sections 605–14 to 605–17 contained shall be construed to prohibit the preparation or use by any party to a transaction of any legal or business form or document used in the transaction.

[3]At the time Defendant-Appellant Kitty L. Atchley (Atchley) allegedly committed the offense in this case, HRS § 605–17 (1993) provided that the first violation of HRS § 605–14 was a violation, but that subsequent violations would constitute a misdemeanor. HRS § 605–17 was amended in 2001 and now provides that any violation of HRS § 605–14 is a misdemeanor. Atchley's prior violation of HRS § 605–14, for which she was fined $1,000, was reflected in a Judgment filed on August 10, 1999.

[4]Ellen Kamaka testified at trial that the Kamakas paid Atchley approximately $350. However, documents the Kamakas submitted at sentencing in support of their restitution claim showed that they paid Atchley approximately $300 for her services plus $160 for the cost of filing their divorce pleadings.

[5]Atchley's term of probation also initially included a condition that she serve 90 days in jail, which was stayed pending a compliance hearing. According to Atchley's brief, after a probation compliance hearing on May 1, 2003, the jail-term condition was removed.

In determining whether a statute is impermissibly vague, we consider judicial decisions clarifying or narrowing the statute. *Wainwright v. Stone,* 414 U.S. 21, 22–23 (1973); *State v. Wees,* 58 P.3d 103, 107 (Idaho 2002). A defendant raising a vagueness claim is assumed to have knowledge of court decisions interpreting the statute. *Winters v. New York,* 333 U.S. 507, 514–15 (1948). Atchley is therefore chargeable with knowledge of the *Fought* decision.

To prevail on her vagueness claim, Atchley must show that HRS § 605–14, as applied to her conduct, was unconstitutionally vague. *State v. Marley,* 54 Haw. 450, 457–58, 509 P.2d 1095, 1101–02 (1973); *State v. Kuhia,* 105 Hawai'i 261, 272, 96 P.3d 590, 601 (2004). In Atchley's case, the evidence showed that in return for a fee, Atchley assisted the Kamakas in preparing and filing form pleadings in the Kamakas' uncontested divorce action. In the course of preparing the forms, Atchley answered the Kamakas' questions and provided explanations on a variety of topics, including: 1) how granting Ellen Kamaka (Ellen) sole as opposed to joint custody of the Kamakas' two children would affect the rights of Richard Kamaka (Richard) to see his children; 2) whether child support payments would be made by Richard through the Child Support Enforcement Agency or directly to Ellen; 3) whether Ellen was eligible for alimony and whether alimony payments would be taxable; 4) how the divorce would affect Ellen's medical coverage under Richard's insurance plan; 5) whether Richard or Ellen would be named as the plaintiff; and 6) the procedures the Kamakas needed to follow to secure a divorce decree. Without the Kamakas' knowledge or consent, Atchley completed certain forms and submitted a letter to the court falsely asserting that Ellen refused to submit financial statements. The Kamakas did not carefully review the documents Atchley filed, but accepted Atchley's assurances that "she knew what she was doing" and would "take care of everything."

In light of Atchley's extensive involvement in preparing the Kamakas' divorce pleadings and her providing the Kamakas' with legal advice, we conclude that HRS § 605–14, as applied to her conduct, was not unconstitutionally vague. In particular, the statute's prohibition against the unlicensed "practice of law" and court decisions interpreting that phrase gave Atchley fair warning that her conduct was illegal. *State v. Richie,* 88 Hawai'i 19, 31–32, 960 P.2d 1227, 1239–40 (1998). Our conclusion is supported by decisions in other jurisdictions which, under analogous circumstances, have rejected claims that statutes prohibiting the unlicensed practice of law were unconstitutionally vague. *E.g., Monroe v. Horwitch,* 820 F.Supp. 682, 686 (1993) ("The preparation of documents in simple divorce actions unequivocally constitutes the practice of law."); *Wees,* 58 P.3d at 108.

II.

In addition to seeking a divorce, the Kamakas were experiencing financial difficulties when they went to see Atchley. Ellen testified that in the context of discussing something related to bankruptcy, Atchley indicated that the Kamakas could call an attorney named Scott Holmes (Holmes). Ellen further testified that she later called Holmes. The State sought to establish that Holmes did not give the Kamakas any advice about their divorce. The State elicited testimony from Holmes that he had a short phone conversation with Ellen about a bankruptcy and that he would not have given the Kamakas advice about their divorce. Atchley did not object to the evidence regarding Ellen's conversation with Holmes.

We reject Atchley's claim that the prosecutor engaged in misconduct in eliciting and the court committed plain error in allowing testimony regarding Ellen's conversation with Holmes. Any attorney-client privilege relating to Ellen's conversation with Holmes was for Ellen, and not Atchley, to assert. Hawaii Rules of Evidence (HRE) Rule 503. Because Atchley did not object, there is no record of whether Ellen had previously waived or would have waived any privilege she had. Moreover, other than indicating that Ellen called Holmes with regard to a bankruptcy, neither Ellen nor Holmes revealed the details of their conversation. The key aspect of Holmes' testimony was that he would not have given the Kamakas any legal advice about their divorce. This portion of Holmes' testimony was not privileged. Under these circumstances, Atchley is not entitled to any relief under the plain error standard of review.

III.

IT IS HEREBY ORDERED that the August 13, 2002, Judgment filed in the Circuit Court of the Second Circuit is affirmed.

Source: Reprinted with permission from ThomsonWest.

OPINION NO. 24—NEW JERSEY COMMITTEE ON THE UNAUTHORIZED PRACTICE OF LAW

Independent paralegals in New Jersey were understandably concerned over the ramifications of Opinion No. 24 of the Committee on the Unauthorized Practice of Law. In essence, it held that paralegals could not render services without being directly employed by an attorney. The Committee felt that the supervision would be per se inadequate and therefore, there could be no "independent" paralegals in New Jersey that were not simultaneously committing UPL just by the nature of their practice. These independent paralegals filed an appeal to the Supreme Court of New Jersey. The Court decided on the issue only of "independent contractor" paralegals employed by an attorney on a temporary or project-based term; the Court did not address those paralegals that rendered legal services directly to the public.

For the full text of this rather lengthy opinion, please visit *In re* Opinion 24, 128 N.J. 114 (1992).

To read NALA's statement to the New Jersey Supreme Court, please visit http://www.nala.org/News.htm and click on the link in the "licensing" column.

NFPA's Response can be viewed at http://backup.paralegals.org/Development/rspd-nj.htm

Part Two

The Attorney-Client Relationship

Chapter 3

Maintaining Competency, Diligence, and Communications

CHAPTER OBJECTIVES

The student will be able to:

- Discuss the attorney's "competing" duties to both follow the directive of the client and render independent legal judgment

- Define "competency" as it relates to the ability to practice law

- Identify the elements of competency as derived through the ABA standards

- Recognize the importance of diligence in the legal profession and the requirements of prompt communications with the client

- Evaluate a situation that could implicate an attorney and/or a paralegal in a professional malpractice action

This chapter examines the roles and responsibilities of all the parties involved in the attorney-client relationship. HOW can an attorney be sure he is able to render competent representation; WHEN must the attorney respond to the client; WHAT constitutes legal malpractice; and WHO is responsible for the failures and harm that may result from unskilled representation?

Just as the paralegal and the attorney have a working relationship wherein both parties need to respect the roles that each play, so the attorney has a working relationship with the client. The attorney's role is to provide guidance along a complex and sometimes treacherous path in achieving a favorable outcome. It is the client's role to decide what would be a favorable outcome. The client is truly the master of the case; ultimately, the decision making rests with the client. An attorney cannot take any actions that are not approved by the client. However, it is the attorney's ethical duty to try to persuade the client to take the best path to achieve the desired result. Sometimes that involves telling the client that her desired result is not possible.

An attorney must delicately address these two obligations to the client: (1) to follow the client's course, and (2) to render independent judgment, sometimes in spite of the first obligation. The paralegal has a central role in this relationship. Often it is the paralegal that serves as liaison between them. In order to facilitate the relationship, the paralegal should be aware of its boundaries.

RENDERING INDEPENDENT LEGAL JUDGMENT

independent legal judgment
The attorney's determination of the best course to pursue to obtain the client's objectives, based upon the attorney's obligation to rely upon her own professional assessment of the legal situation, without undue influences from outside forces.

ABA Model Rule 2.1 states that the attorney's role is an advisor. This obligation to render **independent legal judgment** is what defines the lawyer. All the years of schooling and practice are essentially to lead her to a true assessment of the situation presented by the client. One must always recall that an attorney's first obligation is to the court and the pursuit of justice. This is true even in a transactional matter that is not pursued in litigation. Fairness to all the parties involved is the goal. A client may be the impetus behind the matter, but it is the lawyer that has the knowledge and skill to strategize and manage the case. It is the attorney's ethical duty to expose all the facts to the client, including the unpleasant ones, and make a fair, honest, and objective assessment of the matter to counsel the client properly.

Additionally, as the law itself is not isolated from the principles of morality, socio-economics, or politics, so an attorney's advice does not have to be isolated from them either. A strict answer couched in purely legal terms may not be of value to some clients, who may fail to understand the ramifications of a course of action. The relationship between a lawyer and his client is a fiduciary one. That means that the lawyer must look out for the best interests of the client, even if the client isn't sure what those interests are. It would be hard to imagine that the attorney in an adoption or surrogacy arrangement would not be counseling his client using morality and politics as guideposts for assessing the outcome of the court's decisions.

There is a difference in the "exercise of independent professional judgment" that sets the attorney apart from the paralegal. The very definitions of a paralegal and of the unauthorized practice of law makes the paralegal unable to render her legal conclusions and legal opinions *independently* to the client. This does not mean that the paralegal does not or cannot, independently of the attorney and other influences, render a professional opinion regarding the matter. There may be many occasions in which the paralegal is called upon to analyze and plan the best course of action for a client and report the results *to the supervising attorney*. Both NALA and NFPA have identified the significance of maintaining professionalism in their ethical codes; however, they seem to be in conflict at first blush. Figure 3.1 sets forth their rules. It is important to note that NALA prohibits the paralegal from exercising independent professional judgment vis-à-vis the client—not the attorney.

FIGURE 3.1
Use of Paralegals' Professional Judgment

NALA Guideline 3

Legal Assistants may perform services for an attorney in the representation of the client, provided:
1. The services performed by the legal assistant do not require the exercise of independent professional judgment.

NFPA EC 1.6(a)

A paralegal shall act within the bounds of the law, solely for the benefit of the client, and shall be free of compromising influences and loyalties. Neither the paralegal's personal nor business interest, not those of other clients or third persons, should compromise the paralegal's professional judgment and loyalty to the client.

The exercise of professional judgment by the paralegal is essential to his role of assisting the attorney. Forming theories, rendering opinions, and otherwise applying knowledge to the facts is perfectly acceptable where the final product is given to the supervising attorney. The line is drawn where the paralegal attempts to render this advice to the client without the supervision of an attorney. Recall from the previous chapter that rendering legal advice is the practice of law solely retained by attorneys. Why is this "guard" in place? It is the responsibility of the lawyer to create and maintain the relationship with the client, and the attorney is ultimately the person responsible for the outcome of her decisions. The paralegal may properly relay from the attorney to the client information that consists of the attorney's independent professional judgment, but the paralegal may not directly relay his own opinion to the client.

BALANCE OF AUTHORITY BETWEEN ATTORNEY AND CLIENT

Balancing the lawyer's influence over the outcome of the matter is ABA Model Rule 1.2, which specifically allocates the authority in the attorney-client relationship. The key is a **balance of authority** between lawyer and client. The client is the person who directs the course of action to be taken. It may be helpful to think of the relationship in ownership terms. The client owns the case or matter, and the attorney consults with the client to determine the best way to fix it. Just as people bring their cars to expert mechanics to be fixed, a client brings her troubles to the attorney. Most people do not know the best way to fix their cars, but have a certain idea of how far they are willing to go to solve a problem. The mechanic may not agree with the owner's decision to fix it up no matter what the cost, but as long as the mechanic has been honest in the assessment of the problem and in the cost to fix it, then he is obligated to follow the directive of the owner.

What happens when the client insists on the less desirable or potentially harmful or more costly course? That is where the attorney may find himself in a bind. When a client decides to take a certain course of action that the attorney disagrees with, it is the duty of the attorney to counsel against it. However, if the client insists on following that course, the attorney must follow those wishes. Specifically, the rule states that the client has full authority over the decision to settle a matter. For example, an attorney was advised by the Pennsylvania Ethics Committee that he would not be prohibited by the ethics rules in allowing a client to enter into a settlement agreement whereby she would give up child support in exchange for her ex-husband's giving up a claim of custody. The committee found that under Rule 1.2, the attorney had to follow the wishes of the client insofar as they were reasonable, were made without coercion, and did not prejudice the children's interests. The attorney was not under any obligation to agree with his client's choice. *See* 2000 WL 1616247 (Pa. Bar. Assn. Comm. Leg. Eth. Prof. Resp.) In criminal cases, the client has final say on the plea to be entered, whether to waive a trial by jury, and whether or not the client will testify.

An attorney may also find herself torn between the law and her client's conduct. When should a client's course of conduct be reported to the appropriate agency? Almost everyone feels a little reluctance when writing out the annual tax check to the government; some clients take this a step further and fail to pay taxes at all. When this fact is discovered, what are a lawyer and a paralegal to do? Neither of them may knowingly assist or counsel a client in furtherance of this plan of tax evasion. For instance, attorneys and paralegals cannot effect a transaction that would result in tax evasion or other fraud to escape tax liability. However, once a past transgression has been discovered in confidence, they are not under an obligation to report it. The

balance of authority
The balance between the right of the client to choose the desired outcome of the case and the obligation of the attorney to determine the best legal course to obtain that result.

attorney should counsel his client to pay these taxes; otherwise, the client will be clearly in violation of the law. This is a tricky situation, in which the attorney finds himself as a counselor *during* the questionable conduct. *See* LAWYER'S DUTY DURING CLIENT'S FRAUDULENT CONDUCT, 2001 WL 34004974 (Conn. Bar. Assn.). An attorney must insist that his client cease the unlawful conduct and attempt to rectify the situation without compromising the client's position and the attorney's obligation of confidentiality. The affirmative duty to report criminal or fraudulent conduct to the proper authorities only applies prospectively. Attorneys and paralegals must report only on the future conduct of their clients that they know will be unlawful. A full discussion of this obligation will be undertaken in chapter 4 (Confidentiality).

The test, as demonstrated in the above opinions, is whether or not the attorney believes that the client is making a decision that is relatively reasonable under the circumstances, is not made as the result of force or threat, is not made in furtherance of fraud, and/or does not pose a threat to third-party interests that are not protected. The attorney's agreement with the client's decision is not relevant. Her participation may be limited by law or by his own moral compass so that she declines representation or counsels against such conduct, but she is not responsible for the client's ultimate poor decision making.

COMPETENCY

An attorney is responsible for the establishment of the general parameters of representation and the explanation of the roles that he will play in the relationship with the client. Resting squarely on the shoulders of the attorney is the responsibility of determining whether he is competent to represent that particular client in the matter at hand. Competency is also reflected through the general office of the attorney. This means that the attorney must ensure the competency level of his paralegals, including verifying that the work performed by paralegals under his supervision is performed satisfactorily.

competence
The ability and possession of expertise and skill in a field that is necessary to do the job.

ABA Model Rule 1.1 is not particularly specific with regard to **competence**. It merely asserts that an attorney must possess the legal knowledge and skill to handle the matter, and must be thorough and prepared in the representation. The paralegal codes are no more elucidating than those concerning attorneys; they are set forth in Figure 3.2.

Through cases, ethics opinions, and commentary, the rule becomes more clear. The most enlightening source, however, is the record of malpractice suits. Incompetency not only makes an attorney liable in ethics; it also gives rise to a professional malpractice suit if the plaintiff (former client) can prove the elements of that tort. Competency applies to both attorneys and paralegals, and so will be discussed in both contexts. Indeed, an attorney can be held responsible for the incompetency of her paralegal, and a paralegal may be independently sued for negligence in the execution of his duties. For this reason, the ABA has also written the *Guide for the Utilization of Paralegal Services.*

FIGURE 3.2
A "Competent" Paralegal

NALA Guideline 4

In supervision of a legal assistant, consideration should be given to (1) designating work assignments that correspond to the legal assistant's abilities, knowledge, training and experience.

NFPA EC 1.1(a)

A paralegal shall achieve competency through education, training, and work experience.

What does it mean to be *competent?* Generally speaking, it means that the lawyer or paralegal has the right skills and appropriate knowledge to handle the matter presented. These skills and this knowledge are acquired a number of ways. First, the person's basic legal education should prepare her for the general role of either attorney or paralegal. The educational requirements for both have already been discussed, in chapter 1. But formal education is not the only means of acquiring knowledge; indeed, in the law it is not even adequate. Actual practice on the job is necessary in order to understand the complexities of the legal system, manage the law office, and handle opposing counsel and clients. Furthermore, the law is always changing and evolving; new laws are created constantly to keep pace with societal influences. Even the ways in which lawyers practice law change to reflect new technologies. For this reason, most (40 out of 50) states require that attorneys acquire a certain number of **continuing legal education (CLE)** credits per year after they have been admitted to the bar of those states.

continuing legal education (CLE)
Continued legal competence and skills training required of practicing professionals.

Keeping apace of developments in the law and its practice is so critical to the proper, competent rendering of legal services that in 1986, the ABA promulgated a Model Rule regarding mandatory or minimum continuing legal education as a requisite to practice. It is the ABA's desire that all the states will put these minimums into place so that there is a consistency and assurance of competency across the board. The Model Rule would require 15 hours of CLE each year. This could be satisfied by attending approved CLE courses, teaching, writing for CLE, receiving in-office training, and using other modes, as long as the educational efforts meet conditions set forth in later sections of the Model Rule for CLE. Further, the attorneys must report their CLE credits in order to assure compliance with the minimum requirements. In those states that do have CLE requirements, failure to meet the minimum standards will result in the denial of the right to practice in that jurisdiction where the attorney is delinquent. *See Kentucky Bar Association CLE Commission v. McIntyre,* 937 S.W.2d 708 (Ky. 1997). In this matter, the attorney did not comply with the state's CLE requirements, despite having received several deficiency notices. "The failure to maintain licensing requirements constitutes a serious charge for which suspension is an appropriate remedy for non-compliant members."

Acquiring and maintaining new skills is vital not only for attorneys. The national paralegal associations have also set forth minimum continuing legal education credits required each year for paralegals. As membership in these associations is voluntary, the requirements are not binding on paralegals in general. However, for those paralegals who hold one of the certification designations (CLA/CP, PACE, ALS, PLS, PPC, AACP), the organizations do require CLE credits to be reported by the paralegals in order to maintain their status. NALA requires evidence of completion of 50 hours, of which 5 must be on the subject of legal ethics, of continuing legal education every 5 years. To maintain NFPA's PACE credential, a paralegal must complete 12 hours of continuing legal or specialty education every 2 years, with at least 1 hour in legal ethics. NALS requires 75 hours every 5 years, with at least 5 hours devoted to legal ethics. The newest national certifying body, AAPI, which also requires higher education, mandates 18 hours, of which 2 must be in ethics. The continuing legal education requirement time frames coincide with the organizations' certification renewal periods.

IN CLASS DISCUSSION

What minimum requirements, if any, for paralegal continuing legal education should be required in your state? Do you think that CLE is necessary for practicing paralegals? Why? Does your state offer CLE seminars specifically for paralegals? What types of topics are offered; what topics would you like to see addressed?

In its definition, the ABA identifies two components of competency:

1. Knowledge and skill

2. Thoroughness and preparation

What does each of these elements encompass, and how does one know if they have been satisfied?

Knowledge

It is impossible to assert that every attorney or paralegal knows everything about the law. Even specialists cannot know everything about their particular field. Increasingly, attorneys and the paralegals who work for them are becoming specialized in one field, because the law is becoming more complex. Many attorneys now cross-refer clients to these specialists when they cannot handle the matter competently. Relying on memory of the law is actually an ethical violation! It is imperative that an attorney be certain of the current state of the law, and the only way to do this is to perform the necessary research. Researching is one of the tasks commonly assigned to a paralegal. NALA's Guideline 5 specifically lists research as one of the tasks properly delegated to a paralegal and for which paralegals have competency. Failure to research has been found to be a sanctionable ethical offense by many courts and ethical boards. The requisite knowledge that an attorney or paralegal must have is the knowledge of how to apply the law once it has been found. Knowing how courts are likely to rule given the state of the law and applying it to the particulars of the matter at hand is the test of competency. Knowing *how* to find the answer, not already having the answer, is the essence of proper lawyering.

What this means in practical terms is that an attorney does not necessarily have to have experience in handling a matter in a particular area of law in order to handle that matter. Law schools expose their students to many areas of law in order to assure a certain level of familiarity with the issues involved in the diverse areas of law. General practitioners, those whose offices take on a variety of matters, may often face issues they have never dealt with before. Legal practice is much like a continuing education process, as the law in an attorney's area of concentration may change. The practice of law does not require specialization, and therefore, these attorneys are fully competent to handle the matter as long as they acquire the requisite knowledge during the course of the client's matter. An assessment of the attorney's ability to do the research and analysis will determine whether the case can be undertaken. A more complex specialty or fact pattern of a particular matter may require that the attorney refer the case to another with the relevant competency.

 SPOT THE ISSUE

Natalie is a general practitioner with her own office. She has handled various kinds of cases over the ten years since she graduated law school, but has never drafted a will with a spendthrift trust provision. Natalie recalls how much she liked her estates professor in law school, so she consults her notebooks and casebook from that class to help her draft the will. The client seems pleased with the will, and it is properly executed in Natalie's office.

Has Natalie fulfilled her ethical requirements in taking on this new matter? Why or why not? What details would change your decision? What if Natalie had had her paralegal thoroughly research the issue and draft the will instead of consulting her former coursework?

Skills

An attorney must be able to execute, or follow through with, the knowledge acquired in order to properly represent a client. Knowing how to do something is not quite the same as doing it well. This is where the skill of an attorney becomes relevant with regard to his competency level. Knowing how to perform research is merely the starting point. The skill is in finding the relevant law, identifying the legal issues involved, analyzing the legal ramifications of the legal authority, applying the law to the current fact pattern, composing a viable argument, and writing the necessary documents accurately and persuasively. Further, an attorney is skilled in making decisions as to how best to proceed in a legal matter. A skillful attorney strategizes on if, when, and how to negotiate and how to conduct the trial.

These are finely honed skills that are (or should be) continually improved upon as an attorney practices. They are nebulous, as each matter requires different handling and finesse. While paralegals develop and hone skills complementary to those of attorneys, at its base, a paralegal's skill set is more easily definable. A paralegal should also be able to perform research, draft preliminary documents in legal style, accurately and concisely summarize information, identify material facts, and handle procedure both in the office and with the courts. Perhaps the trademark skills of a paralegal are (or should be) impeccable organization and the ability to manage multiple assignments effectively. As seen in Figure 3.3, NALA lists the basic skills of a paralegal in its ethical guidelines.

NALA's emphasis on the supervision of an attorney underscores the importance of the paralegal's knowledge of the ethical mandates for attorneys. The list is not all inclusive. Both the attorney and the paralegal are responsible for ascertaining the proper delegation of work. Not only must they each know their own limits of competency, they must also understand each other's limitations. It is a cooperative effort.

FIGURE 3.3
Basic Skills of a Competent Paralegal

NALA Guideline 5

Except as otherwise provided by statute, court rule or decision, administrative rule or regulation, or the attorney's rules of professional responsibility, and within the preceding parameters and proscriptions, a legal assistant may perform any function delegated by an attorney, including, but not limited to the following:

1. Conduct client interviews and maintain general contact with the client after the establishment of the attorney-client relationship, so long as the client is aware of the status and function of the legal assistant, and the client contact is under the supervision of the attorney.
2. Locate and interview witnesses, so long as the witnesses are aware of the status and function of the legal assistant.
3. Conduct investigations and statistical and documentary research for review by the attorney.
4. Conduct legal research for review by the attorney.
5. Draft legal documents for review by the attorney.
6. Draft correspondence and pleadings for review by and signature of the attorney.
7. Summarize depositions, interrogatories and testimony for review by the attorney.
8. Attend executions of wills, real estate closings, depositions, court or administrative hearings and trials with the attorney.
9. Author and sign letters providing the legal assistant's status is clearly indicated and the correspondence does not contain independent legal opinions or legal advice.

In *The Verdict* (1982), Paul Newman's character, Frank Galvin, is an alcoholic attorney on the brink of destroying his career. He struggles with his situation during his one last chance to prove his competency as an attorney in a medical malpractice defense matter. How does this attorney overcome his difficulties? Would it be ethical for him to take on this matter or for his firm to give him responsibility for it based upon his demonstrated competency level? Why or why not? If you were his paralegal, what would or should you do? Would it be ethical for you to assist him, knowing about his condition? Why or why not?

Thoroughness

Not only must attorneys and paralegals acquire the requisite knowledge and skills; they also must perform thoroughly the tasks related to them. It is not enough to have *some* of the information; it is vital to have *all* of it. The practice of law is detail oriented. Cases turn on very specific facts; materiality is not necessarily dependent upon the amount of information available. In other words, size doesn't matter in determining the importance of a fact or an issue. It may be easy to overlook an element of the case without a thorough review of the file materials; it may be easy to miss the defining case without thorough research; it may be easy to miss an argument without a thorough examination of the issues; and it may be easy to miscalculate the probable or possible outcomes without a thorough analysis of the relevant law. Truly, "God is in the details" (Ludwig Mies van der Rohe, German Architect 1886–1969). The real challenge for legal professionals is to accomplish the level of thoroughness required in the most efficient manner possible. This is why competency in all skill sets is so important as it relates to time management. A paralegal must learn to manage the amount of time spent on a task while still being thorough. It is a delicate balance between efficiency and thoroughness.

Preparation

After all the preliminary work is done and it's show time for the attorney, she must be prepared. All information must be at her fingertips, accessible and comprehensible.

A survey by the ABA finds that many lawyers are not using technology to its best advantage. Many lawyers are too busy to learn new technologies, or they distrust them to do what they need. This is where paralegals may come in very useful.

Read the following article:

Ed Polls, *Do You Commit Malpractice. . . . When It Comes to Technology?*, MASSACHUSETTS LAWYERS WEEKLY, Nov. 20, 2006, http://www.lawbiz.com/coachs_corner_11-20-06.html

The Polls article contends that lawyers who are not using technology may not be competent and that they are not conforming to the standard of care established in the local legal community.

Visit the above Web site and read the Polls article. How do you think paralegals can support lawyers in realizing their ethical responsibilities as they relate to technology?

For more information:

Technology can be used to better serve clients and enhances a lawyer's level of competency. For this reason the ABA has created its Legal Technology Resource Center. It can be accessed at

http://www.abanet.org/tech/ltrc/home.html

Catherine Sanders Reach, MLIS, *Make Technology Part of Your CLE!*, ABA TECHNOLOGY RESOURCE CENTER, August 2004, is an interesting article about technology and continuing legal education. Please visit http://www.abanet.org/tech/ltrc/publications/techtrain.html

It is usually a matter of teamwork, and the attorney relies on her team to have her prepared to face any situation or contingency. It is not enough to have competently, skillfully, and thoroughly prepared only the client's side of the issues. An attorney must be prepared for what the opposing side will counterargue. Courts have little patience or tolerance for ill-prepared attorneys. Indeed, a Vermont attorney was indefinitely suspended from the practice of law until he could prove that he was fit to practice; in other words, the court found him incompetent. In that case, a judge filed a complaint with the ethics board regarding the attorney's inadequate preparation of legal submissions to the court.

> *All members of the Board agreed with the hearing panel's finding that between 1985 and 1992 respondent repeatedly submitted legal briefs to this Court that were generally incomprehensible, made arguments without explaining the claimed legal errors, presented no substantiated legal structure to the arguments, and devoted large portions of the narrative to irrelevant philosophical rhetoric. The briefs contained numerous citation errors that made identification of the cases difficult, cited cases for irrelevant or incomprehensible reasons, made legal arguments without citation to authority, and inaccurately represented the law contained in the cited cases. All members of the Board also agreed with the hearing panel's conclusions that respondent's briefs were not competently prepared and fell below the minimum standard for brief-writing expected of a practicing attorney....*

In re Shepperson, 164 Vt. 636, 674 A.2d 1273, 1274 (1996).

Clearly, the justice system does not usually tolerate those who "wing it," or have a "good enough" attitude; inadequate preparation is obvious and inexcusable. This applies not only to the substance of the preparation, but also to the adherence to technical requirements of a submission. To adequately prepare, the paralegal should consult all local rules of court with regard to the particulars of documents and appearances, and sufficient time should be allocated in order to comply with those requirements. Competent preparation takes time. Time and paralegal support is apparently what the lawyers in *Bradshaw v. Unity Marine Corp.,* 147 F.Supp.2d 668 (S.D. Tex. 2001), did not have. Both lawyers apparently submitted their pleadings "entirely in crayon on the back sides of gravy-stained paper place mats." The full text of the case appears at the end of this chapter and is well worth the read, simply for the humor of its author, Judge Kent.

DILIGENCE

Connected to the definition of competency is the exercise of **diligence** in pursuing a matter for the client. Having legal knowledge and skill is of no use unless the attorney takes prompt action upon it to preserve his client's interests in the matter. ABA Model Rule 1.3 simply states that an attorney needs to be reasonably diligent and prompt when representing a client, and, as Figure 3.4 illustrates, the paralegal's mandate is no clearer.

The paralegal code is no more elucidating than the ABA Model Rule. This again underscores that the interpretation of reasonable actions and time frames must be determined in light of a particular matter. Each matter must be individually evaluated to determine the boundaries of ethical behavior for diligence.

With rare exception, all matters are subject to deadlines. Delay can cause anything from minor inconvenience, such as the rescheduling of a real estate closing, to annihilation of a claim, such as the lapse of the Statute of Limitations. Diligence relates

diligence
Acting within the legally proscribed time or promptly responding to a client's or party's request.

NFPA EC 1.1(c)

A paralegal shall perform all assignments promptly and efficiently.

FIGURE 3.4
The Diligent Paralegal

not only to legally required time limits but also to the general progress of the matter as it develops in the law office. Procrastination is unacceptable in the practice of law. There are many clients' needs that must be addressed and they often, if not always, overlap. Difficulties and delays will invariably arise; the fact of a delay does not automatically indicate that there has been a lapse in diligence. The most diligent and conscientious paralegals and attorneys find themselves behind schedule and affected by postponements; there are circumstances beyond their control. Diligence does not require that the delays be avoided entirely—only that the paralegal and attorney have put forth their best efforts to facilitate and expedite the matter.

In a "snowball effect" case, an attorney was found to have violated the ethics rules relating to diligence and promptness. *Attorney Grievance Commission of Maryland v. Ficker*, 349 Md. 13, 706 A.2d 1045 (Ct. App. 1998). The constant "putting off" of matters and dealing in a very high volume of cases resulted in an utter collapse of the entire practice. This is what is described as **pervasive neglect**. The court discussed eight separate cases in which the attorney had failed to exercise diligence in pursuit of his clients' interests. Perhaps taken one by one, they would not have had the same impact as all of the transgressions viewed at once. The attorney was in the habit of interviewing clients and then assigning them to either himself or an associate. The problem with this habit was that the assignment came the day before trial. There was no way that either Ficker or his associates could prepare to appear and represent their clients. Failure to file proper motions on the theory that the request could be made in person on the court date was violative of the duty of diligence, in that it subjected the clients, the court, and other attorneys to unanticipated circumstances and further delay. The attorney was found lacking in diligence in almost every aspect of his practice, including following through with reasonable investigation of his clients' claims. A diligent attorney checks facts before cavalierly assuming that the matter is a simple one. *Id.* at 28.

pervasive neglect
Continued disregard for matters pending in the law office, deadlines, and other obligations that seriously impacts clients' interests and indicates an utter lack of diligence.

> *Ficker essentially operated his practice like a taxicab company. . . . What he apparently, and inexcusably, failed to realize is that, while perhaps any competent taxi driver can transport a passenger from one point to another on a moment's notice, legal services cannot routinely be dispensed on that basis with an acceptable degree of competence. As the direct result of Ficker's practices, not only was the court inconvenienced but [the client] was faced with the unacceptable prospect of either falling on his sword or going to trial with a lawyer he never hired and who knew little or nothing about his case.*

Id. at 32.

RESEARCH THIS

Find a case or ethical opinion in your jurisdiction that addresses the issue of "pervasive neglect" culminating in a sanctionable offense violating the duty of diligence.

Additionally, the court noted that the entire office was lacking in any method of tracking cases and clients. Attorneys have a duty to remain diligent, to review cases periodically to ensure that no dates are missed, and that the other parties are current in their obligations in the matter. The directives as far as timing of an attorney's actions can also come from the client. If a client instructs an attorney to take certain steps on her behalf or in connection with a matter, the attorney must do so in as prompt a manner as possible, as much as the attorney may not want to. Failure to abide by a client's directives in a prompt manner is also violative of the duty of diligence. *See In re Caldwell*, 715 N.E.2d 362 (Ind. 1999).

FIGURE 3.5
Docketing and Calendaring

Missing a filing deadline or court appearance can be extremely damaging to a client as well as causing embarrassment and a potential malpractice claim for you. Each firm member should maintain an individual calendar in addition to a master calendar for the entire firm. Answer the following questions to determine how well you are doing in this area.

	Yes	No	N/A
Do we keep individual calendars, i.e., attorney and secretary/paralegal?			
Does your calendar include (as applicable):			
a) statutes of limitations?			
b) all court appearances?			
c) client and other appointments?			
e) real estate closing dates?			
g) all self-imposed, discretionary deadlines (i.e., promises made to others, promises made to you and work deadlines you have set for yourself?)			
Do we maintain a master calendar?			
Do we have a good system for updating and maintaining each calendar in case of scheduling changes?			
Do we use reminder slips (tickler slips) to draw the attorney's attention to an upcoming deadline?			
If the calendar is maintained on the computer, do we frequently print out a copy to use in case of power failures or other computer problems?			

Diligence is perhaps the area where paralegals can help most in the law office. Having the procedural knowledge of court schedules and deadlines, the paralegal can "calendar" important dates. Factual knowledge of the firm's caseload will enable the paralegal to appropriately monitor the status of cases and alert the responsible attorney. There is a great deal of information to keep track of in the law office. The Colorado Bar has created a checklist, set forth in Figure 3.5, for analyzing whether dates or information are falling through the cracks.

One of the most effective tools in use by paralegals and other professionals is the "tickler file system." A tickler file is designed to tickle your memory so that tasks do not get forgotten in the onslaught of activity at work. It keeps track of assignments that need to get done on a certain day and lets you put reminders on a date. Tasks are grouped not only by project, but also by day and month. The system is flexible and lets you re-file tasks as deadlines or priorities change. Essentially, you need a folder or compartment for each day of the month, and then a folder for each subsequent month. In the morning, the folder for that day is taken out; assignments and reminders are already in place so that they can be tackled without resorting to mere memory. At the end of the day, either all tasks are completed and the folder is empty, or an uncompleted task remains and can then be placed in the front of the next day's folder. Color-coding by kind of project or matter and filing the supporting materials with the task can add dimension to the file so that all the information is readily accessible.

COMMUNICATIONS WITH THE CLIENT

Lastly, in order to assert that one is competent, the legal professional has to keep the lines of **communication** open between himself and his client. Recall that the matter really "belongs" to the client. In order for a client to make decisions regarding the

CYBER TRIP

Good "how-to" explanations are located at these sites:

http://www.lifehack.org/articles/productivity/the-tickler-action-file.html (The Lifehack site offers many different organizational and productivity discussions.)

http://www.addresources.org/article_tickler_roehl.php.

A virtual system is available for a small monthly fee at www.myticklerfile.com.

communication
The obligation of an attorney to keep his client informed of the status of the matter, and to respond promptly to the client's requests for information in a candid manner.

FIGURE 3.6

Paralegals' Duty to Communicate

> **NALA Guideline 5**
>
> [A] legal assistant may perform any function delegated by an attorney, including but not limited to: (1) . . . maintain general contact with the client after the establishment of the attorney-client relationship, so long as the client is aware of the status and function of the legal assistant, and the client contact is under the supervisions of the attorney.

handling of the matter, he must be informed as to the status of the matter and the legal ramifications of his decisions. Further, in order to satisfy the demands for diligence, an attorney must promptly answer the inquiries of his client. Attorneys, just like other professionals, are very busy, but, unlike other professionals, they can be sanctioned for failing to respond to their clients. Additionally, attorneys, in helping to steer the ship must adequately explain the legal process and how the client's matter fits within it. The general public is not aware of the intricacies of the legal system and particulars of the laws in their jurisdiction; if they were there would be little need for lawyers!

ABA Model Rule 1.4 sets forth the requirements for communicating with clients. It requires that the attorney consult with the client regarding the means to achieve the client's objectives and other pertinent matters, and to keep the client informed about the status of the matter. NALA has recognized the vital supportive role of the paralegal in keeping the lines of communication open. See Figure 3.6.

These communications must also be made openly and forthrightly. Concealment and falsity are unacceptable as well. It is not good enough just to be talking; that exchange must be made in good faith and support the fiduciary nature of the relationship. While most people do not like to be the bearers of bad news, it is a requirement for attorneys to speak candidly about any issues that have arisen in the course of the matter. It may also be necessary for a paralegal to be that bearer of news as well.

It cannot be stressed enough that the client is in charge of the direction of the matter. It is the client's objectives that must be met or at least attempted, not necessarily the best or most reasonable or most achievable objectives in the estimation of the attorney. The end and the means to the end are the prerogative of the client; the attorney counsels, advises, and in some cases warns, but does not take action without the authority of the client. In a strange manifestation of diligence, an attorney cannot make decisions unilaterally, of her own accord, even if the issue is urgent and time is short. She must communicate with the client and make her best efforts at securing the client's consent. An absent or evasive client simply cannot be helped, even if it is in his best interest to take a specific action.

For example, *In re Samai*, 706 N.E.2d 146 (Ind. 1999) dealt with an attorney who was representing a client in an automobile personal injury matter. Having contacted the insurance company and set a medical examination of his client, the attorney attempted to contact the client again and again. He was unable to locate her and had no further contact. However, being diligent and perhaps not wanting to prejudice his client and to keep the matter moving along, the attorney sent a demand letter for a $5,000 settlement of the claim. The insurance company counteroffered $2,000, which the attorney accepted on behalf of his client. This would have been bad enough, but the attorney aggravated the situation by then using the settlement proceeds to his own benefit. The failure to communicate coupled with the "selfish motive" warranted an 18-month suspension from the practice of law.

It is vital that these communications emanate from the responsible attorney. While it is true that paralegals play a vital role in keeping clients current in the progress of their matters, it is not their role to substitute for the required consultations with the attorney. Further, the attorney and paralegal should maintain communications so as not to mislead the client. In *People v. Milner,* 35 P.3d 670 (Colo. 2001), the attorney's paralegal took over communications with the client and made certain representations and misrepresentations regarding the progress of the case that did not come to fruition due to the lack of diligence of the attorney. The attorney was not affirmatively contacting the client and not affirmatively supervising the paralegal's contact with the client. There was a litany of charges in a variety of individual matters brought against this attorney and paralegal team. Essentially, it was determined that the attorney abandoned her clients, causing serious or potentially serious harm. This was aggravated by her failure to properly supervise the communications between her paralegal and her clients. It should come as no surprise that Milner was disbarred. To avoid such missed or faulty communications, the Colorado Bar's checklist for Client Relations is included as Figure 3.7.

As in any relationship, honest and candid communication is vital. An attorney cannot perform his tasks without input from the client; therefore, the client should be kept informed of all elements of the matter, and it is the task of the attorney to educate the client as to the status of the law and how it will impact the client in order for the client to make the choices necessary to keep the matter going forward. A competent attorney diligently communicates with his client, adverse parties, and the tribunal. While these ethical standards as they are applied are fact specific, there are certain acts or omissions that are clearly violative of the attorney's duties in the attorney-client relationship. Perhaps the best way to evaluate an attorney's conduct is to determine what another responsible attorney would do in the same situation. Reasonable actions are gauged by how most attorneys act in or react to the specific circumstances.

FIGURE 3.7
Client Relations

The relationship with the client is a critical consideration for law office management. Everything that happens in a law firm has a direct or indirect effect on the client. The way a law firm conducts its business will also influence its relationship with its clients.

Law firms are often set up so that the critical element of administrative support is service to the attorney. The attorney, in turn, serves the client. Today, a client-centered law firm involves all personnel directly serving the client. The attorney is a team member involved in providing overall service to the client.

Examine your client relation efforts by asking the following questions:

	Yes	No	N/A
Do we return clients' phone calls and emails within 24–48 hours?			
Do we perform all the work we told the client we would?			
Do we send follow-up letters after a meeting or telephone conversation in which new decisions have been reached?			
Do we complete the work in a timely fashion?			
Do we follow up with clients at least every six weeks even when their cases are inactive?			
Do we acknowledge staff members for good client relations?			
Do we ask the client for feedback as the matter moves along?			

legal malpractice
A civil cause of action wherein a client may sue his attorney for failures in the representation that caused the client actual harm. The client may be entitled to money damages and possibly punitive damages in excess of actual pecuniary loss if the attorney's conduct was egregious.

ethical complaint
A report of suspected unethical activity on the part of an attorney, to the ethical committee of the state bar association or other appropriate tribunal. The committee may investigate to determine if an ethics violation has, indeed, occurred.

LEGAL MALPRACTICE

Lack of competency, diligence, or communication can also give rise to a civil lawsuit with separate and additional penalties: the malpractice claim brought by a client against the attorney. While some of the elements of these two claims are the same, there are different standards of proof required in order to recover for malpractice. In both an **ethical complaint** and a malpractice suit, the claimant needs to prove that *the relationship itself does exist,* and, therefore, the attorney owes the client a duty to protect her interests. Without the relationship, there can be no duty towards that person. The claimant is without a cause of action at that point. Secondly and also similarly, the client must show that *the attorney acted unreasonably* by failing to have (or acquire) the requisite knowledge, and failed to exercise the ordinary skill of a practicing attorney. There is a difference between malpractice and errors in professional judgment that end in an unsuccessful outcome.

> There can be no liability for acts and omissions by an attorney in the conduct of litigation which are based on an honest exercise of professional judgment. This is a sound rule. Otherwise every losing litigant would be able to sue his attorney if he could find another attorney who was willing to second guess the decisions of the first attorney with the advantage of hindsight. . . .

Clary v. Lite Machines Corporation, 850 N.E.2d 423, 431 (Ind. 2006).

The court also determined that an attorney is liable for mistakes in legal research, a task that is often delegated to paralegals.

The difference between the ethical complaint and the malpractice suit is found in the last two elements of a civil cause of action: the attorney must be the *proximate cause* (the third element) of *actual harm to the client* (the fourth and last element). In order to show that he was harmed by the attorney, the client needs to show that he would have been successful in the underlying action. In other words, his loss in the matter must be attributable to the attorney. If the client would have lost no matter how incompetent the attorney, then there is no harm. While the defense of the malpractice suit can assert "no harm, no foul," the ethical boards are equally as concerned with the impact on the client as they are with the actual violation. The fact of the violation is enough to warrant a sanction. No harm to the client needs to be proven in order to bring the attorney before the ethical board; the harm is presumed to be against the profession itself.

PARALEGAL MALPRACTICE

The way legal malpractice suits contrast with lawsuits against paralegals is still relatively uncharted territory. Paralegals *are* practicing law inside the law office, and while they should be held to the standard of care applicable in their jurisdiction, ultimately, they do not have a direct, independent relationship with the client as the attorney does. This is the primary hurdle that generally cannot be overcome in order to hold paralegals liable for legal malpractice. The cause of action requires the fiduciary relationship, which is generally absent in the case of a paralegal. It is absent not because the paralegal does not have a relationship with the client, but because the primary responsibility for that relationship rests with the attorney. *See In re Estate of Divine,* 263 Ill. App. 3d 799, 809, 635 N.E.2d 581, 588 (1994). (The court "refuse[d] to find that [the paralegal] owed [the client] a fiduciary duty simply because she worked for [the] attorney, and we refuse to hold that paralegals are fiduciaries to their employers' clients as a matter of law.")

Attorneys are held responsible for the actions or inactions of their paralegals that cause harm to the clients, under the doctrine of respondeat superior ("let the superior answer"). This means that the supervising attorney is held liable for the malpractice of the paralegal. Essentially, the attorney is in a position to review the paralegal's actions and direct the course of the conduct, and therefore is in a position to avoid the mistake.

> The label "paralegal" is not in itself a shield from liability. A factual investigation is necessary to distinguish a paralegal who is working under an attorney's supervision from one who is actually practicing law. A finding that a paralegal is practicing law will not be supported merely by evidence of infrequent contact with the supervising attorney. As long as the paralegal does in fact have a supervising attorney who is responsible for the case, any deficiency in the quality of the supervision or in the quality of the paralegal's work goes to the attorney's negligence, not the paralegal's.

Tegman v. Accident & Medical Investigations, Inc., 107 Wash. App. 868, 876, 30 P.3d 8, 13 (2001).

This vicarious responsibility for the actions of the paralegal is understood by the malpractice insurance carriers covering attorneys. The policies generally also cover the errors of employees, as long as the employees were acting within the scope of their employment. Problems arise where there is no supervising attorney to hold responsible. Paralegals who are directly working for and representing individuals can and should be held to a certain standard of care for which they can be held liable for breaches of their duty. *See Busch v. Flangas,* 108 Nev. 821, 837 P.2d 438 (1992). (The Court determined that if the paralegal held himself out as having the legal ability to competently prepare all the necessary documents and protect the client's legal interests, he should be subject to a legal malpractice claim for negligent provision of legal services.) Other courts have decided that paralegals could not be held liable for legal malpractice because they are not attorneys and therefore cannot enter into the requisite attorney-client relationship that gives rise to the duty of care. *See Palmer v. Westmeyer,* 48 Ohio App. 3d 296, 303, 549 N.E.2d 1202, 1209 (1988). However, a caveat to that generalization exists when the non-lawyer holds herself out as an attorney. In that case, courts have found that the non-lawyer, by misrepresenting herself, opened herself up to a viable legal malpractice claim. This uses the same line of reasoning as *Busch. See Pytka v. Hannah,* 15 Mass. L. Rptr. 451, 2002 WL 31862712 (Mass. Super. 2002) (not reported in N.E.2d). The court found that all of the facts necessary to uphold a cause of action for legal malpractice were satisfied as against the non-lawyer except for the fact that he was not a member of the bar subject to that particular charge. However, "the allegations still f[e]ll well within charges of negligence, deceit, misrepresentation and breach of contract." *Id.* at 8. The non-attorney defendant was found liable for the client's losses and punitive damages were further assessed. In total, almost one million dollars in damages were assessed against him, and the plaintiff was further granted interest, fees, and costs to be added to that judgment. The unauthorized practice of law can be very costly for those disregarding the rules.

Paralegals, according to the definition of their role in the law office, cannot establish an attorney-client relationship. However, where liability may not attach for legal malpractice, it certainly may lie in an action for the unauthorized practice of law. Any paralegal holding himself out as capable of providing direct services, and therefore outside the scope of an attorney's vicarious liability under malpractice, can be sued for the damages incurred as a result of the unauthorized practice of law.

Summary

An attorney must maintain a working relationship between herself and her client. There are two competing obligations in performing this duty: to follow her own independent legal judgment and to follow the desired course of the client. This requires that the authority and control over the matter must be shared between the attorney and the client.

Both attorneys and paralegals must be competent to handle each type of case presented to them. This means that they have the requisite knowledge and skill and have approached the matter with thoroughness and preparation. These efforts must also be made with diligence; the matter must be pursued promptly in order to preserve the client's interests in the case. In order for the client to make the decisions regarding the case, the attorney needs to maintain communications with the client in a timely manner.

An attorney lacking in any of the above-mentioned attributes may find himself the subject of a legal malpractice action. The private action initiated by the client is separate and in addition to any ethical sanctions and penalties to be imposed by the relevant ethical board. Paralegals, although they are not subject to their own ethical boards with sanction powers, can be sued individually for their lapse in the standard of care attributable to the paralegal profession.

Key Terms and Concepts

Balance of authority
Communication
Competence
Continuing legal education (CLE)
Diligence

Ethical complaint
Independent legal judgment
Legal malpractice
Pervasive neglect

Review Questions

MULTIPLE CHOICE

Choose the best answer(s) and please explain WHY you choose the answer(s).

1. A "competent" attorney has which of the following attributes?
   a. Legal research skills
   b. Knowledge of her ethical obligations
   c. Specialized training in a particular area of law
   d. Excellent oral advocacy skills

    e. A and B

    f. B and C

    g. All of the above

2. Diligence requires that an attorney

    a. Return all phone calls of the client himself

    b. Keep the client informed of the particulars of the case

    c. Write letters to the client once a week

    d. File motions on the due date

3. "Pervasive neglect" means that the attorney

    a. does nothing on a case

    b. has a habit of putting things off until the last minute

    c. has repeatedly failed to maintain diligence in a number of cases

    d. assigns all the work on a matter to her paralegal

EXPLAIN YOURSELF

All answers should be written in complete sentences. A simple yes or no is insufficient.

1. Explain the meaning of "competency." How does a paralegal know whether he is competent to handle a matter?

2. Describe the elements of proper communication with the client (it is more than just returning phone calls!)

3. What does it mean to be thorough and prepared with respect to a legal matter?

4. Do you think paralegals should be held responsible for their supervising attorneys' ethical infractions? Why or why not? Could this cut down on malpractice lawsuits overall? Would that be a benefit to paralegals? How?

5. What are the most important skills of a paralegal?

FAULTY PHRASES

All of the following statements are FALSE. State why they are false and then rewrite each one as a true statement, without just making the statement negative by adding the word "not."

1. In order for an attorney to take on a new kind of matter that she has not previously handled in practice, she must have studied that particular area of law in school.

2. An attorney must always follow the instructions of the client with regard to the handling of the case.

3. An attorney must personally answer all the requests for information from the client.

4. Diligence requires that the attorney or paralegal find all the cases in the jurisdiction that answer the question presented in the matter.

5. As long as the paralegal in the office is keeping the clients happy, the attorney is doing his job.

6. Paralegals cannot be sued for malpractice because their supervising attorneys are responsible for all their work.

7. Paralegals are held responsible for their supervising attorneys' ethical violations under the theory of *respondeat superior*.

PORTFOLIO ASSIGNMENT

Write Away

Compare the following scenarios and write a letter in response to each client. Assume you are a paralegal at a general practice firm and have been given three files to review:

- Client A is getting a divorce and his wife is trying to obtain sole custody of the children.

- Client B wishes to write her will.

- Client C is involved in a complex litigation that is currently in the discovery phase.

You have read all the relevant facts of these cases.

- Client A asks how many times women get custody of the children in these kinds of matters and what his chances are to obtain sole custody.

- Client B asks whether she can have her sister sign as a witness to the will and whether she should set up a trust for her children.

- Client C wants to know how much time is left for submitting answers to interrogatories served on him by the defendant and what his chances are at getting the counterclaim against him dismissed.

United States District Court, S.D. Texas, Galveston Division.
John W. BRADSHAW, Plaintiff,

v.

UNITY MARINE CORPORATION, INC.; Coronado, in rem; and Phillips Petroleum Company, Defendants.
No. CIV. A. G-00-558.
June 27, 2001.
KENT, District Judge.

Plaintiff brings this action for personal injuries sustained while working aboard the M/V CORONADO. Now before the Court is Defendant Phillips Petroleum Company's ("Phillips") Motion for Summary Judgment. For the reasons set forth below, Defendant's Motion is **GRANTED.**

Plaintiff John W. Bradshaw claims that he was working as a Jones Act seaman aboard the M/V CORONADO on January 4, 1999. The CORONADO was not at sea on January 4, 1999, but instead sat docked at a Phillips' facility in Freeport, Texas. Plaintiff alleges that he "sustained injuries to his body in the course and scope of his employment." The injuries are said to have "occurred as a proximate result of the unsafe and unseaworthy condition of the tugboat CORONADO and its appurtenances while docked at the Phillips/Freeport Dock." Plaintiff's First Amended Complaint, which added Phillips as a Defendant, provides no further information about the manner in which he suffered injury. However, by way of his Response to Defendant's Motion for Summary Judgment, Plaintiff now avers that "he was forced to climb on a piling or dolphin to leave the vessel at the time he was injured." This, in combination with Plaintiff's Complaint, represents the totality of the information available to the Court respecting the potential liability of Defendant Phillips. [FN omitted]

Defendant now contends, in its Motion for Summary Judgment, that the Texas two-year statute of limitations for personal injury claims bars this action. *See* Tex. Civ. Prac. & Rem. Code § 16.003 (Vernon Supp.2001). Plaintiff suffered injury on January 4, 1999 and filed suit in this Court on September 15, 2000. However, Plaintiff did not amend his Complaint to add Defendant Phillips until March 28, 2001, indisputably more than two years after the date of his alleged injury. Plaintiff now responds that he timely sued Phillips, contending that the three-year federal statute for maritime personal injuries applies to his action. *See* 46 U.S.C. § 763a.

Before proceeding further, the Court notes that this case involves two extremely likable lawyers, who have together delivered some of the most amateurish pleadings ever to cross the hallowed causeway into Galveston, an effort which leads the Court to surmise but one plausible explanation. Both attorneys have obviously entered into a secret pact—complete with hats, handshakes and cryptic words—to draft their pleadings entirely in crayon on the back sides of gravy-stained paper place mats, in the hope that the Court would be so charmed by their child-like efforts that their utter dearth of legal authorities in their briefing would go unnoticed. Whatever actually occurred, the Court is now faced with the daunting task of deciphering their submissions. With Big Chief tablet readied, thick black pencil in hand, and a devil-may-care laugh in the face of death, life on the razor's edge sense of exhilaration, the Court begins.

Summary judgment is appropriate if no genuine issue of material fact exists and the moving party is entitled to judgment as a matter of law. *See* Fed.R.Civ.P. 56(c); *see also Celotex Corp. v. Catrett,* 477 U.S. 317, 323, 106 S.Ct. 2548, 2552-53, 91 L.Ed.2d 265 (1986). When a motion for summary judgment is made, the nonmoving party must set forth specific facts showing that there is a genuine issue for trial. *See Anderson v. Liberty Lobby, Inc.,* 477 U.S. 242, 250, 106 S.Ct. 2505, 2510, 91 L.Ed.2d 202 (1986). Therefore, when a defendant moves for summary judgment based upon an affirmative defense to the plaintiff's claim, the plaintiff must bear the burden of producing some evidence to create a fact issue some element of defendant's asserted affirmative defense. *See Kansa Reinsurance Co., Ltd. v. Congressional Mortgage Corp. of Texas,* 20 F.3d 1362, 1371 (5th Cir.1994); *F.D.I.C. v. Shrader & York,* 991 F.2d 216, 220 (5th Cir.1993).

Defendant begins the descent into Alice's Wonderland by submitting a Motion that relies upon only one legal authority. The Motion cites a Fifth Circuit case which stands for the whopping proposition that a federal court sitting in Texas applies the Texas statutes of limitations to certain state and federal law claims. *See Gonzales v. Wyatt,* 157 F.3d 1016, 1021 n. 1 (5th Cir.1998). That is all well and good—the Court is quite fond of the *Erie* doctrine; indeed there is talk of little else around both the Canal and this Court's water cooler. Defendant, however, does not even cite to *Erie,* but to a mere successor case, and further fails to even begin to analyze why the Court should approach the shores of *Erie.* Finally, Defendant does not even provide a cite to its desired Texas limitation statute. [FN omitted] A more bumbling approach is difficult to conceive—but wait folks, There's More!

Plaintiff responds to this deft, yet minimalist analytical wizardry with an equally gossamer wisp of an argument, although Plaintiff does at least cite the federal limitations provision applicable to maritime tort claims. *See* 46 U.S.C. § 763a. Naturally, Plaintiff also neglects to provide any analysis whatsoever of why his claim versus Defendant Phillips is a maritime action. Instead, Plaintiff "cites" to a single case from the Fourth Circuit. Plaintiff's citation, however, points to a nonexistent Volume "1886" of the Federal Reporter Third Edition and neglects to provide a pinpoint citation for what, after being located, turned out to be a forty-page decision. Ultimately, to the Court's dismay after reviewing the opinion, it stands simply for the bombshell proposition that torts committed on navigable waters (in this case an alleged defamation committed by the controversial G. Gordon Liddy aboard a cruise ship at sea) require the application of general maritime rather than state tort law. *See Wells v. Liddy,* 186 F.3d 505, 524 (4th Cir.1999) (What the. . .)?! The Court cannot even begin to comprehend why this case was selected for reference. It is almost as if Plaintiff's counsel chose the opinion by throwing long range darts at the Federal Reporter (remarkably enough hitting a nonexistent volume!). And though the Court often gives great heed to dicta from courts as far flung as those of Manitoba, it finds this case unpersuasive. There is nothing in Plaintiff's cited case about ingress or egress between a vessel and a dock, although counsel must have been thinking that Mr. Liddy *must* have had *both* ingress and egress from the cruise ship at some docking facility, before uttering his fateful words.

Further, as noted above, Plaintiff has submitted a Supplemental Opposition to Defendant's Motion. This Supplement is longer than Plaintiff's purported Response, cites more cases, several constituting binding authority from either the Fifth Circuit or the Supreme Court, and actually includes attachments which purport to be evidence. However, this is all that can be said positively for Plaintiff's Supplement, which does *nothing* to explain why, on the facts of *this* case, Plaintiff has an admiralty claim against Phillips (which probably makes some sense because Plaintiff doesn't). Plaintiff seems to rely on the fact that he has pled Rule 9(h) and stated an admiralty claim versus the vessel and his employer to demonstrate that maritime law applies to Phillips. This bootstrapping argument does not work; Plaintiff must properly invoke admiralty law versus each Defendant discretely. *See Debellefeuille v. Vastar Offshore, Inc.,* 139 F.Supp.2d 821, 824 (S.D.Tex.2001) (discussing this issue and citing authorities). Despite the continued shortcomings of Plaintiff's supplemental submission, the Court commends Plaintiff for his vastly improved choice of crayon—Brick Red is much easier on the eyes than Goldenrod, and stands out much better amidst the mustard splotched about Plaintiff's briefing. But at the end of the day, even if you put a calico dress on it and call it Florence, a pig is still a pig.

Now, alas, the Court must return to grownup land. As vaguely alluded to by the parties, the issue in this case turns upon which law–state or maritime--applies to each of Plaintiff's potential claims versus Defendant Phillips. And despite Plaintiff's and Defendant's joint, heroic efforts to obscure it, the answer to this question is readily ascertained. The Fifth Circuit has held that "absent a maritime status between the parties, a dock owner's duty to crew members of a vessel using the dock is defined by the application of state law, not maritime law." *Florida Fuels, Inc. v. Citgo Petroleum Corp.,* 6 F.3d 330, 332 (5th Cir.1993) (holding that Louisiana premises liability law governed a crew member's claim versus a dock

which was not owned by his employer); *accord Forrester v. Ocean Marine Indem. Co.,* 11 F.3d 1213, 1218 (5th Cir.1993). Specifically, maritime law does not impose a duty on the dock owner to provide a means of safe ingress or egress. *See Forrester,* 11 F.3d at 1218. Therefore, because maritime law does not create a duty on the part of Defendant Phillips vis-a-vis Plaintiff, any claim Plaintiff does have versus Phillips must necessarily arise under state law.[FN omitted] *See id.; Florida Fuels,* 6 F.3d at 332–34.

The Court, therefore, under *Erie,* applies the Texas statute of limitations. Texas has adopted a two-year statute of limitations for personal injury cases. *See* Tex. Civ. Prac. & Rem.Code § 16.003. Plaintiff failed to file his action versus Defendant Phillips within that two-year time frame. Plaintiff has offered no justification, such as the discovery rule or other similar tolling doctrines, for this failure. Accordingly, Plaintiff's claims versus Defendant Phillips were not timely filed and are barred. Defendant Phillips Motion for Summary Judgment is **GRANTED** and Plaintiff's state law claims against Defendant Phillips are hereby **DISMISSED WITH PREJUDICE.** A Final Judgment reflecting such will be entered in due course.

II.

After this remarkably long walk on a short legal pier, having received no useful guidance whatever from either party, the Court has endeavored, primarily based upon its affection for both counsel, but also out of its own sense of morbid curiosity, to resolve what it perceived to be the legal issue presented. Despite the waste of perfectly good crayon seen in both parties briefing (and the inexplicable odor of wet dog emanating from such) the Court believes it has satisfactorily resolved this matter. Defendant's Motion for Summary Judgment is **GRANTED.**

At this juncture, Plaintiff retains, albeit seemingly to his befuddlement and/or consternation, a maritime law cause of action versus his alleged Jones Act employer, Defendant Unity Marine Corporation, Inc. However, it is well known around these parts that Unity Marine's lawyer is equally likable and has been writing crisply in ink since the second grade. Some oldtimers even spin yarns of an ability to type. The Court cannot speak to the veracity of such loose talk, but out of caution, the Court suggests that Plaintiff's lovable counsel had best upgrade to a nice shiny No. 2 pencil or at least sharpen what's left of the stubs of his crayons for what remains of this heart-stopping, spine-tingling action.[4]

IT IS SO ORDERED.

[4]In either case, the Court cautions Plaintiff's counsel not to run with a sharpened writing utensil in hand—he could put his eye out.

Source: Reprinted with permission from ThomsonWest.

Supreme Court of North Dakota.
In the Matter of the Application for REINSTATEMENT OF Cheryl L. ELLIS.
Cheryl L. Ellis, Petitioner

v.

Disciplinary Board of the Supreme Court of the State of North Dakota, Respondent.
No. 20060081.
Sept. 13, 2006.
Background: Attorney who had been suspended from the practice of law filed petition seeking reinstatement.
Holdings: The Supreme Court held that:
(1) attorney was eligible for reinstatement to the practice of law;
(2) attorney was required to retake and pass the bar examination as a condition of reinstatement; and
(3) attorney was required to pay the costs of reinstatement proceedings as a condition of reinstatement.
Reinstatement granted with conditions.
Application for Reinstatement.
John T. Goff, Montgomery, Goff and Bullis, Fargo, N.D., for petitioner.
Paul W. Jacobson, Disciplinary Counsel, Bismarck, N.D., for respondent.
REINSTATEMENT GRANTED WITH CONDITIONS
PER CURIAM.

[¶ 1] Cheryl Ellis petitioned for reinstatement to the bar, and Disciplinary Counsel filed objections to the report of a hearing panel of the Disciplinary Board which recommended Ellis be reinstated. We order that Ellis be reinstated to practice law in this state upon the condition she pass the bar examination and pay the costs of the reinstatement proceedings, and we remand to the hearing panel for a determination of those costs.

I

[¶ 2] In 1989, Ellis was suspended from the practice of law for two years, with imposition of all but the first 90 days of the suspension stayed for a one-year probationary period. Ellis was allowed to return to the practice of law after the initial 90 days of her suspension under the supervision of another licensed attorney, and she was ordered to pay costs of the disciplinary proceedings. *See In re Ellis,* 439 N.W.2d 808 (N.D.1989). When Ellis failed to timely pay the ordered costs, the remainder of the two-year suspension was imposed.

[¶ 3] In 1993, further disciplinary proceedings were brought and Ellis was suspended from the practice of law for six months. *See In re Ellis,* 504 N.W.2d 559 (N.D.1993). Ellis was also ordered to pay costs and attorney fees, and was ordered to take the Multistate Professional Responsibility Examination and achieve a score of at least 80.

[¶ 4] In 1994, further disciplinary proceedings were commenced, alleging Ellis had engaged in the unauthorized practice of law in 1992 while her license was suspended. The hearing panel in that proceeding issued a private reprimand to Ellis, but specifically recommended the reprimand not be considered as a "deterring factor" if Ellis later petitioned for reinstatement.

[¶ 5] In September 2005, Ellis petitioned for reinstatement, claiming she had complied with all of the conditions imposed

in the prior disciplinary orders, including service of all suspension time imposed, payment of all ordered costs and fees, and successful completion of the Multistate Professional Responsibility Examination. The Disciplinary Board appointed a hearing panel to consider Ellis's petition for reinstatement. Following a hearing, the hearing panel recommended that Ellis be reinstated and that she not be assessed costs of the reinstatement proceedings. Disciplinary Counsel filed objections to the hearing panel's report, alleging Ellis had failed to demonstrate she met the criteria for reinstatement, challenging the recommendation that Ellis not be assessed costs, and challenging the hearing panel's failure to require Ellis to retake and pass the bar examination as a condition of reinstatement.

II

[¶ 6] A court which has the power to suspend or disbar an attorney also has the power to reinstate upon proper and satisfactory proof that the attorney has become a fit and proper person to be entrusted with the office of an attorney. *In re Hoffman,* 2005 ND 171, ¶ 5, 704 N.W.2d 810; *In re Christianson,* 202 N.W.2d 756, Syllabus No. 1 (N.D.1972); *see* N.D.R. Lawyer Discipl. 4.5. Reinstatement following suspension is not a matter of right, and the suspended attorney has the burden of establishing the averments of her petition for reinstatement by clear and convincing evidence. *Hoffman,* at ¶ 5; *In re Montgomery,* 2001 ND 127, ¶ 5, 612 N.W.2d 278. The petitioner's proof must be of sufficient weight to overcome the former adverse judgment of her character. *Hoffman,* at ¶ 5; *Montgomery,* at ¶ 5.

[¶ 7] We review disciplinary proceedings against attorneys, including reinstatement proceedings, de novo on the record. *Hoffman,* 2005 ND 171, ¶ 5, 704 N.W.2d 810; *Montgomery,* 2001 ND 127, ¶ 5, 612 N.W.2d 278. However, when reviewing a petition for reinstatement we will accord due weight to the findings, conclusions, and recommendations of the hearing panel. *Hoffman*, at ¶ 5; *Montgomery*, at ¶ 5. Each disciplinary case must be judged on its own facts and merits. *Hoffman*, at ¶ 5; *Montgomery*, at ¶ 5.

III

[¶ 8] Disciplinary Counsel requests that we reject the recommendation of the hearing panel to reinstate Ellis to the practice of law, based upon her conduct in 1992 while under suspension and her failure to acknowledge the 1992 violation in her petition for reinstatement.

[¶ 9] In 1992, while under suspension, Ellis worked as a legal assistant to a licensed attorney on a complex bankruptcy matter. An application for discipline was filed alleging Ellis's conduct violated the rules against unauthorized practice of law. The matter was considered by a hearing panel, which went to great lengths to emphasize that Ellis's conduct was in almost all instances appropriate. The hearing panel did find, however, that Ellis committed a technical violation of the rules by meeting face-to-face with the client. The hearing panel noted that, although Ellis did have direct contact with the client, this direct contact was "necessary" because the client was particularly difficult and demanding. The panel therefore concluded that, although Ellis had technically violated the rule against unauthorized practice when she met with the client, there were mitigating circumstances and Ellis did not willfully violate the order suspending her from the practice of law. The hearing panel recommended a private reprimand, but specifically stated: "We recommend that this private reprimand not be a deterring factor in Ellis petition for reinstatement." The hearing panel in this case summarized the circumstances of the 1992 incident:

The Panel found that she performed services in the rol[e] of a "paralegal," that her work was diligent and resulted in substantial benefit to the client, that the client was aware she was not a licensed attorney, that she did not act independently of attorney Sheppard, that she had a good faith belief her services did not constitute the practice of law, and that there was no harm, but instead a benefit to the client.

[¶ 10] Disciplinary Counsel seeks to characterize Ellis's conduct while suspended in 1992 as a serious violation which, 14 years later, continues to demonstrate her unfitness to practice law. Ellis has already faced disciplinary proceedings for this conduct, and the hearing panel at that time emphasized Ellis's appropriate and beneficial conduct, stressing the technical nature of the violation. Most importantly, the hearing panel in the 1992 incident expressly recommended that the private reprimand not be a factor in any subsequent petition for reinstatement. We conclude, as did the hearing panel, this single, unintentional, and relatively minor violation of the rules against unauthorized practice, which occurred 14 years ago, does not preclude Ellis's reinstatement.

[¶ 11] Disciplinary Counsel further argues Ellis's failure to disclose the private reprimand for the 1992 violation in her petition for reinstatement demonstrates Ellis is currently unfit to practice law. Addressing this contention, the hearing panel found:

The hearing in that matter occurred some eleven years prior to the December 22, 2005 [petition] for reinstatement. When confronted with the Panel's recommendation at the hearing,

apparently for the first time, Ellis recalled the hearing but did not recall the outcome. She testified that she had diligently searched the Supreme Court records relating to previous hearings or suspensions. In so doing she would not have come across the files above referenced which are kept in the offices of the Disciplinary Board.

[¶ 12] We agree with the hearing panel that Ellis's failure to disclose the private reprimand in her petition for reinstatement does not preclude her reinstatement. The conduct in question had occurred more than 13 years earlier, and the hearing on the matter had occurred 11 years earlier, at a time when Ellis suffered from severe depression. Furthermore, there was no potential for prejudice from her nondisclosure, inasmuch as the private reprimand would have been included in her disciplinary file and was readily available to Disciplinary Counsel and the hearing panel.

[¶ 13] Ellis has served the entire terms of her previously ordered suspensions, has met all conditions placed upon her by those orders, and has presented evidence that her clinical depression, which was a major factor in her prior disciplinary violations, has been successfully treated. The hearing panel heard the witnesses and determined that Ellis has demonstrated her qualifications for reinstatement by clear and convincing evidence. The hearing panel expressly stated that Ellis's testimony at the reinstatement hearing was "credible and persuasive." This Court will accord due weight to the hearing panel's ability to assess the credibility of witnesses. *Hoffman*, 2005 ND 171, ¶ 5, 704 N.W.2d 810; *Montgomery*, 2001 ND 127, ¶ 5, 612 N.W.2d 278. We conclude Ellis has established her eligibility for reinstatement.

IV

[¶ 14] Disciplinary Counsel requests that, if Ellis is found to be eligible for reinstatement, she be required to pass the bar examination as a condition of reinstatement.

[¶ 15] The primary purpose of the disciplinary process is to protect the public and the integrity of the profession. *In re Korsmo*, 2006 ND 148, ¶ 6, 718 N.W.2d 6. Accordingly, when ordering reinstatement of a suspended attorney the Court may impose conditions upon the petitioner's reinstatement when the Court "reasonably believes that further precautions should be taken to ensure that the public will be protected upon the petitioner's return to practice." N.D.R. Lawyer Discipl. 4.5(H). The Court may therefore require proof of competency, "including certification by the bar examiners of the successful completion of an examination for admission to practice administered subsequent to the order for reinstatement." N.D.R. Lawyer Discipl. 4.5(H)(3).

[¶ 16] We share Disciplinary Counsel's concern that the lengthy period of time since Ellis last practiced law requires precautions to ensure the public's protection. The situation in this case is analogous to relicensure of an attorney who has been on inactive status for a lengthy period of time. In that instance, Admission to Practice R. 7(C) provides:

If the Board determines that the applicant's legal experience during the nonlicensure does not demonstrate sufficient competency in the practice of law, it shall require the applicant to take an attorney's examination.

[¶ 17] In this case, there was no evidence Ellis has practiced law since 1992, or that she thereafter worked regularly in a position utilizing her legal training and experience. Under these circumstances, further proof of competency is required to ensure the public will be protected upon Ellis's return to the practice of law. *See* N.D.R. Lawyer Discipl. 4.5(H). We therefore order that Ellis retake and pass the bar examination as a condition of reinstatement.

V

[¶ 18] Disciplinary Counsel objects to the hearing panel's recommendation that Ellis not be required to pay the costs of the reinstatement proceedings.

[¶ 19] Payment of all or part of the costs of reinstatement proceedings may be imposed as a condition of reinstatement. N.D.R. Lawyer Discipl. 4.5(H)(1). Costs and expenses of disciplinary proceedings are generally assessed against the disciplined attorney. *See* N.D.R. Lawyer Discipl. 1.3(D); *In re Swanson,* 2002 ND 6, ¶ 13, 638 N.W.2d 240. This Court explained the rationale for imposing costs of disciplinary proceedings against the involved attorney in *In re Larson,* 485 N.W.2d 345, 351 (N.D.1992):

The disciplinary system is necessary because some attorneys are unable to conform their conduct to the minimum ethical standards of the profession. It is only fair that attorneys whose unethical conduct creates the need for a disciplinary system contribute their direct share of the costs of maintaining that system.

[¶ 20] While we commend Ellis on the positive changes she has made to reestablish her eligibility to practice law, we are also mindful that it was Ellis's past misconduct which necessitated this entire process. Accordingly, we order that Ellis be required to pay the costs of the reinstatement proceedings as a condition of reinstatement.

VI

[¶ 21] We order that Ellis be reinstated to practice law in this state upon the condition she pass the bar examination and pay the costs of these proceedings, and we remand to the hearing panel for a determination of those costs.

[¶ 22] GERALD W. VANDE WALLE, C.J., DANIEL J. CROTHERS, MARY MUEHLEN MARING, CAROL RONNING KAPSNER, and DALE V. SANDSTROM, JJ., concur.

Source: Reprinted with permission from ThomsonWest.

Chapter 4

Confidentiality

CHAPTER OBJECTIVES

The student will be able to:

- Differentiate between the duty of confidentiality and the attorney-client privilege.

- Identify information that is not protected under either the duty of confidentiality or the attorney-client privilege.

- Understand the situations where disclosure of confidential information may be required.

- Evaluate the attorney's options in light of anticipated perjury by the client.

- Identify the ethical issues regarding unintentional disclosure of confidential client information.

- Discuss the "work product" doctrine.

- Appreciate the special relationship that the paralegal has with clients and their information.

- Understand the proper use of technology to maintain confidential electronic information.

This chapter will examine the duty of confidentiality that pertains to all attorneys in all matters handled on behalf of their clients. WHO holds the privilege, WHY does the duty exist, WHAT is covered by the duty of confidentiality, and WHEN can it be waived by the client or avoided by the attorney? Most important, the text discusses HOW the duty affects the responsibilities of paralegals.

At the very core of the attorney-client relationship is the trust the client has in his attorney to look out for his best interests and to protect him in the matter at hand. The only way to assure a client that the attorney can be trusted is to protect the communications between them. An attorney must gather very private details from a client, details the client would rather personally retain, in order to properly assess the situation and strategize for the plan of action. Without this assurance of confidentiality, the client has no incentive to disclose all the facts to his attorney. The "[a]ttorney-client privilege serves the cause of justice by promoting candor between counsel and client, which candor is encouraged by the promise that the lawyer will not later reveal the client's confidences or use them to advance the cause of another client." *Daniels v. State,* 17 P.3d 75, 84 (Alaska App. 2001). The attorney's obligation to keep these **confidences** is absolute. Therein lies the key; the ethical rule applies to communications

confidences
Any communication from the client to the attorney which the client intends to be kept private from everyone else.

made to an attorney in her capacity as counselor-at-law regarding the representation of the client. The client can feel secure knowing that the information received by the attorney, through any means, from any source, will not be disclosed by the attorney.

DUTY VERSUS PRIVILEGE

The absolute nature of the duty of confidentiality is tempered by the scope of the application of the **attorney-client privilege**. This is an important distinction; the duty belongs to the attorney and requires that she not reveal *any* information relating to the client; the privilege belongs to the client and permits the client to keep *certain* information from being revealed and used against him. Not everything transmitted (i.e., papers, e-mails, telephone conversations, etc.) between the attorney and client is covered by the privilege, but it is all covered by the duty. The duty arises from the moment that a client consults the attorney, whether or not that attorney is ultimately retained, and continues indefinitely. The client does not have to affirmatively request that the information be kept private; this automatically is covered under the duty. However, the privilege is an evidentiary rule. It applies only to communications made in confidence between an attorney and client that are of a sensitive nature relating specifically to the representation and known only to the client and attorney.

> *We note that in order to invoke the attorney-client privilege successfully, the following elements must be satisfied:*
>
> *"(1) the asserted holder of the privilege is or sought to become a client; (2) the person to whom the communication was made (a) is [a] member of a bar of a court, or his subordinate and (b) in connection with this communication is acting as a lawyer; (3) the communication relates to a fact of which the attorney was informed (a) by his client (b) without the presence of strangers (c) for the purpose of securing primarily either (i) an opinion on law or (ii) legal services or (iii) assistance in some legal proceeding, and not (d) for the purpose of committing a crime or tort; and (4) the privilege has been (a) claimed and (b) not waived by the client."*

State v. von Bulow, 475 A.2d 995, 1004 (R.I. 1984) (quoting *United States v. Kelly,* 569 F.2d 928, 938 (5th Cir. 1978)).

This differs from the **duty of confidentiality** in that the duty does not require that the information come from the client with the intent that it be kept a secret; even if the attorney learns of public information about the client, she is still bound not to repeat it. This may not at first seem necessary; however, statements of an attorney made about a client are cloaked with a certain amount of authority. While the public may know the information, it is substantiated when it is repeated by an attorney, someone who has a fiduciary relationship with the person. These privileged communications are, with few strict exceptions, never revealed to any third parties. The purpose of the rules of confidentiality is to preserve the nature of the attorney-client relationship. Paralegals are bound by the same code of silence as explained in Figure 4.1.

attorney-client privilege
The legal relationship established between attorney and client allowing for free exchange of information without fear of disclosure.

duty of confidentiality
An absolute prohibition against the attorney's disclosure of any information gained about his client, regardless of the source of that information. It is much broader than the matter covered under the attorney-client privilege.

NALA Guideline 1

Legal Assistants should:
2. Preserve the confidences and secrets of all clients.

NFPA EC 1.5

A PARALEGAL SHALL PRESERVE ALL CONFIDENTIAL INFORMATION PROVIDED BY THE CLIENT OR ACQUIRED FROM OTHER SOURCES BEFORE, DURING, AND AFTER THE COURSE OF THE PROFESSIONAL RELATIONSHIP.

EC 1.5(a) A paralegal shall be aware of and abide by all legal authority governing confidential information in the jurisdiction in which the paralegal practices.

FIGURE 4.1
Paralegals' Duty of Confidentiality

ABA Model Rule 1.6 pertains to the ethical constraints regarding the dissemination of information about the client. The foremost principle regarding confidentiality is, in most circumstances, to remain silent about any and all information about the client and the representation.

WAIVER

waiver of confidentiality
Authorization by the client, by his words or actions, of the disclosure of otherwise protected information obtained by his attorney.

It is important to understand that the client "owns" the information. Any and all information relating to the client is the client's "property." The client creates the duty of confidentiality on the part of the attorney and paralegal by disclosing information to them, and the client can destroy it as well. The client may choose to waive the protection afforded to him by the rules of confidentiality. A **waiver of confidentiality** may be either implicit or explicit. A client may explicitly authorize her attorney to reveal the otherwise confidential information; this should be done only as a consequence of informed consent. In a situation where a client wishes to disclose certain information, the attorney should explain the legal ramifications of that disclosure. Once information is no longer protected, it can be used against the client.

Implicit waiver exists where the disclosure is necessary under court rules or orders, as it is assumed that a client would and will consent to comply with the law. A client may also waive the confidential nature of a communication made to her attorney if she makes it knowingly in a nonconfidential setting. This may include speaking in front of third parties, speaking in public places without regard for who may overhear, or performing other actions that express the client's disregard for confidentiality and intent to waive the privacy of the information. The deciding factor in making the determination of whether the communication is made in confidence or that confidence has been waived is the intent of the client. The mere presence of third parties or the place or manner of communication is not determinative. It is reasonable to expect that the presence of a close family member or friend with whom the client already has a confidential relationship would not violate the confidentiality of the communication. It is also reasonable that a time when a person needs to seek the advice of counsel is the very time when he also needs the support of another person with whom he has a close relationship. In *Newman v. State,* 384 Md. 285, 291, 863 A.2d 321 (2004), the attorney requested that the defendant's close friend be present in the meetings for a "cool head in the room." In another situation when the confidentiality of the client was preserved, a young man's father was permitted to attend the consultations and meetings with his attorney regarding his DUI charge. *Kevlik v. Goldstein,* 724 F.2d 844 (1st Cir. 1984). The key is whether the client considered the communications in front of the third person to be confidential.

Where this expectation is unreasonable or the client is careless, the confidentiality is broken. In *People v. Harris,* 57 N.Y.2d 335, 343, 442 N.E.2d 1205, 1208 (Ct. App. 1982), the substance of the accused's telephone conversation with her attorney was admissible. The accused spoke knowing that the police officer was still in the room. The court found that the privilege never attached, as the accused did not intend the statement to be confidential in that situation. The officer "did nothing to purposely overhear the conversation or conceal his presence from defendant. Generally, communications made in the presence of third parties, whose presence is known to the defendant, are not privileged from disclosure."

It is important to note that a client may freely communicate with his attorney in the presence of the attorney's staff, including her paralegals, without destroying

SPOT THE ISSUE

Daniel has gotten himself into some hot water; he has been charged with Driving Under the Influence (DUI) and is in need of some legal help. Bob, the bartender at Daniel's local pub, suggests that Daniel call Larry, a lawyer who specializes in DUI defense. As it happens, not long after Bob and Daniel have spoken, Larry walks into the bar and, coincidentally, sits down next to Daniel. Larry and Daniel strike up a friendly conversation, and Daniel reveals that he is in need of an attorney for his DUI defense. Larry, happy to have found another client, volunteers to listen to all the details of Daniel's run-in with the law.

What are the ethical implications of this situation? What details would you add to argue either that no attorney-client confidentiality exists or that it does exist? What is Larry's duty to Daniel? Is this information privileged? Why or why not? On what facts does your answer depend? What if Larry were a paralegal (not an attorney) who worked for a DUI defense firm? Would your answer change? Why or why not?

For guidance, *see* 2003 WL 23146200 (Cal. St. Bar Comm. On Prof'l Responsibility).

the confidential nature of the communications. These personnel are considered agents of the attorney and therefore are considered extensions of the attorney and bound by these rules. The extension of the "cone of silence" extends to those professionals engaged for the purposes of preparing the matter for litigation. Paralegals often meet with clients without the attorney present. This is part of the vital time-saving role that paralegals play in the law office. Clients should feel comfortable in disclosing confidential information to paralegals, knowing that the information is protected under the ethical rules as it is transmitted to the attorney. Further, paralegals have a duty to keep their supervisors informed of the confidential information obtained by them from the client. See NFPA's rule in Figure 4.2. In this way, all the legal service providers in the office can render their best efforts, because they have all the information available and can better understand of the facts of the matter.

The protection of confidentiality extends not only to paralegals, but also to other agents retained by the attorney or paralegal to assist them in preparing the client's matter. For example, in *Commonwealth v. Noll,* 443 Pa.Super. 602, 607, 662 A.2d 1123, 1126 (1995), *appeal denied,* 543 Pa. 726, 673 A.2d 333 (1996), statements made to an accident reconstructionist hired by the attorney were confidential because they were made in order to determine whether the client had a viable lawsuit. Similarly, in *Miller v. District Court,* 737 P.2d 834 (Colo. 1987), a criminal defendant's statements to a psychiatrist retained by the defense attorney were protected, as they related directly to the evaluation and strategy of the defendant's case. This psychiatrist was not to be called to give trial testimony. "The assistance of these agents 'being indispensable to [the attorney's] work . . . . . ., the privilege must include all persons who act as the attorney's agents'." (Citing J. WIGMORE, WIGMORE ON EVIDENCE § 2301, at 583 (1961).

NFPA EC 1.5

(e) A paralegal shall keep those individuals responsible for the legal representation of a client fully informed of any confidential information the paralegal may have pertaining to that client.

FIGURE 4.2

Transmitting Confidential Information to Supervisors

SPOT THE ISSUE

Attorney Smith represents the national dressmakers association ("NDA") by and through its Board of Directors. The board has consulted Attorney Smith with regard to some of the contracts its members are entering into with suppliers. Attorney Smith has asked his paralegal to prepare a memorandum regarding the legality of some of the proposed terms. The board is planning a meeting and has invited the national tailors association ("NTA") as its guest to discuss these matters. The attorney's memo was attached to the meeting agenda and was discussed. One month later, the NDA files a lawsuit against various suppliers based upon these contracts. The suppliers demand that the NDA produce the legal memorandum discussed at the board meeting with the NTA, claiming that the NDA's disclosure at the meeting waived the confidentiality of the document. The NDA refuses to do so, stating that the NTA's participation in the meeting did not break the confidential nature of the document.

Review the following:

Under the common interest rule, individuals may share information without waiving the attorney-client privilege if: (1) the disclosure is made due to actual or anticipated litigation; (2) for the purpose of furthering a common interest; and (3) the disclosure is made in a manner not inconsistent with maintaining confidentiality against adverse parties. Whether the parties shared a "common interest" in the anticipated litigation must be evaluated as of the time that the confidential information is disclosed.

Do you think the legal memorandum is confidential, or has the NTA waived that protection?

Source: *Holland v. Island Creek Corp.,* 885 F. Supp. 4, 6 (D.D.C.1995).

REQUIRED DISCLOSURE

Prevention of Death or Serious Bodily Harm

The second section of ABA Model Rule 1.6 sets the parameters for those instances in which the client does not consent to disclose, but the attorney *may,* in her professional discretion, reveal the information to the appropriate authority. NFPA has a parallel ethical consideration. (See Figure 4.3.)

permitted disclosure
In certain circumstances, the right of an attorney to reveal certain information learned from his client, even without the client's consent.

The first category of **permitted disclosure** relates to the attorney's or paralegal's reasonable belief that the client will likely contribute to the death or substantial bodily harm of another person. The attorney or paralegal must have a reasonable belief that his client will go through with the threat of harm to another before the duty of confidentiality can be violated. The communication regarding a future criminal act is not protected. Of course, the attorney should try to dissuade the client from going through with the malicious act and advise her as to the serious legal ramifications of her potential actions. If the paralegal is the one in possession of this information, the previously discussed ethical consideration imposes a duty upon the paralegal to report the potentially harmful act to the responsible supervising attorney, who can then take the appropriate legal actions.

> *We believe that conscientious lawyers, faced with the decision of whether or not to exercise their discretionary power to make the limited disclosure "necessary to prevent" a threatened crime, should consider a number of factors. The basic considerations would be the*

FIGURE 4.3
Disclosure to Prevent Harm

NFPA EC 1.5

(d) A paralegal may reveal confidential information only after full disclosure and with the client's written consent; or when required by law or court order; or when necessary to prevent the client from committing an act that could result in death or serious bodily harm.

seriousness of the potential injury (especially when the threatened crime involves death or grave bodily injury), its likelihood and imminence, and the apparent absence of any other feasible way in which such prospective harm can be prevented. The lawyer may also appropriately give weight to other factors of potential relevance, including the extent to which the client may have attempted to involve the lawyer in the prospective crime, the circumstances under which the lawyer acquired the information of the client's intent, and any possibly aggravating or extenuating factors. As already noted, however, disclosure under this exception should be limited to what the lawyer believes necessary to prevent the crime.

NY Eth. Op. 562, 1984 WL 50017 at 4 (N.Y. St. Bar Assn. Comm. on Prof'l Ethics).

The determination is not an easy one to make; it is extremely fact sensitive, and can potentially be second-guessed by a reviewing court. There are two competing interests at stake in making this determination; the attorney or the paralegal must choose between protecting her client's trust and confidence and ensuring the personal safety, even the very life, of a third party.

The pivotal issue is whether the legal professional has information prior to the commission of the future act that she reasonably believes will occur. Indeed, an attorney may be compelled to disclose confidential information where it may prevent death or substantial bodily injury to a third party. This was exactly the case in *Henderson v. State,* 962 S.W.2d 544 (Tex. Crim. App. 1997), wherein the attorney for the accused was compelled to produce maps made by the accused that law enforcement believed might lead them to the missing child. The public policy in protecting the well-being of the child outweighed the accused's right in privileged communications to her attorney.

Crime-Fraud Exception

The second possibility of disclosure relates to the "crime or fraud" exception to the attorney-client privilege and the obligation of the legal professionals in the office to keep all the confidences of the client. If the information exchanged between the attorney and the client was used by the client to directly further the client's misconduct, then the attorney may reveal that secret information to the proper authorities. Essentially, the client has waived the privileged nature of the communication by using it toward an end not tolerable by justice system. To misuse an attorney's advice and abuse his trust is to forfeit the privilege. *In re Grand Jury Proceedings (Violette),* 183 F.3d 71, 77 (1st Cir. 1999). The attorney may be totally in the dark with regard to his client's purpose for seeking the advice; if it turns out that the client has misused the information, it is no longer subject to the privilege. Because the privilege is so well established and vital to the performance of an attorney's duty, it is not lightly disregarded. "It does not suffice that the communications may be related to a crime" (*United States v. White,* 281 U.S. App. D.C. Cir. 39, 43, 887 F.2d 267, 271 (1989); nor is it enough to show that the client communicated to her attorney right before her commission of a crime or fraud (*in re Sealed Case,* 107 F.3d 46, 50, 323 U.S. App. D.C. Cir. 233, 237 (1997)). "[T]he court must determine that the communication was itself in furtherance of the crime or fraud, not merely that it has the potential of being relevant evidence of criminal or fraudulent activity." 1 JOHN W. STRONG, MCCORMICK ON EVIDENCE 382 (5th ed. 1999).

Just like the first exception to the privilege for preventing death or substantial bodily harm to another, the "crime-fraud" exception applies prospectively. The privilege is not broken when the client discusses his past criminal or fraudulent activity—that may very well be why he is consulting an attorney in the first place! These rules are prophylactic in nature. They are designed to prevent future or ongoing harm. It is the attorney's duty to try to assist his client to navigate his way through the justice system, not to cover up, assist, counsel, or otherwise provide information to thwart the process. *In re Federal Grand Jury Proceedings 89-10,* 938 F.2d 1578, 1581 (11th Cir. 1991):

> *A determination of whether the crime-fraud exception applies involves application of a two part test:*
>
> *First, there must be a prima facie showing that the client was engaged in criminal or fraudulent conduct when he sought the advice of counsel, that he was planning such conduct when he sought the advice of counsel, or that he committed a crime or fraud subsequent to receiving the benefit of counsel's advice.*
>
> *Second, there must be a showing that the attorney's assistance was obtained in furtherance of the criminal or fraudulent activity or was closely related to it.*

"fishing expedition"
A request by an opposing party for potentially damaging information from the attorney, on the premise that the opposing party needs it to prevent harm, but without specific evidence of an actual threat of harm.

There must be strong evidence of a nexus between information that the legal professional has in her possession and the planned crime or fraud perpetrated by the client. A "**fishing expedition**," a request for disclosure to see what information the attorney may have, is not permitted, as it fails to meet this standard. *See in re Marriage of Decker,* 153 Ill. 2d 298, 606 N.E.2d 1094 (1992). In that case, a woman filed an emergency motion and subpoena for any information relating to the whereabouts of her ex-husband, who may have abducted their child by failing to return the child after visitation. The court first wrestled with the decision of whether the initial burden was met: whether the woman had enough information to lead a reasonable person to believe that the ex-husband's attorney had relevant information regarding his plan to kidnap the child. The second issue revolved around whether an **in camera inspection** of the materials that potentially contained this information was appropriate, to determine whether the "crime-fraud" exception applied and the privileged information should be made known in order to apprehend the ex-husband. The determination that indeed a crime had been committed was not enough to prove that there was any communication between the attorney and client that was related to that plan to carry out the crime. The court opined that a very specific question posed would clarify the determination.

in camera inspection
A proceeding in the judge's chambers during which the judge can examine the proffered evidence outside of the jury's presence to determine the necessity of disclosure of the confidential information.

> *"Did your client ask your advice on how to commit this [specific illegal] act, knowing it to be unlawful?"* The answer to this question would subject the information to minimal disclosure, and an affirmative answer would remove the privilege for that information.

Id. at 325.

Anticipating Perjury

perjury
The willful assertion as to a matter of fact, opinion, belief, or knowledge, made by a witness in a judicial proceeding as part of his/her evidence, either upon oath or in any form allowed by law to be substituted for an oath, whether such evidence is given in open court, in an affidavit, or otherwise, such assertion being material to the issue or point of inquiry and known to such witness to be false.

Perhaps the most abhorrent fraud is that perpetrated against the justice system's search for the truth: **perjury**. While there is no prohibition against presenting all defenses for the accused, the ethical rules that require an attorney from refraining from perpetrating a fraud or crime also prevent an attorney from permitting the client to lie under oath. If an attorney has a reasonable belief that his client will not tell the truth in presenting testimony, he is prohibited from affirmatively offering that evidence into court. If the client insists on presenting oral testimony in court, there are several options open to the attorney. The primary preference is to convince the client either not to take the stand or to refrain from lying. It is the attorney's duty to also explain the ramifications of that course of action. Permitting the client to commit perjury is, in itself, an ethical violation, as it is the **subornation of perjury** which is a criminal offense. Once a client has committed perjury, it is the attorney's duty to report it to the court. Indeed, not only is the disclosure permitted as an exception from the attorney-client privilege; it is required by the ethics rules. The client needs to be made well aware that the attorney will disclose the perjury to the court. This is perhaps the most powerful weapon the attorney has to prevent the commission of perjury. *Nix v. Whiteside,* 475 U.S. 157, 106 S.Ct. 988, 89 L.Ed. 123 (1986).

subornation of perjury
Assistance by an attorney in carrying out a witness's offer of false testimony.

Sam is a criminal defendant indicted for embezzlement and represented by Eddie. During their meetings, Sam reveals that he has recently purchased several vacation condos in Florida and California. He seems very pleased that he has no mortgages, as he has paid in cash for the full purchase price. He sees this as a sound investment strategy. Eddie seems surprised at his ability to come up with that kind of money right on hand as Sam had difficulty making bail. Eddie recalls reading a recent ethics opinion that he found his paralegal filing in the office library:

> [W]e do not believe that the Code intends to encourage attorneys to be unduly naive or disregard the obvious. There are some circumstances in which an attorney may be aware of facts which fall short of actual knowledge but which still impose on him an obligation to make inquiry to determine whether his client is engaged in unlawful conduct. A lawyer may not purposely close his eyes to what he perceives to be circumstances indicative of illegal or fraudulent conduct by a client. Such selective blindness may be a disservice to the client and, in some cases, has led to disciplinary proceedings against the attorney.
>
> Likewise, an attorney need not turn a blind eye to circumstances that would lead a reasonable person to believe that a client intends to commit a crime even though the lawyer does not "know" that this is the client's intent. If a lawyer reasonably concludes after due inquiry that the client has the intention to commit a future crime, then the lawyer is permitted, but not required, to make disclosure to the appropriate authorities to prevent the crime. Once the threshold of reasonable belief of the client's intention to commit a crime is surmounted, in determining whether to make permissive disclosure, the lawyer should consider a number of factors, including "the seriousness of the potential injury to others if the prospective crime is committed, the likelihood that it will be committed and its imminence, the apparent absence of any other feasible way in which the potential injury can be prevented, the extent to which the client may have attempted to involve the lawyer in the prospective crime [and] the circumstances under which the lawyer acquired the information of the client's intent.

What do you think Eddie should do, given this opinion?

Source: NYC Eth. Op. 2202-1, 2002 WL 1040180 (N.Y.C. Assn. B.Comm. Prof.Jud. Auth.)

With enough advance notice of the proposed perjurious testimony, the attorney can choose to apply to withdraw as counsel. This move has potentially positive outcomes for the attorney, but negative repercussions for the client and potentially for the court. While the attorney removes herself from the perils of an ethical violation, she may place another attorney in the same predicament. Additionally, this successive attorney may not be aware of the falsity of the proposed testimony and the intention of the client to commit perjury. To permit withdrawal is to facilitate the commission of perjury; the attorney who is aware of the potential fraud is no longer in the position to prevent it. Further, the court may not permit the withdrawal on the basis that it will prejudice the client's interests. Withdrawal is unlikely if the trial date is very close, as it would not permit the substituted counsel to adequately prepare. The court may also deny the motion to withdraw as counsel if the facts supporting withdrawal are not sufficient to convince the judge that there is the possibility of perjury. In making the motion, the attorney must disclose enough information to illustrate the possibility of perjury without making it clear exactly what parts of the proposed testimony are false—a difficult showing at best.

The "middle ground" between full disclosure and full preservation of confidentiality by withdrawing as counsel is the disassociation from or "nonsponsorship" of the testimony. If the client cannot be dissuaded from potentially committing perjury and insists on giving testimony on his own behalf, the client may give that testimony in a narrative form without the assistance of the attorney's direct examination. While the savvy juror would understand that this testimony is suspect because the attorney is

IN CLASS DISCUSSION

Lou has been indicted for "loan sharking" (lending money to people and charging very, very high interest on those loans). Lou is a rather large man and has been known to intimidate those with whom he deals. He tells his attorney's paralegal, Claude, that he can get plenty of witnesses to testify on his behalf. In fact, Lou's friend is a police officer, and Lou is *sure* he can *persuade* him to give positive testimony.

The police officer agrees to help Lou out and will in fact lie under oath for him without Lou's attorney knowing about the falsity of the testimony. Should Lou's attorney or paralegal be responsible for subornation of perjury in this case?

See ex parte Castellano, 863 S.W.2d 476 (Tex. Crim. App. 1993).

not participating in offering the testimony into evidence, it is better than the alternative. Some courts have suggested that the attorney may conduct direct examination of his client as to the "nonsuspect" portions of the testimony, and then permit a narrative of that portion of the client's testimony which the attorney cannot support, as it is potentially perjury. This would also permit the attorney to include the direct-exam portion of the testimony in his closing argument as properly admitted evidence. This "bifurcation method" of dealing with the client's testimony has been criticized by other courts and the ABA:

> [T]his is the worst approach of all. . . . This [approach] would be far worse for the client than saying nothing, not to mention it would be virtually impossible to control once the client takes the stand. And what about cross? How can you possibly prepare your clients for that? Tell them not to answer any questions that they do not like?

ABA CRIMINAL JUSTICE SECTION, ETHICAL PROBLEMS FACING THE CRIMINAL DEFENSE LAWYER, at 162 (1995).

"[This] suggestion is impractical, as it may call attention to testimony of the defendant that is not argued by trial counsel, and would likely lead to counsel's making an incoherent final argument." *Commonwealth v. Mitchell,* 438 Mass. 535, 550, 781 N.E.2d 1237, 1249 (2003).

With so much at stake, how does an attorney determine whether the client's testimony is perjury that should be reported? Clients may not always be wholly truthful with their attorneys or fully disclose all the facts known to them. The standard upheld by most courts is that an attorney must have a "firm factual basis" and proof beyond a reasonable doubt that the proffered testimony rises to the level of lying under oath.

RESEARCH THIS

Find a case in your jurisdiction that addresses the situation where an attorney or a paralegal is faced with a client who is contemplating committing perjury. How does your state court decide what is the attorney's or paralegal's most appropriate response and means to handle the issue? Remember to look not only at case law, but also at the ethics opinions from the appropriate body.

Prevention of Further Harm

The third exception to the rule of confidentiality is related to the one just above. However, this third rule contemplates that the legal professional has no knowledge of the planned criminal or fraudulent conduct, but learns of it after the fact. In this instance, if the attorney or paralegal can prevent further damage caused by her client's illegal conduct, she must do so. The New Jersey court stated:

> The Rule reads, "and if his client refuses or is unable to do so, he shall reveal the fraud to the affected person or tribunal." No prior case has stated precisely that the word "shall" in the above Rule is intended to be mandatory. "Shall" is defined in Webster's New Collegiate Dictionary as "ought to, must, will have to, used to express a command or exhortation, used in laws, regulations or directives to express what is mandatory." The clear meaning of "shall" in the Rule must be deemed "mandatory"; otherwise, the purpose of the Rule would be frustrated.

NJ Eth. Op. 520, 112 N.J.L.J. 369, 1983 WL 106230 at 4 (N.J. Adv. Comm. Prof. Eth.); *see also* Utah Ethics Advisory Op. 00-06, 2000 WL 1523292 (Utah St. Bar).

The Utah Ethics Board decided that silence in the face of a fraud or crime is equivalent to aiding in it. The attorney must first attempt to convince the client to rectify the situation; if the client is unwilling, then the attorney must reveal the truth to correct the result of the fraud or crime. The attorney has a duty also to the victim, to prevent the nondisclosure of the crime or fraud from getting worse. For example, having discovered his client's embezzlement of corporate funds, the attorney should take some measure to prevent the coming financial disaster as his client siphons the money.

REEL TO REAL

Witness for the Prosecution (1957) stars two cinematic powerhouses, Tyrone Power and Marlene Dietrich, locked in a courtroom battle over witness testimony. Dietrich's character is the wife of the accused murderer of a rich middle-aged widow. The defense's only alibi witness is his wife; however, she has agreed to take the stand on behalf of the prosecution. Evaluate her credibility, her motives for possible perjury, and the prosecution's decision to put her on the stand.

Contemporary powerhouses also clash in *A Few Good Men* (1992). The movie stars the sparring Jack Nicholson and Tom Cruise, giving rise to one of the most quoted-movie lines: "You want answers, I want the truth. You can't handle the truth."

Prevention of or Self-Defense against Professional Malpractice

The fourth exception to the general close-mouthed position of the attorney essentially permits the attorney to look for legal advice in order to herself comply with the applicable rules. This manifests itself in the numerous and varied ethics opinions rendered by courts and ethical boards. An attorney may find herself in a situation where her ethical duties are unclear. In an effort to do the right thing, the attorney writes to the supervising ethical body posing a hypothetical situation that matches the one in which she has found herself. This disclosure of confidential client information is necessary in order for the attorney to comply with her duty to the profession and to properly counsel her client. The paralegal student will notice, upon finding an opinion rendered by a supervising ethical board or committee, that neither the name of the inquiring attorney nor that of her client is ever revealed in a published opinion. They are set forth as anonymous hypothetical situations in order to preserve the confidentiality of the client and ensure that no one can deduce from the facts set forth who the client may be. It is unclear whether paralegals have access to this kind of advice when they are in possession of such information.

Finally, an attorney or paralegal may reveal information necessary to defend himself against allegations of ethical violations or professional misconduct with regard to the representation of that particular client. To deny a legal professional the opportunity to disclose the content of conversations with his client would be to strip him of the ability to counter the contentions leveled against him. This exception to the privilege applies to accusations brought both by the former client and by third parties who allege that the legal professional was a participant in the former client's wrongdoing. This most often manifests itself as a defense to a malpractice claim. Not only attorneys are covered under malpractice claims and the related insurance; paralegals are as well. If a client challenges the attorney's or the paralegal's competence through either a civil claim or an ethical charge, the attorney may testify as to the relationship and produce documents that would otherwise be privileged. The ability to defend oneself and one's professional integrity is important enough that the courts have determined that the disclosure may be made even prior to an indictment. *See in re Friend,* 411 F. Supp. 776, 777 (S.D.N.Y. 1975). In this matter, the attorney applied for court permission to turn over certain client documents to a United States Grand Jury which was investing his former client and which would help to establish that the attorney acted properly in trying to assure his client's compliance with the law. "Although, as yet, no formal accusation has been made against Mr. Friend, it would be senseless to require the stigma of an indictment to attach prior to allowing Mr. Friend to invoke the exception [to the privilege] in his own defense." The disclosure may be made even in a case where the attorney is made subject to public criticism by "bad-mouthing" from the former client where the accusations leveled against the attorney suggest a breach of contract, fiduciary duty, malpractice, or violation of ethics.

> *A lawyer may reveal protected information in self-defense against an accusation of alleged wrongdoing, regardless of whether there is a formal suit, criminal indictment or disciplinary charge. . . . It requires that the allegation be public and specific such that a person would reasonably conclude that the lawyer is subject to a claim or charge for such misconduct and that the claim or charge is looming and will be brought before a body empowered to rule on such claim or charge.*

NYCLA Eth. Op. 722, 1997 WL 232485 (N.Y. Cty. Law. Assn. Comm. on Prof'l Ethics; emphasis added).

Ethics requires that confidences be broken only where the context of the disparaging comments would lead the listener to believe that the client is about to or could bring an action against the attorney and that the action is imminent. Mere gossip or general complaining is not enough to dissolve the duty of confidentiality; the duty of confidentiality is nearly sacrosanct.

UNINTENTIONAL DISCLOSURE

unintentional disclosure
The accidental release of sensitive client information to a third party.

Whereas the preceding discussion focused on the purposeful ability of the legal professional to disclose confidential information, this section addresses those situations where the information is disclosed by accident. How does this **unintentional disclosure** occur? The most common scenario plays out in the failure of general office procedures. Failure to properly manage client files, mailing lists, faxes, and e-mails can all result in an inadvertent disclosure of sensitive documents. Mindful performance of these tasks by every member of the office is essential to maintaining confidential information. Monitoring these processes may be a key role played by paralegals. The discovery process offers the greatest access to confidential information, as the opposing party often has access to the set of client documents held by the attorney. If a close pre-discovery screening of the files for sensitive information has not been performed by either the attorney or, more likely, the paralegal, these documents will be exposed to opposing counsel. It is imperative to identify and remove all the confidential information from the client's files. Careful use of mailing lists, fax and e-mail is also necessary to keep documents and correspondence from reaching the wrong persons. It is often the legal secretary's or paralegal's job to maintain distribution lists of the parties involved in the suit and their corresponding counsel. Lack of clarity or ease of use of these lists makes it possible to transmit confidential information unintentionally. *See People v. Terry,* 1 Misc.3d 475, 764 N.Y.S.2d 592 (N.Y.Co.Ct.2003), wherein the defendant intended to send a letter to his attorney and put the correct name on the envelope; however, the address was mixed up with the District Attorney's office in charge of the prosecution of the case. The letter was then opened and read by the District Attorney. The court determined that the fault truly lay with the District Attorney and his personnel, because it was clearly sent in error and they should not have opened or read the material. The court determined that the inadvertent disclosure did not constitute a waiver by the client who sent the letter and the information contained in it could not be used against the defendant.

What are the ramifications of this accidental disclosure? There are essentially three conclusions:

1. The privilege is lost, as it is considered waived, and the information can be used by the receiving party.
2. The privilege cannot be waived by accidental disclosure by the attorney, because waiver requires intent to disclose by the holder of the privilege, who in this case is the client. Only a knowing disclosure by the client can operate as a waiver of confidentiality.
3. The disclosure may constitute a waiver, depending on the circumstances surrounding it.

This third approach is a "middle ground" between the first two extremes, both of which operate unfairly on one party or another, or compromise the duties of either the sending or receiving attorneys. The circumstances that the court must examine to determine whether the accidental disclosure should act as a waiver of confidentiality or not are these:

1. the degree of care taken by the disclosing party—or, whether the precautions and the office procedures are reasonably and functionally able to prevent accidental disclosures;
2. "the presence of extenuating circumstances, the most obvious being the press of massive discovery going forward under the pressure of deadlines, where even caution in producing documents is likely to generate occasional mistakes" (*Elkton Care Center Associates Ltd. Partnership v. Quality Care,* 145 Md. App. 532, 545 805 A.2d 1177, 1184 (2002));
3. The number and significance of the accidental disclosures;
4. The extent of the disclosure;
5. The time between the disclosure and the attempts to rectify the situation;
6. The overriding interests of justice that may be served by relieving a party of its error.

See Sampson Fire Sales v. Oaks, 201 F.R.D., 351, 360 (M.D.Pa. 2001).

There is a duty upon the receiving party to maintain the overarching ethical principle of client confidentiality, maintain the highest standards of the profession, and ensure fairness in the legal process. An attorney or paralegal receiving this kind of sensitive confidential information should do three things:

1. refrain from viewing the material as soon as she realizes that it is privileged information;

2. notify the sender about the disclosure;

3. follow the instructions regarding the return or destruction of documents or seek a resolution in court.

Only the second task *must* be undertaken as a requirement of the Model Rules of Professional Responsibility. The first and third are moral and ethical considerations that the legal professional may and should consider in making his decision, but he is not bound by the formal rules to follow them. *See* ABA Formal Opinion 06-440 (2006); this opinion formally withdrew the previous opinion, 94-382, which did require all three steps to be taken. However, this retraction does not leave the door open for unscrupulous or questionable activity in obtaining and using privileged or confidential information. Where confidential information is obtained through tortious or criminal conduct, the attorney retaining and using the information may be sanctioned for such an offence. *See Maldonado v. New Jersey,* 225 F.R.D. 120 (D.N.J. 2004). The prosecuting attorney in that case clearly took advantage of the mysterious appearance in the plaintiff's mailbox of a confidential letter written by the defendants and addressed to their attorney.

Even the most innocent situations may pose a threat to a client's confidential information. Friends and family often ask about a paralegal's day: "Hi, honey, I'm home; how was your day?" It is a social norm to talk about things going on at work as you gather for lunch or dinner. A paralegal must be especially careful not to talk about matters in any specific or identifiable way, because many people do not understand the full scope of a legal professional's duty of confidentiality. It may be particularly hard not to discuss a high-profile matter in which the paralegal is involved. Recall that even if the information is publicly known, it is unacceptable for the legal professional to reveal it, as it might color the facts with a certain authority.

> The reality of maintaining these confidences is not so cut and dried. For instance, can you recall how many paralegals were talking with just a little too much detail about their cases at the last paralegal association luncheon/dinner you attended? Or, how about that novice paralegal seeking guidance from you on how to accomplish a paralegal task, but who gave enough information about the client that the person at the next table in the restaurant could identify the client?
>
> Suppose that person who overheard your conversation was from the adversary's lawyer's office and the information revealed client confidences to that person? And finally, imagine attending an interview for a paralegal job and being asked by the interviewing attorney to discuss the kinds of cases in which you have been involved. Wanting the job, wanting to impress the attorney sufficiently to secure the job, yet trying to be careful, you slip–hook, line and sinker—you've divulged a client confidence and lost any chance at ever getting a job with that firm or company.

Susan D. Daugherty, *Loose Lips Sink Ships . . . or Paralegals,* THE NATIONAL PARALEGAL REPORTER ONLINE 1998.

Clearly, paralegals must always be vigilant about their conversations about their work. As a legal professional, it is not always possible to leave work at the office and shed your duties as you "clock out." The ethical obligations remain in force 24 hours a day, seven days a week, no matter whom the paralegal is with or where the paralegal is.

UNPROTECTED COMMUNICATIONS

While clients would like to believe, or mistakenly do believe, that any and all documents in the possession of their attorneys and all communications between themselves and their attorneys are protected by the duty of confidentiality, the truth is that only those that relate to the representation of the client are protectable (not necessarily protected). Documents by the boxload may be brought to the attorney's office in preparation for litigation; however, the change in their location does not change their status from discoverable and unprotected to privileged. All documents that existed prior to the preparation for litigation are "fair game"; merely bringing or sending documents to your attorney does not make them confidential. Communications between the attorney and client that deal solely with a matter of fact are not ordinarily privileged, unless the communication of those facts were shown to be "inextricably linked" to the giving of legal advice. *See State v. Carpenter,* 2001 WL 1561058 (Conn. Super. 2001), wherein the defendant sent letters attached to various documents, including newspaper clippings regarding the crime and possible suspects, to her attorney. The defendant claimed that these documents were privileged because although they dealt with public facts, when viewed in conjunction with the confidential letters, they revealed an ongoing legal strategy and were inextricably linked to the confidential legal advice rendered by her attorney. Letters (or e-mails) sent by clients to counsel as "courtesy copies" (a.k.a. cc's) to make sure the attorney has the information contained in them are not protected by confidentiality rules. These letters are "not sent or received for purpose of giving or receiving legal advice" but are sent merely for informational purposes. *See Isom v. Bank of America, N.A.,* 2006 WL 1140958 (N.C. App. 2006).

Information that may have been intended by its creator to be confidential may not be actually protected by attorney-client confidentiality rules. The court must strike a balance between the sanctity of confidentiality and judicial search for the truth. The court will generally uphold the confidentiality of information, but only if it satisfies the prerequisites for this protection. (See the four conditions set forth in *State v. von Bulow* at the beginning of this chapter.) Information which is not communicated between attorney and client for the purpose of legal representation or seeking legal advice is not covered, despite the intention of the party. *See Cangelosi v. Capasso,* 2006 WL 1875368 (Ill. App. 2.Dist. 2006), wherein a nurse took notes regarding her patient for her own use. She intended that they would be confidential and kept them secret for two years at which time she gave them to an attorney representing that former patient, who was bringing a medical malpractice action. Those notes contained the nurse's factual observations of what she saw and heard during treatment. The notes, although intended to be confidential by their creator, the nurse, were not protected by attorney-client privilege, because the nurse had no relationship with an attorney at the time of their creation and was not preparing the documents for a pending lawsuit, although she suspected that an action could be brought against the doctor.

Physical evidence of a crime is not protected by the privilege. It is impermissible for an officer of the court to fail to turn over relevant physical evidence of a crime.

The attorney should not be a depository for criminal evidence such as a knife, other weapons, stolen property, etc.), which in itself has little, if any, material value for the purposes of aiding counsel in the preparation of the defense of his client's case. Such evidence given to the attorney during legal consultation for information purposes and used by the attorney in preparing the defense of his client's case, whether or not the case ever goes to trial, could clearly be withheld for a reasonable period of time. It follows that the attorney, after a reasonable period, should, as an officer of the court, on his own motion turn the same over to the prosecution.

> *We think the attorney-client privilege should and can be preserved even though the attorney surrenders the evidence he has in his possession. The prosecution, upon receipt of such evidence from an attorney, where charge against the attorney's client is contemplated (pres-*

ently or in the future), should be well aware of the existence of the attorney-client privilege. Therefore, the state, when attempting to introduce such evidence at the trial, should take extreme precautions to make certain that the source of the evidence is not disclosed in the presence of the jury and prejudicial error is not committed. By thus allowing the prosecution to recover such evidence, the public interest is served, and by refusing the prosecution an opportunity to disclose the source of the evidence, the client's privilege is preserved and a balance is reached between these conflicting interests. The burden of introducing such evidence at a trial would continue to be upon the prosecution.

Sowers v. Olwell, 64 Wash. 2d 828, 833–834, 394 P.2d 681, 684–685 (1964).

Again, the court plays a balancing act between the rights of the defendant and the needs of the justice system. After all, the real goal of the law is to ensure fairness not only to the parties involved, but also to society as a whole. These are generalized rules and precepts which require judicious application to specific facts in order to arrive at a fair outcome.

WORK PRODUCT RULE

In fairness, it is only right that a person gets to control that which she has worked on herself and is her own original product. She should not be required to share the fruits of her own labor. This is the guiding principle behind the work product rule. Materials prepared by attorneys and paralegals in connection with their client's representation in anticipation of litigation are protected as "work product," and this type of material is protected against disclosure. It isn't really privileged information, because privilege refers to the client's ownership and the legal professional's fiduciary duty towards him. **Work product** is independently immune from discovery, and that immunity is very rarely pierced. There are two types of "work product":

work product
An attorney's written notes, impressions, charts, diagrams, and other material used by him or her to prepare strategy and tactics for trial.

1. Mental impressions: these are the attorney's thoughts on how to conduct the litigation, including, but not limited to, trial strategies, theories of the case, and structured legal arguments.

2. Informational material: the underlying factual research material, witness interviews, internal legal memoranda, and similar means of compiling data (even the way a nonprotected document was summarized or indexed) are protected, as they are the result of the way in which an attorney or paralegal thinks and approaches the case. The underlying facts are not protected, but the way in which they are organized and analyzed in these documents is protected.

Either type of work is the result of the attorney's brainpower, a compilation of information that has been sifted through the attorney's (or paralegal's) mind. The landmark case on this issue is *Hickman v. Taylor,* 329 U.S. 495, 67 S. Ct. 385, 91 L. Ed. 451 (1947). The United States Supreme Court acknowledged that an attorney's work product was not covered under the attorney-client privilege, yet it was equally protectable.

Historically, a lawyer is an officer of the court and is bound to work for the advancement of justice while faithfully protecting the rightful interests of his clients. In performing his various duties, however, it is essential that a lawyer work with a certain degree of privacy, free from unnecessary intrusion by opposing parties and their counsel. Proper preparation of a client's case demands that he assemble information, sift what he considers to be the relevant from the irrelevant facts, prepare his legal theories and plan his strategy without undue and needless interference. That is the historical and the necessary way in which lawyers act within the framework of our system of jurisprudence to promote justice and to protect their clients' interests. This work is reflected, of course, in interviews, statement, memoranda, correspondence, briefs, mental impressions, personal beliefs, and countless other tangible and intangible ways—aptly though roughly termed by the circuit court of appeals in this case as the "work product of the lawyer." Were such materials open to opposing counsel on mere demand, much of what is now put in writing would remain unwritten. An attorney's thoughts, heretofore inviolate, would not be his own.

Id. at 510–511.

The court in *Surf Drugs, Inc. v. Vermette,* 236 So. 2d 108, 112 (Fla. 1970) acknowledged that the concept of attorney work product is "incapable of precise definition" but that it included, generally, all those things that the attorney does not intend to offer into evidence, but rather creates for her own use in preparation for litigation. The *Surf* court listed other products of the attorney which could not be compelled to be disclosed: the

> *personal views of the attorney as to how and when to present evidence, his evaluation of its relative importance, his knowledge of which witnesses will give certain testimony, personal notes and records as to witnesses, jurors, legal citations, proposed arguments, jury instructions, diagrams and charts he may refer to at trial for his convenience but not to be used as evidence.*

Work product can be anything; its defining characteristic is that it is the result of the attorney's own thought process that will not be introduced as evidence to support his client's case.

PARALEGALS' DUTY TO MAINTAIN CONFIDENTIALITY

The ABA Model Guidelines for the Utilization of Legal Assistant Services state this: "It is the responsibility of a lawyer to take reasonable measures to ensure that all client confidences are preserved by a legal assistant." It is unquestionably necessary that a paralegal and every other employee of the attorney maintain the client's information as a secret. Recall the breadth of the duty of confidentiality: nothing communicated between the attorney and the client may be revealed by the attorney without the permission of the client. It does not matter if the information is available from other sources. With regard to confidentiality, it matters only that the client has spoken to her legal representative in his capacity as such. This holds true for all the employees of the attorney, but has particular applicability to paralegals, as they are the employees most often exposed to client information. A paralegal's role on the legal team makes it essential that she know all the details of the matter; to perform her duties as a paralegal would be impossible without this level of exposure to potentially sensitive information. This may not be the case for other employees of the legal office, who are responsible for the business maintenance of the office, rather than the practice of law, which is the concern of the paralegal. Reflecting the importance of the preservation of client confidences, both NALA and NFPA have incorporated mandates of confidentiality into their standards of professional conduct for paralegals. See Appendixes C and D for the complete text and commentary of these codes.

How does a paralegal put these ideals into practice? A law firm should have well-established policies and procedures for dealing with such information. There are many ways of handling sensitive information: it may include, but is not limited to, keeping files in a secure location; marking or separating privileged information from the general files; proper storage and eventual destruction of closed files; use of security-enabled computers and systems; use of databases that are carefully constructed so that discoverable information is kept separate from confidential information; using private areas for phone calls; and requiring confidentiality agreements with outside vendors. Paralegals are also prohibited from using "inside information" to their own gain. This may occur most frequently in mergers and acquisitions and stock information exchanges to which the paralegal is privy. The Colorado Bar

FIGURE 4.4
Confidentiality Checklist

Clients depend on their lawyer to safeguard the information they provide. The Rules of Professional Conduct provide for only limited situations where this trust may be broken. Since trust is very difficult to reestablish once it has been broken, it is important that you take steps to ensure that every member of the firm does all they can to safeguard client information.

	Yes	No	N/A
Do all new employees sign a confidentiality form acknowledging they have discussed confidentiality with you, read the relevant Rules of Professional Conduct, and will not breach the confidentiality of any client during and after their association with the firm?			
Do we make sure no client files or other confidential materials are ever left in the reception area or other public access areas?			
While conferring in person with clients, do we avoid taking calls or otherwise talking with other clients so as to protect client identities and confidentialities?			
Are the fax machines and copiers located away from where non-firm persons may be able to see confidential materials?			
If we are in an office-sharing arrangement, have we discussed confidentiality with the landlord, other tenants and any employees who may be privy to confidential information (e.g. receptionist, word processor, etc.)?			

Association produced a very helpful checklist so that legal professionals could perform a "self-test" evaluating the care taken in their office to protect client confidentiality. (See Figure 4.4.)

SPECIAL ISSUES WITH TECHNOLOGY

Technology can be both a boon to efficiency and the bane of the law office's existence. Electronic records and communications are at once transient and permanent. As society has become more familiar with technology, its use has skyrocketed; however, with comfort come complacency and carelessness. It is quite easy to hit a button on the computer keyboard and thereby create a confidentiality breach.

What are the specific threats to confidentiality posed by technology? The primary offenders are these:

• *Fax machines.* Fax numbers that are dialed incorrectly or speed dial errors can result in a threat, in that the dialers may accidentally transfer confidential information to third parties. *See Beverly v. Reinert,* 239 Ill. App. 3d 91, 606 N.E.2d 621 (1992). Another interesting point with regard to fax machines emerges in office-sharing situations. In a shared office, who is the "recipient" of the fax? See the ABA article *How to Protect Client Confidences in a Shared Office Suite* at http://www.abanet.org/buslaw/blt/bltmay01_feldman.html

- *Cell phones and other wireless devices.* Conversations are easily intercepted, as this technology relies on radio broadcast signals rather than land lines. Many people use cell phones so frequently that they forget when speaking to clients that they are in public, not in their private offices. Particularly worrisome are PDAs and other handheld electronic devices that hold data as well as function as a phone. See the ABA article *Is One in the Hand Really Worth Two in the Office?* at http://www.abanet.org/buslaw/blt/bltmay01_feldman.html

- *E-mail.* This mode of communication should generally not be used for sensitive information. If communication is necessary via e-mail, after the client's consent to use this kind of communication is obtained, the user should be sure it is encrypted. For various ABA articles on this issue, please visit the ABA's Technology Resource Center, and in particular, the following two articles: *E-mail Encryption Simplified,* at http://meetings.abanet.org/ltrc/index.cfm? data=20051117 and *Playing It Safe with Encryption,* at http://www.abanet.org/tech/ltrc/fyidocs/FYI_Playing_it_safe.html

- *"Metadata."* This is the invisible information contained in an electronic document that does not necessarily appear when the document is viewed or printed. It keeps information about the history and management of a document, such as how, by whom, and when it was created, collected, accessed and modified. This includes the file's name, location in a directory, file format, type, size, permission or security information (who can read, run, or write the data). Some of this may be particularly useful and incriminating, but it can be misleading too, in that some documents may list the form's creator but not the author of that particular modification to it. This is important in tracing the authenticity and context of an electronic document. Sometimes the metadata can be inaccurate, as when a form document reflects the author as the person who created the template but who did not draft the document. The ABA article What's the Meta with MetaData? is informative. It can be accessed at http://www.abanet.org/media/youraba/200601/article01.html

- *Access from the "outside."* Passwords and "firewalls" are necessary with regard to computer access. Databases should be maintained in a way to prevent secure information from being "lifted." For a discussion of the various security measures needed, see the ABA article *Practicing Safe Computing: Security Tips, Products and Services to Protect Your Small Firm* at http://www.abanet.org/genpractice/newsletter/lawtrends/0508/business/safecomputing.html

As technology increases, so will both the attorney's and the paralegal's vigilance in maintaining procedures to ensure the security of client confidences. Convenience and ease of use makes it more tempting to use than other more traditional means of communications. However, traditional and, unfortunately, slower exchanges can be thought out and better controlled. It is perhaps the paralegal's most valuable contribution to the law office to manage the most efficient and protective way to handle these technological issues. Again, the Colorado Bar provides a helpful checklist for dealing with these special issues relating to confidentiality. See Figure 4.5.

It is an onerous but important responsibility to maintain the confidences of the client in almost any and every situation. It is not just for the individual client that the rules of confidentiality exist; it is for the preservation of the integrity of the legal profession (either attorney or paralegal) itself. When the duty is excused, it must be for an imperative reason. It is vital that a paralegal understand the parameters of the duty in order to comply with the ethical obligations that are faced every day at work.

CYBER TRIP

For general articles written about technology and confidentiality, please visit the following sites. This is just a small sampling of the information available on this topic.

- Mary Frances Lapidus, P.C., *Professional Responsibility and Confidentiality Considerations When Using the Internet,* http://www.legalethics.com/?page_id=413

- Charles F. Luce, Jr., *Confidentiality, Cell Phones & E-Mail,* http://www.mgovg.com/ethics/8cel&eml.htm

- Joshua M. Masur, *Safety in Numbers: Revisiting the Risks to Client Confidences and Attorney-Client Privilege Posed by Internet Electronic Mail,* http://www.law.berkeley.edu/journals/btlj/articles/vol14/Masur/html/text.html

FIGURE 4.5
Technology and Confidentiality Checklist

Office technology is nothing more than the tools to best serve your clients. The challenge is to have the knowledge to use these tools fully. Indeed, it may soon be that a lawyer's professional competence will include the use of technology to benefit clients.

	Yes	No	N/A
Do all our lawyers and staff use computers?			
Do we use a networked (if applicable) calendar program?			
Is everyone trained to usefully use our software?			
Is the office locked every night to discourage theft?			
Do we use case management software?			
Do we use e-mail with client permission?			
Is our e-mail marked "Confidential Privileged Communication"?			
Do we back up our data at least weekly?			
Do we attempt periodic "restores" of data (to check if it works)?			
Do we train new employees about our computer system?			
Do we use computer virus filters and a firewall?			
Does our voice mail tell callers to limit their message?			
Do we need a password to access data?			
Do we have confidentiality agreements for cleaning services, contract staff and computer maintenance vendors who have access to our computer systems?			

SURF'S UP

Find several (four or five) lawyer Web sites (any jurisdiction) wherein the visitor can pose a question to the lawyer or firm. What kind of information does the site seek to obtain? Are there any disclaimers regarding confidentiality or the attorney-client relationship? Compare the Web sites. Does one do a better job of protecting the confidentiality of the submitted information than the others? How?

This issue was dealt with in the California State Bar Standing Committee on Professional Responsibility and Conduct, Formal Opinion 2005–168. That Web site contained a link entitled "What are my rights?" The visitor to the site then filled in an electronic form with her name, her contact information, and a statement of facts relating to the divorce she wanted to obtain. The Web site contained the following terms and disclaimers:

Terms

I understand and agree that I may receive a response to my inquiry from an attorney at Law Firm.

I agree that by submitting this inquiry, I will not be charged for the initial response.

I agree that I am not forming an attorney-client relationship by submitting this question. I also understand that I am not forming a confidential relationship.

I further agree that I may only retain Law Firm or any of its attorneys as my attorney by entering into a written fee agreement, and that I am not hereby entering into a fee agreement. I understand that I will not be charged for the response to this inquiry.

Below the foregoing list of "Terms" are two buttons, one which reads "SUBMIT" and the other which reads "CANCEL," with the following statement:

By clicking the appropriate button below, I agree to:

SUBMIT my inquiry pursuant to the foregoing terms.

CANCEL my inquiry.

Must the law firm keep the information received from the wife confidential? How can it do so? Should the firm be precluded from representing the husband in the divorce because it has this confidential information from the wife?

Attorneys have an absolute duty to maintain their clients' confidence and not reveal any information relating to the representation of the client. The attorney-client privilege is narrower in scope, in that it prevents disclosure only of information that is communicated between the attorney and client relating to the representation, or of information that is the work product of the attorney or paralegal. "Work product" refers to either the mental impressions of the attorney or information gathered and formatted by the attorney.

Summary

A client may waive the confidential or privileged nature of the information. An attorney may reveal confidential or privileged information without the client's consent only in limited circumstances:

1. to prevent death or substantial bodily harm to another;
2. to prevent the client from committing a crime or fraud, including perjury;
3. to prevent future substantial financial harm to another;
4. to secure legal advice regarding compliance with the ethical rules;
5. to defend against a malpractice claim;
6. to comply with any other court order or law.

An attorney may unintentionally disclose sensitive client information through a variety of ways and, depending on the means taken to rectify the exposure, there may be a waiver of the privilege. The means to correct the disclosure can include any of the following:

1. the degree of care taken by the disclosing party to avoid the disclosure;
2. extenuating circumstances;
3. the number and significance of the accidental disclosures;
4. the extent of the disclosure;
5. the time between the disclosure and the attempts to rectify the situation;
6. the overriding interests of justice that may be served by relieving a party of its error.

The party on the receiving end of the inadvertent disclosure should, in the broader interest of fairness and justice,

1. refrain from viewing the material as soon as he realizes that it is privileged information;
2. notify the sender about the disclosure;
3. follow the instructions regarding the return or destruction of documents or seek a resolution in court.

There are some communications and documents that are not protected from disclosure to opposing parties. Documents that were in existence prior to the preparation for litigation are discoverable, as are communications solely of fact between attorney and client, unless they are inexorably linked to the giving of legal advice.

As a logical complement to the attorney's ethical duty of confidentiality and the client's right of privilege in those communications, the paralegal is held to the same standard of secrecy. As it is often the paralegal's role to deal with the technology that drives the law office, it is important that the paralegal understand the issues involved with its utilization and the preservation of confidential information.

		Key Terms and Concepts
Attorney-client privilege	"Fishing expedition"	
Confidences	In camera inspection	
Duty of confidentiality	Perjury	

Permitted disclosure

Subornation of perjury

Unintentional disclosure

Unprotected communications

Waiver of confidentiality

Work product

Review Questions

MULTIPLE CHOICE

Choose the best answer(s) and please explain WHY you choose the answer(s).

1. The attorney-client privilege
   a. requires the attorney to keep all his client's secrets.
   b. attaches to all private work prepared by the attorney in preparation for litigation.
   c. restricts the attorney from speaking to anyone about his client's matters.
   d. is the same as the attorney's duty of confidentiality.

2. If a client insists on taking the stand and the attorney thinks the client will commit perjury,
   a. the attorney can permit narrative testimony.
   b. the attorney must withdraw from the case.
   c. the client doesn't have to take an oath.
   d. the attorney can use that testimony in her closing statement.

3. In defense of a professional malpractice claim,
   a. an attorney can hand over all his files to the judge for an in camera inspection.
   b. the attorney may not testify.
   c. the attorney may disclose confidential information about the client.
   d. the attorney may disclose confidential information that relates to the relationship and actions taken in the matter.
   e. all of the above.

EXPLAIN YOURSELF

All answers should be written in complete sentences. A simple yes or no is insufficient.

1. Describe the difference between the attorney's duty of confidentiality and the attorney-client privilege.

2. Explain the exceptions to the attorney's duty of confidentiality; when may an attorney divulge his client's secrets?

3. Explain the "crime-fraud" exception to the duty of confidentiality.

4. What should a paralegal do after receiving unintentionally disclosed confidential information from opposing counsel? What is the attorney ethically bound to do?

5. What is the work product rule? Does it apply to paralegals as well as to attorneys?

FAULTY PHRASES

All of the following statements are FALSE. State why they are false and then rewrite them as true statements, without just making a statement negative by adding the word "not."

1. The attorney-client privilege requires that the attorney not reveal any information about her client relating to her representation.

2. A person who overhears the attorney and client's conversations ruins the privilege, and that eavesdropper can testify as to the private conversation.

3. An attorney must be absolutely sure his client will commit a crime before he can reveal that information.

4. Opposing counsel can seek to obtain privileged documents, and the court must allow them to see the information if they have performed an in camera inspection of the materials.

5. Once confidential information is inadvertently disclosed, opposing counsel may use it in their case.

6. All communications between an attorney and a client are protected by the attorney-client privilege.

7. Electronic communications are not protected by either the rules of confidentiality or attorney-client privilege.

PORTFOLIO ASSIGNMENT

Write Away

Prepare an interoffice memorandum regarding the proper procedures for handling client communications. Be sure to address the various types of communications (both traditionally written and electronic) and indicate what special considerations should be taken into account when dealing with each. As this memorandum will be circulated to all office personnel, be sure to explain why the method of handling the communications has such important ethical considerations.

UNPUBLISHED OPINION. CHECK COURT RULES BEFORE CITING.
Court of Appeals of Michigan.
CHRYSLER CORPORATION, Plaintiff-Appellant,

v.

Paul V SHERIDAN, Defendant-Appellee.
No. 227511.
July 10, 2001.
Before: WHITE, P.J., and WILDER and ZAHRA, JJ.
PER CURIAM.
Plaintiff appeals by leave granted the circuit court's order denying plaintiff's
motion for return of a privileged document. We reverse.

FACTS

Plaintiff filed this suit on December 27, 1994, claiming defendant wrongfully disclosed its trade secrets. A preliminary injunction was entered in 1996, prohibiting defendant from disclosing plaintiff's confidential, proprietary information. On February 23, 2000, the trial court dissolved that injunction. Soon thereafter, plaintiff learned of an affidavit defendant submitted in connection with a separate suit filed in Texas. Plaintiff claimed the substance of that affidavit referred to confidential information that plaintiff had not previously disclosed. On March 8, 2000, plaintiff filed a motion and brief for reconsideration of the court's decision to dissolve the injunction. Plaintiff specifically identified and attached to the brief three exhibits: Exhibit A was a copy of the trial court's February 23, 2000 opinion and order dissolving the preliminary injunction; Exhibit B was a copy of defendant's twenty-one-page affidavit filed in the Texas case; and Exhibit C was a copy of the trial court's March 27, 1996 opinion granting a preliminary injunction. Defendant's affidavit was attached to plaintiff's brief as Exhibit D, and behind defendant's affidavit was a copy of a two-page e-mail written by plaintiff's lead national trial counsel, David Tyrrell. The e-mail was not identified as a separate exhibit and was not referenced in defendant's affidavit, plaintiff's motion for reconsideration or the brief supporting plaintiff's motion for reconsideration.

On March 23, 2000, plaintiff filed an emergency motion for return of the document and for a temporary restraining order, alleging that the e-mail was subject to the attorney-client privilege and that it had been inadvertently attached to the affidavit. Plaintiff requested that the court enter an order stating that no privilege had been waived and that defendant be ordered to return all copies of the document and to refrain from further dissemination and disclosure of the document. After a hearing on the issue, the trial court ruled the e-mail is not privileged and denied plaintiff's motion for its return. In a short opinion and order denying plaintiff's motion for return of any copies of the e-mail, the court stated, in pertinent part:

Here, the document is not marked confidential or privileged. The unrelated attorney who first forwarded the document did not mark it confidential. The in-house counsel of the client forwarded the document without marking it confidential. When received by the court and defense counsel, the document was not marked confidential. Rather, it appears related to the arguments in the motion to which it was attached. When received by Defendant's counsel, the document was further distributed around the country. Assuming the document was subject to privilege and its attachment to the exhibit was an inadvertent error, there was little to notify the recipients that the document may be subject to a privilege. As such, this court finds that the document is not now subject to a privilege and Plaintiff's motion for return of privileged document and restraining order is denied.

The instant appeal followed.

ANALYSIS

A. Standard of Review

The sole issue before us is whether the trial court erred in determining the e-mail document is not subject to the attorney-client privilege. Whether the lower court properly construed the privilege is a legal question we review de novo. *Reed Dairy Farm v. Consumers Power Company*, 227 Mich.App 614, 618; 576 NW2d 709 (1998). If the lower court properly construed the privilege, application of the privilege to the facts of the case is reviewed for an abuse of discretion. *Franzel v. Kerr Mfg*, 234 Mich.App 600, 614; 600 NW2d 66 (1999). An abuse of discretion may be found if we conclude that an unprejudiced person reviewing the facts and law would find no justification or excuse for the trial court's ruling. *Id.* at 617.

B. Common Law Privilege and Waiver

The common law attorney-client privilege attaches to direct communications between a client and his attorney and communications made through their respective agents. *Reed Dairy Farm, supra*. Where the client is an organization, the privilege extends to communications between attorneys and agents or employees of the organization authorized to speak on its behalf in regard to the subject matter of the communication. *Id.* at 619.

Although a communication is subject to the attorney-client privilege, that privilege may be waived. *Franzel, supra* at 616; *Sterling v. Keidan*, 162 Mich.App 88, 91–92; 412 NW2d 255

(1987). In *Franzel,* this Court clarified the following with respect to waiver of the attorney-client privilege:

(1) The attorney-client privilege has a dual nature, i.e., it includes both the security against publication and the right to control the introduction into evidence of such information or knowledge communicated to or possessed by the attorney; (2) This dual nature of the privilege applies where there has been inadvertent disclosure of privileged material; (3) An implied waiver of the privilege must be judged by standards as stringent as for a "true waiver," before the right to control the introduction of privileged matter into evidence will be destroyed, even though the inadvertent disclosure has eliminated any security against publication; (4) A "true waiver" requires " 'an intentional, voluntary act and cannot arise by implication,' " or " 'the voluntary relinquishment of a known right,' "; and (5) Error of judgment where the person knows that privileged information is being released but concludes that the privilege will nevertheless survive will destroy any privilege. [*Franzel, supra* at 613-614, citing *Sterling, supra* (internal citations omitted).]

Thus, regardless whether a party is charged with an intentional or implied waiver of the attorney-client privilege, there can be no waiver without an intentional, voluntary act. Inadvertent disclosure of a privileged communication does not constitute a waiver. *Id.*

C. The E-Mail was Privileged and Production of it Did Not Constitute a Waiver of the Privilege

Proper analysis of this issue requires us first to examine whether the e-mail is protected under the attorney-client privilege. If that question is answered in the affirmative, we must then consider whether the privilege was waived when the copy of the e-mail was attached to plaintiff's motion and brief for reconsideration. It is undisputed the e-mail was drafted by a member of plaintiff's national legal counsel. While neither the e-mail itself nor its copies were expressly marked "confidential" or "privileged," the undisputed facts establish it was distributed to members of plaintiff's legal counsel in confidence. Defendant does not claim Tyrrell sent the e-mail to anyone other than plaintiff's agents or counsel. Nor is there evidence that plaintiff's in-house counsel sent the document to any party other than plaintiff's trial counsel in the present case. The e-mail was specifically addressed to plaintiff's in-house counsel and contains Tyrrell's candid impressions of defendant's suspected knowledge of various issues. It also contains Tyrrell's opinions, conclusions and recommendations in regard to defendant's affidavit and defendant's qualifications as a witness against plaintiff. Under these circumstances, we conclude the e-mail was intended as a confidential communication between plaintiff's agents and counsel pertaining to on-going and future litigation, and is subject to the attorney-client privilege. *Reed Dairy Farm, supra* at 618-619.

We conclude as a matter of law that the production of the e-mail was inadvertent and neither plaintiff nor its counsel waived the privilege by this inadvertent production. Plaintiff's trial counsel in the present case submitted a detailed affidavit

below, asserting the e-mail was inadvertently attached to the motion. The attorney who signed the motion for reconsideration appeared in court on the hearing date prepared to testify that the e-mail was inadvertently attached to the motion for reconsideration, and to submit to cross-examination by defendant and examination by the court. Defendant did not examine the attorney and did not present any evidence to dispute these assertions. Instead, defendant argued that the privilege does not apply or was waived because the e-mail related to the motion for reconsideration. The trial court appears to have accepted defendant's argument, at least in part, as it concluded that the e-mail related to the contents of plaintiff's motion for reconsideration. The trial court abused its discretion in reaching this conclusion.

The content of the e-mail reflects the opinions and factual assertions of plaintiff's counsel in the Texas litigation. The e-mail is not presented in the form of an affidavit. This document, as attached to the motion for reconsideration, is of no evidentiary value to a court. It is not documentary evidence of any kind. Had plaintiff intended to present the opinions or factual assertions of Texas counsel as evidence to support its motion for reconsideration, such information would have been offered by way of an affidavit. Moreover, each of the marked exhibits offered in support of the motion for reconsideration is specifically referenced in the brief supporting the motion. Significantly, the e-mail, which was not marked as an exhibit to the motion, is not referenced anywhere in the motion, the brief or the exhibits supporting the motion. In sum, we conclude that an unbiased person viewing all of the facts presented would not be justified in concluding that the e-mail was intentionally attached to support the motion for reconsideration. The facts and circumstances presented below do not support the conclusion that plaintiff or its counsel no longer intended to maintain the document's confidentiality. *Sterling, supra* at 96. Plaintiff's counsel's inadvertent disclosure of the e-mail did not constitute a waiver of the attorney-client privilege that attached to the document. *Franzel, supra; Sterling, supra.*

We also are not persuaded that the absence of a statement in the e-mail notifying recipients of its confidential or privileged nature defeats the privilege or constitutes a waiver. No authority requires that a document be expressly marked confidential or privileged in order for it to be subject to the attorney-client privilege. As discussed *supra,* the e-mail was a confidential communication between plaintiff's counsel and agents involving legal issues and was subject to the attorney-client privilege. Plaintiff's counsel's inadvertent disclosure of the document did not constitute a waiver of the privilege.

CONCLUSION

Accordingly, we hold that the trial court abused its discretion in denying plaintiff's request for an order declaring that the privilege was not waived.

Reversed.

Source: Reprinted with permission from Thomson West.

United States District Court,
D. Kansas.
David BURTON, Plaintiff,
v.
R.J. REYNOLDS TOBACCO CO. and The American Tobacco Co., Defendants.
No. 94-2202-JWL.
May 1, 1996.
MEMORANDUM AND ORDER
LUNGSTRUM, District Judge.

I. INTRODUCTION

[. . .]

II. FACTS.

The Tobacco Industry Research Committee ("TIRC") was formed in 1954 by members of the tobacco industry, including the defendants, to provide funding for research on the effects of tobacco use. In 1958, the TIRC changed its name to the CTR. The CTR's Scientific Advisory Board ("SAB"), which is composed of scientists, reviews grant proposals and provides funding to research projects they deem worthy. Between 1965 and 1990, the CTR began conducting its own scientific projects separate from the SAB's grant program under the name special projects.

On September 9, 1995, the plaintiff served the defendants with its Third Request for Documents. Request No. 1 sought all documents relating to the CTR special projects division or program. In their response dated October 11, 1995, the defendants objected to this request because it sought privileged or protected documents and because it sought documents relating to subjects other than those matters at issue here, peripheral vascular disease and the alleged addictive nature of cigarettes. Subject to their objections, both defendants produced what they believe are non-privileged CTR Documents in their possession relating to the conditions they believe are at issue in this case. [. . .] Defendant Reynolds represents that these Documents are privileged because they consist of communications between Reynolds and its counsel, communications between its counsel and counsel for other tobacco companies, and internal company communications reflecting privileged information. [. . .]

III. DISCUSSION.

A. Motion to compel.
  1. Timeliness of plaintiff's motion.
                    [. . .]
  2. Relevance.
    The next hurdle for the plaintiff to clear is a showing that the material he seeks is relevant. The plaintiff's claims are based on his assertions that the defendants knew and had a duty to disclose to the public that the nicotine in their cigarettes was addictive, that the defendants knew and had a duty to disclose to

the public that their cigarettes are a vasoconstrictor, and that the defendants knew and had a duty to disclose to the public that their cigarettes contributed to the development of peripheral vascular diseases including atherosclerotic peripheral arterial occlusive. Thus, the relevance analysis must focus on whether the information sought bears on whether the defendants knew during the relevant time period what the plaintiff alleges they knew.

The court believes that the 33 CTR Documents withheld by Defendant Reynolds would be relevant to this case to the extent the plaintiff could link the documents to a showing that the Defendant Reynolds knew during the relevant time period that nicotine is addictive, that its cigarettes are a vasoconstrictor, or that its cigarettes caused peripheral vascular diseases. [citation omitted] [. . .]

The defendants argue that even if they had disclosed the information the plaintiff alleges they had in their possession, the plaintiff would have continued to smoke cigarettes because by 1952 the plaintiff was, in his mind, addicted to the nicotine contained in the defendants' cigarettes and, therefore, could not stop regardless of what information the defendants disclosed. The court disagrees. It may be one thing to recognize retrospectively, as the plaintiff claims, that he was addicted and thus was powerless to quit smoking based on warnings that tobacco use could be harmful to his health. It is quite something different to have been denied, as plaintiff also claims, the information that nicotine truly is addictive, thus depriving him of the impetus to seek professional assistance to overcome his dilemma. Had the defendants disclosed the information the plaintiff alleges the defendants had in their possession, the court believes that a reasonable jury could credit the proposition that the plaintiff, upon realizing that nicotine was addictive and that he had a high likelihood of contracting peripheral vascular disease from smoking, would, more likely than not, have sought medical attention to help him break his nicotine addiction. Thus, the plaintiff's motion to compel does not fail on relevance grounds.

  3. Privileges.
  a. Choice of law.
                    [. . .]
  b. Attachment of privilege.
    Under Kansas law, the attorney client privilege protects communications found by the judge to have been between a

lawyer and his or her client in the course of that relationship and in professional confidence. K.S.A. § 60-426(a). The defendants contend that the CTR Documents are protected by the attorney client privilege because they involve communications between themselves and their lawyers in the course of their legal relationship and in professional confidence.

In order to be protected by work product immunity, the party asserting the privilege must show (1) that the material is a document or tangible thing, (2) that the material was prepared in anticipation of litigation, and (3) that the material was prepared by or for a party or by or for the party's representative. *Jones v. Boeing Co.,* 163 F.R.D. 15, 17 (D.Kan.1995). The defendants contend that the CTR Documents are protected by the work product doctrine because they were prepared in anticipation of litigation.

Under Kansas law, the disclosure of privileged information by an attorney to counsel of actual or potential co-defendants does not constitute a waiver of the attorney client privilege based on the joint defense exception to the general rule that no privilege attaches to communications made in the presence of third parties. *State v. Maxwell,* 10 Kan.App.2d 62, 66, 691 P.2d 1316 (1984). The joint defense privilege encompasses shared communications to the extent that they concern common issues and are intended to facilitate representation in possible subsequent proceedings. *Id.* It is also essential that the co-defendants have exchanged the information in confidence, "not . . . for the purpose of allowing unlimited publication and use, but rather . . . for the limited purpose of assisting in their common cause." *Id.* The defendants contend that the CTR Documents are protected by the joint defense privilege.

[. . .]

c. Waiver.

Intentional disclosure to third parties of privileged information is a waiver of any privilege. *See Monarch Cement Co. v. Lone Star Indus., Inc.,* 132 F.R.D. 558 (D.Kan.1990). The plaintiff contends that the defendants waived any privileges or immunities from disclosure which might have attached to the CTR Documents when they intentionally and knowingly chose to funnel them through the CTR, a third party committed to public disclosure. [. . .] The court agrees with the defendants that, based upon the submissions of the parties, the plaintiff has not met his burden of showing that the defendants waived any privileges.

4. Crime-fraud exception—in camera review.

a. Standard.

During the court's telephone hearing on the plaintiff's motion to compel, plaintiff's counsel took the position that his strongest argument to obtain discovery of the CTR Documents is the so-called crime-fraud exception to the doctrines which otherwise would protect the confidentiality of certain legal communications. The crime-fraud exception's purpose is to assure that the seal of secrecy between lawyer and client does not extend to communications made for the purpose of getting advice for the commission of a fraud or crime. *United States v. Zolin,* 491 U.S. 554, 563, 109 S.Ct. 2619, 2626, 105 L.Ed.2d 469 (1989). [. . .]

Although Kansas courts have enunciated the requisite burden for the party seeking the application of the crime-fraud exception, no Kansas court has addressed whether the requisite burden for a party seeking an in camera review based on the

crime-fraud exception of allegedly privileged documents is any different. In 1989, the United States Supreme Court held, under federal law, that a district court may conduct an in camera review to determine the applicability of the crime-fraud exception if the party requesting such a review makes a showing of a factual basis adequate to support a good faith belief by a reasonable person that in camera review of the documents may reveal evidence to establish that the crime-fraud exception applies. [citations omitted] [. . .]

[. . .] "Such privileges shall not extend (1) to a communication if the judge finds that sufficient evidence, *aside from the communication,* has been introduced to warrant a finding that the legal service was sought or obtained in order to enable or aid the commission or planning of a crime or a tort. . . . " K.S.A. § 60-426(b)(1) (emphasis added). [. . .]

b. Evidence.

The plaintiff argues that lawyers for tobacco companies, including the defendants, were used to facilitate the perpetration of a continuing fraud. Specifically, the plaintiff contends that the lawyers for the tobacco companies used the CTR to deceive the public about the health risks associated with smoking. The plaintiff requests that the court review the CTR Documents in camera to determine whether they evidence this deception. [. . .] The defendants object to these documents based on hearsay, authenticity, and relevance grounds, among others.

The court rejects the hearsay and authenticity arguments because under Federal Rule of Evidence 104(a), it is not bound by the rules of evidence on those subjects in determining the existence of a privilege and because it is sufficiently satisfied with the reliability of the proffered FDA, JAMA, and TIRC evidence to conclude that those items of evidence should be considered for this purpose. Those documents are also relevant to the plaintiff's claims.

[. . .]

The TIRC's Frank Statement essentially states that the members of the TIRC, which includes the defendants, do not believe that their tobacco products are injurious to the public health and that the TIRC will aid and assist in the research effort concerning all areas of tobacco use and health. The excerpts from the FDA Special Supplement discuss tobacco industry documents which the FDA contends reveal that nicotine is a drug, that consumers of tobacco products smoke cigarettes for the pharmacological effects of nicotine, that nicotine creates physical dependency, that nicotine has addictive properties and that tobacco company researchers and top officials are aware of and understand these facts.

The court believes that the plaintiff has carried his burden to make out a prima facie case of fraud based on the Frank Statement and the excerpts from the FDA's Special Supplement. The Frank Statement clearly indicates that the TIRC/CTR was created to research and disclose to the public the effects of tobacco use on people's health. The excerpts from the FDA's Special Supplement give rise to the inference that the members of the CTR knew during relevant time periods that nicotine was addictive and did not disclose that information to the public, which is in direct conflict with the Frank Statement. Moreover, the members of the CTR's silence on the issue of nicotine being addictive raises the inference, based on the Frank Statement, that the tobacco companies believed that nicotine was not addictive. In other words, this is evidence which, left unexplained or uncontradicted, would be sufficient to support the conclusion that the members of the CTR chose not to disclose information about nicotine being addictive to deliberately mislead the public about the effects of tobacco use. *Wallace Saunders Austin Brown & Enochs, Chartered, v. Louisburg Grain Co.,* 250 Kan. 54, 824 P.2d 933 (1992). As a result, the court deems it necessary to conduct an in camera review of Defendant Reynolds' 33 allegedly privileged CTR Documents to determine whether any of them indicate that the defendants knew during the relevant time period that nicotine was addictive and failed to disclose that information despite the CTR's public representation that it would make such disclosures to the public. The motion to compel (Doc. # 214) is retained under advisement to that extent and is referred to United States Magistrate Judge Ronald C. Newman to conduct the review and rule on whether any of the documents are to be produced.

[. . .]

Source: Reprinted with permission from ThomsonWest.

Chapter 5

Conflicts of Interest

CHAPTER OBJECTIVES

The student will be able to:

- Discuss the reasons for conflict rules in attorney-client relationships

- Analyze whether a conflict exists between clients, either current or former

- Explain the prohibited transactions between attorneys and clients in which the conflict is automatically assumed

- Acknowledge an "appearance of impropriety" in an attorney-client relationship even where an "official" conflict is lacking

- Discern between those conflict situations where waiver is proper and permissible and those where it is not

- Discuss "imputed conflicts" and how and when it applies

- Determine whether an "ethical wall" can overcome a potential conflict and describe how one is constructed

This chapter will examine the maze of conflict rules in order to sort out WHO may or may not be taken on as a client and WHAT constitutes a conflict of interest between both former and present clients and between attorneys and clients. If a potential conflict exists, the rules also explain HOW to avoid or deal with the situation.

The same principles that require legal professionals to keep all client confidences also require them to avoid all situations that may compromise these client secrets and maintain trustworthiness and integrity in client representation. The **conflict of interest** rules are really an extension of the confidentiality rules. Because of the knowledge that attorneys and paralegals have about their past and present clients, they are prohibited from either representing another party whose interests are adverse to either the attorney's present or former clients or entering into certain personal, financial, or business relationships and transactions with those clients. The practical consequence of these rules is the attorney's obligation to refuse employment from potential clients whose representation would violate the rules of professional conduct. In some situations, the analysis of the rules' application to the potential representation is clear-cut; in others, the potential representation does not pose an immediate or obvious conflict, and the attorney must analyze the future possible impact of taking on the representation. Even when the actual circumstances do not lead to any negative consequence to either attorney or client, the mere appearance of impropriety may result in a violation of the rules' overarching concern about the preservation of the integrity of the legal

conflict of interest
Clash between private and professional interests or competing professional interests that makes impartiality difficult and creates an unfair advantage.

FIGURE 5.1
Avoidance of
Conflicts of Interest

> **NFPA 1.6**
>
> A paralegal shall avoid conflicts of interest and shall disclose any possible conflict to the employer or client, as well as to the prospective employers or clients.

profession. Clients must be able to trust that an attorney will look out for their individual best interests and have unwavering loyalty to them. Again, this rests directly on the cornerstone of the duty of confidentiality. The ABA Model Rules (and those state codes based upon them) are broken down by (1) type of client and (2) type of relationship involved.

- Rule 1.7 deals with conflicts between current and/or potential clients.
- Rule 1.8 deals with particular conflicts between the current client and a transaction with the attorney.
- Rule 1.9 deals with conflicts involving former clients and potential new clients.
- Rule 1.10 deals with an entire firm's inability to take on a client due to the "infection" from an attorney's individual conflict based upon one of the three preceding rules.
- Rule 1.11 deals with a particular circumstance: when a former government/public attorney reenters the private practice. Due to the scope of public practice, returning to the private sector would be all but impossible if not for the exceptions in this rule.

NALA's Model Standards do not separately address conflicts of interest. Rather, in the Comment to Guideline 1, the avoidance of conflicts is the responsibility of the supervising attorney. It is imperative that the paralegal "take any and all steps necessary to prevent conflicts of interest and fully disclose such conflicts to the supervising attorney."

NFPA does directly address a paralegal's duty to avoid conflicts of interest and essentially parallels the ABA Model Rules in this regard. (See Figure 5.1.)

CURRENT CLIENTS

The most obvious conflict situation arises where there is a direct conflict between the current representation of a client and another potential client's interests. It is simply an acknowledgement that "you cannot serve two masters" with equality and fairness. (See Figure 5.2.)

Legal professionals are bound to represent their clients in an attempt to obtain the best possible outcomes for the clients. This is not possible when one client's interest is adverse to another's. The best the attorney could do would be to meet in the middle at a reasonable compromise. An attorney's role is to be a zealous advocate, not a mediator. Taking actions inconsistent with this role as the "client's champion" is violative of the attorney's duties of confidentiality and competence. How? The attorney or paralegal cannot cordon off the part of his brain that knows secrets about one client and keep it separate from another that knows about adverse

FIGURE 5.2
Loyalty to Client

> **NFPA EC 1.6(a)**
>
> A paralegal shall act within the bounds of the law, solely for the benefit of the client, and shall be free of compromising influences and loyalties. Neither the paralegal's personal or business interest, nor those of other clients or third persons, should compromise the paralegal's professional judgment and loyalty to the client.

client interests. Even the most disciplined professional will be torn as to how to keep this information from affecting the representation of the other client. Additionally, the clients will most likely be unable to accept this arrangement and its potential for disloyalty. How do these conflicts affect competence? It is the attorney's and the paralegal's duty to act as other reasonable professionals in a similar situation; most reasonable attorneys and paralegals do not put themselves in a conflict position.

The ABA Model Rules contemplate that there are situations where a conflict or apparent conflict may exist, yet the attorney and client can still enter into this "conflictual" relationship. Neither of the paralegal codes addresses this issue as it pertains to the establishment of the attorney-client relationship. This decision as to whether or not a conflict does exist and if it can be overcome is ultimately a legal judgment and solely within the purview of the practice of the attorney. Where the ethical rules may perceive a conflict, a client may not. It is acceptable to represent potentially adverse clients where they both consent to this representation. At this juncture, it is important to discuss what the ethical rules perceive as **adverse**. The term does not merely mean a directly contrary position between opposing parties in the same matter. "Adversity" lies in the inability of the attorney to render full and impartial representation of an individual client's best interest. While superficially it may appear that the multiple clients have concomitant interests in the transaction or litigation, the processes, strategies, theories of liability and/or ultimate outcomes may diverge during the representation. The ethical rules seek to avoid this situation as well. The rules address possibilities as well as the apparent probabilities. The mere threat of this type of harm is enough to implicate a conflict of interest. *Ferrara v. Jordache Enterprises, Inc.,* 12 Misc.3d 769, 771, 819 N.Y.S.2d 421, 423 (Kings Cty. 2006). (The driver and passenger were represented by the same counsel in an automobile accident case. While their claims against the defendant are the same, there lies the possibility that the plaintiff-passenger may bring a counterclaim against the plaintiff-driver. Indeed, joining the driver as a defendant is necessary in order to preserve an opportunity for recovery if the defendant in the other vehicle is exonerated.) It is the preservation of independent professional judgment which is paramount. Without these potential conflict prohibitions, the attorney would have the ability to take on potentially (although not actually) disharmonious clients and then have to try to disengage from the representation after work had been started.

> Indeed, the dual representation mandates the disqualification of counsel in regard to his continuing representation of either of these plaintiffs since such continued representation would necessarily result in a violation of the firm's fiduciary obligations to preserve client confidentiality and vigorously represent the clients' interests.

Id. at 770.

In some circumstances, the parties may consent to the adverse multiple representation. This consent must be obtained after the attorney has fully explained the possible ramifications of the multiple representation; this is the concept of **informed consent**. In other situations, despite the attorney's full disclosure of the implications of multiple representation and the clients' informed consent, the multiple representation is prohibited. The courts are generally in agreement that where two or more parties can assert claims against each other in the same litigation, these clients are unable to give informed consent. The attorney, by definition, cannot reasonably, responsibly, and diligently represent these clients without some compromise in loyalty, either actual or perceived. Even where the attorney feels she can act with clinical neutrality, the appearance of impropriety will taint the representation. Further, in truth, clinical neutrality is not the role of the attorney in representing a client. The attorney has an ethical duty of zealous representation which includes a certain conviction or passion for the interests of the individual client. "Because dual representation is fraught with the potential for

adverse
Characteristic of a position or interest that is inconsistent or opposite with another, so that they cannot be reconciled without compromising an important element of one or both positions or interests.

informed consent
Permission that is voluntarily given after having received and understood all relevant information relating to the situation's risks and alternatives.

SPOT THE ISSUE

Two independent businessmen, Charles and Robert, have regularly used Attorney Thomas to draft their commercial leases on their respective properties. Last week, during a meeting, Charles and Robert decided to create a joint-venture agreement to buy and lease commercial real estate together. They now approach Attorney Thomas to draft this agreement. Can he do so? Why or why not? What are the potential problems in this dual representation? What facts, if different, would change the outcome?

irreconcilable conflict, it will rarely be sanctioned even after full disclosure has been made and the consent of the clients obtained." *LaRusso v. Katz,* 30 A.D.3d 240, 244, 818 N.Y.S.2d 17, 20 (2006). The court has the ultimate responsibility for the fairness of the justice system, and the "existence of conflict undermines the integrity of the court." *State v. Davis,* 366 N.J. Super. 30, 38, 840 A.2d 279, 284 (App. Div. 2004).

The current conflict may even exist between the attorney and the client. An attorney must not have a financial or other personal interest in the outcome of the case in which he is representing a client. This is clearly demonstrated where the attorney represents a client in a bankruptcy matter and that client owes the attorney money for unpaid legal fees. The representation is subject to **material limitation** by the attorney's interest and those duties owed to the other creditors of the client. *In the Matter of Disciplinary Proceedings against Krueger,* 288 Wis. 2d 586, 594, 709 N.W.2d 857, 861 (2006). (These proceedings were further exacerbated by the fact that the attorney failed to disclose his status as a creditor of the client on the court papers and collected the fees after they were discharged in bankruptcy in violation of the code. The attorney was suspended from practice for 60 days and was required to pay the costs of the disciplinary proceeding in the amount of $20,489.37).

In determining whether a conflict of interest exists, an attorney must take all these factors into consideration:

- Actual or apparent adversity
- The ability to give informed consent
- The degree of limitation presented by the lawyer's own interests and ethical duties to his clients

Then, the attorney must determine whether a **disinterested lawyer**, one that is unrelated and unaffected by the situation, "would believe that the lawyer can competently represent the interest of each." *Ferrara v. Jordache Enterprises, Inc.,* 12 Misc. 3d 769, 771, 819, N.Y.S.2d 421, 423 (2006). In order to avoid a possible conflict of interest that might be violative of the ethical rules, an attorney must examine the situation from three perspectives:

1. The perspective of the client—in order to determine whether an individual client would feel betrayed by another's representation. This encompasses the element of *direct adversity*.

material limitation
The inability to render neutral and unbiased services or advice.

disinterested lawyer
The standard to which potentially affected attorneys must measure their actions. An attorney must detach himself from any personal interest in the matter and act accordingly.

IN CLASS DISCUSSION

Mary, a newly hired paralegal at the highly regarded Smith and Thompson Law Firm, has just been assigned to participate in the defense of some local teenagers who attempted to carry out a Columbine-like shooting spree at their high school. Luckily, no one was killed, but several students were seriously wounded. Mary is devoutly religious and is adamantly supportive of gun control. She feels deep sympathy for the children and parents affected at the school and is convinced that stricter gun control laws could have prevented the tragedy. What is Mary's best response to this situation at work?

SURF'S UP

Attorneys are increasingly using the Internet to obtain new clients. Many of their Web sites contain forms on which to submit legal questions. What happens when two opposing parties submit the same question simultaneously to the attorney? Can the attorney disclaim the existence of an attorney-client relationship even after she has received confidential communications from both potential clients?

Read the following excerpt from The State Bar of California's Standing Committee on Professional Responsibility and Conduct, Formal Opinion No. 2005–168:

After typing in her contact information, Wife explained that she was interested in obtaining a divorce. She related that her Husband, a Vice-President at Ace Incorporated in Los Angeles, was cohabiting with a co-worker. She also stated that her 13-year-old son was living with her and asked if she could obtain sole custody of him. She noted that Husband was providing some support but that she had to take part-time work as a typist, and was thinking about being re-certified as a teacher. She revealed that she feared Husband would contest her right to sole custody of her son and that, many years ago, she had engaged in an extra-marital affair herself, about which Husband remained unaware. Wife stated that she wanted a lawyer who was a good negotiator, because she wanted to obtain a reasonable property settlement without jeopardizing her goal of obtaining sole custody of the child and keeping her own affair a secret. She concluded by noting she had some money saved from when she was a teacher, and stating, "I like your Web site and would like you to represent me."

[…]

Upon receiving Wife's inquiry, the law firm discovered that Husband had already retained Law Firm to explore the possibility of a divorce from Wife. The next day, an attorney in Law Firm sent Wife an e-mail, which stated:

"We regret we will be unable to accept you as a client because there is a conflict with one of our present clients. Good luck with your case."

We address whether Law Firm may be precluded from representing Husband as a result of the firm's contact with Wife on the ground that Law Firm has obtained material confidential information.

[…]

[W]e discussed situations in which there was some question about whether the attorney had agreed to be consulted, noting that the attorney must "evidence, by words or conduct, a willingness to engage in a confidential consultation with any of the individuals." Here, by providing the link that states, "What are my rights?" in combination with directions to submit facts that related to a legal problem she was "[w]ondering about," Law Firm has invited the consultation with Wife, and has done so for the purpose of considering whether to enter into an attorney-client relationship with the inquirer.

Law Firm has attempted to avoid taking on a duty of confidentiality by requiring each inquirer to agree that (1) by submitting a question, the inquirer is not forming an attorney-client relationship or a "confidential relationship"; and (2) whatever response Law Firm provides will not

constitute legal advice but, rather, "general information." To assess whether Wife's agreement to these terms prevented Law Firm from taking on a duty of confidentiality, we apply the "reasonable belief" test we set forth in California State Bar Formal Opn. No. 2003-161: "If the attorney's conduct, in light of the surrounding circumstances, implies a willingness to be consulted, then the speaker may be found to have a reasonable belief that he is consulting the attorney in the attorney's professional capacity." We do not believe that a prospective client's agreement to Law Firm's terms prevented a duty of confidentiality from arising on the facts before us, because Law Firm's disclosures to Wife were not adequate to defeat her reasonable belief that she was consulting Law Firm for the purpose of retaining Law Firm.

First, our assumption that Law Firm did not form an attorney-client relationship with Wife is not conclusive concerning Law Firm's confidentiality obligations to Wife. An attorney-client relationship is not a prerequisite to a lawyer assuming a duty of confidentiality in such a situation. As we explained earlier, and elaborated fully in California State Bar Formal Opn. No. 2003-161, a lawyer can owe a duty of confidentiality to a prospective client who consults the lawyer in confidence for the purpose of retaining the lawyer. Thus, that an attorney-client relationship did not arise from Wife's consultation with Law Firm did not prevent Law Firm from taking on a duty of confidentiality to Wife.

Second, Wife's agreement that she would not be forming a "confidential relationship" does not, in our view, mean that Wife could not still have a reasonable belief that Law Firm would keep her information confidential. We believe that this statement is potentially confusing to a lay person such as Wife, who might reasonably view it as a variant of her agreement that she has not yet entered into an attorney-client relationship with Law Firm. Cf. Virginia State Bar Ethics Opn. 1794 (June 30, 2004) (Lawyer's use of a disclaimer in non-Internet setting that stated "I understand that my initial interview with this attorney does not create an attorney/client relationship and that no such relationship is formed unless (sic) actually retain this attorney" is not effective in preventing the lawyer from incurring duty of confidentiality to prospective client). Had Law Firm written its agreement with Wife with a plain-language reference that her submission would lack confidentiality, then that would have defeated a reasonable expectation of confidentiality. Accord, *Barton v. District Court* (9th Cir. 2005) 410 F.3d 1104, 1110 (Law firm should have spoken clearly to the laymen to whom its website was addressed about what commitments it did and did not make by a plain English explanation on the Web site).

Without ruling out other possibilities, we note that had Wife agreed to the following, she would have had, in our opinion, no reasonable expectation of confidentiality with Law Firm: "I understand and agree that Law Firm will have no duty to keep confidential the information I am now transmitting to Law Firm."

Continued

Another way in which Law Firm could have proceeded that would have avoided the confidentiality issue entirely would have been to request from Web site visitors only that information that would allow the firm to perform a conflicts check. For example, under the facts presented, Law Firm would first want to ensure that it does not represent the other spouse. Law Firm could explain that it is seeking the information to determine whether representing the visitor might create a conflict with one of its present clients, preventing it from representing the visitor. Law Firm could request that the inquirer provide relevant information such as the names of the parties, children, former spouses, etc., and, given the subject area, any relevant maiden names. Regardless of the precise language used, it is important that lawyers who invite the public to submit questions on their Web sites, and do not want to assume a duty of confidentiality to the inquirers, plainly state the legal effect of a waiver of confidentiality. (See also D.C. Ethics Opn. 302 (providing tentative "best practices" guidance on attorney communications over the Internet to avoid formation of attorney-client relationships, including the use of prominent "click through" disclaimers).) We note that by suggesting a means for lawyers to avoid inadvertently taking on a duty of confidentiality to Web site visitors, we do not mean to suggest that this methodology is the only means for doing so.

In the situation presented, however, Law Firm chose neither to make a plain-language reference to the non-confidential nature of communications submitted to its Web site, nor to first screen visitors for potential conflicts with its existing clients. Having taken the course it did, Law Firm may be disqualified from representing Husband should the court conclude that the information Wife submitted was material to the resolution of the dissolution action.

2. The perspective of the attorney's own conscience—in order to determine whether the representation presents some underlying bias that would place the attorney's interests over those of her client, thereby *materially limiting* her ability to function as the client's advocate.

3. The perspectives of the justice system and public at large—in order to determine whether other, outside attorneys would consider the representation a conflictual one (the *disinterested lawyer standard*), and whether the integrity of the court would be compromised in the eyes of the public if the representation were permitted (in other words, if it would *appear improper*).

There are particular circumstances that present themselves with sufficient predictability and are serious enough to warrant specific treatment, and these are encapsulated in ABA Model Rule 1.8. Most of these situations relate to the intimate knowledge of the client's financial situation and the possibility that the attorney may take advantage of that knowledge in a transaction with the client. Other rules deal with the basic intimate relationship between the attorney and the client.

Business Dealings with the Client

The ABA Model Rules present a general prohibition against both entering into a business transaction with a client and being involved in a business interest that is in conflict with that of the client. This reflects the concern that while the client would be relying upon the expertise of his attorney, the attorney would be looking out for her own best interest in the deal, not that of her client. The conflict lies in the dual role the attorney is attempting to play in the transaction, she is both counsel and party and cannot serve these two masters with equal fairness; her loyalty is divided.

[The rule] specifically limits business transactions between lawyers and clients when the lawyer and client have "differing interests" in the transaction and when "the client expects the lawyer to exercise professional judgment [in the transaction] for the protection of the client. . . ." When these circumstances are present, a lawyer must refrain from entering into the transaction unless the client has consented after full disclosure by the lawyer. Business ventures between lawyers and their clients are normally discouraged.

Iowa Supreme Court Bd. of Professional Ethics and Conduct v. Fay, 619 N.W.2d 321, 325 (Iowa 2000); citing *Committee on Prof'l Ethics & Conduct v. Carty,* 515 N.W.2d 32, 35 (Iowa 1994).

The situations in which an attorney or paralegal may have an adverse interest in another transaction involving his client come up rather often, as the practice of law is closely related to other business services. Attorneys and paralegals may have business relationships with insurance providers, medical professionals, realtors, brokers, accountants, and others to which they customarily refer their clients. These referrals may ordinarily not pose a problem. However, if the attorney or paralegal has an interest in the business to which his client was referred, a potential conflict exists. Legal professionals in their fiduciary capacity may have made the referrals to a proper professional; however, where the attorney or paralegal has a financial stake in the company to which the client was referred, the referral is improper. The attorney or the paralegal has an incentive to refer clients to his monetary gain, rather than to the most competent or appropriate service provider for the client. *See* Fla. Ethics Op. 90–7, 1991 WL 425377 (Fla.St.Bar Assn.). In this matter, an inherent conflict existed where the attorney advised the client to obtain insurance

REEL TO REAL

Both family relations and personal convictions are involved in the conflict between a young lawyer and his client in the 1996 movie *The Chamber,* based on John Grisham's novel. It stars Chris O'Donnell as the young lawyer and Gene Hackman as the racist murderer on death row. The twist lies in the fact that the murderer is the lawyer's own grandfather. While the lawyer despises racism, he defends his grandfather. Is this representation ethically responsible? Why or why not? How could the grandson/lawyer justify his representation?

and then referred the client to an insurance company in which the attorney's partner had a financial interest. This prohibition also pertains to referrals for which the attorney hopes to gain future benefit. An attorney may send clients to a particular professional in the hopes of obtaining that professional as a client or to gain reciprocal referrals. The test is whether a disinterested attorney would look at the situation and determine that the involved attorney was looking out for her client's best interest. (See Figure 5.3.)

This prohibition extends even so far as to exclude an attorney or paralegal from representing a family member in a business transaction with one of his clients. The same kind of conflict exists, as the attorney or the paralegal is torn between loyalties, despite having no direct benefit derived for himself out of the transaction. *In the Matter of Hurd,* 69 N.J. 316, 354 A.2d 78 (1976), an attorney took on dual representation of his long-time family friend and the attorney's own sister in a real estate transaction. The record became unclear whether the parties intended a sale, some other sort of transfer, or loan/mortgage; but what was clear was the fact that the attorney had divided interest. He could not remove himself from his loyalty to his sister, and accepted her version of the arrangement to the detriment of the other client.

NFPA EC 1.6(c)	**FIGURE 5.3**
A paralegal shall avoid conflicts of interest that may arise from family relationships and from personal and business interests.	**Relationships That Cause Conflict**

A strict prohibition would be a burden both for enterprising attorneys and hard-working paralegals and for those residents of smaller communities where the businesses are naturally interdependent. Therefore, the ethics rules do allow for these transactions, provided that several conditions are met. First, the terms of the transaction and the deal as a whole must be fair and reasonable. The standards of "fairness" and "reasonableness" are measured by an objective standard, as if those terms were arrived at by two parties dealing at arm's length with each other, and having the advice of independent counsel. Further, these fair and reasonable terms must be fully disclosed in writing to the client and the client must be able to understand them. This may require the attorney to write the agreement in plainer language than she normally uses when dealing with other legal professionals. There is an additional writing requirement: the client must be advised of the benefit of obtaining a neutral third-party lawyer to render advice regarding the transaction. The requirement that the attorney put this request in writing underscores its importance. Securing advice from another attorney who has no previous relationship to either the involved attorney or the client ensures that at least one attorney is looking out for the client's best interests; this puts the interested attorney and his client on a level playing field. It is a protection against potential over-reaching or advantage-taking. To memorialize these precautions and to ensure that they are indeed undertaken, there is also the requirement that the client give this informed consent in a writing signed by the client. Much of this emphasis on the writing requirement relates to problems of proof. The rules of professional ethics are strictly enforced, and attorneys must comply with all of their seemingly rigorous protocol. A violation of any part of a rule renders the attorney culpable; further, the attorney bears the heavy burden of proof to show that the dealings were fair and reasonable to the client. *See* Cal. Ethics Op. 1995–140, 1995 WL 530133 at 6 (Cal. St. Bar Comm. on Prof'l Resp.). Generally, these transactions between an attorney or paralegal and a client are discouraged; no harm needs to be proven in order to void the agreement for failure to comply with these requirements. If, however, the client has been harmed and the attorney or paralegal has appeared to have benefited in the transaction, it is presumed that the agreement is invalid.

Maintaining Confidentiality in a Conflict Situation

Attorneys and paralegals are privy to sensitive information regarding their clients. It is imperative not only to avoid disclosure of this confidential information, but also, in the absence of disclosure, to avoid using it to one's own advantage. For example, an attorney representing a mother in a child support action obtained information regarding the father's whereabouts and financial status. During his investigation of the mother's file, the attorney also discovered that both the parents were indebted to the local welfare agency for some of the costs associated with the birth of their child. The welfare agency was a client of the attorney in question; therefore, the attorney had to withdraw from the representation of the mother. All would have been well and good had the attorney stopped there. However, the attorney violated the ethics rules when he contacted the welfare agency and gave them information obtained from the mother's file about the father so that the agency could seek collection from him. Of course, the mother was later added as a defendant to that suit as well. The attorney was not ethically permitted to reveal the information obtained from the file to the disadvantage of his client, the mother, without her consent. *See Matter of Anonymous,* 654 N.E.2d 1128 (Ind. 1995). Also implicated is the duty to preserve the confidences of former clients, discussed under ABA Model Rule 1.9. Many of these situations involve several ethical rules. The ethics rules seem relatively duplicative, but this underscores the importance of their essence and inviolability. Overlapping coverage can help to ensure their applicability to almost any questionable situation.

Financial Incentives Prohibited

The ethical rules also prohibit an attorney from obtaining any personal financial interest in the outcome of the client's matter that may affect how the attorney handles the case. This is exclusive of fee arrangements that may be contingent upon a positive resolution of the matter and recovery for the client. The concern is that the attorney will not be able to render neutral, independent professional advice where the attorney has a stake in the outcome. While it may be true that the attorney's advice would benefit both himself and the client, it may just as well be true that there are two or more outcomes possible, some of which would be better for the client and some of which would be better for the attorney at the expense of the client's best interest. It is only human nature to desire the best possible outcome for oneself.

Substantial gifts given by clients to either the attorney or the paralegal are also prohibited "financial incentives." The key to understanding this section is to define a **substantial gift**. Small tokens of appreciation or presents given on holidays or birthdays usually are permitted; after all, legal professionals are people too. It is the elaborate or expensive gift that is prohibited. Why? Those who lavish gifts upon someone usually expect something in return. In some circumstances, these gifts may also be seen as rewards or bribes. Attorneys may not be compensated over and above their initial fee arrangements with their clients. Paralegals may not be compensated for their performance over and above their salaries and regular bonuses. A successful outcome is not grounds for extra compensation; gifts cannot serve as incentive for the attorney or the paralegal to put forth extra efforts to win. An attorney must render zealous representation and the paralegal must render her best efforts to their clients under the ethical rules. There should be no such thing as the ability to work harder to gain a better outcome for a client. A legal professional should always work at the outermost limit of effort and professionalism—the best cannot, by definition, get any better.

The real issue posed by this rule is the meaning of the word "substantial." Courts have not defined this standard in any clear terms and have acknowledged that every case is so fact sensitive that to attempt to define "substantiality" across the board would be ineffectual.

> The issue as to allowance of anything more than a token gift or gift of nominal value is whether or not the proposed gift "represents general standards of fairness." The reason for that conclusion lies in the fact that nowhere in the Rules is there a definition of "substantial." Moreover, there would appear to be no case law nor any published opinion indicating what constitutes a "substantial gift." And, even if there were cases indicating what is considered "substantial," it would not be likely that results reached in one case would help in deciding another.

Pa. Ethics Op. 95–177, 1996 WL 928114 (Pa. Bar Ass'n. Comm. Leg. Eth. Prof'l. Resp.).

> Other factors may also be taken into consideration in determining the nature of the gift. [I]ts value should be assessed at the time the [gift or bequest] is [given or] prepared, and both the size of the [donor's] estate and the financial status of the lawyer should be considered when deciding if the gift is substantial. This analysis could be helpful in that, at least, it tells one that the determination of substantiality takes place at the time of the document preparation.

PA Ethics Op. 90–146, 1990 WL 709667 (Pa. Bar Ass'n. Comm. Leg. Eth. Prof'l. Resp.)

This rule against securing a financial interest in the outcome of the client's matter or accepting a gift is bent in cases where the legal professional's family is involved. The ethical rules allow people to take advantage of having a lawyer or paralegal in the family and, vice versa, permitting them to take care of her family. This includes writing wills or other property transfers for family members, even where the family member/lawyer takes as a beneficiary from the relative/client. In the case of estates

substantial gift
A gift from client to attorney large enough to have a significant impact on the attorney's ability to perform services in a neutral and detached manner.

SPOT THE ISSUE

Walter, a very wealthy and generous friend of Peter, a paralegal, requested that Peter ask his employer attorney to draft Walter's last will and testament. The will bequeathed his sizable estate to his four married sons, but should all four predecease him and leave no surviving children, Peter would receive 25 percent of the estate, and the remainder would go to Walter's alma mater, State University. Upon Walter's death last year, all four sons received their share of the estate because they had all survived their father. Therefore, Peter received nothing. Indeed, Peter had never expected to receive anything under the will, as the contingency (that all four sons would predecease their father and leave no children to take as their heirs) was so improbable. Therefore, the attorney and Peter did not believe that the 25 percent bequest would constitute a substantial gift from Walter, Peter's good friend and client. Is Peter correct? Why? For a hint, see *In re Disciplinary Action Against Boulger,* 637 N.W.2d 710 (N.D. 2001).

or property transfers, the subject matter is of a "substantial" nature; it is more than a mere token of affection or gratitude, but permitted. Other than this familial exception, attorneys and paralegals are not generally permitted to be beneficiaries under their clients' wills. The reason for this is clear: legal professionals, in their fiduciary, confidential, and trusted roles, have substantial influence over their clients. Courts and ethical tribunals have recognized this potential for abuse and have determined that the "receiving" attorney or paralegal must show that she did not unduly influence or take advantage of her client in any way that resulted in the bequest. The courts will presume fraudulent conduct; it is the attorney's burden to show otherwise.

> *[I]f a lawyer accepts a gift from his client he is peculiarly susceptible to the charge that he unduly influenced or overreached the client and that, other than in exceptional circumstances, a lawyer should insist that an instrument in which his client desires to name him beneficially be prepared by another lawyer selected by the client. Indeed, public policy necessitates such a shift in the burden of proof. In its absence, an attorney may freely misappropriate testator's property or make himself a beneficiary in a will knowing full and well that at the death or incapacity of the client all evidence against the lawyer would die with the client. A disciplinary proceeding is not intended for the purpose of punishment, but rather to determine the fitness of an officer of the court to continue in that capacity and to protect the courts and public from unfit persons.*

Matter of Smith, 572 N.E.2d 1280, 1286 (Ind. 1991).

This prohibition against taking substantial gifts from non-relative clients extends to those that are contingent or merely possible. See *In re Boulger,* 637 N.W.2d 710, 712 (N.D. 2001), wherein the court rejected the attorney's argument that the contingencies drafted into the will which would trigger the testamentary gift to him were so unlikely to happen that the conditional bequests were not actually substantial gifts under the ethical rule's prohibition.

Taking advantage of a client's situation also applies when Hollywood calls. Popular media such as books, television shows, and movies are constantly being created with legal issues and lawyers as the central themes and characters. Indeed, not only is it hard to watch an evening of prime time on any of the networks without encountering a legal drama, but also an entire network, Court TV, has arisen in response to the demand. The temptation to cash in on the demand for stories has been expressly prohibited by the ABA Model Rules.

Violation of this ethical provision can be dealt with in the most severe manner permissible under the ABA Standards for Imposing Lawyer Sanctions, Section 7.1. Where an attorney knowingly violates his professional duties to his client with the intent to obtain a benefit for himself at the expense of his client or the justice system, disbarment is generally appropriate. This prohibition extends even to the selling of the attorney's own story as it relates to the representation of his clients.

In signing the option contract for "The Garnett Harrison Story," Harrison [the attorney] violated Rule 1.8(d) of the Rules of Professional Conduct. Such transaction, for which Harrison was paid $10,000, is prohibited as creating a conflict of interest between a lawyer and client. Her clients—at that point, the estate of Dorrie Singley, and Bernice Singley as administratrix—may not have been injured by Harrison's signing of the option contract. However, the potential serious injury to the legal profession is manifest. Realization of personal profit from representation of a client creates an appearance of impropriety which the profession can ill afford. *Therefore, disbarment is proper under this Rule.*

Harrison v. Mississippi Bar, 637 So.2d 204 (Miss. 1994) (emphasis added).

The key to this prohibition is its effect or potential effect upon the legal system, its integrity, and the public's confidence in its truth-finding and justice-rendering role. A legal professional who has a financial interest in the profitability of the client's story as a book or movie also has an incentive to make that story as marketableand appealing as possible. This may be at odds with the outcome that is best or most just for the client. Even if this were not so, there would always be doubts surrounding the motivation for the actions taken by the attorney or paralegal. This **appearance of impropriety** standard applies in many circumstances, under many ethical rules. The legal profession regards the preservation of the dignity of the law as one which is so important that only the possibility of harm can be met with discipline that is equally stringent.

appearance of impropriety
A standard used to evaluate whether actions which are not strictly prohibited are still deemed unethical, because an ordinary citizen would suspect them as inappropriate behavior for a legal professional.

Recall that the client is the "master of the claim" and therefore is ultimately in charge of the direction and settlement of the matter. The attorney's role is to properly steer the course in the legal system to achieve the client's desired result. Any incentives an attorney has to direct the end result towards her own gain are prohibited, even if those incentives are never realized or intended. Again, the attorney must avoid the mere possibility and public perception of them. Another way to acquire a financial interest in the outcome of the client's matter is to lend money to him. The attorney then has her own agenda in settling the matter for the maximum amount possible, which may not be the best outcome for the client, particularly if that client wishes to end the matter quickly.

Another prohibition relates to financial aid to clients. Essentially, it is impermissible to provide assistance to the client in connection with pending or contemplated litigation. There are two exceptions to the "no-loan" rule, and they are strictly enforced. Any money advanced by the attorney's office that does not qualify as court costs or expenses of litigation is prohibited. The attorney's intent in making any other sort of loan, the loan terms, and/or the client's needs are irrelevant to the determination that the ethical rule has been violated. There are many situations where attorneys may be sympathetic to the plight of their clients; however, in all cases, the courts will find an ethical violation. This is based upon the desire to prevent "(1) clients selecting a lawyer based on improper factors, and (2) conflicts of interest, including compromising a lawyer's independent judgment in the case and creating the potentially conflicting roles of the lawyer as both lawyer and creditor with divergent interests." *State ex rel. Oklahoma Bar Ass'n v. Smole,* 17 P.3d 456, 462 (Okla. 2000). The attorney was not permitted to advance living expenses to his worker's compensation client until the final disposition of the case. Dramatically, in *Matter of K.A.H.,* 967 P.2d 91 (Alaska 1998), the attorney was not permitted to advance money to the widow and children of a seaman killed on an Alaskan crab boat so that they could pay rent and move out of their car! Along the same lines, in *Toledo Bar Assn. v. Crossmock,* 111 Ohio St.3d 278, 855 N.E.2d 1215 (2006), the attorney was not permitted to advance funds for medical treatment for his personal injury client. It is not that courts have turned a deaf ear to the financial troubles of clients; they simply have sent a clear message that the integrity of the justice system must be preserved by prohibiting these loans between legal professionals and clients.

Financial influences can come from outside sources, those that are not related to the actual action but have an interest in the outcome. Since the beginning of law practice in America, the "American Rule" with regard to fees has been in place. The American Rule provides that parties pay for their own legal services and costs. The victor in the litigation battle does not also win the costs of retaining the attorney in the recovery. This practice is reflected in the ethics rules, which essentially require that the client pay for her own representation.

As always, there are exceptions to the general prohibition. There are situations where a third party/non-client can agree to pay for the client's legal costs. The first should be familiar: most, not all, actions to be undertaken by an attorney relative to representation can be validated by informed client consent. The client must understand the risks involved in permitting the attorney to accept payment from another source. One of the characteristics of the practice of law is the exercise of independent professional judgment. In potential conflict with this duty is the desire of this third party, who is paying the bills for the client, to have some say in how the matter is pursued—how the money is spent, so to speak. This is impermissible, and therefore any monetary influence a third party may have over the attorney-client relationship is prohibited. Further, the principle of client confidentiality must be maintained. The third party paying for the legal services has not paid for access to the private communications between the attorney and client. Recall NFPA's EC 1.6 (a): "Neither the paralegal's personal or business interest, nor those of other clients or *third persons,* should compromise the paralegal's professional judgment and loyalty to the client" (emphasis added).

This danger of interference with the attorney-client relationship by payment rendered by an outside party surfaces most often in insurance coverage matters. The client is the insured person, while the payer is the insurance company. The insurance company has a vested interest in keeping the cost of handling the insured's matter at a minimum, and the client has the opposite incentive: to get as much work as possible out of the attorney, to obtain the best possible outcome for the matter.

> *The tension between insurer control of defense and settlement of claims and the exercise of an attorney's independent judgment on behalf of an insured exists in part because of the unsettled nature of the insured, insurer, defense counsel relationship. The insured purchases insurance from an insurance company. The insurance company promises to defend claims against the insured and to indemnify the insured for judgments and settlements. The insurance company hires an attorney to defend claims against insureds. The insured agrees to cooperate.*
>
> *The relationship has been described as a "tripartite relationship." The precise nature of the relationship among an insured, an insurer, and defense counsel is enigmatic.*
>
> *There are different views as to whether the insured and insurer are both clients, or whether the insured is a single client and the insurer is a third party payer, or whether the relationship is characterized otherwise. . . . Within this patchwork of views regarding the nature of the relationship among the insured, insurer and defense counsel, questions emerge regarding what is ethical conduct for insurance defense attorneys. The unsettled nature of the relationship stimulates the search for ethical guidance.*
>
> *Whether an insurance defense attorney may abide by an insurer's "litigation management guidelines" without violating ethical duties of the legal profession has been the subject of advisory opinions in this state and other states. The majority view is that certain carrier imposed limitations give rise to ethical problems. . . . In conclusion, it is this Board's view that it is improper under [the ethical rules] for an insurance defense attorney to abide by an insurance company's litigation management guidelines in the representation of an insured when the guidelines interfere with the professional judgment of the attorney. Attorneys must not yield professional control of their legal work to an insurer.*

OH Adv. Op. 2000-3, 2000 WL 1005223 at 2-3. (Ohio Bd. Com. Griev. Disp.) (citations omitted).

In what ways can third-party payers influence the professional judgment of the legal professionals?

> *Guidelines that restrict or require prior approval before performing computerized or other legal research are an interference with the professional judgment of an attorney. Legal*

research improves the competence of an attorney and increases the quality of legal services. Attorneys must be able to research legal issues when they deem necessary without interference by non-attorneys.

Guidelines that dictate how work is to be allocated among defense team members by designating what tasks are to be performed by a paralegal, associate, or senior attorney are an interference with an attorney's professional judgment. Under the facts and circumstances of a particular case, an attorney may deem it necessary or more expedient to perform a research task or other task, rather than designate the task to a paralegal. This is not a decision for others to make. The attorney is professionally responsible for the legal services. Attorneys must be able to exercise professional judgment and discretion.

Guidelines that require approval before conducting discovery, taking a deposition, or consulting with an expert witness are an interference with an attorney's professional judgment. These are professional decisions that competent attorneys make on a daily basis.

Guidelines that require an insurer's approval before filing a motion or other pleading are an interference with an attorney's professional judgment. Motion by motion evaluation by an insurer of an attorney's legal work is an inappropriate interference with professional judgment and is demeaning to the legal profession. If an insurer is unsatisfied with the overall legal services performed, the insurer has the opportunity in the future to retain different counsel.

Id. at 6–7.

This long list of prohibited interferences underscores the importance of the exercise of independent professional judgment and the maintenance of the sanctity of the confidentiality and inviolatibility of the attorney-client relationship—one that is free from "outsider" influence driven by financial interests. A paralegal working with an attorney must be cognizant of these situations. Paralegals are highly involved in insurance cases and must take care to avoid influence from third-party insurance carriers. Where the third party is trying to assert such influence, the paralegal clearly must adhere to the ethical standards to maintain his professional integrity and independence. (See Figure 5.4.)

Multiple Representation

Independence as a theme for the manner in which the attorney must operate also pertains to the situation where the attorney has permissibly represented two or more clients in the same matter. After clearing the initial conflict of interest hurdle and determining that a present conflict does not exist, an attorney still must maintain separability between or among the clients. Each client retains her own cause of action, and the attorney must treat the clients as if they were independent of each other. This means that the end result must also be separable; there are no "two-for-one" deals in making settlements, no volume discounts simply because the attorney is handling more than one client in the matter.

Of course, the most common requirement, informed consent in writing, is also present if the attorney and clients wish to enter into a multiple representation agreement. It is so very important for clients to be fully aware of the potential pitfalls associated with multiple representation and to know their rights with respect to each other. In essence, the client must not fare any worse than she would have if she had obtained independent counsel. The clients must all come to an agreement about the goals and amount of settlement that will be acceptable. Further, once the aggregate settlement has been made, the proceeds need to be divided according to that written agreement reflecting the understanding of the represented clients, and all of those clients must be consulted at the various stages of the settlement procedure. Particularly susceptible to an aggregate settlement without full consultation is the probate of estates. The estate is made up of several persons with an interest in the disposition

NFPA EC 1.6(f)
A paralegal shall not participate in or conduct work on any matter where a conflict of interest has been identified.

FIGURE 5.4
Work Prohibited Where There Is a Conflict

of the entire estate. For example, in *In re Hoffman,* 883 So.2d 425, 433–434 (La. 2004), the attorney settled the matter after consulting with one of the three siblings, albeit the one who was given most of the control over the matter. The court found that the attorney had to give the other siblings an "opportunity to exercise their absolute right to control the settlement decision. . . it is of no moment whether the Walker siblings had actually agreed to divide the settlement funds equally. Prior to accepting the settlement offer, respondent should have resolved with all of his clients the issue of the allocation of the settlement proceeds." It is important to note that the client is not the estate itself in these matters; the clients are the living persons who are retaining the attorney to assist them with a problem in the probate and distribution of the estate. It is to them that the attorney must consult. "Rejecting the lawyer's argument that he was required to consult only with the personal representative of the decedent's estate, whom the lawyer asserted was the "true client,'" the court pointed out that the lawyer "had three clients in the action and owed to each the right of disclosure and consent in accepting and distributing the award'." *Id., citing State ex rel. Oklahoma Bar Ass'n v. Watson,* 897 P.2d 246 (Okla. 1994).

Waiver of Claims against the Legal Professional

While fee agreements will be handled in a later chapter, it is helpful to note here that an auxiliary agreement, one that addresses the attorney's quality of performance, is prohibited under ABA Model Rule 1.8. Attorneys cannot attempt to contractually limit their own or their paralegal's liability for malpractice claims or to settle a malpractice claim unless the client is represented by a disinterested third-party attorney in making the arrangement. In essence, the lawyer cannot escape a claim for malpractice by having his client waive that claim in a pre-representative contract. While these types of agreements, limitation of liability and limitation of damages, are common in ordinary business transactions, they are disfavored in the lawyer-client relationship. For that reason, any proposal that the attorney or paralegal will not be held accountable for acts of malpractice requires that the client knowingly waive these rights with consultation and advice from an independent attorney. The same holds true for any settlement regarding a potential claim for malpractice. The client cannot settle her rights with respect to her claim against the attorney or paralegal absent consultation from an outside disinterested attorney. The courts consider an attorney's accountability so important that it is not necessary for the client to prove that any malpractice occurred; the mere waiver of the right to sue for malpractice is grounds enough for the finding of an ethical violation. *In re Disciplinary Proceeding Against Greenlee,* 158 Wash.2d 259, 143 P.3d 807 (2006) illustrates this point. The client requested written confirmation from the attorney that no further fees were owed, just $1,595 in costs. The attorney agreed to this only if the client agreed to sign a mutual release which included the release of any claims she might have against the attorney. No claim was filed against the attorney; however, the court, deciding the matter as a case of first impression, stated that none need exist because

> *[o]ne of the primary purposes of attorney discipline is the protection of the public from attorney misconduct, and disciplinary rules should be interpreted to advance that purpose. As a general matter, the rule seeks to protect unrepresented clients when a lawyer seeks release of liability in situations where the lawyer's interests either directly conflict or have the potential to directly conflict with the client's interests.*

Id. at 271 (citations omitted).

It is clear that agreements to release the attorney from potential liability at the outset of representation remove the attorney's incentive to do his very best and align himself with his client's best interests. Settling a potential claim after representation without permitting the client to consult outside counsel permits the attorney to take advantage of his established relationship with his client, and is essentially also a violation of the rules forbidding communications with unrepresented persons. The client is essentially unrepresented in the settlement, because the attorney is looking out for his own interest at the cost of the client.

Stake in the Outcome of the Case

Legal professionals should be looking out for their clients' best interests. The best interest of the client may be (1) a protracted litigation or (2) extensive aggressive settlement negotiations rewarded with a large judgment or (3) a quick settlement. Which course is actually most desirous? The client may prefer a swift resolution to a large judgment. The attorney, understandably, wants to take the course that will render the most money in fees. Therefore, at times, the attorney's interest in the outcome of the case may diverge from that of the client. The attorney is bound to take that route which the client most desires. The ethics rules prohibit an attorney or a paralegal from acquiring a stake in the outcome of the case or in the subject matter in contention. This removes another level of temptation to increase the duration, the settlement, or the judgment in order to secure a higher fee.

There are two exceptions to this rule that are necessary in order to protect an attorney's ability to collect the monies duly owed. The first permits an attorney to use client property (including the client's files at the attorney's office) as collateral or security in order to ensure that the fees and expenses will get paid. *See Skarecky & Horenstein, P.A. v. 3605 North 36th Street Co.,* 170 Ariz. 424, 825 P.2d 949 (Ariz. App. 1991). (The law firm's acceptance of a client's assignment of the beneficial interest of a deed of trust, intended to secure payment of attorney's fees in a lawsuit concerning the promissory note secured by that deed of trust, did not violate the ethical rules prohibiting the acquisition of a **proprietary interest** in the cause of action.) These fees and liens are not tied to the cause of action, but rather exist because the lawyer performed work. The second exception permits an attorney to accept matters on a contingent fee basis. This is a common arrangement in personal injury, class action, and other types of damage cases. It is absolutely prohibited in most family law matters and criminal cases. While the fees in a contingency arrangement are usually much higher than those billed hourly, the situation is attractive to clients, as they have no bill for services to pay unless there is a recovery. The only restraint in other kinds of civil cases is the requirement that the contingency fee be reasonable. This usually translates into 33 percent of the recovery; however, there are many other kinds of contingencies that are permissible as long as they are reasonable. The reasonableness is determined on a case-by-case basis. One instance where the fee is unreasonable deals with basing the contingency on the demanded amount in a complaint or, in the case of a defendant, on the reduction in amount from that claimed in the complaint to actual judgment. Plaintiffs often overstate the amount of damages sought; there is no penalty for doing so. Therefore, the contingency based upon these figures is completely unrelated to the actual settlement of the matter and, therefore, commonly found unreasonable.

> *A plaintiff may sue defendant for $1,000,000, but the fact that sum is named in the complaint does not necessarily mean that plaintiff's claim can fairly be said to be for that amount. Plaintiff's counsel often overstate the amount to which their client is entitled, and indeed have little incentive for restraint. Thus, the amount demanded cannot automatically be the number from which the savings resulting from a judgment or settlement can reasonably be calculated.*

ABA Comm. on Ethics and Prof'l Responsibility, Formal Op. 93-373 at 1001:181–82 (1993). *See also Brown & Sturm v. Frederick Road Ltd. Partnership,* 137 Md. App. 150, 768 A.2d 62 (2001). (The proposed compensation, which would have been based upon sales, leases, or development of the farm, bore little relation to the actual work being

proprietary interest
A definite financial stake in the outcome of a case or matter which may influence the attorney to take a path that is not in the best interest of his client, but, rather, will result in a greater monetary recovery for the attorney.

done, and appellants [lawyers] could conceivably have received substantial sums of money for rendering few or no legal services.)

Sexual Relationships Prohibited

The last prohibition relating to the relationship with the client that naturally causes a conflict of interest is extremely personal. Legal professionals must not commence a sexual relationship with a client. It is never a good idea to become romantically involved with anyone you must work with on a professional basis. This rule states the obvious. However, the Pennsylvania Bar Association Committee on Legal Ethics and Professional Responsibility felt it necessary to examine the issue of attorney-client sexual relations in 17 pages of analysis, ultimately concluding that this type of relationship should not be permitted.

> *Several problems arise when an attorney engages in sexual contact with a client. The lawyer-client relationship is grounded on mutual trust. A sexual relationship that exploits that trust compromises the lawyer-client relationship. Also, an attorney is in a fiduciary relationship with a client. Many authorities support the proposition that when an attorney has sexual involvement with a client, the fiduciary relationship the attorney owes to a client is breached.*

1997 WL 671579 at 3.

The only exception is where the relationship came first. This relates back to the benefit of having an attorney in the family. Of course, a person may look to her significant other who is a lawyer for legal assistance. "[A] woman may choose her lover as her lawyer, but not her lawyer as her lover." Linda Fitts Mischler, *Reconciling Rapture, Representation, and Responsibility: An Argument Against Per Se Bans on Attorney-Client Sex,* 10 GEORGETOWN J. LEGAL ETHICS 209, 237 (Winter 1996).

All of these prohibitions, with the exception of the last (romantic) one, relate to all attorneys and paralegals in the firm. Any act that is prohibited to one of them is prohibited to all of them. ABA Model Rule 1.8 sets forth very specific prohibitions in the relationship between an attorney and a current client, so that clarity can prevent potentially disastrous results due to the inherent conflict in these situations. The ABA Model Rule sets forth ten prohibited activities, and NFPA's code reflects much of the same substance. Most of these restrictions have exceptions to them if certain requirements are met. In simple sum, the following behaviors are prohibited:

1. Entering into business transactions with a client, unless a transaction is fair, written in easy-to-understand language, and able to be reviewed by a disinterested attorney, which equates to informed consent.

2. Using information obtained from a client against the interests of that client, unless the client gives informed consent.

3. Accepting a substantial gift from a client, unless the client is a family member.

4. Securing media or literary rights in the client's action.

5. Giving financial assistance to a client, except to advance litigation costs and filing fees.

6. Accepting payment from a third party, unless the attorney notifies the client and the third party neither makes decisions nor obtains client confidences.

7. Making an aggregate settlement on behalf of two or more clients in the same matter without first obtaining informed consent.

8. Limiting liability for malpractice claims.

9. Obtaining a proprietary interest in the cause of action, except to secure a valid attorney lien or create a contingency fee arrangement.

10. Starting a romantic relationship with a client.

All of these rules are designed to ensure that the legal professionals act in their clients' best interests and not for any personal gain that may interfere with the proper management of the case.

FORMER CLIENTS

Current clients are not the only ones to whom legal professionals owe certain duties of loyalty. Former clients are also protected. Without the professionals' preserving of certain aspects of the relationship "to the grave," clients would have little confidence in the relationship. If an attorney or a paralegal were able to use personal and potentially harmful confidential information about a client after the matter was closed, then the client would be reluctant to enter into the relationship at all. Therefore, the ethical rules address how an attorney or a paralegal must conduct herself with regard to the client after the representation has ended. (See Figure 5.5.)

This rule is of importance to paralegals who assist in intake of clients and perform a **conflict check**. See Figure 5.6 for a sample intake form. The "ghost" of the

conflict check
A procedure to verify potential adverse interests before accepting a new client.

NFPA EC 1.6(b)

A paralegal shall avoid conflicts of interest that may arise from previous assignments, whether for a present or past employer or client.

FIGURE 5.5
Conflicts Arising from Prior Employment

All information is protected by the ethical duty of attorney-client confidentiality.

Today's Date: _____

Name: _____

Address: _____

Home telephone: _____   Work telephone: _____

Employer: _____

Birth date: _____   Social Security Number: _____

Married   Divorced   Single   Widowed (circle one)
Children: (Name, sex, age)
How did you learn about this firm/attorney? (Yellow pages, referral, etc.)
_____

SUBJECT MATTER: _____

STATUTE OF LIMITATIONS DEADLINE: _____

OTHER INFORMATION: _____

Previous legal consultations? With whom? _____

Previous medical consultations? (if relevant) With whom? _____

BRIEF STATEMENT OF FACTS: _____
_____.

NAMES OF WITNESSES: _____

What final result/relief is the client looking for? _____
_____

CONFLICT CHECKING:
✓ All business/employment relationships:
✓ Family names/relationships:
✓ Persons or entities involved in this matter:
✓ Persons or entities with whom you have been legally involved, including prior
   lawsuits:

FIGURE 5.6
Initial Client Interview/Intake Form

former client remains in the office of the attorney. If a new client comes in looking for representation, the attorney (or, most likely, the paralegal) will need to check to see if any former clients were involved with this potential client. If there is a conflict between a former client and the new potential client, further inquiry needs to be made. The prohibitions against taking this potential client are not as strict as if the existing client were currently being represented. For the prohibition to stand, the potential client must be looking for representation that relates to the same or substantially similar subject matter as the previous representation of the former client. The rule is based on the premise that a client's confidences remain forever inviolate. For legal professionals to have intimate knowledge of a former client's matters and then be able to turn around and use it to that former client's disadvantage totally eviscerates the principles of confidentiality. If the new client is looking for representation regarding a different matter, the attorney will be permitted to take the case. This is where the rule of current clients (ABA Model Rule 1.9) differs from that of former clients (ABA Model Rule 1.7). There is more latitude in taking a new client that has some sort of conflict with a former client, whereas there is a ban on taking a new client that has some sort of conflict with the current client.

For example, Attorney Able represents Larry Lumberman in his lawsuit against Donald Developer regarding an outstanding balance owed for lumber and supplies to one of Donald's many construction projects. Obviously, during the representation of Larry, Able could not represent Donald in any matter (assuming that Larry did not consent to the concurrent representation). However, after Larry's matter is over and Able has concluded all representation of Larry, Able would be able to take Donald on as a new client in a matter involving the sale of any of the development projects or other matters not related to the collection matter in which he represented Larry.

How do courts determine whether a conflict exists when a former client brings a motion to disqualify his former firm from representing a new client with a potential conflict? The key to understanding this disqualification based upon the subject matter is to determine what "substantially similar" means in this context.

> *The key to making a determination about the former client disqualification is to understand what a "substantially similar" matter is. Thus, an attorney should be disqualified if he has accepted employment adverse to the interests of a former client on a matter substantially related to the prior representation. This test has been honed in its practical application to grant disqualification only upon a showing that the relationship between the issues in the prior and present cases is 'patently clear' or when the issues are 'identical' or 'essentially the same.'*

Bergeron v. Mackler, 225 Conn. 391, 398–399, 623 A.2d 489, 493–494 (1993). (citations omitted; emphasis added.)

Why do courts seem to narrow the definition so that many times the attorney will be able to take on a new client even where that client's interests are directly adverse to those of the former client? It is the legal system's balance in protecting the confidentiality of the former client with the new client's right to freely engage the counsel of her choice. Too many restrictions with regard to former clients would result in too many attorneys being "conflicted out" and unable to render the services the new client desires. Imagine the impact a more stringent rule would have on small-town practices. With only four or five attorneys to choose from, once a client had consulted with all of them on various matters, no one else in the town could engage those attorneys as counsel in any matters against the first client. They all would have some sort of confidences relating to that first client. This is why the ethical rules put the

NFPA EC 1.6(e)

A paralegal shall reveal sufficient non-confidential information about a client or former client to reasonably ascertain if an actual or potential conflict of interest exists.

FIGURE 5.7
Identifying a Conflict

"substantially similar" requirement in place: to allow subsequent clients the most choice in selecting counsel.

The same standard applies to paralegals. In order to determine whether the law office can take on a matter, the paralegals must determine whether they have had any former dealings with the potential new client. In this determination, it is important for paralegals to appreciate the confidentiality responsibility fully. Only as much of the prior client's information as is necessary can be revealed in order to make the conflict determination. (See Figure 5.7.)

Once a potential conflict has been identified, further analysis is required; it involves looking at the question of whether subsequent representation would be "materially adverse" to the former client.

> The court must make a case-specific inquiry to determine the degree to which the current representation may actually be harmful to the former client. This fact-intensive analysis focuses on whether the current representation may cause legal, financial, or other identifiable detriment to the former client. Additionally, we must determine "whether the attorney's exercise of individual loyalty to one client might harm the other client or whether his zealous representation will induce him to use confidential information that could adversely affect the former client.

Simpson Performance Products, Inc. v. Robert W. Horn, P.C., 92 P.3d 283, 288 (Wyo. 2004). (citations omitted.)

The issue to be determined here is whether the legal professional had significant contact with the former client's matter. In making this determination, three factors are generally considered: "(1) factual similarities between the two representations, (2) similarities in legal issues, and (3) the nature and extent of the attorney's involvement with the case and whether he was in a position to learn of the client's policy or strategy." *Ochoa v. Fordel, Inc.,* 146 Cal. App. 4th 898, 908, 53 Cal. Rptr. 3d 277, 285; citing *Adams v. Aerojet-General Corp.,* 86 Cal. App. 4th 1324, 1332, 104 Cal. Rptr. 2d 116 (2001). If the attorney or paralegal had obtained no confidences either through contact with the client or through other legal professionals in the firm, then there is no need for the protections afforded by this rule. The attorney and/or paralegal will generally carry the burden of proof showing that he did not have the opportunity to obtain sensitive client information during his prior association with his former firm. Not only is an attorney prohibited from taking on a new client where the rules apply, but the attorney and the paralegal are also prohibited from using any information obtained from the former representation to the former client's detriment in any way or disclosing the information under any circumstances not permitted by the relevant rules.

Lastly, ABA Model Rule 1.10 functions to subsume all the above prohibitions and apply them to all the attorneys and paralegals associated in a firm. This rule makes it clear that the conflict follows the attorney or paralegal when she changes firms, thereby "infecting" the new firm and clearing the old firm of its previous conflict. The theory behind attributing the "taint" of conflict to every other attorney and paralegal in the firm rests on the fact that attorneys and paralegals talk to one another, both socially in the coffee room and professionally for advice. Therefore, the law assumes that what one legal professional knows, they all know. Such **imputed conflict** does not

imputed conflict
An entire law office can be prohibited from representing a client with whom an attorney or paralegal has an individual conflict. The conflict is attributed to the whole firm.

Ethical Wall
A set of internal office procedures by which a law firm can isolate or screen attorneys and paralegals who present a conflict with matters in the office and can prevent the disclosure of clients' confidential information.

apply in the case where the conflict is personal to the individual attorney or paralegal. Conflicts resulting from personal bias or revulsion or a sexual relationship are not transferred to all the legal professionals in the firm.

Generally, the taint of conflict is removed when the conflicted attorney or paralegal leaves the firm; however, if there are others who may have shared in some way in the former representation, the taint may remain. The purpose of the entire set of ethical rules is reinforced: where there is a possibility that an attorney or paralegal could use information gained from the confidential relationship with a client to the client's detriment, the attorney is prohibited from taking on that representation.

RESEARCH THIS

In your jurisdiction, find one case that disqualified a firm from representing a client due to a conflict with an employed paralegal, and one case in which the court found that no conflict existed, but the paralegal had only a potential conflict. What factors were different in the two cases that led to different results?

In order to comply with all of these ethical requirements, meticulous record keeping is required. Even the most conscientious legal professional will be unable to keep track of all clients and the substance of their representation. (See Figure 5.8.)

From the first day on the job, a paralegal must have a system of keeping track of all clients and matters assigned to her. Ethical compliance is an immediate obligation. Followed to a strict end, this may mean that the more experience a paralegal has, the less able she is to change firms without conflicting herself out. The more clients a paralegal comes in contact with, the more potential conflicts exist. In essence, a paralegal could work herself into a situation where she had little option for changing firms! In order to permit paralegals to advance their careers at other offices, there must be some way of screening out the taint. This screen is usually referred to as either an **Ethical Wall** or a "Chinese Wall" (meaning that it is purportedly as solid and defendable as the Great Wall of China). (See Figure 5.9.)

A paralegal who creates a conflict situation in the firm may be "walled off" from participating in the matter which creates the conflict. This isolation from the matter is similar to the tenets of confidentiality, with its "cone of silence." There are many steps in creating this Wall, and every firm must have a method for putting it into place if necessary. Additionally, if an adversary seeks to disqualify the firm based

FIGURE 5.8
Conflict Records

NFPA EC 1.6(d)

In order to be able to determine whether an actual or potential conflict of interest exists, a paralegal shall create and maintain an effective recordkeeping system that identifies clients, matters, and parties with which the paralegal has worked.

FIGURE 5.9
Ethical Wall

NFPA EC 1.6(g)

In matters where a conflict of interest has been identified and the client consents to continued representation, a paralegal shall comply fully with the implementation and maintenance of an Ethical Wall.

upon a paralegal's taint, the firm must have documented its steps to show that it has done its very best to keep the paralegal and the other members of the firm who are participating in the matter separate from the persons actively working on it. The following steps should be taken to attempt to prevent the transmission of confidential information:

1. The office should have a written statement regarding the importance of confidential information, along with ongoing ethical educational programs to enforce compliance.

2. The "infected" employee may be required to sign a confidentiality agreement wherein he agrees not to disclose any information relating to the conflict situation.

3. An office meeting may be required to inform other employees that they are not to discuss the matter with the "tainted" employee. They may also be required to sign an agreement not to discuss the matter.

4. Files must be kept in a secure location to restrict access. Files that create a conflict situation should be marked as such and kept away from general circulation. The files must be marked so they can be easily identified.

5. Client consent should be obtained where conflict or potential conflict situations arise.

This list is not all-inclusive or exhaustive. The measures taken will depend upon the structure and administration of the particular law office. The main point is to keep the tainted employee away from those who are working on the matter in a way that makes it as if the tainted employee were not present to create the conflict. The sensitive and fiduciary nature of the relationship between the legal professional and the client is held sacrosanct, and any impingement on that is strongly disfavored. Clients must feel that their interests are being advanced with no reservations on the part of the legal professionals who work for them. Conflicts chip away at this trust and must be avoided or mitigated to the furthest extent that they can be.

Summary

The ethics rules regarding conflicts of interest are broad in scope and applicable to every attorney-client relationship or paralegal-client rapport, and last indefinitely. Where there is a doubt as to whether the attorney may take on a new client or should withdraw as counsel, the preferred choice (where there is not a prejudicial effect upon the client) is to defer to the conflicts rules and disengage from the relationship.

There are very specific requirements that must be fulfilled in order to enter into or maintain an attorney-client relationship or generally prohibited transaction. The requirement that is found in almost every rule is the concept of "informed consent." Because attorneys have superior knowledge of the law and legal relationships, they cannot use this to the detriment of their clients who look to them for advice. Clients generally assume that their attorneys and paralegals are looking out for their best interests, and this is generally a good assumption, because the ethics rules impose this burden upon them. However, in this chapter, we have seen that there are certain circumstances for which this premise may not be true. In these instances the client must be informed of the terms and consequences of the proposed arrangement in clear, easy-to-understand terms and must have the ability to consult with outside counsel for advice on those terms.

Simply stated, an attorney owes an uncompromised duty of loyalty to every current and former client. Further, most of these conflicts are imputed to the entire firm for which the attorney works. Essentially, the firm must demonstrate loyalty to the individual client as well. All of these conflicts rules work in concert with the confidentiality rules to ensure that a client feels protected and the fiduciary relationship remains intact and unmarred by any outside interests.

Key Terms and Concepts

Adverse
Appearance of impropriety
Conflict check
Conflict of interest
Disinterested lawyer
Ethical Wall

Imputed conflict
Informed consent
Material limitation
Proprietary interest
Substantial gift

Review Questions

MULTIPLE CHOICE

Choose the best answer(s) and please explain WHY you choose the answer(s).

1. Informed consent
   a. Requires the attorney to tell the prospective client about every current client the attorney represents.
   b. Means the client has waived the conflict of interest.
   c. Restricts the attorney from speaking to anyone about his client's matters.
   d. Is a client's voluntary, written permission, after full disclosure of the risks, for the attorney to take on potentially conflicting clients.

2. The appearance of impropriety standard
   a. Disqualifies attorneys who lack moral character.
   b. Requires an attorney to refuse or withdraw from representation where the representation would make a person question the attorney's motives.
   c. Requires an attorney to submit her potentially disqualifying representation to the ethics board for an opinion as to its validity.
   d. Disqualifies an attorney who has committed an ethics violation in open court.

3. An attorney cannot enter into a business transaction with a client unless
   a. The transaction is fair and reasonable on its terms.
   b. The terms are in writing.
   c. The client has an opportunity to seek independent counsel.
   d. The client gives informed consent.
   e. All of the above.
   f. None of the above; an attorney should never go into business with his client.

EXPLAIN YOURSELF

All answers should be written in complete sentences. A simple yes or no is insufficient.

1. When can an attorney concurrently represent two or more clients that may have a potential conflict?
2. Explain the concept of adversity as it pertains to a conflict of interest.
3. What is the disinterested lawyer standard and when does it apply?
4. Are attorneys always prohibited from accepting gifts from clients?
5. What is an imputed conflict? Does it apply to paralegals as well as to attorneys?

FAULTY PHRASES

All of the following statements are FALSE; state why they are false and then rewrite them as true statements, without just making the statement negative by adding the word "not."

1. An attorney may never represent a present client who has a conflict with a former client.
2. A client can always waive a conflict of interest.
3. Gifts are considered substantial if they exceed $10,000 and, consequently, legal professionals are always prohibited from accepting them. Clients must always pay for their own representation.
4. An attorney can limit the amount of money that a client can recover from a malpractice suit in the retainer agreement.
5. Because courts favor settlement over trial, an attorney is permitted to take on quarreling clients in order to encourage a speedy resolution to the matter.
6. An attorney is ethically prohibited from having any romantic or sexual relationship with her client.

PORTFOLIO ASSIGNMENT

Write Away

The law firm where you are employed has just hired a new attorney. However, Connie, the new attorney, has worked at another law firm, where she represented an opposing party in one of the matters you are currently working on. Your supervising attorney has asked you to prepare an interoffice memorandum explaining the steps that the law office should take to screen Connie and why these steps are necessary. Make sure you are detailed enough that all members of the staff know what they should do in this situation.

Court of Appeals of Arizona, Division 1, Department E.
SMART INDUSTRIES CORP., MFG., and Lutes Enterprises, Inc., Petitioners,

v.

SUPERIOR COURT of the State of Arizona, In and For the COUNTY OF YUMA, The Honorable
H. Stewart Bradshaw, a judge thereof, Respondent Judge,
Darryl and Marilyn ST. GERMAINE, Real Parties in Interest.
No. 1 CA-SA 93-0320.
April 7, 1994.
Review Denied July 28, 1994.

OPINION

JACOBSON, Presiding Judge.

Petitioner Smart Industries, a defendant in the underlying personal injury suit, seeks review of the trial court's denial of its motion to disqualify plaintiff's lawyer after defendant's counsel's former legal assistant was hired by plaintiff's lawyer. [FN omitted] This special action requires us to decide whether the same rules of imputed disqualification that apply to lawyers also apply to nonlawyer personnel who change employment between law firms.

[...]

Factual Background

In December 1990, real parties in interest Darryl and Marilyn St. Germaine (collectively, "the St. Germaines" or "plaintiffs"), through their former lawyer Richard D. Engler, filed a personal injury suit alleging products liability and premises liability against Smart and other defendants. The St. Germaines subsequently retained their present counsel, Don B. Engler, the brother of Richard D. Engler, to represent them in this action. Don Engler is a sole practitioner in Yuma.

Smart retained the law firm of Mower, Koeller, Nebeker, Carlson & Haluck ("Mower, Koeller") to defend it in that litigation. The Yuma office of Mower, Koeller consists of two lawyers and three support staff. Co-counsel Constance Miller and William A. Nebeker of that firm worked on the case. Ms. Miller also worked with her secretary, Janet Gregston, who has been employed "in a secretarial/paralegal capacity" at Mower, Koeller since September 1991. According to Ms. Miller's affidavit, Ms. Gregston's paralegal duties involved extensive work on the St. Germaine/Smart litigation:

[Ms. Gregston] worked extensively [on this case] in numerous confidential settings. . . . [She] was privy to exhaustive client confidences, correspondences between counsel and clients, strategic planning, litigation preparation and documentation, pretrial conferences with clients, lay and expert witnesses. She participated in the preparation of trial exhibits and is shown in one test video which may be presented at trial.

According to counsel for Lutes, Ms. Gregston participated in numerous discussions with co-defendants, clients, and experts, involving strategic planning for a cooperative defense.

On October 8, 1993, approximately 60 days prior to the firm trial date, Ms. Gregston suddenly terminated her employment at Mower, Koeller. [FN omitted] On October 18, 1993, she began new employment as a legal secretary for plaintiff's lawyer Don Engler. According to Mr. Engler's avowal to the court:

[C]ontrary to Mrs. Gregston's duties while in Ms. Miller's employ . . . her duties [in Engler's employ] do not include a broad spectrum of "paralegal" tasks. To the contrary, Mrs. Gregston was employed to perform the specific professional duties of a legal secretary.

This means that Mrs. Gregston is responsible only to prepare those pleadings, motions and correspondence which [Engler] dictates, in conformance with [his] directions. Mrs. Gregston's contact with clients generally, and in this case in particular, is limited to receipt of telephone messages and placing of telephone calls for the undersigned.

Mr. Engler also avowed that he had given "specific and segregated authority" to a separate paralegal with her own secretary for "[a]ll matters relating to discovery, client conferences, preparation of discovery motions for final review . . . , trial exhibits, and pretrial statements . . ." and that "Mrs. Gregston has no responsibility in regards to these matters whatsoever." Similarly, Ms. Gregston's affidavit states that, prior to her employment with Mr. Engler, she was informed that she would not be asked to reveal any confidences she had learned in her prior employment, and to report to Mr. Engler if she were ever questioned by anyone in the office regarding her knowledge gained from her employment at Mower, Koeller. However, Ms. Gregston's initials and signature appear on several pleadings in this case, both in the underlying litigation and in special action papers filed in this court. Thus, it is apparent she is presently performing secretarial work on this case.

On November 15, 1993, Smart filed a motion to disqualify Engler as plaintiff's counsel, based on imputed disqualification of Engler's firm under ER 1.10, Rule 42, Rules of the Arizona Supreme Court, [FN omitted] because of Ms. Gregston's employment by Engler. [FN omitted] The motion relied heavily on the California case of *In re Complex Asbestos Litigation*, 232 Cal.App.3d 572, 283 Cal.Rptr. 732 (Dist. 1 1991).

In response, Mr. Engler argued that ER 1.10 had no application in a nonlawyer context, and that California case law was distinguishable. Furthermore, he contended, he had met the requirements of the applicable ethical rule, ER 5.3, by instructing Ms. Gregston not to divulge confidences. Thus, he concluded, disqualification was not required.

At a hearing on the motion, the trial court questioned its authority to order disqualification based on the conduct of a nonlawyer. The court subsequently ruled as follows:

The issue covered by this order is whether the plaintiff's attorney must be disqualified to continue to act by reason of the fact that he has hired a secretary/legal assistant who formerly worked for counsel for a defendant and who, it is contended, did a great deal of work on this case and has considerable "inside information" about the case.

. . . .

Plaintiff's counsel has contended that he has studiously insulated himself from any possible knowledge his employee might have, and the court accepts this as true.

Were this an attorney there would be absolutely no doubt in the court's mind that disqualification would be proper. This is not an attorney.

Not being an attorney, two thoughts are raised.

The first is that the court really has no method of protecting the privilege of confidentiality which Ms. Miller's client is entitled to enjoy.

The second is that there is no code of conduct in place which would guide a lawyer. The code of conduct is that of the employer.

The upshot of all of this is that the continued representation of the plaintiff by her attorney and a defendant attorney's former employee looks bad. It cannot be but perceived by the public that something fishy is going on. Thus, it smells bad, too.

However bad it may appear, mere appearance of evil is not a sufficient basis for the court to disqualify an attorney. While it may be that he should, ethically, withdraw, the court is not in a position to force the issue.

ORDERED that the motion to disqualify plaintiff's counsel is overruled.

Smart petitioned for special action from this order.

DISCUSSION

A. Standard of Review

Rulings on disqualification motions are within the discretion of the trial court, limited only by the applicable legal principles. *See, e.g., In re Complex Asbestos Litigation,* 283 Cal.Rptr. at 739. Our review is thus limited to a determination whether the trial court abused its discretion. *Id.*

B. Application of Ethical Rules to Disqualification Motions

The trial court apparently questioned its authority to disqualify a lawyer based on the conduct of a nonlawyer, when that conduct falls outside the scope of the disciplinary system. Smart argues that the court's ruling therefore may have constituted a failure to exercise discretion, as much as an abuse of discretion. As a preliminary matter, then, we determine the basis for the trial court's authority to disqualify a lawyer based upon employment of nonlawyer personnel.

A trial court's authority to apply an ethical rule to govern a disqualification motion in a litigation setting derives from the inherent power of the court to control judicial officers in any proceeding before it. *See In re Complex Asbestos Litigation,* 283 Cal.Rptr. at 739. As one court has defined this inherent authority:

Attorney disqualification of counsel is a part of a court's duty to safeguard the sacrosanct privacy of the attorney-client relationship which is necessary to maintain public confidence in the legal profession and to protect the integrity of the judicial process.

Panduit Corp. v. All States Plastic Mfg. Co., 744 F.2d 1564, 1576 (Fed.Cir. 1984).

The trial court's quandary in this case, however, was that the disqualification motion was based on the conduct of a nonlawyer, over whom the Model Rules have no effect in a disciplinary setting. However, as both Smart and the St. Germaines point out, the operation of ER 1.10(b) may be extended to the conduct of nonlawyers through ER 5.3. This duty imposes on a lawyer the duty to supervise a nonlawyer employee, which includes "reasonable efforts to ensure that the person's conduct is compatible with the professional obligations of the lawyer. . . ." ER 5.3(b). The duty of supervision also includes lawyer responsibility for any nonlawyer conduct "that would be a violation of the rules of professional conduct if engaged in by a lawyer," if the lawyer orders, has knowledge of, or ratifies such conduct. ER 5.3(c).

The lawyer's duty of supervision over, and responsibility for, the conduct of a nonlawyer assistant under ER 5.3 clearly encompasses the protection of client confidences communicated to a nonlawyer assistant, such as a paralegal or secretary. *See id.* at 433 n. 8, 844 P.2d at 600 n. 8 (obligations over nonlawyer include insuring client confidentiality). Under these combined principles, we conclude that a trial court has authority, in a litigation setting, to disqualify counsel on the basis of a nonlawyer assistant's conduct that would violate an ethical rule protecting a client's confidential communications to a lawyer. Therefore, to the extent that the trial court's ruling in this case may have been based on the erroneous assumption that it lacked authority to disqualify a lawyer based on the conduct of a nonlawyer, that ruling constitutes a failure to exercise discretion necessary "to safeguard the sacrosanct privacy of the attorney-client relationship which is necessary to maintain public confidence in the legal profession and to protect the integrity of the judicial process." *See Panduit,* 744 F.2d at 1576; *see also* Rule 3(a), Arizona Rules of Special Actions (special actions may address failure of judicial officer "to exercise discretion which he has a duty to exercise").

C. Application of Imputed Disqualification Rules to a Nonlawyer Assistant

Having concluded that a trial court has the authority, in a litigation context, to disqualify counsel based on the conduct of a nonlawyer assistant that is incompatible with the lawyer's ethical obligations, we turn next to the standard to be applied in determining whether disqualification is mandated under the facts of this case.

This is a case of first impression in Arizona. Indeed, we note that very few jurisdictions have considered the issue, either in the context of litigation case law or in ethical opinions. Those that have addressed the issue tend to apply the same standards to nonlawyers as are applied to lawyers under the jurisdiction's applicable disciplinary rules regarding imputed disqualification. (citations omitted)

Thus, if, under the jurisdiction's applicable ethical rules, a lawyer can be saved from imputing disqualification to his or her new firm by appropriate screening mechanisms, then a paralegal's or secretary's potential conflict in the new firm can be avoided by the same mechanisms, sometimes described as "Chinese Walls," or "cones of silence." *See, e.g., Kapco; In re Complex Asbestos Litigation.* However, if the jurisdiction does not recognize such a "screening" option as adequate protection against a lawyer's potential conflict in the new firm, then it usually does not recognize such an exception to the imputed disqualification rule for a nonlawyer assistant. *See, e.g., Glover Bottled Gas Corp.;* Kansas Bar Ass'n Ethical Op. No. 90-555.

Arizona law does not recognize screening devices to avoid imputed disqualification of the new law firm to which a lawyer moves when that lawyer possesses client confidences and the new firm has interests adverse to that client. *Towne,* 173 Ariz. at 369, 842 P.2d at 1382. In *Towne,* we interpreted ER 1.10(b) and the comments thereto, as adopted by our supreme court, to require that, when a lawyer in possession of client confidences moves from one firm to another, that movement imputes absolute disqualification to the new firm in any matter materially adverse to the client. *Id.* at 365, 842 P.2d at 1378. We adopted the trial court's conclusion that the firm and the lawyer had "scrupulously maintained" an ironclad wall to screen him from any adverse representation of the client undertaken by the new firm. [FN omitted] *Id.* at 368, 842 P.2d at 1381. However, we concluded:

Unfortunately, these efforts do not suffice.

. . . .

The language of ER 1.10 is absolute. When, as in this case, the moving lawyer has acquired protected information, the rule admits waiver or consent as the only exception to imputed disqualification of the receiving firm. This mandatory bright line was drawn in deliberate contra-distinction to ER 1.11, which permits a screening solution when lawyers move from government practice to private firms. . . .

. . . .

ER 1.10, as adopted in Arizona, rejects walling off a tainted attorney as an alternative to imputed disqualification of the firm.

Id. at 368-69, 842 P.2d at 1381-82 (citations and footnotes omitted).

We are also reluctant, however, to adopt the reasoning of those jurisdictions that have declined to adopt the "cone of silence" screening defense for lawyers, but then have blindly applied this rule to the analogous nonlawyer situation without first examining whether any distinction exists between the two situations.

In ABA Informal Opinion, the Committee was asked whether, under the Model Rules, a law firm that hires a paralegal who was formerly employed by another lawyer must withdraw from representation in a matter adverse to a client of the former firm about whom the paralegal had obtained substantial information relating to the suit. The employing firm proposed to "screen the paralegal from receiving information about or working on the lawsuit and will direct the paralegal not to reveal any information relating to the representation of the sole practitioner's client gained by the paralegal during the former employment." *Id.* at 318. Although acknowledging that ER 1.10(b) does "not recognize screening the *lawyer* from sharing the information in the employing firm as a mechanism to avoid disqualification of the entire firm" (emphasis added), the Committee nonetheless found screening the *nonlawyer* to be an acceptable alternative to disqualification of the new firm, for the following reasons:

In the case of nonlawyers changing firms, however, additional considerations are present which persuade the Committee that the functional analysis [of the seventh circuit] in *Kapco* is more appropriate than would be a rule requiring automatic disqualification once the nonlawyer is shown to have acquired information in the former employment relating to the representation of the opponent.

It is important that nonlawyer employees have as much mobility in employment opportunity as possible consistent with the protection of client's interest. To so limit employment opportunities that some nonlawyers trained to work with law firms might be required to leave the careers for which they are trained would disserve clients as well as the legal profession. Accordingly, any restrictions on the nonlawyer's employment should be held to the minimum necessary to protect confidentiality of client information.

Id. at 320. We note that a similar "issue of fairness" was recognized by the Kansas Bar Association even though it ultimately rejected screening of nonlawyers as an alternative to disqualification: A rigid rule of "if the employee possess[es] information which if possessed by an attorney is a conflict, the hiring firm is disqualified" raises important questions, not the least of which is the anomalous proposition that the more skilled a legal assistant or other employee becomes to the employer and the more information he or she acquires on cases in the firm, such assistant becomes *less* valuable to other firms with significant caseloads with the current employer. . . . [A] literal reading [of this rigid rule] would stymie a legal assistant's career, or at the very least make them "Typhoid Marys," unemployable by firms practicing in specialized areas of the law where the employees are most skilled and experienced.

KBA Ethics Op. No. 90-005 at 6-7.

Noting this concern for the ability of nonlawyers to change employment, the California court in *Complex Asbestos Litigation* added its concern for the rights of clients to obtain counsel of their own choosing; balanced against those concerns, however, are "the need to maintain ethical standards of professional responsibility," and "the paramount concern" for "the preservation of public trust in the scrupulous administration of justice and the integrity of the bar." 283 Cal.Rptr. at 740. We too agree that all these concerns are relevant and important in determining a disqualification issue; however, we are wary of allowing a literal reading of a rule appropriate for lawyers to become a means of injustice to the parties when applied to nonlawyers if there are valid reasons to draw distinctions between them.

We believe that this reason for treating government lawyers differently in the context of imputed disqualification cases applies equally to nonlawyer assistants, who, unlike lawyers in private practice, generally have neither a financial interest in the outcome of a particular litigation, nor the choice of which clients they serve. Moreover, in our opinion, the public perception of what is expected of lawyers as compared to nonlawyers is different, probably based on the "independent contractor" status enjoyed by lawyers as compared to the "master/servant" role of nonlawyer assistants. Our analysis, thus, is directed to determining the scope and extent of a supervising lawyer's ethical duty under ER 5.3, to insure that a nonlawyer's conduct in this "master/servant" setting is compatible with other ethical obligations.

In ABA Informal Opinion, the Committee construed the lawyer's duty under Model Rule 5.3, to assure that a nonlawyer's conduct is "compatible" with the lawyer's ethical obligations. "Compatible" requirements to preserve confidentiality under Model Rule 5.3 in the supervision of the nonlawyer, but not "identical" to those imposed on lawyers under Model Rule 1.10(b), included the following:

(a) appropriate instruction and supervision concerning the ethical aspects of their employment, particularly regarding the obligation not to disclose information relating to representation of the client;

(b) admonitions to be alert to all legal matters, including lawsuits, in which any client of the former employer had an interest. The nonlawyer should be cautioned:

(1) not to disclose any information relating to the representation of a client of the former employer; and

(2) that the employee should not work on any matter on which the employee worked for the prior employer or respecting which the employee has information relating to the representation of the client of the former employer.

Id. at 320-21 (emphasis and blocked format added).

[5] We conclude that the screening requirements articulated above are sufficient to satisfy a lawyer's duty under ER 5.3 to supervise a nonlawyer employee in a manner that will assure conduct "compatible" with the lawyer's ethical obligations. Thus, satisfaction of these requirements will prevent disqualification of the firm based on a nonlawyer's potential conflict even though a stricter standard is imposed on lawyers by operation of ER 1.10(b). *See Towne.*

Applying these concepts to this case, however, we conclude that Smart is entitled to disqualification of plaintiffs' counsel under the undisputed facts before us. First, there is no question that Ms. Gregston obtained client confidences in her former employment; the St. Germaines do not contend that her involvement in the case was any less than lawyer Miller has alleged. Second, there is no question that these client confidences are substantially related to the representation by her current employer; indeed, she is now on the other side of the same lawsuit, which is pending trial. It is also clear on this record that Smart did not consent to her employment by opposing counsel, nor did Smart waive its objection to her new employment. [FN omitted]

We understand that plaintiffs' counsel instructed Ms. Gregston not to divulge any client confidences gained in her former employment, and, as previously mentioned, we accept as true

counsel's avowals, in both this court and the trial court, that he has insulated himself from any possible disclosure. However, this instruction and insulation do not necessarily satisfy the minimum requirements necessary under ER 5.3 to prevent disqualification. In this case, counsel does not dispute that Ms. Gregston has not been screened from participation in the actual litigation with which she was intimately involved in her former employment; rather, she has initialed and signed pleadings and correspondence in this record. She has also submitted personal affidavits as evidence, in both the trial court and in this court. Counsel's avowal that Ms. Gregston's duties are limited to typing and taking phone messages is not sufficient to remove her from involvement in the case in a manner that would significantly decrease the likelihood of a prohibited disclosure, even inadvertently. *See, e.g.,* Maryland State Bar Ethics Op. 90-17 (secretary whose duties are "limited to typing" must be screened from information about or participation in matters involving clients of her former employer); *see also LaSalle Nat'l Bank v. County of Lake,* 703 F.2d 252 (7th Cir. 1983) (promise not to discuss case was inadequate screening). Furthermore, we observe that counsel's refusal, after a strong suggestion by the trial court to withdraw, to even offer to screen this employee from working on the very matter which gave rise to the problem shows an apparent insensitivity by counsel to the valid concerns of the adverse client that confidences may be disclosed by the nonlawyer who had such a significant involvement on the other side of the case for over two years. [FN omitted] Such conduct by counsel is insufficient to protect the "reputation of the bar as a whole." *Id.* at 259.

Under the facts of this case, we conclude that the trial court should have granted the motion to disqualify plaintiffs' counsel, and abused its discretion in failing to do so. No screening mechanism was utilized to assure Smart that its confidences were preserved, and, at this stage of the litigation, given Ms. Gregston's participation on behalf of the St. Germaines, we cannot fashion any remedial action that counsel could employ to mitigate Smart's perception that its confidences could be compromised, or to satisfy the duties imposed by ER 5.3.

CONCLUSION

For the foregoing reasons, we hold that the trial court abused its discretion in denying Smart's motion to disqualify. We remand this matter to the trial court for entry of an order consistent with this opinion. [FN omitted]

Source: Reprinted with permission from ThomsonWest.

Chapter 6

Fees and Client Property

CHAPTER OBJECTIVES

The student will be able to:

- Evaluate the reasonableness of attorney's fees using the appropriate factors
- Determine whether paralegal fees could be part of an award of fees
- Recognize improper fee-sharing or fee-splitting arrangements and how they apply to employed paralegals
- Discuss the attorney's (and paralegal's) duty to ensure that a client's property is kept securely

This chapter will examine particular issues that affect the attorney-client relationship at its core. HOW MUCH can an attorney reasonable charge for her services? WHEN can she charge the client for legal services performed by the paralegal? WHAT should the law firm do with clients' money and property when it is under the firm's control?

There are few issues that affect the very essence of attorney-client relationships more than money. As the parties consider entering into the agreement, they need to understand not only their individual roles as either the attorney or the client, but also the details relating to the duties and disclosures required from the attorney to assist the client in obtaining the larger goal of representation. These can be discussed in a chronological manner. First, the attorney must set a reasonable fee for her services in order for the client to determine whether or not to enter into the relationship, by weighing the cost with the expected benefit in going forward. Second, the attorney must determine whether the paralegal's tasks will be billable and/or recoverable. Third, there must be strict control over what an attorney does with the fees, monies, and property of the client. Along with the duty of confidentiality (keeping a client's secrets safe), an attorney must also be able to safely keep a client's property. This means that she must have places and procedures already set up before taking on the matter that will require them.

ESTABLISHING FEES

Perhaps one of the most notorious issues surrounding attorneys is the cost of legal services. Indeed, the development of the paralegal profession was a direct response to this issue. While ABA Model Rule 1.5 speaks at length regarding fees, there is no restriction on the amount of fee, as long as it is "reasonable." The issue of fees is not new.

Justice should be administered economically, efficiently, and expeditiously. The attorney's fee is, therefore, a very important factor in the administration of justice, and if it is not determined with proper relation to that fact it results in a species of social malpractice that undermines the confidence of the public in the bench and bar. It does more than that; it brings the court into disrepute and destroys its power to perform adequately the function of its creation.

Baruch v. Giblin, 122 Fla. 59, 164 So. 831 (1936).

The retainer agreement that creates the service contract between the attorney and client varies widely. At its core, it establishes the work to be performed and the fees to be paid. A sample is provided in Figure 6.1. However, there is great diversity in forms; this is illustrated well in the Table of Contents of *Legal Representation and Fee Agreements for the Maryland Lawyer: Forms and Comments,* by Christopher L. Beard, Esq., and Richard C. Goodwin, Esq. (available through the Maryland Institute for Continuing Professional Education for Lawyers, Inc. which can be accessed at: http://www.micpel.edu). (See Figure 6.2.)

Billing

An unavoidable element to the practice of law is the **timesheet** (see Figure 6.3). Attorneys and paralegals watch the clock all day, recording how much time it takes to complete each and every task of the day and to what client it is attributable. Very often there are "work codes" or abbreviations used for tasks that are performed often. Examples are "TC" for telephone call, "DR" for draft, "RR" for receipt and review of correspondence, "LR" for legal research, and so on. Whether that amount of time is actually billed to the client is another matter; this is referred to as the **billable hour**. Supervising attorneys have the discretion to reduce the bill to compensate for inexperience or other factors. For example, the new associate is assigned a relatively complex complaint to draft, not having had much drafting experience. Hoping to impress the partner, the associate spends ten hours on the complaint. At $100 an hour, the actual timesheet reflects $1,000 due for that work; however, the supervising attorney knows that this is not a reasonable amount of time for an average associate to spend on the matter. She, therefore, reduces the amount to five hours on the client's bill, reflecting the real value of the service rendered to the client. The new associate is not in any trouble for this "loss" in billables, as the other five hours are considered part of the learning curve, a known and anticipated "expense" of training a new lawyer or paralegal. The importance of accurate time records cannot be overemphasized. An attorney may lose money that may have been properly earned, but is reduced through a court's intervention as "unreasonable." Essentially, the court is not finding that the time spent or hourly fee is necessarily unreasonable, but that not having accurate time records is unreasonable and is punishable by that reduction. *See In re Trust of McDonald,* 858 S.W.2d 271, 279 (Mo. App. 1993). (The attorney billed $30,000 in fees representing "over 400 hours"; however, he did not keep very good time records. The court found the fee was excessive in the absence of adequate evidence of having spent that time.)

While sloppy or absent time records may result in a reduction of the attorney's fee, inaccurate timesheets result in severe disciplinary action. Padding timesheets and **double-billing** are absolutely unacceptable in the legal profession. Both these practices involve fraud and dishonesty, which are prohibited under the ethical rules and impinge the integrity of the profession itself. Padding time refers to adding extra minutes or hours that were not spent onto those that were spent. As with any ethical violation, the claim that no actual harm occurred is not a valid defense. Even if the supervising attorney reduces the amount of time billed to accurately reflect the actual time spent, or the time doesn't get billed to the client at all as in a contingent fee case, the act of padding is its own violation. Junior associates may feel the pressure to bill as many hours as humanly possible and may even fear for their jobs; however, this does not

timesheet
An accurate, daily record of time spent on each task performed by an attorney or paralegal for each client.

billable hour
Time (totaling one hour) spent on a client's matter for which the client is responsible to pay, as the attorney's effort relates to and benefits the client's matter.

double-billing
Charging two or more clients for the same services and/or same time period.

FIGURE 6.1

Sample Retainer Agreement

Source: 5 FEDERAL PROCEDURAL FORMS § 10:385. Chapter 10. Civil Rights. VII. Attorney's Fees. B. Procedural Forms. Reprinted with permission from Thomson West.

§ 10:385. Retainer agreement–Between client and attorney

Form of Retainer Agreement

1. [Name of client] hereby agrees to retain [name of attorney] as [his/her] attorney to represent [him/her] with respect to all claims against [name of defendant] or any other person (including a corporation or governmental body) arising out of incidents occurring on or about [list of dates of incidents], in which [name of client] was subjected to discriminatory treatment in [specification of nature of discrimination] because of [his/her] [race/color/creed/sex/marital status/national origin].

2. Client hereby authorizes the attorney to retain, associate, join, or dismiss additional attorneys on client's behalf as the attorney deems necessary. Client further authorizes the attorney or other attorney(s) designated by the attorney to conduct any negotiations on client's behalf, and, as the attorney deems necessary, to commence any litigation or other proceedings, including actions in any appropriate forum.

3. It is further understood and agreed that the attorney may employ any qualified person(s) to assist in the preparation of the case to the extent permitted by the law.

4. It is expressly agreed between the attorney and client that the client shall have the obligation to pay a fee from all amounts and other consideration recovered in cash, as well as in kind or otherwise, as a result of a settlement compromise, or judgment, including punitive damages unless an equal or greater attorney fee is awarded by court order or judgment, or by a provision in any settlement agreement reached with any other party expressly providing a sum certain for a reasonable attorney fee.

5. The attorney reserves the right to seek a court award of attorney fees to be paid by the defendant or defendant's attorney and the client agrees to pay the attorney the amount of any such fee actually recovered from the defendant, whether or not this amount exceeds the fee established by reference to paragraph 6, below.

6. The fee shall be determined by applying the following agreed schedule of compensation to any recovery:
   a. [percentage of amount recovered]% on the first $1000 recovered to the attorney;
   b. [percentage of amount recovered]% on the next $19,000 recovered to the attorney;
   c. percentage of amount recovered]% on the next $30,000 recovered to the attorney;
   d. [percentage of amount recovered]% on any amount recovered over $50,000 to the attorney.

   This fee schedule shall apply to any consideration received from the defendant, whether in kind or as a cash recovery or settlement, but shall not preclude the attorney from a greater recovery, if so provided by paragraph 5.

7. It is understood and agreed that the attorney may advance any and all disbursements incurred by the attorney in connection with this representation, including, but not limited to filing and service fees, costs of discovery and investigations, expert witness and subpoena fees, photocopying, printing, and other incidental expenses, etc. The client authorizes the attorney to withhold from any award recovered in connection with this representation, an amount equal to any unreimbursed disbursements or costs, prior to calculating the permissible fee.

8. The permissible fee provided for in the above schedule shall be computed on the net sum recovered after disbursements advanced by the attorney in connection with the institution and prosecution of the claim have first been reimbursed to the attorney by the client.

9. The foregoing fee agreement shall not apply to legal services rendered on any appeal, review proceeding or retrial, and this agreement shall not be deemed to require the attorney to take an appeal.

FIGURE 6.2   **Types of Maryland Attorney Fee Agreements**

Reprinted with permission from *Legal Representation and Fee Agreements for the Maryland Lawyer: Forms and Comments,* by Christopher L. Beard, Esq., and Richard C. Goodwin, Esq. Available through the Maryland Institute for Continuing Professional Education for Lawyers, Inc., which can be accessed at: http://www.micpel.edu/.

MARYLAND ATTORNEY FEE AGREEMENTS

FORMS AND COMMENTS

TABLE OF CONTENTS

Continued

FIGURE 6.2 **Types of Maryland Attorney Fee Agreements** *Continued*

Continued

FIGURE 6.2   **Types of Maryland Attorney Fee Agreements** *Continued*

Continued

FIGURE 6.2 **Types of Maryland Attorney Fee Agreements** *Continued*

FIGURE 6.3

Daily Time Record

TIME CONVERSIONS:

 6 minutes = .1 hour
12 minutes = .2 hour
18 minutes = .3 hour
24 minutes = .4 hour
30 minutes = .5 hour
36 minutes = .6 hour
42 minutes = .7 hour
48 minutes = .8 hour
54 minutes = .9 hour

DATE:

Client	File No.	Task Performed	Supervising Attorney	Time Spent

excuse the padding, even when done with the permission of the supervising attorney. One associate testified that he

[decided] to "pad" my bills in the plaintiff's personal injury contingency fee cases on which I was working by logging time that I did not actually work. I felt this was the most acceptable solution to my dilemma, because (a) bills in plaintiff's personal injury contingency fee cases

are not paid by the client, so there was no real damage done to anyone by a "padded bill," and (b) when my total hours were checked by the partners of the firm, the amount would be high enough to keep my job. While this was not a perfect solution to a tough dilemma, it was the best, in my view, under the circumstances.

In re Lawrence, 884 So.2d 561, 563 (La. 2004) (attorney was suspended for three months).

Double-billing is the practice of charging two clients for the same time period; like being in two places at once, it is humanly impossible to work for two parties at once. In some circumstances this practice can result in charging for more hours than there are in a day! For example, an attorney flying out to a witness deposition may choose to bill Client A, for whom the witness is relevant, for his travel time, OR he may chose to work on another matter entirely, for Client B. Those five hours spent in the plane will be billed to either one of the clients, but not *both*. His timesheets should not show six hours' worth of billing (three to Client A, for the travel, and three to Client B, for the work). Consider what would happen if, after his three-hour deposition, he chose to spend six hours doing research that was relevant to two separate but very similar matters, and billed each client for those six hours. This would result in 25 hours of work in one day! ($5 \times 2 + 3 + 6 \times 2$). This may very well be a hard-working attorney (after all, the real time spent equals 14 hours of billable time), but no one can work 25 hours in a 24-hour day. Some courts have characterized double-billing not only as dishonesty, but also as misappropriation: essentially, stealing from clients. *See Disciplinary Counsel v. Holland,* 106 Ohio St. 3d 372, 835 N.E.2d 361 (2005). (Although the attorney was not ultimately convicted of the charge of grand larceny, he was suspended for one year and was forced to repay the amount he had overcharged.)

Reasonable Fees

Setting of a reasonable fee is "measured" by balancing the following factors. Performing this analysis will not render a mathematically certain rate; it can only really determine whether a fee is truly exorbitant and, therefore, unreasonable. There are many factors to be taken into account when trying to determine whether a fee is reasonable. The first is straightforward: the amount of time and labor required to perform the tasks necessary to representation. Simple tasks cost less than more complicated, time-consuming ones. Aside from being simple or complex, a matter may pose new or unique challenges for the attorney and paralegal that may merit a higher fee. Highly skilled legal professionals can also garner higher fees because the client is paying for that talent. Of course, legal professionals with extensive experience in a particular field or those held in high regard by their peers are also paid for their reputations, as much as for their skill. These are factors that are characteristic of the individual legal professional. There are other factors under the control of the client that may affect the reasonableness of the fee. If the client is highly demanding of exclusive time with the attorney or paralegal and this prevents that professional from working on other matters, the fee may be higher. Additionally,

FIGURE 6.4
Factors to Consider When Establishing Reasonable Fees

The following factors must be considered in determining a reasonable fee:

- Time and labor required to perform the tasks
- Complexity, uniqueness, or novelty of the issues
- Degree of skill of the legal professional
- Reputation and experience of the legal professional
- Preclusion of work on other matters
- Time constraints
- Fees customarily charged in the same area for similar services
- The amount of money and/or risk at stake in the matter
- Whether the fee is contingent

if the client imposes significant time constraints on the attorney, then the fee can be increased. Rush orders always carry a premium. Objective factors are also taken into account when setting a reasonable fee. Attorneys are selling a commodity, and the local market will often determine the range of fees. Most firms or individual attorneys will charge about the same fee for similar legal services. It only makes ordinary business sense to do so. Further, the greater the amount of money at stake, the higher the fee may be to secure it. A multimillion-dollar real estate transaction can be billed out at a higher rate than a modest residential home purchase. Risk is allocated not only to the clients' outcomes but also to how the attorney plans on collecting the fee. Fixed fees based on hourly billing or other reliable and objectively determinable factors carry little risk of loss (aside from client nonpayment). Contingent fees, however, carry the risk that the attorney may not get paid any fees at all if the case is lost. Generally, contingent fees end up being higher than fixed fees, due to this risk taking on the part of the attorney. A basic list of these factors can be found in Figure 6.4.

reasonable fee
A charge for legal services that accurately reflects the time, effort, and expertise spent on a client matter.

A **reasonable fee** is determined by the above factors, and the courts have added several others in reviewing whether an attorney charged a fee that should be fairly recoverable. All of these fee review matters are evaluated on a case-by-case basis, as there is no standardization of attorneys' or paralegals' fees, either nationally or by state. Generally, when speaking of fees, people often simply ask for the hourly rate charged and then multiply it by the anticipated time it will take to complete the tasks at hand. But the base calculation only addresses the first two factors considered above. This is the **lodestar calculation** approach, which only can approximate the amount of fee.

lodestar calculation
A mere guidepost for determining the amount of fee to be charged, by multiplying the time to be spent on the task by the attorney's hourly rate.

It is just a starting point which can guide the rest of the inquiry into whether the fee is reasonable. The elements of novelty and difficulty must also enter into the equation. In this way, an attorney can estimate the amount of time needed to competently prepare for the matter. If time expended were the only measure of reasonableness, attorneys and paralegals would have little incentive to work at their most efficient speed and, ironically, the most experienced legal professionals might receive less compensation for their efforts, because it would take them less time than their novice counterparts.

> The general agreement in all jurisdictions is that the time and labor spent by the attorney in performing services for which compensation is sought is an important factor to be considered in setting a reasonable fee. However, it is also commonly agreed that the time element must be considered in connection with other factors. Fees cannot fairly be awarded on the basis of time alone. The use of time as the sole criterion is of dubious value because economy of time could cease to be a virtue; and inexperience, inefficiency, and incompetence may be rewarded to the detriment of expeditious disposition of litigation.

Oliver's Sports Center, Inc. v. National Standard Ins. Co., 615 P.2d 291 (Okla. 1980).

Factors to Consider

Taking on an entirely new issue of law, one that has never been tested in the courts in the relevant jurisdiction before, or challenging the validity of an existing law takes time as well as courage. Novelty is also rewarded by an increase in attorney's fees.

This will often be tied to the expenditure of a substantial amount of time. See *Rackow v. Illinois Human Rights Comm'n,* 152 Ill. App. 3d 1046, 504 N.E.2d 1344 (1987):

> *Additionally, while . . . counsel did not request it, the administrative law judge applied a multiplier of 1.5 to insure that reasonable attorney fees were awarded, as this was a case of first impression before the Human Rights Commission. He noted that the amount of attorney fees may be large as compared with the relatively small amount of monetary damages, but justified his decision because this was a case of first impression and because the uniqueness of Illinois law under these circumstances required extensive research and analysis.*

Further, spending time on one client's matter may prevent the legal professional from working on matter for another. Despite current emphasis on multitasking, attorneys and paralegals (as well as most other professionals) can and should do only one thing at a time. To reemphasize, working on more than one matter at a time is impermissible "double-billing" under the ethics rules. However, taking one case may not preclude taking another of a similar nature or of a type with which the attorney has a good deal of experience, as these can be dealt with efficiently. Preclusion of other employment depends primarily upon the factors of complexity of the matter and experience of the attorney. On the other hand, some matters may be time intensive and therefore genuinely preclude work on other matters. *See Kittler and Hedelson v. Sheehan Properties, Inc.,* 295 Minn. 232, 203 N.W.2d 835 (1973). In this case, the attorney was required to be absent from his office on extended and frequent international travel in order to properly handle the matter. Also, time limitations imposed by the client or by the circumstances would warrant a higher fee. The shorter the time period in which the legal professional has to operate, the more she must concentrate solely on that matter; the pressure adds an "urgency surcharge."

Attorneys are not immune from the economic principle of supply and demand. The "market" will reach some sort of average range in an area; consumers of the service will not (or should not) bear costs greatly in excess of this range. To determine whether a fee is reasonable, looking at the fee customarily charged in the locality for similar legal services is a good indicator. It is, of course, like all the other factors, not determinative, but merely one point of reference. This factor must be broken down into its elements:

1. How does one arrive at the **customary fee**?
2. What is the relevant locality?
3. What is the degree of similarity between the services?

customary fee
A rate generally charged in a given locality by lawyers of the same level of expertise and area of practice.

First, a court's evaluation of the "customary fee" begins with testimony from attorneys regarding the fees charged by them and their colleagues. Of course, as in any dispute, opinions will be offered on both the high and low sides of the issue. The court can then make some average calculation based upon this testimony. However, the average fees will depend largely on the second factor, the locality. In *Eve's Garden, Inc. v. Upshaw & Upshaw, Inc.,* 801 So.2d 976 (Fla. App. 2001), the attorneys testifying as to the customary fee in the locality used the judicial circuit as the defining jurisdiction. The appellate court did not agree with the trial judge, who noted that the circuit included metropolitan areas in which attorneys often charged higher rates similar to the amount requested by the plaintiffs. The locality in this instance was a rural community and attorneys charged significantly less than attorneys in the metropolitan areas of the circuit. The locality must be sufficiently similar in nature and proximity to the place in which the action is brought. If there are no attorneys in that locality that practice a particular kind of law due to its uniqueness or complexity, then a court may look outward to the prevailing rates where that special attorney normally practices. *See Standard Theatres, Inc. v. State Dept. of Transp., Div. of Highways,* 118 Wis.2d 730, 349 N.W.2d 661 (1984). The next factor really refers to comparing "apples to apples." Not only the locality, but also the nature of the matter must be sufficiently similar. This analysis may include the number of parties, amount in controversy, difficulty of obtaining evidence, witness preparation, amount of documentation needed (either reviewed or prepared), and a host of other factors, in addition to the relevant area of law.

The amount of money at stake or the value placed on the results by the client also plays a part in determining whether the fee is reasonable. Fee agreements can reflect the understanding that the higher the stakes are, the higher the fee is. In some cases, an attorney can be awarded over and above the contingency fee agreement by using a "multiplier" to compensate the attorney for the results obtained for his client. A trial court may determine whether a multiplier is necessary by considering the following factors:

> *(1) whether the relevant market requires a contingency fee multiplier to obtain competent counsel; (2) whether the attorney was able to mitigate the risk of nonpayment in any way; and (3) whether any of the factors set forth in Rowe are applicable, especially, the amount involved, the results obtained, and the type of fee arrangement between the attorney and his client. Evidence of these factors must be presented to justify the utilization of a multiplier.*

Alvarado v. Cassarino, 706 So.2d 380, 381 (Fla. App. 1998).

These factors are weighed with the likelihood of success as seen from the outset of the matter. The riskier the venture, the more apt the court is to employ a multiplier anywhere from 1.5 to 2.5. In the Alvarado case, the trial court applied a contingency risk multiplier of 1.5 to the attorney's fee of $57,570, which resulted in a total recovery by the attorney of $86,355 for his work.

Contrary to this multiplication of the fee for hard, risky work is the court's ability to reduce the recoverable contingent fee because it is not reasonable in the circumstances. In *People v. Egbune,* 58 P.3d 1168, 1173–1174 (Colo. 1999), the attorney and client entered into a 35 percent contingent fee agreement. The matter settled quickly for $17,500 and the attorney collected a fee of $6,122. While this seems mathematically reasonable, the surrounding circumstances rendered it unreasonable. The attorney worked for only three weeks and "did no more than make a few phone calls to the insurance adjuster, meet with his client, examine some medical treatment records and do some research at the law library to determine the reasonable range of settlement for [these types of] claims." The attorney's work did very little to enhance the client's claim, and therefore he was not entitled to such a large share of it.

Attorneys are essentially skilled craftsmen; you pay not only for the time spent on a project but also for the talent of the particular "artist." Delicate or complicated matters may take more finesse rather than more time, and the attorney should be compensated for this effort. This is where the "lodestar" approach fails; adeptness should be ultimately rewarded. One court eloquently stated it this way:

> *The evidence before me bearing upon an attorney's fee is as follows. This is a private anti-trust suit which was not preceded by a public or even another private suit in the same industry. Plaintiff's chief counsel, James D. Saint Clair, Esq., in his thoroughness of preparation, economy of effort, choice of emphasis, quality of examination and cross-examination, presentation of argument, analysis of the law, courtesy to parties, witnesses, opposing counsel, and the Court, and that indefinable distinction with breathes excellence, can stand comparison with any lawyer who has appeared before me in the last dozen years. The success that he achieved, while founded on the merit of plaintiff's case, was by no means inevitable. In hands less gifted and with a lawyer less persuasive to a jury, plaintiff's cause might well have gone a-gley. Here as in earlier cases, plaintiff's counsel has shown that despite his relative youth and his short career at the bar, he is quite capable of holding his own against the most experienced advocates of our profession. With becoming deference to his seniors, but with unflinching courage in examining witnesses, in meeting opposing arguments, and in resisting what he regarded as unsound rulings from the bench, plaintiff's counsel set a model not likely to be surpassed . . . Sometimes the figure may seem high. But so far as price is determined by unique excellence and by social*

IN CLASS DISCUSSION

The real-life drama surrounding Anna Nicole Smith did not get laid to rest at her funeral in February of 2007. The paternity suit filed (and won) by Larry Birkhead resulted in exorbitant legal fees nearing one million dollars. His attorney Debra Opri filed a lawsuit for unpaid legal bills and Mr. Birkhead countersued, claiming Attorney Opri had agreed to represent Mr. Birkhead for free because the publicity would benefit her career. Mr. Birkhead's lawsuit accuses Attorney Opri of charging Mr. Birkhead not only for costs directly associated with his representation but also for her travel expenses, dinners with friends, and entertainment expenses. While Mr. Birkhead is capable of making the payments demanded by Attorney Opri, he maintains that the fee agreement states that he would not be charged for her services. Who do you think is at fault in this situation? What could have been done to avoid the fee disagreement? Is the purported fee arrangement fair? Should this type of arrangement be allowed in celebrity or high-profile cases? Why or why not?

> *usefulness, the advocate is especially worthy of large recompense. . . . Unless excellence in the trial lawyer is properly recompensed, the best men will not spend their time in court, and thus there will dry up the most essential sources of an independent bar.*

Cape Cod Food Products v. National Cranberry Ass'n, 119 F.Supp. 242, 242–243 (D.C.Mass. 1954).

Experience and reputation also garner significant premiums. Usually an attorney with both of these can efficiently handle a certain matter better than another without them. Specialists and boutique firms fall into this category. A *"certified"* specialist, an attorney that has proven her ability to the bar association, may certainly reasonably demand a higher fee.

Last in our discussion is the nature and length of the professional relationship with the client, which factors into the "reasonableness" equation.

> *Under appropriate circumstances, an attorney who is the attorney for a client who has frequent and continuing legal problems may make appropriate adjustment of the amount of the fee charged. What would be a reasonable fee to such a client may not be the same as for a client who sees the lawyer for the first time.*

Peebles v. Miley, 439 So.2d 137, 143 (Ala. 1983).

It may be that the attorney is rewarding client loyalty and/or that the attorney is better able to use efficiencies of scale when dealing with the same client over and over. The background information remains the same, the risk of nonpayment is probably not present (attorneys are not apt to agree to represent a client in a new matter when there are significant outstanding bills), the possibility exists of reusing work product and general familiarity with the issues; all of these factors weigh in favor of a previous client "discount." On the other hand, an attorney may know what is in store for him if he does take on another matter for this client and therefore, being warned of the difficulties that might be encountered yet again, may choose to adjust the fee upward to compensate for the reasonably anticipated hardships in taking on another matter for this client.

certified attorney
An attorney who has been acknowledged to have specialized and demonstrated knowledge in a particular area of law by a bar-recognized legal association.

PARALEGAL FEES

The range of reasonableness is extraordinarily large in determining an attorney's fee. Practically speaking, a better measure is to establish that the fee is not unconscionable and then justify its sum by balancing the above factors. The same approach is taken in determining a paralegal's fee to be awarded in a case. This is not to say that paralegals are directly compensated or earn individual fees payable to them, but rather

FIGURE 6.5

Sample Calculation for Services

Employee	Billable Hours	Rate	Total
Senior Attorney	1,000	$250	$ 250,000
Junior Associate	1,200	$150	$ 180,000
Paralegal	1,500	$100	$ 150,000
Total Compensation =			$ 580,000

that, if an attorney is awarded fees by a court, the attorney may properly include billable hours performed by a paralegal in the total submission for compensation. For an example of this type of submission, see Figure 6.5.

The bill for the paralegal services should be at the prevailing market rate for paralegals in that jurisdiction, not at the cost of the services to the attorney. In other words, even if the paralegal is paid $25 per hour, the attorney can bill at the prevailing rate, which can be significantly higher, as in Figure 6.5. Paralegals' work is part of the "attorney work product" for which the office collects its fee. The United States Supreme Court validated this approach in *Missouri v. Jenkins,* 491 U.S. 274, 109 S.Ct. 2463, 105 L.Ed.2d 22 (1989). The plaintiff, Jenkins, brought a suit against the State of Missouri under a civil rights statute that also permitted the award of attorney's fees. The state argued that the paralegal fees should be calculated at their actual cost to the attorney to prevent a "windfall" to the firm. The Court rejected this argument. "By encouraging the use of lower cost paralegals rather than attorneys wherever possible, permitting market-rate billing of paralegal hours encourages cost-effective delivery of legal services and, by reducing the spiraling cost of civil rights litigation, furthers the policies underlying civil rights statutes." *Id.* at 288.

> The award of paralegal fees is not limited to civil rights proceedings. In any case where a statute or other legal authority permits the prevailing party to recover attorney's fees and costs against the opposition, paralegal fees may be included. This award of fees is contrary to the traditional "American Rule," where each party is responsible for his own attorney's fees. The requirement for submitting expenses to the court for an award is reasonableness, proper justification, and detail in calculating that fee. The Supreme Court of Rhode Island stated it simply: Our legal community, like the majority of jurisdictions in the United States, separately lists the paralegal services that are compensable. Therefore, the trial justice may use his discretion in determining whether the proffered fees are reasonable and whether the paralegal work performed was a necessary element in the proceeding.

Schroff, Inc. v. Taylor-Peterson, 732 A.2d 719, 721 (R.I. 1999) (emphasis added).

It is important to note that the purpose of the billed paralegal work must be sufficiently specified so that the court can make a determination that the paralegal work was a necessary element in preparing the matter. If the type of work is not described adequately, the court can deny reimbursement for those paralegal fees. This, of course, brings the paralegal back to her duty to accurately record her time and work in the daily timesheet.

Applauding paralegals' skills at keeping these necessary records, the court in *Role Models America, Inc. v. Brownlee,* 353 F.3d 962, 974 (Ct. App. D.C. 2004), found that the only properly kept time records were those kept by the paralegals, and therefore all of their fees were recoverable.

> Here, by contrast, the legal assistants' time records, unlike the attorneys' and the law clerk's, provide adequate detail and show that these employees performed suitable tasks. We will therefore award reimbursement for the full number of hours requested for the legal assistants' time, with the exception of the two hours that a legal assistant spent visiting this court to pick up a brief and the time that a legal assistant spent on three separate occasions filing a brief.

RESEARCH THIS

Find the local prevailing rates for paralegal time in your locality. You can look online for paralegal salary surveys or career information sites, con- tact recruiters, or do it the old-fashioned way and interview employers.

FEE ARRANGEMENTS

While all of these factors have weight in determining what a reasonable fee is, and that may be a subject of much debate, there is very little debate over the requirement of clear communication to the client. The ideal is to memorialize the agreement in writing so that all possible future questions will have a baseline to refer to. This fee agreement is the first manifestation of the fiduciary relationship between the parties. The attorney is bound not to procure the agreement by misrepresentation or to "overreach" for the highest fee possible in the matter. The writing protects both parties. Courts will not generally disturb the fee arrangement as agreed to by the parties without evidence of fraud or overreaching by counsel. *Jacobs v. Holston*, 434 N.E.2d 738 (Ohio App. 1980).

> *In order to prove such good faith and fairness, an attorney seeking to enforce a contract for attorney's fees must show:*
> *(1) the client fully understood the contract's meaning and effect,*
> *(2) the attorney and client shared the same understanding of the contract, and*
> *(3) the terms of the contract are just and reasonable.*

Alexander v. Inman, 974 S.W.2d 689, 694 (Tenn. 1998).

It is important to note that it is not just the attorney's fees that must be spelled out in detail. If a paralegal will be working on the matter, that fee must be agreed upon as well. Any costs that will be passed on to the client, such as copying, phone charges, mailing, travel expenses, and other necessary payments made on the client's behalf, must be included in the fee agreement. Simply stated, the client should not be surprised at the charges included on the bill; he may be upset about the amount, but he shouldn't be taken by total surprise.

The ABA Model Rules address in a separate section the validity of **contingency fees**. Because these fees may result in enormous sums of money, far more than the attorney would recover under the "normal" hourly billing method, the rules specifically state that they must be in writing. This writing must be as specific as possible in setting forth how the fee shall be calculated and whether costs are included or

contingency fees
The attorney's fee calculated as a percentage of the final award in a civil case.

SPOT THE ISSUE

Carrie has worked as a paralegal for a construction law boutique firm for a while and, with her help, the firm was recently successful in challenging a state's public bidding process for a local construction project. It was a long and arduous task. The relevant statute pertaining to these kinds of suits permits the challenging/prevailing party to recover costs associated with the suit. The lead attorney has requested $100,000. The trial court denied this amount and significantly reduced the fees to $12,000. The court also denied the fees billed by the paralegal on this matter, as it considered those costs to be part of "overhead" in running the practice. Apparently, the trial court decided that the attorney should have spent only 120 hours on the matter and should be billing $100 per hour for his services. Is the court correct? Why or why not? What factors should the court have taken into consideration? Make an argument using the factors discussed above to receive the full amount requested: $100,000.

CYBER TRIP

The ABA Law Practice Management Section has many articles on the fine art of finances. Here are two of these, relevant to all members of the legal office:

Margaret Spencer Dixon and Debbie Foster, *Capturing More Time . . . And Keeping Your Clients Happy While Doing It,*

http://www.abanet.org/lpm/lpt/articles/bot03071.shtml

Harry Styron, *The Art of Time Entries,*

http://www.abanet.org/lpm/lpt/articles/fin08061.shtml.

The various paralegal associations deal with this issue as well. For Laurel Bielec's article *How to Put More Bite In Your Buck,* visit this site:

http://backup paralegals.org/Reporter/Fall97/bite.htm

excluded in that amount. Additionally, many cases terminate before they are fully tried in court. Therefore, the attorney must stipulate how a fee will be calculated if the matter settles without a trial. The rules of ethics put great emphasis in contingent fee cases on the specificity of the required writings and accountings.

Contingent fees essentially give the attorney a stake in the outcome of the case. The larger the settlement or judgment amount, the larger the fee collected. This incentive for more, more, more is ethically prohibited in cases involving some domestic relations or in any criminal matter. A contingent fee in a domestic relations matter is not per se invalid, whereas any contingency fee in any criminal matter is prohibited. A contingency based upon obtaining the divorce itself or upon the amount of the settlement is prohibited. For example, it is impermissible to charge a contingency fee based upon the amount of alimony received in the divorce or based upon the amount received in the division of property. Contingency fees in other kinds of domestic relations matters are subject to strict scrutiny to evaluate whether they are proper in the circumstances.

> *As a general rule, contingent fee agreements are begrudgingly permitted in domestic relations cases. Because public policy favors marriage and discourages attorneys from promoting bitter divorce battles for financial gain, contingent fees are subjected to enhanced scrutiny and rarely are found to be justified. As a matter of fact, so unsavory are contingent fees in domestic relations cases that a higher quantum of proof is necessary to enforce a contingent fee.*

Alexander at 693.

Generally speaking for domestic relations matters and definitively speaking for defending criminal cases, contingent fees are to be avoided.

FEE SPLITTING/SHARING

On some level all lawyers in a law office share their fees with all the other employees; they are the sole source of office income. There is nothing wrong with this. The fees from individual clients are pooled into the general operating account and from there they lose their individuality. From this general account, salaries and other expenses are disbursed. The prohibition on fee splitting and fee sharing arises where particular, identifiable client proceeds are disbursed to another individual in payment for work performed on that matter. This can come in the form of splitting the particular client's fee with lawyers outside the firm or sharing the fee with non-attorneys inside or outside the firm. This is not to say that paralegal time spent on a matter cannot be billed out and collected in a particular matter. Paralegal fees are considered part of recoverable attorney's fees; it is simply that these fees must not be directly paid to the paralegal out of the individual recovery.

Attorneys can and sometimes should consult with professional colleagues who are not members of their own firm. Perhaps an attorney has come across an issue that cannot be readily and effectively handled within her own firm. Her best option is to consult an attorney who specializes or has expertise in the area she is struggling with. However, the attorney may not seek this assistance without the consent of her client. To do so would be to essentially delegate some work and responsibility without the client's knowing that the matter was being handled in some way by an attorney with whom she did not contract. If the client does consent to the services to be supplied by the other attorney and the proportion of work to be performed by him, the other requirements are:

1. The proportion of work and the proportion of fee are relatively equal. An attorney doing 30 percent of the work should receive roughly 30 percent of the total fee.

2. The attorneys assume joint responsibility for the representation. An attorney cannot contribute to the total "product" without also bearing some blame if it all goes

REEL TO REAL

Both *Regarding Henry* (1991, starring Harrison Ford) and *The Firm* (1993, starring Tom Cruise) deal with attorney's fees indirectly, as both films expose the perils of becoming a slave to wealth. How do these attorneys deal with the pressure to bill for their services? Do you think this accurately reflects the practice of law? In what way? Can you think of a way to cut down on this kind of pressure? How would you have reacted in these situations?

wrong. The contributing attorney becomes a fiduciary of the client as well. It is as if the attorneys have formed a partnership for the purposes of this client.

3. The fee-sharing agreement must be in writing.

4. The total fee is reasonable.

Of course, the attorney who is consulted must still be in good standing. An attorney who hired a suspended attorney to work as a paralegal in the office was himself suspended for three months (reduced from the original recommendation of an 18-month suspension) for sharing legal fees with the suspended attorney who had worked on particular matters. *Attorney Grievance Comm'n of Maryland v. Brennan,* 350 Md. 489, 714 A.2d 157 (1998).

This arrangement is entirely prohibited in the circumstance where a paralegal has worked for the attorney. Paralegals, no matter how much or how well they perform in a case, cannot be allocated a percentage of the recovery based upon the percentage of work done, even where the client consents. This prohibition extends to paralegal contract agencies as well. The court in *In re Watley,* 802 So.2d 593 (La. 2001), determined that the paralegal agency, "We the People," could not collect a percentage of the attorney's fees earned on personal injury cases on which the contract paralegals worked. The payments made into this "paralegal pool" were impermissible under the relevant ethics rules; the agency was still a non-lawyer. The attorney's actions were not shown to have caused direct harm to the represented clients; there were no underlying malpractice actions. The court found that the fee-sharing arrangement had the potential to harm clients. The harm came from the paralegals' and agency's financial interest in the attorney's fees. This financial stake in the outcome of the case could cause the agency or the paralegals to interfere with the attorney's independent legal judgment. *Id.* at 597. Further, attempts to disguise a fee-sharing arrangement as an hourly wage will be closely examined, as they were in *State Bar of Texas v. Faubion,* 821 S.W.2d 203. The independent paralegal/investigator was paid a percentage of the fee recovered in the case based on his "involvement" in the matter. The wage was not actually based upon the number of hours worked, but was calculated as a percentage of the recovery. The paralegal was paid in the form of a salary out of the firm's operating account on regular paydays. This was where the acceptability ended. The amount of his paycheck was in the range of 20 to 33 percent of the fee received in a particular case, depending on the paralegal's time and involvement in the case. Essentially, once payment to the paralegal is tied to a particular case, it crosses the line into unethical fee sharing.

SAFEKEEPING OF PROPERTY

Clients should feel safe in trusting their attorneys to keep not only their interests but also their property (including money) safe. Perhaps the mantra of all attorneys is, or should be, this: Do not mix clients' property with your own. This is the ethical mandate that, when broken, garners the most severe penalties. This is most easily done with personal or real property that is not money. If a client needs the attorney to hold onto some pieces of an estate she is administering, safe deposit boxes at the local bank can be easily secured for the client's benefit, and that is the most reasonable place to safely keep such items. Where attorneys find themselves getting into trouble is in the handling of money. The best practice is absolutely scrupulous accounting and meticulous separation of client funds from attorney funds. Mixing of these two kinds of accounts is impermissible; the mere **commingling** of the funds, even if they are all there or it is a small amount, is an ethical violation.

commingling
A term for mixing a client's funds with the attorney's personal funds without permission; an ethical violation.

Often, attorneys are in possession of client funds that are intended to cover future legal fees incurred on the matter. Retainer fees may be either characterized as a non-refundable payment to engage the attorney or as a prepayment sum to be drawn upon as fees are earned. In the first case, the money was intended to go straight to the attorney's working account. The client has relinquished any interest in that money that is nonrefundable; by accepting the client, the attorney has earned it. On the other hand, client money deposited with the attorney that is intended to be drawn on as the attorney bills for services is still the client's money until it is earned; the attorney must not put any unearned portion in his working account.

Money must be identified as to its source, where it is going, and why; it must be placed in the appropriate account and be used only for its intended purpose. Promptness and accurate record keeping are essential. In the real world in personal accounts, people juggle money from account to account to cover withdrawals and payments, eventually coming out even in the end. It is a rare person who hasn't taken a little out of savings to cover a bill or two in a tight month, or failed to balance the checkbook to the penny every month. However, this is unacceptable practice in a law firm, even without improper motive. Mere sloppiness, the resulting inaccuracies, failure to keep records, and other poor accounting practices can result in severe sanctions. This may be true even when the attorney had the interests of his clients in mind when he made certain improper disbursements, for example, postdating a check or giving more money in settlement than originally agreed on. The absence of dishonest intent is only a mitigating factor in the decision to sanction the attorney for these accounting failures. The fact remains that the violations of the ethical rule to the safekeeping of property were committed. *See Attorney Grievance Comm'n of Maryland v. Mba-Jonas,* 2007 WL 816836 (Md. 2007). To keep track of the office procedures involving these issues, see Figure 6.6.

misappropriation
The unlawful and unethical taking of a client's property for the lawyer's own use, regardless of intent or duration of time the property is kept.

On the opposite side of the spectrum is the knowing **misappropriation** of client funds. Anytime an attorney takes money that should properly be left in a client trust account and uses it for her own purposes she is guilty of misappropriation.

An attorney not only must leave money in the client trust account until it is properly earned and disbursed, but is under an ethical duty to notify the client that the office has received those funds for the client. Further, the disbursement to the client of the monies or property received must be promptly made and an accounting, if requested, be supplied. Significant delay in delivery of the client's money or property is misappropriation as well.

It does not matter for what reason the attorney improperly kept or took the funds: to cover payroll or other office expenses, to pay a court fee on another matter, to take a vacation. All of these reasons are improper, because misappropriation is not related to what the money was intended for; the attorney doesn't have to have a devious plan. Further, it doesn't matter whether the attorney intended only to "borrow" the money and meant to pay the money back, or even that he indeed did pay it back; the money was used for a purpose for which it was not intended. "Intentional misappropriation of a client's funds is always indefensible; it strikes at the very foundation of the trust and honesty that are indispensable to the functioning of the attorney-client relationship

	Yes	No
All expenses of representation are posted to the clients' files on a regular basis (filing fees, travel, other outsourcing).		
Outsourced services' and vendors' prices and invoices are reviewed for accuracy and posted to the proper account.		
All internal costs are posted to the clients' files on a regular basis (postage, long-distance calls, other office overhead attributable to one particular client).		
All entries are reviewed for completeness and accuracy.		
All bills to clients are reviewed and approved by the supervising attorney prior to posting.		
All bills are sent to clients at the same time each month or on other regular schedule.		
All payments are recorded regularly to the clients' files.		
All accounts receivable are updated and followed up on a regular basis.		
All client trust funds are kept in a proper Attorney Trust Account separate from operating funds and accounts.		
All client trust accounts are reviewed for accuracy and updated regularly.		

FIGURE 6.6
Billing and Expense Checklist

and, indeed, to the functioning of the legal profession itself." *In re Discipline of Babilis,* 951 P.2d 207, 217 (Utah 1997).

> *Respondent's restitution of the funds prior to notification of the random audit of his records indicates that he did intend only to "borrow" funds in the sense that he planned to use the funds for his own purposes only temporarily before restoring them. Nevertheless, restitution does not alter the character of knowing misappropriation and misuse of clients' funds.*
>
> *Intent to deprive permanently a client of [his or her] funds . . . is not an element of knowing misappropriation. Nor is the intent to repay funds or otherwise make restitution a defense to the charge of knowing misappropriation. A lawyer who uses funds, knowing that the funds belong to a client and that the client has not given permission to invade them, is guilty of knowing misappropriation. . . . It makes no difference whether the money is used for a good purpose or a bad purpose, for the benefit of the lawyer or for the benefit of others, or whether the lawyer intended to return the money when he took it, or whether in fact he ultimately did reimburse the client; nor does it matter that the pressures on the lawyer to take the money were great or minimal. The essence of Wilson is that the relative moral quality of the act, measured by these many circumstances that may surround both it and the attorney's state of mind, is irrelevant: it is the mere act of taking your client's money knowing that you have no authority to do so that requires disbarment.*

Matter of Blumenstyk, 152 N.J. 158, 162–163, 704 A.2d 1, 3–4 (N.J. 1997).

In every relationship, including that between attorney and client, parties will fight over money. Where there is a dispute over who has the right to certain property, it is the attorney's job to keep that property (including controverted fees) in the client trust account until the court (or other resolution) decides how the property is to be dispersed.

When the controversy is over fees, the attorney can dispense only those funds that are not in dispute. For example, if the client's matter settled for $100,000 and the fee arrangement provides for a 25 percent contingent fee, it may appear at first blush to the client that the attorney should send a check for $75,000 from his client trust account and transfer $25,000 to her own business account. However, the attorney claims that the fee arrangement provides that the costs associated with the prosecution of the claim come off the top first, and then the disbursements are made, according to the contingent fee arrangement. If the costs totaled $10,000, then the client would be entitled to $67,500 and the attorney to $22,500. Under the ethics rules, the unquestioned amounts should be disbursed and the disputed amount ($10,000) should remain in the client's trust account until the matter is settled.

The safekeeping of property rules are really very simple to understand; however, they tend to get attorneys in the most trouble. There is a clear-cut, bright-line mandate: never, never move a client's property unless and until the party is clearly entitled to it without dispute. Further, all property must be accounted for to the last penny and identifiable as to where it came from, for what purpose it was handed into the attorney's hands, which party is entitled to it, and why that party is entitled to it.

Summary

The provisions discussed in this chapter have one thing in common: they all underscore the importance of trust and respect in the way in which attorneys handle their clients. Attorneys must not gouge their clients with exorbitant fees, and must handle client property with scrupulous care.

Key Terms and Concepts

Billable hour	Double-billing
Certified attorney	Lodestar calculation
Commingling	Misappropriation
Contingency fees	Reasonable fee
Customary fee	Timesheet

Review Questions

MULTIPLE CHOICE

Choose the best answer(s) and please explain WHY you choose the answer(s).

1. Timesheets must be filled out
   a. On a daily basis
   b. As soon as after the assignment or meeting is completed
   c. To include both billable and non-billable time
   d. All of the above
2. Double-billing
   a. Is the practice of sending two collection statements to a client per month
   b. Means that the firm will collect twice as much in fees as it originally expected
   c. Is always unethical
   d. Is permitted if the attorney can reuse some work previously completed for another client in the same kind of matter
3. Paralegal fees may be recoverable when
   a. A paralegal has worked over 10 hours on a file
   b. A paralegal has been assigned legal work in a matter
   c. The total amount of fees requested by the attorney is not excessive
   d. The requested amount is a reflection of reasonable time and legal effort spent on the matter

4. Paralegals may be paid
   a. In an amount equal to the percentage of effort they put forth in an individual matter
   b. Bonuses for a good year of work and effort put in on all the cases
   c. Out of the client trust account
   d. By the client directly
5. When fees owed are in dispute, a paralegal
   a. Cannot get paid
   b. Must create a separate client trust account for that disputed amount
   c. Still draws his salary because his money is not tied to an individual case
   d. Must report attorney misappropriation to the ethics board

EXPLAIN YOURSELF

All answers should be written in complete sentences. A simple yes or no is insufficient.

1. Describe an attorney's duty of safekeeping of property. To what kind of property does it attach?
2. What is commingling of funds? Are there any circumstances when it is permitted?
3. When can an attorney split her fee with another professional?
4. What are the factors to be considered in determining whether a paralegal's fee may be recoverable in court?

FAULTY PHRASES

All of the following statements are FALSE; state why they are false and then rewrite them as true statements, without just making a statement negative by adding the word "not."

1. A customary fee is usually determined by what other local law firms charge.
2. All legal matters can use the method of contingency fee billing.
3. A reasonable fee is one that multiplies the number of hours spent on a legal matter by the attorney's hourly wage.
4. An attorney can split a fee with his paralegal for her work performed on the matter.
5. A paralegal sets his own fees in each matter he handles in the law office.
6. All paralegals in the same law office must be billed out at the same rate to every client.

PORTFOLIO ASSIGNMENT

Write Away

Create a table or spreadsheet that will serve as your own timesheet for the next three days. Keep track of every task you perform and how long that takes. The "client" may be yourself, your family, your professors, your boss, etc. The point of this writing assignment is to take a critical look at how you spend your time and decide whether this use is efficient. Once the timesheet has been filled in, review it to determine which tasks should be "billable" and which should not. For example, doing your homework for class is billable work. Your knowledge and skill is being utilized to create "work product." Taking a long shower or watching a movie is not billable time.

2004 WL 253453 (E.D.LA.)
Only the Westlaw citation is currently available.
United States District Court, E.D. Louisiana.
Edith L. STAGNER
v.
WESTERN KENTUCKY NAVIGATION, INC.
No. Civ.A. 02-1418.
Feb. 10, 2004.

[...]

[T]he Court ordered counsel for the defendant to provide the Court with (1) an affidavit attesting to their education, background, skills and experience and (2) sufficient evidence of rates charged in similar cases by other local attorneys with similar experience, skill and reputation no later than January 9, 2004. Defendant's counsel complied and the Court is now ready to rule on the amount of attorney's fees that should be awarded.

[...]

II. ANALYSIS

[...]

The defendant seeks to recover attorney's fees in the amount of $627.50. The defendant contends that Kathy Bilich, paralegal, expended a total of 1 hour on matters regarding the motion to compel at an hourly rate of $60.00. The defendant further contends that Zachary Stump, attorney, expended a total of 2.9 hours drafting and revising the motion to compel at an hourly rate of $110.00, and attorney Danica Benbow spent 1.1 hours in connection with the motion at an hourly rate of $135.00.

[...]

B. Standard

The determination of a reasonable attorney's fee award involves a two-step process. *See Rutherford v. Harris County,* 197 F.3d 173, 192 (5th Cir.1999). The court must first determine the "lodestar" by multiplying the reasonable number of hours expended and the reasonable hourly rate for each participating attorney. *See Hensley,* 461 U.S. at 433. This "lodestar" method serves as the initial estimate of a reasonable attorney's fee. *Blum v. Stenson,* 465 U.S. 886, 888, 104 S.Ct. 1541, 79 L.Ed.2d 891 (1984).

The second step involves the application of twelve factors the Fifth Circuit applies in determining what amount is warranted. *Johnson v. Georgia Highway Express, Inc.,* 488 F.2d 714, 717-719 (5th Cir.1974). These factors are: (1) the time and labor required; (2) the novelty and difficulty of the questions presented; (3) the skill required to perform the legal service properly; (4) the preclusion of other employment by the attorney due to acceptance of the case; (5) the customary fee; (6) whether the fee is fixed or contingent; (7) time limitations imposed by the client or the circumstances; (8) the amount of money involved and the results obtained; (9) the experience, reputation, and ability of the attorneys; (10) the undesirability of the case; (11) the nature and length of the professional relationship with the client; and (12) awards in similar cases.

Once the lodestar is computed by multiplying the reasonable number of hours by a reasonable hourly rate, the court may adjust the lodestar upward or downward depending on its analysis of the twelve factors espoused in Johnson. *See Dodge v. Hunt Petroleum Corp.,* 174 F.Supp.2d 505, 508 (N.D. Tex. 2001). Thus, in light of the Johnson factors, the Court may reduce the award resulting from the lodestar calculation if the documentation of hours worked is inadequate or if the calculation includes hours that were not "reasonably expended." *See Hensley,* 461 U.S. at 433-34.

C. The Lodestar

1. Reasonable Fee

The party seeking attorney's fees has the burden of establishing the reasonableness of the fees by "submitting evidence supporting the hours worked and the rates claimed." *Rode v. Dellarciprete,* 892 F.2d 1177, 1183 (3rd Cir.1990) (citing *Hensley,* 461 U.S. at 433). Thus, counsel for the defendant "must produce satisfactory evidence-in addition to [their] own affidavits-that the requested rates are in line with those prevailing in the community for similar services by lawyers of reasonably comparable skill, experience and reputation." *Blum v. Stenson,* 465 U.S. 886, 896 n. 11, 104 S.Ct. 1541, 79 L.Ed.2d 891 (1984); *Watkins v. Fordice,* 7 F.3d 453, 457 (5th Cir.1993).

The Court must determine the reasonable number of hours expended in the litigation and the reasonable hourly rate for the participating attorneys. *See Louisiana Power & Light Co. v. Kellstrom,* 50 F.3d 319, 324 (5th Cir.1995). The lodestar is then computed by multiplying the number of hours by the reasonable hourly rate. Id.

2. Reasonable Hourly Rate

Attorneys' fees are to be calculated at the prevailing market rates in the relevant community for similar services by attorneys of reasonably comparable skills, experience, and reputation. *Blum v. Stenson,* 465 U.S. 886, 895, 104 S.Ct. 1541, 79 L.Ed.2d 891 (1984). In the instant case, it is uncontested that the relevant community here is the New Orleans, Louisiana legal market.

[...]

Evidence of rates may be adduced through direct or opinion evidence as to what local attorneys charge under similar circumstances. The weight to be given to the opinion evidence is affected by the detail contained in the testimony on matters such as similarity of skill, reputation, experience, similarity of case and client, and breath of the sample of which the expert has knowledge. *Norman,* 836 F.2d at 1299.

a. Zachary Stump

[...]

b. Danica Benbow

[...]

c. Kathy Bilich

Kathy Bilich ("Bilich"), a paralegal with Frilot, Partridge, Kohnke & Clements, L.C., submits that for all of the work she performs on behalf of clients, the firm charges an hourly rate of $60.00. As proof of the reasonableness of the rate, the defendant has only provided the affidavit of Kathy Bilich, the paralegal performing the work.

Bilich states that she graduated high school in 1975, attended Tulane Paralegal School, completing courses for Legal Research and Writing, and she also has a certificate from the University of Colorado for Paralegal Studies. Bilich further states that she has twenty-five years of legal experience.

The defendant has not offered evidence, other than the affidavits, that the rates charged for the services are in line with the prevailing rates charged by attorneys or paralegals of similar experience or education in the community. However, Stagner does not oppose the hourly rates requested by the defendant, the itemization of costs submitted by the defendant, or the hours expended on bringing the motion. Further, as discussed below and based on the Court's own knowledge

i. Attorney rates

[...]

ii. Paralegal rate

It is well established that prevailing parties can recover for fees expended by paralegals working on the file.[10] Kathy Bilich, in her affidavit stated that she was billed at her customary rate of $60.00 per hour. Further, this rate has not been contested by Stagner.

> FN10. The cost of paralegal services are to be included in the assessment and award of attorney's fees if the following criteria are met:
> 1. the services performed must be legal in nature;
> 2. the performance of such services by the paralegal must be supervised by an attorney;
> 3. the qualifications of the paralegal performing the services must be specified in the application or motion requesting an award of fees in order to demonstrate that the paralegal is qualified by virtue of education, training, or work experience to perform substantive work;
> 4. the nature of the services performed by the paralegal must be specified in the application/motion requesting an award of fees in order to permit a determination that the services performed were legal rather than clerical in nature;
> 5. the amount of time expended by the paralegal in performing the services must be reasonable and must be set out in the motion; and
> 6. the amount charged for the time spent by the paralegal must reflect reasonable community standards of remuneration.

See Jones v. Armstrong Cork Co., 630 F.2d 324, 325 n. 1 (5th Cir.1980). See also Fees for Paralegal Services: Are They Recoverable, 461 PLI/Lit 185 (1993); Associated Builders, 919 F.2d at 380.

In Baza v. Chevron Oil Service Co., the Court allowed the paralegals to bill at their customary rates of $50.00 and $60.00 per hour, finding the rates reasonable, within the prevailing market range in New Orleans, and uncontested by opposing counsel. 1996 WL 711506 at *2 (E.D.La. December 10, 1996); see also Jimenez v. Paw-Paw's Camper City, Inc., 2002 WL 257691 at *20 (finding that $60.00 per hour was a reasonable rate for paralegal services). Considering Bilich's education in paralegal studies and her twenty-five years of legal experience, her customary rate of $60.00 per hour is reasonable.

However, in order to recover for paralegal fees, the services rendered by the paralegal must be legal in nature, or work traditionally performed by an attorney. See Armstrong, 630 F.2d 324, 325 n. 1 (5th Cir.1980). Work that is legal in nature includes, for example, "factual investigation, locating and interviewing witnesses, assistance with depositions, interrogatories and document production, compilation of statistical and financial data, checking legal citations and drafting correspondence." Missouri v. Jenkins, 491 U.S. 274, 288, 109 S.Ct. 2463, 105 L.Ed.2d 229 (1989).

The legal activities undertaken by paralegals must be distinguished from other activities that are purely clerical in nature, such as typing, copying, or delivering pleadings. See Lalla v. City of New Orleans, 161 F.Supp.2d 686, 710 (E.D.La.2001). Pure clerical or secretarial work may not be billed at a paralegal rate. Jenkins, Id.

Counsel for the defendant is seeking to recover for one hour of paralegal services for the following: 1.) 0.2 hours for a telephone conference with Dr. Parnell regarding IME; 2.) 0.4 hours for review of the file regarding Stagner's IME and supporting information prepared for motion to compel; 3.) 0.2 hours for telephone conference with Tim Young regarding IME and motion to compel; and 4.) 0.2 hours for telephone conference with Dr. Parnell regarding fees. These time entries reflect work that is legal in nature as opposed to pure secretarial tasks, and counsel for the defendant should be allowed to recover for the services performed by Bilich.

3. Reasonable Number of Hours Expended

*6 The party seeking attorneys' fees must present adequately documented time records to the court. Watkins v. Fordice, 7 F.3d 453, 457 (5th Cir.1993). As a general proposition, all time that is excessive, duplicative or inadequately documented should be excluded from any award of attorney's fees. Raspanti v. United States Dept. of the Army, 2001 WL 1081375, at *6. Attorneys must exercise "billing judgment" by "writing off unproductive, excessive, or redundant hours" when seeking fee awards. Id. (citing Walker v. United States Dep't of Housing & Urban Dev., 99 F.3d 761, 769 (5th Cir.1996). The fee seeker's attorneys are "charged with the burden of showing the reasonableness of the hours they bill and, accordingly, are charged with proving that they exercised billing judgment." Walker, 99 F.3d at 770. When billing judgment is lacking, the court must exclude from the lodestar calculation the hours that were not reasonably expended. Hensley, 461 U.S. at 434.

In reviewing the time sheets submitted by the defendant, seeking to recover fees for a total of five hours expended on the motion to compel, the Court finds that the hours are not excessive, duplicative, or unreasonable.

4. Fees/Costs

Lastly, the defendant seeks to recover attorney fees and costs in the amount of $200.00. This amount is reflective of the cancellation fee charged by Dr. Melvin Parnell for Stagner's failure to appear for the medical exam. […]

The invoice submitted by the defendant indicates that Dr. Parnell charged defendant's counsel $200.00 for Stagner's "no-show office consult", on October 21, 2003.[13] However, these costs cannot be said to have been incurred in bringing the motion to compel. Therefore, the request for reimbursement for the "no-show office consult" is denied.

5. The Johnson Factors

"The lodestar . . . is presumptively reasonable", and should be enhanced or reduced only in exceptional cases. *Watkins v. Fordice,* 7 F.3d 453, 459 (5th Cir.1993) (citing *City of Burlington v. Dague,* 505 U.S. 557, 567, 112 S.Ct. 2638, 120 L.Ed.2d 449 (1992). After carefully reviewing the record, the Court finds that the Lodestar amount is reasonable and finds that no further reduction or enhancement is required. In making this recommendation, the Court has considered and applied the factors articulated in Johnson as required by the Fifth Circuit.

Accordingly,

IT IS ORDERED that the defendant's application for attorney's fees in connection with the previous Motion to Compel Independent Medical Examination (doc. # 29) is GRANTED IN PART and DENIED IN PART as follows:

1.) GRANTED to the extent that the defendant seeks to recover fees for attorney and paralegal time expended in bringing the motion to compel. The defendant is entitled to recover for 1 hour at an hourly rate of $60.00 for paralegal work, 2.9 hours at an hourly rate of $110.00 for work performed by Zachary Stump, and 1.1 hours at an hourly rate of $135.00 for work performed by Danica Benbow, or an amount of $427.50.

2.) DENIED to the extent that the defendant seeks to recover $200.00 for the cancellation fee charged by Dr. Parnell for Stagner's failure to attend the scheduled examination on October 21, 2003.

Source: Reprinted with permission from ThomsonWest.

Chapter 7

Special Clients and Situations

CHAPTER OBJECTIVES

The student will be able to:

- Acknowledge that each client must be individually evaluated for special needs or circumstances

- Differentiate between the organization and the "control group" as a client and recognize the significance of the difference

- Discuss the special considerations involved in dealing with clients with diminished capacity

- Explain the circumstances where an attorney should either decline or terminate representation of the client

This chapter will examine particular issues that affect the attorney-client relationship at its core. WHO is the client when the client is not a real person, but a legal entity such as a corporation? WHY are some clients in need of special care, and WHAT is the attorney's heightened duty toward them? WHEN should an attorney decline or terminate representation of a client?

There are a few special issues that affect the very essence of attorney-client relationships. As both parties consider entering into the agreement, they need to understand not only their individual roles as either the attorney or the client, but also the details relating to the duties and disclosures required from the attorney to assist the client in obtaining the larger goal of representation. Legal professionals must evaluate the client to determine if there are any special considerations relating to that kind of representation. Where the client is actually a business entity, the people who make up that organization must be treated in a manner slightly different from the way the attorney treats a client who is an individual. Similarly, persons who have special needs due to some infirmity should be treated with particular care not necessarily due to other individual clients. Finally, if the attorney feels that taking on the representation is not in either party's best interest or within the attorney's competency, the attorney cannot simply show the client the door. Even absent a formal attorney-client relationship, the attorney still owes certain duties to the declined or terminated client. All of these requirements stem from the same underlying core as the rest of the ethics rules: preservation of the integrity of the legal profession and society's confidence in it.

AN ORGANIZATION AS A CLIENT

A client is traditionally thought of as the person who sits across the desk from the attorney and explains the recent problem plaguing her. However, in many cases, the client is actually not the individual sitting in the chair, but what that individual represents: an organization. These entities are recognized as autonomous legal beings that have collective separate interests from the human beings that run them. ABA Model Rule 1.13 addresses this situation in great detail; neither NALA nor NFPA does so, because both groups defer to the rules of attorney ethics in this matter. The client is the organization, and therefore, the attorney's fiduciary duty is to that organization, not necessarily to its board of directors, president, or shareholders. Of course, the only way for the organization to make its legal needs known to the attorney is through its authorized representatives, those individuals who control the organization and its direction. This group of people is commonly referred to as the "control group."

It is important to remember exactly who the client is and what interests must be protected. The rule of confidentiality attaches to those communications made by the agents of the organization who seek the advice of the attorney and who are acting within their capacity in the organization. Confidentiality is not limited to any one class of persons, like the control group, but rather to the kind of communication made. The United States Supreme Court made this position clear in *Upjohn Co. v. United States,* 449 U.S. 383, 101 S. Ct. 677, 66 L. Ed. 2d 584 (1981): that the attorney-client privilege applies to communications made by corporate employees concerning matters pertinent to their job tasks, regardless of the employee's status or position in the corporation, as long as that communication was made to the corporation's attorney in order for him to formulate and render legal advice to the corporation. In other words, the significance lies not in *who* said it, but rather in *what* was said and *why*.

Tied to confidentiality is the duty of loyalty; the identity of the client is vital in determining a conflict of interest. Corporate America is not set up as insular units of business. An organization is made up of different people playing different roles. Whether an organization is comprised of one shareholder or one thousand, the client remains the one focus of the attorney. This focus must be clearly conveyed to all others with whom the attorney must deal, particularly to those who may be confused as to the role the attorney is playing and the party to whom her loyalty is pledged.

Conflicts of Interest within the Organization

Conflicts are evaluated under the same analysis for organizations as individual personal clients. Multiple representation may be permissible if no actual conflict exists and the clients consent. This means that the organization's directors, officers, members, shareholders, employees, and various other affiliated persons can be represented by that attorney and paralegal. The legal professional must bear in mind the ethical constraints of the relevant conflicts rules. For paralegals, reference should be made to NFPA EC 1.7 and NALA Guideline 1, both of which have been discussed in previous chapters.

Further, many large corporations have subsidiaries that exist as independent business entities. Representing a large conglomerate can impose substantial conflict for attorneys not exclusively employed by that corporation—also known as "outside counsel." How does an attorney determine when a conflict exists when a subsidiary is involved? Is the subsidiary the same as or different from the parent company? The California State Bar opined:

Though the question of whether a parent and its subsidiaries must be treated as the same or different entities for conflict purposes is one of the most frequently arising questions in corporate practice, there are surprisingly few judicial or ethics authorities on the issue presented. Nevertheless, we do not believe that majority or even sole ownership of a subsidiary corporation should be controlling in determining who is the client for conflict purposes unless the subsidiary is merely an alter ego of the parent corporation. Notwithstanding the ownership interest which a person or entity has in a corporation, the ethical rules make clear that the client is the corporation which is represented by the attorney. When the subsidiary involved is a wholly-owned subsidiary, instances will be infrequent, though not impossible, where parent and subsidiary can have interests adverse to each other. Regardless of the ownership of his or her client, the duty of the lawyer to keep paramount the interests of the entity which he or she actually represents is still the same. The fact of total ownership does not change the parent corporation's status as a constituent of the subsidiary. The duties which an attorney owes to a constituent are defined in and go no further than those set out in [the ethics rules] . . . On the facts presented here, the parent is not a party to the suit against the subsidiary, and there is no prospect that it will be made a party. The representation against the subsidiary can therefore have no direct consequences on the parent; the only adversity can be that indirect adversity which might result from the diminution in the value of the parent's stock in the subsidiary if the attorney's suit against the subsidiary is ultimately successful. This possible indirect impact is insufficient to give rise to a breach of the duty of loyalty owed to the parent. The attorney's duty of loyalty does not encompass the obligation to refrain from actions which may have only indirect adverse effects on existing clients in matters unrelated to those which the attorney is handling for such clients.

CA Ethics Op. 1989–113, 1989 WL 253261 (emphasis added).

The attorney must continuously look out for the best interests of the organizational client. The personal interests of the agents must be separated from the proper goals of the organization; this is again an exercise in focusing on the issue of who the client really is: the organization, not any of its constituents. There are occasions where a person associated with the organization may take actions that are detrimental to the organization's interest, may subject the organization to legal process, or may do other substantial injury. If this is the case, then the attorney must first inform a higher or the highest authority in the organization, depending upon the severity of the potential harm and status of the wrongdoer. This is the first step an attorney should take when he has come into knowledge that a member of the organization is committing or omitting some act that will harm the organization's best interests, or intends to do so. It is an internal "whistle-blower" protection for the attorney, and permits the disclosure of information without violation of confidentiality or privilege. While this provision may look as though there is little to keep an attorney quiet after communicating with a member of the organization, the rule has a rather high standard for a protected disclosure.

This is similar to the standard that applies to individual clients: the attorney must know or suspect with reasonable certainty that the member is going to cause harm to the organization. Additionally, the harm threatened must be so substantial as to rise to the level of imperiling the organization by violating a legal obligation or the law. Poor business judgment or imprudence cannot be avoided by counsel's intervention using this rule. The principle of disclosing the least amount of confidential information possible to avoid the potentially disastrous consequences applies here as well. The first line of defense is to ask the "offender" in the organization to reconsider her position on the matter. Should that approach fail, then the attorney must go to a higher-ranking member and request that remedial measures be taken.

Permitted Disclosures

So far, the damage control has occurred "in house." However, where the questionable conduct emanates from the highest officer(s) able to act, or where these officers have been notified but refuse to act in the best interest of the organization, the attorney can disclose the relevant information to the appropriate outside authority. The act or omission involving the highest authority in the organization must be a clear violation of law before the attorney can act to disclose confidential information to others, to prevent the reasonably certain and substantial harm to the organization.

Once litigation or other proceedings have been instituted against the organizational client, of course the normal attorney-client confidentiality and privileges apply. The attorney is not required to disclose information that relates to the defense of the organization against charges of wrongdoing. The reporting requirement applies to actions or inactions taken by the organization during the normal course of business.

There are certain sectors that are more heavily regulated, for good reason, than others. The Securities and Exchange Commission (SEC) tolerates very little in the way of questionable business practices. The commission places additional reporting requirements on the attorneys and paralegals for businesses governed by its regulations. Section 307 of the Sarbanes-Oxley Act of 2002 ("SOX") required the Securities and Exchange Commission (the Commission) to issue rules setting forth minimum standards of professional conduct for attorneys appearing and practicing before the SEC. This section functions as another avenue to guide attorneys practicing in this area. It essentially underscores the ABA Model Rule 1.13.

The first part of section 307 of SOX equates to ABA Model Rule 1.13(b); it requires the "attorney to report evidence of a material violation of securities law or breach of fiduciary duty or similar violation by the company or any agent thereof, to the chief legal counsel or the chief executive officer of the company (or the equivalent thereof)." The second part equates to Rule 1.13(c) and states that

> *if the counsel or officer does not appropriately respond to the evidence (adopting, as necessary, appropriate remedial measures or sanctions with respect to the violation), [it requires] the attorney to report the evidence to the audit committee of the board of directors of the issuer or to another committee of the board of directors comprised solely of directors not employed directly or indirectly by the issuer, or to the board of directors.*

These ethical rules and regulations, in part a response to scandals like Enron, have caused attorneys for businesses to question whether they are acting as trusted counselors or governmental informants. The SEC requires the attorney to report mere evidence of the violation, whereas the Model Rules require knowledge on the part of the attorney that a violation has occurred or will occur.

Legal Professionals' Protections after Disclosure

If an attorney does "blow the whistle" on her employer, the ethics rules provide protection for the attorney. If an attorney believes that she has been fired or forced to withdraw for making a justified disclosure to protect the organization from harm, then she can take whatever steps she feels are professionally necessary to protect herself. This protective rule applies also to paralegals who feel it necessary to report misconduct.

The ABA Model Rules afford an attorney a means to defend herself against **retaliatory discharge**: her employer cannot fire her because she made the requisite disclosures to the appropriate authorities. In addition, the attorney may properly withdraw from representing the organization. In the instance where the company is the sole client of the attorney, the unemployment is deemed to be a **constructive discharge** rather than a resignation. This would equate to a wrongful termination claim against the client. Under normal circumstances, this is unacceptable in the attorney-client relationship. The fiduciary duties owed to the client prohibit this potentiality; it is incongruous to expect almost absolute trust from the client and to uphold the attorney's duty of loyalty with the ominous threat of suit at the hands of the fiduciary. However, as an employee of an organization, the attorney is entitled to

retaliatory discharge
A client's firing of the attorney for the attorney's failure to pursue the client's unethical or imprudent course in handling its legal affairs.

constructive discharge
An attorney's cessation of the performance of legal work due to the client's insistence on pursuing unethical or imprudent means to achieve its desired result in the legal matter.

the same economic protection that other contractually bound employees enjoy. This includes employment protection. Losing this client could mean losing an attorney's entire livelihood.

The attorney-plaintiff in *O'Brien v. Stolt-Nielsen Transportation Group, Ltd.,* 48 Conn. Supp. 200, 209, 838 A.2d 1076, 1083 (2003) claimed that he was constructively discharged from employment at the company because he was "ethically and legally barred from rendering legal services to, and remaining in, the management of Stolt-Nielsen while the company's alleged illegal activities continued." The attorney followed the requisite course of reporting the questionable actions to the highest authorities in the company, but the company failed to stop the activity. The attorney-plaintiff sought not only money damages but also a declaratory judgment that would allow him to reveal confidential client information to the court and law enforcement authorities.

This step, requesting the court's permission to reveal the information, is necessary in such an instance of revealing past acts of the client. However, if the attorney had knowledge of an ongoing crime or fraud, that information could be revealed under the "prevention of a crime-fraud" exception of the ethical rules. This serves as a reminder that while in-house counsel and other attorneys dealing with organizations as a client have a special rule that applies to them, it works in concert with the other rules covering all attorneys.

CLIENTS WITH DIMINISHED CAPACITY

In a perfect world, clients not only present the attorney with all the relevant information, but also are capable of understanding the legal situation and agree with the attorney's well-reasoned advice. The fact that this very seldom happens can pose problems for attorneys working with "average" clients. The problems and efforts increase when an attorney finds himself working with a client with **diminished capacity**. This can mean that the client is a minor, is physically or mentally ill or impaired, or has some other disability that affects her capacity to appreciate the situation, comprehend the attorney's advice, and/or make a reasoned decision. The attorney must try to overcome these challenges to maintain as normal a relationship as possible with this type of client and, of course, act in the best interest of the client. ABA Model Rule 1.14 addresses the issues in dealing with this type of client. The most difficult task in this respect may be that the client takes a position that is not in his best interest and the attorney must "disobey" the directives of the client.

diminished capacity
A client's incapability to understand legal ramifications of her decisions, as a result of immaturity, or of some mental or physical infirmity.

Acting in the best interests of the client may not be possible without the assistance of other professionals, or at least of family members. The least drastic and invasive actions should be attempted first; an example would be a consultation with the family to suggest creating a power of attorney to take charge of the affected client's interests. Should that prove unsuccessful or ineffective, evaluation and counseling from a professional may be necessary. Lastly, **guardianship/conservatorship** should be sought. It is a delicate situation and introduces another person's opinion as to what is best for the client. The goal is to permit the client to retain as much independence and dignity as possible in the handling of his legal affairs.

guardianship/conservatorship
An appointed third party who has the legal authority and fiduciary duty to care for a diminished person and/or his property. Also known as a *conservator*.

Indeed, even making the decision to seek protection for the client is not easy:

The most difficult task is determining whether under Rule 1.14(b) you must take protective action with respect to your client. You must believe that your client cannot act in her own best interests, but this should not be based upon what you believe are ill-considered judgments alone. If you feel that you have doubts about your client's ability to act in her own best interests, it may be appropriate to seek guidance from an appropriate diagnostician. [. . .]

Before you attempt any protective action, you must determine that other, less drastic, solutions are not available. Examples of less drastic solutions in the ABA Formal Opinion are: "involvement of other family members who are concerned about the client's well-being, use of a durable power of attorney or a revocable trust where a client of impaired capacity has the capacity to execute such a document, and referral to support groups or social services that could enhance the client's capacities or ameliorate the feared harm." These types of avenues should be examined and explored prior to taking protective action.

After a thorough review of the situation, your professional judgment may lead you to believe that protective action is necessary. This could mean applying for the appointment of a conservator (voluntary or involuntary) or guardian ad litem.

While Rule 1.14 does allow a lawyer to take protective action on behalf of a client, it is not a mandate a lawyer must follow. Obviously, many lawyers would feel uncomfortable filing for protective action for their client. Termination of representation is permissible, but must be performed "without material adverse effect on the interests of the client."

Conn. Ethics Op. 97–19, 1997 WL 700686 (Conn. Bar Assn.)

Lastly, in dealing with a client of diminished capacity, all the rules of confidentiality take on an added dimension, as the attorney needs to consult with outside parties in order to effectuate proper representation. In this regard, the attorney may reveal only client confidences that are directly related and absolutely necessary for the third party to know in order to assist the attorney in making the best decisions for the client.

SPECIAL CIRCUMSTANCES

Declining Representation

Attorneys do not have to take on prospective clients who may pose difficulties, for whatever reason; they may decline to represent a person. While the underlying reasons for declination are not subject to any rules, the way in which the person is treated is. Primarily, any person who approaches an attorney in any setting and seeks legal advice about any situation, whether or not the attorney is competent in that area, is considered a **prospective client**, and shall be treated according to the ethical rules. The governing ABA Model Rule is 1.18. The key to understanding when the ethical rules kick in is determining whether the person knows she is speaking to an attorney and intends to communicate with him about a legal issue. It is a very broad interpretation and is designed to safeguard the integrity of the profession. It is well known and well established that attorneys must keep communications secret. Extending this protection to any person who seeks advice, a "prospective client," ensures that people will feel comfortable seeking legal assistance.

prospective client
Any person who knowingly seeks the advice of an attorney relating to legal matters.

The rules specifically state that any communications made in this initial consultation are held confidential, as if they were made by an actual client. This duty of confidentiality does not depend on whether the attorney takes on the person as an actual client or whether any fees were paid. The moment the prospective client opens her mouth, the ethical "cone of silence" applies. The duties to this "prospective client" are the same as those that apply to former clients, as discussed in chapter 5, "Conflicts of Interest."

Further, declination of representation is *mandated* where taking on the prospective client would create a conflict of interest with a current client. The conflict would arise where the prospective client's interests are materially adverse to those of the current or former client in the same or a substantially related matter. Once an attorney has obtained enough information from the initial communications from the prospective client to determine that a conflict exists, he must prevent the prospective client from further revealing information and decline the representation. No other member of that firm may take on that prospective client, according to the imputed disqualification rule of conflicts.

As in the previously discussed conflicts rules, an attorney would be able to overcome the conflict and take on the representation only if the parties affected knowingly waived the conflict in writing or the affected attorney were properly screened from the matter if the firm decided to take on the representation. Of course, notice of these precautions must be given to a prospective client. This provision allows the prospective client to be represented by the firm of his choice.

Mandated Termination of Representation

On the other hand, if the attorney has already taken on a matter which has gone sour, the attorney may properly withdraw from that representation only as long as the ethical requirements are met. There are two categories of withdrawal or declination of representation: when it is *mandatory* for the attorney to withdraw and when it is *permissible* to withdraw. **Mandatory withdrawal** occurs if an attorney finds herself in a situation where

1. the rules of professional ethics will be violated if the attorney continues to represent the client, or

2. the attorney is impaired by a physical or mental condition that materially interferes with her ability to represent the client, or

3. the attorney is fired by her client.

In a mandatory withdrawal, the attorney has no discretion as to whether the relationship needs to end; it must end. The attorney can no longer represent that particular client.

The first enumerated provision underscores the importance of understanding the ethical rules and their application in any situation. It is impermissible to violate the ethical rules; therefore, if the representation will result in an ethical violation, the representation is prohibited. The second provision addresses the condition of the attorney. Practicing the law is not easy; the stress and fast pace can put a strain on an attorney's general well-being. Add to this any personal, physical, and mental problems the attorney may be experiencing, and this strain can result in a diminished fitness to practice. The disability suffered by the attorney must be influencing the legal tasks required in his practice. In other words, the performance of the attorney must be directly caused by and compromised by the disability. Without this causal connection, the attorney may continue without threat of a violation of his ethical duties. The simple fact that an attorney is under stress, overworked, or dealing with a myriad of problems, either mental or physical, does not mean that he has diminished capacity to practice law. The disability must impact the lawyer's fitness to practice law.

There is a tension here: how is a compromised attorney to recognize when she needs to decline work, withdraw, or seek help? Unfortunately, an attorney may not realize that she is unable to perform at the appropriate competency level, and an ethical violation may result. However, the fact that the attorney did not purposefully neglect or falter in his practice, but rather suffered under a disability, will mitigate the sanction imposed. The ABA has set forth in Rule 9.32 of the Standards for Imposing Lawyer Sanctions the circumstances under which a mental disability, including a chemical dependency, will be considered. The affected attorney must be able to show:

1. medical evidence that she is impaired by a chemical or mental disability, and that

2. the misconduct was caused by the chemical dependency or mental disability, and that

mandatory withdrawal
Withdrawal of an attorney from representation where that representation will result in a violation of ethical rules, or the attorney is materially impaired, or the attorney is discharged.

3. she has sustained a meaningful and successful period of rehabilitation from the chemical dependency or mental disability, and that

4. this recovery has stopped the misconduct, and that

5. the recurrence of the misconduct is unlikely.

It is not enough that an attorney suffers from a disability that causes him to falter in his legal and ethical duties to his clients. He also must show that he is willing and able to recover from the disability, that the recovery is substantial in *both time and effect, and that the recovery will affect positively how the attorney resumes* his practice. Indeed, after the period of rehabilitation, the attorney must apply to the bar to show the extent of recovery in order for the bar to assess whether the attorney should, indeed, be reinstated.

CYBER TRIP

A springboard to your state's code as it relates to a disabled or dependent legal professional should start at

www.mhhe.com/paralegalportal

How do you recognize if your professional colleagues are suffering from mental disabilities or abusing substances in a way that may impair their abilities to conform to their ethical obligations? Visit these general information sites:

http://www.helpguide.org/mental_emotional_health.htm

http://helpguide.org/mental/drug_substance_abuse_addiction_signs_effects_treatment.htm

http://www.sacsconsulting.com/book/book.htm

Even prescription drugs can be dangerous, as this Web site shows:

http://www.fda.gov/fdac/features/2001/501_drug.html

The compassionate nature of the disciplinary board was aptly demonstrated in *Lawyer Disciplinary Bd. v. Dues,* 218 W. Va. 104, 624 S.E.2d 125 (2005). In the time frame of just two years, Attorney Dues suffered a heart attack, underwent triple bypass surgery, was admitted to the hospital on three occasions for various physical ailments, and had a prostate operation. All of these physical problems led to severe depression, and Attorney Dues began psychiatric treatment. It was only after these problems occurred that Attorney Dues was found to have committed 39 violations of his professional duties. He presented "unchallenged medical evidence that his legal deficiencies were directly connected to the serious depression that flowed from his physical problems." *Id.* at 113. The court empathized and opined: "the unique facts of this case convincingly demonstrate that, in addition to his clients, Mr. Dues was also a tragic victim in this matter. He was the victim of a mental disease that 'the legal community has been slow to recognize . . . as a legitimate disease that merits attention'." *Id.* citing Todd Goren & Bethany Smith, *Depression as a Mitigating Factor in Lawyer Discipline,* 14 Geo. J. Legal Ethics 1081, 1082 (2001).

RESEARCH THIS

Find the Lawyer's Assistance program in your jurisdiction. Make note of its mission statement and contact information. What services do they offer?

For a refreshing comedic break, watch *All of Me* (1984), starring Steve Martin and Lily Tomlin. Tomlin's character is a wealthy heiress who, in preparing for her death, arranges to have her soul transferred into a younger woman's body. However, her soul ends up in the body of her lawyer, played by Martin. Would this unconventional problem be considered grounds for an attorney to withdraw from representation of clients under the theory of mental impairment?

Stress can be a killer, not only of productivity, but of sanity. Surf the Internet to find ways to handle the pressures associated with an overload of work. Technology and the Internet can be a "virtual" lifesaver. It is important to test drive many different ways of handling your own to-do list. Find the appropriate program to do just that. It may be already on your computer, like Outlook® or other calendaring programs. Blackberries® and other mobile devices keep tasks manageable. Don't let technology burden your paralegal career—use it to enhance your productivity and lower your mental stress levels so that you can perform at your best.

On the other hand, where an attorney uses the fact of having a disability to escape responsibility, the disciplinary board is not sympathetic. An attorney diagnosed with bipolar II disorder was suspended from practice for three years for his 22 ethical violations. The attorney's conduct involved dishonesty in lying to clients and judges and falsifying documents in order to cover up his mistakes in practice. His treating psychiatrist testified that dishonesty is not a symptom of bipolar II disorder. The violations could not be connected to the underlying mental disease, and, therefore, the disability could not have caused the attorney's improper actions. Consequently, the disability was not a mitigating factor in deciding how to sanction the attorney. *Lawyer Disciplinary Bd. v. Scott*, 213 W. Va. 209, 215, 579 S.E.2d 550, 556 (2003).

Lastly, an attorney must withdraw if her client terminates the relationship. The attorney is essentially employed by the client at the client's will. If the client wishes to "fire" his attorney, that is his prerogative. "Public policy strongly favors a client's freedom to employ a lawyer of his choosing and, except in some instances where counsel is appointed, to discharge the lawyer during the representation for any reason or no reason at all." *Hoover Slovacek LLP v. Walton,* 206 S.W.3d 557, 562 (Tex. 2006). However, the attorney will be able to recover the value of her services rendered to the client prior to the termination by the client. Attorneys are entitled to collect the proper fees for their time and effort, even if the fee arrangement was originally contingent. The firing of the attorney does not allow the client to obtain free counsel. If the attorney must resort to the court for collection of her fee, a reasonable fee will be determined and awarded to the attorney in a contingent fee case. It is not based upon the actual settlement or judgment obtained by the former client. Fees can also be collected by securing an attorney lien on the proceeds of the matter. The right to place such a lien is dependent upon the circumstances surrounding the client's termination of the attorney. If the attorney was discharged for cause (the attorney violated some duty owed to the client), then the attorney has no right to place a lien on the matter; on the other hand, if the client terminated the relationship without cause, the attorney does have the right to place the lien. *See Friedman v. Park Cake, Inc.,* 825 N.Y.S.2d 11 (N.Y. App. Div. 2006).

Permissive Termination of Representation

The attorney has the option of withdrawing in many other situations that arise in practice. The operative language in ABA Model Rule 1.16 is that the attorney *may* withdraw, but does not have to, in the following situations:

1. there is no material, adverse effect on the client's interests if the attorney chooses to withdraw;

2. the lawyer reasonably believes the client will use, will continue to use, or has used the attorney's services to perpetrate a crime or fraud;

3. the attorney is repulsed by or has a fundamental disagreement with the client's actions or decisions in the matter;

4. the attorney has previously notified the client of the client's failures to fulfill his obligations under the retainer agreement and the client has continuously and substantially failed to satisfy those obligations. The attorney may withdraw after such warning has been given;

IN CLASS DISCUSSION

Evaluate the "disabilities" suffered by two attorneys in capital murder cases. If you were on the appellate panels, would you have ruled the same way? Should these attorneys have withdrawn? Should they have been ethically sanctioned for their failure to withdraw in these situations? Note that in both trials, the defendants had co-counsels (each was represented by another attorney who assisted the counsel in question).

In the first case, the applicant's first claim is that he was actually or constructively denied counsel because of his retained attorney's persistent habit of napping during the trial.

> He argues that when Mr. Benn slept through significant portions of his trial, applicant was totally deprived of that counsel's assistance. Applicant notes that in *United States v. Cronic,* the Supreme Court held that a defendant's Sixth Amendment rights are violated "if the accused is denied counsel at a critical stage." Under Cronic and its progeny, a defendant is denied counsel not only when his attorney is physically absent from the proceeding, but when he is mentally absent as well, i.e., counsel is asleep, unconscious, or otherwise actually non compos mentis. This prong of Cronic is epitomized by the "inert" or "potted plant" lawyer who, although physically and mentally present in the courtroom, fails to provide (or is prevented from providing) any meaningful assistance. In this situation, courts presume prejudice based upon the actual or constructive denial of counsel "when such absence threatens the overall fairness of a trial."

See Ex parte McFarland, 163 S.W.3d 743, 752 (Tex. Crim. App. 2005) (citations omitted).

In the second, the attorney (Mr. Portwood) not only admitted to a problem with alcohol abuse (drinking 12 shots of rum per night during the trial, contrary to the findings of the court below), he was later pulled off another death penalty case and sent to a detoxification facility. The attorney later died of a liver-related illness. The defendant's appeal to the Supreme Court of the United States was denied, and Mr. Frye was executed in August of 2001.

> Frye also contends, in connection with his ineffective assistance claim, that Portwood's asserted alcohol dependency rendered him incapable of providing constitutionally effective assistance up to and during the sentencing phase of the trial. We are indeed troubled by Portwood's acknowledgment of a decades-long routine of drinking approximately twelve ounces of rum each evening. However, the district court found that Portwood "never consumed alcohol during the work day and never performed any work on the case when he had consumed alcohol." Frye, 89 F.Supp.2d at 701. We agree with our sister circuits that, in order for an attorney's alcohol addiction to make his assistance constitutionally ineffective, there must be specific instances of deficient performance attributable to alcohol. In this case, there is no evidence of specific instances of defective performance caused by Portwood's alcohol abuse. Furthermore, it is significant that Frye was not represented by Portwood alone—he had the benefit of two court-appointed lawyers assisting in his defense.

Frye v. Lee, 235 F.3d 897, 907 (4th Cir. 2000) (citations omitted).

5. the attorney will suffer unreasonable financial burden by continuing to represent the client;

6. actions or inactions by the client have rendered the representation unreasonably difficult; or

7. other good cause exists which justifies withdrawal.

Many of these factors are present in any one case. Most, if not all of the time, finances play some part in the **permissive withdrawal** of the attorney. Either the client refuses to pay bills as they come due or the representation itself has become too expensive to go forward (factors 4 and 5 above). Generally, withdrawal will require the attorney to make a motion to the court to obtain permission to terminate the relationship. At that time, the court will first examine whether the client will be adversely affected by the withdrawal. There is a presumption that the longer an attorney has represented the client and the closer it is to the time of trial, the more likely it is that a client will be adversely affected. Withdrawals on the eve of trial, without exceptional excuse, are not granted. If the request to withdraw is not granted, the attorney must continue to represent his client to the best of his ability.

In making the application to withdraw, the attorney must only disclose as much information as is necessary to effectuate the withdrawal; the attorney must keep as much client information secret as possible pursuant to his ethical duty of confidentiality. "In this case the motion was filed early on in the appeal, and withdrawal will not unduly disrupt the proceedings. We see no need for this counsel to explain why he wishes to withdraw in more detail, as such an explanation could be detrimental to the client or protected by the attorney-client privilege." *Horan v. O'Connor*, 832 So.2d 193, 194 (Fla. App. 2002). In that matter, the attorney withdrew from representation due to "irreconcilable differences" that arose between the attorney and the client, "rendering the [attorney] unable to ethically and fairly represent [client] in this matter." *Id.*

Similarly, where an attorney determines that a case lacks merit, the economic incentives to pursue the matter dissipate, adding insult to injury. This is particularly true in a contingency fee case. *See Elton v. Dougherty*, 931 So.2d 201 (Fla. App. 2006), wherein the attorney decided that the case lacked merit and he was no longer willing to advance costs necessary to proceed. The client could not afford to pay the costs, and, therefore, the court found "that the attorney's and client's interests were in insurmountable conflict."

No matter what the reason, economic or otherwise, the attorney must preserve the client's rights and advise him of any issues that he needs to be aware of before full termination of the relationship. Former clients are still protected by attorneys' ethical obligations. An attorney must do all she can to make sure that the client is not harmed by the withdrawal, and facilitate the transfer of the matter to another attorney if necessary. The disengaging attorney must surrender client files and property and return unearned legal fees. These protections are of utmost importance when timing is critical, as when the Statute of Limitations is running. There is no bright line rule

permissive withdrawal
The attorney's chosen termination of representation of the client in certain circumstances that comply with the attorney's ethical obligations to the client.

SPOT THE ISSUE

Ronald, a relatively new client, has just learned that Leonard, the lawyer handling his matter, has delegated many substantial legal tasks to Connie, his very competent paralegal. Ronald voiced his unsubstantiated and uneducated opinions about the way that Leonard was handling the matter. He thought that Leonard should do all the work, since Leonard was the one who signed the retainer agreement. Ronald disparaged Connie's abilities to perform the tasks assigned to her. Ronald stubbornly refused to go to another lawyer; he wanted only Leonard to work on the matter. What options does Leonard have in dealing with Ronald?

as to how close to trial or to the end of the filing period for the cause of action is too close, making it impermissible for counsel to withdraw.

Every case is determined on its own facts and parties involved. Where a few weeks may be enough time for a simple legal issue, it may not be for a complex matter. Or, with regard to the parties, the time required for a savvy businessperson familiar with legal affairs to obtain new counsel may not be enough for another individual.

> *The letter of termination, moreover, while it referred to the two-year statute of limitations and "suggest[ed]" plaintiff contact another lawyer immediately, did not specify the critical date. Finally, a fact-finder could also conclude that the period of time left to plaintiff before the statute of limitations had run was unreasonably short, particularly in view of the preceding six-month period following [the attorney]'s receipt of Dr. Stein's favorable report. In this regard, we note that medical malpractice cases are ordinarily difficult representations and are not lightly or casually undertaken by serious and responsible lawyers. It is by no means clear that plaintiff could have obtained a new lawyer who, in three weeks, would have been able to review her file, make the necessary evaluations, and agree to file a complaint, particularly after knowing that her previous lawyer, who had represented her for twenty-one months, had suddenly declined to continue.*

Gilles v. Wiley, Malehorn & Sirota, 345 N.J. Super. 119, 127, 783 A.2d 756, 761 (App. Div. 2001).

The attorney must take the individual client's capacity to deal with the situation at hand into consideration when withdrawing from the representation. Recalling the discussion of clients with special needs due to diminished capacity, the protection of the client's interests during and after withdrawal becomes paramount. The key to handling this potentially delicate situation is to understand the capacity of the disabled client to comprehend the ramifications of the withdrawal. While letters of disengagement may work for clients of normal functioning, a client with special needs may need more explanation. The attorney's benevolent intent is immaterial if the communication is ineffective. In *Cuyahoga Cty. Bar Assn. v. Newman,* 102 Ohio St.3d 186, 808 N.E.2d 375 (2004), the attorney represented a gentleman who had been injured in an accident, leaving him physically and mentally disabled. He helped this client for years and free of charge, as he considered him a friend. Of course, the attorney asserted that he did not mean to financially harm his disabled client. The attorney sent his client a letter in which he stated that he would not be acting as his attorney for a certain matter involving a commercial lease. The court found that the brief letter of withdrawal was insufficient to give the client proper notice given the capabilities of his client, and that the attorney knew or should have known that the client would not be able to understand the significance of the letter. Not only was the withdrawal improper because it was ineffectual under the ethical rules; the attorney, in fact, had violated his ethical obligations by "abandon[ing] his client's interests during the course of a professional relationship and caus[ing], at least in part, the client's personal liability for defaulting on the lease." *Id.* at 190. This brings us to the lesson learned in this section: write a carefully crafted letter of disengagement, specifically noting all deadlines and ramifications of withdrawal, and have the client confirm his understanding of it.

Let us return to the reasons why an attorney may choose to withdraw. The crime or fraud factor most often relates to false statements made in legal documents or to client perjury. In those cases the attorney has the option of withdrawing if the client persists in this course of conduct despite admonitions from the attorney. Pursuit of unmeritorious claims is not only punishable by ethical sanctions, but also penalized under the civil rules' "frivolous claims" prohibition; in that instance, the attorney should be permitted to withdraw. For example, in *Pritt v. Suzuki Motor Co., Ltd.,* 204 W. Va. 388, 513 S.E.2d 161 (1998), the attorney learned that his client was faking the extent of his injuries and that the activities in which the client was engaging were completely inconsistent with the plaintiff's theory of the case. The attorney was permitted to withdraw due to the client's use of the attorney's services to perpetrate fraud on the court. In *Staples v. McKnight,* 763 S.W.2d 914 (Tex. App. 1988), the attorney would be permitted to withdraw if she believed and could show reasonable basis for her belief that her client intended to commit perjury.

Whether a client's actions or suggestions for conducting the case are repugnant or not is highly fact sensitive. What is clear is that inconsiderate or distasteful conduct towards other parties or counsel is ground for withdrawal. The North Carolina Court opined that while an attorney should zealously represent the interests of her clients, taking unfair advantage of a colleague who is suffering from an ailment or disability is inconsiderate or repugnant. The attorney can avoid the client's propositions to use offensive tactics and is, on the contrary, ethically obligated to "treat [. . .] with courtesy and consideration all persons involved in the legal process. . . . If the client is insistent and the client-lawyer relationship is no longer functional because of the disagreement about tactics, the lawyer may withdraw from the representation pursuant to Rule 1.16(b)(4). 2003 N.C. Ethics Op. 2, 2003 WL 24306941.

While the ethical rules speak to ideals, they are not confined to them. The practice of law involves the practical issues of running a business as well. For that reason, factors (4) and (5) above speak to the financial and operational issues that occur in representation. Clearly, the client has an obligation to pay certain costs and fees associated with the matter; additionally, the client has an obligation to stay in communication with the attorney. Nonresponsiveness to efforts by the attorney to consult with the client is a "breach" of the client's "duty" to help move the case forward. *Benefield v. City of New York,* 824 N.Y.S.2d 889 (2006). If these obligations are not met, the attorney has the right to withdraw as counsel. Similarly, if the attorney's practice, indeed, his very livelihood, is placed in jeopardy due to the financial stresses of handling the matter, the attorney may be able to withdraw. In a case of first impression, the Appellate Division of New Jersey weighed the public policy considerations involved in permitting a firm to withdraw as counsel under a contingent fee arrangement in a large, costly, and prolonged tobacco litigation. Weighing against such a withdrawal, the trial court opined and the appellate court agreed:

> *The fact that no competent counsel appears willing to invest the time and energy on such basis clearly reflects that withdrawal will have "material adverse effect on the interests" of plaintiffs. The question before us therefore is whether the representation of plaintiffs in this case will cause such an unreasonable financial burden as to permit withdrawal of counsel under [Rule] 1.16(b)(5). . . . This argument [of unreasonable financial burden] is not compelling in the context of a contingency fee relationship which, by its nature, involves uncertainty and risk and requires the parties to make predictions as to (1) the likelihood of recovery, (2) the length of time until recovery and (3) the probable size of recovery. Given their litigation experience, lawyers are in a better position than clients to make these predictions.*

Smith v. R. J. Reynolds Tobacco Co., 267 N.J. Super. 62, 75–77, 630 A.2d 820 (App. Div. 1993).

The court recognized that the firm took on this risk, and determined that to permit withdrawal on the ground that maintaining the litigation had become too costly would "stigmatize" such risky yet socially important claims. "As for plaintiffs, the disappointment at having been abandoned midstream is likely to undermine faith in the legal system and to reinforce the notion that access to the courthouse is a function of wealth." *Id.* at 78. However, on the other hand:

> *Denial of the present motion would serve only to discourage lawyers confronted with requests by clients to pursue ground-breaking claims on their behalf. While the risk of bearing litigation costs and the costs of lawyer and paralegal time without compensation will always exist in such cases if, as here, the lawyer's compensation is contingent, denying permission to*

withdraw here would threaten otherwise courageous counsel with the need to contemplate that no matter how bleak and desperate the financial costs of carrying litigation costs had become, the firm would be required to stagger on and complete the course. For a court to require such heroic undertakings would also add to the threat of imposed litigation costs that defendants can often dictate in a case through cost-generating and delay-producing moves in the course of the litigation. If anything, such a decision would only add to the incentives of defendants to engage in such practices.

Id. at 81.

This extensive examination of the financial burdens and risks on the part of both attorneys and clients underscores the case-sensitive nature of such requests to withdraw as counsel. The legal system balances all the factors as described in ABA Model Rule 1.16, to determine the most just result for the parties involved and for the maintenance of confidence in the system as a whole. Clients should not feel as though attorneys can desert them midstream without a means to reach their goals.

Summary

The provisions discussed in this chapter have one thing in common: they all underscore the importance of trust and respect in the way in which attorneys handle their clients. An attorney must identify his client and act only in the client's best interest despite outside influences, from either those who would take advantage of a disabled client or the directors of an organizational client. Where an organization is the client, the duty of loyalty is owed to the organization as a whole, not to an individual member. All clients, prospective, current, or past, must be respected and their information kept confidential to the extent required under the rules. Respect for the client's best interest may manifest itself in declining representation or withdrawing from representation if representation would result in an ethical violation. There are certain situations which require an attorney to withdraw:

1. the rules of professional ethics will be violated if the attorney continues to represent the client, or
2. the attorney is impaired by a physical or mental condition that materially interferes with her ability to represent the client, or
3. the attorney is fired by her client.

There are certain situations in which the attorney may choose to withdraw or to continue representation. These exist where

4. there is no material, adverse effect on the client's interests if the attorney chooses to withdraw;
5. the lawyer reasonably believes the client will use, will continue to use, or has used the attorney's services to perpetrate a crime or fraud;
6. the attorney is repulsed by or has a fundamental disagreement with the client's actions or decisions in the matter;
7. the attorney has previously notified the client of the client's failures to fulfill his obligations under the retainer agreement and the client has continuously and substantially failed to satisfy those obligations. The attorney may withdraw after such warning has been given;
8. the attorney will suffer unreasonable financial burden by continuing to represent the client;
9. actions or inactions by the client have rendered the representation unreasonably difficult; or
10. other good cause exists which justifies withdrawal.

Whether the issue involves special clients or special circumstances, paralegals and attorneys must act in the best interests of each client and do their best to deal with the situation at hand with all the ethical mandates in mind. All of the matters dealt with in this chapter pose challenges for legal professionals. It is the purpose of the ethical rules to provide parameters in which to deal with them.

Constructive discharge
Diminished capacity
Guardian/Conservator
Mandatory withdrawal

Permissive withdrawal
Prospective client
Retaliatory discharge

Key Terms and Concepts

MULTIPLE CHOICE

Review Questions

Choose the best answer(s) and please explain WHY you choose the answer(s).

1. Where the attorney represents an organizational client,
    a. he also represents all the shareholders of that corporation.
    b. he may represent other members of the organization if there is no conflict of interest.
    c. he can share confidential corporate information only with the board of directors.
    d. all subsidiary companies of the organization are also clients of the attorney for the parent company.
    e. All of the above

2. An attorney must maintain an organization's confidential information unless
    a. she chooses to represent the organization's employees instead.
    b. the SEC requests all the records of the company.
    c. the organization chooses to pursue a criminal or fraudulent activity.
    d. she has been retaliatorily discharged as counsel.

3. An attorney may permissively withdraw from representation
    a. only with the court's approval at a hearing or at trial.
    b. if he is fired by the client.
    c. if the client continues to pursue an ill-advised course of action.
    d. when the attorney is found guilty of ethical misconduct.

4. An attorney who has agreed to represent a client with diminished capacity must obtain a guardian when
    a. the client is unable to make her own decisions in her representation.
    b. the family of the disabled client asks the attorney to obtain one.
    c. the client has made poor decisions regarding her representation.
    d. the client is completely unable to understand the ramifications of her decisions regarding her representation.

EXPLAIN YOURSELF

All answers should be written in complete sentences. A simple yes or no is insufficient.

1. Who is the client when the attorney handles matters for a corporation?
2. What are the duties owed to a client with diminished capacity?

3. When MUST an attorney withdraw or decline representation of a client?

4. Describe a situation in which an attorney should withdraw for mental impairment or disability. What can you as a paralegal do in this circumstance?

FAULTY PHRASES

All of the following statements are FALSE; state why they are false and then rewrite them as true statements, without just making the statement negative by adding the word "not."

1. All employees of a corporation who have relevant information about the legal matter at issue are protected under attorney-client privilege.

2. A client with diminished capacity does not have the same rights of attorney-client privilege as other clients.

3. An attorney must take on all clients who come to his office who present him with a problem in the area of law in which he specializes.

4. An attorney must decline to represent a potential client who suffers from diminished capacity because the potential client cannot act for herself.

5. An attorney who drinks alcohol or uses drugs should withdraw from the representation of clients.

6. An attorney can appeal her client's decision to terminate the representation if the attorney is fired right before trial.

7. An attorney may cease to work on a client's matter until he is paid for his work.

PORTFOLIO ASSIGNMENT

Write Away
Draft a letter of disengagement to your client, Sly Stone. Explain why the law firm can no longer represent him. Use any of the reasons explained in this chapter and be sure to include enough details to justify the termination of the relationship. Also make note of any important steps that Mr. Stone should take after receiving the letter. Provide for return of any client property, if necessary.

CORPORATE CLIENTS

44 Pa. D. & C.3d 513, 1987 WL 46863 (Pa.Com.Pl.)
Court of Common Pleas of Pennsylvania, Allegheny County.
Monah

v.

Western Pennsylvania Hospital
No. G.D. 86-8881.
February 23, 1987

WETTICK, A.J.

This is a medical malpractice action in which plaintiffs' negligence claims include the negligent monitoring of the patient following surgery in the recovery room of defendant, Western Pennsylvania Hospital. Plaintiffs have filed a motion to compel Western Pennsylvania Hospital to produce a written statement of the head nurse in the recovery room. The nurse is an eyewitness to the events in the recovery room at the time that plaintiff suffered a cardiac and respiratory arrest.

The nurse is an employee of Western Pennsylvania Hospital. Her statement was prepared prior to the commencement of the lawsuit at the request of in-house counsel for the hospital. For purposes of this motion to compel, we assume that this statement was prepared to assist counsel in evaluating the hospital's potential liability and that counsel did not reveal the contents of this statement to any third persons. Western Pennsylvania Hospital contends that this statement is protected by the attorney-client privilege because this was a statement by an employee of the corporation to corporate counsel while both were acting in the course of their employment. Plaintiffs, on the other hand, contend that the attorney-client privilege does not extend to factual statements of an employee who is only a witness to an incident.

The law is settled that the attorney-client privilege extends to corporations. *Upjohn Co. v. United States,* 449 U.S. 383, 101 S. Ct. 677 (1981). Because a corporation is capable of communicating with its attorneys only through its agents, it is necessary to determine which communications between corporate counsel and employees or other agents of the corporation come within the scope of the attorney-client privilege.

All communications between corporate employees and corporate counsel should not be protected. For example, a corporation should not be able to assert the attorney-client privilege to protect a statement of an employee injured in the course of his employment made to corporate counsel at counsel's request in a FELA action by this employee against the corporation arising out of the incident described in the statement; or to protect statements by fellow laborers, sympathetic to the injured employee, made to corporate counsel; or to protect statements that an employee made to corporate counsel as part of a corporate investigation to determine whether the employee had been embezzling corporate funds. In these situations, the employees making the statements have none of the attributes of a client making a statement to his or her counsel and counsel has none of the responsibilities to these employees that an attorney owes to a client.

There is no Pennsylvania appellate court case law that has considered the issue of what statements made by employees to corporate counsel are protected by the attorney-client privilege. Furthermore, the issue has not arisen frequently in other jurisdictions because most jurisdictions protect attorney work product from discovery and this protection encompasses most statements that corporate employees make to corporate counsel. However, this issue has been thoughtfully addressed by a sufficient number of appellate courts so that the different approaches available to a court have been carefully examined. The opinions in *Consolidation Coal Co. v. Bucyrus-Erie Co.,* 432 N.E. 2d 250 (Illinois Supreme Court, 1982), *Leer v. Chicago, Milwaukee, St. Paul and Pacific Railway Co.,* 308 N.W.2d 305 (Minnesota Supreme Court, 1981) cert. denied 455 U.S. 939 (1982), and *Marriott Corp. v. American Academy of Psychotherapists Inc.,* 277 S.E.2d 785 (Georgia Court of Appeals, 1981), thoroughly review the development of the case law.

Prior to 1981, most jurisdictions followed one of two tests. The first test–the control group test–was initially adopted in *City of Philadelphia v. Westinghouse Electric Corp.,* 210 F. Supp. 483 (E.D., Pa., 1962). This test extends the attorney-client privilege only to corporate employees who will be directly involved in making any decision that may be based on the advice of counsel. The rationale for the test is that the employee, by virtue of his or her position with the corporation, will be acting as the corporation when he or she is consulting with counsel. This test focuses on the status of the employee within the corporate hierarchy.

"[I]f the employee making the communication, of whatever rank he may be, is in a position to control or even to take a substantial part in a decision about any action which the corporation may take upon the advice of the attorney, or if he is an authorized member of a body or group which has that authority, then, in effect, he is (or personifies) the corporation when he makes his disclosure to the lawyer and the privilege would apply. In all other cases the employee would be merely giving information to the lawyer to enable the latter to advise those in the corporation having the authority to act or refrain from acting on the advice." *Id. at 485.*

This test has been criticized because it fails to protect confidential communications that are essential in order for corporate counsel to provide legal advice. Top level executives frequently do not have the information necessary for counsel to render legal advice to the corporation. They will be reluctant to authorize counsel to obtain such information from lower level employees who have direct knowledge of the corporate operations if this information is not protected. This, in turn, will prevent corporations from utilizing counsel to learn how to obey the law according to the critics of the control group test. *Marriott Corp. v. American Academy of Psychotherapists Inc., supra.; Upjohn Co. v. United States, supra*

The second test–the subject-matter test–was initially formulated in *Harper and Row Publishers Inc. v. Decker,* 423 F.2d 487 (7th Cir., 1970*)*; af-by an equally divided court, 400 U.S. 348 (1971). Under this test, the communication of an employee who is not a member of the control group with corporate counsel is privileged if the employee made the communication at the direction of a supervisor and if the subject matter upon which the lawyer's advice was sought by the corporation and dealt with in the communication was within the performance of the employee's duties. This test has been criticized because it protects almost all communications between a corporate employee and corporate counsel. In response to this criticizm, the Court of Appeals for the Eighth in *Diversified Industries Inc. v. Meredith,* 572 F.2d 596 (1978*)* (en banc), adopted a third test–the Weinstein test–which is a refined subject matter test initially proposed by Judge/Professor Weinstein. Under the Weinstein test, the attorney-client privilege will be available to a corporation if the following requirements are met:

"(1) [T]he communication was made for the purpose of securing legal advice, (2) the employee making the communication did so at the direction of his corporate superior, (3) the superior made the request so that the corporation could secure legal advice, (4) the subject matter of the communication is within the scope of the employee's corporate duties, and (5) the communication is not disseminated beyond those persons who, because of the corporate structure, need to know its contents." *Id.* at 609.

In 1981, in the case of *Upjohn Co. v. United States, supra,* the United States Supreme Court rejected the use of a narrow control group test because this test fails to protect confidential communications of employees who are not members of the control group made to counsel in order for counsel to acquire the information necessary to give informed advice. In this case, outside counsel was retained by the board of directors of the corporation to learn whether corporate funds had been paid to foreign governments to secure governmental business for the corporation. The ultimate purpose of counsel's investigation was to give legal advice to the board of directors. At counsel's request, the control group instructed management employees outside of the control group to provide information to counsel.

The Internal Revenue Service issued a summons for the production of this information which these corporate employees had furnished counsel. The corporation raised, inter alia, the attorney-client privilege as a basis for its refusal to provide any information furnished to corporate counsel. The court of appeals rejected the corporation's contention, holding that any information supplied by an officer or agent not responsible for directing the corporation's activities in response to legal advice which counsel furnished was outside the scope of this privilege. The United States Supreme Court reversed, stating that the narrow control group test sanctioned by the court of appeals cannot control the development of this area of the law. The court concluded that the information was protected because of the need by corporate counsel, if he or she is to adequately advise the client, to obtain relevant information from middle and lower level employees. The court did not propose a substitute test but, instead, stated that the scope of the privilege will be determined on a case-by-case basis.

While the Upjohn case is not binding on state courts, the case will be carefully considered by any state court that is addressing the issue of the applicability of the attorney-client privilege to communications by corporate employees to corporate counsel. The result in Upjohn appears to be consistent with the goals and purposes of the attorney-client privilege. The Upjohn case dealt with information which counsel obtained from management employees as to corporate practices that they may have pursued on behalf of the corporation. Counsel's inquiries did not involve incidents which a corporate employee may have witnessed but, instead, dealt with policies made or followed by employees on behalf of the corporation.

This court's conclusion that the result in Upjohn is consistent with the attorney-client privilege as recognized by the Pennsylvania courts does not mean that the control group test should be completely abandoned. In fact, it would appear that the Upjohn court's dissatisfaction with the Sixth Circuit's ruling stemmed from its use of a rigid control group test that did not bring within the scope of the attorney-client privilege employees who are apparently acting as the corporation (although possibly outside the scope of any specific direction from upper management).

An important rationale for the Upjohn holding was that the application of the attorney-client privilege to the communications that were involved "puts the adversary in no worse position than if the communications had never taken place." 101 S. Ct. at 685. In the present case, the application of the attorney-client privilege to the communication by the head nurse to corporate counsel would place plaintiffs in a worse position than if the communication had never taken place.

This nurse is a potential witness for plaintiffs. If she would testify on behalf of plaintiffs, Western Pennsylvania Hospital would be in a position to impeach her testimony through the use of a statement that was never made available to plaintiffs. Thus, if this court were to protect this statement, we would be creating a situation in which Western Pennsylvania Hospital could use this witness without any fear that her statement could be used to impeach her testimony while plaintiffs, if they called this nurse as a witness, would run the risk of impeachment based upon a statement that they have never seen.

The attorney-client privilege was initially developed to protect people, not corporations. If the nurse was the client of the attorney who obtained her statement, the attorney-client privilege would bar the attorney from using this statement to impeach the nurse. Thus, if this court were to protect this statement, we would be placing the corporation in a better position than if it were an individual.

While there may be situations in which the attorney-client privilege should be applied in a manner that places the corporation in a better position than an individual client, this result must be supported by strong policy considerations. These policy considerations do not exist where the communication from the employee to corporate counsel involves only the factual description of a witness to an incident that resulted in injury or death. There is no need to protect this information in order for a corporation to conduct its business affairs because the communication does not involve matters concerning confidential corporate practices. If the purpose for the communication is to assess the corporation's liability, the communication need not be protected because the same information may be obtained by plaintiff through discovery. If the purpose for the communication is to obtain evidence that will be unavailable to the plaintiff, the communication should not be protected.

The choice of the test to be applied to communications of corporate employees to corporate counsel depends on the manner in which the court balances the competing interests of the corporation in protecting employee communications with counsel and of the litigant in obtaining full discovery of the relevant facts in order that the law's protections are extended to those persons whom the law seeks to protect. In the case of *Consolidated Coal Co. v. Bucyrus-Erie Co., supra* (which was decided after and gave consideration to Upjohn), the court concluded that a broad control group test strikes the proper balance between the state's broad discovery policies which are essential to a fair disposition of the lawsuit and the needs of the corporation to obtain legal advice. Thus, the court held that a factual report of an engineer who had examined the pieces of the machine in question was not protected by the attorney-client privilege.

A similar approach was followed by the Minnesota Supreme Court in *Leer v. Chicago, Milwaukee, St. Paul and Pacific Railway Co., supra* (which also was decided after and gave consideration to the Upjohn opinion). In that case, the corporate railroad was seeking to protect statements of other members of a switching crew who had observed the accident in which plaintiff, a switchman, was injured. The court concluded that the attorney-client privilege should not extend to suppress statements of witnesses to the incident because of the state policy favoring a liberal construction of the discovery rules. The court ruled that "when an employee is merely a witness to an accident and not a party to a subsequent action, communications made with him in a general investigation do not create an attorney-client relationship." 308 N.W.2d at 309.

This court recognizes that other jurisdictions have more broadly construed the attorney-client privilege to protect the statements of employees who witnessed an accident made to corporate counsel in connection with pending or threatened litigation. *See State of Missouri ex. ref. Missouri, Highways and Transportation Commission v. Legere,* 706 S.W.2d 560 (Missouri Court of Appeals, 1986); *Macey v. Rollins Environmental Services,* 432 A.2d 960 (Superior Court of New Jersey, 1981). This court declines to follow these cases because these communications do not need to be protected in order for corporate counsel to properly prepare a defense or to give legal advice to the corporation. Furthermore, an extension of the attorney-client privilege to such communications is inconsistent with the broad discovery provisions of the Pennsylvania Rules of Civil Procedure governing discovery of trial preparation material, such as Pa.R.C.P. 4003.3 which protects from discovery only the mental impressions, conclusions, or opinions respecting the value or merit of a claim or defense or respecting strategy or tactics with respect to a representative of a party other than the party's attorney, and rule 4003.5 which does not protect the facts known or opinions held by a regular employee of a party who may have collected the facts or rendered the opinions under the direction of counsel for a party. In jurisdictions, such as Pennsylvania, which do not protect factual information obtained in anticipation of litigation, a broad construction of the attorney-client privilege as to communications to corporate counsel from corporate employees who are witnesses to the incident would create an unfair result. The rules of discovery would permit the corporation to obtain each statement that counsel for an adverse party obtained from a corporate employee who witnessed the incident while the attorney-client privilege would protect from discovery each statement that corporate counsel obtained from the same employee.

For these reasons, the court enters the following

ORDER

On this February 23, 1987, it is hereby ordered that plaintiffs' motion to compel is granted and that the statement of the recovery room nurse shall be produced within 20 days.

Source: Reprinted with permission from ThomsonWest.

Part Three

Attorneys' Roles in the Justice System

Chapter 8

Advocacy and Litigation Issues

CHAPTER OBJECTIVES

The student will be able to:

- Differentiate between meritorious claims and defenses and potentially frivolous ones and provide an explanation of the choice.

- Acknowledge the importance of expediting litigation despite the temptation to use dilatory practices.

- Discuss the obligation of honesty in presenting information to a tribunal and identify when certain disclosures must be made in order to effectuate justice.

- Identify the rules pertaining to communications with opposing and third parties.

- Evaluate an attorney or paralegal's actions during the litigation process in light of their obligations of fairness.

This chapter will examine the legal professional's role as an advocate and/or litigator. HOW are the participants in the litigation process obligated to act towards one another and towards the justice system? To WHOM may a lawyer or paralegal speak in either a transactional or a litigious matter? WHAT can the legal professional communicate to others? Most important, this section of the ABA Model Rules emphasizes the foundations of justice and fairness as the reason WHY attorneys and paralegals are required to act in a certain way in presenting claims and defenses in the adversarial process.

In the previous five chapters (chapters 3 through 7), the duties of the attorney to her client have been explored. In the following four chapters (chapters 8 through 11), the responsibilities of the attorney to the justice system will be explained. It is important to bear in mind that both transactional matters and litigation are components of the justice system; however, most frequently the adversarial nature of legal representation presents itself in litigation. There may be times when the client, the justice system, and/or the employment situation of the attorney may cause a problem or conflict for the attorney. The purpose of the ethics rules in this area is to guide the attorney through the problem's resolution, which will undoubtedly favor the maintenance of the integrity of the profession and the administration of justice. The question posed in this part of the text is this: How can the attorney balance her responsibilities in order to ensure that her actions comport with all of the applicable ethical rules?

For the same reason discussed previously, the paralegal must be able to understand why a firm or an attorney is acting in a certain manner in order to do his part to ensure compliance. A paralegal cannot do that which an attorney cannot do under the ethics rules. Often, the paralegal is involved in preparing the submissions to the tribunal, and, therefore, takes an active role in ensuring that the attorney fulfills her duties of honesty and fairness to everyone and every entity with whom she comes in contact.

advocacy
Engage in the profession of taking on clients to actively support their cause.

adversarial model
The American system of retaining separate independent and oppositional counsel to engage in zealous representation of individual clients.

There are particular issues that arise in the context of **advocacy**. The "in-your-face" **adversarial model** under which the American system operates, and indeed, has been honed to a sharp edge, tempts both the attorney and the client to take any advantage. However, justice is not served by "pot-shots" taken at an adversary; justice is served by exposing truths in their proper light. Already the paralegal student can see the conflict within the trial attorney's psyche: how to protect his client's vulnerability without misleading the tribunal and without overly assisting his adversary.

The ABA Model Rules are presented relatively chronologically and will be discussed in that order. The attorney and paralegal must

1. Present plausible causes of action and defenses to those claims in the pleading or other initial papers to the tribunal (ABA Model Rule 3.1)

2. Keep the litigation moving through the system by not purposefully causing delay in the preparation for trial (ABA Model Rule 3.2)

3. Be honest with the court in all matters, even when that honesty may compromise the client's interest (ABA Model Rule 3.3)

4. Deal fairly with all parties involved in the litigation (ABA Model Rule 3.4)

5. Remain neutral and respectful to the justice system and its processes (ABA Model Rule 3.5)

6. Refrain from revealing to the media certain information covering the litigation which may have an adverse impact on the proceedings (ABA Model Rule 3.6)

7. Treat all "non-clients" with respect, keeping an eye on the justice system's overriding interest in fairness (ABA Model Rules 4.1–4.4)

MERITORIOUS CLAIMS AND DEFENSES

After the attorney has decided to pursue litigation as the means to achieve her client's goals, she must file a complaint with the court or other proper tribunal competent to hear the matter. Recall that the client may determine the ultimate end to be achieved, but it is the attorney who must direct the course to that end. Therefore, she is responsible for the content of all presentations to the court—after all, the client retained her for just that reason. The attorney knows (or should know) the proper course of conduct and submission to the tribunal. To impress the importance of proper submissions upon practicing attorneys, they are held to be responsible for the content of the documents that they have prepared. Pleadings, motions, and other papers sent to the court for its consideration must be signed by an attorney who will vouch for their credibility. This is not to say that the allegations contained therein are absolutely true, but rather that the attorney has made a reasonable inquiry into the plausibility of the facts and legal arguments set forth. The signature requirement for court submissions makes someone, usually the attorney, accountable, and without the signature, the paper will be stricken. The court must be assured that it is not wasting its time on a matter that an attorney will not stand behind.

NALA Guideline 5

1. Locate and interview witnesses, so long as the witnesses are aware of the status and function of the legal assistant.
2. Conduct investigations and statistical and documentary research for review by the attorney.
3. Draft legal documents for review by the attorney.
4. Draft correspondence and pleadings for review by and signature of the attorney.

FIGURE 8.1
Duties Properly Delegated to Paralegals

good faith
An attorney must reasonably believe in the validity of the claim(s) asserted and present them for a proper purpose for adjudication by the tribunal.

CYBER TRIP

See this Web site for full access to all the Rules of Federal Procedure:

http://www.law.cornell.edu/rules/frcp/

The Federal Judiciary's PDF document includes helpful forms at the end:

http://judiciary.house.gov/judiciary/civil99.pdf

For a discussion of the 2007 amendments to the Federal Rules of Civil Procedure, see Michael C. Dorf's article, *Meet the New Federal Rules of Civil Procedure: Same as the Old Rules?*

http://writ.news.findlaw.com/dorf/20070718.html

Locate both your state's civil court rules and your county's local rules of procedure. Start at the McGraw-Hill Paralegal Portal:

www.mhhe.com/paralegalportal

Paralegals are involved in these processes of collecting information from the client and witnesses and drafting the initial documents submitted to the court. Indeed, NALA's Guideline 5 sets forth these duties as some of those properly delegated to a paralegal. (See Figure 8.1.)

As the paralegal's work will form the foundation of the attorney's work product submitted to the opposing party and the tribunal, it is imperative that the paralegal scrupulously adhere to the ethical requirements that underpin the adversarial system.

How does an attorney make the determination as to whether or not the cause of action has merit and is properly submitted to a tribunal for adjudication? In this situation, an attorney has two sources of guidance: ABA Model Rule 3.1 and the Federal Rules of Civil Procedure Rule 11. It is very important to note that most cases are *not* handled in federal court. The Federal Rules are discussed in this text as an example only. Paralegals and students must always check the rules in their relevant jurisdictions. ABA Model Rule 3.1 prohibits an attorney from bringing any issue before the court for which he cannot make a good faith argument in law and that he cannot support with some factual basis. Essentially, it prohibits nonsense or baseless claims. The true key to understanding this rule is to understand the **good faith** requirement imposed upon the attorney. This is where Federal Rule 11 is helpful. Most states have enacted similar rules pertaining to frivolous claims. Subsection (b) of Federal Rule 11, "Representations to Court," presents the situations in which the attorney would not be acting in good faith in presenting the issue to the tribunal. The attorney can be said to be acting in good faith only if, after a reasonable inquiry into the matter, he asserts that

1. it is not being presented for any improper purpose, such as to harass or to cause unnecessary delay or needless increase in the cost of litigation;

2. the claims, defenses, and other legal contentions therein are warranted by existing law or by a non-frivolous argument for the extension, modification, or reversal of existing law or the establishment of new law;

3. the allegations and other factual contentions have evidentiary support or, if specifically so identified, are likely to have evidentiary support after a reasonable opportunity for further investigation or discovery; and

4. the denials of factual contentions are warranted on the evidence or, if specifically so identified, are reasonably based on a lack of information or belief.

It is helpful to take each of these instances of good faith in turn. First, the attorney must promise that he is not bringing the matter to court just to bully another party. Mere unsubstantiated threat to sue is a violation of the attorney's duty to use the justice system only for proper purposes; actual misuse of the justice system is a more serious sanctionable offense violating both relevant rules of conduct. Further, even if the matter is properly brought before the court, it is impermissible to use any procedure in the court rules to achieve an improper purpose. For example, an attorney may not bring motion after motion which essentially seeks the same result just so the other party is forced to take time out of case preparation in order to answer them, and as a consequence the matter is delayed. More specifically, an attorney would be hard pressed to justify this sequence of motions as a "good faith" tactic: first, a motion for a more definite statement on the pleadings; second, another motion for the same; then, a motion to dismiss for failure to state a cause of action; then, a motion to dismiss on the pleadings; then, a summary judgment motion; and so on. All of these in rapid succession would not advance the proper purpose of these motions, but rather cause delay and frustration for the opposing counsel. This may also play out in the discovery phase of litigation, where an attorney drowns the opposition in superfluous and repetitive requests for production of information. A paralegal should be on alert for a supervising attorney's aggressive tactics in this regard. The court may also find that only part of the claim brought before the court is without merit, and dismiss that element of the matter. See, for example, *Hudson v. Moore Business Forms, Inc.,* 836 F.2d 1156 (9th Cir. 1987), wherein the plaintiff filed suit against her former employer alleging wrongful discharge and sex discrimination. Her employer counterclaimed, alleging that she had breached her employment duties of loyalty and good faith in performing her work. While the employer's claim of $200,000 in compensatory damages may have been a reasonable request for extension of the law of tort damages in an employment context, the $4 million sought in punitive damages was found to be wholly frivolous. The request for $4.2 million in damages was determined to have no plausible factual or legal basis and was made for the improper purpose of harassing the plaintiff and discouraging others from bringing similar suits against the employer.

Second, legal professionals must know not only the law, but also the boundaries of the law and when and if those borders should be crossed. Attorneys and paralegals have an obligation to the legal system to uphold those laws which are just and to advocate for change where the law or interpretation of the law is not just or equitable. To confine legal professionals by maintaining that any challenge to existing law is **frivolous** is to abrogate the very nature of our legal system. Laws change and develop over time in order to address the contemporary needs of society. Without challenges to the existing laws, past legal horrors like segregation and discrimination would still be in place. However, merely a desire to avoid the proper application of a just law to the present situation because it adversely impacts the client is not a good faith argument to have it changed. This truly "good faith" argument for change may be unconventional given the relevant precedent, however:

> *Rule 11 must not be construed so as to conflict with the primary duty of an attorney to represent his or her client zealously. Forceful representation often requires that an attorney attempt to read a case or an agreement in an innovative though sensible way. Our law is constantly evolving, and effective representation sometimes compels attorneys to take the lead in that evolution. Rule 11 must not be turned into a bar to legal progress.*

Operating Engineers Pension Trust v. A-C Co., 859 F.2d 1336, 1344 (9th Cir. 1988).

Third, conjecture and hypothesis based upon legal theory are not the sole basis for a claim; there must also be supporting facts that can be applied to the legal standards set forth in the law. The fact-finder, usually the jury, must be able to hear evidence that could convince them that the party has a **viable claim**; without evidence there can be no claim. This does not mean that the attorney must have her hands on all the supporting documentation at the time the pleadings are filed, but rather that she is satisfied that there exist such facts and evidence to support the claim. The standard applied in this situation is whether another attorney similarly situated would feel that the matter has enough factual support to bring the matter before the court. The attorney must make a reasonable inquiry as to the merits of the case before proceeding.

frivolous
Having neither factual merit nor legal purpose.

viable claim
A claim for which the fact-finder can supply a redress in law by applying the relevant legal standard to the presentable and substantiated facts.

In deciding whether an attorney signing a pleading made a reasonable inquiry into the facts and law of a case, the court uses an objective standard, asking what a reasonable attorney should have done under the circumstances that existed at the time of the challenged filing. Applying this objective standard, a court should consider these factors in determining whether an attorney made a reasonable inquiry to the facts:

> *whether the signer of the documents had sufficient time for investigation; the extent to which the attorney had to rely on his or her client for the factual foundation underlying the pleading, motion, or other paper; whether the case was accepted from another attorney; the complexity of the facts and the attorney's ability to do a sufficient pre-filing investigation; and whether discovery would have been beneficial to the development of the underlying facts.*
>
> *An attorney may rely upon his or her client for the factual basis for a claim when the client's statements are objectively reasonable, but this does not mean that an attorney always acts reasonably in accepting a client's statements. Whether it is reasonable to rely on one's client depends in part upon whether there is another means to verify what the client says without discovery. A party and attorney may not rely on formal discovery after the filing of a suit to establish the factual basis for the cause of action when the required factual basis could be established without formal discovery. In addition, in deciding whether to rely on one's client for the factual foundation of a claim, an attorney must carefully question the client and determine if the client's knowledge is direct or hearsay and is plausible; the attorney may not accept the client's version of the facts on faith alone. Allegations by a client of serious misconduct of another may require a more serious investigation. While the investigation need not be to the point of certainty to be reasonable and need not involve steps that are not cost-justified or are unlikely to produce results, the signer must explore readily available avenues of factual inquiry rather than simply taking a client's word.*

Wisconsin Chiropractic Ass'n v. State of Wisconsin ChiropracticExamining Board, 269 Wis. 2d 837, 853–854, 676 N.W.2d 580, 589–590 (WI App 2004) (citations omitted).

The Wisconsin court's point regarding client statements cannot be overemphasized, particularly for paralegals. Clients will, understandably, slant their recounting of the underlying facts to best support their claims, and it is often the paralegal's responsibility to perform client intake interviews, or at least attend them in order to take notes. Understanding the motivation for the client's accounting of the situation and evaluating his reliability and truthfulness is critically important at this early stage.

The last subsection of Rule 11 deals with properly defending against allegations. Just as a plaintiff may not wantonly hurl accusations at a defendant, so a defendant cannot recklessly deny them. While the burden of proving the essential elements of the cause of action lies with the plaintiff (generally speaking), the defendant cannot deny those factual elements that either are indeed known to her to be true or for which she has no knowledge as to the truth of the matter asserted.

 IN CLASS DISCUSSION

While many people thought the case brought against McDonald's alleging damages because Big Macs made the plaintiff fat was absolutely ridiculous, it was not frivolous under either ABA Model Rule 3.1 or Federal Rule 11 standards. The plaintiff was claiming that although he knew that Big Macs were not healthful, the marketing of the product caused him to consume too many and therefore caused him harm. This may appear to be a case of "assumption of the risk"; if the plaintiff is aware of the danger and proceeds anyway, there should be no recovery against the other party who presented the risk of harm. Why, then, did the attorney for the plaintiff file suit when everyone knows that fast food is not good for you and will make you fat if you eat too much of it? It looks like a loser from the start, doesn't it? Or does it? Didn't hundreds of plaintiffs win millions of dollars alleging the very same thing with respect to cigarettes?

SURF'S UP

Late hours and work overload may cause some attorneys to lash out in papers which, of course, will never be filed—very similar to those letters that we write to purge ourselves of tension and stress and then promptly shred or burn. But unforgiving technology doesn't let you retract that scathing e-mail that got sent because you inadvertently pushed the "enter" or "send" button. Similarly, a Colorado attorney, blowing off some steam onto yet another dreaded motion, probably did not intend to send the motion in Figure 8.2 by electronic filing.

FIGURE 8.2
Motion for Extension
Source: www.abovethelaw. com

EFILED Document

DISTRICT COURT, WATER DIVISION 7, COLORADO 1060 2nd Ave. Durango, CO 81301	CO La Plata County District Court 6th JD Filing Date: Mar 4 2007 11:28 AM MST Filing ID: 14001012 Review Clerk: Paula Petersen
IN THE MATTER OF THE APPLICATION FOR WATER RIGHTS OF THE SOUTHWESTERN WATER CONSERVATION DISTRICT, Applicant.	▲ COURT USE ONLY ▲
ATTORNEY FOR OPPOSER: REDACTED Denver, CO 80222 REDACTED	Case No.: 01 CW 54

MOTION FOR RULE 6(b)(2) EXTENSION TO RESPOND TO BILLS OF COSTS

Certificate of Compliance with Conferral Requirement

The undersigned certifies that opposing counsel do not consent to the extension.

Opposer Citizens Progressive Alliance ("CPA"), through its attorney undersigned and pursuant to Rule 6(b)(2), C.R.C.P., respectfully requests another one-day extension, to Monday, March 5, 2007, to respond to the Applicant's (and other opposers') bills of costs. As grounds therefore, the undersigned states that she had almost completed this response on the due date, which was Friday, March 2, but suspended her work in order to take a friend out to dinner for his birthday. When she came back, she was unable to finish it, due to the wine. :-) The response is filed herewith.

WHEREFORE, <u>inebriation constituting excusable neglect.</u> and no prejudice inuring to the other parties, the court should grant the present extension, as it is in the interest of justice.

EXPEDITING LITIGATION

Misusing the system to gain an unfair advantage may begin as described above; by contrast, later in the process, after a valid claim has been asserted, the abuse may take the form of overt disregard for and explicit impediments to the procedural deadlines imposed by the court rules. ABA Model Rule 3.2 requires that attorneys, and therefore their paralegals, make reasonable efforts to keep the litigation moving at a pace consistent with their obligations to the client and the legal system. Not only must legal professionals keep track of the timeline for litigation in a passive manner; they must also actively try to advance the resolution of the matter.

> *That rule imposes an affirmative duty on lawyers to make reasonable efforts to expedite litigation. The caveat—consistent with the interests of the client—insures that a lawyer's efforts to expedite litigation do not conflict with the client's legitimate interests. The comments [to the ethics rule], however, make it clear that "delaying tactics" are discouraged.*

Matter of Shannon, 179 Ariz. 52, 67, 876 P.2d 548, 563 (1994).

The Shannon disciplinary matter highlights the balancing act that attorneys must play in managing the progress of their cases. Hastiness, like excessive delay, is rarely congruous with good lawyering. Somewhere between these two extremes, the proper approach can be found. Paralegals play a vital role in finding and maintaining that balance through essential calendaring and case management systems. It is sometimes proper to request extensions of time in order to be thorough or due to extenuating circumstances not under the attorney's control or influence. However, prolonging the matter in order to gain strategic or financial advantage or simply to wear down the opposition's patience is unacceptable. The "reasonable lawyer" standard is used in determining whether the delay is tolerable. The essential question is whether another attorney or paralegal acting in good faith in carrying out her duties and obligations would take a similar course of action. The reasoning behind the request for an extension must have some purpose other than delay or advantage-taking. As in many areas of life, judging the conduct by the standard of the "Golden Rule"—treat others as you want to be treated—provides the best guidance.

CANDOR TOWARD THE TRIBUNAL

The underlying foundation of the entire justice system is honesty: "[c]andor and truthfulness are two of the most important moral character traits of a lawyer." *Attorney Grievance Com'n of Maryland v. Myers,* 333 Md. 440, 635 A.2d 1315 (1994). The attorney previously had been suspended for three years for an intentional misrepresentation to the court. At this hearing, the court stressed the importance of truthfulness and disbarred the attorney for this second offense involving misrepresentation to the court. Although history and the notorious media have not always held up that ideal, attorneys, aware of the severe sanctions possible, generally comply. To ensure that attorneys understand the sanctity of this principle, ABA Model Rule 3.3 is very specific as to the attorney's duties and makes it clear that in all situations where there is a conflict, candor toward the tribunal outweighs the attorney's duty to keep his clients' confidences. Figure 8.3 lists the various obligations of a legal professional to maintain honesty in the administration of justice.

FIGURE 8.3

Ensuring Honesty and Truthfulness before a Tribunal

Attorneys and paralegals are obligated to

1. refrain from making any statement of fact or law that the legal professional knows is false.
2. correct any previously made false statement of material fact.
3. disclose controlling legal authority (statutes, cases, rules, etc.) that is known by the legal professional and is directly adverse to the position of the client and which has not been disclosed to the tribunal by opposing counsel.
4. refrain from offering evidence that the legal professional knows to be false. An attorney may refuse to offer evidence that the attorney reasonably believes to be false, although the attorney cannot prohibit a criminal defendant from testifying in his own behalf if he chooses to exercise that right.
5. correct any false evidence submitted, once the attorney becomes aware of its falsity.
6. prevent or remediate criminal or fraudulent conduct of his client, where those activities are related to the proceedings.

Knowing
Believing with a reasonable and substantial probability (it is not necessary to be absolutely certain).

The key to understanding these obligations and their applicability is the definition of **knowing**. Where is the line to be drawn between knowledge and ignorance? There is a grey area of uncertainty between these two states of mind; how should the determination be made that an attorney or a paralegal "knew" a fact or statement of law was false? Since the purpose of the ethical rules is to protect the public and maintain the respectability of the profession, the courts have decided to err in favor of the public and the integrity of the legal system and hold that a negligent submission to a tribunal is a knowing misstatement subject to sanction. Attorneys are trained to make reasonable investigations into facts and law; they are required to make inquiry into the veracity of the underlying basis of their submissions to the tribunal. When they do not do so, they are making not an intentional misrepresentation, but rather a negligent declaration which they know is unsupported and therefore could be false. This knowledge of potential falsity and the potential to mislead or deceive is enough to achieve the "knowing" standard of the ethics rules. "By making no inquiry into the truth or falsity of her statement regarding the . . . incident, [the attorney] 'knowingly' misrepresented the facts." *In re Dodge,* 141 Idaho 215, 108 P.3d 362 (2005). Once the attorney formulates the intent to deceive by making a false statement to the tribunal, ABA Model Rule 8.4 comes into force. Professional misconduct is defined as engaging in conduct involving dishonesty, fraud, deceit, or misrepresentation. Similarly, NFPA prohibits such conduct in EC 1.3(b). (See Figure 8.4.) Violations such as fraud and misrepresentation by their legal definitions require the intent to deceive another regarding a material fact. Dishonesty may not require a specific intent to make a false statement regarding a material fact only. Any false statement impinges upon the trustworthiness and honesty of the legal professional. Every statement by an attorney to the court should be deliberately made, and this deliberateness should not depend upon the importance of that fact. It also does not matter if the court actually relied upon that false statement in making its decision, or whether any harm may have resulted from it. The mere fact of making a false statement to the court which the attorney knew was not necessarily true or verified is enough to form the basis of a sanction.

> *If an attorney does not know if an assertion is true or cannot point to a reasonably diligent inquiry to ascertain the truth of the statement, the attorney can remain silent, profess no knowledge, or couch the assertion in equivocal terms so the court can assess the assertion's probative value. The standard of affirming facts to the court cannot be the negligence standard, which is the argument presented to the Court by [the attorney]. . . . It is not unrealistic to expect an attorney making a representation to the court purporting to come from personal knowledge to take reasonable steps to assure she is speaking truthfully.*

Id. at 219–222.

materiality
Having a reasonable and recognizable importance in the process of evaluating a situation, such that its omission might affect the determination of fact or law.

Materiality does impact the legal professional's obligation when it comes to correcting a previously made statement. If, at the time that the legal professional made the submission to the court, it was true or the legal professional reasonably believed it to be true, but later, the legal professional discovers that it was incorrect, the attorney must make a supplemental disclosure to the court correcting the statement that is now known to be false. All litigants are entitled to a fair hearing and to judgments

FIGURE 8.4

Impropriety of Dishonesty

NFPA EC 1.3(b)

A paralegal shall avoid impropriety and the appearance of impropriety and shall not engage in any conduct that would adversely affect his/her fitness to practice. Such conduct may include, but is not limited to: violence, *dishonesty,* interference with the administration of justice, and/or abuse of a professional position or public office. (emphasis added) based upon a complete and truthful record. The obligation to supply the tribunal with correct information may last even beyond the final judgment, although the usual limit is the termination of the matter, by either settlement or final judgment, or the end of the time period for review on appeal. In *Washington v. Lee Tractor Co., Inc.,* 526 So.2d 447, La. App. 1988, the plaintiff sued the tractor company for personal injuries he sustained after falling off the tractor sold to the plaintiff's employer and used by the plaintiff in his course of work. The defendant tractor company obtained summary judgment in its favor based upon an affidavit from the tractor company's president that asserted that the tractor was not sold by his company and therefore was not liable for the plaintiff's personal injuries. The tractor company believed this information to be true at the time the affidavit was made. One month later, the tractor company found the invoice indicating the sale of the tractor. The lawyers for both sides agreed to reinstate the lawsuit; however, plaintiff's counsel informed the defendant that the suit would not be pursued. Approximately nine months later, plaintiff hired new counsel who contacted defense counsel to go forward with the reinstatement. Defense counsel at this time refused to honor the former agreement to reopen the matter. On application to the court, plaintiff was able to reopen the case and the summary judgment was annulled. The court found defense counsel's actions unacceptable and unethical because the summary judgment was obtained by knowingly false evidence and counsel is bound "to correct a false statement of material fact" (RPC 3.3), and the Rules

> place a distinct burden on an attorney who discovers the existence of false evidence to take 'reasonable remedial measures', and that such duty is unlimited in time, and do not abate at the end of the proceeding. . . .
>
> In essence, failure to correct false evidence, even if originally offered in good faith, is violative of this rule. . . . The failure to rescind the falsely obtained summary judgment has deprived Mr. Washington of his action against Lee. Defendant would not otherwise have been entitled to the summary judgment on the grounds for which it was prayed, without the supporting affidavit. By failing, and then refusing to have the summary judgment rescinded, and thus correct the record, the judgment has been allowed to stand. The result is unconscionable as the plaintiff is left without a remedy through no fault of his own. Therefore, we hold that these events constitute a [violation of the ethical rules].

Washington at 448–449.

There could be no more important fact than that which forms the basis for judgment, like the affidavit in the Washington case. The obligation applies to material facts only. What, then, does "material" mean? A fact is considered "material" if

> (a) a reasonable man would attach importance to its existence or nonexistence in determining his choice of action in the transaction in question; or
> (b) the maker of the representation knows or has reason to know that its recipient regards or is likely to regard the matter as important in determining his choice of action, although a reasonable man would not so regard it.

Watts v. Krebs, 131 Idaho 616, 620, 962 P.2d 387, 391 (1998) (quoting *Edmark Motors, Inc. v. Twin Cities Toyota,* 111 Idaho 846, 848, 727 P.2d 1274, 1276) (Ct. App.1986) (citing Restatement (Second) of Torts § 538(2)) (1977).

Essentially, if the submitted fact would have impacted the decision in any way and the attorney making the representation knew that the average "reasonable" person would regard that fact as an important factor—*or* if perhaps a "reasonable" person would not perceive the submitted fact as important, but the legal professional knows or suspects that the person will place importance on the fact and base some of her decision upon that fact (whether logically or not)—the legal professional has a duty to correct or update that decision maker by informing her of any changes in the original submission.

The third listed obligation seems almost counterintuitive to the adversarial system; however, attorneys and paralegals are ethically bound to reveal to the court the legal authority in the **controlling jurisdiction** in the matter, whether or not the authority is adverse to the attorney's position. It would be nearly impossible, relatively redundant, and ineffectual to mandate that all law that may impact the matter before the court be revealed and discussed. Indeed, a legal professional's skill set includes the ability to analyze and artfully choose not only the relevant legal authority to present to the court, but also the most persuasive authority, because it is most factually similar to the matter at hand. Clearly, the law that is most persuasive is that which comes from the controlling jurisdiction, where a decision has been made by a higher court within the jurisdictional hierarchy. Of course, the attorney or paralegal will willingly reveal the authority that bolsters her cause. If authority exists that is not favorable to the attorney's case, she must not ignore it. The duty of the attorney in that case is, in zealous advocacy for her client, to argue that the adverse authority is distinguishable from the matter at hand or was based upon an improper application of the law and therefore should not be applied. "The concept underlying this requirement of disclosure is that legal argument is a discussion seeking to determine the legal premises properly applicable to the case." *In re Thonert,* 733 N.E.2d 932, 934 (Ind. 2000). Indeed, this "open discourse" is appreciated by the courts and was remarkably noted in *Seidman v. American Express Company,* 523 F. Supp. 1107, 1110 (E.D. Pa. 1981): the trial court "commended" the defense attorney for calling attention to a case that was handed down after the defense's oral argument that severely undercut the position defendant had taken at oral argument.

The courts are apt to take a more expansive view of what legal authority should be disclosed, rather than a narrow view—again, in an effort to make a determination on the merits of the case and to properly ascertain a just and fair result.

The legislative history of Professional Conduct Rule 3.3(a)(3) and the commentaries on the rule show that "directly adverse" does not mean "controlling." It refers to a broader range of cases and statutes.

The meaning of "directly adverse" is explained in Formal Opinion No. 280 issued by the American Bar Association's Committee on Professional Ethics and Grievances. The Committee had been asked to clarify the "duty of a lawyer . . . to advise the court of decisions adverse to his client's contentions that are known to him and unknown to his adversary." The Committee wrote:

> We would not confine the [lawyer's duty] to "controlling authorities' "—i.e., those decisive of the pending case—but, in accordance with the tests hereafter suggested, would apply it to a decision directly adverse to any proposition of law on which the lawyer expressly relies, which would reasonably be considered important by the judge sitting on the case.

The Committee then defined the duty of disclosure:

> The test in every case should be: Is the decision which opposing counsel has overlooked one which the court should clearly consider in deciding the case? Would a reasonable judge properly feel that a lawyer who advanced, as the law, a proposition adverse to the undisclosed decision, was lacking in candor and fairness to him? Might the judge consider himself misled by an implied representation that the lawyer knew of no adverse authority?

Tyler v. State, 47 P.3d 1095, 1104–1105 (Alaska App. 2001).

The implication for attorneys and paralegals is clear: perform complete and thorough research and deal with it all, the good and the bad, in an honest, albeit persuasive, manner. This may mean that the paralegal will have to present her supervising attorney with cases that he doesn't necessarily want to hear about, but must be able to face and deal with. What if the other side has not been so diligent? What if opposing counsel

controlling jurisdiction
The legal system in which the tribunal sits whose higher courts' opinions are binding authority upon the lower courts.

has failed to find the law that is supportive of its side? The first attorney is required to essentially do the opposition's work for it. Yes, the ideal is to have adversaries that are vigorously defending their positions with their own arguments and legal support; however, "the old idea that litigation is a game between the lawyers has been supplanted by the more modern view that the lawyer is a minister of justice." *In re Greenberg,* 104 A.2d 46, 49, 15 N.J. 132, 138 (1954). Counsel cannot take advantage of the sloppy lawyering of opposing counsel. Adverse authority in the controlling jurisdiction must be presented to the court.

Even more egregious than failing to disclose, which is essentially a sin of omission, is actively and knowingly offering false evidence, a sin of commission. The rules and violations thereof are much clearer; either the evidence is substantiated and verifiable or it is not. The Greenberg case, *supra,* stated clearly that while attorneys should be able to argue perceptions of the facts and what they might indicate and submit those to the jury for its consideration, an attorney must not "present his inferences from the facts as if they were the very facts themselves. When he is indulging, as he has every right to do, in inferences or reasoning from the facts, he must say so […] and to be effective he should state the facts in the record from which he is making inferences." *Greenberg* at 47–48. A simple example of the difference between fact and inference is as follows: upon awakening, a person notices that her driveway is wet; she may infer that it rained during the night, but she has no factual basis without consulting the weather authority that it did in fact rain during the night. This prohibition applies not only to matters in an attorney's professional trial files, but also to those in her personal affairs that may end up in court. An attorney who sued in small claims court based on a simple breach of an equipment purchase submitted a letter he had written regarding the matter to settle the dispute. He was caught in a fabrication of evidence; he claimed to have sent this letter to the company that was suing him with a courtesy copy to the attorney representing the company. As it turns out, on the date that the letter was dated, the current attorney for the company was still in law school! The attorney, in an attempt to extricate himself from the knowing submission of false evidence, argued that it was merely a "petty business dispute" arising out of his poor temper in a personal matter which did satisfactorily settle out of court and therefore was not material to any disciplinary action. The court opined that "[t]his interpretation of the events grossly understate[d] their seriousness." *In the Matter of Barratt,* 663 N.E.2d 536, 539 (Ind. 1996). The attorney was suspended from practice for an entire year; this demonstrated the court's acknowledgment of the seriousness of the violation, as it reflected deleteriously upon the integrity of the profession and adversely upon the attorney's fitness to practice law. The lesson here for all legal professionals is to be scrupulous in all dealings with others.

The attorney must not only maintain his own honesty, but actively prevent others under his control from submitting false evidence. If the attorney is or becomes aware of a false submission from either his client or his witness, he must take action to correct it. The corrective action may go as far as withdrawing as counsel and disclosing the falsehood to the tribunal. The drafters of the Model Rules were not insensitive to the harshness of such a result. In comment 11 to Rule 3.3, they acknowledged that the client would naturally and understandably feel betrayed by the attorney's or paralegal's disclosure of the client's false testimony. However, the more evil of the two alternatives is the legal professional's assistance in the deception of the court. The truth-finding mission of the justice system can be served only by imposing this absolute obligation upon those who serve the system. Above all, the attorney must remain true to his highest role as an officer of the court, and the paralegal must steadfastly support that function.

Nowhere is this tension between loyalty to the client and duty to the court more strongly felt than in the criminal context. Criminal defendants have been given certain

due process
The ensuring of appropriateness and adequacy of government action in circumstances infringing on fundamental individual rights.

constitutional protections in judicial proceedings not afforded to civil matters due to the severity of punishment that can be imposed upon those found guilty of a crime. Where life and liberty, both constitutional protections, are threatened, the court has the highest duty to ensure fairness and just adjudication based upon the merits, and to afford the opportunity for the defendant to avail herself of all proper defenses. **Due process** may require that the defendant be given an opportunity to testify on her own behalf, and the United States Supreme Court has considered it a corollary to the Fifth Amendment right not to present evidence against oneself: i.e., if a defendant has the right not to speak, she should have the right to speak if she so chooses. In the landmark case *Nix v. Whiteside,* 475 U.S. 157, 106 S. Ct. 988, 89 L. Ed. 2d 123 (1986), the United States Supreme Court was presented with a case wherein the criminal defendant claimed a violation of his Sixth Amendment right to assistance of counsel when his attorney told him not to state in his own defense testimony that he saw "something metallic" (alluding to the fact that the defendant believed his murder victim to have had a gun but did not in fact see one); the attorney also told the defendant that if he insisted in presenting that testimony, the attorney would have to disclose the perjured testimony to the court. The Supreme Court found that the Sixth Amendment does not and cannot extend to subornation of perjury. "The Model Rules do not merely *authorize* disclosure by counsel of client perjury; they *require* such disclosure." *Id.* at 168 (emphasis in the original). The only deprivation in this case was the defendant's loss of his proposed submission of perjury; this, in the Court's view, is not only a good thing, but reasonable and proper under the Professional Rules of Conduct, and did not, therefore, deny or impair the defendant's Sixth Amendment right to effective assistance of counsel. "The right to counsel includes no right to have a lawyer who will cooperate with planned perjury. A lawyer who would so cooperate would be at risk of prosecution for suborning perjury, and disciplinary proceedings, including suspension or disbarment." *Id.* at 173.

The recurrent theme throughout these ethical obligations is the overarching duty of fairness in the justice system. To take advantage of the lack of actual knowledge of the court, jury, or adversary by submitting false legal authority, facts, or other evidence is to undermine the purpose of the system itself: to render justice based upon the truth. One court characterized this behavior as an attempt at "victory of unbridled egotism and arrogance over the judicial process and the rule of law." *Candolfi v. New York City Transit Authority,* 156 Misc.2d 964, 969, 595 N.Y.S.2d 656 (N.Y. City Civ. Ct. 1992).

This theme of candor and justice is extended to opposing parties and counsel as well. The thrust of ABA Model Rule 3.4 is the openness of the exchange of evidence or other relevant material between attorneys and the honest communication of information. In short, it is really about fighting fair. Fairness can be achieved only through full access to the truth. Attorneys and paralegals are prohibited from obstructing access to evidence and from destroying, altering, or falsifying evidence or any other material or document that may have evidentiary value. Evidence can also come in the form of testimony. Legal professionals must not advise or assist a witness to offer false testimony.

In a situation where one party has control of the evidence or information necessary to properly prepare for the resolution of the matter, opposing counsel must be given an opportunity to examine that evidence. Clearly, parties may wish that certain documentation indicating weakness, or worse, acknowledging fault, remained hidden; however, this cannot be the case where the legal system insists upon determining matters upon their merits. The infamous shredding, destruction, or modification of materials before responding to discovery requests is unacceptable and almost invariably, the parties get caught. Particularly horrendous is manipulation of the evidence by the attorney himself, not just at his suggestion. For example, in the case of *Bank of*

Hawaii v. Kunimoto, 91 Haw. 372, 984 P.2d 1198 (1999), counsel for the defendant in a bankruptcy judgment went into receivership; creditors were looking for payment on the 1.6 million dollar judgment. The receiver requested, properly, financial information and an accounting of all assets either previously or before owned. In an attempt to protect their client, the attorneys withheld certain stock issuance information which they alleged was not relevant because it had been transferred to the defendant's father years before. However, counsel knew that the receiver was entitled to the information and the court had ordered the defendant's father and sister to testify in court as to the stock. Despite this, counsel accepted the transfer of title of the stock in question to their firm in purported payment for legal fees and then, still aware that the court and receiver were interested in this stock, the firm sold it to liquidate the asset and kept the proceeds. The court found that counsel "recklessly or knowingly deceived the Court, withheld material, responsive information and documents regarding the CPB stock, and recklessly or knowingly disregarded, if not the letter, then certainly the spirit of Court orders and Court proceedings regarding the CPB stock." *Id.* at 386. The court ordered the disgorgement of the $90,000 from the sale to the receiver. In addition, counsel, who were acting under a limited admission to the Hawai'i bar (pro hac vice), were ordered to disclose the fact that their status was terminated in this matter and to give the reasons for their termination should they ever apply to any court in Hawai'i again.

An attorney or a paralegal who engages in this type of dishonest conduct, offering false or falsified evidence, is not fit to practice. An attorney and a paralegal must remain loyal first to the proper functioning of the justice system, and secondly, to their client. In an attempt to "get the heat off his client," an attorney had false bills of sale witnessed by another one of his clients after he noticed that the witness line was left blank for stolen equipment. He then submitted them to the court as proof that his client was not acting as a "fence" in the subsequent sale of the goods. Digging himself deeper, the attorney testified at his grievance hearing that he was unaware, at the time he prepared the receipts, that the equipment was stolen. An unlikely story, given that he previously had defended this client on larceny charges. The attorney's violation by altering and/or creating false evidence in violation of the subsequent subsection is

> regarded as misconduct of the most serious sort:
>
> Fundamental honesty is the base line and mandatory requirement to serve in the legal profession. The whole structure of ethical standards is derived from the paramount need for lawyers to be trustworthy. The court system and the public we serve are damaged when our officers play fast and loose with the truth. The damage occurs without regard to whether misleading conduct is motivated by the client's interest or the lawyer's own.

Iowa Supreme Court Board of Professional Ethics and Conduct v. Romeo, 554 N.W.2d 552, 554 (Iowa 1996).

Even mere hinting to a witness to alter her testimony is prohibited. Where an attorney knew that testimony might be damaging to his client, he told the grand jury witness: "Look, do me a favor. Just don't hurt the old guy, will you?" *Matter of Verdiramo,* 96 N.J. 183, 184, 475 A.2d 45, 46 (1984). The attorney was merely trying to protect his client, whom he characterized as "a genuinely nice human being who screwed up what checks went into what account." *Id.* The motive behind the attorney's misconduct is irrelevant.

> Attempted subornation of perjury is an inexcusable and reprehensible transgression. It is an obstruction of the administration of justice. Respondent's actions project a public image of corruption of the judicial process. . . . Professional misconduct that takes deadly aim at the public-at-large is as grave as the misconduct that victimizes a lawyer's individual clients. Because such a transgression directly subverts and corrupts the administration of justice, it must be ranked among the most egregious of ethical violations.

Id. at 185–186.

Whether the attorney actively engaged in the fraud upon the court, as in the Romeo disciplinary matter, or merely suggested that he would rather not see his client hurt by a full account of the truth in a witness's testimony, the attorney violated his obligation of honesty just the same. Any contravention of the rules subjects the attorney to severe discipline.

The openness and forthrightness required also pertains to dealings with third persons (non-clients and non-attorneys). To instruct witnesses or others holding relevant materials not to disclose that information is to obstruct access to potential evidence and is impermissible for the same reasons discussed above. The only two exceptions here apply to those persons in a close and potentially confidential relationship with the client and that kind of information which, if withheld, would pose no harm to the party seeking it. The first exception is easily understood: information from a client's spouse or another person who stands in an intimate relationship with the client and to whom the initial disclosures from the client would have been presumed to be secret or protected due to the relationship should be held safe. This protects the expectations of the client when the information was shared with the third party. There are certain parties to whom it is expected that private discloses will or must be made in order to facilitate the purpose of the relationship. Second, if the person from whom information is sought will not be adversely affected by the refusal to disclose the information, then that person may properly refuse to divulge the information. This will come up in the context where an informal request is made to a person not a party to the litigation and the information sought could be obtained through other means. If, however, a subpoena (formal request) has been issued, the attorney may not counsel the third party to fail to respond, because that would subject the third party to court sanctions (an adverse effect resulting from the refusal to render up the requested information). An attorney can advise another to refrain from voluntarily giving out the information only where there will be no adverse consequence. As officers of the court, attorneys and paralegals are expected to obey the orders and rules of procedure and other obligations to the letter. If an attorney decides that he has a valid and ethical basis upon which to rest his refusal to comply with an order or rule, he must present his excuse for refusal to comply openly to the court. In this way, the court can make the final determination of whether the attorney is properly maintaining his duties to both client and court. An attorney is not permitted to merely self-diagnose the problem and, once it is concealed from the court, take action upon it. An attorney is not the final arbiter of the conflict of duty; he has an obligation to expose the issue to the tribunal.

The rules of civil procedure for discovery underscore the theory that full, open, and honest disclosure of information is vital to just adjudication. They set forth mandates that opposing counsel exchange documents, answer interrogatories, conduct depositions, and the like within a certain time period. In this way, the matter can move forward at a predictable pace and the parties are fully aware of all supporting documentation for their claims and defenses. Again, in this area, paralegals are indispensable. Case management and calendaring are of the utmost importance. All discovery requests must be reasonably made and answered. Very often this duty falls upon the paralegal to accomplish in accordance with the rules of court procedure and ethical obligations of diligence and candor.

In a series of egregious failures to comply with the rules of discovery, including failure to supply opposing counsel with requested information, failing to make any requests for discovery until after the court-appointed time, and making motions for extensions of discovery time just in case he decided to make formal discovery requests, an attorney subjected himself to serious ethical sanctions. In his practice, the attorney felt that he was better able to serve his clients by keeping costs down and doing only as much informal discovery as necessary. He would interview witnesses on his own and not rely on information gathered through opposing counsel. In the same vein, he failed to make appropriate disclosures to opposing counsel. The court appointed another independent attorney to supervise the violator; this monitoring attorney would have access to all the violator's paperwork regarding the management of his practice. Specifically, and probably humiliatingly, the monitoring attorney would meet with the violator twice a month and the violator would have to report "whether he has failed to timely respond to requests for discovery, to motions to compel, or to orders to show cause." He also had to "maintain a comprehensive calendar of court appearances, discovery deadlines, and other pleading deadlines." *In re Boone,* 269 Kan. 484, 7 P.3d 270, 284 (2000). The courts have the ability to fashion appropriate remedies to ensure that attorneys do not flout their obligations under both the rules of procedure and the rules of ethics.

Particularly damaging is dishonesty or deceitful tactics in open court. Juries can be unduly influenced by the dramatics of the courtroom, and the matter of admissibility of evidence is enough to confuse an experienced attorney, let alone a layperson. Further, it is simply human nature to draw conclusions, whether substantiated or not, and nearly impossible to disregard a statement once heard; one court characterized the damage of an attorney's misconduct in front of the jury as "like trying to un-ring a bell." *Love v. Wolf,* 226 Cal. App. 2d 378, 392, 38 Cal. Rptr. 183 (1964). In order to provide the fact-finder with a clear stream of evidence to consider, all matters not relevant or unsupported by admissible evidence should not be brought up in open court. The record should be "clean" for the jury to consider the evidence fairly.

> *It is fair to say that the average jury, in a greater or less degree, has confidence that these obligations [of candor], which so plainly rest upon the prosecuting attorney, will be faithfully observed. Consequently, improper suggestions, insinuations, and, especially, assertions of personal knowledge are apt to carry much weight against the accused when they should properly carry none.*

Berger v. U.S., 295 U.S. 78, 88, 55 S. Ct. 629 (1935).

The ABA Model Rules require attorneys to refrain from making any remarks that are not supported by the information properly before the court.

While trial advocacy is an art, there are some boundaries that must not be crossed. Attorneys are granted considerable latitude when crafting their opening and closing arguments, as well as in how they phrase their questions on examination of witnesses.

> *Aggressive advocacy is not only proper but desirable. Our jurisprudence is built upon a firm belief in the adversary system. Moreover, in a long trial, as this one was, vigorously prosecuted and defended, frayed tempers leading to intemperate outbursts are a to-be-expected byproduct. Skilled advocates are not always endowed with "high boiling points." Juries, characteristically composed of average men and women, may be assumed able to withstand substantial blandishments without surrendering their ability to reason soberly and fairly. Recognizing these factors, reviewing courts are not, and should not be, overly eager to reverse for conduct which is merely moderately captious.*
>
> *But there is a limit. The misconduct here was intentional, blatant, and continuous from opening statement, throughout the trial, to closing argument. It was committed by a seasoned and experienced trial lawyer and the record leaves no doubt it was carefully contrived and calculated to produce a result.*

Love, supra, at 393–394.

During trial, testimony procured from cross-examination must refer only to evidence that has been or will be admitted for consideration to the jury. An attorney may become a master at the **leading question** designed to elicit the desired answer from the opposing side's witnesses. However, cross-examination questions may not refer to supposed facts that are not supported by evidence received in court. Infamous

leading question
The phrasing of an interrogatory so as to suggest the desired answer.

tactics like these—"Isn't it true that . . . " and "Did you know that . . . "—may refer only to that which is substantiated by supporting evidence. The attorney cannot use the question to suggest that certain facts exist when indeed they do not. "These 'did you know that' questions designed not to obtain information or test adverse testimony but to afford cross-examining counsel a device by which his own unsworn statements can reach the ears of the jury and be accepted by them as proof have been repeatedly condemned." *supra,* at 391 (citations omitted).

Similarly, the closing arguments of counsel must refer only to the facts presented during the trial that were properly admitted before the court. This would exclude unsubstantiated allusions of counsel during testimonial evidence, as discussed above.

> *[I]t is first necessary to reiterate certain well established principles of law concerning closing arguments. The purpose of a closing argument is to assist the jury in arriving at a verdict, with all facts presented fairly. Considerable latitude of expression on anything that is in evidence must be allowed counsel. The closing arguments of counsel must be confined to those matters that are in evidence or admitted and uncontroverted. When counsel oversteps the boundaries of proper argument, the trial judge need not wait for opposing counsel to object but under appropriate circumstances the court can halt the improper argument. [...] It is the duty of the court to control counsel within reasonable bounds and to restrict the argument to the evidence in the case.*

Foerster v. Illinois Bell Tel. Co., 20 Ill. App.3d 656, 661–662, 315 N.E.2d 63, 67 (1974) (citations omitted).

Clearly, if an attorney is prohibited from alluding to inadmissible evidence, she is just as clearly prohibited from expressing her personal opinions on the credibility of a witness (insinuating or declaring outright that the witness is a liar) or on the justness of the cause (characterizing the claim or defense as ridiculous) or on the guilt or innocence of the litigant (usurping the very job of the jury). Where "the assistant prosecutor referred to defense evidence as "lies," "garbage," "garbage lies," "[a] smoke screen," and "a well conceived and well rehearsed lie," there was a clear violation of the rule. *State v. Smith,* 14 Ohio St.3d 13, 14, 470 N.E.2d 883, 885 (1984). Paralegals attending trial and sitting at counsel table assisting their supervising attorneys must take care not to use body language to send negative signals to the jury. Commentary upon the evidence and to suggest what a jury may infer for itself from the properly admitted evidence is proper; reaching beyond this is unethical. Argument is not the same as assertion. Essentially, if attorneys were able to present their own opinions on the matters considered by the court, they would be acting as unsworn witnesses themselves. An attorney is not permitted, as a general rule, to act as a witness in a case where he is also acting as an advocate. See ABA Model Rule 3.7 (Lawyer as Witness).

Closely allied to the requirement of honesty in a tribunal is the idea that the third persons (non-parties) involved in the litigation should remain unbiased and be able to openly evaluate the merits of the case properly presented to them. Attorneys and paralegals are prohibited from seeking to influence anyone involved with the justice system. This includes judges, jurors, prospective jurors, bailiffs, clerks, and other court personnel. The tasks of judges and jurors in the justice system require that they maintain a respectful distance and neutrality in all matters before them. Attorneys frequently appear before the same judges in the various cases they handle. It is important for both parties to retain a respectful distance and decorum despite the familiarity that may develop between them. These players in the system have a mutual obligation to ensure that they do not take advantage of their respective roles and circles of influence. In a rather startling matter, a judge met with an attorney who was frequently before him in court and asked why the attorney didn't "turn [his] two hundred and fifty thousand dollar case into a million" and, of course, give the judge his share of the increased collected fee. *Committee on Legal Ethics of the West Virginia State Bar v.*

Hobbs, 190 W.Va. 606, 607, 439 S.E.2d 629, 630 (1993). But the judge was not the only one sanctioned in this matter. The duty to remain neutral and abide by all the relevant ethical rules is mutual. Even though the attorney voluntarily came forward after the judge was indicted on other matters, the hearing court found that the attorney had expected to gain an advantage in this or other matters.

> *In this case, the ethics violations are serious. Secret payments of money to a presiding judge are a direct attack on one of the most vital areas of our legal system. To paraphrase In re Barron, 155 W.Va. 98, 102, 181 S.E.2d 273, 275 (1971) (disbarment for bribing a juror), we find it difficult to consider an offense which is more destructive or corruptive of the legal system of West Virginia than secret payments, however categorized, to a presiding judge. Protection of the public against members of the Bar who are unworthy of the trust and confidence essential to the attorney/client relationship is a primary purpose of professional discipline.*

Hobbs at 611.

This attempt to influence any official, not just a judge, in the litigation will most likely result in disbarment, due to the grave implications it has on the effective administration of justice. *See Matter of Kassner,* 93 A.D.2d 87, 461 N.Y.S.2d 11, (N.Y.A.D.1983), *app. denied,* 59 N.Y.2d 604, 464 N.Y.S.2d 1025, 451 N.E.2d 504 (1983), wherein the attorney was disbarred after attempting to bribe the judge's secretary in an attempt to gain a favorable verdict. This rule against improper influence is intuitive and, fortunately, crops up infrequently in practice, although it makes for wonderful plot complications in television dramas and movies. Remember, any action that is prohibited for an attorney cannot be performed by a paralegal; the ethical obligations are the same.

The interaction with the judge, juror, or other official need not be so drastic as bribery or other extreme conduct. In order to preserve the inviolability of the process, any **ex parte** communications with these types of persons are prohibited. NFPA EC 1.2(a) specifically prohibits paralegals from making such communications. (See Figure 8.5.) Ex parte communications are those that are made by an attorney to the tribunal without opposing counsel present that relate to the substance of the matter. General inquiries about court dates or other procedural questions are not generally considered prohibited communications. The types of communication that are prohibited, with exceptions for emergencies, are those that attempt to gain an unfair advantage. Secret communications do not correspond with candor toward the tribunal. All exchanges of information must be made openly and with the participation of both sides. Both sides should at all times be able to present and respond at the same time. This ensures that no unfair advantage can be taken. It does not matter whether the attorney actually gained any unfair advantage or not due to the ex parte communication. The simple fact that the exchange took place and could have had some effect on the legal rights of the parties in the matter before the court is enough. The violation does not depend upon how the judge reacts to the improper communication; the attorney's actions are determinative of the issue. *See In re Complaint of Thompson,* 325 Or. 467, 473, 940 P.2d 512, 515 (1997). In this way, there is a "bright-line" rule prohibiting the ex parte communication, and therefore, an attorney can clearly determine his obligation under the rule and conduct himself accordingly. The rule against ex parte communication applies even when the attorney does not talk about the facts of the matter before the court:

> *Even though petitioner did not discuss the merits of his case with the juror, the record amply supports the trial judge's conclusion that petitioner attempted indirectly to influence her. By initiating a friendly conversation, buying drinks, and discussing his personal history and religious*

Ex parte
A legal professional's communication regarding the substance of the matter without opposing counsel present.

NFPA EC 1.2(a)

A paralegal shall not engage in any ex parte communications involving the courts or any other adjudicatory body in an attempt to exert undue influence or to obtain advantage or benefit of only one party.

FIGURE 8.5
Ex Parte Communications

*beliefs, petitioner attempted to arouse sympathy on his behalf. "The harm inherent in deliberate contact or communication can take the form of subtly creating juror empathy with the party. . . . " (*Rinker v. County of Napa *(9th Cir. 1983) 724 F.2d 1352, 1354.)*

Petitioner's conduct may in itself have been criminal. At the very least, it was grossly unethical. As an attorney, petitioner must have been aware that any outside influences on the jury's deliberative processes are inimical to our system of justice.

*"In a criminal case, any private communication, contact, or tampering, directly or indirectly, with a juror during a trial about the matter pending before the jury is, for obvious reasons, deemed presumptively prejudicial, if not made in pursuance of known rules of the court and the instructions and directions of the court made during the trial, with full knowledge of the parties." (*Remmer v. United States *(1954) 347 U.S. 227, 229 [98 L. Ed. 654, 656, 74 S. Ct. 450, 451].) Thus, it is unethical for an attorney to communicate with a juror outside the courtroom during the course of a trial. Petitioner's blatant violation of this rule plainly demonstrates an unfitness to practice law.*

In re Possino, 37 Cal.3d 163, 170, 207 Cal. Rptr. 543 (1984).

The prohibition of ex parte communications is not limited to attorneys or paralegals who are directly involved in either prosecution or defense of matter. In *People v. Honeycutt,* 20 Cal.3d 150, 141 Cal. Rptr. 698 (1977), a juror contacted his own attorney for advice during deliberations in a criminal case. Not only is the juror guilty of misconduct, but, ethically, so is the outside attorney who is communicating with the juror. Paralegals are also prohibited from consulting with anyone involved in a proceeding. Friends and family may ask for advice, commentary, or explanation when they are involved as jurors in the legal system. This is understandable. However, it is imperative that paralegals refrain from offering any information. These ex parte communications, whether they come from a participating attorney, outside attorney, judge, or other official, have the potential to compromise the proceedings. The juror would be receiving information not properly admitted into evidence; this would constitute an obstruction of justice and a knowing violation on the part of the attorney of the ethical mandate to refrain from interfering with the judicial process.

This obligation of noninterference does not end with the termination of the litigation in all circumstances. As discussed above, attorneys may find themselves before the same judge in another case, so they must remain at a professional distance at all times. This is not the case with jurors. Once the matter is over, the attorney is unlikely to see them in the legal context again. However, the ethical rules still prohibit talking to jurors even *after* the case has concluded under some circumstances. An attorney or a paralegal must not communicate in any way with a juror after discharge of the jury where such communications are

1. prohibited by court order or other law or rule

2. unwanted by the juror, where the juror has told that to the legal professional

3. in furtherance of misrepresentation, coercion, duress, or harassment

The second and third subsections are self-explanatory with regard to their impropriety. Under what circumstances would a communication be prohibited by law or court order? There are two major reasons for seeking to communicate with jurors post-trial: (1) to determine whether there has been any improper conduct during the jury deliberations to form a ground to challenge the verdict based upon jury misconduct, and (2) to determine on what basis the verdict was reached.

In the first instance, the attorney must apply for leave of court to contact the jurors to evaluate the potential for a challenge to the jury's conduct, and the attorney must demonstrate in a sworn affidavit some specific evidence of misconduct. "Federal courts have generally disfavored post-verdict interviewing of jurors. We have repeatedly refused to 'denigrate jury trials by afterwards ransacking the jurors in search of some new ground, not previously supported by evidence, for a new trial.'" *Haeberle v. Texas Intern. Airlines,* 739 F.2d 1019, 1021 (5th Cir. 1984), citing, *United States v. Riley,* 544 F.2d 237, 242 (5th Cir.1976), *cert. denied,* 430 U.S. 932, 97 S. Ct. 1554, 51 L. Ed. 2d 777 (1977).

The second reason may have arguable implications in First Amendment rights (freedom to speak and associate with other members of the public); however, the privacy interests of the jurors to be free of harassment and the respectability of the jury system outweigh the "curiosity" of attorneys and litigants. *Haeberle* at 1022.

Impartiality and Decorum

As is the custom with ethics rules, there is a final "catch-all" provision in both the ABA Model Rules and the NFPA Rules. Attorneys and paralegals are prohibited from disrupting or disrespecting the decorum of the tribunal. (See Figure 8.6.)

Where no specific rule applies, but the attorney or paralegal has clearly engaged in some improper conduct that has negative consequences on the trial, the disciplinary board can rest its findings in this provision. For example, in *Disciplinary Counsel v. LoDico,* 106 Ohio St. 3d 229, 833 N.E.2d 1235, 1237 (2005), two judges found the attorney in contempt for his "pervasive and continuing pattern of misconduct in their courtrooms." His behavior was egregious and the antics hard to comprehend outside of a TV courtroom drama series.

> *[The attorney]'s misconduct began even before the jury was impaneled, with inappropriate, loud, and rude statements that wrongly impugned the integrity of a prospective juror during voir dire. Respondent was cautioned about his conduct in the courtroom early in the trial proceedings. [...] Rather than curtailing his misconduct, however, respondent continued his behavior, at one point throwing money and credit cards on the bench in anticipation of a sanction and telling the Judge, '[G]o ahead and fine me'." [...] Disregarding [the] Judge's orders, he spoke loudly at sidebars in an apparent effort to ensure that the jury heard his statements, including his suggestions that witnesses were lying. [...] [Attorney]'s pattern of misconduct in [the] courtroom appears to have been an effort to create "an atmosphere of utter confusion and chaos, quoting the trial court's contempt charge." Rather than advancing the pursuit of justice, [the attorney] advanced obstruction, obfuscation, and opprobrium.*

Id. at 233–234, citing *Mayberry v. Pennsylvania* (1971), 400 U.S. 455, 462, 91 S. Ct. 499, 27 L. Ed. 2d 532.

Trial Publicity

Some rules address the conduct within the confines of the individual tribunal in order to maintain the dignity of the justice system, and others focus on the perception of

NFPA EC 1.3(a)	**FIGURE 8.6**
A paralegal shall refrain from engaging in any conduct that offends the dignity and decorum of proceedings before a court or other adjudicatory body and shall be respectful of all rules and procedures.	**Decorum in Proceedings**

the matter as portrayed to the public at large. The relationship between attorneys and the media is mutually impactful, but not necessarily mutually beneficial, in high-profile cases. A legal professional is not prohibited from making statements outside the courtroom (extrajudicial statements); however, she must be careful in what she does say, as public sentiment is a powerful weapon inside the jury deliberations. The ABA Model Rules do permit basic facts to be disseminated because the public also has a right to know what is going on.

> *The judicial system, and in particular our criminal justice courts, play a vital part in a democratic state, and the public has a legitimate interest in their operations. See, e.g.,* Landmark Communications, Inc. v. Virginia, *435 U.S. 829, 838–839, 98 S. Ct. 1535, 1541–1542, 56 L. Ed. 2d 1 (1978). "[I]t would be difficult to single out any aspect of government of higher concern and importance to the people than the manner in which criminal trials are conducted."* Richmond Newspapers, Inc. v. Virginia, *448 U.S. 555, 575, 100 S. Ct. 2814, 2826, 65 L. Ed. 2d 973 (1980). Public vigilance serves us well, for "[t]he knowledge that every criminal trial is subject to contemporaneous review in the forum of public opinion is an effective restraint on possible abuse of judicial power. . . . Without publicity, all other checks are insufficient: in comparison of publicity, all other checks are of small account."* In re Oliver, *333 U.S. 257, 270-271, 68 S. Ct. 499, 506–507, 92 L. Ed. 682 (1948).*

Gentile v. State Bar of Nevada, 501 U.S. 1030, 1035, 111 S. Ct. 2720, 2724, 115 L. Ed. 2d 888 (1991).

Indeed, the Sixth Amendment of the United States Constitution requires a public trial in criminal cases, as the Framers understood the need to ensure fairness to the accused and to ensure the community's confidence in the judicial system. The Framers did not set a priority between the First and Sixth Amendments probably because the factors in each case must be delicately balanced to secure justice in that particular circumstance. There are certainly more factors to consider when celebrities are involved or during a particularly notorious crime.

ABA Model Rule 3.6 sets forth the kinds of information that can be disseminated. The real danger lies not in the factual content of the statement, but rather in the connotations, implications, and inferences that can be drawn by the public because the information is coming from an attorney. The information may be imbued with authority because of its source. It matters who the messenger is in this circumstance. Therefore, statements other than the most basic information are prohibited. Attorneys are confined to

1. stating the type of claim asserted and/or any defenses available
2. identifying their client (unless there is a legal prohibition or exception, as in the case of minors)
3. stating information available from public records
4. stating that there is an investigation in progress
5. advising of the progress or stage of litigation and any court scheduling
6. requesting assistance in obtaining information regarding the matter
7. warning the public about any danger posed by the person or people involved in the matter
8. advising of the status of the criminal arrest, investigation, and officers involved (if applicable)

All of these types of information should seem relatively familiar, as they are regularly reported on news broadcasts. If you pay attention to interviews with attorneys, you will notice which information they readily make public and which is not commented on at all.

IN CLASS DISCUSSION

Evaluate whether the commentary to the press was appropriate under the ethical rules regarding trial publicity—whether it may have been prejudicial or was consistent with Constitutional protections.

In July of 1993, Rothman was retained by Mr. C. and his son, a minor, to seek redress against the popular singer, Michael Jackson, for alleged torts against the boy. Rothman contacted Jackson and began to negotiate on behalf of the C. family, but did not immediately file a lawsuit, as the family wished the matter kept confidential.

While negotiations were proceeding, a psychological evaluation of the boy, which had been filed with the Los Angeles County Department of Children's Services, as required by California's child abuse reporting laws was "leaked" by a person or persons unknown. However, no claim has been made that Rothman or his clients were responsible for the leak. In any event, whoever caused the leak, its result was what Rothman characterizes as a "firestorm" of publicity, for Jackson is a celebrity among celebrities, and the charges contained in the psychological evaluation were sensational.

The defendants responded to this negative public exposure by calling a press conference on August 29, 1993, and by making other statements to the media thereafter, in which the defendants not only denied the charges against Jackson, but made countercharges that Rothman and his clients had knowingly and intentionally made false accusations against Jackson in order to extort money from him. Extortion is, of course, a crime and the charge was inevitably damaging to Rothman's professional reputation. Moreover, as an additional consequence of the extortion charges, Rothman felt compelled to withdraw from his representation of the C. family, causing him significant economic damage, as the C.'s eventually retained other counsel who negotiated a settlement with Jackson that was never disclosed to the public, but was reputed to be over $25 million.

See Rothman v. Jackson, 49 Cal. App. 4th 1134, 1138–1139 (1996).

RESEARCH THIS

Tabloids, pop culture magazines, TV broadcasts—they are all littered with celebrity goings-on, and the juiciest morsels often relate to legal battles. Find the truth behind the sensational headlines. Pick a current high-profile legal battle that is garnering a lot of media attention and perform your own unbiased legal research on the matter. Evaluate the ethical implications of the public commentary on the matter.

The United States Supreme Court rendered an opinion regarding the potential impact of these restrictions not just on an attorney's ethical obligations, but also on the attorney's First Amendment right to free speech. The ethical obligations prohibit an attorney from statements to the press that he knows or reasonably should know will have a substantial likelihood of materially prejudicing the trial. Essentially, information that goes beyond the basic can be considered to be prejudicial to the litigant's right to a fair trial.

The "substantial likelihood of material prejudice" standard is a constitutionally permissible balance between the First Amendment rights of attorneys in pending cases and the State's interest in fair trials. Lawyers in such cases are key participants in the criminal justice system, and the State may demand some adherence to that system's precepts in regulating their speech and conduct. Their extrajudicial statements pose a threat to a pending proceeding's fairness, since they have special access to information through discovery and client communication, and since their statements are likely to be received as especially authoritative. The standard is designed to protect the integrity and fairness of a State's judicial system and imposes only narrow and necessary limitations on lawyers' speech.

Gentile at 1031.

Even if the press could report the occurrences as public information gained from open access to the court proceedings, the attorney and his staff may be prohibited from discussing the same information. The key to understanding this principle is to understand the perception of the public. The source of the information is just as critical as the information itself. It is the difference between getting your news from the *Wall Street Journal,* the publication of record with an impeccable reputation for accuracy and integrity, and getting it from one of the "tabloid" magazines that thrive on scandal and creatively captioning paparazzi snapshots of the rich and famous. Attorneys are presumed, whether correctly or not, to have insider information, and what they say is given authority and taken to be true. They are not neutrals to the matter, as they are allied with either the prosecution or the defense and are ethically bound to zealously advocate for their respective positions. This may either cause what they say to be slanted in itself or cause their speech to be unduly influential. Understandably and consistently with the other rules, all attorneys associated in a firm are bound to conform their actions to the obligations of each individual attorney. This also holds true for the paralegals and other support staff in the firm. What an attorney is prohibited from doing, so are all employees and agents of the attorney.

SPOT THE ISSUE

Prosecutors owe a dual loyalty: to the public as their champion against those who threaten their security and peace, and to the criminal justice system. They are often called upon to comment on criminal investigations and recent apprehensions.

Paul, a prosecutor, recently attended a press conference and made several statements to the media regarding the anticipated prosecution in two separate murders that had the town up in arms.

He described Suspect #1's confession and the circumstances surrounding his custodial statements to police:

The police were able to obtain a confession completely consistent with the suspect's constitutional rights; he confessed within just a few hours with incredible details that only the murderer would have known. He was then provided the opportunity to rest and . . . he slept, and commented that it was one of the best nights of sleep he had gotten in a long time.

"This morning at dawn, he was taken up to the crime scene, was videotaped by police, and went over in detail by detail every step of what he did to the victim. Suspect #1 provided a full and detailed account of the assault and murder.

As for Suspect #2, the prosecutor stated this:

The County Police were able to determine definitively that indeed it was Suspect #2 who had committed the second notorious murder. They were able to do so by following him. They conducted surveillance for over 24 hours. And then when they actually found him, he was wearing a very unique shoe, a very unique boot, and the print of that boot matched the print that was found at the scene of the crime, and then further questioning revealed, in fact, he was the person that had done it. We have a confession from the perpetrator as well as scientific and forensic evidence to corroborate that confession. We have found the person who committed the crime at this point and the case against Suspect #2 will be a strong case.

For guidance, see *Attorney Grievance Commission of Maryland v. Gansler,* 377 Md. 656, 835 A.2d 548 (2002).

An exception exists where an attorney is put in a defensive position due to another person's statement regarding the matter. By making a potentially harmful comment, that party has "opened the door" for the attorney to respond as appropriate in order to protect her client's interests in receiving a fair trial. the response must be purely remedial in nature and cannot divulge information beyond that which has been released publicly by the other party or the press.

Truthfulness in Statements to Others

Of course, it is not only inside the courtroom that an attorney represents the honor of the justice system; in all his dealings, including those with non-clients and those not participating in the litigation, he must act with the same candor and respect. The various parts of ABA Model Rules 4.1 through 4.4 ("Transactions with Persons Other than Clients") essentially reiterate and underscore this duty to uphold the reputation and respect of the justice system with everyone.

Relying on everything that was discussed regarding trial publicity, it is merely an extrapolation of the principle that statements made by legal professionals have a certain added authority, and, therefore, they are obligated to be careful in making statements to others. Misstatements of law or fact are not permissible in any context. Delegation or blame placed on another person involved in the misrepresentation does not absolve the attorney of her responsibility to ensure that communications to third persons are not misleading or false. Encouraging or instructing a client to make a false statement to a third party is still violative of the ethics rules, as if the attorney had made the statement himself, because it is clothed in his authority when made in the context of a legal matter. *See In re Mitchell,* 822 A.2d 1106 (D.C. Ct. App. 2003), wherein the attorney apparently instructed the client to inform the third party creditor to the client that the personal injury suit was "on appeal" and therefore the attempt at collecting the debt from the lawsuit proceeds was not yet ripe. This was a false statement in an attempt to avoid payment. It doesn't matter that the falsification was through his client, nor would it matter if the misrepresentation were through another third party. The attorney may be held responsible if he knew that the false statement was made. There is also the continuing obligation to correct any prior statements that either were unknowingly incorrect at the time they were made or were true at the time but have become incorrect.

> *Making a false statement includes the failure to make a statement in circumstances in which nondisclosure is equivalent to making such a statement. Thus, where a lawyer has made a statement that the lawyer believed to be true when made but later discovers that the statement was not true, in some circumstances failure to correct the statement is equivalent to making a statement that is false.*

Carpenito's Case, 139 N.H. 168, 173, 651 A.2d 1, 4 (1994) (emphasis added).

Persons Represented by Counsel

Respect for third persons extends to acknowledging the fact of their representation by another attorney or the fact that they should be represented by another attorney in the matter for which the attorney seeks to speak to them. There are specific rules addressing the propriety of communicating with persons represented by counsel and rules for when they are not. If a person is represented by counsel, legal professionals are not permitted to communicate with her. All communications must be made through the represented person's attorney. There are two exceptions to this general prohibition: the attorney may have permission from the other attorney to contact his client directly, or there may be a court order or rule that permits this direct communication.

It is very important to note that paralegals, support staff, and other persons working with the attorney (whether or not an agency relationship exists) must respect these

FIGURE 8.7

**Communication with
Represented Persons**

NFPA EC 1.2(b)

A paralegal shall not communicate, or cause another to communicate, with a party the paralegal knows to be represented by a lawyer in a pending matter without the prior consent of the lawyer representing such other party.

rules as well. (See NFPA EC 1.2(b) in Figure 8.7.) This was the case in *In re Conduct of Burrows*, 291 Or. 135, 629 P.2d 820 (1981). A rape and robbery suspect was approached by the prosecuting attorney to turn into an informant regarding the local drug scene in exchange for a reduction or dismissal of the other pending charges. The suspect met with the prosecutor and police officers in the prosecutor's office and they told him they would not discuss the rape matter because he was represented by an attorney. After the meeting and in the presence of the prosecutor, the police told the suspect not to mention the undercover work to his attorney in the rape case; the prosecutor said nothing. The police worked with the suspect for months without ever contacting the suspect's attorney. The court found that the prosecutor was guilty of communicating with a represented person about the subject matter of the case. In his defense, the prosecutor first claimed that the role of drug informant was not the "subject of the representation"; however, the court found this to be too limited an interpretation. The suspect's activities in cooperation with the police had a direct impact on the charges levied against him. The suspect received a more favorable plea agreement on the charges for which he was represented as a consequence of his cooperation with the police.

> It is entirely possible, if not probable, that an accused needs competent legal counsel representation during the evolution of an agreement for leniency in exchange for cooperation with law enforcement agencies. . . . In short, we think that where it was clear that [suspect]'s undercover drug activities were likely to, or at least were expected to, impact the pending criminal charges, the subject matter of the communications necessarily involved the pending criminal charges.

Id. at 143.

Having determined that there indeed was communication regarding the "subject of representation," the prosecutor then argued that it was not himself that was communicating with the represented suspect.

> Further, we are not aware of any rule of law or principle which enables an attorney to excuse his failure to obtain an opposing attorney's consent by delegating the task to non-lawyers who, albeit deceptively, failed to follow through with their instructions. It would be difficult to hypothecate a set of circumstances which better illustrate the folly and danger of a principle of ethics which would permit a lawyer to excuse his misfeasance or nonfeasance by delegating to, and then later blaming, a non-lawyer. The overzealous and at times deceptive conduct of one or more of the police officers involved in this episode aptly illustrate the point.
>
> In any event, by the time the police officers were instructed to inform [the suspect's attorney], two proscribed meetings had been held and the die was practically cast. [The suspect's attorney] merely would have been presented with a fait accompli.
>
> In our opinion, both attorneys violated [the rule] by communicating, or causing others to communicate, with [the suspect] without obtaining [the suspect's attorney]'s consent.[...]
>
> We also find that [the prosecutor] acted to conceal the communications by his failure to countermand the police officers' suggestion to [the suspect] that he not tell [the suspect's attorney].

Id. at 143–144.

Any communications that could not be made by the attorney, could also not be made by any person with whom she is working. To allow an attorney to delegate or assign away her ethical responsibility is impermissible, as it would give the attorney a loophole to avoid compliance with the ethical rules.

NFPA EC 1.7

A paralegal's title shall clearly indicate the individual's status and shall be disclosed in all business and professional communications to avoid misunderstanding and misconceptions about the paralegal's role and responsibilities.

FIGURE 8.8
Disclosure of Paralegal's Status

Persons Not Represented by Counsel

Particularly susceptible are those persons who are not represented by an attorney and who are then contacted by an outside legal professional. Why? Because the roles of attorneys are not always clear to those not accustomed to legal affairs. A legal professional cannot state or imply that he is unbiased in the matter. He is not a neutral mediator in his role as advocate for an individual client. Recall that legal professionals are ethically bound to represent their clients to the best of their ability. This is incongruous with an assertion of neutrality. Both attorneys and paralegals have an affirmative duty to either avoid or correct misunderstandings regarding their role in a matter. (See Figure 8.8.)

Essentially, the "best practice" of this rule boils down to only speaking to an unrepresented person only in order to advise her to seek her own counsel. However, the rule does not act as a "gag order." If the unrepresented person consents to speak to the attorney after being advised of both the interests represented by the attorney and the advisability of obtaining independent counsel, then the attorney may communicate with that person without fearing a violation of the rule. The only proscription is against giving legal advice to an unrepresented person who may have interests adverse to those of the attorney's client. Receiving legal advice may indeed threaten to irreparably compromise the unrepresented person's legal position. What are the dangers? Any statements made by the unrepresented person may be admitted against them later if those comments are deemed "statements against interest"—or, in a worst-case scenario, a settlement could be made concerning a legal matter contrary to the actual rights and liabilities in the matter.

Recall that the line between client and third party becomes blurred in the instance where the attorney represents an organization. The legal entity of the business is the party to which the attorney owes his loyalty, despite the fact that the communications are made solely through real persons. Information may be gathered through either current or former employees by the organization in order to properly represent the entity. There are a myriad of dangers here for those unrepresented persons, as they may feel that their interests are aligned with those of their employer where the matter does not involve a direct suit between them, but rather, the employee is acting as a third-party witness to the underlying facts. Recognizing that a balance needs to be struck between the need to protect those persons not represented by counsel and the need to obtain information for the organizational client, the court in *In re Environmental Ins. Declaratory Judgment Actions,* 252 N.J. Super. 510, 600 A.2d 165 (Law Div. 1991), set forth strict requirements for the attorneys making contact with the company's employees. The attorneys were required to first send a letter "to that employee explaining who they were and who they represented, what their purpose was and what their rights were with respect to agreeing to being interviewed. Then, once the contact was made to conduct the interview, the court mandated the following:

> *No interview of any former employee shall be conducted unless the following script is used by the investigator or attorney conducting the interview:*
> *1. I am a (private investigator/attorney) working on behalf of _____. I want you to understand that _____ and several other companies have sued their insurance carriers. That said action is pending in the Union County Superior Court. The purpose of the lawsuit*

> *is to determine whether _____ insurance companies will be required to reimburse _____ for any amounts of money _____ must pay as a result of environmental property damage and personal injury caused by _____. I have been engaged by _____ to investigate the issues involved in that lawsuit between _____ and _____, its insurance company.*
>
> 2. *Are you represented by an attorney in this litigation between _____ and _____?*
>   *If answer is YES, end questioning.*
>   *If answer is NO, ask:*
> 3. *May I interview you at this time about the issues in this litigation?*
>   *If answer is NO, end questioning.*
>   *If answer is YES, substance of interview may commence.*

Id. at 523–524.

It may seem incredibly controlling of the court to require such formal actions by the attorneys before interviewing third parties, but that is how seriously the court takes its responsibilities to monitor conduct and ensure fairness to all members of the public, regardless of their manner of involvement in a legal matter. It is significant to note that the court recognized that it may not be the attorney herself making the contact with the unrepresented person, but an investigator. The court intended that any person acting on behalf of and/or at the direction of the attorney be bound by the same rigorous requirements of disclosure. Of course, paralegals play a significant role in the fact-gathering stage of litigation and are therefore also bound by such mandates of fairness in disclosure. The "best practice" note for paralegals is to immediately identify oneself as the paralegal for the attorney in the matter and state which party that supervising attorney represents.

Respect for Others

The last rule is the "catch-all." Attorneys are required to treat all persons with respect to maintain the integrity of and confidence in the justice system. Attorneys and their agents, like paralegals, cannot forget that they are representing the legal system to the general public. Tactics designed solely to embarrass, delay, or burden a third party violate the legal professional's ethical responsibility to both individuals and tribunals.

Misuse of the position of attorney or paralegal by using tactics that are intended to harass a non-client in order to gain advantage over that non-client is prohibited. Any person who is not a client, including another attorney, is covered under this catch-all. Attorneys send confrontational letters to each other in order to obtain their desired results; however, stepping over the line by making that confrontation public is not permitted, as there is no other purpose but to embarrass the other attorney. *See In the Matter of Comfort,* 2007 WL 1649925 (Kan.) The attorney not only sent a "sharp-worded," if not "vitriolic," letter to the opposing counsel advising him of a potential conflict of interest on the opposing counsel's part (and also insinuating other ethical violations), but he also "published" it to nine city officials. The court found the attorney in violation of his ethical obligations because opposing counsel was a non-client and therefore covered under the prohibition against misuse of his position. There was no other reason for sending copies of the letter to the various city officials than to embarrass opposing counsel.

The spirit of this rule is abstention from taking unfair advantage of anyone other than a client. This is not to say that attorneys may take advantage of their clients; those actions are even more egregious and are covered under other rules in a much more formal and detailed manner. Until now, the discussion regarding communications with others has focused on actions or failures to act where there is a duty. But what happens when information is simply sent to an attorney's office without any request by the attorney or the paralegal? The attorney or paralegal is merely the passive recipient of the communication and has done nothing in contravention of the ethical requirements. Reinforcing the idea that legal professionals should "do the right thing" with respect to third persons, any information that (1) is mistakenly sent to the attorney's office and (2) may be used to the attorney's advantage and (3) is known to be sensitive and confidential must be reported to the sender. The attorney or receiving paralegal must let the sender know that the "cat may be out of the bag" with regard to certain information. Additionally, the attorney cannot then use that information to her advantage. By giving notice to the sender, the legal professional can alert the sender to this possibility, and therefore the sender can react appropriately. Of course, the initial recipient of this inadvertent communication may be the paralegal, who is often the manager of information in the firm. In order to ensure that the attorney complies with the ethical obligations to treat all third parties with respect, the paralegal will need to bring the inadvertent disclosure to the attorney's attention. The motto of this ethical requirement is to "fight fair" with all potential players, not just those directly involved in the litigation. This rule closes the loophole where the information received is not already covered by attorney-client privilege. Clearly, where opposing counsel mistakenly sends confidential information to the other attorney, the privilege rules attach to cover that situation. Where third parties, like witnesses, send information, this rule is required to cover the situation and guarantee the respect for the third party's interests.

The overall principle here was best summed up over two hundred years ago by Thomas Jefferson in a letter to George Hammond: "It is reasonable that everyone who asks justice should do justice." From the commencement of litigation, an attorney should work within the standards set forth by the courts to ensure a just and fair result, not merely the one that the client desires. The initial papers filed with the court should accurately, truthfully, and in good faith represent the facts and law applicable to the client's position. Once litigation has commenced, the attorney has the duty to assist in moving it forward to a proper and legally satisfactory resolution even where the client's interests may be subordinated to those of truth-seeking. The attorney must always be mindful of his chief allegiance to the justice system and its processes.

Summary

Respect for the legal profession manifests itself in respect for the other legal professionals, all parties involved in the matter, and those persons not directly affected by the outcome. Each individual matter should be handled in a manner that reflects positively on the adversarial and adjudicatory process. There are seven means to achieve this result specifically discussed in the ABA Model Rules and also reflected in NFPA's Ethical Code. They require

1. presentment of meritorious claims and defenses. The legal professional must have a good faith belief that the pleading contains plausible causes of action and defenses to those claims.

2. keeping the litigation moving through the system by not purposefully causing delay in the preparation for trial.

3. being honest with the court in all matters, even when that honesty may compromise the client's interest. This may require disclosure of confidential information or adverse legal authority.

4. dealing fairly with all parties involved in the litigation.

5. remaining neutral and respectful to the justice system and its processes, particularly in dealing with court personnel and jurors.

6. refraining from revealing certain information to the media covering the litigation that may have an adverse impact on the proceedings.

7. treating all "non-clients" with respect, keeping an eye on the justice system's overriding interest in fairness in communicating with other persons.

Key Terms and Concepts

Adversarial model	Good faith
Advocacy	Knowing
Controlling jurisdiction	Leading question
Due process	Materiality
Ex parte	Viable claim
Frivolous	

Review Questions

MULTIPLE CHOICE

Choose the best answer(s) and please explain WHY you choose the answer(s).

1. A frivolous claim
   a. extends or modifies existing law.
   b. is always permissible as a defense in a criminal case.
   c. is sanctionable unless supported by a belief that it is necessary.
   d. unduly burdens the process of litigation

2. An attorney's ongoing duty of candor to the tribunal requires
   a. the attorney to submit all the case law found during his research process.
   b. the paralegal to call and update the court before trial if any facts change.
   c. the attorney to present only information which he reasonably believes to be true.
   d. All of the above

3. If an attorney wants to speak to a third-party witness, she must
   a. call him and identify himself as an attorney for the opposition.
   b. determine whether or not he is represented by counsel.
   c. subpoena the witness to testify.
   d. submit written interrogatories to opposing counsel.

EXPLAIN YOURSELF

All answers should be written in complete sentences. A simple yes or no is insufficient.

1. Explain an attorney's duty to reveal contrary legal authority to the court.
2. Why is it impermissible for an attorney to speak about a matter he is handling in public?
3. Describe the kind of courtroom behavior that would result in an ethical complaint against the attorney.
4. A frivolous claim is best described as. . . .

FAULTY PHRASES

All of the following statements are FALSE; state why they are false and then rewrite them as true statements, without just making a statement negative by adding the word "not."

1. An attorney must always perform an independent factual investigation to support all her client's claims prior to filing suit.

2. An attorney cannot ask for extensions of time, because he has an ethical duty to expedite litigation.

3. An attorney is obligated to reveal all her sources of law under her duty of candor to the tribunal.

4. A lawyer's inviolate duty of confidentiality outweighs his duty of candor to the tribunal.

5. Attorneys can express their opinions on the value of the evidence presented at trial in their closing arguments.

6. After trial an attorney is permitted to ask the jurors how they deliberated and rendered the verdict.

7. An attorney can simply ignore her client's perjured testimony; she is not in violation of the rules unless she directed the false testimony.

8. Ex parte communications are permitted where the attorney is familiar with the judge.

 PORTFOLIO ASSIGNMENT

Write Away

Draft a memorandum for all paralegals in your office that explains their ethical obligations regarding their code of conduct in a courtroom or other tribunal when they accompany the supervising attorney. Make sure you include enough details and cover all possible situations that may arise in contentious litigation.

Commission for Lawyer Discipline v. Benton, 980 S.W.2d 425 (Tex. 1998).
Supreme Court of Texas.
COMMISSION FOR LAWYER DISCIPLINE, Petitioner,
v.
Barry Robert BENTON, Respondent.
No. 97-0228.
Argued Feb. 5, 1998.
Decided July 14, 1998.
Rehearing Overruled Dec. 31, 1998.

This is a disciplinary action arising out of an attorney's letter attacking the integrity of jurors who rendered a verdict against his clients. The Commission for Lawyer Discipline of the State Bar of Texas charged the attorney with violating Rule 3.06(d) of the Texas Disciplinary Rules of Professional Conduct, which regulates lawyers' post-verdict communications with jurors. The trial court found that the attorney had violated Rule 3.06(d) and imposed a probated suspension. The court of appeals reversed on constitutional grounds and dismissed the action. 933 S.W.2d 784, 941 S.W.2d 229 (Seerden, C.J., concurring on motion for rehearing). We reverse the judgment of the court of appeals and remand the cause to the trial court for a new punishment hearing.

I

Respondent Barry Benton represented the plaintiffs in a personal injury action that was tried to a jury in October 1991. The jury found the defendant liable but awarded Benton's clients no damages. In February 1992, after the trial court had granted the plaintiffs' motion for new trial, Benton sent the following letter to all members of the jury, with a copy to his clients:

Re: Florentino and Mary Esther Salas vs. Rene and Rosemarie Abete

Dear [juror]

It has been over four months since you sat on the jury in the above-referenced case and returned a verdict that Mr. and Mrs. Florentino Salas suffered no damages as a result of the bike accident involving Mr. Salas and the Abete's dog.

I was so angry with your verdict that I could not talk with you after the trial. I could not believe that 12 allegedly, [sic] good people from Cameron County, who swore to return a verdict based on the evidence, could find that the Salases were not damaged. The only evidence admitted at trial was that Mr. Salas was hurt. The Abete's lawyer, paid for by State Farm Insurance Company, admitted that Mr. Salas was injured. There was no evidence introduced that Mr. Salas was not injured. Yet by your answers, you found that Mr. Salas was not injured.

The only reason I can see as to why you ignored the evidence is that you were affected by the "Lawsuit Abuse" campaign in the Valley. Why else would a jury breach its oath to render a true verdict based on the evidence? I want to say that when you make a finding in a trial which is not based on the evidence you are perverting our civil justice system and hurting everyone in the community. Who knows, maybe someday you will need the aid of our civil justice system and it will be as corrupted for you as you made it for the Salases. The next time you think of government as crooked, remember your contribution to the corruption of good government. You knew Mr. Salas was injured, but swore that he was not.

Your cold and unfair conduct does not matter now. Judge Hester reviewed the evidence admitted at trial and decided that your verdict was obviously unjust and granted the Salases a new trial. The first trial now was nothing more than a waste of everyone's time and the county's money. The Salases and myself are very relieved that our justice system may still provide a fair resolution to their claim, despite your verdict.

If you wish to discuss anything in this letter, please feel free to contact me.

These facts came to the attention of the State Bar District Grievance Committee. The committee held an investigatory hearing and concluded that Benton had violated Rule 3.06(d), which provides:

After discharge of the jury from further consideration of a matter with which the lawyer was connected, the lawyer shall not ask questions of or make comments to a member of that jury that are calculated merely to harass or embarrass the juror or to influence his actions in future jury service.

[...]

Although he admitted to violating Rule 3.06(d) by attempting to influence the discharged jurors' actions in future jury service, Benton argued that the rule was unconstitutional. In his first amended original answer, he argued that Rule 3.06(d) violated the United States and Texas Constitutions in that it violated his right to free speech, was overbroad and vague, and denied him equal protection of the law. The trial court accepted Benton's stipulation that he had violated the rule, but held an evidentiary hearing on punishment. The trial court rendered judgment suspending Benton from law practice for six months with the suspension fully probated for one year subject to the conditions that, among other things, he apologize to the jurors and perform community service.

Benton appealed on the same four constitutional grounds that he asserted in the trial court. [...]

II

Because the question of whether Rule 3.06(d) inhibits constitutionally protected speech will affect our analysis of Benton's vagueness challenge, we will begin by considering Benton's claim that the free speech guarantees of the federal and state constitutions prohibit the Commission from disciplining him for sending the letter. [...] it requires us to resolve a conflict between the expressive rights of attorneys and the public's right to impartial jury trials—a right described in Texas's Declaration of Independence as "that palladium of civil liberty, and only safe guarantee for the life, liberty, and property of the citizen," and prominently enshrined in both constitutions. *See U.S. Const. amends.* VI, VII; Tex. Const. art. I, §§ 10, 15; id. art. V, § 10.

[...]

The Supreme Court's most recent pronouncement on the First Amendment standard applicable to lawyers' professional speech is *Gentile v. State Bar of Nevada,* 501 U.S. 1030, 111 S. Ct. 2720, 115 L .Ed. 2d 888 (1991). [...] The Supreme Court held that the rule's "substantial likelihood of material prejudice" standard was sufficiently protective of lawyers' free speech rights to pass constitutional muster. [...]

Of course, a lawyer is a person and he too has a constitutional freedom of utterance and may exercise it to castigate courts and their administration of justice. But a lawyer actively participating in a trial . . . is not merely a person and not even merely a lawyer.

He is an intimate and trusted and essential part of the machinery of justice, an "officer of the court" in the most compelling sense.

As is the case with most fiduciary positions, the privileged place attorneys hold in the justice system gives them a special capacity to harm that system. When lawyers connected to a pending case make remarks about that case, the public is far more likely to regard them as authoritative than other speakers. Lawyers not only have special expertise not shared by laypeople, but they have access to confidential information through discovery and client communications known only to them. *See id.* (opinion of Rehnquist, C.J.). Thus, such remarks have enhanced potential to prejudice the pool of potential jurors. Moreover, the basic fact that our system gives lawyers the dominant role in the presentation of cases at trial gives them immense influence over how jurors decide those cases.

[...]

Under the Gentile standard, the application of Rule 3.06(d) to Benton's letter does not violate the First Amendment because the letter created a substantial likelihood of material prejudice to the administration of justice. Benton asserts that post-verdict juror communications, unlike the pretrial publicity in Gentile, do not threaten the right to a fair trial because the jurors have already rendered their verdict. [...]

The abusive and insulting comments in Benton's letter threatened to damage the jury system in at least two ways. First, the testimony at Benton's punishment hearing established that the letter discouraged jury service. One of the jurors to whom Benton sent the letter testified that although he had felt it was an honor to serve as a juror in the underlying personal injury case, he intended to express bias in future voir dire proceedings in order to avoid being chosen for jury service again. The sole reason for this change, he stated, was that he did not want to receive another letter like Benton's. Another juror's testimony illustrated the wide-ranging indirect impact a communication like Benton's can have on the jury system by affecting what discharged jurors tell potential future jurors about their service. That juror testified that she was formerly very involved in voter registration efforts, but that she stopped that activity after receiving Benton's letter because if people asked her about the possibility of being called for jury duty as a result of registering to vote, she would have to tell them about her negative experience with Benton and she felt it would cause them not to register.

Second, the fear of receiving abusive post-verdict communications like Benton's letter threatens to affect jurors' service while the trial is still in progress. [...] the threat of verbal attacks by disappointed lawyers creates an atmosphere of intimidation during trial that can affect jurors' impartiality. An outcome affected by extrajudicial statements violates litigants' fundamental right to a fair trial.

[...]

III

Benton also argues that Rule 3.06(d) is unconstitutionally overbroad. An overbroad statute "sweeps within its scope a wide range of both protected and non-protected expressive activity." *Hobbs v. Thompson,* 448 F.2d 456, 460 (5th Cir.1971). When a statute prohibits speech or expressive conduct, the overbreadth doctrine allows a person whose own expression is unprotected to challenge the statute on the ground that it also prohibits protected speech. [...] However, a statute will not be invalidated for overbreadth merely because it is possible to imagine some unconstitutional applications. [...]

Rule 3.06(d)'s prohibition on comments calculated merely to harass or embarrass a former juror is not substantially overbroad. The Fifth Circuit has upheld restrictions on post-verdict communication more broadly worded than Rule 3.06(d) based on the possibility that the prohibited speech might lead to harassment.

Nor is the rule's ban on comments calculated to influence discharged jurors' actions in future jury service substantially overbroad. Our discussion today has focused primarily on the dangers to the jury system from rude and abusive speech, but polite comments calculated to influence future actions in jury service may pose a substantial threat to the administration of justice in a different way. [...]

Our holding that Rule 3.06(d) is not substantially overbroad does not foreclose lawyers who believe the rule violates the First Amendment as applied to them from challenging it. We simply conclude that "whatever overbreadth may exist should be cured through case-by-case analysis of the fact situations to which [the rule's] sanctions, assertedly, may not be applied." *Id.* at 615–16, 93 S. Ct. 2908.

[...] To survive a vagueness challenge, a statute need not spell out with perfect precision what conduct it forbids. "Words inevitably contain germs of uncertainty." *Broadrick,* 413 U.S. at 608, 93 S. Ct. 2908. Due process is satisfied if the prohibition is "set out in terms that the ordinary person exercising ordinary common sense can sufficiently understand and comply with." *Un* 413 U.S. 548, 579, 93 S. Ct. 2880, 37 L.Ed.2d 796 (1973). [...] The vagueness doctrine requires different levels of clarity depending on the nature of the law in question. Courts demand less precision of statutes that impose only civil penalties than of criminal statutes because their consequences are less severe. [...]

Although in colloquial usage "harass" may sometimes have the same meaning and hence the same vagueness as "annoy," we are bound to construe it to avoid constitutional infirmity if possible. [citations omitted] [...]

Because Benton did not engage in a course of conduct—that is, repeated communications—directed at any individual, but merely sent a single letter to each discharged juror, he did not violate the "harass" provision of Rule 3.06(d) as we have interpreted it. We need not decide whether this provision would be unconstitutionally vague as applied to communications that fall within our limiting construction but that occurred before we announced the construction.

D

We agree with Benton, however, that "embarrass" is fatally vague. Unlike "harass," "embarrass" is a term seldom used and, to our knowledge, never defined in statutory law. Although we have found no authority discussing the constitutionality of the word "embarrass," we believe it is comparable to "annoy." The Supreme Court held in Coates that the word "annoy" was unconstitutionally vague, "not in the sense that it requires a person to conform his conduct to an imprecise but comprehensible normative standard, but rather in the sense that no standard of conduct is specified at all." *Id.* at 611 n. 1, 614, 91 S. Ct. 1686.

Similarly, the problem is not that one cannot understand what "embarrass" means in the abstract, but that one cannot tell with any sort of accuracy what speech will trigger embarrassment in the 'average' listener. Thus, Rule 3.06(d)'s "embarrass" provision runs afoul of the notice aspect of the vagueness doctrine, because "men of common intelligence must necessarily guess" at what speech might embarrass a juror. [...]

The unconstitutionality of one part of a statute does not require us to invalidate the entire statute unless the unconstitutional provision is not separable from the remainder. Except for the words "or embarrass," Rule 3.06(d) is constitutional and remains in effect. [...]

VI

The final issue before us is how our narrowing construction of "harass" and our holding that "embarrass" is unconstitutionally vague affect the trial court's judgment. [...] We have limited Rule 3.06(d) so as to render it constitutional by striking the term "embarrass" and narrowing the term "harass."

[...]

But since it is possible that the trial court increased the punishment based on the belief that Benton's letter violated all three provisions of Rule 3.06(d) instead of only one, justice demands that we remand this cause to give the parties an opportunity to present argument to the trial court on how, if at all, our holdings today affect the previously imposed punishment. For the foregoing reasons, we reverse the judgment of the court of appeals and remand this cause to the trial court for a new hearing on punishment.

Source: Reprinted with permission from ThomsonWest.

Chapter 9

Law Firms: Understanding the Structure and Management of the Practice

CHAPTER OBJECTIVES

The student will be able to:

- Differentiate between the ethical responsibilities of partners, supervising attorneys, and paralegals

- Acknowledge the importance of professional independence, free from monetary incentives or restrictions, in the practice of law

- Define and discuss the issues surrounding multijurisdictional practice of law

- Evaluate the paralegal's roles and responsibilities in maintaining ethical standards appropriate to the firm

This chapter will examine HOW law firms are structured; this hierarchical structure defines WHO is ultimately held responsible for the ethical breaches within a law firm. In order to ensure the professional independence of the attorney, the rules stipulate the parties with WHOM fees may be shared and WHAT restrictions may be placed upon an attorney's right to practice law. Although, clearly, paralegals cannot practice law outside of the work they perform in their own law firm, attorneys are also restricted as to WHERE they may practice outside their jurisdiction of admission.

It is not enough that an attorney comply with his own individual ethical obligations as if he were "an island." Most lawyers do not practice in isolation; even solo practitioners usually have some sort of office assistance. Due to the sensitive nature of the work that attorneys perform, it is necessary for them to maintain controls over everyone that works on the attorneys' matters to ensure that there are no leaks of information or failures in performance of the requisite actions on the cases. It may seem that this is an exercise in micromanagement; however, with proper training and reporting procedures, all persons employed by the supervising attorney can feel satisfied that they are not the "weak link in the chain." The first rules discussed in this chapter address the responsibility of partners, managers, and other **supervising attorneys** toward the firm, clients, and other parties when another person acts on behalf of the firm. The second set of rules addresses the concern of placing certain ethical responsibilities upon an attorney where that individual lawyer is acting in a business relationship outside of her firm, but still in a legal context.

SUPERVISORY RESPONSIBILITY FOR OTHER ATTORNEYS

As in any business, there is a certain organizational hierarchy and accompanying responsibility and accountability. For a general representation of the structure of a large law office, see Figure 9.1. The personnel farther down the chart have less ethical responsibility for the acts of others. Of course, every member of the law office has full ethical responsibility for his own acts. Senior and managing partners, rewarded with large hourly fees and other perks of experience, are conversely burdened with the extra responsibility to oversee and ensure compliance with all members' ethical duties. Yes, they are their "brothers' keeper." It is not enough to know that they are maintaining their own cases and clients properly; it is their duty to ensure that the entire firm acts according to the ethical code. The ABA Model Rules specifically set out the responsibility of partners regarding each kind of employee of the firm: copartner, subordinate associate, or non-lawyer assistant.

FIGURE 9.1

Structure of a Law Office

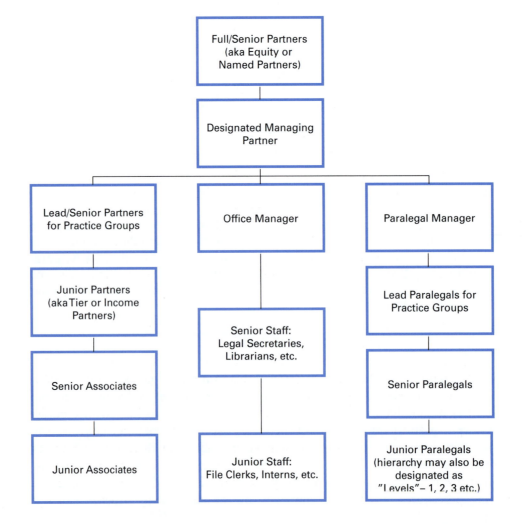

A partner may be held accountable for actions or omissions of her equal. One might assume that after many years in practice and after gaining the status of partner, an attorney may enjoy autonomy—the right to handle her matters in the way she sees fit. This is true, but only to a certain extent. While partners are not in the habit of looking over each other's shoulders (they simply do not have time or energy for that), all partners in the law firm must make sure there are protocols in place that will effectuate ethical compliance, similar to quality control measures in other businesses.

> *The measures required to fulfill the responsibility prescribed in paragraphs (a) and (b) can depend on the firm's structure and the nature of its practice. In a small firm, informal supervision and occasional admonition ordinarily might be sufficient. In a large firm, or in practice situations in which intensely difficult ethical problems frequently arise, more elaborate procedures may be necessary.*

In re Myers, 355 S.C. 1, 8, 584 S.E.2d 357, 361 (2003), citing Comment to Rule 5.1.

Ethical compliance is so important that these supervising attorneys can be held responsible for even **negligent misconduct**; the acts or omissions need not rise to the level of reckless or knowing conduct, although the sanctions may be less severe for negligence. *See In re Froelich*, 838 A.2d 1117, 1118 (Del. 2003), wherein the attorney did not have a system in place for verifying whether the documents prepared by an outside paralegal company were accurately handled. He was unaware of the number of outstanding checks from real estate closing until his wife, a certified paralegal, reviewed the materials and informed him of the problem. The attorney made immediate attempts at rectifying the situation. Due to his voluntary disclosure and efforts at rectifying the issues, the court found him merely negligent and publicly reprimanded him.

As could be expected, many of the problems in the partnership deal with money, from the more mundane accounting practices to the flagrant misappropriation of funds.

> *Although a managing partner cannot guarantee absolutely the integrity of the firm's books and records, it is the managing partner's responsibility to implement reasonable safeguards to ensure that the firm is meeting its obligations with respect to its books and records. As the Lawyers' Fund points out, meeting these responsibilities need not pose an onerous burden for the managing partner. It is, however, a serious responsibility.*
>
> *[…] Finally, even if we concluded there was no evidence that [the attorney] explicitly or implicitly directed the invasion of client trust funds, we still find clear and convincing evidence on this record that [the attorney] engaged in knowing misconduct. We agree with the Lawyers' Fund's assertion that the "sustained and systematic failure" of a managing partner to supervise a firm's employees to ensure compliance […] may not be characterized as simple negligence. A lawyer who accepts responsibility for the administrative operations of a law firm stands in a position of trust vis-à-vis other lawyers and employees of the firm. The managing partner must discharge those responsibilities faithfully and diligently.*

In re Bailey, 821 A.2d 851, 864–865 (Del. 2003).

All the ethical requirements regarding supervision of any employee have the same underlying theory. However, a supervising attorney is held more responsible for the acts and omissions of a subordinate lawyer and less responsible for those of his partners. Generally, partners are absolved of responsibility for their fellow partners' actions where there is no knowledge of the wrongdoing and where there are procedural safeguards in place. This is not necessarily the case where a **subordinate attorney** is involved. *In Kus v. Irving*, 46 Conn. Supp. 35, 736 A.2d 946 (Conn. Super. 1999), the court noted that the liability rules for partnerships were applicable and the ethical rules did not expand the liability as between law partners. As the other partners had no knowledge of the one partner's wrongdoing, they were protected from liability under the general business partnership rules. The court noted that a different conclusion would result if the other partners had supervisory authority over the miscreant attorney. The more experienced supervising attorney can be held liable for negligent acts of the subordinate lawyer because the ABA Model Rules impose not only a

negligent misconduct
Acts that are not done intentionally, but that do not comply with the standard of ordinary care and thought needed to fulfill the relevant ethical obligations.

subordinate attorney
An attorney who must report to a supervising attorney, who then takes ultimate responsibility for the work product's compliance with the firm's ethical practices.

FIGURE 9.2
Holding the
Supervising Attorney
Responsible

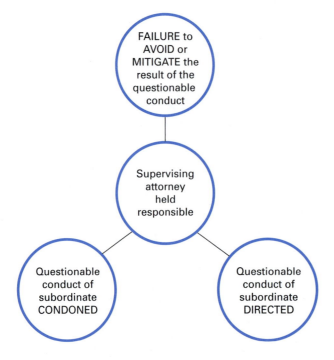

general safeguarding obligation as discussed above, but also require that the supervising attorney makes reasonable efforts to oversee that class of lawyers. It is not enough to let the procedural processes in place at the office function as all the supervision the subordinate lawyer is subject to; supervision requires a more active role. The additional supervision requirements work in tandem to ensure that the subordinate lawyer learns how to work within the ethics rules because these requirements place the burden on the supervising attorney to guarantee the supervision. Becoming a competent, ethical attorney requires this kind of "apprenticeship." The court found it "troubling" that there "was the lack of a review mechanism which allowed an associate's work to be reviewed and guided by a supervisory attorney." *In re Cohen,* 847 A.2d 1162, 1166 (D.C. 2004). The real issue was that the supervisory attorney, although she may not have had actual knowledge of ethical violations, should have exercised prudence and competence and therefore, *"reasonably should have known"* about the status of the matters handled by the subordinate lawyer. *Id.* at 1167 (emphasis added).

These rules do not necessarily impose vicarious liability, "passive" responsibility, under a respondeat superior theory, but rather impose an active ethical duty upon the supervising attorney. The mere fact of the professional relationship does not create the responsibility. Part of a senior attorney's duty is to actively supervise lawyers that report to her. This responsibility can be broken down into three obligations, as shown in Figure 9.2. It is clear that liability will attach where the supervising attorney has actually ordered the offensive conduct. The subordinate lawyer is not absolved of responsibility if it is a clear ethical violation, but the supervising attorney does not absolve herself of responsibility because it was not she herself who violated the ethical rules. Accountability cannot be delegated; the supervising attorney will remain "on the hook." If, as a result of the supervision, the senior attorney learns of the violation and either condones it by doing nothing (**ratification**) or fails to act to prevent or lessen the consequences of the violation (avoidance, or **mitigation**), she is just as guilty of the **malfeasance** as the acting attorney. Essentially, the failure to act to remediate the violative actions of the subordinate attorney is an unethical omission with sanctionable consequences.

By placing some responsibility on the senior management of a firm, the rule prevents those attorneys who have the most influence over the atmosphere of the firm from turning a blind eye to the behavior of the firm's attorneys. While partners are not required to guarantee that

ratification
The adoption, as one's own, of the words or actions of another person.

mitigation
The lessening of the harmful effects of a course of action.

malfeasance
A wrongful, unethical, or tortious act.

other attorneys in their firm will not violate the Rules of Professional Conduct, ignoring their supervisory responsibilities can lead to sanctions for those running the firm.

Undoubtably, the supervision of attorneys by other attorneys in their firm is one of the most effective methods of preventing attorney misconduct. However, that supervision must be reasonably competent or it is meaningless and that failure in itself can encourage unethical behavior. In situations where supervising attorneys fail to make reasonable efforts to ensure their subordinates follow the Rules of Professional Conduct, if the disciplinary proceedings only punished the individual attorney who committed the violation, the environment that fostered the attorney's unethical conduct would be allowed to continue.

In re Anonymous Member of South Carolina Bar, 346 S.C. 177, 187, 552 S.E.2d 10, 14–15 (2001).

Clearly, this method of self-policing and the resulting accountability for all attorneys in a law firm maintains the integrity of the entire justice system and the confidence of the public in entrusting their most sensitive legal matters to it. Each ethical obligation builds upon another one, becoming more specific as to the duty to ensure that the law firm operates within the boundaries of ethics. Procedures must be implemented to ensure a means to monitor the activities of the attorneys in the firm; a supervisory attorney must take an active role in guiding the conduct of subordinate lawyers to ensure that they conform to the ethical rules; and finally, any attorney may be liable for the unethical acts of another lawyer in the firm if she has either ordered the violative conduct or knowingly ratified the conduct. A supervisory attorney will be liable for a subordinate attorney's unethical conduct if she knows of it and fails to act to either stop it or lessen the impact of it.

SUPERVISORY RESPONSIBILITY FOR NON-LAWYERS

Just as attorneys are responsible for assuring that the other lawyers in the firm act in a manner that comports with the relevant ethical codes, so they must ensure that all non-lawyers employed by them follow the ethical rules that bind attorneys. Indeed, the ABA Model Rules explain the supervising attorney's responsibility for non-lawyers using the very same language they use regarding subordinate lawyers. To permit non-lawyer assistants to act in a way that is impermissible for the attorney is to completely undercut the ethical rules and render them useless, as the attorney could circumvent them by delegating a task to a non-lawyer in his employ. This rule applies to all persons retained by the attorney to assist them in his practice. It applies not only to the paralegals and legal secretaries, but also to the investigators and experts retained. "Ethical considerations are as applicable to representatives of lawyers as to lawyers themselves. Further, not to impose these rules when a lawyer's [representative] acts improperly would render the rules relatively meaningless." *In re Environmental Ins. Declaratory Judgment Actions,* 252 N.J. Super. 510, 515, 600 A.2d 165, 168 (Law Div. 1991).

There is a range of roles and skills that the support system of non-lawyers renders to the attorney. The extent of supervision needed depends upon the role and knowledge of the assistant. What is certain is that the attorney cannot delegate ultimate responsibility for the legal functions of these persons and must account for their ethical performance. Further, when attorneys delegate legal work to these **paraprofessionals**, clients must always understand their role in the rendering of the legal services. Without this comprehension, the client is not in a position to evaluate to whom she should be speaking and to what extent that paraprofessional can render assistance to the client. The client would be unable to alert the attorney to any issues that might pose an ethical issue during the course of the paraprofessional's work if this understanding were not accomplished. Without the client's input, the attorney could not comply with her obligations to supervise and to fix any problem that the non-lawyer assistant had created. See

paraprofessional
A person with the appropriate education, knowledge, and training to perform specialized work under the supervision of another professional who has the ultimate responsibility for the collaborative work.

CYBER TRIP

Every business needs to ensure the ethical practices of its employees to ensure that they comply with the mission statement of the office. Having standards of practice and procedures for supervising their implementation is essential. An exceptionally helpful article can be found on NALA's Web site:

The Corporate Human Resource Guide to the Legal Assistant/Paralegal Profession, http://www.nala.org/HRbrochure.htm

The following Web sites offer advice applicable to all fields.

Ethics Resource Center:

http://www.ethics.org

Nan DeMars:

http://www.officeethics.com

Free Management Library:

http://www.managementhelp.org/ethics/ethxgde.htm#anchor33077

What's Workplace Ethics?:

http://www.workplaceethics.ca/work.html

IN CLASS DISCUSSION

Arnold Jones usually handles family law and wills; however, on occasion he will handle some personal injury claims on behalf of his injured clients. As the majority of his practice does not consist of handling the money or property of his regular clients, he delegates the day-to-day management of both his trust and his operating bank account activities to his paralegal, Annie, whom he has employed for over 15 years. Arnold has given Annie authority to use his signature stamp to deposit money to both his trust and his operating accounts and to write checks from both accounts. Annie's office duties also include opening Arnold's mail, including his bank statements. Every year, Arnold uses an outside, professional accountant to reconcile transactions or activities involving his operating and trust bank accounts.

The office received two checks for a recent settlement in a personal injury matter: one from the insurance company and the other from the defendant directly for medical expenses. Annie endorsed the client's signature on the two checks, because Arnold usually obtains this kind of permission from his personal injury clients. This practice ensures that the settlement monies are available in a shorter time frame for disbursement. In conjunction with this, Annie used Arnold's signature stamp to make a deposit into the trust account.

This time, Annie knew that she would not be able to pay her rent. She decided to endorse the medical expense check over to herself because she didn't think anyone would miss that smaller check and she could repay the trust account before the accountant checked it. Arnold knew nothing of these transactions.

Should Arnold be held responsible for Annie's actions? Why or why not? Would you suggest different procedures in this office in order for it to comply with the ethical requirements?

Source: This scenario is loosely based on *State ex rel. Oklahoma Bar Ass'n v. Mayes,* 977 P.2d 1073 (Okla. 1999).

Mays v. Neal, 327 Ark. 302, 314, 938 S.W.2d 830, 834 (1997), wherein the court stated: "In sum, we must conclude, [...], that [the attorney] failed to properly delegate his legal work and responsibilities and failed to properly supervise work delegated to his assistants. If he had, he would have been in the position at the least to have tried to resolve the questions that continued to resurface during his legal representation of [the client]".

Interestingly, ABA Model Rule 5.3 (Responsibilities Regarding the Non-Lawyer Assistant) was used to defeat the attempt to regulate the paralegal profession independently. Recall from chapter 2 the discussion surrounding *In re Opinion 24,* 128 N.J. 114, 607 A.2d 962 (1992) as it relates to the unauthorized practice of law. ABA Model Rule 5.3 supplements the attorney's obligations to prevent the UPL by his support personnel by also requiring that there be procedures in place to ensure compliance with the rules. These may include ethics training in-house or sponsoring the non-lawyer's attendance at continuing legal education seminars. The paralegal, as the closest paraprofessional to the attorney, and one who is "extremely aware of the potential ethical dilemmas of the legal profession," is also responsible for his own conduct to a degree. *In re Opinion No. 24 of Committee on Unauthorized Practice of Law,* 128 N.J. 114, 131, 607 A.2d 962, 971 (1992).

> *Although fulfilling the ethical requirements of RPC 5.3 is primarily the attorney's obligation and responsibility, a paralegal is not relieved from an independent obligation to refrain from illegal conduct and to work directly under the supervision of the attorney. A paralegal who recognizes that the attorney is not directly supervising his or her work or that such supervision is illusory because the attorney knows nothing about the field in which the paralegal is working must understand that he or she is engaged in the unauthorized practice of law. In such a situation an independent paralegal must withdraw from representation of the client. The key is supervision, and that supervision must occur regardless of whether the paralegal is employed by the attorney or retained by the attorney.*

Id. at 127.

The court felt that the proper supervision of an attorney negated the need for a separate body to oversee, certify, or otherwise regulate the paralegal profession. The court stressed that the crux of the question regarding paralegals and the practice of law is the direct supervision of the attorney to ensure that all ethical requirements have been fulfilled. Essentially, the supervising attorney must make sure that the paraprofessional, whether employed or retained as an independent contractor, is performing all her duties as if she were an attorney. This is a clear instance of the interrelatedness of the ethics rules and underscores the importance of accountability.

This obligation of supervision is not relieved just because the supervising attorney has the utmost confidence in the abilities of her non-lawyer assistant. The rule regarding ethical supervision does not assume that the lawyer's assistant does not have the requisite knowledge or competence. It must assume that she does. Indeed, if the attorney were to delegate work to the assistant, she could do so only if the assistant were competent and capable of handling that aspect of the matter. Instead, this rule is designed to provide security and accountability on the part of the supervising attorney; an attorney never has the excuse that it was someone else's fault because that attorney did not do the actual work that was unacceptable even where that "someone else" had the requisite skill and knowledge to complete the task. This is the reason some states have amended their particular local ethics rules to forbid the hiring of a disbarred attorney as a legal assistant in almost any capacity (i.e. paralegal, office manager, etc.). There is a great temptation to let this disbarred attorney work without the same amount of supervision that another non-lawyer assistant would receive, because the supervising attorney knows that the disbarred attorney has the training and education to do the job assigned. This is an unacceptable practice.

> *These rules recognize that lawyers generally employ non-lawyers in their practice, including secretaries, investigators, clerks, and paralegals, and that such individuals assist the lawyer in the efficient rendition of the lawyer's professional services. However, a lawyer is completely responsible for the work product of his non-lawyer assistants and must give the assistants appropriate instruction and supervision concerning the ethical aspects of their employment. While appropriate delegation of tasks to non-lawyer assistants is allowed and encouraged, a lawyer may never permit non-lawyer assistants to engage in activities that constitute the practice of law or to hold themselves out as lawyers. The key to appropriate delegation is proper supervision by the lawyer, which includes adequate instruction when assigning projects, monitoring of the progress of the project, and review of the completed project. It is the lawyer's responsibility to see that his non-lawyer employees understand these limitations.*
>
> *Applying these principles to the instant matter, there is little doubt that respondent failed to adequately supervise [the disbarred attorney]. The record demonstrates that respondent gave [the disbarred attorney] a free hand to meet with clients, handle legal fees, correspond with attorneys and insurance adjusters, render legal opinions, and negotiate settlements. Unquestionably, the evidence in the record in support of Counts I and II proves in a clear and convincing fashion that respondent violated Rules 5.3 and 5.5(b). Furthermore, respondent engaged in conduct prejudicial to the administration of justice when he permitted a legal pleading to be "notarized" with his "signature" by [the disbarred attorney], then filed into the public record.*

In re Comish, 889 So.2d 236, 244–245 (La. 2004) (citations omitted).

The court made it very clear that the supervising attorney had to actively oversee the disbarred attorney's work, not just be available for the disbarred attorney to consult with him where the disbarred attorney felt he needed assistance with handling a matter. The contact with clients is perhaps the most serious of the ethical violations because of the resulting harm that may occur. Another court severely sanctioned the supervising attorney because he had been warned of the potential harm. *See In re Gaff,* 272 Ga. 7, 524 S.E.2d 728 (2000). In sum, any non-lawyer assistant must be supervised; the degree of review will vary depending upon the experience and track record of the person in question, but there must be that ultimate accountability on the part of the supervising attorney.

RESEARCH THIS

Find a case in your jurisdiction, either state or federal, that discusses an attorney's failure to properly supervise a non-attorney member of the staff (paralegal, secretary, or other). What was the sanction imposed upon the attorney? Do you think it was fair in the situation? Why or why not?

PROFESSIONAL STATUS OF THE PARALEGAL

Many law offices consider paralegals to be indispensable professionals and integral to the structure and function of their organizations. Attorneys rely on paralegals' knowledge, skill, and training to accomplish complex legal tasks that otherwise would have to be performed by the attorneys. While attorneys are unquestionably considered professionals, there has been a considerable amount of debate as to the status of paralegals as "white-collar professionals" under the United States Department of Labor (DOL) regulations of the Fair Labor Standards Act. The distinction made between exempt and non-exempt employees serves to distinguish those employees who are covered by minimum wage and overtime regulations and those who are not. White-collar professionals are exempt. Employers are not required to pay a minimum wage or overtime pay to these professionals. The criteria for exempt status as a professional can be generally stated as follows:

1. The employee is salaried at a certain minimum. His wages are not subject to reductions or variations depending on the quality of the work or the amount of time worked in a week.

2. The employee is performing non-manual work that requires the exercise of discretion and independent judgment related to the management of the business of the employer.

3. The work requires advanced knowledge acquired through prolonged specialized intellectual instruction.

These three requirements for exempt status are the characteristics of a good paralegal. However, the DOL did not find that the paralegal profession as a whole qualified under all three conditions. The two most important factors discussed, which still form the basis for controversy, are "the exercise of discretion and independent judgment related to the management of the business" and "knowledge acquired by a prolonged course of specialized intellectual instruction."

The DOL asserted that paralegals do not exercise independent judgment because their work consists of using a set of skills and well-established techniques to formulate a course of action. These decisions are also confined to clearly defined parameters of action. The definition of discretion and independent judgment must relate to the management and business operations of the employer in order for an employee to qualify as exempt. The DOL relied on the ABA's rules against the unauthorized practice of law to support this position:

> *[A] delegation of legal tasks to a lay person is proper only if the lawyer maintains a direct relationship with the client, supervises the delegated work, and has complete professional responsibility for the work produced. The implication of such strictures is that the paralegal employees you describe [in the request for a formal opinion from the DOL] would not have the amount of authority to exercise independent judgments with regard to legal matters necessary to bring them within the administrative exception.*

Additionally, an exempt employee must have acquired specialized academic training as a prerequisite for entrance into the profession. "The best prima facie evidence that an employee meets this requirement is possession of the appropriate academic degree." Herein lies the problem for paralegals. As discussed previously, paralegals are not required to have a particular undergraduate degree or graduate certificate in order to be employed as paralegals. Paralegals can have degrees in various fields of study; a great deal of their knowledge is acquired through hands-on working experience, as in an apprenticeship. "The learned professional exemption also does not apply to occupations in which most employees have acquired their skill by experience rather than by advanced specialized intellectual instruction." 29 C.F.R. §541.301(d).

It is important to note that the DOL recognizes that every paralegal's employment situation and job responsibilities can differ in the amount of discretion and independent judgment exercised. Further, many paralegals do hold advanced specialized degrees, and the educational background of each paralegal can be analyzed to determine whether it comports with the exempt status requirements. The DOL's formal opinion in 2005 was based on an inquiry into six different paralegals. Their education ranged from little formal postsecondary education to a masters in business administration (MBA) degree and national paralegal certifications. None of these paralegals met the requirements for exempt status. However, in *Austin v. CUNA Mut. Ins. Soc.,* 240 F.R.D. 420 (W.D. Wis. 2006), a "law specialist" sued her employer for failure to pay overtime. The employee argued that she and others in similar positions were nonexempt employees and therefore were entitled to overtime pay for hours worked in excess of 40 per week. To qualify for the position of "law specialist" within the Office of General Counsel, an applicant "needed a general college degree, a paralegal education or equivalent experience." *Id.* at 423. The plaintiff, Austin, had a bachelor's degree in legal assistance and criminal justice and at the time of suit had worked as a paralegal for more than 25 years. At CUNA the paralegal plaintiff was responsible for managing cases where claims against the insurance had been filed. After a restructuring, her duties increased

> *to include maintaining the litigation team's "Knowledge Management" database. To maintain the Knowledge Management database, plaintiff was required to read briefs from outside counsel and opinion letters from in-house lawyers, summarize the content of the brief or opinion letter, and index the summary by topic so it could be found again if similar issues arose in later cases."*

Id. at 427.

The court found that this type of work was included in the kind that requires the exercise of discretion and independent judgment directly related to management or general business operations. This kind of work includes, but is not limited to, the following:

> *work in functional areas such as tax; finance; accounting; budgeting; auditing; insurance; quality control; purchasing; procurement; advertising; marketing; research; safety and health; personnel management; human resources; employee benefits; labor relations; public relations; government relations; computer network, internet and database administration; legal and regulatory compliance; and similar activities.*

Id. at 428–429, citing 29 C.F.R. § 541.201(b).

Employees who act as advisers or consultants to their employer's clients or customers perform work that is considered to be "directly related to management or general business operations." *Id.,* citing 29 C.F.R. § 541.201(c). Austin's work in assuring that her employer's insurance policies were properly administered and the contested claims were managed with outside counsel was considered "directly related to the [employer's]

CYBER TRIP

The full text of section 541 of title 29—"Defining and delimiting the exemptions for executive, administrative, professional, computer and outside sales employees"—can be found at:

http://www.access.
gpo.gov/nara/cfr/
waisidx_06/29cfr541
_06.html

The full text of the letter from the Department of Labor regarding the application of non-exempt status can be found on the DOL Web site:

http://www.dol.gov/
esa/whd/opinion/
FLSA/2005/2005_12_
16_54_FLSA.htm

NFPA's position can be accessed at:

http://www.parale
gals.org/display
common.cfm?an=1
&subarticlenbr=800

general business operations and crucial to its functioning. Therefore, under this element, performing work directly related to the management of the employer, the legal specialist was considered exempt.

The second element discussed, independence of the employee, also was decided in the employer's favor. The paralegal was found to be exempt from overtime. The court was careful to explain that

> [a]lthough the exercise of discretion and independent judgment implies that the employee has authority to make an independent choice, free from immediate direction or supervision, the term "discretion and independent judgment" does not require that the decisions made by an employee be free from review or that the employee have unlimited authority.

Id. at 430, citing 29 C.F.R. § 541.202(c).

The number of times that the employee actually deviates from the standard practice of her employer is not determinative of her actual authority to do so. Austin had the discretion to reject outside counsel's recommendations on a particular matter if she disagreed with them. The fact that she rarely did so was not dispositive of that factor. The paralegal had the authority to act independently and to exercise discretion in handling cases worth up to $50,000. The fact that the paralegal could commit her employer to such a sum of money without supervisory approval was indicative of her independent authority. On this element as well, the paralegal was found to be exempt from overtime.

ATTORNEYS' INDEPENDENCE OF BUSINESS JUDGMENT

The ethical rules also prescribe the way in which lawyers may associate with other lawyers and non-lawyers in order to preserve the independence of the profession. Attorneys must always maintain their first loyalty to their clients; any interference that may result from a business association or fee payment arrangement is not permitted. While ABA Model Rule 5.4 has many subsections, its essence underscores the integrity of the individual attorney and the firm, which must remain free of outside influences. A point previously discussed must be underscored here: an attorney cannot share his fee with any non-lawyer; legal fees earned are a result of legal work that only an attorney can render. The reasoning behind all the restrictions on fee sharing is that no outside person without legal training should have any say in or any reward for legal services rendered. There are certain situations that may look like fee-sharing but are not; they are merely a function of the business of the office. A law firm may

1. pay money into the estate of a deceased attorney of the office over a reasonable period of time pursuant to an employment or benefit agreement.

2. pay money to the estate or representative of a deceased, disabled, or disappeared attorney for the purchase of that attorney's practice.

3. Include non-lawyer employees in a firm retirement plan or other compensation plan, even where that plan is based on a profit-sharing arrangement. This practice encourages attorneys to take care of all their employees, regardless of their status as "attorney" or lack of it.

4. Share fees with a nonprofit organization that employed or otherwise recommended or retained the attorney in that matter for which the court awarded the fees. This exception encourages an attorney's predilection to charity.

SPOT THE ISSUE

Wanda is an attorney engaged in labor, wage, and hour practice with her paralegal William. They are trying to stir up more business and so send out this letter:

Dear Members of the Labor Union:

We are so sure that we can champion your cause for fair labor practices in the courts of this state that we will gladly donate 20 percent of our portion of any recoveries made by your individual members back into the union.

Signed, Wanda and William

Wanda also had William contact the Employers' Association and make essentially the same offer.

What, if any, ethical problems are involved with these letters?

RESTRICTIONS ON PARTNERSHIP

No attorney may include any non-lawyer in a partnership where the enterprise entails the practice of law. All partners must be attorneys, in order to preserve the integrity of the practice and to keep it free of any influences from the non-lawyer partners who may have different business goals and views from the attorney and who are not constrained by the professional rules of ethics as attorneys are. This is not to say that attorneys cannot enter into business relationships with non-lawyers at all; what the ethical rule prohibits is a business wherein legal services are rendered. An attorney is free to form any other association with any other person for any other legitimate business purpose—just not a purpose which would involve the practice of law.

Finally, to further ensure that the attorney maintains her independent business judgment, without threat of compromise due to monetary incentive, the ethics rules disapprove of an attorney's accepting payment from any person other than her client. If that type of financial arrangement is made, the attorney cannot be influenced in any way by the desires of the third-party payor in making decisions about the case. This is true even where the attorney is in-house counsel for a company. This potential conflict arises quite often in the insurance context. The client is the insured policyholder; however, payment comes from the insurance company. There is tension, because the insured's claim may not be in the best financial interest of the insurance company. The attorney must do her best to follow the procedures set forth by the insurance company, but the company cannot in any way direct the course of the representation of the insured.

REEL TO REAL

Watch *A Civil Action* (the 1998 film starring John Travolta, Robert Duvall, and William H. Macy) and keep your eye out for factors that may cloud an attorney's independent judgment and cause him to pursue a case to a bitter end.

What do you think the triggers were to lead to this result? Do you think this happens in real life? Why or why not? What would you have done differently?

> *Because a defense attorney is ethically obligated to maintain an independence of professional judgment in the defense of a client/insured, an insurance company possesses no right to control the methods or means chosen by the attorney to defend the insured. As one court stated, an insurance company cannot control the details of the attorney's performance, dictate the strategy or tactics employed, or limit the attorney's professional discretion with regard to the representation [of the insured].*

Barefield v. DPIC Companies, Inc., 215 W.Va. 544, 558, 600 S.E.2d 256, 270 (2004).

The practice of law is considered exclusive territory for attorneys, and any potential threat to compromise their independent trained and skilled judgment is discouraged. It is ultimately the attorneys who have responsibility, and they are the only ones accountable under the ethics rules for breaches of the clients' trust.

MULTIJURISDICTIONAL PRACTICE

Attorneys

Clients can be located anywhere, particularly with the modern trend of globalization; almost every business is national on some scale. Corporate counsel has a particularly tough job trying to keep up with the interstate goings-on of their clients. As discussed in chapter 1, each state must admit the attorney before its bar. Anyone not licensed in that particular state who practices there commits the unauthorized practice of law, even if that person is an attorney licensed in another state. Further, an attorney licensed in the state cannot assist another in practicing in that state where the other attorney is not licensed.

Recognizing the impossibility of counsel's being admitted in every state where the client may be involved in legal issues, the ABA Model Rules provide two ways for the preferred and retained attorney to practice outside of the state in which he is licensed. The first admits the attorney to practice law in that jurisdiction *pro hac vice* (for this time only), in litigation or on another temporary basis. It is as if the attorney is a member of the bar of the other state for that matter alone.

There are certain attendant qualifications that must be satisfied in order for the out-of-state attorney to properly represent her client in the non-admitted jurisdiction. First and foremost, the attorney must be in good standing in her home state. This is a protective measure and easily understood: the non-admitted jurisdiction does not want a substandard attorney practicing and potentially harming its own citizens. If the attorney was not good enough to practice in her home state, she surely isn't good enough to practice outside of it. Secondly, the out-of-state attorney must associate with an attorney who is admitted in the jurisdiction in which the out-of-state attorney wishes to practice. This is an "insurance policy" of sorts for the outside jurisdiction; one of its own has vouched for the credentials of the out-of-state attorney and will remain actively involved in the representation in the matter. In this way the court can be assured that the out-of-state attorney can be made aware of the local rules of procedure, standards of conduct, and local laws.

Attorneys may, in good faith, perform preliminary work in preparation for the legal work in the outside jurisdiction without fear of committing the UPL. Courts have understood that in order to evaluate the need for admission into another state, there must be some investigation into the potential cause of action. Therefore, meetings, interviews, and document reviews are permitted without a temporary admission in that state. The object of the court is not to hamper the process and client representation, but rather to protect the integrity of the court system. The rules are designed to permit these activities—but only if they are related to a proceeding in which the out-of-state attorney is involved with the client in her home state. If the matter involves appearances before the court, then the attorney should seek formal admission by motion for pro hac vice status. Other tribunals do not have such a formal status. If the attorney regularly handles construction arbitrations in her home state for her client, she may be able to handle the same in another state for that client. The standard applied is whether those out-of-state activities "arise out of or are otherwise reasonably related to the lawyer's practice" where she is admitted to practice. RESTATEMENT (THIRD) OF LAW GOVERNING LAW Comment (3) (2000).

> *Transactional and similar out-of-court representation of clients may raise similar issues, yet there is no equivalent of temporary admission pro hac vice for such representation, as there is in litigation. Even activities that bear close resemblance to in-court litigation, such as representation of clients in arbitration or in administrative hearings, may not include measures for pro hac vice appearance. Some activities are clearly permissible. Thus, a lawyer conducting activities in the lawyer's home state may advise a client about the law of another state, a proceeding in another state, or a transaction there, including conducting research in the law of the other state, advising the client about the application of that law, and drafting legal documents intended to have legal effect there.*

RESTATEMENT (THIRD) OF LAW GOVERNING LAW § 3 (2000).

There is, of course, another "catch-all" for legal services that do not fit in to either pro hac vice or other temporary admission categories. If the out-of-state attorney needs to perform legal services for his client and these services are reasonably related to the duties he performs in his home state, then he may reasonably expect that his activities out of state will be permissible. The goal of this rule is really to preserve efficiency. Requiring a client to retain outside counsel in another jurisdiction and then educating that counsel regarding the matter and the client's background may delay the proceedings and unduly burden the client.

Directly addressing the issues of national and global organizational clients, the ABA Model Rules provide that in-house counsel can operate in the non-admitted jurisdiction to provide the kind of services that are needed by the organization and that the attorney normally provides in the home jurisdiction. Recall that the client is only the organization and the attorney cannot represent the officers or employees individually in another jurisdiction, even if such representation would be related to the business entity which the attorney does represent. The ABA Model Rules on Multijurisdictional Practice really apply to in-house corporate lawyers, government lawyers, and others who are employed to render legal services to an organizational employer doing business in many different jurisdictions. The lawyer's ability to represent the employer outside the jurisdiction in which the lawyer is licensed generally serves the interests of the employer and does not create an unreasonable risk to the client and others, because the organizational client is in the best position to evaluate that individual lawyer's qualifications to perform the extrajurisdictional work. There may also be situations where the attorney is permitted to practice in that outside jurisdiction due to some other procedural rule or by federal law.

Paralegals

Because paralegals are not licensed as of yet in any state, they are not subject to the same restrictions as attorneys. They may freely move from state to state and practice their craft under the supervision of any admitted attorney. The paralegal's ethical obligations remain the same: to adhere to the local ethics rules and avoid the unauthorized practice of law in any jurisdiction. There may come a time when this issue becomes complicated, if some states license paralegals and some do not. This will potentially pose a practical obstacle to moving to another jurisdiction. As of now, however, this is not the case. Voluntary certifications do not affect a paralegal's right to practice across jurisdictions.

RESTRICTIONS ON THE RIGHT TO PRACTICE

Independence is the cornerstone of an attorney's practice. Outside influences are not permitted to sway the manner in which the attorney handles himself, his clients, or his advocacy. Clients are free to choose whichever attorney they feel most comfortable with and whom they trust with their matters. Acknowledging that business competition is a fact of life in the practice of law as well, ABA Model Rule 5.6 seeks to balance the clients' interest in selecting the attorney of choice, an individual attorney's interest in maintaining his livelihood, and the law firm's interest in its business.

covenant not to compete
An employment clause that prohibits an employee from leaving his job and going to work for a competitor for a specified period of time in a particular area.

Broadly speaking, no lawyer or firm can restrict another lawyer's right to practice law in any setting. This means that a **covenant not to compete** is unenforceable against attorneys. When an attorney leaves a firm, he cannot be told if, where, when, and with whom he may practice law. His professional autonomy is intact. The only agreement an attorney and the firm can make is one that restricts retirement benefits should the attorney seek to disengage from the firm. This is purely a business condition and does not relate to the practice of the individual lawyer, but rather restricts potential benefits that would accrue towards retirement based upon the profitability of the firm which the attorney is leaving. Any other financial disincentives to the departing attorney to restrict his practice, whether in client base, time, or geographic scope, are invalid.

> *Indirect financial disincentives may interfere with this right just as much as direct covenants not to compete. A provision offering financial disincentives may force lawyers to give up their clients, thereby interfering with the client's freedom of choice. [...] [w]e recognize that we may be holding attorneys to a higher standard than the commercial sector in general. While an indirect financial disincentive against competition or a reasonable covenant not to compete may have vitality in a commercial setting, we believe the strong public-policy concerns surrounding client choice warrant prohibition of lawyer restrictions.*

Whiteside v. Griffis & Griffis, P.C., 902 S.W.2d 739, 744 (Tex. App. 1995).

Just as the firm cannot restrict an attorney's right to practice in order to protect its business activities, a client cannot hold that kind of power over an attorney's right to practice. The ethical rules do not allow a client to hold this kind of power over an attorney. This restriction may take the form of an agreement that the settlement will be entered into only as long as the attorney agrees not to represent other similarly situated clients against the restriction-requesting opposing party. In this situation, the opposing party has restricted the right of an attorney to take on other clients against her. This is what happened in *In re Conduct of Brandt,* 331 Or. 113, 10 P.3d 906 (2000). The defendant offered to settle the matter with plaintiffs' counsel only if plaintiffs' counsel would agree to then leave those clients after the settlement was final and be retained by the defendant. Essentially, the defendant was trying to buy out the plaintiffs' attorneys and make it impossible for them to bring future claims against the defendant. The court found that the discussion during settlement negotiations of future employment that would disqualify the plaintiff's attorney in the future from representing that type of client by virtue of a conflict of interest once he was retained by the defendant was violative of Rule 5.6(b).

> *First, permitting such agreements restricts the access of the public to lawyers who, by virtue of their background and experience, might be the very best available talent to represent these individuals. Second, the use of such agreements may provide clients with rewards that bear less relationship to the merits of their claims than they do to the desire of the defendant to 'buy off' plaintiffs' counsel. Third, the offering of such restrictive agreements places the plaintiff's lawyer in a situation where there is conflict between the interests of present clients and those of potential future clients.*

Id. at 131, citing, ABA Comm. on Ethics and Prof'l Responsibility, Formal Op. 371 (1993).

This restriction on the attorney's right to choose which future clients he would take on is an unacceptable restriction on his right to practice law. Attorneys, as a whole, are fiercely independent, and their judgment cannot be permitted to be clouded with financial concerns and potential negative ramifications for their livelihood.

While the business of the practice of law is similar in many ways to other businesses, there are certain conditions that the attorneys in law firms must consider in order to remain faithful to their ethical obligations. There are added burdens on supervising attorneys to ensure not just the quality of the work being done in their firms, but also the ethical manner in which those legal tasks are performed. Due to the nature of their relationship with their clients, attorneys must be vigilant to ensure that there are no "cracks" in the system into which some work could fall; they would be held accountable for the mistake. The practice of law is relatively unforgiving of mistakes, as each one, even little ones, may have a substantial impact on the rights and liabilities of clients. That is also the reason attorneys must maintain their independence from outside influences. Those who are not attorneys do not understand the ethical implications of every element of the practice of law and are not held responsible for any transgression. Therefore, the attorney must depend upon his individual professional judgment alone in handling a matter for a client. Clients have every right to expect this duty of care from their attorneys and have a right to freely choose which attorney will represent their interests. This is the reason no outside influences, monetary incentives, or other restrictions on attorney access is permitted.

Summary

It is important for paralegals to understand the organizational structure of the law firm in order to implement best ethical practices. Supervising attorneys have the greatest responsibility for ensuring ethical compliance in the law office. Paralegal managers have the same sort of duty with regard to the supervised paralegals. The hierarchical structure of the branches within the office may seem duplicative with regard to ethical responsibility; however, that organization serves to ensure that the highest ethical standards of conduct are followed.

Office organization and ethical responsibility also affect the employment status of the personnel. Clearly, attorneys are white-collar employees exempt from wage and overtime mandates from the Department of Labor. Exempt employees

1. are salaried at a certain minimum. Their wages are not subject to reductions or variations depending on the quality of the work or the amount of time worked in a week.

2. perform non-manual work that requires the exercise of discretion and independent judgment related to the management of the business of the employer.

3. have advanced knowledge acquired through prolonged specialized intellectual instruction.

Paralegals have generally been considered "blue-collar," non-exempt employees. This has advantages and disadvantages, for the individual earning the overtime and for the profession as a whole and its public perception as a true "profession."

Ethics in a law office must be free from monetary incentives or other restrictions. It is imperative that attorneys maintain their independence in order to properly function as ethical professionals. This independence takes the form of rules regarding partnerships and prohibiting attorneys from forming business partnerships with non-lawyers or giving outside third parties control over the decision-making process of the attorney.

The globalization of business has also affected the practice of law. Attorneys are traditionally licensed in only one or two states, whereas businesses are often national in scale. This creates problems associated with multijurisdictional practice. Paralegals are not confined in a state-specific licensure scheme, so they are not restricted to any geographical area of practice.

Key Terms and Concepts

Covenant not to compete
Malfeasance
Mitigation
Negligent misconduct

Paraprofessional
Ratification
Subordinate attorney
Supervising attorney

Review Questions

MULTIPLE CHOICE

Choose the best answer(s) and please explain WHY you choose the answer(s).

1. An attorney may share legal fees with a paralegal in the following circumstances:
   a. pursuant to a written fee agreement with attorney's firm
   b. after a reasonable time after attorney's death
   c. never
   d. as long as the paralegal agrees to accept whatever portion is deemed fair and appropriate by the attorney that reflects the value of the paralegal's services

2. A supervisory attorney is responsible for the conduct of
   a. all subordinate employees.
   b. her partners.
   c. all attorneys and support staff to whom she assigns/delegates work.
   d. only full-time attorneys, not any independent contractors like freelance paralegals.

3. Multijurisdictional practice
   a. requires that an attorney pass the bar exam in every jurisdiction in which she intends to practice.
   b. is never permitted by unadmitted attorneys.
   c. requires that the attorney make a motion to be admitted pro hac vice.
   d. is becoming more prevalent, and there are many ways to deal with the issues.

EXPLAIN YOURSELF

All answers should be written in complete sentences. A simple yes or no is insufficient.

1. Describe the circumstances under which an attorney could apply for pro hac vice status in a matter.
2. When may an attorney share legal fees with a non-attorney?
3. Explain the difference between an attorney's responsibility for unethical conduct of one of his partners and the attorney's responsibility for one of the paralegals in the firm.
4. When is it permissible for an attorney to accept payment for legal services from a third-party non-client?
5. Should a law firm be able to require its paralegals to sign a covenant not to compete as part of their employment contracts?

FAULTY PHRASES

All of the following statements are FALSE; state why they are false and then rewrite them as true statements, without just making a statement negative by adding the word "not."

1. An attorney cannot be responsible for another lawyer's misconduct if the supervising attorney did not specifically direct that course of action.
2. A supervising attorney will not be ethically sanctioned for the actions of a subordinate if no harm was caused to the client.
3. An attorney may form a business with a non-attorney if only a small portion of that business involves the practice of law.
4. Covenants not to compete are enforceable against former attorney-employees as long as they are reasonable.
5. An attorney may practice in a jurisdiction in which she is not licensed as long as it is the kind of matter in which she customarily engages in her home jurisdiction.
6. A paralegal in another jurisdiction can assist an out-of-state attorney to prepare a legal matter for submission to the court.
7. A supervising attorney has no ethical obligation to correct the mistakes of his paralegal.

 PORTFOLIO ASSIGNMENT

Write Away

Prepare a persuasive brief for submission to your local paralegal association explaining your position on the impact "non-exempt" (blue-collar) or "exempt" (white-collar) status has on the paralegal profession as a whole. There is no right or wrong answer, as good arguments can be made for the impact of either status on both the public's perception of the profession and an individual paralegal's opinion about her chosen career. Be sure to include enough detail in your argument to support your position.

State Bar of Michigan
Standing Committee on Professional and Judicial Ethics
Opinion Number R-1
*1 December 16, 1988

SYLLABUS

A lawyer having direct supervisory authority over a nonlawyer shall make reasonable efforts to ensure that the person's conduct is compatible with the professional obligations of the lawyer.

A lawyer cannot adequately supervise the quality of legal services rendered by six civilian and eighteen prison paralegals to a prospective client population of 4,500 prisoners located in prisons throughout the State of Michigan, including the Upper Peninsula.

TEXT

The director of a legal services organization (LSO) is considering submitting a bid on a legal assistance program which the Michigan Department of Corrections may start pursuant to a recent federal court order. Under the program, LSO would provide assistance, not in-court representation, in post-conviction and conditions of confinement cases to prisoners at six locations in four Michigan prisons. The staff would consist of one lawyer/director, six civilian paralegals and eighteen prisoner paralegals. The duties of the lawyer/director would include the hiring, training and supervision of the six civilian and eighteen prisoner paralegals at six separate locations throughout the state. While the duties would include other aspects of administering the program, it is the hiring, training and necessary supervision of the paralegals which generate concern. The civilian paralegals would be entrusted with a variety of responsibilities which would include visiting and assisting prisoners in segregation units, responding in writing to requests for legal assistance and supervising an average of three prisoner paralegals and an unknown number of prisoner law library clerks. The prisoner paralegals would be entrusted with duties which would include providing legal research and drafting assistance to civilian paralegals and conducting conferences with prisoner clients.

Estimates of new caseloads range to 1,718 persons per year. Additionally, there are currently 226 open cases. Case estimates are difficult because, first, the prisoner population at any prison constantly changes, thus even though capacity for a given facility may be 500 prisoners, several thousand persons could pass through the facility each year. Second, the percentage of persons requesting assistance fluctuates depending on the quality and speed of the responses. The more efficient and better staffed the LSO becomes, the greater the number of requests.

May the lawyer/director of LSO ethically accept the responsibility of supervising 24 or more nonlawyers or any number of nonlawyers in so many locations? May civilian paralegals under the lawyer/director's control provide on-site supervision over the work of prisoner paralegals?

Any issue addressed relative to the activities of paralegals operating under the supervision of licensed lawyers must be viewed with *MRPC 5.3* and *5.5* in mind. *MRPC 5.5* forbids a lawyer from assisting a person who is not a member of the bar in the performance of activity that constitutes the unauthorized practice of law. The comment following *MRPC 5.5* specifies that paragraph (b) does not prohibit a lawyer from employing the services of paraprofessionals and delegating functions to them, so long as the lawyer supervises and retains responsibility for the delegated work.

What constitutes the unauthorized practice of law in a particular jurisdiction is a matter for determination by the courts of that jurisdiction. Questions of law are beyond the scope of the Committee's jurisdiction. The inquirer is referred to the following resources: *State Bar v Cramer,* 399 Mich 116 (1976); Vol 59 No 3 MBJ 173 (1980); Vol 62 No 8 MBJ 624 (1983); and Vol 56 No 8 MBJ 704 (1977).

MRPC 5.3 further defines and enhances the responsibility of the supervising lawyer by providing that not only does that lawyer have a responsibility not to aid in the unauthorized practice of law, but also must assure that the nonlawyer over whom he or she has direct supervisory authority does not engage in conduct incompatible with the professional obligations of the lawyer, or engage in conduct that would be a violation of the Michigan Rules of Professional Conduct if engaged in by a lawyer. The comment following *MRPC 5.3* notes that the measures employed in supervising nonlawyers should take account of the fact that they do not have legal training and are not subject to professional discipline. It also says a lawyer should give nonlawyers personal assistance, appropriate instruction, and supervision concerning the ethical aspects of their employment, particularly regarding the obligation not to disclose information relating to representation of the client, and that the lawyer should be responsible for the work product of the nonlawyer.

Given the parameters set forth in *MRPC 5.3* and *5.5*, for the lawyer/director to assume the responsibilities as outlined would be to invite a violation of *MRPC 5.5* and could lead to a violation of *MRPC 5.3*. While it appears as though the legal assistants under the terms of the plan described would not be expected to engage in the practice of law by making court appearances or providing actual, technical representation, there is a distinct possibility and, in all likelihood, a probability that they will be engaged in advising clients of their legal rights. The proposed legal assistance program will utilize the Technical Assistance Manual on Offender Legal Service prepared by the American Bar Association's Commission on Correctional Facilities and Services as a guide in delivering services. The manual repeatedly stresses two things--the exigencies under which prisoners are operating in securing even the most basic legal services and the role of the lawyer in providing those services. It discusses in detail such prisoner problems as illiteracy, confusion, unsophistication and lack of access to the system. It also expressly contemplates the extreme reliance of such individuals upon the advice provided by the lawyer. Under the proposal submitted here for examination, it is clear that for all practical purposes, it would be the paralegals (civilian and prisoner) upon whom the bulk of the reliance for advice would be placed. This system does not provide the quality legal service to which the clients are entitled and the Michigan Rules of Professional Conduct require of lawyers.

The reasoning behind the adoption of the rules forbidding the unauthorized practice of law operates to substantiate the opinion that the activities proposed under the plan would present an unavoidable ethical dilemma. Initially, it must be remembered that paralegals are not subject to state licensure, nor are they subject to the requirements and regulations imposed upon the members of the legal profession. A nonlawyer who undertakes to handle legal matters is not governed as to integrity or legal competence by the same rules that govern the conduct of the lawyer. A lawyer is not only subject to license regulation, but also is committed to high standards of ethical conduct. The public is best served in legal matters by a highly trained and regulated profession committed to such standards. Only lawyers are subject to the special fiduciary duties in the lawyer-client relationship and to the regulations of an effectively policed profession.

Moreover, a layperson who seeks legal service often is not in a position to judge whether he or she will receive proper professional attention. The entrustment of a legal matter may well involve the confidences, the reputation, the property, the freedom or even the life of the client. Proper protection of members of the public demands that no person be permitted to act in the confidential and demanding role of a lawyer unless he or she is subject to high standards. In this instance, those who seek the legal services are particularly disadvantaged, and additional care must be taken to assure that the reliability of the assistance they receive is not impaired.

Given the fact that the lawyer/director would be expected to hire, train and supervise a minimum of six civilian and eighteen prisoner paralegals at six separate locations, it is difficult to perceive how the lawyer/director could provide the direct supervision required for each client and realistically assume full responsibility to each and every client for the actions or nonactions of the legal assistants. Moreover, given the number of paralegals and their locations as well as the potential caseload, it is our opinion that it would be physically impossible for the lawyer/director to provide the supervision required to avoid violating *MRPC 5.5* or *MRPC 5.3*. Additionally, the direct supervision of the prisoner paralegals and an unknown number of prisoner law library clerks by civilian paralegals would be direct contravention of the requirement that they be directly supervised by a lawyer.

Finally, the ABA manual recommends a lawyer to prisoner ratio of one lawyer to four hundred prisoners per year, divided between a variety of "advice only" and more time consuming court action cases. In the plan being considered, the lawyer to client ratio would be one lawyer to 1,944 prisoners. That ratio is incompatible with the appropriate delivery of legal services and the stated purpose of the program to provide meaningful assistance to the prison population.

For the foregoing reasons, the inquirer's participation as supervising lawyer in the LSO as presently structured would violate *MRPC 5.3* and *5.5*.

Source: Reprinted with permission from ThomsonWest.

Chapter 10

Advertising and the Solicitation of Clients

CHAPTER OBJECTIVES

The student will be able to:

- Understand the reasons for stricter restrictions on attorney advertising
- Discuss the kinds of advertising that are and are not acceptable under the rules and identify those advertisements that are "borderline"
- Distinguish between salesmanship and false and misleading legal advertising
- Identify situations where solicitations are prohibited
- Describe the proper use of the terms "specialization" and "certification"

This chapter will examine WHAT an attorney or paralegal may say to a client in soliciting business, to WHOM the legal professional may speak in drumming up more business, HOW the advertisements and solicitations for new business must comply with certain ethical requirements, and WHY these requirements are different from those for normal commercial advertising.

Honesty and advertising—not two words one usually puts together in the same sentence. However, when it comes to attorneys' attempts at gaining clientele, they must go hand in hand. An attorney's commercial advertisement will never air during the Super Bowl, when the funniest and wittiest marketing powerhouses are out for the American consumer. However, in the short time that attorney advertising has been permitted, it has come a long way; whether for better or for worse is not yet evident.

OVERCOMING THE BAN ON ATTORNEY ADVERTISING

Historically, attorneys were not permitted to advertise their services *at all*. The first ABA Model Code of Ethics, written in 1908, prohibited any means of advertising other than printed business cards with the attorney's contact information. The legal profession, through many different associations, courts, and individuals, has sought to maintain the integrity and honor of this noble profession. The codes of conduct were slow to change; until the late 1970s, only listings in the Yellow Pages that contained contact information, basic personal background information, and area of

**Very Reasonable Fees
for Legal Services**

- Uncontested divorce or legal separation – $300 + $25 filing fee
- Preparation of a "how-to" kit for filing your own uncontested divorce papers – $100
- Adoption in an uncontested severance proceeding – $350 + $25 publication cost

FIGURE 10.1

**Sample Legal
Advertisement**

practice were permitted. See Figure 10.1 for a very typical example of the type of advertisement in question. The United States Supreme Court, in its landmark decision regarding attorney advertising, *Bates v. State Bar of Arizona,* 433 U.S. 350, 367, 97 S. Ct. 2691, 2700 (1977), acknowledged "that an advertising diet limited to such spartan fare would provide scant nourishment." The crux of the issue in *Bates* was the publication of a fee schedule in the attorneys' advertisements for legal services. The Court examined the origins of the "no advertising" rule and determined that it was no longer relevant and could not withstand a Constitutional First Amendment challenge for freedom of speech, albeit **commercial speech**.

> It appears that the ban on advertising originated as a rule of etiquette and not as a rule of ethics. Early lawyers in Great Britain viewed the law as a form of public service, rather than as a means of earning a living, and they looked down on "trade" as unseemly. Eventually, the attitude toward advertising fostered by this view evolved into an aspect of the ethics of the profession. But habit and tradition are not in themselves an adequate answer to a constitutional challenge. In this day, we do not belittle the person who earns his living by the strength of his arm or the force of his mind. Since the belief that lawyers are somehow "above" trade has become an anachronism, the historical foundation for the advertising restraint has crumbled.

Id. at 371–372.

Word of mouth, reputation in the community, and other referral systems had worked when the geographic practice areas of attorneys were relatively limited. But just as every segment of the economy has grown and become specialized, attorneys must reach out to find those with whom they can do business. The Supreme Court found the opposition without merit in their main arguments against permitting attorney advertising. While attorneys do charge different rates for different clients and matters depending on many variables unique to each case, the general advertisement will not necessarily be misleading because of "the inherent lack of standardization in legal services." *Id.* at 373. The advertisement will not be able to completely address the particular concerns of each client and will not be able to give full background regarding the competency of the attorney, but that is not an excuse to ban that kind of speech altogether. The very nature of advertisement has those problems inherent in it for any service. "A rule allowing restrained advertising would be in accord with the bar's obligation to facilitate the process of intelligent selection of lawyers, and to assist in making legal services fully available." *Id.* at 377. The Supreme Court took a very balanced approach in protecting lawyers' interest in obtaining clients by the right exercise of free speech and the need to regulate these advertisements so as to protect the public from those who might take this opportunity to mislead the public for increased profits.

commercial speech
A category of expression that has only limited protection under the United States Constitution because its purpose is not the dissemination of an idea, but rather the garnering of monetary rewards through commerce.

REEL TO REAL

John Grisham's 1997 film *The Rainmaker* (starring Matt Damon and Danny DeVito, and directed by Frances Ford Coppola) portrays a young, freshly admitted attorney's struggle to start his career and obtain clients. Pay attention to the ethical interplay between Damon's character and DeVito's as they take on clients.

MODERN RESTRICTIONS ON ATTORNEY ADVERTISEMENT AND SOLICITATION

solicitation
An attorney's attempt to gain business, usually directed at a specific individual or group and involving an invitation to consult with the attorney regarding legal matters.

The current ABA Model Rules permit advertising and certain types of **solicitation** (invitations to consult with the attorney on a matter). Each jurisdiction has a set of rules based upon these general principles, but the ways in which the individual state courts have interpreted them can vary widely. At the core, an attorney is prohibited from making a false or misleading statement with regard to the lawyer or his services. Advertisements and solicitations must not misstate a fact or law or omit a fact such that the statement is rendered misleading.

"Materially Misleading" Communication

materially misleading
Characterized by false information upon which a member of the intended audience would rely in making a decision.

The rules of advertisement and solicitation apply to any and every kind of communication: oral, written, or electronic. The key to their application is the understanding of what constitutes a **materially misleading** communication. As in other contexts, a statement is material if it is one upon which a person would base some or all of his decision. If it doesn't make a difference to that person, then it isn't material. Different audiences, the targets of the advertising and solicitation, may consider different factors to be material, so it is important to examine the circumstances surrounding the communication as well. "[B]ecause the public lacks sophistication concerning legal services, misstatements that might be overlooked or deemed unimportant in other advertising may be found quite inappropriate in legal advertising." *Bates, supra,* at 383. Unlike the typical commercials for consumer products that the public is used to seeing and hearing, legal advertisements must remain relatively conservative. They cannot use such normal marketing language as "best" or "premier"; nor can they make any comparative or statistical claims based upon their track record or client information. What attorneys cannot do in marketing their services really is an exhaustive list of "shall-nots." If the advertisement presents self-praise, creates unjustified expectations in a potential client based upon past success stories, offers an opinion as to the quality of the attorney's services, implies that the attorney's services are better than those of others, omits the name of the firm or the attorney, or contains unverifiable information, it is misleading under the multitude of court cases dealing with this issue.

NFPA addresses specific misrepresentations that may tempt a paralegal to bolster her résumé or credentials. NFPA EC. 1.7(d) and (e). NALA's Guideline 1, although not specifically tailored to this particular issue, provides that legal assistants should disclose their status as legal assistants. (See Figure 10.2.)

Advertisements can be found to be misleading for a number of reasons. One advertisement that was found to be misleading came from the Florida law firm of Pape and Chandler. It featured an image of a pit bull. The court forced them to change their logo because the image of the pit bull was "inherently deceptive because there is no way to measure whether the attorneys in fact conduct themselves like pit bulls so as to ascertain whether this logo and phone number convey accurate information. […] In addition, the image of a pit bull and the on-screen display of the words "PIT-BULL" as part of the firm's phone number are not objectively relevant to the selection

FIGURE 10.2
**Disclosure of Status
of Paralegal**

NFPA EC 1.7

(d) A paralegal shall not practice under color of any record, diploma or certificate that has been illegally or fraudulently obtained or issued or which is misrepresentative in any way.

(e) A paralegal shall not participate in the creation, issuance or dissemination of fraudulent records, diplomas or certificates.

of an attorney. The referee found that the qualities of a pit bull as depicted by the logo are loyalty, persistence, tenacity, and aggressiveness. We consider this a charitable set of associations that ignores the darker side of the qualities often also associated with pit bulls: malevolence, viciousness, and unpredictability." *The Florida Bar v. Pape,* 918 So.2d 240, 244–245 (2005). The actual advertisement and its "tamer" replacement can be accessed at this address: http://www.papeandchandler.com. The Florida court "would not condone an advertisement that stated that a lawyer will get results through combative and vicious tactics that will maim, scar, or harm the opposing party, conduct that would violate our Rules of Professional Conduct. […] Yet this is precisely the type of unethical and unprofessional conduct that is conveyed by the image of a pit bull and the display of the 1-800-PIT-BULL phone number" *Id.* at 246. Essentially, all the glitz and tools of the marketing industry are to be kept out of legal advertisement. To keep tabs on all of these new requirements and secure enforcement, attorneys must keep copies of all their advertisements on file for three years.

IN CLASS DISCUSSION

Review a recent attorney advertisement from a divorce law firm. The first billboard placed by the law firm had larger-than-life photos of a female torso practically bursting out of a lace bra and black thong and an extremely toned and muscular male torso. The firm was required to replace the ads with a less provocative ad. The second is the "more tame" replacement. It features photos of a female in a see-through negligee and thigh-high stockings and a male unbuttoning his shirt, again to reveal very toned abs. In neither advertising campaign were the faces of the models shown. The firm's slogan remained unchanged and reads, "Life is Short. Get a Divorce." The law firm defends its advertisements and clearly plans to continue this line of advertising. See http://www.fgalawfirm.com/ for more information about the Fetman, Garland and Associates law firm. Also note that attorney Fetman is the female model for the ads and has plans to pose for *Playboy* magazine. Are these advertising tactics ethical under the relevant rules? Why or why not?

Technology

The ways in which attorneys market their services are changing with both industry and the technology. In January 2007, the New York State Unified Court System adopted new advertising rules for the state's attorneys. These changes attempt to address a host of issues related to common marketing tactics and modes of communication, particularly concerning the use of the Internet. The new rules cover computer-accessed communication, which they define as

> any communication made by or on behalf of a lawyer or law firm that is disseminated through the use of a computer or related electronic device, including, but not limited to, web sites, weblogs, search engines, electronic mail, banner advertisements, pop-up and pop-under advertisements, chat rooms, list servers, instant messaging, or other internet presences, and any attachments or links related thereto.

Further, New York proposed Disciplinary Rule 2–101 prohibits the use of pop-ups unless they are contained solely on the firm's individual Web site. As to the "catchiness" of the attorney's advertisement, endorsements or testimonials from clients with pending matters are prohibited, as are portrayals of a judge or a fictitious law firm. No mottos, nicknames, trade names or other titles that are not directly related to the business of the law firm and/or mislead, are to be used, nor are attorneys permitted to use celebrity voice-overs in their commercials. Full disclosure of the fact that an advertisement uses actors or dramatizations must be prominently made; it must clearly display the label "ATTORNEY ADVERTISEMENT."

IN CLASS DISCUSSION

Discuss the following scripts from the television advertisements of law firms. Which do you think violate ABA Model Rule 7.1, prohibiting false or misleading communications? Why? Describe the elements of the commercial that are potentially misleading. What could you change about them to make them comply with the ethical constraints? (Ignore the fact that the name of the law firm has been omitted; assume there is one in the actual commercial.)

1. The advertisement, known as the "Strategy Session," depicts a conference room where actors portraying insurance adjusters are discussing a claim. An older man, the "senior adjuster," asks a younger man, the "junior adjuster," how the claim should be handled. The junior adjuster describes the claim as " . . . a large claim, serious auto accident" and suggests they try to deny and delay to see if the claimant will "crack." The senior adjuster then asks which lawyer represents the victim, whereupon the junior adjuster responds: "The XYZ Law Firm." A metallic sound effect follows and the senior adjuster, now looking concerned, states: "The XYZ Law Firm? Let's settle this one." At this point in the advertisement, a well-known actor appears on screen and advises viewers, "[T]he insurance companies know the name The XYZ Law Firm." He invites individuals who have been injured in an auto accident to tell the insurance companies they "mean business" by calling The XYZ Law Firm. The actor provides the firm's telephone number, which also appears at the bottom of the screen. *See In re Keller,* 792 N.E.2d 865 (Ind. 2003).

2. In four of the television commercials, former clients of the firm appear, talking about actual situations in which they have employed the law firm. In one of the presentations, a client says that the firm "fought the law all the way to the state Supreme Court and we won." A client in another presentation says, "They really fought for me. They were aggressive and settled things quickly. I never expected the large settlement they won for me." A third client says, "They made things happen. And they got results. If you have the right attorneys, you can fight City Hall." The fourth former client says, "They fought for me and got me a very good judgment. Take my word for it, they're the best." The attorney adds at the end of the commercial: "There's no charge unless we win your case. What could be fairer?" *See Disciplinary Counsel v. Shane,* 81 Ohio St. 3d 494, 692 N.E.2d 571 (1998).

3. The following two commercials are from the same law firm:
   a. The "Divorce Case" scene shows a couple discussing a division of their property. After they agree to split everything "right down the middle," the husband uses a power saw to cut through a table and a sofa while their dog looks on soulfully, possibly with some concern that he may suffer the same fate. The announcer then states:

      "When a marriage gets in trouble, everyone wants to be fair. But that's not always so easy. Our law offices can help you through those difficult times. Because we understand that people facing a divorce don't need any more problems than they already have."
   b. The "Bankruptcy Case" shows a man sitting in his living room in front of a television set with a bowl of popcorn. Two men come in and proceed to strip the room of all its furnishings, including the television set and finally the bowl of popcorn. The announcer then states: "When financial tragedy strikes you, you don't have to lose everything; there are laws to protect you. Bankruptcy laws. Our law offices can help you protect yourself, because the law is designed to serve ordinary people. So are our law offices."

See Grievance Committee for Hartford-New Britain Judicial Dist. v. Trantolo, 192 Conn. 15, 470 A.2d 228 (1984).

The old adage "Let the Buyer Beware" is not applicable in the area of legal services. The courts and bar associations have unequivocally decided that the buyer in this case, the client, deserves extra protection from the potential **overreaching** of attorneys in their quest to increase their client bases. Many of the disciplinary boards of the states have contended with the issue of which communications will be permitted and which ones go too far and put the public at risk of misunderstanding the services provided by the advertising attorney. In discussing the content and method of delivery, the courts have come far since the days of an all-out ban. Indeed, as each new method of delivery has become available and widely used, the court has reevaluated the ethical rules pertaining to the content of legal advertising.

overreaching
Taking unfair commercial advantage of another by going beyond normal and reasonable means to obtain the desired result.

The trial court found that the prohibition of "drawings, animations, dramatizations, music or lyrics" in attorney advertising did not pass constitutional muster under the United States Supreme Court's attorney advertising decisions. The factual finding underlying that conclusion was that such techniques, while they may be factually deceptive, are not inherently so. The trial court found what the record overwhelmingly supports, namely that the use of these techniques "are only inherently misleading in the sense . . . [of] inducing action more on the basis of emotion than rational thought." The trial court explicitly determined that, despite this emotional aspect of these techniques, their prohibition would "preclude the effective use of legal services advertising and constitute more extensive regulation than necessary to serve the governmental interests in precluding false, misleading, and undignified advertising." Prohibiting these techniques would result in "tombstone" ads that would not "accomplish the intended purposes of attention-getting, recall assistance (memory storage), and supplying substantive legal services information to the public." At the same time, the trial court stressed that its factual finding assumed not only that ads would be required to be truthful and not misleading, but also that the requirement that ads be presented in a dignified manner would be maintained. Clearly concerned with the irrational aspect of creative advertising, the trial court also noted that "careful monitoring and measurement of the effect on the public of the use of the techniques is obviously necessary and desirable."

Petition of Felmeister & Isaacs, 104 N.J. 515, 522–523, 518 A.2d 188, 191–192 (1986).

RECOMMENDATIONS AND REFERRALS

"Money changes everything" is an adage true in legal advertising as well as in other areas. Protecting the integrity of the profession from "buying" clients is ABA Model Rule 7.2. The ethical rules recognize that legal professionals will have to pay for commercial advertisements. This is against the normal prohibition forbidding attorneys to pay for referrals. The advertising medium is not referring or in any way endorsing the use of the attorney. All media, such as television, newspapers, and other public means of dissemination, charge for the advertising time and space they provide. The rules, therefore, must allow the attorney to pay for such advertisements without violating the "no payment for referral" rule. Lawyers may not give anything of value to individuals for their assistance in getting the word out about the attorneys' services. This means they are not to give out cash, bonuses, awards, or presents or to barter their services for anyone who recommends their legal services.

The exception on the "bartering" for services is that an attorney may recommend that his clients seek the professional services of another lawyer or other professional.

This professional referral is constrained; the attorney may have a mutual referral agreement ("you scratch my back, I'll scratch yours") with the other attorney or professional only if the agreement is not exclusive and the client is made aware of the agreement. This serves two purposes. First, the nonexclusivity rule assures that clients have a meaningful choice among professionals and that the referring attorney gives the best referral to the most appropriate professional, not the one to whom she is bound by agreement. Such agreements cannot interfere with the attorney's independent professional judgment. Second, the client's awareness of the reciprocal referral agreement is necessary so that the client is able to decide for himself whether to seek independent counsel or the service of another professional, knowing that the attorney may have some favorable bias toward the referred professional.

An attorney referral system can be a type of clearinghouse to funnel potential clients to the appropriate attorney in practice and geographical area. It makes all the difference whether the advertising system is for-profit or not-for-profit. The only acceptable referral system is a non-profit one, as the monetary compensation for referral is not permitted. There is a difference between a true referral system and a paid group advertisement, wherein a specific group of lawyers combine their resources to advertise their services. As long as the advertisement clearly indicates that the group commercial is not an attorney referral service and indicates the participating attorneys, the commercial is permissible. In *Alabama State Bar Ass'n v. R.W. Lynch Co., Inc.,* 655 So.2d 982, 983 (Ala. 1995), the defendant advertising agency produced an "Injury Helpline" television marketing program. Several law firms or solo attorneys jointly purchased advertising to be included in the pool of attorneys listed on the "Injury Helpline" commercial. The 30-second commercial expressly states: "Advertising paid by sponsoring attorneys. Not a lawyer referral service." The attorneys' or firms' names and addresses appear on the commercial, and a 1-800 toll-free telephone number is provided for the viewer to call. The calls are received by an answering service and the caller needs to supply only her name, telephone number, and zip code. The court found this to be an acceptable form of group advertisement and that it was not a referral service. The distinction was important because the advertising agency was run for profit. This allows the potential clients to ascertain whether they will be assisted in making their choices based on need (as in a true referral service) or simply directed to an answering service that then transferred their calls to the lawyer who paid for the right to service clients in that geographic area. Where there may be any confusion on the part of the consumer, the attorney is to err on the side of caution and make sure that if it is a paid advertisement, that fact is explicitly and prominently indicated.

> *When advertising is done through a vehicle which is not explicitly referenced as an advertisement, and is not readily known to consumers as a place of pure advertising (as, for example, the Yellow Pages would be), there is a possibility that the presentation and language could lead a reasonably informed consumer to believe that the listing has some sort of professional or authoritative imprimatur, as a kind of endorsement, such as an authorized lawyer referral service might give (e.g., a web page presented as "anti-trust lawyers.coím," as a hypothetical). Such a presentation could, intentionally or inadvertently, thus mislead consumers into believing it was other or more than simply a paid advertisement, and carried greater weight.*

N.J. Atty. Advert. Op. 36, 15 N.J.L. 48, 182 N.J.L.J. 1206 (2005) (The Committee on Attorney Advertising was presented with a question regarding Web site advertising.)

Whether an attorney seeks clients through advertising or referral, the real harm to the consumer is in the monetary incentive to generate further business. Further, a referral system could not advertise any of the participating attorneys' services in a manner that would violate any of the other rules regarding communications of legal services. Essentially, the advertisement or not-for-profit referral service may not deliver

CYBER TRIP

Compare these sites:

http://www.abanet.org/legalservices/lris/directory/

www.LegalMatch.com

http://www.legalservices4less.com

http://www.selectcounsel.com

http://united defensegroup.com

http://www.requestlegalhelp.com

the information about the attorneys' services in a manner in which the legal professional himself would be prohibited from doing so.

An interesting case was brought before Maryland's Attorney Grievance Commission involving the work of a paralegal and her assistance in gaining clientele for her employer. The paralegal, who was very successful in the thriving personal injury firm that she wished to leave, contacted an attorney whose personal injury practice could use some bolstering. The paralegal assured the attorney that she could help because of her work experience and the fact that she had "lots of contacts and friends." Her new employment contract gave her an $80,000 a year salary and included a term that she would need to increase the firm's practice by acquiring one hundred personal injury files within a year. The paralegal's former firm brought charges against the paralegal and her new firm, alleging that she stole closed client file information and was unethically soliciting former clients for the new attorney. The trial court found that

> *[The attorney] knowingly hired [the paralegal] not for her legal or secretarial skills but with the primary motive/purpose of obtaining the personal injury clients that could be delivered through [the paralegal]'s access to the white copy of the information forms from [her prior employer] and/or her own personal client contacts. Rule 7.2(c), the advertising rule, is the most appropriate one to apply to this violation. While this particular form of payment for referrals is a matter of first impression now before this Court, it is analogous to paying 'runners' or 'bird dogs' for referrals as discussed under 7.2(c). These are similar practices for which the Court has previously disciplined lawyers. [The paralegal] brought no specific qualifications that would justify such an exorbitant compensation package; thus, it is clear that she was being compensated for her services in bringing in clients.*

Attorney Grievance Comm'n of Maryland v. Wills, *348 Md. 633, 639, 705 A.2d 1121, 1124 (Md. Ct. App. 1998)*.

However, the Appellate Court of Maryland could not find that the sending of letters to the former clients associated with the paralegal's prior firm was in violation of the ethical rules pertaining to advertising or solicitation. While the salary was very high, it could be paid for both her paralegal skills and her advertising services. She merely prepared proper letters for distribution to potential clients. The letters themselves were not in violation of the rules for advertising and solicitation and, therefore, if the paralegal were performing a function that the attorney could ethically perform, even though those services were linked to paying her for her time in preparing advertisements, the paralegal was not in any violation either. The trial court's decision was reversed and the complaint dismissed.

RESEARCH THIS

Find and compare two cases in your jurisdiction that deal with the propriety of attorney advertising: one which held that the advertising material was in compliance with your local rules and one holding that it was not. What were the defining factors that led to these opposite conclusions? What could you change about each one to get the opposite result? (i.e., what would have put the valid advertisement "over the line" and what would have kept the unethical one within the regulations?)

DIRECT CONTACT WITH PROSPECTIVE CLIENTS

Televised commercials, radio spots, and letters are all ways to reach out impersonally to potential clients. There is significantly more danger associated with in-person solicitation of clients. The directness, influence, pressure, immediacy, and surrounding circumstances may overpower the consumer into making a less than well-thought-out decision regarding the retention of the particular attorney. For this reason, legal professionals are prohibited from contacting potential clients "live." This is set forth in ABA Model Rule 7.3. The contact is considered "in person" or "live" if the communications can be made instantaneously between the attorney and client. This includes use of the telephone and electronic means of communication.

As in almost every other rule, there are exceptions to the general prohibition against contacting a prospective client in person. The first exception permits in-person or other "live" contact only if the other party is an attorney or if the contacting legal professional already has a relationship of some sort with the potential client. It guards the potential client's privacy first of all, but most of all it protects the potential client's ability to reflect upon the decision. The danger of pressure from one attorney to another is significantly less than that of pressure on a lay consumer who contacts a legal professional. Presumably, other attorneys are not influenced by the "silver-tongued" solicitor and understand their right to take the time to make an informed decision about retaining the contacting attorney. The second group excepted from this rule already knows the attorney and/or paralegal and therefore has reason to have and expect contact with her. An attorney or a paralegal has more to lose if certain strong-arm tactics are used with family, close friends, and former clients. Indeed, the attorney and/or the paralegal may be motivated to help these individuals not by monetary gain, but by a sense of duty and loyalty.

ambulance chasers
A derogatory term used to describe attorneys that make direct in-person or mailed solicitation to injured persons very shortly after the accident, so that they seem to be waiting at the ambulance door for them.

Most of the case law in this area of in-person solicitation involves the notorious "**ambulance chasers,**" those attorneys or their agents who contact victims shortly after their incidents in an effort to be retained. The danger here lies in the fact that the legal professional may engage in overreaching not only in selling his services immediately, but also in taking advantage of the potential client's vulnerability during this time. Attorneys and courts have taken this issue very seriously, as it potentially infringes not only on an attorney's right to pursue his livelihood, but also on the First Amendment right of freedom of speech (albeit commercial speech) which is entitled to less protection than other kinds of expression not fueled primarily for pecuniary gain. Two United States Supreme Court cases address this very issue of in-person solicitation. In the first, *Ohralik v. Ohio State Bar Association,* 436 U.S. 447, 98 S. Ct. 1912, 56 L.Ed.2d 444 (1978), the attorney/acquaintance of the family of the injured visited her in the hospital and, over the course of a few days spent talking with her and her family, secured a contingent fee contract to represent her personal injury claim. The injured client fired the attorney a few days after signing the contract. The Court found that while the First Amendment does protect "restrained advertising" to address society's interest in obtaining information about the availability of legal services, each state has a countervailing interest in protecting its citizens against overreaching by attorneys in securing their services. *Id.* at 455. The Court found that "in-person solicitation of professional employment by a lawyer does not stand on a par with truthful advertising about the availability and terms of routine legal services." *Id.* Therefore, there is no comparison between the advertisement in *Bates, supra,* wherein a print advertisement set forth standard fees, and the in-person solicitation of business. While both advertise the availability of legal services, there are significant and material differences.

> *Unlike a public advertisement, which simply provides information and leaves the recipient free to act upon it or not, in-person solicitation may exert pressure and often demands an immediate response, without providing an opportunity for comparison or reflection. The aim and effect of in-person solicitation may be to provide a one-sided presentation and to encourage speedy and perhaps uninformed decisionmaking; there is no opportunity for intervention or counter-education by agencies of the Bar, supervisory authorities, or persons close to the solicited individual.*

Ohralik at 457.

Whereas printed informational material, like *Bates,* offers potential clients the opportunity to make a reliable and informed decision, direct in-person or live solicitation does not.

If the person with whom the attorney would like to make contact has made it known, either directly or through circumstance, that she does not wish to be contacted,

SPOT THE ISSUE

Ernie, the insurance salesman, contacted Sally after Ernie saw her advertisement regarding Sally's insurance malpractice firm. Ernie asked Sally if Sally might consider hiring him to assist in finding plaintiffs for Sally's prospective class action suit against a large insurance company. Ernie said that other attorneys had utilized his services in the past. Sally hired Ernie as a paralegal in her firm and since he had such an extensive insurance background, simply gave him a client package which contained a client intake form, a set of questionnaires, and Sally's retainer agreement. Ernie contacted 100 potential clients and successfully signed 63 as clients using the supplied retainer agreement.

Discuss the possible ethical violations. For a hint, *see Mississippi Bar v. Turnage*, 919 So.2d 36 (Miss. 2005).

the attorney must not solicit employment from that person. The rule is clear in its directive: "No means no." However, the rule also prohibits solicitation, either impersonal or face-to-face, that involves coercion, duress, or harassment. It is much harder to discern this situation. One circumstance is clear: overzealousness in trying to be the first one to see the victim is in violation of that prohibition. In order to protect the public from these evils proscribed by the rule, most, if not all, states ban attorneys from contacting victims in personal injury or wrongful death matters for 30 days. This gives the victim some "breathing room" to regain reason and objectivity regarding the incident. The courts, bar associations, and disciplinary boards are constantly trying to maintain or improve the public's perception of the legal profession. In an effort to adopt appropriate ethical rules to assist in this endeavor, the Florida Bar undertook a two-year study of the effects of lawyer advertising on public opinion. As a result of this study, the Florida Bar instituted a 30-day blackout period during which an attorney could not solicit the accident victims or their families. A lawyer referral service (Went For It, Inc.) challenged the constitutionality of the rule changes. The United States Supreme Court, once again, found that the public's interest in remaining free from overreaching or unduly influential communications from attorneys seeking employment outweighs the free speech concerns of the attorneys involved in purely commercial speech.

> *While it is undoubtedly true that many people find the image of lawyers sifting through accident and police reports in pursuit of prospective clients unpalatable and invasive, this case targets a different kind of intrusion. The Bar has argued, and the record reflects, that a principal purpose of the ban is protecting the personal privacy and tranquility of [Florida's] citizens from crass commercial intrusion by attorneys upon their personal grief in times of trauma. The intrusion targeted by the Bar's regulation stems not from the fact that a lawyer has learned about an accident or disaster (as the Court of Appeals notes, in many instances a lawyer need only read the newspaper to glean this information), but from the lawyer's confrontation of victims or relatives with such information, while wounds are still open, in order to solicit their business. In this respect, an untargeted letter mailed to society at large is different in kind from a targeted solicitation; the untargeted letter involves no willful or knowing affront to or invasion of the tranquility of bereaved or injured individuals and simply does not cause the same kind of reputational harm to the profession unearthed by the Bar's study.*

Florida Bar v. Went for It, Inc., 515 U.S. 618, 630, 115 S. Ct. 2371, 2379, 132 L.Ed.2d 541 (1995).

There are technical requirements that apply to the above substantive provisions. The first attempts to protect the public by requiring a standard **disclaimer** on any and all attorney communications that seek to gain employment for the lawyer. The label "Advertising Material" must be prominently displayed, either printed or stated, as appropriate to the method of transmission. The second qualifies the

disclaimer

A term which limits claim or denial.

substantive rules by providing an exclusion for prepaid or group legal plans. These potential clients may be solicited by the organization itself, as they are subscribers to the plan and on some level have consented to the direct solicitation for services. However, the participating attorney cannot herself contact these subscribers, and the attorney cannot be an owner or director of that organization. This underscores the dangers in direct attorney solicitation and the evils associated with paying for legal referrals.

FIELDS OF PRACTICE AND SPECIALIZATION

general practice firm
An attorney or firm that will handle almost any type of legal matter that is presented by clients.

The last two ABA Model Rules on this subject are very specific in application and concern how the attorney represents himself or his firm to the public at large. Traditionally, most lawyers were involved in **general practice firms**, but there has been an increasing trend toward specialization in the profession. Attorneys and **boutique firms** are concentrating on one particular or a related group of legal matters. In order for any potential client to identify which attorney she should contact for assistance, it is necessary to permit these attorneys and firms to advertise their areas of legal practice.

boutique firm
An attorney or firm that handles only certain types of legal matters that are usually highly detailed and related to each other and that require specialized knowledge and experience.

This applies to the advertising rules in that an attorney may place an advertisement indicating that he is willing to take on a particular kind of case or class of plaintiffs without violating the rule against solicitation. *In Zauderer v. Office of Disciplinary Counsel of Supreme Court of Ohio,* 471 U.S. 626, 639–640, 105 S. Ct. 2265, 2276, 85 L.Ed.2d 652 (1985), the United States Supreme Court held that where an advertisement was truthful and not misleading as to the facts of the type of litigation and that the attorney was handling such matters for other similarly situated plaintiffs, there was no ethical violation:

> The advertisement did not promise readers that lawsuits alleging injuries caused by the Dalkon Shield [an intrauterine birth control device] would be successful, nor did it suggest that [the attorney] had any special expertise in handling such lawsuits other than his employment in other such litigation. Rather, the advertisement reported the indisputable fact that the Dalkon Shield has spawned an impressive number of lawsuits and advised readers that [the attorney] was currently handling such lawsuits and was willing to represent other women asserting similar claims.

The heart of the analysis as to the permissibility of advertising the area of concentration is the deceptive or misleading standard used in the other advertising rules.

specialization
An attorney who has chosen to practice in a certain area of the law and has developed a concentration in this kind of legal matter.

It is extremely important to distinguish between an area of practice as a **specialization,** (an attorney who chooses to concentrate in a specific area) and a **certified specialist** in a particular area of law. A certified specialist must apply to her own state in order to be authorized to use such a moniker. Each state is in control of the areas in which it offers ABA-accredited certification programs, just as each state is in control of its own bar admission standards. There are a few national certification programs, such as the National Board of Trial Advocacy. These certifying boards all have some elements in common: they all have demanding standards for the applicants; require extensive experience in the area of specialization; and require continuing legal education, an exam, recommendations from judges, and other such credentials. Thus, it is very different for an attorney to say she specializes in one area of the law rather than to claim to be a specialist in a type of practice. The attorney who concentrates in an area of law should make it very clear that she is not a specialist certified by any state or national body. To blur the line between the two is to invite an ethical infraction regarding the advertisement of the lawyer's services.

certified specialist
An attorney who has applied for and obtained state and bar acknowledgement of extensive knowledge and expertise in an area of law through demonstrable evidence of testing scores and experience.

In 1990, the United States Supreme Court decided that an attorney had a First Amendment constitutional right to advertise his certification in a specialized area.

The Court opined that while opinions as to the quality of an attorney's legal work are impermissible under the ethical rules, a designation from an accredited certifying body as to the background qualifications of an attorney are not, as they are verifiable statements that can indicate a certain level of quality that has been achieved. The state bar that opposed the attorney's right to list this credential on his letterhead contended that the statement may be misleading to potential clients.

> *To the extent that potentially misleading statements of private certification or specialization could confuse consumers, a State might consider screening certifying organizations or requiring a disclaimer about the certifying organization or the standards of a specialty. A State may not, however, completely ban statements that are not actually or inherently misleading, such as certification as a specialist by bona fide organizations such as NBTA.*

Peel v. Attorney Registration and Disciplinary Comm'n of Illinois, 496 U.S. 91, 112, 110 S. Ct. 2281, 2292–2293, 110 L.Ed.2d 83 (1990).

Similarly, paralegals who have earned a certified status through a paralegal association/organization as discussed in the first chapter have a right to use that designation. Relying on *Peel*, the New York State Bar Association determined that the "certified" status of a paralegal employed at the firm is subject to the same inquiry as the status of an attorney. As long as the association bestowing the credential is a bona fide organization, the standards for certification are objectively clear and the title is not misleading, the credential can be used.

FIRM NAMES AND LETTERHEAD

The most public and widespread "advertisements" for attorneys are their firm name and their letterhead; these two are "everywhere" and project a certain image (or at least the attorneys hope that they do). For a paralegal, the most important thing to remember is that the firm's reputation is carried on every piece of letterhead that leaves the office. No matter how trivial the correspondence, the paralegal should ensure that it is well written, free of errors, uses the appropriate tone, and is formatted correctly.

Traditionally, firm names are composed of the "list" of equity partners in order of seniority; however, this is not required under ABA Model Rule 7.5. **Trade names**, such as "Toxic Tort Tamers, Inc.," could be employed, as long as they passed muster under the other advertising rules regarding deceptive or misleading tactics. Most important, the trade name must not insinuate that the firm is in any way a governmental entity or associated with governmentally sponsored legal services or charitable organizations. It seems clear from the various cases handling violative trade names that the use of words like "legal services," "legal clinic," "claim service," and "consumer law center" are all potentially misleading, as they may suggest a relationship with those organizations that truly do provide free or no-cost legal aid services by and through governmental and charitable agencies. New Jersey went so far as to opine:

trade name
The title of a company that it uses in commerce to identify it and distinguish it from others in the field.

> *A law firm name may include additional identifying language such as "& Associates" only when such language is accurate and descriptive of the firm. Any firm name including additional identifying language such as "Legal Services" or other similar phrases shall inform all prospective clients in the retainer agreement or other writing that the law firm is not affiliated or associated with a public, quasi-public or charitable organization. However, no firm shall use the phrase "legal aid" in its name or in any additional identifying language.*

Matter of Vincenti, 152 N.J. 253, 272, 704 A.2d 927, 937 (1998).

Most of the time, firm names are made up of the list of named partners in the firm. Without any other indication on the letterhead, the law firm is presumed to practice solely in the jurisdiction where the office is located. However, as clients' matters became more complicated and the effects of globalization were felt, attorneysbecame licensed in more than one jurisdiction to better serve their clients' interests, and the firms opened up offices in different states. Where it is the case that attorneys in the firm are able to practice in various office locations, the letterhead must indicate where each attorney is licensed. Failure to identify the jurisdictional limitations of the attorneys in the firm is an ethical violation.

> *Even where there is one office located in a single jurisdiction, the attorneys are bound to indicate where they are licensed to practice if they are not so licensed in the state where the one office is located. A Virginian attorney found himself in violation of this rule because, while he worked out of the Maryland office with his partner, he did not take any of the Maryland related cases. The Virginian attorney did not list his jurisdictional limitation and the court felt that this would be misleading because clients would believe he was licensed where he maintained an office. It is as if he were holding himself out as a Maryland attorney, when in fact, he was not.*

Attorney Grievance Comm'n of Maryland v. Johnson, 363 Md. 598, 605, 770 A.2d 130, 135 (2001).

Some states take the name of the firm very seriously and protect the public by requiring that all the attorneys whose names are used in a law firm's name be members of the bar of that state.

> *The purpose of the rule is obvious. It is reasonable to expect that those listed in a law firm name are licensed to practice in this State. If those persons are not so licensed, the firm name is deceptive to consumers of legal services. To the extent law firm names with unlicensed lawyers defeat consumers' reasonable expectations, the disciplinary rule protects the public against deception*

On Petition for Review of Opinion 475 of Advisory Committee on Professional Ethics, 89 N.J. 74, 77, 444 A.2d 1092, 1094 (1982).

The New Jersey Supreme Court would not permit the national firm "Jacoby & Meyers" to open a New Jersey office because neither Mr. Jacoby nor Mr. Meyers were admitted to the New Jersey Bar. Interestingly, there is no prohibition in continuing to use a long-dead partner's name in the firm name in which he participated; in actuality this provides a consistency of identification and an indicator of service. For example, the largest U.S. law firm, Baker & McKenzie, has long since lost both founding partners, but continues using that name with enormous success, employing over three thousand attorneys.

If a lawyer also happens to hold a public office, her name cannot be used in the firm's name. The prohibition prohibits an attorney or firm from appearing to hold any sway with a government official. Therefore, if one of the named partners is a government official, there is an inherent conflict.

Finally, the list of attorneys in the firm name is presumed to be the partners in a duly organized law firm. Partners owe each other certain duties of loyalty and are responsible for each other's actions, as discussed in the previous chapter. For attorneys to present their names as if they were associated in a partnership or other professional corporation when they are, in fact, not so related, is misleading and in violation of advertising rule 7.5 (d). Such a violation was found in *In re Weiss, Healy, & Rea,* 109 N.J. 246, 536 A.2d 266 (1988), where eight in-house attorneys for an insurance company sought to "assemble" under the name of "Weiss, Healy & Rea." These attorneys worked together and shared information as to strategic decisions in the defense of the insurance company's insureds. However, they were all employees of the company and did not share in any profits, losses, or other expenses in the group; all of this was covered under the company.

> *We believe that the message conveyed by the firm name "A, B & C" is that the three persons designated are engaged in the general practice of law in New Jersey as partners. Such partnership implies the full financial and professional responsibility of a law firm that has pooled its resources of intellect and capital to serve a general clientele. The partnership arrangement*

implies much more than office space shared by representatives of a single insurer. Put differently, the designation "A, B & C" does not imply that the associated attorneys are in fact employees, with whatever inferences a client might draw about their ultimate interest and advice. The public, we believe, infers that the collective professional, ethical, and financial responsibility of a partnership-in-fact bespeaks the "kind and caliber of legal services rendered".

Id. at 252.

New Jersey also dealt with an interesting question regarding the use of partners' names in more than one law firm. The facts were as follows:

> *The Committee has received an inquiry from a law firm practicing under the name "A, B, C, D & E" which would like to merge and form a separate firm with a sole practitioner in another part of the State to be known as "A & X" or "A, B & X." Well-established in its geographical area, the inquiring firm does not wish to change its name. Nor does it wish to add the sole practitioner's name as it believes the firm name is already too long and would become unwieldy. However, because of his reputation, the firm believes it advisable that the sole practitioner's name be included in the name of the newly formed firm.*
>
> *[...] The inquiring firm's formation of a second firm for the limited purpose of advancing the sole practitioner's name circumvents the rule. The newly formed firm would be owned in its entirety by the inquiring firm. It would in no way function as a separate, distinct, autonomous firm. Rather, it would be but an appendage or satellite office of the parent firm. Moreover, all of the members of the original firm would be members of the newly formed firm and listed as such on its letterhead. Therefore, these lawyers and the inquiring firm would be practicing under more than one name, which is prohibited by RPC 7.5(a).*

It is clear that where attorneys seek to affiliate themselves for any other reason than the formation of a recognized business partnership under which they will practice as an independent group of attorneys, they will be in violation of the ethics rules. The firm name and letterhead must accurately reflect the true nature of the business relationship between the attorneys.

While it is clear that a paralegal's name will never appear in a firm name, paralegals may be listed on the letterhead with their appropriate designations as "paralegal" and any earned certifications after their names. The legal community has recognized the "growing presence of formally trained and/or experienced legal assistants and paralegals in the practice of law" and therefore acknowledged the desirability of including them on letterhead and allowing them to distribute business cards. Fla. Ethics Op. 86–4 (Fla. St. Bar Ass'n 1986). A New York Ethics Committee found that "[s]ince paralegals may have to deal with clients and members of the court system and the public while performing their duties, it will often be convenient for them to identify themselves and their affiliation by means of a business card." NYCLA Ethics Op. 673 (N.Y. Cty Law Ass'n Comm'n Prof'l Ethics 1989. NFPA has addressed this issue in its Ethical Consideration 1.7(c). (See Figure 10.3.)

There are so many titles that a paralegal can use—the designations vary from firm to firm and in different geographic regions. The vast majority of states hold that listing paralegals on letterhead and issuing them firm business cards is acceptable, even beneficial to the public. The prime consideration when including a paralegal on the firm letterhead or on business cards is to avoid misleading the recipient as to the paralegal's status. However, as the New York State Bar Association pointed out, the inquiry is whether "the various titles clearly demonstrate that the paralegal is not an attorney." NY Ethics Op. 640 (N.Y. St. Bar Ass'n Comm'n Prof'l Ethics 1992).

FIGURE 10.3
Paralegals' Use of Letterhead and Business Cards

NFPA EC 1.7(c)

A paralegal shall not use letterhead, business cards or other promotional materials to create a fraudulent impression of his/her status or ability to practice in the jurisdiction in which the paralegal practices.

The committee determined that titles such as "paralegal" and "senior paralegal" are clearly permissible, as they unambiguously indicate that the person is not an attorney. However, the term "paralegal coordinator" is not permitted without further clarification, because it is not clear whether the person responsible for overseeing the paralegals is a paralegal himself or an attorney in charge of this task. The term "legal associate" is not permissible at all, because the title "associate" refers only to non-partner attorneys in the firm. These titles are merely examples, not an all-inclusive list. Other designations may be used, as long as they clearly define the status of the paralegal as a non-lawyer.

All public representations made by an attorney in any form—solicitation, advertisements, firm names, letterhead, and others—must be made in an honest and forthright manner. Any practice that could be deemed misleading or action that would constitute overreaching by the attorney can be sanctioned under the ethics rules. The purpose behind these strict rules is to ensure that the public retains its confidence in the legal profession. The old-fashioned notion of the noble profession in which attorneys should only "live to serve" without any need for efforts to attract clients has long passed, and the commercial aspects of the practice have been recognized. Attorneys are permitted to promote their services to potential clients. The time, place, and manner of those efforts can be regulated without the impingement of the attorneys' right to freedom of commercial speech. Advertising and solicitation of clients require, as many of the other ethical constructs do, a balancing of the attorneys' needs and duties with those of clients and the public.

Summary

The practice of law is also a business which depends on attracting clients through general public advertisements and targeted solicitation to individuals or a class of persons. As in every other aspect of legal practice, there are ethical rules to delineate what legal professionals may say to the public in advertisements and solicitations. The statements may not be false or misleading. This prohibition also extends to advertisements that are overly aggressive or suggestive. Paralegals are prohibited specifically from enhancing their credentials under color of record or degree. Technology plays an important role in the delivery of legal advertisements, and there are restrictions placed upon television advertisements and Web site content to avoid overdramatization or overreaching by a legal professional. In-person solicitation is the most restricted form of attorney commercial contact, as it has the greatest risk for undue influence by the legal professional. Also potentially unduly influential is the use of certification and specialization designations. Paralegals must be particularly careful to clearly convey their status and title, both in using certifications and on the general firm letterhead and their own business cards. Always bear in mind that whatever an attorney cannot do in the advertising context, a paralegal cannot do either.

Key Terms and Concepts

"Ambulance chaser"
Boutique firm
Certified specialist
Commercial speech
Disclaimer
General practice firm

Materially misleading
Overreaching
Solicitation
Specialization
Trade name

MULTIPLE CHOICE

Choose the best answer(s) and please explain WHY you choose the answer(s).

1. An attorney may use the title "certified trial attorney"
   a. only on his letterhead and business cards, but not in his advertising.
   b. only after applying for and passing the requirements set forth by the appropriate association approved by the ABA.
   c. if his practice is limited to litigation only.
   d. all of the above
   e. none of the above
2. Advertising is materially misleading if
   a. recipients will believe the claims made by the attorney.
   b. no reasonable person could believe the claims made by the attorney.
   c. a recipient believes that the attorney can guarantee a winning result in her case.
   d. the court determines that the facts contained in the advertisement is important to the public.
3. An attorney may solicit clients
   a. by bulk mail flyers indicating her areas of concentration of practice.
   b. through her paralegal.
   c. via the Internet and Web site directories.
   d. all of the above
   e. none of the above

EXPLAIN YOURSELF

All answers should be written in complete sentences. A simple yes or no is insufficient.

1. Why is attorney advertising more heavily controlled than other forms of commercial speech?
2. Describe in your own words what "materially misleading" advertising is.
3. How can an attorney become a certified specialist? Is that the only time she can advertise her area of concentration?
4. Explain the proper use of paralegals in obtaining new clients.

FAULTY PHRASES

All of the following statements are FALSE; state why they are false and then rewrite them as true statements, without just making a statement negative by adding the word "not."

1. A law firm's name must always be composed of the equity partners' surnames.
2. As long as the victim is a relative, an attorney may solicit legal business at the hospital.
3. Every attorney must become certified in his area of specialty.
4. As long as the advertisement has a disclaimer, the content of the ad cannot be considered materially misleading.
5. The Constitution protects the content of commercial speech as it pertains to all attorney advertisements.
6. Paralegals' names should not appear on the firm's letterhead.

7. All the members of a boutique firm are certified specialists in that area of law.

8. A satisfied client may not recommend her attorney to a friend without violating the attorney solicitation rules.

 PORTFOLIO ASSIGNMENT

Write Away

Create the following for your law firm, which consists of 20 attorneys and 5 paralegals. Two of the named partners are certified by the American Board of Certification (see http://www.abcworld.org/abchome.html for details); the firm specializes in bankruptcy law; and you, one of the paralegals, hold a national paralegal certification.

1. A Yellow Pages advertisement

2. A bulk mailing to everyone in the town

3. A mailing directed at persons who are currently in foreclosure on their homes

4. A PowerPoint (or other visual) presentation outlining the concept for a television advertisement

Iowa Supreme Court Bd. of Professional Ethics & Conduct v. Wherry,
569 N.W.2d 822 (Iowa 1997)
Supreme Court of Iowa.
IOWA SUPREME COURT BOARD OF PROFESSIONAL ETHICS & CONDUCT, Appellee,
v.
James C. WHERRY, Appellant.
No. 97–777.
Oct. 22, 1997.

HARRIS, Justice.

In Bates v. State Bar of Arizona, 433 U.S. 350, 382–83, 97 S. Ct. 2691, 2708–09, 53 L.Ed.2d 810, 835 (1977), states were denied authority to prohibit advertising by practicing lawyers. The question in this appeal, as we see it, comes down to whether, having submitted to the rule in *Bates,* states can adopt and enforce lawyer advertising rules to assure that, in addition to being reasonable, the advertising is forthright and accurate.

Attorney James C. Wherry was admitted to practice in 1991 and maintains a general practice in Davenport. Wherry has consistently advertised his practice in the areas of bankruptcy, domestic relations, wills, and social security appeals. He has never filed a report showing his eligibility to indicate areas of practice with the commission on continuing legal education as required by DR 2–105(A)(4) of the Iowa code of professional responsibility for lawyers.[1] We have said a lawyer who advertises a practice in a specific field without compliance with DR 2–105(A)(4) acts unethically. *Committee on Prof'l Ethics & Conduct v. Morris,* 490 N.W.2d 806, 808 (Iowa 1992).

Wherry's advertisements in various telephone directories in violation of this rule prompted the present complaint by the board of professional ethics and conduct. Wherry testified he has continuing legal education hours and experience required to report eligibility for bankruptcy, but has taken no steps to do so. For the other areas he advertises, he had not met the practice time or the continuing legal education requirements. He had drawn only one or two wills before publishing an advertisement referring to wills. He had not obtained any continuing legal education in the areas of domestic relations, wills, or social security.

Wherry's noncompliance has been no mere oversight. He seems determined to confront our advertising rules; the

1. DR 2–105(A)(4) provides that a lawyer who wishes to advertise an area of practice must first comply with certain steps:
   Prior to communication of a description or indication of practice permitted by DR 2–105(A)(2) [listing various areas of practice], a lawyer shall report the lawyer's compliance with the following eligibility requirements each year in the written report required to be submitted to the Commission on Continuing Legal Education:
   (a) The lawyer must have devoted the greater of 200 hours or twenty percent of the lawyer's time spent in actual law practice to each separate indicated field of practice for each of the last two calendar years; and
   (b) The lawyer must have completed at least ten hours of accredited Continuing Legal Education courses of study in each separate indicated field of practice during the preceding calendar year.

violations involved here follow a prior proceeding in which he was privately admonished by the board in 1993 for similar noncompliance.

I. As a preliminary claim, Wherry contends DR 2–105(A)(4) is permissive, not mandatory. He concedes the rule states that an attorney must comply with the eligibility requirements before advertising. But he contrasts this with the introductory language in DR 2–105(A)(2) which he says is made to only apply to lawyers who in fact "limit" practice to certain fields of the law.

DR 2–105(A)(2), before listing the areas of practice appropriate for specialty advertising, does refer to lawyers who limit practice to those areas or who wish to practice primarily in them. But no language in the rule provides the escape Wherry suggests because the rule is subject to the general authority for all lawyer advertising which allows informational but prohibits solely promotional advertisements. To distinguish between informational and promotional advertising, DR 2–101(C) then provides:

Content (Informational). The following information shall be presumed to be informational and not solely promotional:

. . . .

(2) Fields of practice, limitation of practice or specialization, but only to the extent permitted by DR 2–105.

Compliance with DR 2–105(A)(4) is clearly required for all Iowa lawyers who advertise specific fields of practice. The requirement is not confined to those lawyers who would limit their practice as Wherry suggests.

II. Until two decades ago, state supreme courts were free to prohibit lawyer advertising. *In Virginia Pharmacy Board v. Virginia Citizens Consumer Council, Inc.,* 425 U.S. 748, 770–71, 96 S. Ct. 1817, 1830, 48 L.Ed.2d 346, 363–64 (1976), the United States Supreme Court for the first time extended first amendment protection to commercial speech. The following year Bates held that lawyer advertising is commercial speech and entitled to limited first amendment protection. *Bates,* 433 U.S. at 383, 97 S. Ct. at 2709, 53 L.Ed.2d at 835.

The limited protection for commercial speech is less than afforded other forms of expression such as political speech. *Board of Trustees v. Fox,* 492 U.S. 469, 477, 109 S.Ct. 3028, 3033, 106 L.Ed.2d 388, 402 (1989). Commercial speech by members of the learned professions, because it poses special problems, may justify more restrictions than would be appropriate for other commercial speech. *In re R.M.J.,* 455 U.S. 191, 202, 102 S. Ct. 929, 937, 71 L.Ed.2d 64, 73 (1982). Advertising by the legal profession may warrant even more restrictions than advertising by those of other learned professions. *Edenfield v. Fane,*

507 U.S. 761, 775, 113 S.Ct. 1792, 1802–03, 123 L.Ed.2d 543, 558 (1993).

The subject of commercial free speech rights for lawyers wishing to advertise was recently analyzed in *Florida Bar v. Went For It, Inc.*, 515 U.S. 618, 115 S. Ct. 2371, 132 L.Ed.2d 541 (1995), where it was said:

> [W]e engage in "intermediate" scrutiny of restrictions on commercial speech, analyzing them under the framework set forth in *Central Hudson Gas & Electric Corp. v. Public Service Comm'n of N.Y.*, 447 U.S. 557, 100 S. Ct. 2343, 65 L.Ed.2d 341 (1980). Under Central Hudson, the government may freely regulate commercial speech that concerns unlawful activity or is misleading. Commercial speech that falls into neither of these categories, like the advertising at issue here, may be regulated if the government satisfies a test consisting of three related prongs: first, the government must assert a substantial interest in support of its regulation; second, the government must demonstrate that the restriction on commercial speech directly and materially advances that interest; and third, the regulation must be "narrowly drawn."

Florida Bar, 515 U.S. at 624, 115 S. Ct. at 2376, 132 L.Ed.2d at 549 (citations omitted).

We think our advertising rule easily satisfies the three-prong test. Iowa government, particularly its judicial branch, has a clear responsibility to protect the public interest in informed selection of legal representation. False claims of expertise are a real danger to those who need and are searching for legal services. [citations omitted].

DR 2–105(A)(4) is our carefully considered attempt to protect the public interest in making this informed decision. It does so by requiring a minimum of specialized training by those who pose in their advertising as specialists in a listed field. If we are to be criticized for our efforts, it might well be for drawing our requirements too narrowly—that is, for not requiring much more training. The rule was designed by striking a balance between—on the one hand—the public's right to have a lawyer qualified in the field advertised and—on the other hand—in not making the training requirements more onerous than we felt absolutely necessary to justify the advertised claims. The rule offers only limited protection, but the limitation was thought necessary in order to satisfy the third prong of the Central Hudson test. We think the rule is a reasonable accommodation. *See Edenfield*, 507 U.S. at 767, 113 S. Ct. at 1798, 123 L.Ed.2d at 553 ("[L]aws restricting commercial speech, unlike laws burdening other forms of protected expression, need only be tailored in a reasonable manner to serve a substantial state interest in order to survive First Amendment scrutiny.").

III. Wherry contends his advertisements are not misleading, that readers would not take them to mean he holds himself out as an expert, only that he performs professional services in the listed fields of practice. We are satisfied however that the advertisements were misleading because they would be taken by many readers as a claim of expertise in the listed fields. The record, as well as common sense, supports this view.

The record contains a summary of findings by the special master in the 1988 proceedings before our special commission which studied the subject and recommended approval of the challenged rule. A finding, which we accepted, was that "the public, in relying on listings of fields of practice, assumes that the attorney has additional education and expertise in the advertised field of practice." We adopted the rule in the hope it would bring a measure of reality to this assumption. Other courts have reached the same conclusion. [citations omitted]

[4] Those reading Wherry's advertisements implying experience in wills were misled because, at the time, he had only drawn one or two. He was similarly lacking in most of the fields mentioned in his advertisements. We thus conclude that advertising by an Iowa lawyer in fields of practice without the training required in accordance with our rule is misleading. We disagree with Wherry's contention that it is only potentially misleading. So saying, we do not suggest Wherry's view would make his case stronger because we are authorized to protect the public from advertisements that are only potentially misleading. [citations omitted].

Wherry relies on *In re R.M.J.*, a case we find not in point. R.M.J. involved an absolute ban on advertising fields of practice except by language specified by the rule. *In re R.M.J.*, 455 U.S. at 193, 102 S. Ct. at 932, 71 L.Ed.2d at 68. Our ban is not so absolute. Iowa lawyers, after meeting the eligibility requirements, are free to advertise within reasonable limits.

IV. Wherry also contends rule DR 2–105(A)(4) violates two clauses of the United States Constitution and is also preempted by federal bankruptcy law. First he asserts DR 2–105(A)(4) violates article I, section 8 of the United States Constitution (commerce clause). Because Wherry derives at least twenty percent of his employment from Illinois, he contends the regulation imposes a substantial and excessive burden on interstate commerce. Wherry does not show how his right to practice in interstate commerce is affected by the challenged rule. He continues to practice in both Iowa and Illinois. Wherry can claim the rule restricts his ability to advertise but such a restriction does not impose a substantial and excessive burden on interstate commerce. He maintains his office in Iowa and eighty percent of his practice occurs here. We reject the challenge.

He further asserts the professional responsibility rule is preempted by "any of the various interstate telephone and communication acts." Wherry also claims the rule is an unconstitutional regulation of bankruptcy in violation of article I, section 8 of the United States Constitution. He cites no authority for either proposition. We find none and reject them both.

V. Wherry next asserts DR 2–105(A)(4) violates equal protection as guaranteed by the fourteenth amendment of the United States Constitution, an assertion we also reject.[2] The rule treats all lawyers the same, and all lawyers are subject to it. Equal protection requires only that those in similar positions be treated alike. *Bruns v. State*, 503 N.W.2d 607, 610 (Iowa 1993). In rejecting the argument on this basis, we do not imply that the equal protection analysis is even applicable when a commercial speech issue was justiciable in the claim, a matter we do not decide. *See United States v. Edge Broad. Co.*, 509 U.S. 418, 424, 113 S. Ct. 2696, 2702, 125 L.Ed.2d 345, 353 (1993); *Posadas de Puerto Rico Assocs. v. Tourism Co.*, 478 U.S. 328, 331, 337–38, 106 S. Ct. 2968, 2971, 2975, 92 L.Ed.2d 266, 274, 278 (1986).

2. Wherry seems to make a separate argument that the challenged rule lacks a rational basis. Although he did not so state, we assume the argument stands on his equal protection claim and falls with it.

VI. The closest question is with the recommended sanction—a public reprimand. In view of his prior private admonition for violating the same rule, Wherry's obdurate stand cannot be ascribed to a lack of experience. Neither can it be attributed alone to his desire to mount a constitutional test. A "safe harbor" was available to him. *Committee on Prof'l Ethics & Conduct v. Humphrey,* 355 N.W.2d 565, 569 (Iowa 1984) (safe harbor administrative system available for challenging advertising rules), vacated on other grounds, 472 U.S. 1004, 105 S. Ct. 2693, 86 L.Ed.2d 710 (1985).

With some reservations, we adopt the recommendation. For any future violations, we will take into consideration both Wherry's admonition and this reprimand.

James C. Wherry is reprimanded for his unprofessional conduct in violating DR 2–105(A)(4) of the Iowa code of professional responsibility for lawyers.

ATTORNEY REPRIMANDED.

Source: From Westlaw. Reprinted with permission from ThomsonWest.

Chapter 11

Maintaining the Integrity of the Profession

CHAPTER OBJECTIVES

The student will be able to:

- Discuss the role that both attorneys and paralegals play in maintaining the distinguished character of the practice of law

- Define and discuss the "appearance of impropriety" standard as it applies to attorney and paralegal conduct

- Compare the obligation for truthfulness in all aspects of an attorney's life with those of other professionals

- Explain an attorney's and a paralegal's obligation to report professional misconduct to the proper authorities

This final chapter will explore and review the overarching ethical principles that mandate HOW legal professionals should act at all times, no matter WHERE they are or WHOM they are with. Loyalty to the justice system takes precedence over all other professional obligations, and attorneys are required to report the misconduct of others in the profession in order to maintain the integrity of the profession and ensure that the public trust is truly earned and protected. Similarly, paralegals find themselves under reporting obligations pursuant to their own code of ethics.

The last set of rules deals with the general behavior of attorneys with respect to their various roles as counselors and as officers of the court. No matter what they do or in what capacity they act, all attorneys must behave in a manner that will honor the profession and the rule of law. Attorneys do not necessarily "clock out" when they leave the office; they remain representatives of the legal profession while they are in public, and those around them are conscious of their position. It is a demanding role to play, but this has been so since the origin of this "noble profession." Trust and confidence are not "on and off" characteristics; once instilled, they must be constantly nurtured and maintained by every attorney and judge at all times. This chapter will explore the overarching ethical requirements that attempt to ensure that attorneys act in compliance with all the specific rules previously discussed. It should be the aspiration of all paralegals also to adhere to these codes of conduct. While there is no uniform, enforceable ethical code for all paralegals, there are models and guidelines that should motivate the actions of all legal professionals.

DUTY OF HONESTY TO ADMISSIONS OR REVIEW BOARDS

The rules of ethics come full circle in ABA Model Rule 8.1. Where an attorney begins is a good indicator of where she will end. The boards of bar examiners in every jurisdiction take their jobs very seriously in setting standards and evaluating candidates for admission to practice law. Every bar candidate and every attorney sponsoring or recommending that candidate must be truthful in all the representations made in the application. There is an ongoing duty to correct or supplement any information that changes during the pendency of the application. This honesty and forthrightness is a continuing obligation throughout the attorney's career, during both normal practice and any disciplinary matters. The obligation of bar candidates and attorneys in both applications and disciplinary matters is trifold. First, and most obviously, no false statements of material fact can be made in connection with either proceeding. Second, silence can be misleading. The party before the board of bar examiners or disciplinary council cannot fail to speak where the candidate or attorney knows the board or council is mistaken about a material fact. "Letting it slide" may allow the party to avoid negative consequences, but it is not in compliance with the duty of candor to the tribunal. Third, the candidate or the attorney must comply with any proper demand for information pertaining to the bar admission or disciplinary action. This may pose a delicate situation where the information sought may be the object of privilege and protected under the rules of confidentiality. Recall that confidentiality generally trumps all other rules requiring disclosure. The reason is the ultimate objective of the profession: to instill trust in the profession from the public and clients.

The confidentiality rule not only will protect disclosure of information requested by a disciplinary authority, but also is the only privilege an attorney can assert that will permit the attorney to refuse to disclose client information in a proceeding against the attorney. Even where a private citizen could assert a free speech protection, an attorney may not be granted that immunity. Political elections are fraught with mudslinging, and campaigns surrounding the election of judges to the bench are not immune from such attacks among the candidates. In a charge of making false statements in connection with a judicial election, the opposing attorney/candidate asserted a "journalistic" First Amendment right in that he was entitled both to speak publicly about his opponent, as he "had the intent to disseminate to the public the information obtained through [his] investigation," and to keep his journalistic sources confidential. *In re Charges of Unprofessional Conduct Involving File no. 17139,* 720 N.W.2d 807, 816 (Minn. 2006). The disciplinary board requested that the attorney reveal the source of his information that formed the basis of his defamatory statements about his judicial opponent. Despite the attorney's assertion that he had the right to keep his sources confidential (although not through attorney/client privilege), the court found that the attorney must disclose his sources in compliance with ABA Model Rule 8.1(b). The disciplinary board had shown that its "request [was] rationally related to the charges of professional misconduct or to a lawyer's defense to those charges and whether the request is unduly burdensome in light of the gravity and complexity of the charges. In this case, the identities of respondent's sources are extremely relevant—indeed, critical—to the ethical violation alleged." *Id.* at 814. Further, the protections generally afforded to all journalists claiming First Amendment privilege may be pierced where there is an inherent improbability of truth behind the statement, and the journalist may be compelled to disclose the sources so that they can be evaluated. Therefore, for two reasons, one based upon the obligation to disclose nonprivileged information under the rules of confidentiality and the other constituting an exception to the journalistic privilege, the information had to be disclosed in the disciplinary matter.

RESPECT FOR THE LEGAL SYSTEM

The profession encompasses participants other than attorneys, and attorneys' conduct must also remain respectful of these persons. The deference that the attorneys must show to the system is manifested through their conduct towards judges and other legal officers of the judicial system. To improperly affront the working members of the judiciary or other court officials or their conduct in the public eye is to insult the system itself and undermine its integrity. A distinction again must be made here between proper exercise of the First Amendment free speech rights of lawyers and improper disparagement for purposes not related to acceptable criticism of the function of the individual or office. Attorneys are often disappointed in the outcome of their matters before judges or magistrates; however, airing their displeasure in a public forum is not acceptable where the attorney goes beyond the facts of the rendered decision. In *In re Disciplinary Action Against Graham,* 453 N.W. 2d 313 (Minn. 1990), the animosity between attorneys grew into one's conspiracy theory that the opposing attorney and the judge had fixed the outcome of a case. To support his allegations, the attorney accused the judge of substantial procedural irregularities that favored the opposing attorney's position. To expose the purported conspiracy to "decide the upcoming case [...] without regard to the law and facts," the complaining attorney wrote a letter to the U.S. Attorney alleging the judicial misconduct. *Id.* at 317–318. Had any of this been true or made in proper political criticism based upon genuine or ascertainable facts, the attorney would not have been disciplined; indeed, he would have been in compliance with his ethical obligations to report actual, known misconduct. However, by his own testimony, he made these statements believing they were probably true but not having the certain knowledge he had claimed in his letter to the U.S. Attorney. Additionally, while he had accused the judge of improperly using political friendships and stated that these other persons had knowledge of the judge's improper intentions, the attorney could not identify any others purportedly involved in the matter. As a consequence, the disciplinary board found that his allegations were "false, frivolous, and made in reckless disregard of their truth or falsity." *Id.* at 319. The First Amendment protects the expression of even unpopular views and protects the speaker against liability for defamation when he criticizes public officials for their official conduct. An abuse of this privilege will not be tolerated in the legal profession.

> *This court certifies attorneys for practice to protect the public and the administration of justice. That certification implies that the individual admitted to practice law exhibits a sound capacity for judgment. Where an attorney criticizes the bench and bar, the issue is not simply whether the criticized individual has been harmed, but rather whether the criticism impugning the integrity of judge or legal officer adversely affects the administration of justice and adversely reflects on the accuser's capacity for sound judgment. An attorney who makes critical statements regarding judges and legal officers with reckless disregard as to their truth or falsity and who brings frivolous actions against members of the bench and bar exhibits a lack of judgment that conflicts with his or her position as an officer of the legal system and a public citizen having special responsibility for the quality of justice.*

Id. at 322.

The standard applied to attorneys in their exercise of free speech in criticizing judges and other elements of the legal system is higher than that of private citizens, because, in short, attorneys "know better." Attorneys have proven themselves worthy of public confidence by demonstrating competence and responsibility that others do not possess. The "reasonableness" standard applied in a review of an attorney's conduct will be that of another reasonable attorney, not just a reasonable person in general. This does not mean that an attorney is prohibited from making any derogatory statements at all regarding judges and their capacity to render accurate and just opinions. "Restrictions on attorney speech burden not only the attorney's right to criticize judges, but also hinder the public's access to the class of people in the best position to comment on the functioning of the judicial system." *In re Green,* 11 P.3d 1078, 1085 (Colo. 2000). An African-American attorney wrote three letters to the judge and opposing counsel accusing the judge of being a racist and a bigot in the way in which the attorney was treated by the judge. While these are strong words, the attorney had factual basis for making these allegations and they were substantiated personal opinion. As the comments were "opinion based upon fully disclosed and uncontested facts . . . [the court could] not, consistent with the First Amendment and the first prong of the New York Times test, discipline Green for his subjective opinions, irrespective of our disagreement with them." *Green* at 1086. It is important to note that these comments were made to a limited audience—only the judge and opposing counsel—although it is not clear whether the court would have been able to rule any differently had the comments been made available to the public at large. The attorney did not make them with any recklessness as to their truth or falsity and therefore the statements were not violative of the ethical rule. There may have been an argument under the "catch-all" rule discussed later in this chapter.

DUTY TO REPORT MISCONDUCT

How does this code of personal conduct affect paralegals? The answer is stated eloquently in NFPA's Preamble to its Model Code of Conduct.

> *Paralegals have recognized, and will continue to recognize, that the profession must continue to evolve to enhance their roles in the delivery of legal services. With increased levels of responsibility comes the need to define and enforce mandatory rules of professional conduct. Enforcement of codes of paralegal conduct is a logical and necessary step to enhance and ensure the confidence of the legal community and the public in the integrity and professional responsibility of paralegals.*

Paralegals play an essential role in the delivery of legal services to clients, and their conduct, just like that of attorneys, reflects upon their competency to hold the public trust. Honesty, integrity, and trustworthiness are personal characteristics that cannot be left at the door. A paralegal's work is influenced by her own personal ethical fiber, and the actions taken by a paralegal outside the office reflect upon the workings of the legal system as a whole. It may be a demanding profession; however, the importance of the work requires this level of personal character. Attorneys and paralegals are responsible for the public confidence in the legal system and hope in the attainment of justice.

How do the ethical boards learn of these breaches of conduct by attorneys and paralegals? Clients, other attorneys, and court personnel can bring an ethical complaint against an attorney who has shown that he may not be fit to practice due to some action or statement. However, as the profession is **self-policing** (this means that it disciplines its own members), it must rely on its own members to report the misconduct. In order to be sure that lawyers do not have an incentive to shield each other from investigation into their activities, the ethical rules mandate that a lawyer with knowledge of another's misconduct must report it or be found to have violated the rules herself. It is unethical not to report a known violation of the rules by another attorney.

The same is true for paralegals holding an NFPA certification credential. NFPA affirmatively requires paralegals to report the misconduct of any other legal professional

self-policing
The profession's practice of relying on its own members to report misconduct by others, and to mete out punishment for infractions.

FIGURE 11.1

A Paralegal's Duty to
Report Misconduct

> **NFPA EC1.3(d)**
>
> A paralegal shall advise the proper authority of non-confidential knowledge of any action of another legal professional that clearly demonstrates fraud, deceit, dishonesty, or misrepresentation. The authority to whom the report is made shall depend on the nature and circumstances of the possible misconduct (e.g., ethics committees of law firms, corporations and/or paralegal associations, local or state bar associations, local prosecutors, administrative agencies, etc.). Failure to report such knowledge is in itself misconduct and shall be treated as such under these rules.

to the proper authorities, as stated in NFPA EC1.3(d). (See Figure 11.1.) This is broad in scope and significant in practice. This canon requires a paralegal to report known misconduct not only of other paralegals, but also of the attorneys. This could mean that the paralegal is reporting on her supervisory lawyer or partner! This is exactly what happened in the case of *Paralegal v. Lawyer,* 783 F.Supp.230 (E.D. Pa. 1992) (As the case stemmed from a then-unresolved disciplinary matter, the "names have been changed to protect the presumptively innocent.") A paralegal brought a wrongful discharge case against her employer. She claimed that she was fired because she reported his misconduct (backdating a letter to avoid another disciplinary complaint). The court found that the paralegal had a viable cause of action for wrongful termination. She was protected after properly disclosing her supervising attorney's misconduct. The backdating of documents to avoid discipline is clearly indicative of fraud, deceit, and an unfitness to practice law.

Knowledge

knowledge

The near certainty of belief that a fact is most likely true.

The imposition of a sanction against a nonreporting legal professional depends upon the establishment of **knowledge** and the subsequent failure to report what the attorney "knew." First, it should be noted that the information must be nonprivileged. An attorney or paralegal cannot be required to report misconduct for which he is representing the accused colleague; that information is protected as a client confidence. Any other result would be illogical; it would mean that every professional legal malpractice attorney would have to report many of his clients if there were a reasonable basis for the claim against them! Where an attorney, who does not stand in a relationship requiring confidentiality, has "a firm opinion that the conduct in question more likely than not occurred" and that conduct is an ethical violation, the attorney has the duty to report the incident to the appropriate authority. *In re Riehlmann*, 891 So.2d 1239, 1244 (La. 2005). The question remains: At what degree of probability does the duty to report arise? Case law has suggested that it arises with less than absolute certainty but more than mere speculation or conjecture. Case law is also inconsistent from state to state as to what actual knowledge is: it can range from having real facts at hand upon which to make the conclusion that a violation has occurred to reasonable belief based upon the circumstances surrounding the incident. The essence is what a reasonable attorney would presume another would conclude when presented with the same facts and circumstances. This may be tricky ground. A practical approach was espoused:

> *[A] lawyer's conduct will be assessed according to a legal standard that assumes a lawyer can "know" the truth of a situation, even if he cannot be absolutely sure. Even the criminal law, after all, does not require absolute certainty; it requires only a conclusion that is beyond a reasonable doubt. As noted in § 402, the law of lawyering as set forth in the Terminology section of the Rules of Professional Conduct permits a disciplinary authority to "infer from circumstances" that a lawyer knows what a reasonable person would know. More than this, the law takes account of a lawyer's legal training and experience in assessing his or her state*

of mind. A lawyer is an adult, a man or a woman of the world, not a child. He or she is also better educated than most people, more sophisticated and more sharply sensitized to the legal implications of a situation. The law will make inferences as to a lawyer's knowledge with those considerations in mind.

Attorney U v. Mississippi Bar, 678 So.2d 963, 971 (Miss. 1996), citing GEOFFREY C. HAZARD, JR., and W. WILLIAM HODES, THE LAW OF LAWYERING § 404 (1993).

Substantial Question of Fitness to Practice Law

Even more difficult than determining when an attorney or paralegal has reportable knowledge of an incident is deciding when that incident raises a **substantial question** as to the legal professional's honesty, trustworthiness, or fitness to practice. After an attorney or paralegal becomes aware of another's potential violation of the ethics rules or other action that reflects poorly upon the other's capacity to practice law, the legal professional with the knowledge must determine how serious the actions or inactions of the one suspected are and whether they impact the ability to perform legal duties to the standard required. While there are no bright-line rules regarding the reporting obligation, it is clear that criminal activity is grounds to suspect that another legal professional is unfit to practice law. How can an attorney or paralegal claim to uphold and defend the laws when she herself has broken them? These criminal activities do not have to be connected to the practice of law. For example, an attorney was found to be operating a vehicle under the influence and during his arrest, he refused to cooperate with police officers by forbidding them to test his blood for alcohol. "Such conduct, when committed by an officer of the court, constitutes a failure to maintain personal integrity, reflects upon one's fitness to practice law, and brings the bench and the bar into disrepute." *In re Hoare,* 155 F.3d 937, 940 (8th Cir. 1998). Convictions of criminal activity are self-reporting and another legal professional does not necessarily have to worry about his duty to report the violation under this rule. However, where the criminal activity is not known to the authorities, there will be an obligation to report that activity to the ethical tribunal. Behavior that involves lying, cheating, or evasiveness generally rises to the reportable level. This may include questionable billing practices like double-billing and padding and inaccurate record keeping. It may also be unrelated to the individual's practice of law. Where an attorney acts in a position that can be held by anyone, for example, as the personal representative of an estate, she will still be held to the higher standards of an attorney.

> *Like the referee, we cannot agree with [the attorney]'s contention that our rules and professional ethics do not apply to an attorney who acts, at some time or another, as a client rather than as an attorney. Conduct while not acting as an attorney can subject one to disciplinary proceedings. As this Court has stated before, "'an attorney is an attorney is an attorney.'" Even in personal transactions and when not acting as an attorney, attorneys must "avoid tarnishing the professional image or damaging the public." We agree with the referee that this claim is simply untenable. The practice of law is a privilege which carries with it responsibilities as well as rights. That an attorney might, as it were, wear different hats at different times does not mean that professional ethics can be "checked at the door" or that unethical or unprofessional conduct by a member of the legal profession can be tolerated.*

The Florida Bar v. Brake, 767 So.2d 1163, 1168 (Fla. 2000), citing *Florida Bar v. Della-Donna,* 583 So.2d 307, 310 (Fla.1989).

However, a given interaction with the legal system may not result in a disciplinary action, where that incident does not bring into question that attorney's honesty or trustworthiness. It is always a fact-sensitive inquiry, though, as the same conduct may bring about discipline in one instance and not in another depending upon the surrounding circumstances. For example, failure to pay child support may be due to

substantial question
A serious doubt as to an attorney's fitness to practice law because her actions or inactions reflect negatively on her character.

personal financial difficulties rather than an intentional plan to evade obligations to a former spouse. *See The Florida Bar v. Taylor,* 648 So.2d 709 (Fla. 1995).

For paralegals certified under one of the state programs or a paralegal association, the duty to refrain from criminal conduct is the same. For example, North Carolina's certification plan contains this statement: "(c) Notwithstanding an applicant's satisfaction of the standards set forth in Rule .0119(a) or (b), no individual may be certified as a paralegal if: [. . .] (3) the individual has been convicted of a criminal act that reflects adversely on the individual's honesty, trustworthiness or fitness as a paralegal." Florida's newly enacted Registered Paralegal Program similarly provides: "The following individuals are ineligible for registration as a Florida Registered Paralegal or for renewal of a registration that was previously granted: [. . .] (2) a person who has been convicted of a felony in any state or jurisdiction and whose civil rights have not been restored."

RESEARCH THIS

Find out how to report attorney misconduct to the appropriate authority in your jurisdiction.   Make note of the contact information and filing requirements, if any.

Reporting Judicial Misconduct

Upholding the dignity of the legal system is also a responsibility of the judges who sit on the bench, not just a duty binding legal practitioners. Therefore, judges are held to professional standards of conduct, and if a member of the judiciary should demonstrate a lack of fitness in her office, an attorney has an obligation to report that misconduct as well. Judges are the figureheads of the legal system and have their own Code of Judicial Conduct that they must follow. Discourteous conduct may be a trait of overly zealous attorneys, but that kind of behavior is not tolerated on the bench. "Thus, the ideal judge is a person who has by habit and practice achieved self-control and acquired the virtue of being able to will and act as a just person ought to act." *Matter of Hocking,* 451 Mich. 1, 6, 546 N.W.2d 234, 237 (1996). "It is clear, however, that every graceless, distasteful, or bungled attempt to communicate the reason for a judge's decision cannot serve as the basis for judicial discipline." *Id.* at 12. The true nature of the exchange and the effect it may have upon the administration of justice must be examined. In this case, two separate incidents formed the basis of the judicial complaint. In the first, the attorney accused the judge of rudeness and improper sentencing in a sexual assault case. The judge expressed frustration at the jury's verdict and made improper remarks regarding the victim. The court found that "[t]he comments were tasteless and undoubtedly offensive to the sensibilities of many citizens. They do not display a mindset unable to render fair judgment." *Id.* at 14. In another instance, the court found that the judge "had instigated a confrontational exchange" with the attorney in front of him. He communicated indirectly that he had already made up his mind about the matter and "challenged" the attorney to defend her position. Additionally, the aggressive nature of the exchange, caustic tone, and personal abuse to the attorney was "clearly prejudicial to the administration of justice. *Id.* at 23. In this particular instance, the attorney was in compliance with her ethical obligations to file a report with the grievance commission against the judge. The true test derived from comparing these two incidents in the Hocking matter is the ability of the judge to remain *fair* in handling the parties, the attorneys, and the disposition of the case.

Pat Parkins has worked as a paralegal for the Godwin, Bailey and Ulmer Law Firm for years and knows a great deal about the practice and the expectations of the firm. Archie, the new associate, is under a tremendous amount of pressure to bill more hours and get more clients. He has begun to binge drink at lunch with potential new clients. One day at lunch, in a loud, obviously drunken voice, he began to complain about a well-known and well-respected judge. Pat was the only employee of the firm that was there to hear this. Three days after that incident, Archie was grumbling about his workload at the local pub with Pat. He claimed that the firm was giving him all the cases in front of this judge just to punish him; after all, the firm had this judge in its "back pocket" and the firm would ultimately win no matter how Archie performed, so this was all just "busy work." Pat knows that other pub patrons heard this comment. What should Pat do? Does Pat have any ethical obligations under your state's rules of professional conduct? What about under the paralegal association's rules of conduct? Is Pat obligated to say anything? If so, to whom?

Confidentiality Exception

The final element of the requirement to report misconduct is the exception for confidentiality. There is a significant, questionable grey area in this situation. Where an attorney or paralegal learns through a client of another's misconduct that rises to the level of a reportable violation of the obligation of honesty and trustworthiness, must the reporting professional obtain the client's consent before he is able to disclose the misconduct of the other professional? It is clear that embezzlement of client funds is an offense which reflects negatively on the attorney's honesty and fitness to practice law. If an attorney came upon this knowledge of another lawyer's embezzlement of client funds in any manner other than a client confidence, there would be no question that ABA Model Rule 8.3 would impose an obligation to report that misconduct. *See In re Ethics Advisory Panel Opinion No. 92–1,* 627 A.2d 317 (R.I. 1993). However, it is precisely in that manner in which the attorney learned of the misconduct; a client sought out another attorney in order to recoup the embezzled funds from the first lawyer. The client withheld consent for the second attorney to disclose the misconduct and therefore, under the rule of confidentiality, the second attorney could not report the misconduct using the client's confidential information that he acquired as a result of the client's representation. The exceptions to the confidentiality rule do not apply in this situation. The disclosure would not be made either to prevent the client from committing a criminal act or to establish a claim or defense of the lawyer based upon conduct in which the client was involved.

The Rhode Island court found that the rules of confidentiality overruled the rules of reporting misconduct. Other courts may take a different view depending on the language and interpretation of the state's code of conduct. The court in *In re Himmel,* 125 Ill. 2d 531, 533 N.E.2d 790 (1988), came to a different conclusion regarding a client's request not to report a prior attorney's misconduct. It hinged upon the court's definition of "privileged information" received by his client. The court determined that the client had disclosed this same information to third parties and, therefore, did not have an expectation that the information would come under the attorney-client privilege. It is important to note that the court took the narrower view of the confidential nature of the attorney-client communication and held that only evidentiary privilege applied, not the more general rule of confidentiality. This means that only communications made between the attorney and client for purposes of the representation for which no other source of the information existed would exclude the information from being disclosed. The more general rule of confidentiality does

IN CLASS DISCUSSION

Courtney has filed for divorce from her husband Allen, who is an attorney. He has chosen to represent himself at the divorce proceedings.

At the final court hearing, Allen testifies that he is currently an outpatient in the local hospital's alcohol and drug addiction program. He admits that he has used cocaine recently, but that he has not used it since entering the program two weeks ago. Courtney wins full custody of the children and Allen is required to pay substantial child support.

What duty does Courtney's lawyer have to report Allen's admitted use of cocaine to the appropriate ethical authority? If Allen loses his position at his law firm, he will be unable to pay this support.

See ILL ADV.OP. 94–18, 1995 WL 932094 (Ill. St. Bar Assn.)

not rest upon how the attorney came to know of the information: he may not disclose the information if he obtained it from any source; it matters only that it pertains to his client. Taking the former, narrow view that privileged information only is excluded from the rule requiring disclosure, the court stated that the attorney having the non-privileged information regarding another lawyer's misconduct must divulge that information to the ethical authority. It is no defense that the client did not give his consent to the disclosure: "A lawyer may not choose to circumvent the rules by simply asserting that his client asked him to do so." *Id.* at 539. This much narrower view is not the one favored by most courts, and the Washington Supreme Court took pains to point out the following: "[We] cannot tolerate for a moment, neither can the profession, neither can the community, any disloyalty on the part of a lawyer to his client. In all things he must be true to that trust, or, failing it, he must leave the profession." *In re Disciplinary Proceeding Against Schafer,* 149 Wash. 2d 148, 66 P.3d 1036 (2003) (citing *United States v. Costen,* 38 F. 24 (C.C.D. Colo.1889)).

Conversely, disclosure where it is not warranted and in violation of the rules requiring the maintenance of confidentiality opens the reporting attorney or paralegal up to sanctions of his own. The attorney, Schafer, not only disclosed information obtained through his former client to the tribunal; he also published newspaper articles and forwarded investigatory information to the FBI and the IRS regarding the prior questionable business investments of his former client and his former client's business partner, who just happened to presently be a sitting judge with whom the reporting attorney did not get along. The court found that the reporting attorney went too far in disclosing more information than was necessary in order to reveal the misconduct by the judge, and certainly broadcast it to too large an audience. Rule 8.3 permits disclosure to the appropriate tribunal, not the world at large in a willful and spiteful exposé. While the court found that the end result, the removal of a corrupt judge, served the public good, the means to bring about that end were not justified, and the attorney was suspended from practice for six months. Viewing these cases as part of the broader picture, it comes down to a case-sensitive balancing act based on the principle of maintaining the integrity of the profession.

SURF'S UP

Famous attorneys have famous clients, and somehow the relationship always ends up in the rolls of infamy. Cruise the 'Net and you will find plenty of attorneys for the rich and famous who set up their own promotional Web sites to capitalize on their fame. What impact does this have on the integrity of the profession? Do you think this kind of notoriety is good for the reputation of the justice system?

For an example, see http://www.debraopri.com

THE CATCH-ALL RULE OF CONDUCT

The last rule to be discussed is the "catch-all" for the behavioral control of attorneys. ABA Model Rule 8.4 essentially reiterates and reinforces all the rules that have come before it, and plugs any possible loopholes that a clever attorney might try to find.

The primary mandate of this all-encompassing rule binds an attorney and her agents to all the applicable rules of professional conduct. Not only is an actual violation of the rules a sanctionable offense; so is an attempt to circumvent the obligations under the ethical rules. The rules apply not only to the attorney but to all those who work with him, as he cannot ask a non-attorney to do anything that would violate the rules in order to escape responsibility for the infraction. In a constitutional challenge alleging that ABA Model Rule 8.4(a) is invalid and unconstitutional because it is too vague for the prohibitions to be understood, the court found that argument without merit. Attorneys are well aware of their "shall" and "shall not" obligations under the ethics rules. Any violation, attempted violation, or third-party solicitation to violate the rules on behalf of the attorney is sanctionable. In *Rogers v. Mississippi Bar,* 731 So.2d 1158, 1166 (Miss. 1999), the court found that the "moonlighting" attorney was improperly taking legal matters from his firm when he worked on them privately after hours, without disclosing this arrangement to the firm. It is under this language as well that paralegals need to be familiar with the ethical rules governing attorneys in their jurisdictions. A paralegal cannot be asked to perform any task that the attorney herself would be prohibited from undertaking under the rules. To do so would be to "knowingly assist or induce another" to violate or attempt to violate the ethical obligations imposed by the relevant code of professional conduct. This is also reflected in NFPA EC1.3(e). (See Figure 11.2.)

Criminal Activity

Criminal activity is expressly proscribed. To commit an act that is prohibited by the very laws that the attorney has sworn to uphold, to disobey the rule of law before the tribunal of which the attorney is a member, is impermissible and will be sanctioned as professional misconduct, regardless of the fact of conviction or acquittal of the act.

> *The lawyer's offense causing disciplinary violation need not be criminal, but rather one that reflects adversely on the profession. The practice of law is an honorable profession and no lawyer should ever do any act or acts that would in any way reflect poorly upon the honorable profession of law. [. . .] Fitness to practice law includes maintaining good moral character. It is a long standing principle that for one to be worthy to practice law, the person must have a good moral character upon entering the profession, and must maintain such character all through his or her professional life. Any act by an attorney that brings the profession or the authority of the courts and administration of the law into disrespect or disregard, such as dishonesty, personal misconduct, questionable moral character, or unprofessional conduct is potential grounds for disbarment. Rather, the public is entitled to rely on an attorney's admission to the practice of law as a certification of the attorney's honesty, high ethical standards, and good moral character.*

Grigsby v. Kentucky Bar Ass'n, 181 S.W.3d 40, 42 (Ky. 2005) (citations omitted).

In that matter the attorney, through a plea bargain, was convicted of a misdemeanor offense of possession of a controlled substance. The court looked past the

---

NFPA EC1.3(e)

A paralegal shall not knowingly assist any individual with the commission of an act that is in direct violation of the Model Code/Model Rules and/or the rules and/or laws governing the jurisdiction in which the paralegal practices.

FIGURE 11.2

A Paralegal's Duty to Refrain from Assisting in a Violation of Ethics Rules

REEL TO REAL

In the classic film-noir *Force of Evil* (1948), attorney Joe Morse (played by John Garfield) wants to use his position and knowledge to consolidate all the small-time numbers racket operators into one big powerful operation, even though his brother, a small-time operator, opposes him. How does this movie embody the maxim "Power corrupts"? Why is legal power so dangerous? Consider what President John Adams had to say on the subject: "Because power corrupts, society's demands for moral authority and character increase as the importance of the position increases."

plea bargain arrangement to the actual facts of the situation and found that the original felony charges should form the basis of the sanction. It does not affect the ethical board's sanction power that an attorney has served his criminal time in prison or has otherwise been punished for his conduct. Attorneys are admonished to avoid all illegal conduct and maintain only the highest standards in their lives, both professional and personal. "Obedience to the law exemplifies respect for the law." *Toledo Bar Ass'n v. Abood,* 104 Ohio St. 3d 655, 821 N.E.2d 560, 563 (2004).

Dishonesty, Fraud, or Misrepresentation

The rule further addresses the lack of personal character and integrity, sometimes referred to in a term of art as acts of "moral turpitude." There can be no enumeration of the various and sundry ways in which a person can exhibit a deficiency of the morals and values that are demanded by the legal profession. That is why there is this need for the "catch-all" sections. False notarization and submission of inaccurate bills for reimbursement from public funds are two ways in which a county attorney found himself in trouble and sanctioned by a one-year suspension. He knowingly and selfishly performed these acts of dishonesty and therefore was found unfit to practice. *In re Kraushaar,* 268 Kan. 451, 997 P.2d 81 (2000).

REEL TO REAL

Perhaps one of the most "over-the-top" portrayals of a senior partner was Al Pacino's role in *The Devil's Advocate* (1997). There is no character so lacking in morals and integrity as Lucifer himself. He lures young attorneys (like the character played by Keanu Reeves) into becoming his minions and turns them into his corrupt gargoyles. Do you agree or disagree with this kind of portrayal of attorneys? How does it affect the public's perception of the profession? Do you think it reflects on the paralegal profession as well? How?

Conduct Prejudicial to the Administration of Justice

Clearly, the suppression of evidence or otherwise hindering of the process of the legal system is prejudicial to its administration. But less drastic and indirect methods of encumbering the system are sanctionable as well if they are performed by attorneys. As officers of the court, attorneys enjoy a special symbiotic relationship with the justice system and should at all times act in the best interest of its functioning and maintain its dignity. In preserving the integrity of the system, attorneys uphold the honor of their chosen profession as well. Public commentary regarding unfairness of a particular proceeding should be undertaken with extreme caution.

Did respondent's mailing of his letter 19 days after his discipline to more than 281 addressees constitute conduct prejudicial to the administration of justice? It did. His minimal research may have supported the existence of certain previous relationships between insurance industry clients and some group of members of the Disciplinary Board; he may truly have realized too late that he should have hired counsel to represent him in his disciplinary proceeding; he may have had previous unpleasant dealings with his own insurance company and suspected an insurance company's involvement in alerting the disciplinary office to his behavior. Even if he was correct in all of these respects, even if his personal animosity toward the insurance industry was somehow justified, his wholesale indictment of the Kansas disciplinary process as "stacked against him" was not. Rule 8.4(d) can be violated by conduct unbecoming an officer of the court, even if a legal proceeding has ended and even if the lawyer stops somewhere short of spreading outright lies.

Members of the Disciplinary Board serve as judges or commissioners in the Kansas disciplinary process. Our society has a substantial interest in protecting them and other actors in the process from unfounded attacks, and it may do so without running afoul of a disciplined attorney's First Amendment rights. There is a line between just and unjust criticism. Respondent crossed it. This is evident from his plainly selfish motive. He displayed no desire to improve the disciplinary system, only to excuse its focus on him.

In re Pyle, 156 P.3d 1231, 1247–1248 (Kan. 2007).

Misuse may not rise to the level of abuse, but the ethical rules make it clear that even small infractions may be significant if they reflect upon the dignity of the tribunal and respect for all the parties involved in the proceedings. Attacking the ability of opposing counsel, threatening to bring disciplinary actions and appeals if the attorney's requests are not met, and other overtly offensive conduct that manifests a disrespect for others are all actions which, while not an express violation of one of the enumerated ethical rules, are a violation of ABA Model Rule 8.4 (d). Courts have been warning attorneys through case law to exhibit civility and good manners. *In re McAlvey,* 69 N.J. 349, 354 A.2d 289 (1976). Perhaps this statement puts it most eloquently and succinctly: "Care with words and respect for courts and one's adversaries is a necessity, not because lawyers and judges are without fault, but because trial by combat long ago proved unsatisfactory." *In re Converse,* 258 Neb. 159, 602 N.W.2d 500, 508 (1999). Attorneys, like all other people, can be hostile when faced with a stressful situation like litigation, and they will be forgiven the isolated incidents of heated moments of anger or frustration. However, when attorneys have prepared for the insult and have had sufficient time to reflect on the inflammatory nature of their speech or actions, they should be held accountable. These catch-all rules give the court the latitude to discipline them for such outrageous lapses in better judgment that interfere with the proper and rational administration of justice. Discourteous conduct "tears at the fabric of the legal profession, which can expect to have no better reputation for trustworthiness in the community than that of its worst actors." *In re Porter,* 320 Or. 692, 707, 890 P. 2d 1377, 1386 (1995).

Improper Influence over the System

Justice can be obtained only where there has been an opportunity for both sides to fairly and equally present their cases before a neutral tribunal. Any interference with the neutrality of the court negatively affects the public perception of the function of the legal system. To suggest that the outcome of the case can be influenced by anything other than the evidence presented and fair deliberation of the merits is to undermine the system. This is the harm that subsection (e) of the ABA Model Rule 8.4 seeks to avoid by making it a sanctionable offense to suggest that an attorney or her agent can influence the outcome of a matter by means other than those permitted. Bribery, a classic example of such impermissible influence, is also considered criminal conduct punishable under subsection (b). Relationships between attorneys and judges may arise as they work in close proximity to each other, sometimes on a fairly regular basis. While there is no prohibition against such associations, they become improper when the judge and the attorney develop a personal, intimate relationship and then must work together. The justice system can work only when a neutral judge is listening to the adversaries before her without personal bias. If there is a personal relationship, a judge may properly recuse herself from the matter in order to preserve the integrity of the pending matter. This is exactly what a judge did in *Disciplinary Counsel v. Cicero,* 78 Ohio St. 3d 351, 678 N.E.2d 517 (1997). However, the attorney violated subsection (e) by boasting to opposing counsel and other members of the bar that he was in a sexual relationship with the judge and that any continuances sought in the matter would be denied, as he and the judge would be going away together for the holidays. *Id.* To insinuate that the judge would prefer the attorney's company over the fair administration of justice was entirely unacceptable and warranted a one-year suspension for the attorney from the practice of law.

Accessory to Judicial Misconduct

The practice of law is participatory. There are many actors on the justice system's stage, and each one must respect the obligations of the part they play. The last subsection acknowledges that while judges are in a position superior to that of attorneys, they too can be fallible, and an attorney must not assist the members of the bench in committing a violation of the Code of Judicial Conduct. This may be particularly tempting when the violation tends to help the attorney in the matter before the judge, and it may be tempting also where there is little chance of detection or challenge. However, it is to be avoided at all costs; further, as previously discussed, the attorney has a reporting obligation to the relevant ethical board if the attorney knows of the judge's ethical violation. In the case of *In re Wilder,* 764 N.E.2d 617 (Ind. 2002), the town attorney attempted to file a temporary restraining order against the town's commissioners to prohibit them from taking a certain action. The attorney filed the papers and met with the judge ex parte and after 5:00 p.m. to obtain the judge's signature on the order. The signed papers were then served the next morning upon the commissioners. While this may seem to be merely a procedural irregularity, the court found that the judge violated the judicial code by signing the order without finding that there would be irreparable and immediate harm if he did not do so at that moment without notice to the opposing party. The judge was suspended for three days. However, the attorney was also subject to discipline, because he knew that the application for the TRO required notice, and by obtaining the judge's signature without complying with the "exigent circumstances" showing required under the court rules, he was assisting the judge to commit an act of impropriety. As the attorney was found to be equally culpable of the questionable conduct, he was equally sanctioned by a three-day suspension.

PRO BONO ACTIVITIES

pro bono publico
Literally, "for the public good." Describing legal services provided to the public by legal professionals voluntarily and without payment.

In order to maintain the confidence and trust of the public and to better serve the interests of justice, legal professionals should strive to provide **pro bono publico** services in their communities. By doing so, paralegals can provide access to justice and make the difference that the paralegal profession was designed to address. Not only has NFPA incorporated this aspiration to public service in its Model Code, it is deeply committed through its Pro Bono Committee. The association has also incorporated this mission into its ethical code. (See Figure 11.3.) Certified members should aspire to dedicate 24 hours of pro bono service per year in their communities. Attorneys are encouraged by the ABA Model standard to provide 50 hours of pro bono services.

1.4	**A paralegal shall serve the public interest by contributing to the improvement of the legal system and delivery of quality legal services, including pro bono publico services.**

Ethical Considerations

EC 1.4(a)	A paralegal shall be sensitive to the legal needs of the public and shall promote the development and implementation of programs that address those needs.
EC 1.4(b)	A paralegal shall support efforts to improve the legal system and access thereto and shall assist in making changes.
EC 1.4(c)	A paralegal shall support and participate in the delivery of Pro Bono Publico services directed toward implementing and improving access to justice, the law, the legal system or the paralegal and legal professions.
EC 1.4(d)	A paralegal should aspire annually to contribute twenty-four (24) hours of Pro Bono Publico services under the supervision of an attorney or as authorized by administrative, statutory or court authority to:

1. persons of limited means; or
2. charitable, religious, civic, community, governmental and educational organizations in matters that are designed primarily to address the legal needs of persons with limited means; or
3. individuals, groups or organizations seeking to secure or protect civil rights, civil liberties or public rights.

The twenty-four (24) hours of Pro Bono Publico services contributed annually by a paralegal may consist of such services as detailed in this EC1.4(d), and/or administrative matters designed to develop and implement the attainment of this aspiration as detailed above in EC 1.4(a), (b), (c), or any combination of the two.

FIGURE 11.3

A Paralegal's Pro Bono Publico Activities

 CYBER TRIP

In order to stay current with the latest developments and opinions of those in the forefront of the paralegal field, please visit these sites often for updates:

McGraw-Hill's State-Specific Paralegal Portal at:

www.mhhe.com/ paralegalportal

Almost 900 different Law Discussion Boards, which can be accessed through this "clearinghouse":

http://chat.lawinfo.com

Numerous legal blogs, accessed through:

http://legalblogwatch.typepad.com/legal_blog_watch

and

http://www.law-library.rutgers.edu/resources/lawblogs.php

LexisNexis' free Research site:

http://research.lawyers.com

A list of new and intriguing Web sites, compiled by Robert Ambrogi, Esq. for the legal profession:

http://www.legaline.com/lawsites.html

And, of course, the authoritative ABA Web site on paralegal issues:

http://www.abanet.org/legalservices/paralegals

These services can be provided directly to a person of limited means or to charitable, religious, civic, community, governmental, and educational organizations that serve that population. Further qualifying for pro bono service is work for organizations whose goals are to protect civil rights or civil liberties of citizens, either individually or as a whole. All of this work improves the legal profession as well.

Volunteerism is a noble goal, and professionals are in a unique position to use their special skills to aid those in need. Indeed, one cannot be an advocate for the justice system if one does not act to improve the justice system for all citizens. Legal professionals have a responsibility to promote overall justice and fairness in their communities. The quality of justice should not depend on the ability to pay for legal services.

As attorneys and paralegals are entrusted with matters of great consequence, with their clients' confidence, judges' trust, and societal expectations, they must always seek to act in accordance with those elements. This may place a burden on the profession, but attorneys enjoy a certain status in the justice system which demands such standards. Paralegals are essential in the delivery of these services as well. Their conduct, not just their work product, must support the legal profession as a whole. Failing to comport with these ethical mandates in both personal and professional activities may increase the cynicism of the public in the fair administration of justice. As officers of the court, legal professionals have a duty to project the very characteristics that attorneys must rely upon when they are before the tribunal. The legal profession started as a "gentleman's calling" to serve society, and attempts should be made to preserve the dignity of the system so that every citizen can feel that she will, if need be, get her fair day in court and be treated with courtesy while trying to navigate the system. Further, the system can only operate as well as its least productive or civilized member. It is for these reasons that the legal profession has burdened attorneys with a duty to comport themselves in accordance with the integrity of the profession. This is precisely why the paralegal profession needs to be cognizant of its own development and reputation to ensure its steady and healthy growth. Preprofessional and continuing legal education is vital to the nurturing of the public's perception and confidence in the profession.

Summary

This chapter examined the overarching principles that unify the entire set of ethical rules that bind all legal professionals. Both attorneys and paralegals must comport themselves with strict professional and personal ethical standards. These broad categories of duties to the legal system and administration of justice are as follows:

1. being honest toward reviewing or admission boards or other legal authorities to maintain the character of the profession
2. displaying respect for the legal system and its participants
3. reporting misconduct to the proper authorities, where the legal professional has knowledge of the act or omission that raises a substantial question of fitness to practice law
4. understanding the code and restraints on judicial conduct and refraining from aiding in judicial misconduct
5. refraining from criminal, dishonest, or deceitful activities or any other conduct that is prejudicial to the administration of justice

Key Terms and Concepts

Knowledge

Pro bono publico

Self-policing

Substantial question

MULTIPLE CHOICE

Choose the best answer(s) and please explain WHY you choose the answer(s).

1. A bar candidate must disclose
   a. all information about herself.
   b. any changes in her situation that are relevant to her application.
   c. nothing that is not specifically asked on the bar application.
   d. only that information that is requested during the oral character and fitness interview.

2. If an attorney wants to speak out against a judicial official,
   a. he must first obtain the court's permission.
   b. he must file his intended statement with the ethics board in his jurisdiction so they can rule whether he is permitted to say those things.
   c. he must remain respectful and truthful but he is free to criticize.
   d. all of the above

3. To raise a "substantial question" as to a lawyer's fitness to practice law, the reporting attorney
   a. should have independent factual proof of the purported misconduct.
   b. should be reasonably sure that the conduct in question occurred.
   c. has to prove that the lawyer was convicted of a crime of moral turpitude.
   d. all of the above

EXPLAIN YOURSELF

All answers should be written in complete sentences. A simple yes or no is insufficient.

1. Explain the concept of a self-policing profession.
2. Describe a situation in which a paralegal should report her supervising attorney's misconduct.
3. Why are paralegals held to the same ethical standards as attorneys?
4. Define acts of "moral turpitude."

FAULTY PHRASES

All of the following statements are FALSE; state why they are false and then rewrite them as true statements, without just making a statement negative by adding the word "not."

1. An attorney has an obligation to report misconduct only of subordinate lawyers.
2. Before reporting professional misconduct, an attorney must be absolutely sure and have supporting facts relating to his allegations.
3. An attorney has the same free speech protections as other citizens when criticizing the judiciary as a branch of the government.
4. The crime for which the attorney was convicted must relate to dishonesty in order for it to be considered an ethical violation.
5. Judges are held to a slightly lower standard for moral conduct because they are not engaged in the active practice of representing clients.
6. Judges are permitted to conduct themselves as they see fit in their own courtrooms, as long as they can control the attorneys appearing before them.

7. An attorney's duty of confidentiality will always be overtaken by her duty to report misconduct of another attorney.

8. A paralegal's duty to maintain the integrity of the justice system is not as high as that of attorneys and judges.

PORTFOLIO ASSIGNMENT

Write Away

Compose a position statement regarding your views on the future of the paralegal profession. What are the most important characteristics that need to be cultivated in the field? How will this be possible? How do the ethical mandates fit into your position? Do they need to be expanded? Made more specific? Please provide examples or hypotheticals where appropriate.

CA Eth. Op. 2003–162, 2003 WL 23146201 (Cal. St. Bar Comm. Prof'l Resp.)

*1 ISSUE: WHAT ETHICAL ISSUES ARE RAISED WHEN A CALIFORNIA ATTORNEY PUBLICLY ADVOCATES CIVIL DISOBEDIENCE, INCLUDING VIOLATIONS OF LAW, IN FURTHERANCE OF HER PERSONALLY HELD POLITICAL, MORAL, OR RELIGIOUS BELIEFS, AND SIMULTANEOUSLY PRACTICES LAW?

Formal Opinion Number 2003–162
2003

DIGEST

While attorneys have rights under the First Amendment to express political, moral, and religious beliefs and to advocate civil disobedience, attorneys must follow their professional responsibility when acting upon their beliefs and when advising clients. At a minimum, attorneys' performance of their professional duties to clients must not be adversely affected by the attorneys' personal beliefs or exercise of First Amendment rights. In selecting areas of legal practice, types of cases and particular clients, attorneys should be cognizant of the possibility that their moral, social, and religious beliefs, and their exercise of their First Amendment rights, could adversely affect the performance of their duties to clients.

AUTHORITIES INTERPRETED

Rules 3–110, 3–210, and 3–310 of the Rules of Professional Conduct of the State Bar of California.

Business and Professions Code sections 6067, 6068, subdivisions (a) and (c), and 6103.

STATEMENT OF FACTS

An attorney (Attorney) maintains a law practice emphasizing business transactional work, estate and tax planning services, and tax controversy matters. She believes sincerely that the entire state and federal tax system is immoral, and has joined an association (Association) that opposes taxation of individuals and family businesses.

She has spoken at Association conferences and advocated resistance to the state and federal tax systems. In these speeches, she has proposed that individuals and small businesses refuse to report to the Franchise Tax Board and the Internal Revenue Service any transaction or event that might lead to the imposition of income, capital gains, or estate taxation, and has advocated that they also refuse to pay taxes.

Attorney has never represented Association, but she receives a substantial number of client referrals from her speeches on behalf of and through her contacts in the organization. While she has publicly advocated civil disobedience, Attorney advises lawful behavior in counseling her clients.

What ethical considerations govern Attorney's activities?

DISCUSSION

I. Is it ethically permissible for Attorney to publicly advocate the refusal to pay taxes?

The facts do not identify the existence of a law prohibiting advocacy of violations of state or federal tax laws. Even if there were such a law, it might well violate the First and Fourteenth Amendments guarantees of free speech and assembly. A state may not forbid or proscribe the advocacy of a violation of law except where such advocacy is directed to inciting or producing imminent lawless action and is likely to incite or produce such action. (*Brandenburg v. Ohio* (1969) 395 U.S. 444 [89 S. Ct. 1827].)

Attorney's status as a lawyer does not change the analysis. To the extent speech is constitutionally protected, Attorney has the First Amendment right to advocate political and social change through the violation of law, even though the First Amendment rights of lawyers are limited in certain respects. (See *Standing Committee on Discipline v. Yagman* (9th Cir. 1995) 55 F.3d 1430 and *In re Palmisano* (7th Cir. 1995) 70 F.3d 483, cert. denied, 116 S. Ct. 1854 (1996) [both dealing with the special problem of discipline for attorneys who publicly criticize judges].)

The Committee notes, however, the distinction between advocating and engaging in violations of law. Attorneys are subject to discipline for illegal conduct even if their conduct occurs outside the practice of law and does not involve moral turpitude. As the California Supreme Court stated in the seminal case of *In re Rohan* (1978) 21 Cal.3d 195, 203 [145 Cal. Rptr. 855], explaining why discipline was appropriate for an attorney's criminal conviction of willful failure to file tax returns: "An attorney as an officer of the court and counselor at law occupies a unique position in society. His refusal to obey the law, and the bar's failure to discipline him for such refusal, will not only demean the integrity of the profession but will encourage disrespect for and further violations of the law. This is particularly true in the case of revenue law violations by an attorney." (See also *In re Kelley* (1990) 52 Cal.3d 487 [276 Cal. Rptr. 375] [discipline imposed for two drunk driving convictions, the second while on probation from the first]; *In re Morales* (1983) 35 Cal.3d 1 [96 Cal. Rptr. 353] [discipline imposed for failure to withhold or pay taxes and unemployment contributions].)

II. Is it ethically permissible for Attorney to advise her clients not to pay taxes that are due under applicable law?

It is important to distinguish between Attorney's exercise of her First Amendment rights and her performance of her duties as a lawyer for clients. By virtue of her participation in and speech on behalf of the Association, Attorney has been retained by clients because of the political and social views she publicly has taken regarding the payment of taxes. Although a lawyer may advocate political and social change through the violation of tax laws, she may not advise a client to violate the law unless she believes reasonably and in good faith that such law is invalid and there is a good-faith argument for the modification or reversal of that law.[1]

III. Does Attorney have an ethical duty to disclose her relationship with Association and her position on taxation to prospective and existing clients?

An attorney may not accept or continue the representation of a client, if the attorney has any of the several potential or actual conflicts of interest listed in *Rule 3–310 of the California Rules of Professional Conduct*, absent "written disclosure" to and, in many instances, "informed written consent" from, the client or potential client. Together, the written disclosure requirements in paragraphs (B)(1) and (B)(2) of *Rule 3–310* apply when a lawyer has or had "a legal, business, financial, professional or personal relationship with" a party or witness in the same matter in which the lawyer represents the client.[2] Paragraph (B)(4) of the rule applies when a lawyer "has or had a legal, business, financial, or professional interest in the subject matter of the representation." As the Association is neither a party or witness in the matters of Attorney's tax clients, no disclosure pursuant to paragraphs (B)(1) or (B)(2) would be required. Similarly, as the Association is not the subject matter of the Attorney's representation of tax clients, no disclosure pursuant to paragraph (B)(4) would be required either.

We recognize that paragraph (B)(3) might appear at first glance to be applicable to Attorney. This part of the rule states that a lawyer shall not accept or continue the representation of a client without providing written "disclosure" to the client or potential client where the attorney has or had a "legal, business, financial, professional, or personal relationship with another person or entity" which the attorney "knows or reasonably should" know would be "substantially affected by resolution of the matter." However, there are no facts that implicate paragraph (B)(3). Whether Attorney "knows or reasonably should know" that the Association would be "substantially affected by the resolution of the matter" depends on the totality of the circumstances. These

circumstances might include such things as the scope and object of the client's engagement of Attorney.

IV. Can Attorney competently represent clients in business and taxation matters?

Attorney has publicly advocated that others resist state and federal tax laws by refusing to report transactions and events on which taxation could be imposed, and by refusing to pay taxes. While her constitutional rights of speech and assembly may permit her such advocacy, they do not alter her duties to her clients.

These duties include the obligation to provide competent representation found in *Rule 3–110 of the California Rules of Professional Conduct*.[3] *Business and Professions Code section 6067* requires that attorneys admitted to practice in California take an oath that includes a promise "faithfully to discharge the duties of an attorney to the best of his [or her] knowledge and ability."

Attorney's personal views and public comments regarding taxation do not necessarily render her unable to competently represent a client in a tax matter. Indeed, it is possible that because of her strong beliefs Attorney has a particularly sophisticated knowledge of the substantive law and the procedures that could be pertinent to her work on tax matters. Despite this possibility, it is important to recognize that the duty of competence includes an emotional component. *Rule 3–110* prohibits intentional, reckless or repeated incompetence and defines "competence" as the application of "the 1) diligence, 2) learning and skill, and 3) *mental, emotional and physical ability reasonably necessary for the performance of legal services*." (Italics added.) Thus, if Attorney's mental or emotional state prevents her from performing an objective evaluation of her client's legal position, providing unbiased advice to her client, or performing her legal representation according to her client's directions, then Attorney would violate the duty of competence. (See *Blanton v. Woman care* (1985) 38 Cal.3d 396, 407–408 [212 Cal. Rptr. 151]; *Considine v. Shadle, Hunt & Hagar* (1986) 187 Cal.App.3d 760, 765 [232 Cal. Rptr. 250]; Cal. State Bar Formal Op. No. 1984–77; and L.A. Cty. Bar Ass'n Formal Op. No. 504 (2001).[4]

This opinion is issued by the Standing Committee on Professional Responsibility and Conduct of the State Bar of California. It is advisory only. It is not binding upon the courts, the State Bar of California, its Board of Governors, any persons or tribunals charged with regulatory responsibility or any member of the State Bar.

---

1. *Rule 3—210 of the California Rules of Professional Conduct* prohibits a member from advising a client to violate the law "unless the member believes in good faith that such law . . . . . is invalid." Similarly, *Rule 3–200 of the Rules of Professional Conduct* prohibits a member from accepting or continuing employment if he or she knows that the client's purpose is "to present a claim or defense in litigation that is not warranted under existing law, unless it can be supported by a good faith argument for an extension, modification, or reversal of such existing law." Further, subdivision (a) of *California Business and Professions Code section 6068* requires that California attorneys support the Constitution and laws of the United States and of this state. Subdivision (c) of section 6068 requires that an attorney maintain such actions or proceedings only as they appear to him or her legal or just. Each of these rule and statutory provisions identifies a duty of an attorney; *California Business and Professions Code section 6103* in turn provides that an attorney may be disciplined for violation of his or her duties as an attorney.

2. "Disclosure" is defined as "informing the client . . . of the relevant circumstances and of the actual and reasonably foreseeable adverse consequences to the client. . . ." *(Rules Prof. Conduct, rule 3–310(A)(1).)* Disclosure permits clients to make knowing and intelligent decisions about their representation when their attorneys have potential or actual conflicts of interest.

3. *Rule 3–110 of the California Rules of Professional Conduct* provides:
   (A) A member shall not intentionally, recklessly, or repeatedly fail to perform legal services with competence.
   (B) For purposes of this rule, "competence" in any legal service shall mean to apply the 1) diligence, 2) learning and skill, and 3) mental, emotional, and physical ability reasonably necessary for the performance of such service.
   (C) If a member does not have sufficient learning and skill when the legal service is undertaken, the member may nonetheless perform such services competently by 1) associating with or, where appropriate, professionally consulting another lawyer reasonably believed to be competent, or 2) by acquiring sufficient learning and skill before performance is required.

4. We express no opinion as to whether or not there may be a duty to communicate to clients the possible impact of her views on taxation, or the knowledge of the taxing authorities of those views, on the outcome of the representation.

Source: From California Ethics Opinion. Reprinted with permission from ThomsonWest.

Appendix A

LINKS TO ETHICAL CODES FOR PARALEGALS AND ATTORNEYS

Please note that this list is not intended to be all-inclusive. The paralegal links included are those of associations that are statewide in scale and that have published their own sets of ethics rules for member paralegals. There are many other local paralegal associations that are associated with either the NALA or NFPA and have simply adopted these respective codes of professional responsibility. Please check the Web sites of the NALA and NFPA for their locally affiliated associations.

Also included are the direct links to the individual states' Rules of Professional Conduct for Attorneys. In each case, the legal authority that has sponsored the Web link (i.e., the state bar association, the court system, or other) is indicated, but all rules emanate from the judicial branch of the state government.

Also note that if any direct links are inactive, please return to the ROOT link of the Web site to find the active link. For example, the ROOT link of http://www.abanet.org/cpr/links.html is simply http://www.abanet.org

National

- The American Bar Association:

  http://www.abanet.org/cpr/links.html

- National Federation of Paralegal Association:

  http://www.paralegals.org/displaycommon.cfm?an=1&subarticlenbr=932 (these list NFPA Member Associations by States / Regions.)

- National Association of Legal Assistants:

  http://www.nala.org/Affiliated_Associations_Info.HTM (these list NALA Member Associations by States.)

Alabama

- Alabama Association of Paralegals:

  http://www.aaopi.com/Ethics.htm

- Alabama State Bar Association—Rules of Professional Conduct:

  http://www.alabar.org/public/ropc.cfm

Alaska

- Alaska Association of Paralegals:

  http://www.alaskaparalegals.org/aap_ethics.htm

- Alaska Court System—Rules of Professional Conduct:

  http://www.state.ak.us/courts/prof.htm

Arizona

- Arizona Paralegal Association:

  http://www.azparalegal.org/resources/resourcescodeofethics.html

- Arizona State Bar Association—Ethics Rules:

  http://www.myazbar.org/Ethics/rules.cfm

Arkansas

- Arkansas Association of Legal Assistants:

  http://www.aala-legal.org/index.html

- Arkansas Office on Professional Ethics:

  http://courts.state.ar.us/professional_conduct/index.cfm

California

- California Alliance of Paralegal Associations:

  http://www.caparalegal.org/ethics.html

- The State Bar of California—Rules of Professional Conduct:

  http://www.calbar.ca.gov/state/calbar/calbar_generic.jsp?cid=10158&id=3422

Colorado

- Rocky Mountain Paralegal Association:

  http://www.rockymtnparalegal.org

- Colorado Bar Association—Rules of Professional Conduct:

  http://www.coloradosupremecourt.com/pdfs/Regulation/Colorado%20RPC%202007.pdf

- Colorado Bar Association—Guidelines for the Utilization of Paralegals:

  http://www.cobar.org/group/index.cfm?category=106&EntityID=CLAS

Connecticut

- Central Connecticut Paralegal Association:

  http://www.ctparalegals.org/Ethics_Central_Connecticut_Paralegal_Association.htm

- State of Connecticut Judicial Branch—Rules of Professional Conduct:

  http://www.jud.ct.gov/pb.htm

Delaware

- Delaware Paralegal Association:

  http://www.deparalegals.org/pdf/final_code_of_ethics.pdf

- The Delaware Lawyers' Rules of Professional Conduct:

  http://courts.delaware.gov/Rules/?DLRPCwithComments_Oct2007.pdf

District of Columbia

- National Capital Area Paralegal Association:

  http://www.ncapa.com/mc/page.do?sitePageId=45963&orgId=ncapa

- The District of Columbia Bar—Rules of Professional Conduct:

  http://www.dcbar.org/new_rules/rules.cfm

Florida

- Paralegal Association of Florida, Inc.:

  http://www.pafinc.org

- Florida Bar Association:

  http://floridabar.org

Georgia

- Georgia Association of Paralegals:

  http://www.gaparalegal.org

- State Bar of Georgia:

  http://www.gabar.org/handbook/part_iv_after_january_1_2001_-_georgia_rules_
  of_professional_conduct

Hawaii

- Hawaii Paralegal Association:

  http://www.hawaiiparalegal.org

- Hawaii Rules of Professional Conduct:

  http://www.state.hi.us/jud/ctrules/hrpcond.htm

Idaho

- Idaho State Bar—Rules of Professional Conduct:

  http://www.isc.idaho.gov/irpc0304_cov.htm

Illinois

- Illinois Paralegal Association:

  http://www.ipaonline.org/displaycommon.cfm?an=1&subarticlenbr=1

- Illinois Court—Rules of Professional Conduct:

  http://www.isc.idaho.gov/irpc0304_cov.htm

Indiana

- Indiana Paralegal Association, Inc.:

  http://indianaparalegals.org/Code%20of%20Ethics.htm

- Indiana Rules of Court—Rules of Professional Conduct:

  http://www.state.in.us/judiciary/rules/prof_conduct/index.html

Iowa

- Iowa Association of Legal Assistants:

  http://www.ialanet.org/about_IALA.asp

- Iowa Judicial Branch—Rules of Professional Conduct:

  http://www.judicial.state.ia.us/Professional_Regulation/Rules_of_Professional_Conduct

Kansas

- Kansas Association of Legal Assistants:

  http://www.accesskansas.org/kala/code_of_ethics.pdf

- Kansas Paralegal Association:

  http://www.ksparalegals.org/ethics.html

- Kansas Judicial Branch—Rules of Professional Conduct:

  http://www.kscourts.org/rules/Rule-List.asp?r1=Rules+Relating+to+Discipline+ of+Attorneys

Kentucky

- Kentucky Bar Association:

  http://www.kybar.org/Default.aspx?tabid=237

Louisiana

- Louisiana State Paralegal Association:

  http://www.la-paralegals.org/ethics.htm

- Louisiana Attorney Disciplinary Board:

  http://www.ladb.org/Publications/ropc2006-04-01.pdf

Maine

- Maine Board of Overseers of the Bar:

  http://www.mebaroverseers.org/Home/Code%20of%20Professional% 20Responsibility.html

Maryland

- Maryland Association of Paralegals:

  http://www.mdparalegals.org

- Maryland Standing Committee on Rules of Practice and Procedure:

  http://www.courts.state.md.us/rules

Massachusetts

- Massachusetts Paralegal Association:

  http://www.massparalegal.org/xyzzy/mp/pdf/06182004_ethics.pdf

- Massachusetts Supreme Judicial Court Rules of Professional Conduct:

  http://www.mass.gov/obcbbo/rpcnet.htm

Michigan

- State Bar of Michigan- Rules of Professional Conduct:

  http://www.michbar.org/professional/pdfs/mrpc.pdf

Minnesota

- Minnesota Paralegal Association:

  http://mnparalegals.org/about.php

- Minnesota Rules of Professional Conduct:

  http://www.mncourts.gov/rules/professionalConduct/MRPC.DOC

Mississippi

- Mississippi Paralegal Association:

  http://msparalegals.org/rules.htm

- Mississippi Supreme Court Rules of Professional Conduct:

  http://www.mssc.state.ms.us/rules/RuleContents.asp?IDNum=7

Missouri

- Missouri Paralegal Association:

  http://www.missouriparalegalassoc.org

- Missouri State Court Rules of Professional Responsibility:

  http://www.courts.mo.gov/page.asp?id=707

Montana

- Montana Association of Legal Assistants:

  http://www.malanet.org

- Montana Rules of Professional Conduct:

  http://www.montanaodc.org/Portals/ODC/docs/rules_of_professional_conduct.Pdf

Nebraska

- Nebraska Association of Paralegals:

  http://www.neala.org

- Rocky Mountain Paralegal Association:

  http://www.rockymtnparalegal.org

- Supreme Court of Nebraska—Rules of Professional Conduct:

  http://www.supremecourt.ne.gov/rules/pdf/rulesprofconduct-34.pdf

Nevada

- Nevada Paralegal Association:

  http://www.nevadaparalegal.org/Home/tabid/492/Default.aspx

- Nevada Rules of Professional Conduct:

  http://www.leg.state.nv.us/CourtRules/RPC.html

New Hampshire

- Paralegal Association of New Hampshire:

  http://www.panh.org/by-laws.htm#ARTICLE_III__

- New Hampshire Supreme Court Rules of Professional Conduct:

  http://www.courts.state.nh.us/supreme/orders/20072507.pdf

New Jersey

- Paralegal Association of New Jersey:

  http://www.njpara.org

- New Jersey Rules of Professional Conduct:

  http://www.judiciary.state.nj.us/rules/apprpc.htm

New Mexico

- State Bar of New Mexico—Rules Governing Paralegal Services:

  http://www.nmbar.org/AboutSBNM/ParalegalDivision/
  PDrulesgovparalegalservices.html

- State of New Mexico Rules of Professional Conduct:

  http://www.conwaygreene.com/nmsu/lpext.dll?f=templates&fn=main-h.htm&2.0

New York

- Empire State Alliance of Paralegal Associations:

  http://www.geocities.com/empirestateparalegals

- New York Lawyers' Code of Professional Responsibility:

  http://www.nysba.org/Content/NavigationMenu/ForAttorneys/
  ProfessionalStandardsforAttorneys/lawyerscodeupdatedNov07.pdf

- North Carolina North Carolina Paralegal Association:

  http://www.ncparalegal.org/mc/page.do?sitePageId=52916&orgId=ncpa

- North Carolina State Bar Rules of Professional Conduct:

  http://www.ncbar.com/rules/rpcsearch.asp

North Dakota

- North Dakota Supreme Court Rules of Professional Conduct:

  http://www.ncbar.com/rules/rpcsearch.asp

Ohio

- Paralegal Association of Central Ohio:

  http://www.pacoparalegals.org/about_us.htm

- Supreme Court of Ohio Task Force on Rules of Professional Conduct:

  http://www.sconet.state.oh.us/Atty-Svcs/ProfConduct/default.asp

Oklahoma

- Oklahoma Paralegal Association:

  http://www.okparalegal.org/standards.htm

- State Bar of Oklahoma—Rules of Professional Conduct:

  http://www.okbar.org/ethics/ORPC07.pdf

Oregon

- Oregon Paralegal Assocation:

  http://www.oregonparalegals.org/e107_plugins/custompages/About%20OPA.php

- Pacific Northwest Paralegal Association:

  http://www.pnwpa.org

- Oregon Rules of Professional Conduct:

  http://www.osbar.org/_docs/rulesregs/orpc.pdf

Pennsylvania

- Keystone Alliance of Paralegal Associations:

  http://keystoneparalegals.org/PDFs/Edu_standard.pdf

- The Disciplinary Board of the Supreme Court of Pennsylvania—Rules
  of Professional Responsibility:

  http://www.padisciplinaryboard.org/documents/Pa%20RPC.pdf

Rhode Island
- Rhode Island Paralegal Association:

  http://www.paralegals.org/displaycommon.cfm?an=1&subarticlenbr=910
- Rhode Island Rules of Professional Conduct:

  http://www.courts.ri.gov/supreme/pdf-files/Rules_Of_Professional_Conduct.pdf

South Carolina
- South Carolina Judicial Department—Rules of Professional Conduct:

  http://www.judicial.state.sc.us/courtReg/newrules/NewRules.cfm

South Dakota
- South Dakota Paralegal Association:

  http://www.sdparalegals.com/index.html
- Rocky Mountain Paralegal Association:

  http://www.rockymtnparalegal.org
- South Dakota Rules of Professional Responsibility:

  http://www.sdbar.org/Rules/Rules/PC_Rules.htm

Tennessee
- Tennessee Paralegal Association:

  http://www.tnparalegal.org/about.html
- Tennessee State Bar Association—Rules of Professional Conduct:

  http://www.tba.org/ethics2002.html

Texas
- The Texas Center for Legal Ethics and Professionalism: Code of Ethics for Legal Assistants:

  http://www.txethics.org/reference_ethics.asp
- State Bar of Texas: Paralegal Division:

  http://txpd.org/page.asp?p=Ethics%20Brochure
- Texas Disciplinary Rules of Professional Conduct:

  http://www.texasbar.com/ContentManagement/ContentDisplay.cfm?ContentID=13942

Utah
- Legal Assistants Association of Utah:

  http://www.laau.info/CANONS%20OF%20ETHICS%20FOR%20LEGAL%20ASSISTANTS%20080103.rtf
- Rocky Mountain Paralegal Association:

  http://www.rockymtnparalegal.org
- Utah State Court Rules:

  http://www.utcourts.gov/resources/rules

Vermont

- Vermont Rules of Professional Conduct:

  http://www.vermontjudiciary.org/PRB1.htm

Virginia

- Virginia Alliance of Paralegal Associations:

  http://www.vaparalegalalliance.org

- Virginia State Bar Professional Guidelines and Rules of Professional Conduct:

  http://www.vsb.org/site/regulation/guidelines

Washington

- Washington State Paralegal Association:

  http://www.wspaonline.com/default.htm

- Washington State Court Rules: Rules of Professional Conduct:

  http://www.courts.wa.gov/court_rules/?fa=court_rules.list&group=ga&set=RPC

West Virginia

- Association of West Virginia Paralegals:

  http://www.awvp.org/4436/11901.html

- West Virginia State Bar Rules of Professional Conduct:

  http://www.wvbar.org/BARINFO/rulesprofconduct/index.htm

Wisconsin

- Rules of Professional Conduct for Attorneys:

  http://www.legis.state.wi.us/rsb/scr/5200.pdf

Wyoming

- Legal Assistants of Wyoming:

  http://www.lawyo.com/LAW/default.htm

- Rocky Mountain Paralegal Association:

  http://www.rockymtnparalegal.org

- Wyoming Judicial Branch—Rules of Professional Conduct for Attorneys at Law:

  http://courts.state.wy.us/CourtRules_Entities.aspx?RulesPage=AttorneysConduct.xml

Appendix B

HOW TO PREPARE THE CASE BRIEF

The paralegal student needs to understand the importance of briefing cases and why this needs to be done properly. After the paralegal has completed collecting the relevant cases through research, the information needs to be summarized and analyzed. A briefed case is the first step in the writing process toward the final trial brief. A case brief is a tool in that it serves as a "cheat sheet"; if a case is briefed properly, no one should have to reread the original case opinion. Some judges have a propensity for verbosity and the use of esoteric language. A paralegal's task is to see through that and simplify and clarify the opinion for future use in the office.

How is the paralegal to accomplish this feat? The following is a relatively standard format for case briefing. Remember to write clearly, use your own words, and be concise.

1. The Facts

- You must identify what the material facts are: what's important. This should read like a story.

  There are two types of facts:
  - Occurrence facts—what happened between the parties that gave rise to the lawsuit.
  - Procedural facts—what happened to the case once it started its journey through the legal system. Most of the time, this involves how/why the case ended up at the appellate level.
- You must learn what is important to a case. For example, the weather conditions are irrelevant in a contract dispute, but they can be vital to a car accident.
  - Pay attention to what the court itself focuses on. These are the facts that make a difference as to how the law is applied in the case.
- Identify the role that each party plays. Are there a buyer and a seller? A realtor and a construction manager? Avoid using the actual names of the parties; it will only confuse and/or annoy the reader.

2. The Issue(s)

- This is NOT the guilt or innocence of a party. It doesn't matter what actually happened to the parties; what matters is how their situation was analyzed by the court.
- What is the correct legal standard to apply and was it applied properly at the trial level?
- You are looking for the reason WHY a certain legal standard was applied in that case, and HOW the result was achieved.
  - In this way, the researcher can determine how that same precedent can or should be applied in the instant case.

- It is most helpful to pose the issue as a question. Very frequently starting the question with "Whether. . . ." is appropriate and helps to focus the reader.
- Break the issue down into its component parts. This may mean that you will have a set of numbered issues.

3. The Holding

- Identify the legal standard relied upon by the court.
- Identify how the court resolved the legal issue before it. Judges will look for statutory authority first; if there is none, then the judge will apply fundamental ideals of right and wrong (equity).
- This should be a short statement; essentially, it answers the question posed in the ISSUE section. Do not try to explain the answer here; that is for the next section.
- If you have more than one question posed in the ISSUE section, you should answer each one separately here.

4. Reasoning (the most important part of the brief!)

- The court gives the reasons *why* the outcome (holding) is what it has determined. It will explain how the legal standard applies in that case. It is important to always apply the law to the facts. This is essential for you to do, to determine how your case will turn out.
- Be sure to mention the relevant law relied upon by the court. Use phrases like "Pursuant to. . . .", "In accordance with. . . .", etc.
- The court may rely on several different theories in making its determination; be sure to discuss all of them. Keep a well-defined format with clear headings to assist the reader in identifying all the pertinent reasoning.
- Treat this section as an educational discussion. Remember that you do not want your reader to have to reread the original case.
- Also note how the court ultimately treated the case: its "Judgment." Did it affirm, reverse, or remand the case?

An effective case brief should ensure that the reader has all the necessary information without having to refer to the text of the case. Also, please proofread, the spell-checker is not a mind reader.

The following is an example of a Case Brief based upon *Herbert V. Haytaian,* 292 N.J.Super. 426, 678 A.2d 1183 (1996). The text of the case follows the brief. The reason why this case was chosen is to demonstrate the skill of analytical reading as well. The "red herring" issue of sexual harassment may cloud the true ethical issue regarding a conflict of interest if the reader is not careful.

Beth HERBERT, Plaintiff-Appellant,

v.

Garabed HAYTAIAN, Individually and in his official capacity, and The State of
New Jersey, Defendants-Respondents.
Argued May 30, 1996.
Decided July 25, 1996.

HUMPHREYS, J.A.D.

Plaintiff alleges that the defendant Garabed Haytaian ("Haytaian") sexually harassed her from July 1994 to October 1995 while he was Speaker of the New Jersey General Assembly and she was employed in the Assembly Majority Office. She seeks compensatory and punitive damages and other relief from the State and Haytaian.

In March 1993, Neil Mullin ("Mullin"), at the request of Haytaian, agreed to undertake an investigation of alleged sexual harassment of State employees in the bi-partisan State Office of Legislative Services ("OLS"). Judge Ferentz found that this undertaking created an appearance of impropriety and entered an order disqualifying Mullin and his law firm from representing the plaintiff in this action. We granted plaintiff's motion for leave to appeal.

Mullin contends that: (1) he never represented Haytaian or the New Jersey Assembly Majority Office; and (2) during the time of his alleged representation of the State, he did not and "temporally" could not have participated in or acquired confidential information about this case.

After thorough consideration of the record and the arguments of counsel, we conclude that under the Rules of Professional Conduct ("RPC") both an actual conflict of interest and an appearance of a conflict of interest are present. The order of disqualification is affirmed.

I. In January 1993, defendant Haytaian was the Vice-Chairman of the New Jersey Legislative Services Commission ("Commission") in addition to his position as the Speaker of the New Jersey General Assembly. The Commission is the governing body of the OLS. The OLS is an agency of the Legislature which assists the Legislature in performing its functions. Haytaian also served as Chairman of the Budget and Personnel Committee ("Committee") of the Commission. The Committee has jurisdiction over OLS personnel matters.

In January 1993, Haytaian received an anonymous letter, allegedly from an OLS employee. According to the letter, a supervisory OLS employee was romantically involved with several women in the office resulting in problems for the other employees. The letter writer charged that there was "favoritism" and a "very hostile atmosphere" in the office. The letter writer stated that "someone may be able to sue the Legislature for allowing this to go on."

Barbara S. Hutcheon ("Hutcheon"), Chief Counsel for the New Jersey Assembly Majority Office, states the following in her certification. Haytaian directed her to retain outside counsel to conduct an investigation regarding the charges in the letter. On February 11, 1993, she contacted Mullin with respect to retaining his services as special counsel. She advised Mullin that, before she could discuss the matter with him, he would have to agree that the conversation would be confidential and protected by the attorney-client privilege; and that all "further discussions" between Mullin and her, "or work performed by [Mullin]" would also be privileged. Mullin agreed and also agreed to conduct the investigation.

She told Mullin that he was to conduct an investigation into allegations of a hostile work environment and sexual harassment which had been directed to the attention of Haytaian, and that Mullin was to render legal advice to the Committee in order to safeguard its interests and the interests of Haytaian and the Legislature.

Thereafter she disclosed to Mullin both Haytaian's concerns and the concerns of the Committee regarding "the existence of the allegations and the need to respond to them." She explained to Mullin that Haytaian, who was not an attorney, had particular concerns. Specifically he was very concerned about the consequences of the allegation that a hostile work environment existed and about his duty and that of the Committee. She further disclosed to Mullin the Speaker's concerns regarding the need for outside counsel and the circumstances leading to the decision to hire outside counsel rather than proceeding in a different manner. Legal fees were also discussed.

By letter dated February 12, 1993, she forwarded to Mullin the anonymous letter and the subsequent correspondence between the Legislature and OLS. She also forwarded a copy of the Legislative Services Act of 1978, which established both the Commission and OLS, and a copy of the OLS staff directory. She thanked Mullin in the letter for "undertaking this matter."

She and Mullin discussed by telephone a number of other confidential matters including the specifics of the allegations and her views about their merits. They also discussed: (1) the identities of the parties involved; (2) the reasons why the Commission was hiring special counsel; (3) the proposed strategy devised by Haytaian and the Committee to deal with the matter including the persons involved in devising the strategy and the alternatives that were considered; and (4) the plans regarding how the Committee should handle such allegations including what steps it should take to prepare to handle such matters in the future.

On March 1, 1993, she spoke with Mullin again by telephone and sought his legal advice as to the legal obligations and duties of Haytaian and the Committee to investigate the anonymous allegations. Mullin advised her that, because of the gravity of the matter and the legal consequences of the failure to act, the Committee and Haytaian should conduct an investigation. She and Mullin also discussed "(1) the steps to be taken in starting the investigation, (2) the manner in which the interviews would be handled, and (3) what was to be disclosed regarding the nature of the investigation."

Mullin asked for written confirmation of his retention. A letter dated March 1, 1993 was sent to Mullin. Haytaian signed the letter in his capacity as Chair of the Committee. Haytaian said in the letter:

This letter will serve to confirm that you have agreed to undertake a matter on behalf of the Budget and Personnel Committee of the Legislative Services Commission, as previously outlined.

Hutcheon again spoke to Mullin to discuss the specific strategies that should be put in place to carry out the investigation, i.e., the timing of the interviews, the identity and number of witnesses to be interviewed, the preparation and the contents of the report and the results of the work.

Haytaian wrote a second letter to Mullin also dated March 1, 1993 in which Haytaian states: "This letter will serve to confirm that you have agreed to undertake the above-referenced matter on behalf of the Budget and Personnel Committee of the Legislative Services Commission on the following terms and conditions." One of the terms and conditions was that "this arrangement will be ratified by the full Legislative Services Commission at their next regularly scheduled meeting."

Haytaian asked Mullin in the letter to:

Please confirm your willingness to undertake the engagement of these terms by signing and returning the enclosed copy of this letter.

I am certain you recognize the importance of this matter and can appreciate the Legislature's desire to apply a prudent manage[ment] approach to its use of special counsel.

The following appears on the bottom of the letter, "I hereby agree to the terms and conditions of the above letter." Mullin signed the bottom of the letter and returned it to Haytaian.

Mullin wrote a "PERSONAL AND CONFIDENTIAL" letter to Haytaian dated March 3, 1993, "RE: Investigation of Harassment Allegation." Mullin stated in the letter that "I will proceed as follows, if it meets with your approval."

Mullin then stated at length how he would proceed. The letter contains the following:

5. The notes I keep will be attorney work product material. Likewise, I will transmit my report in the capacity of attorney to client, so the report too will be privileged and confidential. If the investigation identifies a substantial problem, I will, at your direction, prepare a final report documented with sworn or verbatim statements that will provide a basis for administrative action.

6. I will provide a legal framework as well as a factual framework for my conclusions both in the preliminary phase and the final phase. I will cite relevant case law for purposes of evaluating whether there is any misconduct and whether there is any exposure to the General Assembly as an institution.

Mullin also stated in the letter that, at the conclusion of the investigation, he would "write a preliminary report suggesting whether or not there appears to be unlawful harassment or a polluted work environment." Mullin closed his letter by stating: "Thank you for retaining our firm."

The Commission later decided that special counsel was not needed, and Hutcheon so advised Mullin on March 11, 1993. She asked that he return the documents sent to him previously and he did. She further states:

In all my conversations and dealings with Mr. Mullin, I engaged him as any client would engage his or her attorney. My understanding was that we had an attorney-client relationship. Thus, I was candid in everything I related to Mr. Mullin about the subject of representation. I understood, and believed that Mr. Mullin understood, that all matters we discussed were and remain privileged and confidential.

Mullin states in his certification that he "never represented, as counsel, the State of New Jersey or Garabed Haytaian." He states he never met Hutcheon or Haytaian and that neither he nor his firm have been paid for any professional services in connection with the matter. He states that he had only four phone calls with Hutcheon "of any substance" and did not receive any confidential information relevant to the current suit. Mullin maintains that his contacts with Hutcheon were "preliminary consultations" and that none of the documents support the passing of any confidences. In addition, plaintiff argues in her brief that Mullin could not have been retained without the approval of the Attorney General and the Governor, see N.J.S.A. 52:17A-11 and -13, and the approval was not given.

In January 1996, plaintiff, represented by the Mullin firm, filed this action against the State of New Jersey and Haytaian. Plaintiff alleges in her complaint that from June or July 1994 to October 1995 Haytaian subjected her to "severe and pervasive sexual harassment" and that this "created a hostile, intimidating and offensive working environment."

She also alleges in her complaint that both of the defendants "failed to remediate the sexually hostile work environment"; and that the State of New Jersey is liable under the doctrine of *respondeat superior* because it "delegated to [Haytaian], … the authority to control the work environment, was negligent or reckless, intended the conduct or the consequences, or the conduct violated a non-delegable duty."

Plaintiff contends in her complaint that the acts of the defendants constitute sexual harassment in violation of the Law Against Discrimination, N.J.S.A. 10:5-1 *et seq.* Plaintiff maintains she sustained "severe mental anguish, humiliation, pain and damage to her career and reputation."

Defendants contend that plaintiff's counsel had a press conference to announce the filing of the complaint. Mullin has been quoted in the newspaper as charging that the State has reacted to plaintiff's allegations with "institutional arrogance."

At oral argument on the State's disqualification motion, Mullin admitted that, in connection with the motion, he had disclosed to plaintiff as much of the information in the anonymous letter as was needed "so [plaintiff] could write a certification to help me defend her." He justified the disclosure because plaintiff "has a right to defend herself."

II. Mullin contends that because he was not ultimately retained, an attorney client relationship was not created. We disagree. It is indisputable that Mullin was consulted by Hutcheon on conducting an investigation of sexual harassment of employees in a State office, and that he agreed to undertake the investigation. It is reasonable to conclude that, during his telephone conversations with Hutcheon, which took place over a period of a month, Mullin received confidential information and the views and concerns of Hutcheon and Haytaian on the following subjects: (1) sexual harassment of State employees in OLS and perhaps in State government generally; (2) a hostile work environment in OLS and perhaps in State government generally; and (3) how the OLS and perhaps State government generally were responding or had failed to respond to sexual harassment and a hostile work environment. It is also reasonable to conclude that, during these conversations, Mullin expressed his own views and advice on these subjects.

Under these circumstances, an attorney-client relationship was clearly established. The creation of an attorney-client relationship does not rest on whether the client ultimately decides not to retain the lawyer or whether the lawyer submits a bill. When, as here, the prospective client requests the lawyer to undertake the representation, the lawyer agrees to do so and preliminary conversations are held between the attorney and client regarding the case, then an attorney-client relationship is created. In *Bays v. Theran*, 418 Mass. 685, 639 N.E.2d 720, 723-724 (1994), the court said:

'An attorney-client relationship need not rest on an express contract. An attorney-client relationship may be implied 'when (1) a person seeks advice or assistance from an attorney, (2) the advice or assistance sought pertains to matters within the attorney's professional competence, and (3) the attorney expressly or impliedly agrees to give or actually gives the desired advice or assistance.' ... Such a relationship may be established through preliminary consultations, even though the attorney is never formally retained and the client pays no fee.'

[(Citations omitted).]

[...]

The existence of the attorney-client relationship places upon Mullin the responsibilities set forth in *RPC*. Under *RPC* 1.9 Mullin cannot represent a party in "a substantially related matter" in which that party's interests are "materially adverse to the interests of the former client" nor can he "use information relating to the representation to the disadvantage of the former client" except when permitted by *RPC* 1.6 or when the information becomes generally known. *See RPC* 1.9; *see also Reardon v. Marlayne, Inc.*, 83 N.J. 460, 474, 416 A.2d 852 (1980).

Further:

Where such substantially related matters are present or when a reasonable perception of impropriety exists, the court will assume that confidential information has passed between attorney and former client, notwithstanding the attorney's declarations to the contrary. The presumption of access to and knowledge of confidences may not be rebutted.

[*Reardon, supra*, 83 N.J. at 473, 416 A.2d 852.]

In applying these principles, the need to maintain the highest standards of the profession must be balanced against the rights of litigants to freely choose their attorneys. However, "[o]nly in extraordinary cases should a client's right to counsel of his or her choice outweigh the need to maintain the highest standards of the profession." *Dewey v. R.J. Reynolds Tobacco Co.*, 109 N.J. 201, 220, 536 A.2d 243 (1988); *G.F. Industries v. American Brands*, 245 N.J.Super. 8, 15, 583 A.2d 765 (App. Div.1990).

In *Dewey* the Court said:

We cannot conceive of any situation in which the side-switching attorney or his new firm would be permitted to continue representation if, unlike the situation before us, the attorney had in fact *actually* represented the former client or had acquired confidential information concerning that client's affairs.

[*Dewey, supra*, 109 N.J. at 220, 536 A.2d 243.]

The Court also said:

If the court concludes that the side-switching attorney has not represented the former client, then it must determine whether the attorney whose disqualification is sought has 'acquired information protected by *RPC* 1.6 and *RPC* 1.9(a)(2) that is material to the matter.' *RPC* 1.10(b). The burden at that point shifts to that attorney to show that no protected information has been acquired. *See* ABA Model Rule 1.10 comment, G. Hazard and W. Hodes, *The Law of Lawyering, supra*, at 617. Again, a hearing should be held only when it is indispensable to resolution of the issue.

[*Id.* at 222, 536 A.2d 243.]

New Jersey strictly construes *RPC* 1.9. *See G.F. Industries, supra*, 245 N.J.Super. at 13, 583 A.2d 765. Consequently, "[i]f there be any doubt as to the propriety of an attorney's representation of a client, such doubt must be resolved in favor of disqualification." *Reardon, supra*, 83 N.J. at 471, 416 A.2d 852.

The two matters here are substantially related. Plaintiff charges in her complaint that a hostile work environment exists in her employment by the State of New Jersey. She seeks compensatory and punitive damages against both defendants. If she proves a hostile work environment, then she may be able to recover from the State more than merely "equitable damages." *See Lehmann v. Toys 'R' Us, Inc.*, 132 N.J. 587, 619–620, 626 A.2d 445 (1993).

To prove that the State had a hostile work environment, plaintiff will likely attempt to show that the State was negligent in failing to have in place, and to have publicized and enforced: "anti-harassment policies, effective formal and informal complaint structures, training, and/or monitoring mechanisms." *See Lehmann, supra*, 132 N.J. at 621, 626 A.2d 445.

The Court said in *Lehmann* that an employer may be vicariously liable for compensatory damages "if the employer negligently or recklessly failed to have an explicit policy that bans sexual harassment and that provides an effective procedure for the prompt investigation and remediation of such claims." *Id.* at 624, 626 A.2d 445. An employer may also be liable if the employer knows or should know of sexual harassment and "fails to take effective measures to stop it. . . ." *Id.* at 623, 626 A.2d 445; *see also Payton v. N.J. Turnpike Auth.*, 292 N.J.Super. 36, 46, 678 A.2d 279 (App.Div.1996). The court said in *Payton* that a "core inquiry" is whether the employer had an effective, properly enforced anti-harassment program. *Payton, supra*, 292 N.J.Super. at 46, 678 A.2d 279. The timeliness of an employer's response to an employee's complaint is an important element in determining the effectiveness of an anti-harassment program. *Ibid.* Further, the employer may be liable for punitive damages where the "'wrongdoer's conduct is especially egregious'" and there is "participation by upper management or willful indifference." *Lehmann, supra*, 132 N.J. at 624-625, 626 A.2d 445 (citation omitted).

Mullin's conversations with Hutcheon should be helpful to plaintiff in learning: (a) Whether the State had effective anti-harassment policies, structures, training, monitoring, investigatory and remedial procedures in place in 1993, the year before Haytaian's alleged harassment of plaintiff began; (b) If not then in place, did the State afterwards act promptly to put them in place; (c) Did the State know or should it have known of sexual harassment in State offices and fail to take effective measures to stop it; (d) Was there participation by "upper management" or "willful indifference" regarding especially egregious wrongful conduct, in which case punitive damages may be recovered. Thus, Mullin's confidential conversations with Hutcheon should significantly assist plaintiff in establishing the State's potential liability for not just equitable damages but for compensatory and punitive damages as well. Under these circumstances, Mullin's representation of plaintiff is "materially adverse" to the State. *See RPC* 1.9.

The existence of a conflict is also shown by Mullin's conduct in opposing the disqualification motion. He has admitted that he gave plaintiff confidential information obtained from his former client in order to permit plaintiff to defend herself against the disqualification motion. This was a clear breach of his duty to his former client to preserve the former client's confidences. His conduct shows that, if the interests of his former client and present client conflict, he gives preference to the interests of his present client. This conduct is exactly what the *RPC* were designed to prevent.

Moreover, "the attorney's obligation to preserve the client's confidences" is of "fundamental importance." *Dewey, supra,* 109 N.J. at 217, 536 A.2d 243. As stated in *Reardon:*

The ethical obligation of every attorney to preserve the confidences and secrets of a client is basic to the legitimate practice of law. . . . Persons who seek legal advice must be assured that the secrets and confidences they repose with their attorney will remain with their attorney, and their attorney alone. Preserving the sanctity of confidentiality of a client's disclosures to his attorney will encourage an open atmosphere of trust, thus enabling the attorney to do the best job he can for the client.

[*Reardon, supra,* 83 N.J. at 470, 416 A.2d 852.]

Clearly, an actual conflict of interest is present here.

Aside from the actual conflict, an appearance of impropriety is present. Mullin cannot represent plaintiff if his representation creates an appearance of impropriety, i.e., an "ordinary knowledgeable citizen acquainted with the facts would conclude that the multiple representation poses substantial risk of disservice to either the public interest or the interests of one of the clients." *RPC* 1.7(c)(2); see also *RPC* 1.9(b).

The appearance of impropriety must be something more than a fanciful possibility. It must have a reasonable basis. The conclusion must be based upon a careful analysis of the record. *See McCarthy v. John T. Henderson, Inc.,* 246 N.J.*Super.* 225, 232-233, 587 A.2d 280 (App.Div.1991). "Under any circumstances the disqualification of an attorney in pending litigation does a great disservice to the affected client." *Dewey, supra,* 109 N.J. at 221, 536 A.2d 243.

We have carefully analyzed the record and are satisfied that an appearance of impropriety is present. Mullin was asked by Haytaian on behalf of the State to undertake an investigation of sexual harassment in a State office under Haytaian's oversight. Mullin likely received confidential information as to sexual harassment and the possible existence of a hostile work environment in that office. He also likely received confidential information about the knowledge, concerns and views of Haytaian on those subjects. A few years later Mullin represents a plaintiff in an action charging Haytaian and the State with sexual harassment and creating and permitting a hostile work environment. Such a setting is permeated with the appearance of impropriety. The fact that different State offices are involved is not significant. The "average citizen" is not likely to perceive "any distinctions or appreciate the bureaucratic structuring of responsibility." *See In re Petition for Review of Opinion No. 569,* 103 N.J. 325, 331, 511 A.2d 119 (1986).

Avoiding the appearance of impropriety is extremely important to our legal system. As stated in *Reardon:*

The public display of an attorney representing conflicting interests, regardless of the attorney's good faith, may prevent the prospective client from completely confiding in his attorney. . . . It likewise would tend to erode the public's confidence in the bar.

[*Reardon, supra,* 83 N.J. at 470, 416 A.2d 852 (citation omitted).]

The appearance of impropriety here is clear. Mullin would be disqualified for that reason even if no actual conflict existed.

In sum, the facts show both an actual conflict of interest and an appearance of impropriety. Disqualification must follow in order to uphold the high ethical standards of the New Jersey legal system.

Affirmed.

SAMPLE CASE BRIEF

Herbert V. Haytaian, 292 N.J.Super. 426, 678 A.2d 1183 (1996)

Facts

Defendant, the Speaker of the NJ General Assembly, was accused of sexually harassing the Plaintiff, a co-worker at the Office of Legislative Services ("OLS"). Ironically, the Defendant had previously commissioned an investigation of sexual harassment claims by State employees. The Plaintiff, at the direction of the Defendant, contacted outside counsel to undertake this investigation. The Plaintiff discussed the issues involved in the sexual harassment investigation in telephone conversations and letters with the attorney and gave him access to the files of the OLS. The Plaintiff, Defendant and outside counsel considered this material and communications to be confidential. The OLS later concluded that it was not in need of outside counsel and therefore, terminated its "relationship" with the attorney and requested the return of its documents.

Three years later, the Plaintiff contacted the attorney's firm to represent her in an action against the Defendant and State alleging sexual harassment at the OLS. The State moved to disqualify the attorney due to a conflict of interest and appearance of impropriety.

Issues

Can an attorney who was consulted but never ultimately retained or paid by a first party can later represent a plaintiff in a suit against the first party? When is the attorney-client relationship formed in a "consultation" arrangement? What are the factors to be considered in making that determination?

Holding

The fact of formal employment by signing a retainer letter or receiving payment is not the determinative factor in determining whether the parties have entered into an attorney-client relationship. An attorney-client relationship is created when a party seeks advice or assistance from an attorney and the attorney agrees to render that advice. Further, even if no actual conflict was created the public policy to uphold the integrity of the justice system was compromised due to an "appearance of impropriety" in the later representation.

Reasoning

The court determined that the attorney's access to the confidential information of the Defendant when he consulted with the OLS by and through the Plaintiff created an attorney-client relationship. The Defendant sought the advice of the attorney regarding the identical issue for which the Plaintiff sought to retain the attorney. The OLS and the attorney were ready and willing to enter into a retainer agreement regarding the sexual harassment investigation. The fact that the attorney was not ultimately retained nor paid is of no consequence with regard to his obligation to maintain the confidences of the Defendant, the first party to consult with the attorney in this matter.

> An attorney-client relationship need not rest on an express contract. An attorney-client relationship may be implied "when (1) a person seeks advice or assistance from an attorney, (2) the advice or assistance sought pertains to matters within the attorney's professional competence, and (3) the attorney expressly or impliedly agrees to give or actually gives the desired advice or assistance."

The attorney acquired sensitive information from the Defendant regarding the subject of the lawsuit now against it. This kind of information was transmitted through the letters, telephone calls, and transfer of documents. "Persons who seek legal advice must be assured that the secrets and confidences they repose with their attorney will remain with their attorney, and their attorney alone. Preserving the sanctity of confidentiality of a client's disclosures to his attorney will encourage an open atmosphere of trust, thus enabling the attorney to do the best job he can for the client."

The court argued that even if no actual conflict was found, that the appearance of impropriety would prevent the attorney from taking on the Plaintiff as a subsequent client against this Defendant. "The public display of an attorney representing conflicting interests, regardless of the attorney's good faith, may prevent the prospective client from completely confiding in his attorney…. It likewise would tend to erode the public's confidence in the bar."

The attorney was disqualified from representing the Plaintiff.

Appendix C

NALA MODEL STANDARDS AND GUIDELINES FOR UTILIZATION OF LEGAL ASSISTANTS

Introduction

The purpose of this annotated version of the National Association of Legal Assistants, Inc. Model Standards and Guidelines for the Utilization of Legal Assistants (the "Model," "Standards" and/or the "Guidelines") is to provide references to the existing case law and other authorities where the underlying issues have been considered. The authorities cited will serve as a basis upon which conduct of a legal assistant may be analyzed as proper or improper.

The Guidelines represent a statement of how the legal assistant may function. The Guidelines are not intended to be a comprehensive or exhaustive list of the proper duties of a legal assistant. Rather, they are designed as guides to what may or may not be proper conduct for the legal assistant. In formulating the Guidelines, the reasoning and rules of law in many reported decisions of disciplinary cases and unauthorized practice of law cases have been analyzed and considered. In addition, the provisions of the American Bar Association's Model Rules of Professional Conduct, as well as the ethical promulgations of various state courts and bar associations have been considered in the development of the Guidelines.

These Guidelines form a sound basis for the legal assistant and the supervising attorney to follow. This Model will serve as a comprehensive resource document and as a definitive, well-reasoned guide to those considering voluntary standards and guidelines for legal assistants.

I

Preamble

Proper utilization of the services of legal assistants contributes to the delivery of cost-effective, high-quality legal services. Legal assistants and the legal profession should be assured that measures exist for identifying legal assistants and their role in assisting attorneys in the delivery of legal services. Therefore, the National Association of Legal Assistants, Inc., hereby adopts these Standards and Guidelines as an educational document for the benefit of legal assistants and the legal profession.

Comment

The three most frequently raised questions concerning legal assistants are (1) How do you define a legal assistant; (2) Who is qualified to be identified as a legal assistant; and (3) What duties may a legal assistant perform? The definition adopted in 1984 by the National Association of Legal Assistants answers the first question. The Model sets forth minimum education, training, and experience through standards which will assure that an individual utilizing the title "legal assistant" or "paralegal" has the qualifications to be held out to the legal community and the public in that capacity. The Guidelines identify those acts which the reported cases hold to be proscribed and give examples of services which the legal assistant may perform under the supervision of a licensed attorney.

These Guidelines constitute a statement relating to services performed by legal assistants, as defined herein, as approved by court decisions and other sources of authority. The purpose of the Guidelines is not to place limitations or restrictions on the legal assistant profession. Rather, the Guidelines are intended to outline for the legal profession an acceptable course of conduct. Voluntary recognition and utilization of the Standards and Guidelines will benefit the entire legal profession and the public it serves.

II

Definition

The National Association of Legal Assistants adopted the following definition in 1984:

> *Legal assistants, also known as paralegals, are a distinguishable group of persons who assist attorneys in the delivery of legal services. Through formal education, training, and experience, legal assistants have knowledge and expertise regarding the legal system and substantive and procedural law which qualify them to do work of a legal nature under the supervision of an attorney.*

In recognition of the similarity of the definitions and the need for one clear definition, in July 2001, the NALA membership approved a resolution to adopt the definition of the American Bar Association as well. The ABA definition reads as follows:

> *A legal assistant or paralegal is a person qualified by education, training or work experience who is employed or retained by a lawyer, law office, corporation, governmental agency or other entity who performs specifically delegated substantive legal work for which a lawyer is responsible. (Adopted by the ABA in 1997)*

Comment

These definitions emphasize the knowledge and expertise of legal assistants in substantive and procedural law obtained through education and work experience. They further define the legal assistant or paralegal as a professional working under the supervision of an attorney as distinguished from a non-lawyer who delivers services directly to the public without any intervention or review of work product by an attorney. Such unsupervised services, unless authorized by court or agency rules, constitute the unauthorized practice of law.

Statutes, court rules, case law and bar association documents are additional sources for legal assistant or paralegal definitions. In applying the Standards and Guidelines, it is important to remember that they were developed to apply to the legal assistant as defined herein. Lawyers should refrain from labeling those as paralegals or legal assistants who do not meet the criteria set forth in these definitions and/or the definitions set forth by state rules, guidelines, or bar associations. Labeling secretaries and other administrative staff as legal assistants/paralegals is inaccurate.

For billing purposes, the services of a legal secretary are considered part of overhead costs and are not recoverable in fee awards. However, the courts have held that fees for paralegal services are recoverable as long as they are not clerical functions, such as organizing files, copying documents, checking docket, updating files, checking court dates, and delivering papers. As established in *Missouri v. Jenkins,* 491 U.S.274, 109 S.Ct. 2463, 2471, n.10 (1989) tasks performed by legal assistants must be substantive in nature which, absent the legal assistant, the attorney would perform.

There are also case law and Supreme Court Rules addressing the issue of a disbarred attorney serving in the capacity of a legal assistant.

III
Standards

A legal assistant should meet certain minimum qualifications. The following standards may be used to determine an individual's qualifications as a legal assistant:

1. Successful completion of the Certified Legal Assistant (CLA)/Certified Paralegal (CP) certifying examination of the National Association of Legal Assistants, Inc.;

2. Graduation from an ABA approved program of study for legal assistants;

3. Graduation from a course of study for legal assistants which is institutionally accredited but not ABA approved, and which requires not less than the equivalent of 60 semester hours of classroom study;

4. Graduation from a course of study for legal assistants, other than those set forth in (2) and (3) above, plus not less than six months of in-house training as a legal assistant;

5. A baccalaureate degree in any field, plus not less than six months in-house training as a legal assistant;

6. A minimum of three years of law-related experience under the supervision of an attorney, including at least six months of in-house training as a legal assistant; or

7. Two years of in-house training as a legal assistant.

For purposes of these Standards, "in-house training as a legal assistant" means attorney education of the employee concerning legal assistant duties and these Guidelines. In addition to review and analysis of assignments, the legal assistant should receive a reasonable amount of instruction directly related to the duties and obligations of the legal assistant.

Comment

The Standards set forth suggest minimum qualifications for a legal assistant. These minimum qualifications, as adopted, recognize legal related work backgrounds and formal education backgrounds, both of which provide the legal assistant with a broad base in exposure to and knowledge of the legal profession. This background is necessary to assure the public and the legal profession that the employee identified as a legal assistant is qualified.

The Certified Legal Assistant (CLA) /Certified Paralegal (CP) examination established by NALA in 1976 is a voluntary nationwide certification program for legal assistants. *(CLA and CP are federally registered certification marks owned by NALA.)* The CLA/CP designation is a statement to the legal profession and the public that the legal assistant has met the high levels of knowledge and professionalism required by NALA's certification program. Continuing education requirements, which all certified legal assistants must meet, assure that high standards are maintained. The CLA/CP designation has been recognized as a means of establishing the qualifications of a legal assistant in supreme court rules, state court and bar association standards and utilization guidelines.

Certification through NALA is available to all legal assistants meeting the educational and experience requirements. Certified Legal Assistants may also pursue advanced certification in specialty practice areas through the APC, Advanced Paralegal Certification, credentialing program. Legal assistants/paralegals may also pursue certification based on state laws and procedures in California, Florida, Louisiana and Texas.

IV
Guidelines

These Guidelines relating to standards of performance and professional responsibility are intended to aid legal assistants and attorneys. The ultimate responsibility rests with an attorney who employs legal assistants to educate them with respect to the duties they are assigned and to supervise the manner in which such duties are accomplished.

Comment

In general, a legal assistant is allowed to perform any task which is properly delegated and supervised by an attorney, as long as the attorney is ultimately responsible to the client and assumes complete professional responsibility for the work product.

ABA Model Rules of Professional Conduct, Rule 5.3 provides:

With respect to a non-lawyer employed or retained by or associated with a lawyer:

(a) partner in a law firm shall make reasonable efforts to ensure that the firm has in effect measures giving reasonable assurance that the person's conduct is compatible with the professional obligations of the lawyer;

(b) lawyer having direct supervisory authority over the non-lawyer shall make reasonable efforts to ensure that the person's conduct is compatible with the professional obligations of the lawyer; and

(c) lawyer shall be responsible for conduct of such a person that would be a violation of the rules of professional conduct if engaged in by a lawyer if:

1. the lawyer orders or, with the knowledge of the specific conduct ratifies the conduct involved; or

2. the lawyer is a partner in the law firm in which the person is employed, or has direct supervisory authority over the person, and knows of the conduct at a time when its consequences can be avoided or mitigated but fails to take remedial action.

There are many interesting and complex issues involving the use of legal assistants. In any discussion of the proper role of a legal assistant, attention must be directed to what constitutes the practice of law. Proper delegation to legal assistants is further complicated and confused by the lack of an adequate definition of the practice of law.

Kentucky became the first state to adopt a Paralegal Code by Supreme Court Rule. This Code sets forth certain exclusions to the unauthorized practice of law:

For purposes of this rule, the unauthorized practice of law shall not include any service rendered involving legal knowledge or advice, whether representation, counsel or advocacy, in or out of court, rendered in respect to the acts, duties, obligations, liabilities or business relations of the one requiring services where:

(a) The client understands that the paralegal is not a lawyer;

(b) The lawyer supervises the paralegal in the performance of his or her duties; and

(c) The lawyer remains fully responsible for such representation including all actions taken or not taken in connection therewith by the paralegal to the same extent as if such representation had been furnished entirely by the lawyer and all such actions had been taken or not taken directly by the attorney. Paralegal Code, Ky.S.Ct.R3.700, Sub-Rule 2.

South Dakota Supreme Court Rule 97-25 Utilization Rule a(4) states:

> *The attorney remains responsible for the services performed by the legal assistant to the same extent as though such services had been furnished entirely by the attorney and such actions were those of the attorney.*

Guideline 1

Legal assistants should:

1. Disclose their status as legal assistants at the outset of any professional relationship with a client, other attorneys, a court or administrative agency or personnel thereof, or members of the general public;
2. Preserve the confidences and secrets of all clients; and
3. Understand the attorney's Rules of Professional Responsibility and these Guidelines in order to avoid any action which would involve the attorney in a violation of the Rules, or give the appearance of professional impropriety.

Comment

Routine early disclosure of the paralegal's status when dealing with persons outside the attorney's office is necessary to assure that there will be no misunderstanding as to the responsibilities and role of the legal assistant. Disclosure may be made in any way that avoids confusion. If the person dealing with the legal assistant already knows of his/her status, further disclosure is unnecessary. If at any time in written or oral communication the legal assistant becomes aware that the other person may believe the legal assistant is an attorney, immediate disclosure should be made as to the legal assistant's status.

The attorney should exercise care that the legal assistant preserves and refrains from using any confidence or secrets of a client, and should instruct the legal assistant not to disclose or use any such confidences or secrets.

The legal assistant must take any and all steps necessary to prevent conflicts of interest and fully disclose such conflicts to the supervising attorney. Failure to do so may jeopardize both the attorney's representation of the client and the case itself.

Guidelines for the Utilization of Legal Assistant Services adopted December 3, 1994 by the Washington State Bar Association Board of Governors states:

> *"Guideline 7: A lawyer shall take reasonable measures to prevent conflicts of interest resulting from a legal assistant's other employment or interest insofar as such other employment or interests would present a conflict of interest if it were that of the lawyer."*

In Re Complex Asbestos Litigation, 232 Cal. App. 3d 572 (Cal. 1991), addresses the issue wherein a law firm was disqualified due to possession of attorney-client confidences by a legal assistant employee resulting from previous employment by opposing counsel.

In Oklahoma, in an order issued July 12, 2001, in the matter of *Mark A. Hayes, M.D. v. Central States Orthopedic Specialists, Inc.*, a Tulsa County District Court Judge disqualified a law firm from representation of a client on the basis that an ethical screen was an impermissible device to protect from disclosure confidences gained by a non-lawyer employee while employed by another law firm. In applying the same rules that govern attorneys, the court found that the Rules of Professional Conduct pertaining to confidentiality apply to non-lawyers who leave firms with actual knowledge of material, confidential information and a screening device is not an appropriate alternative to the imputed disqualification of an incoming legal assistant who has moved from one firm to another during ongoing litigation and has actual knowledge of material, confidential information. The decision was appealed and the Oklahoma Supreme Court determined that, under certain circumstances, screening is an appropriate management tool for non-lawyer staff.

In 2004 the Nevada Supreme Court also addressed this issue at the urging of the state's paralegals. The Nevada Supreme Court granted a petition to rescind the Court's 1997 ruling in *Ciaffone v. District Court.* In this case, the court clarified the original ruling, stating "mere opportunity to access confidential information does not merit disqualification." The opinion stated instances in which screening may be appropriate, and listed minimum screening requirements. The opinion also set forth guidelines that a district court may use to determine if screening has been or may be effective. These considerations are:

1. substantiality of the relationship between the former and current matters
2. the time elapsed between the matters
3. size of the firm
4. number of individuals presumed to have confidential information
5. nature of their involvement in the former matter
6. timing and features of any measures taken to reduce the danger of disclosure
7. whether the old firm and the new firm represent adverse parties in the same proceeding rather than in different proceedings.

The ultimate responsibility for compliance with approved standards of professional conduct rests with the supervising attorney. The burden rests upon the attorney who employs a legal assistant to educate the latter with respect to the duties which may be assigned and then to supervise the manner in which the legal assistant carries out such duties. However, this does not relieve the legal assistant from an independent obligation to refrain from illegal conduct. Additionally, and notwithstanding that the Rules are not binding upon non-lawyers, the very nature of a legal assistant's employment imposes an obligation not to engage in conduct which would involve the supervising attorney in a violation of the Rules.

The attorney must make sufficient background investigation of the prior activities and character and integrity of his or her legal assistants.

Further, the attorney must take all measures necessary to avoid and fully disclose conflicts of interest due to other employment or interests. Failure to do so may jeopardize both the attorney's representation of the client and the case itself.

Legal assistant associations strive to maintain the high level of integrity and competence expected of the legal profession and, further, strive to uphold the high standards of ethics.

NALA's Code of Ethics and Professional Responsibility states "A legal assistant's conduct is guided by bar associations' codes of professional responsibility and rules of professional conduct."

Guideline 2

Legal assistants should not:

1. Establish attorney-client relationships; set legal fees; give legal opinions or advice; or represent a client before a court, unless authorized to do so by said court; nor
2. Engage in, encourage, or contribute to any act which could constitute the unauthorized practice of law.

Comment

Case law, court rules, codes of ethics and professional responsibilities, as well as bar ethics opinions now hold which acts can and cannot be performed by a legal assistant.

Generally, the determination of what acts constitute the unauthorized practice of law is made by state supreme courts.

Numerous cases exist relating to the unauthorized practice of law. Courts have gone so far as to prohibit the legal assistant from preparation of divorce kits and assisting in preparation of bankruptcy forms and, more specifically, from providing basic information about procedures and requirements, deciding where information should be placed on forms, and responding to questions from debtors regarding the interpretation or definition of terms.

Cases have identified certain areas in which an attorney has a duty to act, but it is interesting to note that none of these cases state that it is improper for an attorney to have the initial work performed by the legal assistant. This again points out the importance of adequate supervision by the employing attorney.

An attorney can be found to have aided in the unauthorized practice of law when delegating acts which cannot be performed by a legal assistant.

Guideline 3

Legal assistants may perform services for an attorney in the representation of a client, provided:

1. The services performed by the legal assistant do not require the exercise of independent professional legal judgment;

2. The attorney maintains a direct relationship with the client and maintains control of all client matters;

3. The attorney supervises the legal assistant;

4. The attorney remains professionally responsible for all work on behalf of the client, including any actions taken or not taken by the legal assistant in connection therewith; and

5. The services performed supplement, merge with, and become the attorney's work product.

Comment

Paralegals, whether employees or independent contractors, perform services for the attorney in the representation of a client. Attorneys should delegate work to legal assistants commensurate with their knowledge and experience and provide appropriate instruction and supervision concerning the delegated work, as well as ethical acts of their employment. Ultimate responsibility for the work product of a legal assistant rests with the attorney. However, a legal assistant must use discretion and professional judgment and must not render independent legal judgment in place of an attorney.

The work product of a legal assistant is subject to civil rules governing discovery of materials prepared in anticipation of litigation, whether the legal assistant is viewed as an extension of the attorney or as another representative of the party itself. Fed. R.Civ.P. 26 (b) (3) and (5).

Guideline 4

In the supervision of a legal assistant, consideration should be given to

1. Designating work assignments that correspond to the legal assistant's abilities, knowledge, training, and experience;

2. Educating and training the legal assistant with respect to professional responsibility, local rules and practices, and firm policies;

3. Monitoring the work and professional conduct of the legal assistant to ensure that the work is substantively correct and timely performed;

4. Providing continuing education for the legal assistant in substantive matters through courses, institutes, workshops, seminars and in-house training; and

5. Encouraging and supporting membership and active participation in professional organizations.

Comment

Attorneys are responsible for the actions of their employees in both malpractice and disciplinary proceedings. In the vast majority of cases, the courts have not censured attorneys for a particular act delegated to the legal assistant, but rather, have been critical of and imposed sanctions against attorneys for failure to adequately supervise the legal assistant. The attorney's responsibility for supervision of his or her legal assistant must be more than a willingness to accept responsibility and liability for the legal assistant's work. Supervision of a legal assistant must be offered in both the procedural and substantive legal areas. The attorney must delegate work based upon the education, knowledge, and abilities of the legal assistant and must monitor the work product and conduct of the legal assistant to ensure that the work performed is substantively correct and competently performed in a professional manner.

Michigan State Board of Commissioners has adopted Guidelines for the Utilization of Legal Assistants (April 23, 1993). These guidelines, in part, encourage employers to support legal assistant participation in continuing education programs to ensure that the legal assistant remains competent in the fields of practice in which the legal assistant is assigned.

The working relationship between the lawyer and the legal assistant should extend to cooperative efforts on public service activities wherever possible. Participation in pro bono activities is encouraged in ABA Guideline 10.

Guideline 5

Except as otherwise provided by statute, court rule or decision, administrative rule or regulation, or the attorney's rules of professional responsibility, and within the preceding parameters and proscriptions, a legal assistant may perform any function delegated by an attorney, including, but not limited to the following:

1. Conduct client interviews and maintain general contact with the client after the establishment of the attorney-client relationship, so long as the client is aware of the status and function of the legal assistant, and the client contact is under the supervision of the attorney.

2. Locate and interview witnesses, so long as the witnesses are aware of the status and function of the legal assistant.

3. Conduct investigations and statistical and documentary research for review by the attorney.

4. Conduct legal research for review by the attorney.

5. Draft legal documents for review by the attorney.

6. Draft correspondence and pleadings for review by and signature of the attorney.

7. Summarize depositions, interrogatories, and testimony for review by the attorney.

8. Attend executions of wills, real estate closings, depositions, court or administrative hearings, and trials with the attorney.

9. Author and sign letters providing the legal assistant's status is clearly indicated and the correspondence does not contain independent legal opinions or legal advice.

Comment

The United States Supreme Court has recognized the variety of tasks being performed by legal assistants and has noted that use of legal assistants encourages cost-effective delivery of legal services, *Missouri v. Jenkins,* 491 U.S.274, 109 S.Ct. 2463, 2471, n.10 (1989). In *Jenkins,* the court further held that legal assistant time should be included in compensation for attorney fee awards at the market rate of the relevant community to bill legal assistant time.

Courts have held that legal assistant fees are not a part of the overall overhead of a law firm. Legal assistant services are billed separately by attorneys, and decrease litigation expenses. Tasks performed by legal assistants must contain substantive legal work under the direction or supervision of an attorney, such that if the legal assistant were not present, the work would be performed by the attorney.

In *Taylor v. Chubb,* 874 P.2d 806 (Okla. 1994), the Court ruled that attorney fees awarded should include fees for services performed by legal assistants and, further, defined tasks which may be performed by the legal assistant under the supervision of an attorney including, among others: interview clients; draft pleadings and other documents; carry on legal research, both conventional and computer aided; research public records; prepare discovery requests and responses; schedule depositions and prepare notices and subpoenas; summarize depositions and other discovery responses; coordinate and manage document production; locate and interview witnesses; organize pleadings, trial exhibits and other documents; prepare witness and exhibit lists; prepare trial notebooks; prepare for the attendance of witnesses at trial; and assist lawyers at trials.

Except for the specific proscription contained in Guideline 1, the reported cases do not limit the duties which may be performed by a legal assistant under the supervision of the attorney.

An attorney may not split legal fees with a legal assistant, nor pay a legal assistant for the referral of legal business. An attorney may compensate a legal assistant based on the quantity and quality of the legal assistant's work and value of that work to a law practice.

Conclusion

These Standards and Guidelines were developed from generally accepted practices. Each supervising attorney must be aware of the specific rules, decisions and statutes applicable to legal assistants within his/her jurisdiction.

Addendum

For further information, the following cases may be helpful to you:

Duties

Taylor v. Chubb, 874 P.2d 806 (Okla. 1994)

McMackin v. McMackin, 651 A.2d 778 (Del.Fam Ct 1993)

Work Product

Fine v. Facet Aerospace Products Co., 133 F.R.D. 439 (S.D.N.Y. 1990)

Unauthorized Practice of Law

Akron Bar Assn. v. Green, 673 N.E.2d 1307 (Ohio 1997)

In Re Hessinger & Associates, 192 B.R. 211 (N.D. Calif. 1996)

In the Matter of Bright, 171 B.R. 799 (Bkrtcy. E.D. Mich)

Louisiana State Bar Assn v. Edwins, 540 So.2d 294 (La. 1989)

Attorney/Client Privilege

In Re Complex Asbestos Litigation, 232 Cal. App. 3d 572 (Calif. 1991)

Makita Corp. v. U.S., 819 F.Supp. 1099 (CIT 1993)

Conflicts

In Re Complex Asbestos Litigation, 232 Cal. App. 3d 572 (Calif. 1991)

Makita Corp. v. U.S., 819 F.Supp. 1099 (CIT 1993)

Phoenix Founders, Inc., v. Marshall, 887 S.W.2d 831 (Tex. 1994)

Smart Industries v. Superior Court, 876 P.2d 1176 (Ariz. App. Div.1 1994)

Supervision

Matter of Martinez, 754 P.2d 842 (N.M. 1988)

State v. Barrett, 483 P.2d 1106 (Kan. 1971)

Hayes v. Central States Orthopedic Specialists, Inc., 2002 OK 30, 51 P.3d 562

Liebowitz v. Eighth Judicial District Court of Nevada, Nev Sup Ct., No 39683, November 3, 2003 clarified in part and overrules in part Ciaffone v. District Court, 113 Nev 1165, 945. P2d 950 (1997)

Fee Awards

In Re Bicoastal Corp., 121 B.R. 653 (Bktrcy.M.D.Fla. 1990)

In Re Carter, 101 B.R. 170 (Bkrtcy.D.S.D. 1989)

Taylor v. Chubb, 874 P.2d 806 (Okla.1994)

Missouri v. Jenkins, 491 U.S. 274, 109 S.Ct. 2463, 105 L.Ed.2d 229 (1989) 11 U.S.C.A.'330

McMackin v. McMackin, Del.Fam.Ct. 651 A.2d 778 (1993)

Miller v. Alamo, 983 F.2d 856 (8th Cir. 1993)

Stewart v. Sullivan, 810 F.Supp. 1102 (D.Hawaii 1993)

In Re Yankton College, 101 B.R. 151 (Bkrtcy. D.S.D. 1989)

Stacey v. Stroud, 845 F.Supp. 1135 (S.D.W.Va. 1993)

Court Appearances

Louisiana State Bar Assn v. Edwins, 540 So.2d 294 (La. 1989)

In addition to the above referenced cases, you may contact your state bar association for information regarding guidelines for the utilization of legal assistants that may have been adopted by the bar, or ethical opinions concerning the utilization of legal assistants. The following states have adopted a definition of "legal assistant" or "paralegal" either through bar association guidelines, ethical opinions, legislation or case law

Legislation	**Guidelines**	**Bar Associations (Cont.)**
California	Colorado	Massachusetts
Florida	Connecticut	Michigan
Illinois	Georgia	Minnesota
Indiana	Idaho	Missouri
Maine	New York	Nevada
Pennsylvania	Oregon	New Mexico
Supreme Court Cases or Rules	Utah	New Hampshire
	Wisconsin	North Carolina
Kentucky	**Bar Association Activity**	North Dakota
New Hampshire		Ohio
New Mexico		Oregon
North Dakota	Alaska	Rhode Island
Rhode Island	Arizona	South Carolina
South Dakota	Colorado	South Dakota
Virginia	Connecticut	Tennessee
Cases	Florida	Texas
	Illinois	Virginia
Arizona	Iowa	Wisconsin
New Jersey	Kansas	
Oklahoma	Kentucky	
South Carolina		
Washington		

Appendix D

NFPA MODEL CODE OF ETHICS AND PROFESSIONAL RESPONSIBILITY AND GUIDELINES FOR ENFORCEMENT

Preamble

The National Federation of Paralegal Associations, Inc. ("NFPA") is a professional organization comprised of paralegal associations and individual paralegals throughout the United States and Canada. Members of NFPA have varying backgrounds, experiences, education, and job responsibilities that reflect the diversity of the paralegal profession. NFPA promotes the growth, development, and recognition of the paralegal profession as an integral partner in the delivery of legal services.

In May 1993 NFPA adopted its Model Code of Ethics and Professional Responsibility ("Model Code") to delineate the principles for ethics and conduct to which every paralegal should aspire.

Many paralegal associations throughout the United States have endorsed the concept and content of NFPA's Model Code through the adoption of their own ethical codes. In doing so, paralegals have confirmed the profession's commitment to increase the quality and efficiency of legal services, as well as recognized its responsibilities to the public, the legal community, and colleagues.

Paralegals have recognized, and will continue to recognize, that the profession must continue to evolve to enhance their roles in the delivery of legal services. With increased levels of responsibility comes the need to define and enforce mandatory rules of professional conduct. Enforcement of codes of paralegal conduct is a logical and necessary step to enhance and ensure the confidence of the legal community and the public in the integrity and professional responsibility of paralegals.

In April 1997 NFPA adopted the Model Disciplinary Rules ("Model Rules") to make possible the enforcement of the Canons and Ethical Considerations contained in the NFPA Model Code. A concurrent determination was made that the Model Code of Ethics and Professional Responsibility, formerly aspirational in nature, should be recognized as setting forth the enforceable obligations of all paralegals.

The Model Code and Model Rules offer a framework for professional discipline, either voluntarily or through formal regulatory programs.

§1.	NFPA MODEL DISCIPLINARY RULES AND ETHICAL CONSIDERATIONS
1.1	**A PARALEGAL SHALL ACHIEVE AND MAINTAIN A HIGH LEVEL OF COMPETENCE**
	Ethical Considerations
EC 1.1(a)	A paralegal shall achieve competency through education, training, and work experience.
EC 1.1(b)	A paralegal shall aspire to participate in a minimum of twelve (12) hours of continuing legal education, to include at least one (1) hour of ethics education, every two (2) years in order to remain current on developments in the law.
EC 1.1(c)	A paralegal shall perform all assignments promptly and efficiently.
1.2	**A PARALEGAL SHALL MAINTAIN A HIGH LEVEL OF PERSONAL AND PROFESSIONAL INTEGRITY**
	Ethical Considerations
EC 1.2(a)	A paralegal shall not engage in any ex parte communications involving the courts or any other adjudicatory body in an attempt to exert undue influence or to obtain advantage or the benefit of only one party.
EC 1.2(b)	A paralegal shall not communicate, or cause another to communicate, with a party the paralegal knows to be represented by a lawyer in a pending matter without the prior consent of the lawyer representing such other party.
EC 1.2(c)	A paralegal shall ensure that all timekeeping and billing records prepared by the paralegal are thorough, accurate, honest, and complete.
EC 1.2(d)	A paralegal shall not knowingly engage in fraudulent billing practices. Such practices may include, but are not limited to: inflation of hours billed to a client or employer; misrepresentation of the nature of tasks performed; and/or submission of fraudulent expense and disbursement documentation.
EC 1.2(e)	A paralegal shall be scrupulous, thorough and honest in the identification and maintenance of all funds, securities, and other assets of a client and shall provide accurate accounting as appropriate.
EC 1.2(f)	A paralegal shall advise the proper authority of non-confidential knowledge of any dishonest or fraudulent acts by any person pertaining to the handling of the funds, securities or other assets of a client. The authority to whom the report is made shall depend on the nature and circumstances of the possible misconduct, (e.g., ethics committees of law firms, corporations and/or paralegal associations, local or state bar associations, local prosecutors, administrative agencies, etc.). Failure to report such knowledge is in itself misconduct and shall be treated as such under these rules.

1.3	**A PARALEGAL SHALL MAINTAIN A HIGH STANDARD OF PROFESSIONAL CONDUCT**
	Ethical Considerations
EC 1.3(a)	A paralegal shall refrain from engaging in any conduct that offends the dignity and decorum of proceedings before a court or other adjudicatory body and shall be respectful of all rules and procedures.
EC 1.3(b)	A paralegal shall avoid impropriety and the appearance of impropriety and shall not engage in any conduct that would adversely affect his/her fitness to practice. Such conduct may include, but is not limited to: violence, dishonesty, interference with the administration of justice, and/or abuse of a professional position or public office.
EC 1.3(c)	Should a paralegal's fitness to practice be compromised by physical or mental illness, causing that paralegal to commit an act that is in direct violation of the Model Code/Model Rules and/or the rules and/or laws governing the jurisdiction in which the paralegal practices, that paralegal may be protected from sanction upon review of the nature and circumstances of that illness.
EC 1.3(d)	A paralegal shall advise the proper authority of non-confidential knowledge of any action of another legal professional that clearly demonstrates fraud, deceit, dishonesty, or misrepresentation. The authority to whom the report is made shall depend on the nature and circumstances of the possible misconduct, (e.g., ethics committees of law firms, corporations and/or paralegal associations, local or state bar associations, local prosecutors, administrative agencies, etc.). Failure to report such knowledge is in itself misconduct and shall be treated as such under these rules.
EC 1.3(e)	A paralegal shall not knowingly assist any individual with the commission of an act that is in direct violation of the Model Code/Model Rules and/or the rules and/or laws governing the jurisdiction in which the paralegal practices.
EC 1.3(f)	If a paralegal possesses knowledge of future criminal activity, that knowledge must be reported to the appropriate authority immediately.
1.4	**A PARALEGAL SHALL SERVE THE PUBLIC INTEREST BY CONTRIBUTING TO THE IMPROVEMENT OF THE LEGAL SYSTEM AND DELIVERY OF QUALITY LEGAL SERVICES, INCLUDING PRO BONO PUBLICO SERVICES**
	Ethical Considerations
EC 1.4(a)	A paralegal shall be sensitive to the legal needs of the public and shall promote the development and implementation of programs that address those needs.

EC 1.4(b)	A paralegal shall support efforts to improve the legal system and access thereto and shall assist in making changes.
EC 1.4(c)	A paralegal shall support and participate in the delivery of Pro Bono Publico services directed toward implementing and improving access to justice, the law, the legal system or the paralegal and legal professions.
EC 1.4(d)	A paralegal should aspire annually to contribute twenty-four (24) hours of Pro Bono Publico services under the supervision of an attorney or as authorized by administrative, statutory or court authority to: 1. persons of limited means; or 2. charitable, religious, civic, community, governmental and educational organizations in matters that are designed primarily to address the legal needs of persons with limited means; or 3. individuals, groups or organizations seeking to secure or protect civil rights, civil liberties or public rights. The twenty-four (24) hours of Pro Bono Publico services contributed annually by a paralegal may consist of such services as detailed in this EC-1.4(d), and/or administrative matters designed to develop and implement the attainment of this aspiration as detailed above in EC-1.4(a) B (c), or any combination of the two.
1.5	**A PARALEGAL SHALL PRESERVE ALL CONFIDENTIAL INFORMATION PROVIDED BY THE CLIENT OR ACQUIRED FROM OTHER SOURCES BEFORE, DURING, AND AFTER THE COURSE OF THE PROFESSIONAL RELATIONSHIP**
	Ethical Considerations
EC 1.5(a)	A paralegal shall be aware of and abide by all legal authority governing confidential information in the jurisdiction in which the paralegal practices.
EC 1.5(b)	A paralegal shall not use confidential information to the disadvantage of the client.
EC 1.5(c)	A paralegal shall not use confidential information to the advantage of the paralegal or of a third person.
EC 1.5(d)	A paralegal may reveal confidential information only after full disclosure and with the client's written consent; or, when required by law or court order; or, when necessary to prevent the client from committing an act that could result in death or serious bodily harm.
EC 1.5(e)	A paralegal shall keep those individuals responsible for the legal representation of a client fully informed of any confidential information the paralegal may have pertaining to that client.
EC 1.5(f)	A paralegal shall not engage in any indiscreet communications concerning clients.

1.6	**A PARALEGAL SHALL AVOID CONFLICTS OF INTEREST AND SHALL DISCLOSE ANY POSSIBLE CONFLICT TO THE EMPLOYER OR CLIENT, AS WELL AS TO THE PROSPECTIVE EMPLOYERS OR CLIENTS**
	Ethical Considerations
EC 1.6(a)	A paralegal shall act within the bounds of the law, solely for the benefit of the client, and shall be free of compromising influences and loyalties. Neither the paralegal's personal or business interest, nor those of other clients or third persons, should compromise the paralegal's professional judgment and loyalty to the client.
EC 1.6(b)	A paralegal shall avoid conflicts of interest that may arise from previous assignments, whether for a present or past employer or client.
EC 1.6(c)	A paralegal shall avoid conflicts of interest that may arise from family relationships and from personal and business interests.
EC 1.6(d)	In order to be able to determine whether an actual or potential conflict of interest exists a paralegal shall create and maintain an effective record-keeping system that identifies clients, matters, and parties with which the paralegal has worked.
EC 1.6(e)	A paralegal shall reveal sufficient non-confidential information about a client or former client to reasonably ascertain if an actual or potential conflict of interest exists.
EC 1.6(f)	A paralegal shall not participate in or conduct work on any matter where a conflict of interest has been identified.
EC 1.6(g)	In matters where a conflict of interest has been identified and the client consents to continued representation, a paralegal shall comply fully with the implementation and maintenance of an Ethical Wall.

1.7	**A PARALEGAL'S TITLE SHALL BE FULLY DISCLOSED**
	Ethical Considerations
EC 1.7(a)	A paralegal's title shall clearly indicate the individual's status and shall be disclosed in all business and professional communications to avoid misunderstandings and misconceptions about the paralegal's role and responsibilities.
EC 1.7(b)	A paralegal's title shall be included if the paralegal's name appears on business cards, letterhead, brochures, directories, and advertisements.
EC 1.7(c)	A paralegal shall not use letterhead, business cards, or other promotional materials to create a fraudulent impression of his/her status or ability to practice in the jurisdiction in which the paralegal practices.
EC 1.7(d)	A paralegal shall not practice under color of any record, diploma, or certificate that has been illegally or fraudulently obtained or issued or which is misrepresentative in any way.

EC 1.7(e)	A paralegal shall not participate in the creation, issuance, or dissemination of fraudulent records, diplomas, or certificates.
1.8	**A PARALEGAL SHALL NOT ENGAGE IN THE UNAUTHORIZED PRACTICE OF LAW**
	Ethical Considerations
EC 1.8(a)	A paralegal shall comply with the applicable legal authority governing the unauthorized practice of law in the jurisdiction in which the paralegal practices.
§2.	**NFPA GUIDELINES FOR THE ENFORCEMENT OF THE MODEL CODE OF ETHICS AND PROFESSIONAL RESPONSIBILITY**
2.1	**BASIS FOR DISCIPLINE**
EC 2.1(a)	Disciplinary investigations and proceedings brought under authority of the Rules shall be conducted in accord with obligations imposed on the paralegal professional by the Model Code of Ethics and Professional Responsibility.
2.2	**STRUCTURE OF DISCIPLINARY COMMITTEE**
EC 2.2(a)	The Disciplinary Committee ("Committee") shall be made up of nine (9) members including the Chair.
EC 2.2(b)	Each member of the Committee, including any temporary replacement members, shall have demonstrated working knowledge of ethics/professional responsibility-related issues and activities.
EC 2.2(c)	The Committee shall represent a cross-section of practice areas and work experience. The following recommendations are made regarding the members of the Committee. 1) At least one paralegal with one to three years of law-related work experience. 2) At least one paralegal with five to seven years of law-related work experience. 3) At least one paralegal with over ten years of law-related work experience. 4) One paralegal educator with five to seven years of work experience; preferably in the area of ethics/professional responsibility. 5) One paralegal manager. 6) One lawyer with five to seven years of law-related work experience. 7) One lay member.

EC 2.2(d)	The Chair of the Committee shall be appointed within thirty (30) days of its members' induction. The Chair shall have no fewer than ten (10) years of law-related work experience.
EC 2.2(e)	The terms of all members of the Committee shall be staggered. Of those members initially appointed, a simple majority plus one shall be appointed to a term of one year, and the remaining members shall be appointed to a term of two years. Thereafter, all members of the Committee shall be appointed to terms of two years.
EC 2.2(f)	If for any reason the terms of a majority of the Committee will expire at the same time, members may be appointed to terms of one year to maintain continuity of the Committee.
EC 2.2(g)	The Committee shall organize from its members a three-tiered structure to investigate, prosecute and/or adjudicate charges of misconduct. The members shall be rotated among the tiers.

2.3	**OPERATION OF COMMITTEE**
EC 2.3(a)	The Committee shall meet on an as-needed basis to discuss, investigate, and/or adjudicate alleged violations of the Model Code/Model Rules.
EC 2.3(b)	A majority of the members of the Committee present at a meeting shall constitute a quorum.
EC 2.3(c)	A Recording Secretary shall be designated to maintain complete and accurate minutes of all Committee meetings. All such minutes shall be kept confidential until a decision has been made that the matter will be set for hearing as set forth in Section 6.1 below.
EC 2.3(d)	If any member of the Committee has a conflict of interest with the Charging Party, the Responding Party, or the allegations of misconduct, that member shall not take part in any hearing or deliberations concerning those allegations. If the absence of that member creates a lack of a quorum for the Committee, then a temporary replacement for the member shall be appointed.
EC 2.3(e)	Either the Charging Party or the Responding Party may request that, for good cause shown, any member of the Committee not participate in a hearing or deliberation. All such requests shall be honored. If the absence of a Committee member under those circumstances creates a lack of a quorum for the Committee, then a temporary replacement for that member shall be appointed.
EC 2.3(f)	All discussions and correspondence of the Committee shall be kept confidential until a decision has been made that the matter will be set for hearing as set forth in Section 6.1 below.
EC 2.3(g)	All correspondence from the Committee to the Responding Party regarding any charge of misconduct and any decisions made regarding the charge shall be mailed certified mail, return receipt requested, to the Responding Party's last known address and shall be clearly marked with a "Confidential" designation.

2.4	**PROCEDURE FOR THE REPORTING OF ALLEGED VIOLATIONS OF THE MODEL CODE/DISCIPLINARY RULES**
EC 2.4(a)	An individual or entity in possession of non-confidential knowledge or information concerning possible instances of misconduct shall make a confidential written report to the Committee within thirty (30) days of obtaining same. This report shall include all details of the alleged misconduct.
EC 2.4(b)	The Committee so notified shall inform the Responding Party of the allegation(s) of misconduct no later than ten (10) business days after receiving the confidential written report from the Charging Party.
EC 2.4(c)	Notification to the Responding Party shall include the identity of the Charging Party, unless, for good cause shown, the Charging Party requests anonymity.
EC 2.4(d)	The Responding Party shall reply to the allegations within ten (10) business days of notification.
2.5	**PROCEDURE FOR THE INVESTIGATION OF A CHARGE OF MISCONDUCT**
EC 2.5(a)	Upon receipt of a Charge of Misconduct ("Charge"), or on its own initiative, the Committee shall initiate an investigation.
EC 2.5(b)	If, upon initial or preliminary review, the Committee makes a determination that the charges are either without basis in fact or, if proven, would not constitute professional misconduct, the Committee shall dismiss the allegations of misconduct. If such determination of dismissal cannot be made, a formal investigation shall be initiated.
EC 2.5(c)	Upon the decision to conduct a formal investigation, the Committee shall: 1) mail to the Charging and Responding Parties within three (3) business days of that decision notice of the commencement of a formal investigation. That notification shall be in writing and shall contain a complete explanation of all Charge(s), as well as the reasons for a formal investigation and shall cite the applicable codes and rules; 2) allow the Responding Party thirty (30) days to prepare and submit a confidential response to the Committee, which response shall address each charge specifically and shall be in writing; and 3) upon receipt of the response to the notification, have thirty (30) days to investigate the Charge(s). If an extension of time is deemed necessary, that extension shall not exceed ninety (90) days.
EC 2.5(d)	Upon conclusion of the investigation, the Committee may: 1) dismiss the Charge upon the finding that it has no basis in fact; 2) dismiss the Charge upon the finding that, if proven, the Charge would not constitute Misconduct; 3) refer the matter for hearing by the Tribunal; or 4) in the case of criminal activity, refer the Charge(s) and all investigation results to the appropriate authority.

2.6	**PROCEDURE FOR A MISCONDUCT HEARING BEFORE A TRIBUNAL**
EC 2.6(a)	Upon the decision by the Committee that a matter should be heard, all parties shall be notified and a hearing date shall be set. The hearing shall take place no more than thirty (30) days from the conclusion of the formal investigation.
EC 2.6(b)	The Responding Party shall have the right to counsel. The parties and the Tribunal shall have the right to call any witnesses and introduce any documentation that they believe will lead to the fair and reasonable resolution of the matter.
EC 2.6(c)	Upon completion of the hearing, the Tribunal shall deliberate and present a written decision to the parties in accordance with procedures as set forth by the Tribunal.
EC 2.6(d)	Notice of the decision of the Tribunal shall be appropriately published.
2.7	**SANCTIONS**
EC 2.7(a)	Upon a finding of the Tribunal that misconduct has occurred, any of the following sanctions, or others as may be deemed appropriate, may be imposed upon the Responding Party, either singularly or in combination: 1) letter of reprimand to the Responding Party; counseling; 2) attendance at an ethics course approved by the Tribunal; probation; 3) suspension of license/authority to practice; revocation of license/authority to practice; 4) imposition of a fine; assessment of costs; or 5) in the instance of criminal activity, referral to the appropriate authority.
EC 2.7(b)	Upon the expiration of any period of probation, suspension, or revocation, the Responding Party may make application for reinstatement. With the application for reinstatement, the Responding Party must show proof of having complied with all aspects of the sanctions imposed by the Tribunal.
2.8	**APPELLATE PROCEDURES**
EC 2.8(a)	The parties shall have the right to appeal the decision of the Tribunal in accordance with the procedure as set forth by the Tribunal.

Definitions

"**Appellate Body**" means a body established to adjudicate an appeal to any decision made by a Tribunal or other decision-making body with respect to formally heard Charges of Misconduct.

"**Charge of Misconduct**" means a written submission by any individual or entity to an ethics committee, paralegal association, bar association, law enforcement agency, judicial body, government agency, or other appropriate body or entity, that sets forth non-confidential information regarding any instance of alleged misconduct by an individual paralegal or paralegal entity.

"Charging Party" means any individual or entity who submits a Charge of Misconduct against an individual paralegal or paralegal entity.

"Competency" means the demonstration of: diligence, education, skill, and mental, emotional, and physical fitness reasonably necessary for the performance of paralegal services.

"Confidential Information" means information relating to a client, whatever its source, that is not public knowledge nor available to the public. ("Non-Confidential Information" would generally include the name of the client and the identity of the matter for which the paralegal provided services.)

"Disciplinary Hearing" means the confidential proceeding conducted by a committee or other designated body or entity concerning any instance of alleged misconduct by an individual paralegal or paralegal entity.

"Disciplinary Committee" means any committee that has been established by an entity such as a paralegal association, bar association, judicial body, or government agency to: (a) identify, define and investigate general ethical considerations and concerns with respect to paralegal practice; (b) administer and enforce the Model Code and Model Rules and; (c) discipline any individual paralegal or paralegal entity found to be in violation of same.

"Disclose" means communication of information reasonably sufficient to permit identification of the significance of the matter in question.

"Ethical Wall" means the screening method implemented in order to protect a client from a conflict of interest. An Ethical Wall generally includes, but is not limited to, the following elements: (1) prohibit the paralegal from having any connection with the matter; (2) ban discussions with or the transfer of documents to or from the paralegal; (3) restrict access to files; and (4) educate all members of the firm, corporation, or entity as to the separation of the paralegal (both organizationally and physically) from the pending matter. For more information regarding the Ethical Wall, see the NFPA publication entitled "The Ethical Wall—Its Application to Paralegals."

"Ex parte" means actions or communications conducted at the instance and for the benefit of one party only, and without notice to, or contestation by, any person adversely interested.

"Investigation" means the investigation of any charge(s) of misconduct filed against an individual paralegal or paralegal entity by a Committee.

"Letter of Reprimand" means a written notice of formal censure or severe reproof administered to an individual paralegal or paralegal entity for unethical or improper conduct.

"Misconduct" means the knowing or unknowing commission of an act that is in direct violation of those Canons and Ethical Considerations of any and all applicable codes and/or rules of conduct.

"Paralegal" is synonymous with "Legal Assistant" and is defined as a person qualified through education, training, or work experience to perform substantive legal work that requires knowledge of legal concepts and is customarily, but not exclusively performed by a lawyer. This person may be retained or employed by a lawyer, law office, governmental agency, or other entity or may be authorized by administrative, statutory, or court authority to perform this work.

"Pro Bono Publico" means providing or assisting to provide quality legal services in order to enhance access to justice for persons of limited means; charitable, religious, civic, community, governmental and educational organizations in matters that are designed primarily to address the legal needs of persons with limited means; or individuals, groups or organizations seeking to secure or protect civil rights, civil liberties or public rights.

"Proper Authority" means the local paralegal association, the local or state bar association, Committee(s) of the local paralegal or bar association(s), local prosecutor, administrative agency, or other tribunal empowered to investigate or act upon an instance of alleged misconduct.

"Responding Party" means an individual paralegal or paralegal entity against whom a Charge of Misconduct has been submitted.

"Revocation" means the recision of the license, certificate or other authority to practice of an individual paralegal or paralegal entity found in violation of those Canons and Ethical Considerations of any and all applicable codes and/or rules of conduct.

"Suspension" means the suspension of the license, certificate or other authority to practice of an individual paralegal or paralegal entity found in violation of those Canons and Ethical Considerations of any and all applicable codes and/or rules of conduct.

"Tribunal" means the body designated to adjudicate allegations of misconduct.

Source: Reprinted by permission from The National Federation of Paralegal, Associations, Inc., www.paralegals.org.

Glossary

A

access to justice The full opportunity of all persons to use all the legal resources available to the public, without regard for their ability to pay or knowledge of the legal system or experience in dealing with lawyers.

acquisition of clients The approaching of people in need of legal services and the obtaining of their consent to represent them in a legal matter; this may be done only by an attorney.

adversarial model The American system of retaining separate independent and oppositional counsel to engage in zealous representation of individual clients.

adverse Characteristic of a position or interest that is inconsistent or opposite with another, so that they cannot be reconciled without compromising an important element of one or both positions or interests.

advocacy Engage in the profession of taking on clients to actively support their cause.

"ambulance chasers" A derogatory term used to describe attorneys that make direct in-person or mailed solicitation to injured persons very shortly after the accident, so that they seem to be waiting at the ambulance door for them.

appearance of impropriety A standard used to evaluate whether actions which are not strictly prohibited are still deemed unethical, because an ordinary citizen would suspect them as inappropriate behavior for a legal professional.

attorney-client privilege The legal relationship established between attorney and client allowing for free exchange of information without fear of disclosure.

attorney-client relationship The legal relationship established between attorney and client. This relationship has many protective and confidential aspects and is unique in the legal context.

B

balance of authority The balance between the right of the client to choose the desired outcome of the case and the obligation of the attorney to determine the best legal course to obtain that result.

billable hour Time (totaling one hour) spent on a client's matter for which the client is responsible to pay, as the attorney's effort relates to and benefits the client's matter.

boutique firm An attorney or firm that handles only certain types of legal matters that are usually highly detailed and related to each other and that require specialized knowledge and experience.

C

certificated Describing a person who has completed a certain course of study and thus earned a certificate from the issuing institution.

certification The recognition of the attainment of a degree of academic and practical knowledge by a professional.

certified attorney An attorney who has been acknowledged to have specialized and demonstrated knowledge in a particular area of law by a bar-recognized legal association.

certified specialist An attorney who has applied for and obtained state or national bar acknowledgement of extensive knowledge and expertise in an area of law through demonstrable evidence of testing scores and experience.

commercial speech A category of expression that has only limited protection under the United States Constitution because its purpose is not the dissemination of an idea, but rather the garnering of monetary rewards through commerce.

commingling A term for mixing a client's funds with the attorney's personal funds without permission; an ethical violation.

communication The obligation of an attorney to keep his client informed of the status of the matter, and to respond promptly to the client's requests for information in a candid manner.

competence The ability and possession of expertise and skill in a field that is necessary to do the job.

confidences Any communication from the client to the attorney which the client intends to be kept private from everyone else.

conflict check A procedure to verify potential adverse interests before accepting a new client.

conflict of interest Clash between private and professional interests or competing professional interests that makes impartiality difficult and creates an unfair advantage.

conservatorship *See* guardian.

constructive discharge An attorney's cessation of the performance of legal work due to the client's insistence on pursuing unethical or imprudent means to achieve its desired result in the legal matter.

contingency fees The attorney's fee calculated as a percentage of the final award in a civil case.

continuing legal education (CLE) Continued legal competence and skills training required of practicing professionals.

controlling jurisdiction The legal system in which the tribunal sits whose higher courts' opinions are binding authority upon the lower courts.

covenant not to compete An employment clause that prohibits an employee from leaving his job and going to work for a competitor for a specified period of time in a particular area.

customary fee A rate generally charged in a given locality by lawyers of the same level of expertise and area of practice.

D

diligence Acting within the legally prescribed time or promptly responding to a client's or party's request.

diminished capacity A client's incapability to understand legal ramifications of her decisions, as a result of immaturity, or of some mental or physical infirmity.

disbarment Temporary suspension or permanent revocation of an individual's license to practice law.

disclaimer A term which limits claim or denial.

disinterested lawyer The standard to which potentially affected attorneys must measure their actions. An attorney must detach himself from any personal interest in the matter and act accordingly.

double-billing Charging two or more clients for the same services and/or same time period.

due process Ensures the appropriateness and adequacy of government action in circumstances infringing on fundamental individual rights.

duty of confidentiality An absolute prohibition against the attorney's disclosure of any information gained about his client, regardless of the source of that information. It is much broader than the matter covered under the attorney-client privilege.

E

ethical complaint A report of suspected unethical activity on the part of an attorney, made by that attorney's client to the ethical committee of the state bar association. The committee may investigate to determine if an ethics violation has, indeed, occurred.

ethical sanctions Methods of disciplining attorneys who commit a breach of the ethical code of conduct.

Ethical Wall A set of internal office procedures by which a law firm can isolate or screen attorneys and paralegals who present a conflict with matters in the office and can prevent the disclosure of clients' confidential information.

ex parte A legal professional's communiucation regarding the substance of the matter without opposing counsel present.

F

fiduciary One who owes to another the duties of good faith, trust, confidence, and candor.

fiduciary relationship A relationship based on close personal trust that one party is looking out for the other's best interests.

"fishing expedition" A request by an opposing party for potentially damaging information from the attorney, on the premise that the opposing party needs it to prevent harm, but without specific evidence of an actual threat of harm.

freelance paralegal Paralegal in business for him- or herself who contracts with an attorney or law firm to perform specific tasks for a designated fee.

frivolous Having neither factual merit nor legal purpose.

G

gatekeeping function A restriction of entry into a profession to ensure that certain standards are met prior to admission. It serves to protect both the professionals inside and the public at large against unqualified persons performing the tasks associated with that profession.

general practice firm An attorney or firm that will handle almost any type of legal matter that is presented by clients.

good faith An attorney must reasonably believe in the validity of the claim(s) asserted and present them for a proper purpose for adjudication by the tribunal.

guardianship/conservatorship An appointed third party who has the legal authority and fiduciary duty to care for a diminished person and/or his property. Also known as a *conservator.*

I

imputed conflict An entire law office can be prohibited from representing a client with whom an attorney or paralegal has an individual conflict. The conflict is attributed to the whole firm.

in camera inspection A proceeding in the judge's chambers during which the judge can examine the proffered evidence outside of the jury's presence to determine the necessity of disclosure of the confidential information.

independent legal judgment The attorney's determination of the best course to pursue to obtain the client's objectives, based upon the attorney's obligation to rely upon her own professional assessment of the legal situation, without undue influences from outside forces.

independent paralegals See legal document preparer (LDP)

informed consent Permission that is voluntarily given after having received and understood all relevant information relating to the situation's risks and alternatives.

K

knowing Believing with a reasonable and substantial probability (it is not necessary to be absolutely certain).

knowledge The near certainty of belief that a fact is most likely true.

L

leading question The phrasing of an interrogatory so as to suggest the desired answer.

legal advice Generally, the provision of guidance regarding the meaning or application of the law or the rendering of an opinion on the possible outcome of a legal matter.

legal documents Papers that are filed in furtherance of a court action or secure a legal right or grant legal recourse to a party.

legal document preparer (LDP) A legal professional who offers her services directly to the public. LDPs generally restrict their activities to assisting in preparing legal forms based upon the information obtained from their clients; they do not and cannot render legal advice or represent their clients in legal matters. In jurisdictions where there aren't separate formal designations for the profession of LDP, they are generically called "independent paralegals."

legal malpractice A civil cause of action wherein a client may sue his attorney for failures in the representation that caused the client actual harm. The client may be entitled to money damages and possibly punitive damages in excess of actual pecuniary loss if the attorney's conduct was egregious.

licensure The requirement of governmental approval before a person can practice a specific profession.

lodestar calculation A mere guidepost for determining the amount of fee to be charged, by multiplying the time to be spent on the task by the attorney's hourly rate.

M

malfeasance A wrongful, unethical, or tortious act.

management of the law practice Oversight of the purely business aspects of the law firm, as well as ensuring that the protocols conform to the ethical requirements placed upon the attorneys and support staff.

mandatory withdrawal Withdrawal of an attorney from representation where that representation will result in a violation of ethical rules, or the attorney is materially impaired, or the attorney is discharged.

material limitation The inability to render neutral and unbiased services or advice.

materiality Having a reasonable and recognizable importance in the process of evaluating a situation, such that its omission might affect the determination of fact or law.

materially misleading Characterized by false information upon which a member of the intended audience would rely in making a decision.

misappropriation The unlawful and unethical taking of a client's property for the lawyer's own use, regardless of intent or duration of time the property is kept.

mitigation The lessening of the harmful effects of a course of action.

moral turpitude An act or behavior that gravely violates the sentiment or accepted standard of the community.

multijurisdictional practice The practice of law by an attorney outside the state in which that attorney was originally licensed, because the clients' interests are interstate or national in scale.

N

negligent misconduct Acts that are not done intentionally, but that do not comply with the standard of ordinary care and thought needed to fulfill the relevant ethical obligations.

negotiation and settlement The alternative means to terminate a legal matter rather than full trial on the merits. As the settlement has the same force as a final adjudication, an attorney must perform the tasks associated with it.

O

overreaching Taking unfair commercial advantage of another by going beyond normal and reasonable means to obtain the desired result.

P

paralegal manager A position in a law firm held by a paralegal who generally recruits, interviews, and hires new paralegals and helps to train them.

paraprofessional A person with the appropriate education, knowledge, and training to perform specialized work under the supervision of another professional, who has the ultimate responsibility for the collaborative work.

perjury The willful assertion as to a matter of fact, opinion, belief, or knowledge, made by a witness in a judicial proceeding as part of his/her evidence, either upon oath or in any form allowed by law to be substituted for an oath, whether such evidence is given in open court, in an affidavit, or otherwise, such assertion being material to the issue or point of inquiry and known to such witness to be false.

permissive withdrawal The attorney's chosen termination of representation of the client in certain circumstances that comply with the attorney's ethical obligations to the client.

permitted disclosure In certain circumstances, the right of an attorney to reveal certain information learned from his client, even without the client's consent.

pervasive neglect Continued disregard for matters pending in the law office, deadlines, and other obligations that seriously impacts clients' interests and indicates an utter lack of diligence.

practical skills The ability to put theory into practice by performing the tasks necessary to achieve a desired result.

private reprimand The minimum censure for an attorney who commits an ethical violation; the attorney is informed privately about a potential violation, but no official entry is made.

pro bono publico Literally, "for the public good." Describing legal services provided to the public by legal professionals voluntarily and without payment.

probation A court-imposed criminal sentence that, subject to stated conditions, releases a convicted person into the community instead of sending the criminal to prison. Or, in the case of discipline of an attorney for unethical conduct, the monitoring of an attorney's conduct for compliance with ethical rules, sometimes accompanied by additional requirements.

proprietary interest A definite financial stake in the outcome of a case or matter which may influence the attorney to take a path that is not in the best interest of his client, but, rather, will result in a greater monetary recovery for the attorney.

prospective client Any person who knowingly seeks the advice of an attorney relating to legal matters.

public reprimand A published censure of an attorney for an ethical violation.

R

ratification The adoption, as one's own, of the words or actions of another person.

reasonable fee A charge for legal services that accurately reflects the time, effort, and expertise spent on a client matter.

representation in court The right to speak and be heard by the court in a legal matter; a duly licensed attorney is the only person, other than the defendant or plaintiff, who is acknowledged to have this right.

retaliatory discharge A client's firing of the attorney for the attorney's failure to pursue the client's unethical or imprudent course in handling its legal affairs.

S

self-policing The profession's practice of relying on its own members to report misconduct by others, and to mete out punishment for infractions.

solicitation An attorney's attempt to gain business, usually directed at a specific individual or group and involving an invitation to consult with the attorney regarding legal matters.

specialization An attorney who has chosen to practice in a certain area of the law and has developed a concentration in this kind of legal matter.

subordinate attorney An attorney who must report to a supervising attorney, who then takes ultimate responsibility for the work product's compliance with the firm's ethical practices.

subornation of perjury Assistance by an attorney in carrying out a witness's offer of false testimony.

substantial gift A gift from client to attorney large enough to have a significant impact on the attorney's ability to perform services in a neutral and detached manner.

substantial legal task Duties that take legal analysis and application of specialized knowledge, as opposed to clerical jobs.

substantial question A serious doubt as to an attorney's fitness to practice law because her actions or inactions reflect negatively on her character.

supervising attorney A partner or manager having ultimate responsibility for the work product of other attorneys and paralegals in the firm.

suspension The prohibition of an attorney from practicing law for a specified period of time.

T

timesheet An accurate, daily record of time spent on each task performed by an attorney or paralegal for each client.

trade name The title of a company that it uses in commerce to identify it and distinguish it from others in the field.

U

unauthorized practice of law (UPL) Practicing law without proper authorization to do so.

under the supervision of an attorney A term used to describe the work of a paralegal, which must be assigned, reviewed, and approved by a responsible attorney who takes responsibility for the content of the work.

unintentional disclosure The accidental release of sensitive client information to a third party.

unprotected communications Information that must be disclosed to the opposing party if requested during the discovery phase of litigation.

V

viable claim A claim for which the fact-finder can supply a redress in law by applying the relevant legal standard to the presentable and substantiated facts.

W

waiver of confidentiality Authorization by the client, by his words or actions, of the disclosure of otherwise protected information obtained by his attorney.

work product An attorney's written notes, impressions, charts, diagrams, and other material used by him or her to prepare strategy and tactics for trial.

Index